Computer Communications and Networking Technologies

Michael A. Gallo
Florida Institute of Technology

William M. Hancock
Exodus Communications Incorporated

BROOKS/COLE
™
THOMSON LEARNING

Australia • Canada • Mexico • Singapore • Spain • United Kingdom • United States

BROOKS/COLE

THOMSON LEARNING

Publisher: *Bill Stenquist*
Acquiring Editor: *Kallie Swanson*
Marketing Team: *Christopher Kelly, Samantha Cabaluna*
Editorial Assistant: *Grace Fujimoto*
Production Coordinator: *Kelsey McGee*
Production Service: *The Book Company/Dustine Friedman*
Manuscript Editor: *Frank Hubert*
Permissions Editor: *Sue Ewing*
Technology Project Editor: *Sherrill Meaney*

Cover and Interior Design: *Roy R. Neuhaus*
Cover Image: *Photo Disc*
Interior Illustration: *Impact Publications*
Indexer: *Steve Rath*
Photo Researcher: *Myrna Engler*
Print Buyer: *Vena M. Dyer*
Typesetting: *Carlisle Communications, Inc.*
Cover Printing, Printing and Binding: *R.R. Donnelley & Sons/Crawfordsville*

Brooks/Cole is an imprint of the Wadsworth Group, a division of Thomson Learning, Inc. Thomson Learning™ is a trademark used herein under license.

For more information about this or any other Brooks/Cole products, contact:
BROOKS/COLE
511 Forest Lodge Road
Pacific Grove, CA 93950 USA
www.brookscole.com
1-800-423-0563 (Thomson Learning Academic Resource Center)

Printed in United States of America

10   9   8   7   6   5   4   3   2   1

Library of Congress Cataloging-in-Publication Data

Gallo, Michael A.
    Computer Communications and Networking Technologies/Michael A. Gallo,
    William M. Hancock.
        p.   cm.
    Includes bibliographical references and index
    ISBN : 0-534-37780-7
1. Computer networks. 2. Telecommunication. I. Hancock, Bill, (date) II. Title

TK5105.5 .G33 C35 2001   00-062169
004.6—dc21

To my father-in-law, Dr. Ralph Alberg, and to the memory of my mother-in-law, Elaine Alberg—two wonderful people who taught me about love and life.

—MAG

To Margenia—my partner, friend, confidant, woman of infinite affection, infinite patience, and a really cool Mom.

—WMH

Contents

5   Data Link Layer Concepts and IEEE LAN Standards 139

6   Network Hardware Components (Layers 1 and 2) 170

III   Local and Wide Area Networking Technologies   311

9   Ethernet and IEEE 802.3 Networks   312

12 Integrated Services Digital Network (ISDN) 393

13 Frame Relay 416

IV Related Networking Concepts, Applications, and Technologies

16 Dialup and Home Networking 482

Preface

Computer Communications and Networking Technologies presents a comprehensive introduction to the study of its topic. Our book provides a discussion of the scope and dynamics related to (a) the manner in which computers communicate with each other, (b) how computers are grouped together to form networks, (c) the various networking concepts and issues that are key to the successful implementation of computer networks, and (d) the different networking implementation strategies and technologies currently available.

We wrote this book to provide an alternative to the current body of networking and data communications titles, which are too general, too specific, or too technical. For example, general networking books are usually narrow in scope and provide readers with a limited overview of topics without providing sufficient detail that will enable them to understand key network concepts thoroughly. On the other hand, several networking titles provide sufficient detail and coverage but limit their discussions to specific technologies (e.g., Ethernet or the Internet). Finally, technically-based network books are designed expressly for network engineers or computer scientists and present the material from a systems perspective, contain pseudocode or programming assignments, and provide detailed mathematical concepts or derivations involving calculus, probability theory, or queuing theory. Although many of these books are excellent for their respective audiences, they do not address adequately the educational needs of nontechnical students who endeavor to learn and understand—in sufficient detail—the "big picture" of computer networks.

Consequently, *Computer Communications and Networking Technologies* was written expressly for nonengineering students who are taking a first course in computer networks. It is most appropriate for students in two-year postsecondary schools, such as community colleges or professional trade/vocational schools, or for students in four-year colleges or universities. Thus, first- or second-year undergraduate students majoring in computer science, computer information science, or telecommunications will benefit most from using this textbook. Students from other fields, including mathematics, any of the sciences, business, and liberal arts, who are taking a computer-networking course as an elective, will also benefit from this textbook. Finally, engineering or engineering technology students, as well as computer and network professionals, will find this book a valuable resource that can help them fill in the gaps or tie together loose ends that might have accumulated during their years of study or field experience.

Given this target audience, our goal was to impart the highly technical information and issues involving computer communications and networking technologies in a manner that would be accessible to nearly all levels of readers. We believe we have succeeded in this goal. The topics and issues discussed in the book are explained fully and in an uncomplicated manner. Furthermore, our discussions are of considerable depth and of sufficient rigor for the target audience. Given its format and level of coverage, the book can be equated to a snorkeling adventure: We primarily stay at the surface to examine the features, attributes, technical issues, and concepts of computer networks and networking technologies. Occasionally, we hold our joint breath and dive under the surface to explore a particular concept more fully. We do not, however, examine in detail the underlying mathematical foundations of any particular topic (such an undertaking is better left for a scuba diving expedition). Instead, we offer a glimpse into this world through various figures, appendixes, and boxed text items. In this way, all students, including those with only an algebra background, will benefit from the presentation. Thus, students will not only acquire a thorough understanding of computer communications and networks, but will also have an appreciation for many of the issues and problems related to computer networking.

Organizational Structure

We have organized the material in *Computer Communications and Networking Technologies* in four major parts.

- **Part I: Computer Communications and Networking Basics.** This part represents the basic foundations of networking and comprises the first three chapters. Chapter 1 provides an overview of the various topics encompassing computer communications and networking. It treats many of the concepts it presents from a general perspective, and subsequent chapters elaborate them. The main purpose of this chapter is to get students initially engaged in the study of networking. Chapter 2 extends many of the concepts discussed in Chapter 1 and presents new networking terms and concepts. Chapter 3 provides a discussion of basic analog and digital communications concepts. Nearly all of the information contained in these first three chapters represents the foundation of computer communications and networking and is used throughout the remaining three parts of the book.
- **Part II: Physical, Data Link, and Network Layer Concepts.** The second part of the book comprises Chapters 4 through 8 and contains detailed coverage of various network standards and protocols. Chapter 4 discusses the physical concepts and issues related to networking. Chapter 5 addresses IEEE LAN standards and examines how data frames are constructed, how nodes control the flow of data during a transmission, and how data integrity is maintained via error control. Chapter 6 contains a separate discussion of various network hardware components. Chapter 7 provides information about internetworking and routing concepts. Chapter 8 is devoted to the Internet and the TCP/IP protocol suite including TCP/IP's two transport protocols, UDP and TCP. This part of the book provides students with the core networking concepts that are fundamental to the various local and wide area computer networks and networking technologies presented in Part III.

- **Part III: Local and Wide Area Networking Technologies.** Chapters 9 through 15 examine specific LAN or WAN protocols, technologies, and services. Although most students' perception of computer networks revolves around the Internet and Ethernet, this is not the reality they will face when working in the field. Yes, nearly every organization has an Internet connection, and yes, nearly every organization has a local area Ethernet network. However, many organizations also have fully operational first-generation networks such as token ring or outdated second-generation networks such as FDDI. Furthermore, some of these same organizations also have frame relay, ATM, or ISDN connections. Given the diversity of networking technologies that exist in the field, we have provided separate chapters on the common ones students will most likely encounter. These include Ethernet (Chapter 9), Token Ring (Chapter 10), FDDI (Chapter 11), ISDN (Chapter 12), Frame Relay (Chapter 13), SMDS (Chapter 14), and ATM (Chapter 15).
- **Part IV: Related Networking Concepts, Applications, and Technologies.** The final three chapters provide information about several related networking topics: dialup and home networking (Chapter 16), network security issues (Chapter 17), and network convergence (Chapter 18), the merging of the technologies and applications discussed in all the previous chapters. Among the topics discussed in Chapter 18 is the current trend toward multiservice networking, which integrates traditional voice, video, and data applications.

Each chapter concludes with an End-of-Chapter Commentary. These commentaries consist of transitional material that identifies other chapters in the book containing additional information related to the current discussion. In a sense, they provide a notion of "where we are presently, where we were, and where we are going." As a result, students are able to link key concepts and issues from the current chapter to other chapters.

A Chapter Review is provided at the end of each chapter. This section consists of a bulleted-item list that summarizes the salient aspects of the chapter, a vocabulary check that contains key words and phrases introduced in the chapter, approximately 400 review exercises throughout, and suggested readings and references. Finally, five appendixes and a comprehensive 700-word glossary complement the book's nucleus. Appendix A contains information about vendor Ethernet prefixes. Appendix B presents a detailed example of how parity is used for single-bit error correction. Appendix C has guidelines for installing unshielded twisted-pair cable. Appendix D provides information about designing and analyzing networks as well as how to deal with network politics. Appendix E contains a brief overview of X.25.

Although the chapters are structured logically to follow each other and build on previously learned knowledge, this does not preclude their being read in any order. We wrote the chapters to be independent of each other. Throughout every chapter, key terms or concepts that were presented in an earlier chapter or discussed in a later chapter are explained in the current context with either a forward or backward reference that specifies the appropriate chapter or chapters where the term or concept is discussed more completely. These cross-references enable students to take a break from the current discussion so they can either refresh their knowledge of previously presented material or jump ahead to gain further insight into a specific topic. Thus, the cross-references effectively facilitate a deeper understanding of a given concept in the current context. Finally, throughout the entire presentation, illustrations, tables, and special boxed text items are included to promote further knowledge.

To the Instructor

This textbook is designed for use in a one-semester or one-quarter course. Ample material is included to provide you with a great amount of flexibility for its use. Clearly, the chapters you cover will be determined to a large extent by how the course is structured. Following are three suggestions for presenting this material based on one of the authors' teaching experiences.

Perspective	Suggested Chapters	Comments
A less technical approach that focuses on general concepts, the Internet, Ethernet, and home networking	• Part I: Chapters 1 and 2 • Part II: Chapters 4 through 8 • Part III: Chapter 9 • Part IV: Chapter 16	1. One week per chapter, except three weeks for Chapter 8 and two weeks for Chapter 9. 2. Combine selected material from Chapter 6 with Chapters 5 and 7.
A more technical approach that focuses on different networking technologies	• Part I: Chapters 1, 2, and 3 • Part II: Chapters 4 through 8 • Part III: Chapters 9 through 15	1. One week per chapter. 2. Combine selected material from Chapter 6 with Chapters 5 and 7.
A middle-of-the-road approach that provides a comprehensive overview of most text material	• Part I: Chapters 1 and 2 • Part II: Chapters 4 through 8 • Part III: Chapters 9, 12, 13, 15 • Part IV: Chapters 16 and 17	1. One week per chapter, except two weeks for Chapter 9. 2. Combine selected material from Chapter 6 with Chapters 5 and 7. 3. Combine selected material from Chapter 8 throughout all presentations.

Accompanying the textbook is an instructor's resource and solutions manual, which contains chapter outlines and answers to all of the chapter exercises. Additionally, sample chapter examinations with solutions are provided to facilitate test construction. You may find more support online at www.brookscole.com.

To the Student

Computer Communications and Networking Technologies serves as an excellent foundation on which future and current network managers and administrators can build a solid knowledge base of data communications standards and present and emerging network technologies. After reading this book, you will have accrued a greater understanding of and appreciation for networks and networking. This book will help you understand basic networking terminology, components, applications, protocols, architectures, standards, and implementation strategies. Please note that this is *not* a "how-to" book. We do not provide specific information relative to network management or configurations. Thus, the material contained here will not help you perform such tasks as setting up a domain name server, configuring a network printer, or installing or managing an office network. However, your knowledge, appreciation, comprehension, and awareness of the concepts involved in such activities will be more acute after reading this book. To quote a former student who was taught using earlier drafts of this material in a data communications and networking course: "The material cleared a lot of things up for me. It tied together a lot of loose ends I had for 10 years as a network administrator."

Additionally, a companion textbook published by Digital Press, *Networking Explained*, is available as a supplementary resource. *Networking Explained* covers essentially the same material contained in this textbook except it employs an easy-to-follow question-and-answer format. We structured the question–answer format to emulate a conversation between a networking professional and the reader. The questions are representative of those asked by individuals who are interested in computer networks and who wish to gain additional understanding of the subject. Users of *Networking Explained* have found the conversational tone engaging, informative, and entertaining.

Acknowledgments

Many people contributed considerably, either directly or indirectly, in the preparation of this material. It is therefore justifiable that these individuals be acknowledged. First of all, we are grateful to the authors of the articles, books, RFCs, and other reference material listed at the end of each chapter. These publications served as invaluable resources for confirming that our illustrations and material are accurate, complete, and up-to-date. Next, we thank the many reviewers of the manuscript for their suggestions and thought-provoking comments. They did a yeoman's job and their constructive criticisms strengthened the quality of this book greatly. They include Prasad Aloni of Drexel University, Ron Fulle of Rochester Institute of Technology, Arnold Meltzer of George Washington University, Krishna Sivalingam of Washington State University, Eugene Styer of Eastern Kentucky University, and Michael Whitman of Kennesaw State University.

It is with pleasure that we also acknowledge and thank the editorial staff of Brooks/Cole. In particular, an especially warm "thank you" is extended to our editor, Kallie Swanson, who, on a routine follow-up to a several years' earlier submission, actively solicited this project. We are also extremely appreciative of the collaboration among Kallie, publisher Bill Stenquist of Brooks/Cole, and associate editor Pam Chester and former publisher Phil Sutherland of Digital Press. Through a unique, cooperative arrangement between the two publishing companies, we were permitted to use our trade book, *Networking Explained*, which is published by Digital Press, as the basis for much of the material contained within this textbook. A note of gratitude is also extended to production editor Dustine Friedman of The Book Company and to production coordinator Kelsey McGee of Brooks/Cole, who were together responsible for the overall production of this book. We are particularly grateful to copy editor Frank Hubert.

This book also benefited from the contributions of many former students at Rollins College and Florida Institute of Technology, as well as from participants of seminars and workshops we conducted at various regional and national conferences.

Finally, we extend our personal gratitude to our wives, Jane and Margenia, for their support, patience, understanding, and love throughout this entire project.

Michael A. Gallo
William M. Hancock

COMPUTER COMMUNICATIONS AND NETWORKING BASICS

Chapter

1 Overview of Computer Communications and Networking

This chapter gives an overview of the various topics surrounding computer communications and networking. Many of the concepts presented here are done so from a general perspective and are elaborated in subsequent chapters. We begin with a discussion of what we mean by the title of this book: *Computer Communications and Networking Technologies.* We then give a formal definition of computer networks along with a description of the various terms related to this definition. Section 1.3 introduces different types of networks, including local and wide area networks, as well as information about various network topologies such as point-to-point and broadcast designs. Section 1.4 briefly surveys several key networking concepts (addressing, routing, reliability, interoperability, and security), and Section 1.5 gives a formal presentation on network standards. Section 1.6 provides an overview of the current state of the telecommunications industry. In this section, we contrast the terms data communications and telecommunications and introduce specific telecommunications terminology that is relevant to data communications. We conclude the chapter with information about the book's organization and provide a general outline of the chapters that follow.

1.1 What Does Computer Communications and Networking Technologies Mean?

The title of this book is *Computer Communications and Networking Technologies.* What exactly does this mean? Let us examine this title in a piecemeal fashion. The first part of the title, "computer communications," refers to the electronic transmission of data from one system to another; it describes the manner in which computers exchange information with each other. A common title that conveys similar meaning is data communications. Although used interchangeably, some people restrict the term *data* to include only basic and raw facts, and use the term *information* to imply the organization of these facts into meaningful form for humans.

The second part of the title, "networking," refers to the concept of connecting a group of systems for the express purpose of sharing information. The systems that are connected form a network. The concept of networking involves many issues, including:

- *communication methodology and protocols,* which describe the rules network members must follow so they can understand each other's communication;
- *topology and design,* which describe how systems are connected;
- *addressing,* which describes how systems locate each other within a network;
- *routing,* which describes the manner in which data are transferred from one system to another across a network;
- *reliability,* which addresses data integrity issues to ensure that received data are exactly what was sent;
- *interoperability,* which refers to the degree in which software and hardware products developed by different vendors are able to communicate successfully with each other over a network;
- *security,* which pertains to the safekeeping or protection of all components of a network; and
- *standards,* which establish specific rules and regulations to be followed.

The last part of the title, "technologies," refers to the various networking schemes that have been devised. Examples of some common networking technologies that you might have heard of include Ethernet, token ring, asynchronous transfer mode (ATM), frame relay, and ISDN (integrated services data network). These and other networking technologies are the subject of entire chapters later in the book.

Applications of general network concepts and networking abound. For example, in the broadcasting industry, radio, television, and cable companies all have independent networks consisting of individual stations called affiliates. Through these networks, programs such as news, sports, movies, and special features are shared among the affiliates. One of the earliest and best-known communications networks is the telephone network. This network is commonly referred to as the plain old telephone system (POTS) or the public switched telephone network (PSTN). The latter expression describes the traditional analog-based telephone system used in the United States that was originally designed for voice transmissions. (The concept of analog communications is discussed in Chapter 3.) One computer communications network most of us are familiar with today is the Internet, which is really a collection of networks, that is, a network of networks. Both PSTN and the Internet are discussed in more detail in later chapters.

1.2   What Is a Computer Network?

In any computer networking scenario, there are three underlying presumptions. First, a network must consist of members; second, members must be connected to each other in some manner; and third, all members of the network must clearly understand each other's communication for effective communication to take place. In the world of computer networks:

- The connected entities of a network are called *computers or other devices* (although many times they are generically called *nodes*);
- The link through which communication takes place is called a *network medium;* and
- The rules that govern the manner in which data are exchanged between devices are achieved through a *common network protocol.*

Collectively, these three concepts lead to the following formal definition of a computer network:

> *A computer network is a collection of computers and other devices (nodes) that use a common network protocol to share resources with each other over a network medium.*

Let's examine these concepts of members, medium, and protocol a little more closely.

Network Members: Devices, Nodes, and Hosts

In the most generic sense, the term *device* is used to represent any entity that is connected to a network. Such entities may be terminals, printers, computers, or special network-related hardware units such as communication servers, repeaters, bridges, switches, routers, and various other special purpose devices, most of which will be discussed in detail in later chapters. Devices also can be local or remote. The device originating communication across a network is called the *local device* or *sending device,* and any device within the network that is accessed from this local device is called the *remote device* or *receiving device.* In a telephone network, for example, the telephone handsets we all use are devices. So is the interconnecting hardware at the phone company that allows handsets to talk to each other. A network requires many diverse types of devices in order to work. Other words commonly used interchangeably with the term device include *node, station,* and *appliance.* All four terms refer to any equipment that can access a network. (See Chapter 2 for additional information about network appliances.)

An important basic concept to remember is that nearly all network devices employ some method that enables them to be uniquely identified. This is generally up to the network protocol (described later), but many devices are shipped with internal identifiers that are unique to the devices when they are manufactured. This is similar to a serial number on a television or other consumer electronics appliance. For instance, a device that has an Ethernet card or connection will be assigned a vendor-supplied address that cannot be used by any other device. This keeps the device unique and allows a great deal of flexibility in the configuration of the device by network protocols when the system is being connected to the network.

You will notice, however, that in the previous paragraph we said that "nearly all" devices have some method of identifying themselves to the network. In some cases, especially with network security technologies, devices may be added to a network that do not have an address and do not support any protocols, yet they are monitoring the network for activity and reporting security problems via consoles on the device itself. These types of devices are called "transparent" or "stealth" devices and are typically seen on advanced systems that use firewalls and intrusion detection systems.

When describing network members, we prefer to distinguish between devices and computers. As network devices, computers are called *hosts* (or *servers*) or *workstations* (also called *desktops* or *clients*). This terminology refers to computer systems that have their own operating systems (e.g., Windows). Thus, a workstation might be a personal computer such as an Apple Macintosh or any of the many Intel-based machines (commonly called IBM-PCs or compatibles); a graphic workstation such as those manufactured by Sun Microsystems, Silicon Graphics, IBM, Hewlett-Packard, Compaq Computer Corporation; a super-minicomputer such as Compaq's VAX or an IBM AS/400 system; a super-microcomputer such as Compaq's Alpha; or perhaps a mainframe such as an IBM ES-9000.

Network Media and Communication Protocols

To share information or receive a service via a network, group members must be able to communicate with each other. This implies two specific network criteria: connectivity and language. *Connectivity* refers to a physical link or connection among members; *language* refers to a specific vocabulary and mutually agreed upon rules of communication that members must follow.

Media The physical environment used to connect members of a network is referred to as a *medium* (the plural of which is *media*). Network media facilitate communication by providing an environment for communication to take place. Network media come in two broad categories: cable and wireless. Examples of cable include twisted-pair, coaxial, and fiber-optic cable. Examples of wireless include radio waves (including microwave and satellite communication) and infrared radiation. Network media are discussed in more detail in Chapter 4.

Protocols   The language used by members of a network is called a *network communication protocol.* Protocols facilitate understanding of a communication by providing members with a common language. From a general perspective, a network communications protocol is an accepted or established set of procedures, rules, or formal specifications governing specific behavior or language. For example, when eating in a fancy, expensive restaurant, patrons are usually required to observe a specific dress protocol (e.g., men typically have to wear a jacket and tie). Other restaurants, such as the ones frequented by the authors, may have different dress protocols: no shoes, no shirt, no service. If you were to meet the Queen of England, once again you would need to observe a certain protocol. When applied to computer communications and networking, a network protocol is a formal specification that defines how nodes are to "behave" or communicate with each other. Among other things, network protocols define data formatting, data integrity, and data transmission. In short, a network protocol specifies the vocabulary and rules of data communication.

Let's summarize the concepts of media and protocols. Without a link, sharing of information among members cannot be achieved, and without a specified language, communication cannot be understood. Thus, the physical link provides an environment in which communication takes place, while a common language ensures that communications are understood. This is similar to a telephone conversation between one person who speaks only Italian and another who speaks only Russian. If a telephone circuit (i.e., network link) for this conversation is not available, then these two individuals cannot speak to each other (i.e., they cannot exchange data). Given a circuit, the two individuals can now speak and hear each other's voices (i.e., transmission), but communication cannot take place because neither individual is capable of understanding the other's message—they speak different languages. Networking happens when a common wiring infrastructure connects nodes that share a common communication infrastructure—just like human communication.

A good example of a network protocol that you might be familiar with is the individual protocols that are part of the TCP/IP suite. TCP/IP stands for Transmission Control Protocol/Internet Protocol, which serves as the basis of the Internet. (See Chapters 2 and 8 for additional information about TCP/IP and the Internet.) Although TCP/IP specifies two particular protocols (TCP and IP), it is used to name the set of protocols that includes not only TCP and IP, but also many others. This set of protocols is called the TCP/IP *suite.* Another protocol that is part of the TCP/IP suite is FTP, or File Transfer Protocol, which specifies how to do file transfers. HTTP, the Hypertext Transport Protocol, is used for the World Wide Web (WWW) and defines how servers need to transfer documents (Web pages) to clients (Web browsers). Three protocols used for electronic mail (e-mail) with which you might already be familiar are the Post Office Protocol (POP), the Simple Mail Transfer Protocol (SMTP), and the Internet Mail Access Protocol (IMAP). All of the foregoing are network protocols that are also part of the TCP/IP suite. Today's networks employ a great multitude of protocols, ranging from very simple to quite complex. Protocols are the glue that binds together computer networks because they define how specific operations are to be performed.

When a bunch of related and interoperating protocols are put together in a package on a system, we call it a suite.

Examples of other protocol suites include: AppleTalk, which is a network protocol suite used by Apple Computer, Inc., originally in its line of Macintosh computers and now available in many other operating systems; the set of protocols that are part of Microsoft Corporation's Windows 2000 operating systems; and Digital Equipment Corporation's (now Compaq) DECnet, which uses a network protocol called Digital Network Architecture (DNA). DECnet is designed for VAX or Alpha computers running the Open-VMS operating system and for older DEC systems running legacy DEC OSs such as RSX-11M, RT-11, RSTS/E as well as some more popular operating systems such as MS-DOS, Windows, and some UNIX variants. Computer networks are also occasionally named by their protocols. For example, a network that consists of devices supporting AppleTalk is referred to as an AppleTalk network. Similarly, a TCP/IP network implies a set of devices linked together that uses the TCP/IP suite as its set of rules for communication.

1.3   Types of Computer Networks

There are many different types of computer networks. The differences among them are usually based on perspective. For example, computer networks frequently are classified by the geographical area they encompass (e.g., local area networks and wide area networks), their topologies (e.g., point-to-point or broadcast), or the type of communications path they use and the manner in which data are transmitted across this path (e.g., circuit-switched and packet-switched).

Classifying Networks by the Area They Encompass

Computer networks frequently are classified by the geographical area they encompass. One classification is local area network. Another is wide area network. There are also metropolitan area networks, global area networks, personal area networks, and storage area networks.

A *local area network* (LAN) generally interconnects computing resources within a moderately sized geographical area. This can include a room, several rooms within a building, or several buildings of a campus. Since the term "moderately sized" is not well defined, some people quantify a LAN's range by restricting it from a few feet to several miles or kilometers. One professional organization, the Institute of Electrical and Electronics Engineers (IEEE), quantifies LAN length as 10 km or less in radius. Examples of LANs include Ethernet/802.3, token ring, and Fiber Distributed Data Interface (FDDI) networks. These are discussed in Chapters 9, 10, and 11, respectively.

In contrast to a LAN, a *wide area network* (WAN) interconnects computing resources that are widely separated geographically (usually over 100 km). This includes towns, cities, states, and countries. Following the quantification of a LAN's range, a WAN would span an area greater than 5 miles (8 km). A WAN can be thought of as consisting of a collection of LANs. Examples of WANs include the Integrated Services Data Network (ISDN), frame relay, Switched Multimegabit Data Service (SMDS), and Asynchronous Transfer Mode (ATM) networks. These are discussed in Chapters 12, 13, 14, and 15, respectively.

Some people make further distinctions between LANs and WANs. One such distinction is *metropolitan area network* (MAN), which interconnects computing resources that span a metropolitan area. For example, consider a large business organization with buildings located throughout a local county or city. If each building has its own independent LAN, and if these LANs were connected to one another, the resulting network could be considered a MAN since all of the buildings are located within the same metropolitan area, namely, the local county. MANs generally refer to networks that span a larger geographical area than LANs but a smaller geographical area than WANs.

Some organizations also refer to PANs as Home LANs or HLANs.

Another classification is *personal area network* (PAN), which refers to the small computer networks that are found in private homes. The relatively low cost of computers and the resulting growing number of multicomputer homes are driving the need for PANs as home computer users begin to realize the convenience of interconnecting their computers. For example, PANs can interconnect multiple home computers to the same printer, thereby eliminating the need to purchase separate printers for each computer. PANs can also enable home-based computer users to use a file server on which application software and user data can reside but are accessible from any machine connected to the home network. PANs also provide all members of a household with convenient access to home-based shared computing resources from their private rooms (e.g., a child's bedroom, home office, or kitchen).

In 1996, IBM's Almaden Research Group introduced a device about the size of a wireless pager that clipped to the belt of the user and possessed the basics of a small PC. Unique to the system was the way that information was transferred to the device. The unit had two electrodes that were attached to the wearer's skin and used the salinity conductivity of the skin to enable the wearer to provide low-speed network services via tactile feedback (touch). If the wearer were to touch another wearer of the same equipment, the two units would be able to exchange information through the conductivity of the hosts' skin. Further developments included the use of an external device that could receive information such as medical data from the wearer when touched by the wearer or when the wearer was touched by an intermediary person who was also in contact with the receiving device. IBM termed this technique a PAN, which really emphasizes the "personal" in personal area network. IBM intends to embed this technology into personal medical appliances and possibly other areas of information technology such as student assistant databases.

Still another classification is *global area network* (GAN), which refers to a collection of WANs that span the globe. For example, many businesses such as McDonald's Restaurants have operations in many different countries throughout the world. The interconnection of these individual business locations makes up a GAN.

Finally, there is *storage area network* (SAN), which is a network dedicated exclusively for storing data. Given the continuous growth in the number of home pages, e-mails, and network users, the demand for storage capacity has become a real concern. One way of addressing an organization's storage needs is through a SAN in which dedicated storage servers provide unlimited access via a secure network infrastructure.

Classifying Networks by Their Topology

Another way of classifying networks is by their *topology,* which describes the basic design of a network. Network topology is very much like a road map. It details how key network components such as nodes and links are interconnected. A network's topology is comparable to the blueprints of a new home in which components such as the electrical system, heating and air conditioning system, and plumbing are integrated into the overall design. There are three general interconnection schemes: point-to-point, broadcast, and multidrop.

Point-to-Point Networks

A *point-to-point network* consists of nodes that can only communicate with adjacent nodes. It's like looking into a telescope and seeing only one planet out the eyepiece. *Adjacent nodes* are nodes that are next to each other (Figure 1.1). Adjacency is typically expressed by stating the number of hops required for data to travel from the source node to the destination node. A *hop* is a connection to or from an intermediate node on the path from the source to the destination. Adjacent nodes are always one hop from each other. Thus, one hop implies two directly connected nodes. In a more complex form, a point-to-point network might consist of thousands of nodes connected to adjacent nodes, with these adjacent nodes connected to other adjacent nodes and so on. If a node needs to communicate with a nonadjacent node, it does so indirectly via other adjacent nodes. The source node first transmits a message to its adjacent node. This message is then passed serially through each intermediate node until it finally reaches the destination node. Passing data through an adjacent node to another node is typically called *bridging* or *routing* depending on the passing technique used to transfer the information. (Bridging is discussed in Chapter 6; routing is discussed in Chapter 7.) Several network topologies are based on the point-to-point design. Three very common point-to-point topologies are star, loop, and tree.

Star A key characteristic of a star network is the presence of a central processing hub, which serves as a wire center for connecting nodes. A *simple star* configuration is shown in Figure 1.2(a). In order for nodes to communicate with each other, all data must pass through the hub. Consequently, a hub represents a single source of failure. A typical star configuration is shown in Figure 1.2(b). This is a 10BASE-T network (a

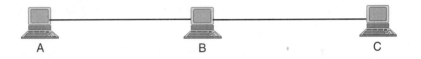

A   B   C

FIGURE 1.1 Example of a point-to-point network design. A characteristic of point-to-point networks is adjacency—nodes can only communicate with nodes they are next to. Thus, node A can only communicate with node B, and node C can only communicate with node B. If nodes A and C need to communicate with each other, they do so using node B, which is adjacent to both A and C.

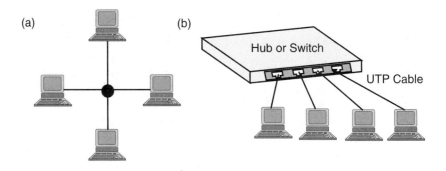

FIGURE 1.2 A simple star configuration (a) involves a wiring center (or hub) to which all nodes are connected and through which all data must pass. The hub represents a single source of failure because, if it fails, then all connected nodes will not be able to communicate. A typical hub configuration is shown in (b).

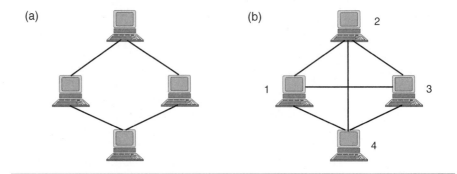

FIGURE 1.3 A loop design (a) is a modified star configuration. Instead of using a wiring hub, nodes are connected directly by dedicated wiring. If every node has a link to every other node, then we have a complete loop (b). (A complete loop is also called fully meshed.) Note that in a complete loop the number of links each node has is one fewer than the number of nodes in the network. Loops are more reliable than stars because the potential for a single source of network failure is removed.

type of Ethernet) consisting of nodes connected to an "Ethernet switch" via unshielded twisted-pair cable (UTP). (10BASE-T networks, Ethernet switches, and UTP cable are discussed in detail in Chapters 4 and 8.)

Loop   A loop network is a modified version of a star. In a loop, nodes are connected via dedicated wiring instead of through a centralized hub. An example of a simple loop is shown in Figure 1.3(a). This involves only one connection between any two nodes. Note that a single link failure does not cause the entire network to fail. Thus, loops are more reliable than stars. A highly reliable and more expensive loop design involves each node being connected to every other node. This is called a *complete loop* and is shown in Figure 1.3(b). In a complete loop, every node is adjacent to every other node.

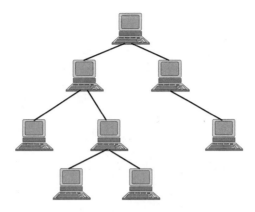

FIGURE 1.4 A simple tree topology consists of nodes interconnected in a hierarchical configuration.

A complete loop is also referred to as a *fully meshed* design, and a partial loop is commonly called a *partially meshed* design.

Tree A tree topology is a hierarchical configuration. It consists of a root node or hub that is connected to second-level nodes or hubs. These level-2 devices are connected to level-3 devices, which in turn are connected to level-4 devices and so forth. A simple tree topology is shown in Figure 1.4. One application of a tree topology is IEEE 802.12, known as 100VG-AnyLAN (see Chapter 9), in which hubs are cascaded to form a hierarchical topology. An example of this network is shown in Figure 1.5.

Broadcast Networks

A *broadcast network* consists of nodes that share a single communications channel. This topology is similar to the old telephone party line concept. (Yes. We are dating ourselves; we are old people, relatively speaking, of course.) In contrast to a point-to-point design, data sent by one machine are received by all other nodes connected to the shared channel. Hosts receiving a transmission check to see who is the recipient of the message and determine if it is intended for them. This is done by examining the message's *destination address.* (The concept of addressing is discussed in the next section.) Hosts that are not the intended recipient discard the message. Thus, only the destination node responds. As an illustration, consider a classroom setting with a teacher and 23 students. If the teacher asks one student a question, all 23 students hear the question but only the chosen student responds. This is analogous to a broadcast network.

Compare this to point-to-point communication. Let us assume that one student, Patty, wants to tell her boyfriend, John, who is sitting two rows over and three seats behind Patty, to wait for her after class. To get this message to John, Patty turns to Jane and says, "Tell John to wait for me after class." Jane turns to the person next to her and says, "Tell John to wait for Patty after class." This message continues being passed

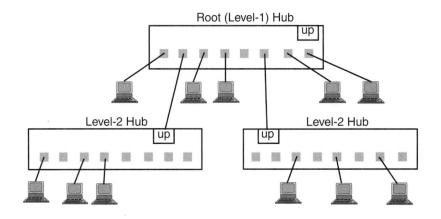

Root (Level-1) Hub

Level-2 Hub

Level-2 Hub

FIGURE 1.5 An example of a two-level hierarchical topology in a 100VG-AnyLAN network. Each hub has at least one uplink port, which connects to a higher-level hub; every port can be used as a downlink port to connect to an end node or a lower-level hub.

FIGURE 1.6 Typical bus configuration. An example of a topology based on a broadcast design.

from one person to the next until it finally reaches John. This is an example of a point-to-point design. Broadcast networks employ several topologies. Two in particular are bus and ring. Satellite communication systems are also broadcast-based.

Bus A typical bus configuration is shown in Figure 1.6. It should be quite apparent from this how a bus design is a broadcast topology. The design clearly shows all the nodes connected to the same channel. An example of a bus-based network is early co-axial Ethernet networks (see Chapter 9).

Ring In a ring configuration, all nodes are connected to the same ring, which serves as the shared medium. Ring-based networks can be designed physically as a star (Figure 1.7a) or as a simple loop (Figure 1.7b). The star design is formally referred to as a *logical ring over a physical star,* and the simple loop design is formally referred to as a *logical ring over a physical ring.* In a classic ring topology, messages are passed from node to node around the ring. The direction of rotation can either be clockwise or counterclockwise (or both) depending on the technology. Note that although data are passed from node to node, rings are not a point-to-point topology because nodes share the same communications channel. Thus, logically, the topology of a ring involves nodes

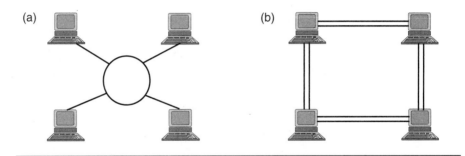

FIGURE 1.7 Ring-based networks represent a topology based on a broadcast design. Rings can be configured as a logical ring over a physical star (a) or as a logical ring over a physical ring (b).

sharing the same communications channel, but physically, the communications are point-to-point. As is the case for the bus topology and for all broadcast systems, ring networks require some method for governing simultaneous ring access.

Satellite In a satellite communication system, data transmissions from a land-based antenna to the satellite are generally point-to-point. However, all nodes that are part of the network can receive the satellite's *downlink* transmission, which is a broadcast from the orbiting satellite to one or more ground stations. Consequently, satellite communication systems are classified as broadcast systems. For example, many schools in the United States have satellite downlink capabilities. Whenever an educational program is broadcast via a satellite system, school sites wishing to receive this transmission simply tune their receivers to the proper frequency. A satellite network is shown in Figure 1.8.

In a broadcast design, there are three different types of messages. The first is a *unicast* message, which is destined to only one recipient. The second is a *multicast* message, which is destined to a group of recipients. It is important to note that a node "knows" that it is in a multicast group by its networking software "telling" it to listen to the multicast messages for the group. In many cases, the sending system to the multicast group does not know which nodes are actually members of the group. The third is a *broadcast* message, which is destined to all hosts connected to the network. A broadcast message is a special multicast message. Distinguishing among the different types of messages is protocol-dependent. Some protocol suites do not use broadcast and only use multicast. Others do not use multicast and use broadcast for group addressing needs.

Another feature of broadcast networks is the concept of *contention*. Since all nodes share the same communication channel, they must contend for the channel when they transmit. Consequently, broadcast-based networks require some sort of method for governing those cases when two or more nodes attempt to transmit data at the same time. Many protocols have been developed for resolving such squabbles among nodes. An overview of some of the more popular protocols is given in Chapter 4, and more detailed descriptions are provided in subsequent chapters.

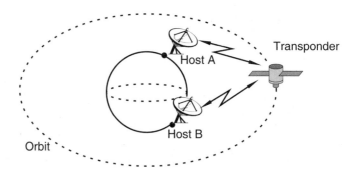

FIGURE 1.8   Typical satellite configuration. Nodes use an antenna to send and receive data.

Multidrop Networks

In some types of networks, especially factory networks and those used to control real-time activities (e.g., power company networks), a particular design concept called a *multidrop network* is frequently used. Multidrop networks typically employ a master–slave concept, with one node being assigned the network master and all other nodes being slaves. In this setting, the master controls the network functions and the slaves request network access from the master. Nodes are connected to a common cable plant similar to a bus design, but unlike bus networks, multidrop nodes are assigned a specific number for communication purposes. This number also is used to establish priority of when a system is permitted to communicate with the master control system. This allows total control over the prioritization of traffic on the network as well as total control over the use of the network. Multidrop networks are popular only in factories because they are not terribly fast networks and would not work well in offices where users might want to share large disk drives and applications. They are typically used for command-and-control operations and some light data transfer of material information or tracking information (e.g., bar codes). Multidrop networks are also often seen on older (circa early 1980s) legacy dumb terminal networks to reduce network costs. An illustration of a multidrop design is given in Figure 1.9.

Switched Networks

In addition to geographical area and topology, networks also can be classified by the type of communications path they use and the manner in which data are transmitted across this path. Two particular classifications are circuit-switched and packet-switched. Switched networks involve a partially or fully meshed topology (see Figure 1.3) and use special network devices called switches to interconnect the links between source and destination nodes.

In a *circuit-switched network,* a dedicated, physical circuit is first established between the source and destination nodes before any data transmission takes place. Furthermore, this circuit remains in place for the duration of a transmission. The public telephone system is an example of a circuit-switched network. When we place a telephone call, a direct physical communications path is established between our telephone

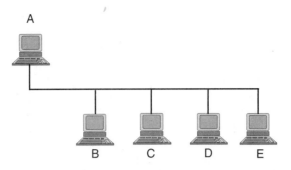

FIGURE 1.9 In a multidrop network topology, all nodes are connected to a common medium. Using a master–slave concept, where one node is the designated master and all other nodes are slaves, the master controls all network functions and the slaves request network access from the master. In this illustration, node A is the master, and nodes B, C, D, and E are slaves.

set and the receiver's telephone set. This path is a point-to-point connection that inter-connects the telephone company's switches, which are located throughout the tele-phone network. Once established, the circuit is dedicated exclusively to the current transmission. After the transmission is completed, this dedicated circuit is then released and made available for another communication transmission. Thus, circuit-switching promotes link sharing since the same circuits can be used for different transmissions, although not at the same time. As an illustration, consider the fully meshed, point-to-point design shown in Figure 1.3(b). If a communications path between nodes 1 and 3 is established by interconnecting links 1-2-4-3, then these links collectively form a dedicated, physical circuit between the two nodes, and this circuit is monopolized by these two nodes for the duration of their communications. However, once their transmission ends, the circuit is released and the individual links that made up this circuit can now be used to construct a new dedicated circuit between two other nodes (e.g., 4-1-2).

In a *packet-switched network,* messages are first partitioned into smaller units called *packets,* which are then sent to the destination node one at a time via intermediate switches. A packet represents the smallest unit of data that can be transferred within a given network. Each packet carries the destination node's address as well as a sequence number. When a packet arrives at an intermediate switch, the switch examines the packet's destination address to determine which path the packet should take to the next switch. This switching technique in which data are stored on one node of a point-to-point link and then forwarded to the next node repeatedly en route to the destination node is called *store-and-forward.* The concept of a store-and-forward transmission requires that the entire contents of a transmitted message (or packet) be received by each intermediate node before it is forwarded to a succeeding node.

Packet-switched networks also promote link sharing by using either virtual circuits or a datagram transport scheme. In *virtual-circuit packet-switching,* instead of using a dedicated, physical circuit for every node-to-node communication, nodes share a communications channel via a *virtual circuit.* A virtual circuit is a logical communications path instead of a physical one. That is, it is a nondedicated logical connection through a shared medium that gives the high-level user the appearance of a dedicated, direct physical connection from the source node to the destination node. In this transport mechanism, individual packets follow the same communications path in sequence as if they were traveling along a dedicated circuit. The difference is that links within this circuit also can be used for other transmissions at the same time. For example, in Figure 1.3(b), node 1 can be communicating with node 3 along the 1-2-4-3 path, and at the same time, node 4 can be communicating with node 2 along the 4-1-2 path. Both paths represent virtual circuits that use the 1-2 link at the same time. Contrast this with circuit-switching in which the circuit is dedicated and the individual links comprising the circuit cannot be used simultaneously to construct any other circuit.

In addition to virtual circuits, packet-switched networks can also use a *datagram* transport mechanism for path selection. In *datagram packet-switching,* packets are transmitted independently of one another at any time. Thus, it is possible for different packets from the same message to be transported across different communications paths. Furthermore, the packets are not necessarily transmitted in a specific order, which implies that the specified destination node is responsible for reassembling them in the correct order. (This is why packets also carry sequence numbers.) Most modern-day computer networks, including the Internet, are packet-switched.

1.4 Network Addressing, Routing, Reliability, Interoperability, and Security

As we noted earlier, the concept of computer networking involves many factors, including addressing, routing, reliability, interoperability, and security. A brief discussion of these concepts follows.

Addressing

The concept of addressing involves assigning a network node a unique address that allows other systems or devices to locate it. It is similar to a house's street address—knowing the street helps to find where we want to go, but having the house number means we will eventually find the exact location of our destination. Another analogy is the phone system. Each phone (a node) has an area code and a number (an address). The area code provides information about the node's location within the global telephone network, and the telephone number is the device's specific identification number within that locale. Systems and call "routers" at the phone company are programmed to provide information to other network devices to get the call from our phone handset to the proper destination (the phone number we are calling).

As an example of addressing, consider an Ethernet/IEEE 802.3 address, which consists of 48 bits (eight bytes) represented as 12 hexadecimal digits and partitioned into six groups of two. For example, 08:00:20:01:D6:2A is a valid Ethernet/802.3 address. If the second hexadecimal digit (from the left) of a destination address is 0 or an even digit (2, 4, 6, 8, A, C, E), then the message is unicast. Thus, 08:00:20:01:D6:2A is a unicast address because its second digit is 8, which is even. If this second hexadecimal digit is odd (1, 3, 5, 7, 9, B, D, F), then the message is multicast. Ethernet broadcast messages, which are special multicast messages, use the address FF:FF:FF:FF:FF:FF. (See Box 5.2 and Appendix A for additional information about Ethernet/802.3 addresses.)

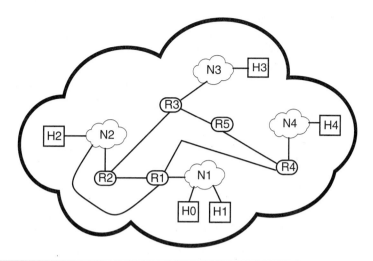

FIGURE 1.10 A network and associated subnetworks (subnets) are typically pictured as clouds. Shown in this figure are four interconnected subnets, N1 through N4; five hosts, H0 through H4; and five routers, R1 through R5. As an example of routing, note that data packets originating on H1 and destined for H2 can take several paths through the network. One path is through R1 only. A second path is R1-R2. Still a third path is via R1-R4-R5-R3-R2.

Routing

The concept of routing involves determining the path a data packet takes as it travels between source and destination nodes. Routing is usually performed by special dedicated hardware units called routers. An illustration of routing is shown in Figure 1.10, which depicts a network and its related segments called subnetworks (subnet for short). Note that in networking circles, networks are pictured as clouds. Shown here are four interconnected subnets (N1–N4), five hosts (H0–H4), and five routers (R1–R5). As an example of routing, note that data packets originating on H1 and destined for H2 can take several paths through the network. One path is through R1 only. A second path is R1-R2. Still, a third path is via R1-R4-R5-R3-R2. The "best" route packets should take is a function of a specific criterion (or criteria), which is called a *metric*. Common routing metrics include distance, number of router hops (recall the concept of hops from our earlier discussion of point-to-point networks), and bandwidth, which specifies the capacity of the link. For example, if the metric used is number of hops, then the best path for Figure 1.10 is through R1 since this involves only one hop. However, if the metric is distance and, of the three possible paths, the shortest distance was through R1-R2, then this becomes the best route. The concepts of routing, switching, routing metrics, and routing protocols and algorithms are all discussed in subsequent chapters.

Reliability

Reliability refers to data integrity, which has to do with ensuring that the data received are identical to the data transmitted. Computer networks are nontrivial systems and are not infallible. In fact, most networks are highly fragile and easily disrupted. Thus, it is important that they be designed with the capability to resolve errors. A common error-control strategy is to provide enough information in the transmitted data to enable the destination node to detect an error. This is called *error detection.* Once a destination node has detected an error, it can then do one of two things: request a retransmission from the sending node or determine what the correct data should be and change them accordingly. Both methods are forms of *error correction.* We call the first *error correction through retransmission* and the second *autonomous error correction.* Note that error correction implies error detection. Autonomous error correction is very expensive to implement. Hence, most networks today are designed with error-detection capabilities, and error correction is done by having the destination node request the sending node to retransmit the data in question. The two most popular error-detection strategies—parity check and cyclic redundancy check (CRC)—are discussed in Chapter 5.

Interoperability

Interoperability refers to the degree in which products (software and hardware) developed by different vendors are able to communicate successfully with each other over a network. During the heyday of proprietary (private, vendor-specific, or in-house) networks, interoperability really wasn't an issue as long as one stayed with a specific vendor's products and protocols. Occasionally, a third-party vendor would set up shop and develop an application that had more bells and whistles (called *valued-added features*) than your vendor was offering. In order to do so, though, this third-party vendor had to receive permission from the primary vendor, which usually implied paying a licensing fee. Today, however, with TCP/IP being an "open" standard and with the Internet's extremely rapid growth, vendors who want to write and sell TCP/IP-based applications are free to do so without fear of violating any proprietary copyrights. Although the protocol specifications for the TCP/IP suite of applications are freely available, the interpretation of these protocols by different vendors is not always the same. This, coupled with the fact that there is no governing body to oversee the development of TCP/IP-based products, sometimes leads to incompatible products.

Although this is no longer the problem it once was, network managers still need to be cognizant of it. This is especially true for network managers who are responsible for the applications that run across their network, and at whom fingers will point when things go wrong. Most computer vendors strive for interoperability with other vendors' products. In fact, one of the largest networking trade shows in the world is called Networld+Interop (for interoperability). Each year at Networld+Interop, competing vendors convene to display their products and to demonstrate how they can interoperate with other vendors' products. Still, the issue of interoperability is paramount, especially in a heterogeneous networking environment in which disparate computer systems are interconnected. Thus, care should be exercised when network products from different vendors are being considered for a network.

Security

Network security refers to the proper safeguarding of everything associated with a network. This includes data, media, and equipment. Security involves administrative functions such as *threat assessment* ("What do you have and who would want it?"), technical tools and facilities such as cryptographic products, and network access control products such as *firewalls,* which are special hardware devices that serve to protect an internal network from the outside world. Security also involves making certain that network resources are used in accordance with a prescribed policy and only by people who are authorized to use these resources. Chapter 17 is dedicated to network security issues.

1.5 Network Standards

A veritable plethora of network standards has been developed defining such things as hardware interfaces, communication protocols, and network architectures. Network standards establish specific rules or regulations to be followed. Standards also promote interoperability among different hardware and software vendors' products. Standards are developed in several ways. First, they can be developed through formal standards organizations. These organizations can be classified into four major categories: (a) national, (b) regional, (c) international, and (d) industry, trade, and professional. A list of some of the influential organizations within these categories is given in Table 1.1.

TABLE 1.1 Network Standards Organizations

National Standards Organizations
(Generally responsible for standards within a nation and usually participate in that nation's international activity)
- American National Standards Institute (ANSI)
- British Standards Institute (BSI)
- French Association for Normalization (AFNOR)
- German Institute for Normalization (DIN)

Regional Standards Organizations
(Restrict their activity to a specific geographical region but generally influence standards outside their regions)
- Committee of European Posts and Telegraph (CEPT)
- European Committee for Standardization (CEN)
- European Computer Manufacturers' Association (ECMA)

International Standards Organizations
(Promote standards for worldwide use)
- International Standards Organization (ISO)
- International Telecommunications Union (ITU)—consists of ITU-T, which is responsible for communications, interfaces, and other standards related to telecommunications; and ITU-R, which is responsible for allocating frequency bands in the electromagnetic spectrum for telecommunications and for making recommendations relating to radio communications. (*Note:* ITU-T is the former CCITT–Consultative Committee for International Telephony and Telegraphy.)

Industry, Trade, and Professional Standards Organizations
(Restrict their activity to member interest areas but generally influence other areas)
- Electronic Industries Association (EIA)
- Telecommunications Industries Association (TIA)
- Institute for Electrical and Electronics Engineers (IEEE)
- Internet Engineering Task Force (IETF)

(Source: adapted from Conrad, 1988.)

TABLE 1.2 The Network Standardization Process

Planning Phase
- Proposals submitted by vendors or organizations are examined.
- A determination is made whether there is a need to establish a standard.
- If a need is found, the development of a project is authorized and assigned to a technical committee.

Development Phase
- Committee prepares a working paper describing the scope of the proposed work.
- Liaisons with other standards groups are established.
- A draft proposal of the standard is produced.
- Draft is voted on and all negative comments are addressed.
- Draft is submitted to parent organization for discussion and approval.

Approval Phase
- All members of the organization vote on draft.
- Draft is made available to the public for review.
- Draft is ultimately approved as a standard.

Publication Phase
- The new standard is published.

(Source: adapted from Conrad, 1988.)

Standards organizations are composed of delegates from the government, from academia, and from vendors who will be developing products based on the proposed standards. The formal standards process, which is designed to ensure that a consensus is reached, is often lengthy and sometimes can take years before a proposed standard is approved. The process also is politically charged. A summary of this process is given in Table 1.2. Standards can be viewed from four different perspectives. There are de jure standards, de facto standards, proprietary standards, and consortia standards.

De Jure Standards

De jure standards are approved by a formal, accredited standards organization. (*De jure* is Latin for "by right, according to law.") Examples include modem protocols developed by the International Telecommunications Union (ITU), the EIA/TIA-568 Standard for Commercial Building Telecommunications Wiring developed by the Electronic Industries Association (EIA) and Telecommunications Industries Association (TIA), and standards for local area networks developed by the Institute for Electrical and Electronic Engineers (IEEE). (These standards are discussed in subsequent chapters.)

De Facto Standards

De facto standards are those that have come into existence without any formal plan by any of the standards organizations. Rather, they are developed through the industry's acceptance of a specific vendor's standard, which is placed in the public domain. (*De facto* is Latin for "from the fact.") One example is Network File System (NFS), a de facto file-sharing protocol standard developed by Sun Microsystems. Sun placed the specifications of this protocol in the public domain so that other vendors could implement it. This resulted in widespread use of NFS and established NFS as a de facto standard. NFS is now implemented on a variety of UNIX systems (including those from Sun, IBM, Silicon Graphics, Compaq, and HP), as well as Macintosh and Intel-based systems. Another de facto standard is Java, a Web-based programming language developed by Sun Microsystems.

Proprietary Standards

Proprietary standards are those developed in a manufacturer-specific manner. This implies that their specifications are not in the public domain and are only used and accepted by a specific vendor. In the early days of networking, proprietary standards were the rule of the day. Although such standards are now frowned upon, many still exist. Some of the best-known are from IBM (e.g., IBM's Systems Network Architecture, or SNA). Novell's IPX protocol, which is based on Xerox's XNS protocol, is also proprietary in nature. Proprietary standards lock a customer into a vendor-specific solution and make it difficult for customers to use products (software or hardware) from other vendors (see Box 1.1).

Consortia Standards

Consortia standards are similar to de jure standards in that they too are the product of a formal planning process. The difference is in the planning process and development of such standards, which are not conducted under the auspices of a formal standards organization. Instead, specifications for standards are designed and agreed upon by a group of vendors that has formed a consortium for the express purpose of achieving a common goal. These vendors pledge their support for the standards being developed by the consortium and also develop and market products based on this mutually agreed upon set of standards. Examples of consortium-based standards include Fast Ethernet, the

BOX 1.1 Open Standards versus Closed Standards

- Open is for everyone.
- Closed is vendor specific.
- Open means that everyone has a chance to implement and benefit from the same standards.
- Closed means that the vendor feels that its standard has value and will not share the technology with other vendors.

- Open allows for the creation and modifications of standards by committee.
- Closed means that the vendor can effect repair or modifications without agreement of other vendors and without comment from customers.
- Open implies that any modifications take a long time.
- Closed implies that modifications are made in a timely manner but they are nonstandard.

early efforts for Asynchronous Transfer Mode (ATM Forum), and Gigabit Ethernet, all of which are discussed in later chapters of this book.

A key decision many network managers face is determining which standard to accept. Obviously, we want to try to avoid proprietary standards and adopt de jure standards. Unfortunately, this is not so easy because standards are starting to fall victim to the relatively short life cycle of a technology. Even worse, the standards organizations (especially the big ones like ISO, ITU, ANSI, IEEE, and others) must reaffirm, remove, or change a standard within 5 years of its creation. This can result in multiple versions of a standard depending on which year is being addressed. Further, a standard developed today for directory services (which is known in the business as X.500) may be completely rewritten and different 4 years hence when the next meeting of the ITU comes around to discuss the standard. A concept for a standard exists for a long time; however, the actual technical detail may last only a short time depending on the standard.

As an example, consider the changes in modem technology. Within a 36-month period in the 1990s, data transmission rates for modems increased from 9600 bits per second (bps) to 14,400 bps to 28,800 bps to 33,600 bps to 56,000 bps. (The concept of modems and data rates is discussed in Chapter 3.) The standards on which each new modem technology was based were originally proprietary. Although users (in most cases) were given vendor assurances that their modems would be compliant with the forthcoming de jure standard, users still faced a purchasing dilemma: Should I invest in the newer technology now, even though it is proprietary, or should I wait for the technology to be approved by a formal standards organization before I commit my resources? Unfortunately, there is no easy answer to this question. As a result, we should be cognizant of the relatively short life cycle of technology and understand that technology will always experience different stages of maturity as it evolves. This situation, coupled with the lengthy process of formal standardization, means we cannot rely solely on de jure standards to achieve interoperability. The realistic approach to achieving interoperability will most likely involve a combination of de jure, de facto, proprietary, and consortia standards.

Internet Standards Development

Internet standards are initially developed by the Internet Engineering Task Force (IETF), which, according to The Tao of IETF (see `http://www.ietf.org/tao.html`), "is a loosely self-organized group of people who make technical and other contributions to the engineering and evolution of the Internet and its technologies." The Internet standards development process involves the generation of special documents called Request for Comments (RFCs), which initially were written comments about resolving certain Internet-related problems. Today, however, RFCs are formal documents that comprise two subseries. The first contains For Your Information (FYI) documents, which provide, in a less technical manner, general overviews and introductory information about various Internet topics. The second subseries, STD, references those RFCs that specify Internet standards. Before an RFC is published, it is first developed as an Internet draft, which enables the Internet community to read and comment on proposed Internet-related documents before they are officially published as an RFC. Internet drafts are considered temporary documents and have a shelf life of only 6 months; hence, they are not archived. To facilitate the dissemination process and to maintain a spirit of openness, RFCs and current Internet drafts are available online at `http://www.rfc-editor.org`.

It should be noted that approved Internet standards are promoted internationally by ISO. However, corresponding RFC-STDs never become international standards, although the ISO may take information from them. The IETF is not a traditional standards organization since it only recommends the standardization of protocols and protocol usage in the Internet. Nevertheless, we list IETF in Table 1.1 because many of the protocol specifications it produces do become standards. (See Chapter 8 for additional information about Internet governance and administration.) For more information about the Internet standards process, see RFC 2026, "The Internet Standards Process—Revision 3."

1.6 The Telephone System and Data Communications

Current technology has taken the analog world we see and hear and converted it to digital form. Today, we have digital telephones, digital cameras, digital radio, digital television (e.g., high-definition TV), and digital video. Nearly every type of analog data can now be expressed in digital form and is being integrated into today's computer networks. The transmission of these data via WANs is being carried by the telephone network, which is also known as the plain old telephone system (POTS) or the public switched telephone network (PSTN). As a result, it is important to understand some of the history and terms associated with telephone networks because they have a direct impact on today's wide area computer communications systems and networks.

The Invention of the Telephone

The invention of the telephone is officially credited to Alexander Graham Bell, when, in 1876, he was awarded a patent for the telephone set. Bell based his invention on the telegraph system. His basic premise was that if he could convert sound into electricity, then the electrical energy generated could be manipulated into a coded message similar to telegraph messages, which were represented as a series of dots and dashes (e.g., Morse code). According to Fagen (1975), Bell endeavored to develop a communications device that made electrical current vary in its intensity the way air varies in density when sound passes through it. If successful, Bell believed that he would be able to telegraph the sound of speech.

Prior to developing a working model of a telephone set, Bell wrote a patent for his invention to protect his ideas and methodologies, and on February 14, 1876, his patent application was filed with the U.S. patent office. Bell's patent application was filed only a few hours before another person, Elisha Gray, officially filed his Notice of Invention to patent the telephone himself. Some people believe that Gray actually invented the telephone but was too late in submitting his notice. This belief is fueled by two key, unsubstantiated events. First, the primary principle on which Bell's invention was based, namely, variable resistance, was not provided within the main text of his patent application. Instead, this principle was written in the margin, leading to the speculation that Bell was apprised of Gray's notice and was permitted to modify his own application. Second, one week after Bell's patent was registered, he and his assistant, Thomas Watson, completed a working telephone model. Interestingly, this model was based on a liquid transmitter that was neither described in Bell's official patent nor ever used by Bell prior to this time. The liquid transmitter concept, however, was described in Gray's patent application. Although Gray filed a lawsuit against Bell for stealing his idea, he lost his case, and the rest is history.

For more information about the telephone's invention, see `http://phworld.tal-on.com/history` and Fagen (1995).

The Evolution of the Telephone Industry and AT&T

See Casson (1910) for an excellent treatise on the early development of the telephone industry.

Within 16 months of receiving his patent approval, Bell formed the Bell Telephone Company in 1877. Although this company was the only telephone company in existence at the time, it nevertheless competed with the Western Union Telegraphic Company, which wanted to monopolize all wire-based communications business. To this end, Western Union formed the American Speaking Telephone Company and hired (among others) Elisha Gray. Western Union's marketing platform was that it had on staff the original inventor of the telephone. In 1878, Western Union, which was buying Bell exchanges, sued the Bell Company for patent infringement, claiming that Elisha Gray was the original inventor of the telephone. Within a year of this suit, and in an unexpected move, Western Union settled with the Bell Company after its lawyers were convinced that the Bell patent was valid. As part of this settlement, Western Union agreed to admit that Bell was the original inventor of the telephone and that his patents were valid. Western Union also agreed to retire from the telephone business. In return, the Bell Company agreed to buy Western Union's telephone system, pay Western Union a royalty of 20% on all telephone rentals, and keep out of the telegraph business. Around this same time, the New England Telephone Company was formed as another competitor to the Bell Telephone Company, but it later merged with Bell in 1879. The new company was named the National Bell Telephone Company and, in 1880, changed its name to the American Bell Telephone Company.

In 1885, the American Telephone and Telegraph (AT&T) Company was formed as a subsidiary to the American Bell Telephone Company. This new subsidiary linked all local telephone companies together throughout the country and owned all telephones and long-distance lines. The company also was responsible for protecting all related patents and served as the headquarters of invention, information, capital, and legal protection for the entire Bell organization. In 1893, competition within the telephone industry began anew when Bell's initial patent expired. In 1899, the American Bell Telephone Company reorganized one final time when it transferred all of its assets, sans AT&T stock, to AT&T. Thus, the Bell Company was now officially known as the American Telephone and Telegraph Company. In an effort to stave off competition during this period, AT&T bought a controlling interest in Western Union. Its efforts to squash the competition worked, and by the mid-1930s, AT&T controlled more than 80% of local calls within the United

States, more than 90% of the country's telephone plant, and more than 95% of the long-distance lines. AT&T's relentless dominance and superiority were bolstered through its research and development arm, Bell Laboratories, as well as its manufacturing facilities, which were provided by Western Electric.

AT&T's de facto monopoly of the telephone business did not go unnoticed, however. On more than one occasion, AT&T was investigated for antitrust actions by various federal agencies. In 1913, it was the Department of Justice, which dropped its antitrust actions after AT&T agreed to stop acquiring independent telephone companies and divest its Western Union stock. Then, in 1934, it was the newly formed Federal Communications Commission (FCC), which had to postpone its actions because of World War II. In 1956, however, the Department of Justice picked up where the FCC left off. The final outcome of this suit, known as the 1956 Consent Decree, effectively made the Bell system a regulated monopoly for telecommunications services. It also prohibited AT&T from getting involved in unregulated businesses. As a result, the telephone system was perceived by the public as a single entity, and there was no need to distinguish between companies that provided local dial tone service and those that provided long-distance services. Thus, voice calls and data transmissions that crossed geographical boundaries (e.g., cities, municipalities, county lines, state borders) simply used the AT&T telephone network.

The AT&T Breakup of 1984

In 1974, the U.S. Department of Justice once again filed a lawsuit against AT&T. This suit was eventually settled in 1981, when AT&T agreed to divest itself of its local Bell operating companies (BOCs). Specifically, AT&T was divided into two groups: carriers that provide local service and carriers that provide long-distance service. Complete divestiture took place on January 1, 1984, and was based on an accord formally known as the Modified Final Judgement (MFJ), which was a modification of the 1956 Consent Decree. As a result of the MFJ, the individual BOCs became known as local exchange carriers (LECs) and were permitted to provide local residential telephone service; AT&T was allowed to provide long-distance service. Furthermore, seven *regional* Bell operating companies (RBOCs) were formed from these original BOCs. The seven RBOCs were Ameritech, Bell Atlantic, BellSouth, NYNEX, Pacific Telesis, Southwestern Bell, and US West. Thus, the RBOCs consisted of LECs that were operating within an RBOCs specific geographical area.

An area of concern that emerged from the 1984 AT&T divestiture was the issue of revenue from the long-distance calling market. AT&T did not want the LECs to have control over both the local and long-distance calling markets. This problem was resolved by establishing 195 *local access and transport areas* (LATAs), which comprised specific geographical and administrative areas controlled by the LECs. Federal regulations restricted LECs to providing only local telephone and telecommunications services within the same LATA. Calls that crossed a LATA were handled by *interexchange carriers* (IECs or IXCs), which provided long-distance telephone and telecommunications services (e.g., AT&T, Sprint, and MCI World-

Com). In other words, an LEC provided *intra*-LATA services and an IEC provided *inter*-LATA services. Thus, voice calls originating in one LATA and destined for another LATA were initially handled by the first LATA's LEC, which then handed the call (i.e., circuit) over to an IEC for inter-LATA transport. The IEC, in turn, handed the call over to the LEC that had control over the destination LATA. Tariffs related to long-distance calls were based on which networks the calls were carried (the LEC's or the IEC's). Thus, it was not uncommon for a long-distance call from New York City to Los Angeles to be less expensive than a call between two cities within the same state and only 50 miles from each other. The NY–LA call might be carried exclusively by an IEC, but the intrastate circuit might have to cross one or more LATA boundaries.

This situation was not restricted to voice calls. Since the telephone network is commonly used for data communications, the LECs and IECs play the same roles for data communications as they do for voice transmissions. As a result, circuit costs associated with data communication networks are a function of LATAs. Circuits established within the same LATA are less expensive than those that have to cross LATA boundaries. The 1984 breakup of AT&T also established clearly defined points of demarcation, called DEMARCs, which separated the customer's premise from the telephone company's network. The DEMARC also specified who owns what equipment—the customer or telephone company—where the equipment is placed, and where tariffs and service rates begin and end. (This will be discussed in more detail in later chapters.)

The Telecommunications Act of 1996

In 1996, the telephone and telecommunications businesses were reformed one more time when President Clinton signed into law the Telecommunications Act of 1996. As a result of this act, LECs and IECs may now get into each other's businesses. That is, LECs are permitted to provide long-distance services, and IECs may provide local calling services. This blurs the distinction between LECs and IECs. The Telecommunications Act also fostered the creation of other telecommunications companies to spur competition for telecommunications services. The logic behind this is that competition reduces prices and provides choices for consumers.

Along with the new law came new terminology. The LECs that existed prior to the Telecommunications Act are now referred to as *incumbent LECs* (ILECs), and the new telecommunications service providers formed as a result of the Telecommunications Act are known as *competitive LECs* (CLECs). Today, ILECs and CLECs offer a wide range of telecommunications services, including local dial tone, long-distance calling, Internet access, and cable TV. The CLECs are also permitted to co-locate their equipment with ILECs' equipment and typically lease ILECs' circuits for delivering their services. Some CLECs have developed their own networks independent of ILEC or IEC networks.

Another result of the Telecommunications Act is an increase in mergers and acquisitions among telecommunications service providers. For example, during the 1998–1999 time frame, RBOCs Bell Atlantic and NYNEX merged into a single company that kept the Bell Atlantic name. Then Bell Atlantic merged yet again in mid-2000, this time with GTE. This newly combined business now operates under the name Verizon Communications, which also includes the combined companies of Bell Atlantic Mobile, Airtouch Cellular, and PrimeCo. The net effect of these mergers transforms the "old" Bell Atlantic into the nation's largest local telephone company and wireless provider. Separately, Ameritech and Southwestern Bell Corporation (SBC) also merged into a single company that kept the SBC name. In fact, of the original seven RBOCs, only four remain.

In the long-distance market, two IECs—WorldCom and Sprint—announced plans to merge in 2000, but their proposal ran afoul of U.S. antitrust regulators. The original Bell, AT&T, has also been quite active. Most notable are AT&T's acquisitions of former cable giant Tele-Communications, Inc. (TCI) and cable company MediaOne. This now makes AT&T the nation's largest provider of cable TV and high-speed Internet access, in addition to being the nation's largest long-distance telephone vendor. (Is it possible that the former telephone monopoly might soon monopolize high-speed Internet services over cable TV lines?) AT&T also acquired McCaw Cellular—now called AT&T Wireless—and AT&T WorldNet continues to be one of the nation's leading analog dialup Internet service providers. The Telecommunications Act also enables traditional cable companies to become CLECs and provide local dial tone service and Internet access in addition to cable TV. Finally, "old media" are beginning to merge with "new media" companies as witnessed by the recent merger of Time Warner Cable (TWC) and America OnLine (AOL).

See `http://www.whitehouse.gov/WH/EOP/OP/telecom/telecom-top.html` For additional information about the Telecommunications Act of 1996.

The bottom line is that the clean and pronounced division among telecommunications service providers and the types of services they deliver is no longer in place today. Telephone carriers do not just provide telephone service, cable television providers do not just offer cable TV broadcasts, and Internet service providers do not just offer Internet access. The world of telecommunications is dynamic in nature, and today's network managers must be knowledgeable and cognizant of the constant changes that are unfolding in this industry.

Data Communications versus Telecommunications

Before ending this chapter, we thought it would be helpful to distinguish between two terms frequently used when discussing computer communications and networking, namely, data communications and telecommunications. *Data communications* refers to the electronic transmission and receipt of any type of information that can be processed by a computer. Computer-processed data are represented using 0s and 1s. This representation is formally called *binary notation,* and the individual symbols, 0 and 1, are referred to as *binary digits,* or *bits* for short. Data expressed in binary form are considered *digital* in nature.[1]

Thus, data communications implies the transmission and receipt of digital data. *Telecommunications,* on the other hand, is a general term that denotes the transmission and receipt of any data type, including traditional analog data such as voice, radio, television,

---

[1] The opposite of digital data is *analog data.* Conventional telephone, radio, and television transmissions are examples of analog data. See Chapter 2 for more information about the terms bits, digital, and analog.

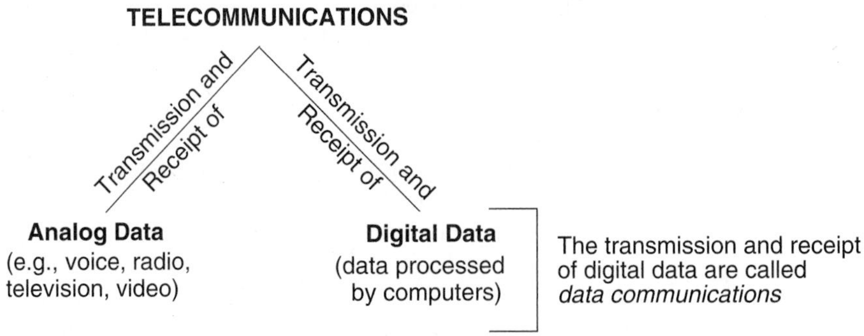

TELECOMMUNICATIONS

FIGURE 1.11 Telecommunications is a general term that indicates the electronic transmission of any data type, including analog (e.g., voice, radio, and television) and digital (i.e., data processed by computers). Since data communications involves the transmission and receipt of digital data, data communications is considered a subset of telecommunications.

and video, as well as digital data. As a result, data communications is considered a subset of telecommunications (Figure 1.11).

1.7   Organization of the Book

Given its title, *Computer Communications and Networking Technologies,* this book provides a discussion of the scope and dynamics related to (a) the manner in which computers communicate with each other, (b) how computers are grouped together to form networks, (c) the various networking concepts that are key to the successful implementation of computer networks, and (d) the different networking implementation strategies and technologies that are available. In presenting this information, we organized the material around the following four major parts:

- **Part 1: Computer Communications and Networking Basics**   This part represents the basic foundations of networking and comprises the first three chapters. Chapter 2 extends many of the concepts discussed in this overview chapter and presents new networking terms and concepts. Chapter 3 provides a discussion of basic analog and digital communications concepts. Nearly all of the information contained in these first three chapters represent the foundation of computer communications and networking and are used throughout the remaining three parts of the book.
- **Part 2: Physical, Data Link, and Network Layer Concepts**   The second part of the book comprises Chapters 4 through 8 and provides detailed coverage of various network standards and protocols. Chapter 4 discusses the physical concepts and issues related to networking; Chapter 5 addresses IEEE LAN standards and examines how data frames are constructed, how nodes control the flow of data during a transmission, and how data integrity is maintained via error control. Chapter

6 contains a separate discussion on various network hardware components; Chapter 7 provides information about internetworking and routing concepts; and Chapter 8 is devoted to the Internet and the TCP/IP protocol suite including TCP/IP's two transport protocols, UDP and TCP.

- **Part 3: Local and Wide Area Networking Technologies**   Chapters 9 through 15 make up the third part of the book, which examines specific LAN or WAN protocols, technologies, and services. These include: Ethernet (Chapter 9), Token Ring (Chapter 10), FDDI (Chapter 11), ISDN (Chapter 12), Frame Relay (Chapter 13), SMDS (Chapter 14), and ATM (Chapter 15).

- **Part 4: Related Networking Concepts, Applications, and Technologies**   The last part of the book consists of the final three chapters and provides information about several related networking topics. These include dialup and home networking (Chapter 16), network security issues (Chapter 17), and network convergence (Chapter 18), which involves the merging of the technologies and applications discussed in all the previous chapters, including traditional voice, video, and data applications.

Each chapter concludes with an End-of-Chapter Commentary, which consists of transitional material that identifies other chapters in the book containing additional information related to the current discussion. A Chapter Review Materials section is also provided at the end of each chapter. This section consists of a Summary of the information presented, a Vocabulary Check that contains key words and phrases introduced in the chapter, Review Exercises, and Suggested Readings and References. A Glossary and several appendixes are also provided at the end of the book. Appendix A contains information about vendor Ethernet prefixes. Appendix B contains a detailed example of how parity is used for single-bit error correction. Appendix C has guidelines for installing unshielded twisted-pair cable. Appendix D provides information about designing and analyzing networks as well as how to deal with network politics. Appendix E contains a brief overview of an early packet-switching technology called X.25.

End-of-Chapter Commentary

This chapter provided a brief overview of some of the fundamental concepts related to computer communications and networking. The concepts presented in this chapter are discussed in greater detail and depth in later chapters. For example, Chapter 4 is devoted entirely to the topic of network media; Chapters 5, 7, and 8 provide detailed descriptions of several current networking protocols; the various network designs and topologies discussed in this chapter are highlighted in Chapters 9 through 15 as part of our examination of local and wide area network technologies; the concepts of addressing, routing, reliability, and interoperability are placed in a much more meaningful context in Chapter 8 when we discuss the Internet; and Chapter 17 is devoted to network security.

CHAPTER REVIEW MATERIALS

SUMMARY

• A surface-level perspective of several different networking concepts was presented in this chapter. The intent was to provide a general overview of these concepts and then develop them more fully in later chapters.

• Computer communications and networking technologies involve the study of (a) computer-based communication networks, (b) key factors necessary to effect such communications, and (c) various technologies that define specific networks such as Ethernet.

• All networks (computer or otherwise) include members who belong to the network, a medium that links the members together, and a protocol that all members must observe to communicate with each other.

• Computer networks are generally described by the geographical areas they serve; common descriptions include local and wide area networks (LANs and WANs). Others include metropolitan area networks (MANs), personal area networks (PANs), global area networks (GANs), and storage area networks (SANs).

• Another method of describing networks is by their topology. A point-to-point topology is characterized by the concept of adjacency, and designs based on this concept include star, loop, and tree. Broadcast networks share a common medium, and nodes must contend for this medium to transmit

data. Designs based on this topology include bus, ring, and satellite networks.

• In addition to design criteria, key elements of all computer communications and networking include the concepts of addressing, routing, reliability, interoperability, and security. Addressing involves assigning a network node a unique address so other systems or devices can locate it; routing involves identifying the path data must travel through a network en route from source to destination; reliability relates to data integrity and involves the process of ensuring that the message received is exactly what was sent; interoperability involves the degree to which disparate computer systems (i.e., those from different vendors) can correctly communicate with each other; and security involves the proper safeguarding of everything associated with a network.

• Four different types of standards are de jure, de facto, proprietary, and consortia; de jure is the most desirable and proprietary the least.

• The conventional analog-based telephone network serves as the basic foundation on which today's modern digitally based data communications networks are designed.

• Data communications is a subset of telecommunications, which involves the transmission and receipt of analog (e.g., voice, radio, television) or digital data.

VOCABULARY CHECK

addressing	contention	firewall
appliance	datagram packet-switching	global area network (GAN)
broadcast	de facto standards	hop
bus design	de jure standards	host
circuit-switched network	device	incumbent local exchange carrier (ILEC)
computer network	error correction	
consortia standards	error detection	interoperability

local area network (LAN)
loop
medium
metropolitan area network
  (MAN)
multicast
multidrop design
network protocol
network security
network standards
network topology
node
packet

packet-switched network
personal area network (PAN)
plain old telephone system
  (POTS)
point-to-point network
proprietary standards
protocol suite
public switched telephone network (PSTN)
regional Bell operating company
  (RBOC)
ring
routing

satellite communication system
star
storage area network (SAN)
store-and-forward
TCP/IP
threat assessment
tree
unicast
virtual circuit
virtual-circuit packet-switching
wide area network (WAN)

REVIEW EXERCISES

1. In our discussion of the title of this book, we provided several applications of general network concepts and networking, including those found in the broadcasting industry, professional organizations, and the telephone network. Identify and discuss other applications or examples of computer communications and networking.

2. Three essential components of any type of network are members, media, and protocols. Identify and discuss these components from the perspective of the networks you listed in problem 1.

3. What roles do network media and protocols have in a computer network?

4. Identify and discuss the communications protocol being observed during a U.S. presidential press conference or during a military briefing.

5. One of the protocols we listed that is part of the TCP/IP protocol suite is the Post Office Protocol (POP), which is the electronic mail program on which the popular program, Eudora, is based. Research this protocol and describe how it operates.

6. Describe the difference between WANs and GANs and give an example (other than the ones in the book) of each.

7. Of the various point-to-point designs described, which do you think is the "best"? As part of your answer, examine the relationship among network design factors such as cost, reliability, and need.

8. What advantages does a fully meshed design have over other point-to-point designs?

9. Give a practical, noncomputer analogy of a broadcast network.

10. Of the various bus designs described, which do you think is the "best"? As in problem 7, your response should include a discussion of cost, reliability, and need.

11. Explain the difference among unicast, multicast, and broadcast messages.

12. Explain the concept of contention and give an example of this concept in a noncomputer networking context.

13. Explain the concept of store-and-forward and give an example of this concept in a noncomputer networking context.

14. The term *virtual* is used frequently in the computer and networking industry. Examples of expressions that include this term include virtual terminal, virtual reality, and virtual circuit. Explain what you think *virtual* means generally and in the context of the given phrases.

15. Why do you think the concept of addressing is important in computer networks?

16. Explain the concept of routing. What function do you think routing has on a bus network?

17. Explain the difference(s) between error correction and error detection. Give an example of a network that requires autonomous error correction.

18. What does interoperability mean? Why is it important in the field of computer networks?
19. Why are networking standards important?
20. What advantages does an organization gain by making a network utility (e.g., Java) available to the public in hopes of it becoming a de facto standard instead of maintaining it as a proprietary standard?
21. Write a report on ITU standards organization. Include a brief history of ITU, what standards it is responsible for developing, how often it reviews or develops standards, who makes up ITU committees, and its relationship with other standards organizations such as ANSI. (*Suggestion:* Visit ITU's Web site at `http://www.itu.int` for information.)

SUGGESTED READINGS AND REFERENCES

BATES, R. J., and D. Gregory. 1998. *Voice and Data Communications Handbook.* New York: McGraw-Hill.

BRADNER, S. 1996. The Internet Standards Process—Revision 3. *RFC 2026,* October.

CASSON, H. N. 1910. *The History of the Telephone.* A. C. McClurg.

CONRAD, J. W. 1988. Open Systems Interconnection. In *Handbook of Communication Systems Management,* ed. J. W. Conrad. 237–251. Boston: Auerbach Publishers.

FAGEN, M. 1975. *A History of Engineering and Science in the Bell System. Volume 1: The Early Years, 1875–1925*, ed. New York: Bell Telephone Laboratories.

GALLO, M., and W. Hancock. 1999. *Networking Explained.* Boston: Digital Press.

HANCOCK, B. 1989. *Network Concepts and Architectures.* Wellesley, MA: QED Information Sciences.

HORVAK, R. 2000. *Communications Systems and Networks,* 2nd ed. Foster City, CA: M&T Books.

STALLINGS, W. 1997. *Local and Metropolitan Area Networks.* 5th ed. Upper Saddle River, NJ: Prentice-Hall.

——. 2000. *Data and Computer Communications.* 6th ed. Upper Saddle River, NJ: Prentice-Hall.

STAMPER, D. A. 1991. *Business Data Communications.* 3rd ed. Redwood City, CA: Benjamin/Cummings.

TANENBAUM, A. S. 1996. *Computer Networks.* 3rd ed. Upper Saddle River, NJ: Prentice-Hall.

2

Essential Terms and Concepts

CHAPTER OBJECTIVES

After studying this chapter, you will be able to do the following:

1. Describe the difference between a network application (e.g., e-mail) and its corresponding application protocol (e.g., the Post Office Protocol, POP).
2. Describe the differences among decentralized, centralized, and distributed computing.
3. Describe the differences between distributed computing and networking.
4. Explain the concept of client/server computing.
5. Contrast the client/server network model and the peer-to-peer model.
6. Explain the Web-based networking model.
7. Contrast serial and parallel communications.
8. Contrast synchronous, asynchronous, and isochronous communications.
9. Describe the differences among simplex, half-duplex, and full-duplex communications.
10. Distinguish between analog and digital communications.
11. Distinguish between analog and digital data.
12. Describe the characteristics of analog and digital signals.
13. Explain the concept of simple harmonic motion and relate it to analog communications.
14. Understand the concept of bandwidth and the units used to measure it.
15. Contrast bandwidth and throughput.
16. Recognize that data rate and baud rate are not synonymous.
17. Describe the concept of electrical noise and identify its sources.
18. Determine the bandwidth or signal-to-noise ratio of a communications channel using Shannon's limit.
19. Describe the concept of multiplexing and contrast the commonly used multiplexing strategies.
20. Describe the concept of switching and contrast circuit-switching and packet-switching.
21. Explain the concept of a virtual circuit.
22. Contrast connection-oriented and connectionless service.
23. Understand the concept of a network architecture.
24. Describe the seven layers of the OSI model.
25. Explain the current role of the OSI model.

Have you ever read a calculus book, legal contract, or sheet of music and understood the information being presented? Without being versed in mathematics, law, or music, these subjects are usually foreign to the uninformed. The reason is that these subjects are based on their own language consisting of special symbols, vocabulary, and terms defined for a specific context. Consequently, understanding these subjects involves first learning the vocabulary and language associated with them. Without this knowledge, effective communication and understanding with others versed in these subjects cannot occur, possibly resulting in confusion, misunderstanding, unacceptable practices, or undesirable results. The subject of computer communications and networking is not unlike mathematics, law, or music. It too has its own special language. In this chapter, we present some of the essential terms and concepts related to computer networks. Understanding these terms and concepts is critical because they serve as the foundation of our study of networks and will be used and expanded upon in subsequent chapters.

In Section 2.1, we extend our discussion of protocols from Chapter 1 by examining the differences between network applications and application protocols. In Section 2.2, we describe different computer communications and networking models, including centralized, distributed, client/server, peer-to-peer, and Web-based systems. Section 2.3 contains information about various communication service methods such as serial, parallel, synchronous, and asynchronous communications, as well as information about simplex and duplex data transmission modes. In Section 2.4, we present an overview of analog and digital communications. Section 2.5 discusses the speed and capacity of a communications channel, including the concepts of bandwidth, data rate, throughput, and noise. Section 2.6 presents the concepts of multiplexing and switching and includes a discussion of common multiplexing and switching strategies. The last section of the chapter examines the concept of network architecture and provides information about the OSI reference model.

2.1 Network Applications and Application Protocols

In Section 1.2, we learned that a network communications protocol is an accepted or established set of procedures, rules, or formal specifications governing specific behavior or language. Thus, a network protocol specifies the vocabulary and rules of data communication. Furthermore, for effective communication to take place among network members, all members must support the same protocols. In this section, we expand on this discussion and contrast network applications and their related protocols.

Ignoring protocols for a moment, most computer networks support similar network-related applications such as e-mail. Although the function of these applications across different networks is similar, the manner in which they are implemented is protocol-dependent. For example, e-mail messages can be exchanged between hosts connected to a TCP/IP network because they speak the same language. Similarly, e-mail messages can be exchanged between hosts of an SNA network because, once again, they speak the same language. However, e-mail messages cannot be exchanged directly between a host connected to a TCP/IP network and a host connected to an SNA network because they may use different *application protocols* for electronic mail. Consequently, although different networks might be functionally equivalent in that they support similar applications (e.g., TCP/IP and SNA networks both support electronic mail), the manner in which these functions are implemented is not the same. As an example, UNIX systems support the e-mail protocol called the Simple Mail Transfer Protocol (SMTP), which is part of the TCP/IP protocol suite. IBM mainframe systems support a different e-mail system called Officevision. By default, these two protocols cannot interoperate directly even though UNIX and IBM mainframe computers are typically connected to the same network. However, Officevision installations can be configured to communicate not only "native" with its own protocols, but also to simultaneously support TCP/IP and SMTP so that UNIX and IBM mainframe users can exchange e-mail. A network may have many protocols and many applications. Not all of them necessarily talk directly with each other. Software entities called *gateways* (explained later) allow conversion (like a linguistic translation) between some application protocols. In other areas, the problems are solved simply by supporting more than one application protocol at the same time. While this sounds complex, usually a little care in the planning cycle makes everything work well when activated for use.

An important point to all of this is that there is a difference between an application such as e-mail and the protocol that defines and allows it to interoperate with other e-mail servers on a network. To help understand this better, consider the hierarchy in Figure 2.1. At the root layer, we have a network protocol suite (TCP/IP). The next layer shows three network

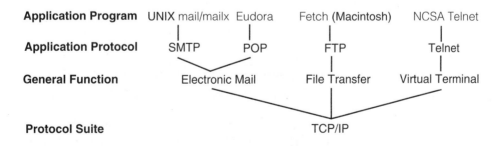

FIGURE 2.1 A protocol suite contains specific network applications (e.g., e-mail), which in turn are defined by specific application protocols (e.g., SMTP). These application protocols are part of specific application programs (e.g., UNIX mail) that provide a user with an interface to interact with an application. The application protocol also defines the manner in which an application is to be implemented between two hosts connected to a network.

applications that are part of this suite (e-mail, file transfer, and virtual terminal). The third layer contains the protocols that define these applications (SMTP and POP for e-mail, FTP for file transfer, and Telnet for virtual terminal). The last layer identifies a specific program that users can use for these applications. A similar tree diagram can be drawn for IBM mainframes or any other protocol suite. In short, a network protocol suite provides the specifications for network applications such as e-mail. These applications have specific protocols that define how the application is to be implemented on the network. The application protocols also include specific user programs that we use to interact with the application.

To illustrate this further, let's use e-mail as an example. E-mail is a network application that involves creating, sending, receiving, and storing messages electronically. These activities are performed by using a "mail program," which provides a utility for users to compose, read, save, delete, and forward e-mail messages (among others). This mail program is an application program that resides on a host. A mail program is also concerned with issues such as how a host accepts or rejects mail, how mail is stored on a system, how a user is notified of the arrival of new mail messages, and so forth. A mail program does not, however, manage the network exchange of e-mail messages between two hosts. Rather, the method by which e-mail is transferred from one host to another is handled by an electronic mail protocol such as SMTP, IMAP, or POP, which are e-mail application protocols that are part of the TCP/IP protocol suite.

Other network applications are similar to e-mail. They consist of an application program that provides the user with an interface to interact with the application, and they contain a related application protocol that defines the manner in which an application communicates over a network. Thus, file transfer programs provide users with an interface for copying files to or from a remote host, and virtual terminal programs provide users with an interface for establishing a login on a remote host. These applications also have corresponding protocols (FTP and Telnet, respectively) that define the rules local and remote hosts must follow to run the application across the network.

Although each application program has an associated network application, there is not a one-to-one correspondence between an application program and network application. Some network applications support more than one application protocol. For example, the TCP/IP-based public domain package NCSA Telnet supports both the virtual terminal protocol (Telnet) and the file transfer protocol (FTP). As another example, consider the software product from Netscape Communications (now part of America Online—AOL), Netscape Communicator. This product supports several protocols, including those for network news (NNTP), e-mail (SMTP, POP, and IMAP4), the World Wide Web (HTTP), and file transfers (FTP).

It is important to note that, although nodes have to use the same application protocol, users are not restricted in their use of application programs. This is because an application program simply provides the user with an interface to interact with the application. Behind this application is an associated protocol that is transparent to the user. As long as the application's corresponding protocol understands another application's protocol, everything should work out. Thus, you might use Eudora as your desktop (or client) e-mail package, but someone else might choose to use the e-mail program that is part of Netscape Communicator, called Messenger, and still a third person might use the e-mail application that is part of Microsoft's Outlook. It doesn't matter—all these applications support protocols that understand each other when properly configured.

2.2 Computer Communications and Networking Models

In the early days of computer networking, data communications generally took place via one of three general models: *decentralized, centralized,* or *distributed.* As computer communications concepts evolved, new networking models were developed. Two in particular are *client/server* and *peer-to-peer,* and today a third, *Web-based,* is rapidly gaining favor. In the study of computer communications and networking, these terms usually emerge and are often misunderstood. Although the first three terms are grounded in old (circa 1970s) management information systems (MIS) vocabulary and are more applicable to the use of computing, not networking, resources, we nevertheless provide a brief description of them for instructional purposes. We also provide a discussion of the client/server, peer-to-peer, and Web-based models, which are the most prevalent models on which network communications and applications are based.

Decentralized Systems

In a decentralized environment, users maintain their own systems, and there is no electronic exchange of resources or information among these separate systems. Decentralization provides user or departments with computing independence; that is, it moves control of the system closer to the end user. Thus, departments do not have to conform to the mandates of a central group and can allocate resources and set priorities in a manner compatible with departmental needs. These attributes are very appealing to users and make a strong case for decentralization.

User–departmental independence, however, can also result in duplication of data, which can lead to data inconsistencies within an organization. To illustrate the concept of decentralization and some of its related problems, consider the computing needs of a college's Student Records and Accounting Departments. In a decentralized environment, the Student Records Department would use a computer to maintain a database of students' grades, home addresses, courses taken, student numbers, and so forth. Independent of this database, the Accounting Department would have its own database consisting of typical accounting information—including some of the information being maintained by Student Records (e.g., students' addresses, which are needed for billing purposes). Thus, both departments maintain duplicate information. If a student were to move and notify Student Records of her new address, when the Records Department updates its database, this change would not be reflected in the Accounting Department's database at the same time and, in many instances, not before a considerable amount of time passes. The two departments now have inconsistent data.

In addition to data redundancy and inconsistencies, decentralization also can be expensive to implement in terms of increased costs for hardware, maintenance, support, and operations since each department has its own system. Decentralization also promotes low productivity. For example, without any type of communications link among departmental systems, updates to databases that contain redundant information would have to be done manually by the individual departments. Thus, if a clerk in the Accounting Department wants to update the department's database to reflect a student's change of address, the clerk would have to receive a paper copy (or possibly a disk) from Student Records and enter this information into the Accounting Department's database. This is a duplication of effort. Moreover, if the Accounting Department mailed a bill to the old address before the update occurred, the bill could get lost, payment by the student could be delayed, and accounting personnel time could be wasted following up on the status of this particular account. A decentralized system does not satisfy our definition of a computer network and hence should not be thought of as a network.

Centralized Systems

In a centralized environment, a single computer houses all the data of an organization, and users have access to these data via terminals, which are end devices that contain a keyboard and display for sending and receiving data via a communications link. In some circles (none to which we belong), a centralized environment is commonly referred to as a *terminal network* because it consists of a collection of terminals connected to a centralized system making data available electronically throughout the enterprise. Consequently, if in our previous example, Student Records were to update student information, all such updates would be housed in a centralized database that is accessible by all other departments of the college. This type of configuration, where terminals connect and communicate to a master computer system, is also commonly called a mainframe environment. Other more derogatory terms include "the great big green dumb terminal farm" (a lot of IBM mainframe terminals have green phosphor screens and are rather large), the "large pile of bits," "Godzilla computing," and other more creative and profane terms.

Centralized computing offers several advantages over decentralized computing. First, all operations and management of a system are now under the auspices and control of a single department, typically MIS. Second, it usually costs less to purchase and maintain a large centralized system than several smaller decentralized systems. Third, by incorporating centralized resources, data redundancy and inconsistencies are reduced or eliminated. Finally, centralized systems promote and ease data sharing among users.

Centralized systems have their share of negative features as well. First, centralized communication systems are not as reliable as decentralized systems because the former represent a single point of failure. If a centralized system or any of its components fail, the entire enterprise is affected. This is not the case with decentralized systems since all the computers are independent of each other. Second, a centralized environment does not always satisfactorily meet or address the computing needs of individual departments or users. Since the system is shared by all departments and users, response times are not always adequate. Also, because the operation of the system is centralized, special departmental programming needs are not always met with satisfaction. Finally, expansion and growth of a large system usually require a Herculean effort since there are so many components and modules that need attention. A centralized system does not satisfy our definition of a computer network, and although some people think of it as a network, we do not.

Distributed Systems

A distributed system consists of independent computers connected to one another. The primary difference between a distributed system and a computer network is that in a distributed environment resources are made available to the user in a transparent manner. What this means is that, in theory, users are unaware that the computers are inter-

---

Terminals have no internal processing capabilities and hence should be distinguished from a computer or host. To use a terminal over a network, an interconnection device or system would be required to allow applications to communicate with the terminal.

connected. From a user's perspective, a distributed system appears as if it were a single system. Using specially designed software, all functions of a distributed system are handled without users ever having to explicitly request a specific service. In a networked environment, though, users must explicitly identify what it is they want done.

To illustrate this difference, consider the task of editing a file that resides on a remote system. In a distributed environment, a user would simply "call up" the file to be edited and the system would make the file available. In a computer network, however, the user must first know on what remote host the file resides and then either (a) transfer the file to the local host (which involves running a file transfer program) or (b) establish a login to the remote host on which the file is located (which involves running a virtual terminal program to log into the remote host). Thus, in a distributed system, the file appears local to the user regardless of where the file actually resides within the system, whereas in a computer network, the user must be cognizant of the file's residence and then explicitly perform some function to gain access to the file. Although not exactly a computer network, there is considerable overlap between distributed systems and computer networks. Suffice it to say that a distributed system represents a special case of a network, with the major distinction being the software as opposed to the hardware.

The key to the inherent transparency of a distributed system is specially designed software generically called a *network operating system* (NOS). Examples include IBM's LAN Server, Banyan's VINES, and Novell's IntranetWare. In each of these cases, the NOS is independent of a computer's native operating system—it is loaded "on top" of the computer's operating system and provides the computer with networking capability based on a particular protocol.

A distributed system can also be thought of as a hybrid of decentralized and centralized systems. In a distributed environment, users of a department are able to control their processing needs using their departmental computer. Furthermore, any departmental data that are required by the entire organization can also be communicated to a central site. So in our running example, Student Records can update its student database using its own system and also communicate any of this updated information to the college's centralized computer, thus making the information available collegewide.

The primary differences among decentralization, centralization, and distributed systems can be expressed more concretely by what Schaeffer (1987) refers to as the user–manager "Happiness Factor," which is graphically depicted in Figure 2.2. To illustrate this factor, consider an office building with no heating or air conditioning (decentralization) versus one with centralized heating and air conditioning (centralization) versus one that utilizes zoned heating and air conditioning (distributed). In the first example, office workers are in control over how much warm or cool air is delivered into their offices. They can do this by opening or closing windows or vents, bringing in space heaters, or installing window air conditioners. Here, workers are happy because they are in control, but managers of the building are unhappy. In the second example, a single thermostat controls the heating or cooling of the building. As a result, office workers have no control over how warm or cool their offices get. The amount of heated or cooled air might be sufficient, inadequate, or too much. In this scenario, building managers are happy, but workers are not. In the last example, each office has its own thermostat, which in turn is part of the overall building system. Zoned heating and air conditioning promote both local autonomy within the offices and still provide some degree of central control. Thus, both workers and managers are happy.

If a computer's native operating system includes built-in network support, then a NOS refers to that particular OS. Examples include Sun Microsystems' Solaris Operating System, Hewlett-Packard's HP-UX Operating System, and Microsoft's Windows 2000 Server incarnations. You can think of the NOS in this context as meaning *networkable* operating system.

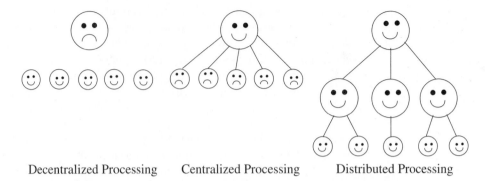

Decentralized Processing   Centralized Processing   Distributed Processing

FIGURE 2.2 In a decentralized environment, users are "happy" but managers are not; in a central-ized environment, managers are "happy" but users are not; in a distributed environment, both man-agers and users are "happy." Source: adapted from Distributed Processing, by F. Kaufman, p. 14. Copyright © 1977 Coopers and Lybrand. Found in *Data Center Operations: A Guide to Effective Planing, Processing, and Performance*, 2e, by H. Schaeffer, p. 272. Copyright @ 1987 Prentice-Hall.

Client/Server Model

Most network communications and applications today are based on a paradigm called the *client/server model*. This model describes network services (e.g., file transfers, ter-minal connections, electronic mail, and printing) and the programs used by end users to access these services. The client/server model can be thought of as dividing a network transaction into two parts: The client side (or front end) provides a user with an inter-face for requesting services from the network, and the server side (or back end) is re-sponsible for accepting user requests for services and providing these services transparent to the user. Both terms—client and server—can be applied either to appli-cation programs or to actual computing devices. A typical example of a client/server model is the common scenario in which an end user using an application program (Word) on a PC prints this document on a network printer. Thus, the user must access a specific network service (printing). In this context, the application program becomes a client when it relays the print request to the printer, while the printer is the server, which accepts and services this request. This is similar to being served in a restaurant. We are the client who issues a request (we order a plate of pasta), and our waiter or waitress is the server who services our request (he or she brings us the pasta).

A TCP/IP client/server interaction works as follows and is illustrated in Figure 2.3:

- A server process (i.e., program) is started on a host. This process notifies the host that it is ready to accept client requests. The server process then waits for a client process to contact it to request a specific network application service.
- Independent of the server process, a client process is started. This process can be in-voked either on the same system that is hosting the server process or on another computer that is connected to the same network to which the computer supporting the server process is connected. Regardless of which system is involved, a client pro-cess is usually initiated by a user through an application program. A request for ser-vice is sent by the client process to the host that is providing the requested service, and the server program running on that host responds to the request.

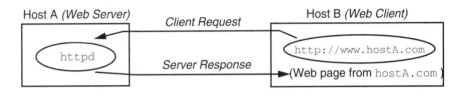

FIGURE 2.3 Example of an HTTP client/server process. Host A is running a Web server process, and host B is running a Web client process (i.e., a Web browser). When a user on host B opens a location (i.e., a Web address or URL), a connection is established to the machine at that address. The server accepts this request and services it by transferring the requested document to the client machine that made the request.

- When the server process has fully honored the client's request, the server returns to a "wait" state and waits for another client request from the same or another client.

In the margin:

On operating systems such as Windows 2000, Open VMS, and OS/400, different nomenclature is used for the same concept.

In TCP/IP, server processes on some systems (e.g., UNIX) are commonly referred to as *daemons* and are designated by the letter *d* at the end of a program's name. For example, the virtual terminal program *telnet* represents the client side, and its companion *telnetd* (pronounced "telnet dee") is the server side. Similarly, the file transfer program has both a client and a server side, *ftp* and *ftpd*. For example, in Figure 2.3, host A is running an HTTP server process (HTTPD), and a user on B is requesting a specific document from this server using a Web browser such as Microsoft's Internet Explorer or Netscape's Communicator. The Web browser is the application that supports the HTTP client protocol. When the server receives the request, it processes it by transferring the requested Web page or document to the client.

Computer systems that run specific server programs are commonly referred to by the application service they provide. For instance, a host that accepts and provides mail service is known as a *mail server;* a computer that provides users access to files remotely is known as a *file server;* a computer running HTTPD is known as a *Web server;* and a computer that runs a network news protocol (e.g., NNTP) is known as a *news server.*

Peer-to-Peer Model

Peer-to-peer is another model on which some network communications and applications are based. In a peer-to-peer environment, each networked host runs both the client and server parts of an application. (Contrast this to a client/server environment in which a host is capable of running only client-based applications, only server applications, or both client and server applications, thereby acting as a server for one application but a client for another application.) This is accomplished by installing the same NOS on all hosts within the network, enabling them to provide resources and services to all other networked hosts. For example, each networked host in a peer-to-peer environment can allow any other connected host to access its files or print documents on its printer while it is being used as a workstation. Once again, the key distinction between peer-to-peer computing and client/server computing is that the former requires each networked host to run both client and server parts of all applications. Examples of peer-to-peer network operating systems include Apple's MacOS, Artisoft's LANtastic, Novell's Personal

NetWare, and Microsoft's Windows NT/95/98/2000. Peer-to-peer networks are relatively inexpensive to purchase and operate and are fairly easy and straightforward to configure. They represent a cost-effective model for small organizations or departments that want to enjoy some of the benefits of networking but do not have the requisite resources (financial, human, or equipment). However, peer-to-peer networks can be less reliable than client/server-based networks. They usually also require the use of more powerful workstations for certain activities (e.g., sharing a database) than a client/server-based network.

It is important to point out that in a peer-to-peer networking model, access to a networked machine can only occur if the target host has been configured for this access. It's just like Apple Macintoshes, which support AppleTalk. If you go into the Control Panel and invoke "file sharing," you can make your Macintosh accessible to any other machine connected to the same network that also is running AppleTalk. In Windows, you select My Computer, followed by the disk you are interested in sharing, and then right-click the mouse. If your network Control Panel applet has been configured for file sharing, you will see the word "Sharing" in the menu and you simply select it and then set up the parameters for sharing that will be allowed. (If sharing is already enabled on Windows 95/98/2000, you will see a picture of a hand holding the device icon.) This is the concept of peer-to-peer networking—it enables users to easily share resources on a network.

Network printing is implemented in a similar manner. For example, a locally connected printer in Windows 2000 can be configured as a network device. During the initial configuration process, the "Add Printer Wizard" provides two radio buttons: Shared and Not Shared. Selecting Shared makes the printer accessible networkwide. (You also have to give it a name and identify the operating systems that will print to this printer so the proper device drivers are installed.) Now, assuming users have the proper access permissions, this printer appears as an available resource whenever users browse network resources in Windows Explorer.

Unlike peer-to-peer networking, in the client/server model, a network service can only be provided if a server program responsible for servicing a request is running on a particular host. For example, look back at Figure 2.3. If host A was not running the HTTPD process, then the request from host B would not be honored. This is why PCs used to access Internet services such as e-mail or the World Wide Web are relatively secure from being compromised by "outside" users. These machines usually run client versions of Internet-related applications. For example, Eudora from Qualcomm is an Internet-based mail client program that requests mail service from a mail server. It makes a connection to another machine running the server process to retrieve mail for a user. If you are running Eudora on your PC, Eudora users on other machines cannot connect to your machine just because you are running Eudora as well; your machine is not running an appropriate mail *server* program (Eudora is a client, not a server). Although some PC- or Macintosh-based Internet applications can be configured as servers (e.g., there are mail, ftp, gopher, and WWW server applications available for PCs and Macintoshes), most users only run the client side of these applications. As a result, without a server process running on a system, a network connection to that system cannot be made by another machine.

One note of caution, however. Client systems are becoming more complicated and capable as operating systems evolve. This means that the potential for compromise of a client system by a network hacker is becoming more of a reality everyday. Technologies such as cable modems and DSL connections (see Chapter 16) mean that a system is "always on" the Internet and accessible at all times to hackers and other unauthorized entities. While a client is less likely to get hacked than a server, it does happen—so don't be complacent about protecting your client system from network attacks. (See Chapter 17 for additional information about network security.)

Web-Based Model

A relatively new communications model that has emerged as a result of the Internet involves the World Wide Web (WWW or Web for short). From a communications model perspective, the Web can be viewed as a collection of Internet-based clients and servers that speak the same language, namely, the Hypertext Transfer Protocol (HTTP). The Web is accessible through Web browsers such as Netscape's Communicator or Microsoft's Internet Explorer. With the introduction of a programming language called Java in the mid-1990s by Sun Microsystems, animated and interactive Web pages can be designed in addition to the standard fare of displaying text and images. A direct result of the Web's evolution is a *Web-based* communications model, which fosters the notion of *the network is the computer,* a phrase coined in the late 1980s by Sun Microsystems' president, Scott McNealy. "The network is the computer" implies that by making resources available to users via a network, the network essentially becomes the single most powerful computer accessible. Thus, the network gives users access to more computing power than their desktop models. Although this communications model is still client/server based, it deserves separate recognition because of its potential for reshaping the manner in which resources are provisioned to the end user.

Web-based communications generally involves the use of specially designed network-based devices, commonly called *network appliances, netappliances, information appliances,* or *Internet appliances.* Unlike traditional desktop personal computers, network appliances usually support a single dedicated application, such as Web browsing or e-mail, and in some cases, do not have keyboards or monitors. Nevertheless, network appliances are powerful computing devices designed for the average consumer who wants Internet access but does not want to be burdened with the attending problems and maintenance issues often related to personal computer ownership. Network appliances also usually rely on *application service providers* (ASPs) (also known as *content service providers* or CSPs) to furnish users with computing resources via the Internet. Examples of network appliances include: handheld devices such as the PalmPilot; two-way "smart pagers" that can send and receive e-mail and provide Web access; "smart phones," which are specially designed corded desktop phones or wireless devices that provide standard voice communications as well as Internet access for e-mail service and Web browsing; and TV set-top boxes such as WebTV, which make Web access and e-mail service available to consumers via standard television sets. Other network appliances that are currently being developed or deployed as of this writing include: automobile dashboard-installed Internet connections and service; refrigerators with an indoor screen-based PC and modem for Internet access, which will enable the device to monitor food quantities and automatically order food from Internet-based grocers; and Internet-enabled fax machines that can send and receive e-mail.

See `http://devices.internet.com` for additional information about the rapidly evolving consumer network appliance marketplace.

In addition to consumer-based network appliances, there are business-based network appliances, which promote the concept of *thin client computing.* Collectively called *network computers* (NCs), these devices are inexpensive ($500 or less) network access units with functionality that allows some applications to be executed, but they are not as complete as what would typically be found on a traditional PC or workstation. Notice that although the term "computer" is part of its name, NCs are not really computers; NCs have a specialized, proprietary (and highly restricted) operating system and are usually diskless (i.e., most have no hard disk drives for local storage). NCs are stripped-down systems that use the network to access their applications dynamically. For example, if you need a word processor, a copy of a word processing application is downloaded from an application service provider's network server to your NC and stored in the NC's memory (RAM). Any documents you create are uploaded to and saved on the ASP's server. The idea behind NCs is to offer businesses a tremendous reduction in cost of ownership for each desktop location where a more expensive traditional terminal or PC would otherwise be used. By incorporating a massive server, or server "farm," with user NCs, companies can save money compared with purchasing fully loaded PCs for each user and dealing with their management and maintenance. In one sense, network computers have the "feel" of centralized computing—what goes around comes around. What do you call a computing device that relies on the network for its application? The answer of course is a terminal. The NC concept is very reminiscent of the era when terminals (dumb or otherwise) were connected to a mainframe. The old MIS people called this a network, but we know better now. It also is similar in concept to diskless UNIX workstations and X-terminals for those readers who are familiar with these two device types.

Emerging File-Sharing Model: Servant

Before we end this section, we need to mention one other type of network communications model that is emerging as a result of the music-sharing software program, Napster. Napster, which is electronically distributed by Napster, Inc., an Internet startup company founded in May 1999 (see `http://www.napster.com`), is a piece of software that resides on a PC host. A user configures Napster to specify which audio files residing on the user's hard drive may be downloaded. When this host is connected to the Internet, an active Napster process enables the host to link to all other Napster-running PC hosts that are connected to the Internet at that time and share audio files. Napster searches the hard drives of all the interconnected hosts running Napster, tells the user what files are available for downloading, and then enables the user to download a file(s) from a remote user's machine. Note that in this scenario, the local and remote systems are both client and server, similar to the peer-to-peer model. In this model, however, all the hosts running Napster are concurrently servers and clients, and one term used to denote a Napster-active host is *servant,* which is a combination of server and client. Thus, unlike the peer-to-peer model, which is one-to-one, or the client/server model, which is one-to-many, the servant model is many-to-many.

The servant concept, which effectively eliminates the need for centralized servers—the mainstay of the current client/server model—is expected to be expanded into a general file-sharing model that will enable all interconnected hosts to exchange any file, regardless of data type, residing on their hard drives. For example, following Napster's lead, servant-type programs are currently available that enable users to freely exchange video files. Before any paradigm shift from a client/server model to servant model becomes widely implemented, however, legal issues involving copyrights and intellectual property ownership must be resolved. For example, the Recording Industry Association of America and several musicians sued Napster in mid-2000 for copyright infringement. The lawsuit's basis is that Napster's file swapping software enables users to exchange audio files directly to their local PCs free of charge, which effectively usurps music publishers and musicians from receiving licensing fees or royalties. Napster claims that it does not violate copyright laws, because the company (and its product) serves only as a conduit among users. Although the result of this lawsuit was still unknown as of this writing, the Napster case demonstrates yet another instance in which new technology is challenging current laws as well as the entire royalty-based financial model for intellectual properties.

2.3   Communication Service Methods and Data Transmission Modes

In addition to the different models of communications, there are several methods in which data can be transmitted between source and destination nodes. These include *serial* and *parallel* communications, *synchronous, asynchronous,* and *isochronous communications,* and *simplex* and *duplex communications.*

Serial and Parallel Communications

Serial communication (also referred to as *serial transmission*) is a data transmission method in which the bits representing a character of data are transmitted in sequence, one bit at a time, over a single communications channel. Serial transmission is limited to the speed of the line. *Parallel communication* (also called *parallel transmission*) refers to the simultaneous transmission, each on a separate channel, of all the bits representing a character. In contrast to serial communications, a parallel link transmits a group of bits at one time. The number of bits varies from device to device. Consequently, assuming the line speeds were the same, in the same amount of time required to transmit one bit of information to a remote node over a serial line, we can transmit eight bits (or more) of data over a parallel line (Figure 2.4).

Serial Communication	Parallel Communication
$0 \rightarrow 1 \rightarrow 0 \rightarrow 0 \rightarrow 0 \rightarrow 1 \rightarrow 0 \rightarrow 1 \rightarrow$	$0 \rightarrow$
(1 channel transmits 1 bit at a time)	$1 \rightarrow$
	$0 \rightarrow$
	$0 \rightarrow$
	$0 \rightarrow$
	$1 \rightarrow$
	$0 \rightarrow$
	$1 \rightarrow$
	(8 parallel channels transmit 1 bit)

FIGURE 2.4 Serial and parallel communications. Here, the character E, which is 01000101 in binary, is transmitted 1 bit at a time (serial communication) and 8 bits at once in parallel.

Although parallel communication is capable of transmitting data more quickly than serial communication, it does have its limitations. For instance, parallel communication requires a relatively complex communication link, which is achieved through the use of large multiwire copper cables. Also, the longer the parallel link, the worse the degradation of the electrical signal from the most distant nodes. Consequently, in most networking applications, parallel communication is limited to peripherals directly connected to a system and for communication between systems that are relatively close (in many cases, within a few yards or meters of each other). Serial communication, on the other hand, with its simpler data path, is typically slower but enables data transmission to occur over existing communications systems that were not originally designed for such transmission. As a result, serial communications are seen nearly everywhere, including in terminal-to-systems connections, via leased phone lines for data transfers, dialup lines, satellite links, and high-speed fiber-optic lines.

The speed problems typically seen with serial communications are quickly evaporating, however, as higher-speed signaling technologies are introduced. Universal Serial Bus (USB) provides a multimegabit serial interface that not only replaces the need for a parallel port on a PC but can interconnect up to 128 devices at a much higher data transmission rate. Other technologies, such as Firewire, promise to keep serial communications very viable in the future at gigabit rates.

Synchronous, Asynchronous, and Isochronous Communications

In serial transmission, a receiver must be informed when a complete unit of data has been transmitted. For example, in Figure 2.4, a single character, E, was initially transferred. What happens if a second character (say, X) is transferred immediately after the first character? How does the receiving node identify the beginning (or ending) of a character when all it is seeing is a stream of bits (0s and 1s)? Obviously, without some way of identifying the beginning (or ending) of a character, the transmitted data would be indecipherable, resulting in some sort of communication breakdown.

Three methods can be employed to resolve this problem: We can synchronize the sending and receiving nodes so that the receiving node always knows when a new character is being sent, or we can insert within the bit stream special "start" and "stop" bits that signify the beginning and end of a character. The former technique is called *synchronous communication* and the latter is called *asynchronous communication*. We can also prenegotiate the data rate between devices and provide a continual bit-oriented data delivery rate. This is called *isochronous communication*.

Synchronous communication implies that communication between two nodes is monitored by each node. That is, all actions resulting in data transmission (and general link conditions) are closely synchronized between the nodes. If data are to be transmitted or received, then the nodes are aware of this transmission almost immediately and prepare for the exchange based on ordered data rates and sizes. Thus, the sending and receiving nodes are "in sync" with each other. Synchronous communication is also tied to the clocking inherent on the link.

Asynchronous communication (commonly referred to as *async*) is achieved by surrounding the data by special *start* and *stop bits*.[1] Hence, asynchronous communication is

---

[1] This process is commonly called *data encapsulation*. Thus, the data stream is encapsulated by start and stop bits.

sometimes called *start–stop transmission*. A direct consequence of the inclusion of these start–stop bits in the bit stream is that data can be transferred at any time by the sending node without the receiving node having any advance notification of the transfer. Thus, a receiving node does not necessarily know when a data string is being sent or the length of the message. An example of async communications is a computer terminal (sender) connected to a system (receiver). The system does not know when someone will begin entering data on a terminal. As a result, the system must always be in a "ready" state. Async communication lines remain in an idle state until the hardware on the line is ready to transmit data. Since the line is idle, a series of bits have to be sent to the receiving node to notify it that data are coming. At the conclusion of a transmission, the node has to be notified that the transmission is complete so that it can return to an idle state; hence, the stop bits. This pattern continues for the duration of the time the link is operative.

The difference between synchronous and asynchronous communications is sometimes better understood from the perspective of a mugging on a television crime drama. In an asynchronous mugging, you know the actor is going to be attacked and hence are ready for it, but you don't know when it will occur. In a synchronous mugging, you not only know the actor is going to be mugged, but you also know when, so again, you are ready for it. The term asynchronous is commonly used in the context of distance education: Through distance education technologies, education can be delivered "asynchronously," namely, at any time or place.

Isochronous communications was originally intended to service the requirements of constant and complete delivery of video communications over a transmission medium. For example, television signaling in the United States requires that 30 frames per second of video be delivered to the receiver for full-motion video. Not 29, not 31, but exactly 30. By establishing in the communications path that a session is going to require a specific bandwidth on the path and also communicating what the data rate will be, a continual and uninterrupted flow of data can be realized. This is critical for the delivery of applications such as video, which requires a constant bit rate (CBR) of information to be sent and delivered over the communications interface. Isochronous communications makes this happen. Networks such as ATM, SONET, and a special full-duplex version of Ethernet have isochronous capabilities. To extend the previous mugging analogy, isochronous is like being mugged all the time, but the mugger and muggee have agreed on the mugging interval and constancy before the mugging actually started.

From a computer networking perspective, most terminals, dialup modems, and local links are asynchronous in nature. Synchronous communication tends to be more expensive than asynchronous because of the need for sophisticated clocking mechanisms in the hardware. However, synchronous communication can eliminate up to 20% of associated overhead inherent in asynchronous communication. This allows for greater data throughput (i.e., the amount of real data that can be transferred in a given period) and better error detection. Synchronous communications are typically seen in higher-speed connections.

At this writing, isochronous communications are not very commonly used but are becoming more widespread as convergence of video, voice, and data over the same communications media pick up implementation commonality and speed. As companies adopt multipurpose networking, isochronous communications will be critical to deal with video and other CBR applications. (See Chapter 18 for additional information about convergence technologies.)

Simplex and Duplex Communications

Serial, parallel, synchronous, asynchronous, and isochronous communications represent different techniques for transferring data. Associated with these techniques are three different modes of data transmission used for communication purposes; each corresponds to a specific type of circuit—simplex, half-duplex, and full-duplex. These modes specify the protocols that sending and receiving nodes follow when transferring data. Figure 2.5 contains a summary of these three transmission modes.

Simplex communications imply a simple method of communicating. In a simplex communications mode, data may flow in only one direction; one device assumes the role of sender and the other assumes the role of receiver. Furthermore, these roles may not be reversed. An example of simplex communication is a television transmission—the main transmitter sends out a signal (broadcast), but it does not expect a reply since the receiving devices cannot issue a reply back to the transmitter. It's like a very boring person telling you his or her life story, and you can neither interrupt nor get away from it.

In *half-duplex transmission,* data may travel in either direction, but only one unit can send at *any one time.* While one node is in send mode, the other is in receive mode. Half-duplex communication is analogous to a conversation between two polite people—while one talks, the other listens, but neither talks at the same time. An example of a half-duplex communication is a Citizens Band (CB) transceiver. Users of a CB transceiver can either be senders or receivers but not both at the same time. Another example of half-duplex communication is a very polite game of tag between two people. Only two can play, only one can be "it" at a time, and you know who is going to be "it" next, don't you?

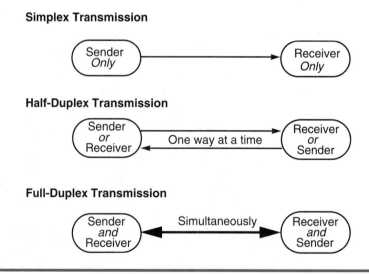

FIGURE 2.5 Three different transmission modes. Simplex is a "fixed" one-way transmission; half-duplex is a two-way transmission, but only one way at a time; full-duplex is a simultaneous two-way transmission.

A *full-duplex transmission* involves a link that allows simultaneous sending and receiving of data in both directions. Imagine, if you can, two people talking at the same time and each one understanding the other one perfectly. Compound this idea with the added benefit of not having to talk about the same thing. This is the realization of full-duplex communications—two separate but parallel transmissions occurring simultaneously. A full-duplex line can be thought of as the combination of two simplex lines, one in each direction working simultaneously.

2.4 Analog and Digital Communications

Two more terms that are frequently used when discussing computer communications and networking are *analog* and *digital*. An overview of the basic concepts related to analog and digital communications is provided here. This brief overview is then expanded on in Chapter 3, which is devoted entirely to analog and digital communications concepts, including analog-to-digital and digital-to-analog conversion methods.

Analog Communications

The term *analog* refers to any physical device or signal that can continuously vary in strength or quantity, for example, voltage in a circuit. The term *analog communication* refers to any method of communication based on analog principles. Typically, this term is associated with voice transmission because voice transmission facilities such as the telephone were initially analog-based. Analog communication is used in phones (both landline and cellular), modems, fax machines, cable television, and lots of other devices and network services. The other type of physical communication is *digital communication,* which we'll talk about later.

To help explain analog communications, we need to be familiar with the concept of *harmonic motion,* which has nothing to do with Nostradamus. Harmonic motion, which is also called *simple harmonic motion* because it is a very simple concept, can best be described by considering an object attached to a spring that is suspended from a ceiling (Figure 2.6). If

FIGURE 2.6 An object is attached to a spring that is suspended from a ceiling. When pulled and released, the spring oscillates up and down. This oscillation is called simple harmonic motion.

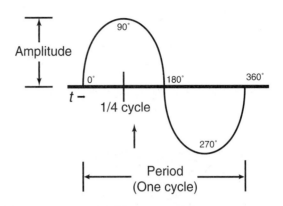

FIGURE 2.7 One cycle of a sine curve.

you pull on the attached weight and release it, the spring begins oscillating up and down. In a frictionless environment, this up and down motion would continue forever. This idealized motion is called simple harmonic motion, which is the basic model for vibratory or oscillatory motion and can occur in many different types of wave motion. Examples include mechanical oscillators, such as mass–spring systems similar to that shown in Figure 2.6, and pendulums; periodic motion found in the earth sciences, such as water waves, tides, and climatic cycles; and electromagnetic waves, such as alternating electrical currents, sound waves, light waves, radio waves, and television waves.

In any computer communications system, data are transmitted across a medium from sender to receiver in the form of electrical signals. In analog communications, signals flow across a wire in the form of electromagnetic waves. When viewed by an oscilloscope, these signals appear as continuous waves called sinusoidal waves, which resemble a sine curve (Figure 2.7). Sinusoidal waves are characteristic of anything that oscillates, and they have the following three attributes: *amplitude,* which is the level of voltage on a wire (or the intensity of a light beam when dealing with fiber-optic cable); *frequency,* which is the number of oscillations, or cycles, of a wave in a specified length of time; and *phase,* which is the point a wave has advanced within its cycle. A frequency rate of one cycle per second is defined as 1 hertz (abbreviated Hz) in honor of Heinrich Rudolph Hertz (1857–1894), a German physicist who in the late 1880s was the first to produce radio waves artificially. Thus, hertz is a measure of frequency in cycles per second.

The reciprocal of frequency is called *period,* which is the amount of time it take to complete a single cycle, that is, seconds per cycle.

As an illustration of these terms, consider the act of speaking over the telephone. If we speak softly or whisper, the amplitude (volume) decreases. If we speak loudly or scream, the amplitude increases. If we speak in a high-pitched voice, the frequency changes to more cycles per second than if we speak in a low-pitched voice, which requires fewer cycles per second (Figure 2.8). AM/FM radio, television speakers, public address systems, and most important of all, traditional telephones are all examples of analog devices, although there is a fast-growing trend toward a full-digital telephone system both in business and wireless networks. In data communications, data are represented in analog form by varying the voltage of the wave (called amplitude modulation, abbreviated AM), by varying the frequency (called frequency modulation,

---

Heinrich Rudolph Hertz (1857–1894)

Born in Hamburg, Germany, and educated at the University of Berlin, Heinrich Rudolph Hertz was a physicist who confirmed experimentally British physicist James Clark Maxwell's electromagnetic theory by demonstrating the nature of electromagnetic wave propagation. Hertz's studies led to the discovery of radio waves (also known as electromagnetic waves), which are a form of electromagnetic radiation. Hertz demonstrated that these waves travel at the speed of light and possess many other properties of light, including reflection, refraction, and polarization. Hertz's discovery led directly to radio, television, and radar. The unit of frequency, the hertz (Hz), which is a measure in cycles per second, was named in honor of him.

Interestingly, Maxwell and Hertz (as did many late 19th- and early 20th-century scientists) believed that electromagnetic waves were like sound waves and, thus, propagated through some previously unknown medium (as sound waves propagate through air). This invisible medium was called the *luminiferous ether* (or ether for short). The existence of the ether was eventually disproved by the German-born American physicist Albert Michelson and American chemist Edward Morley in 1881 and 1887. Neither Maxwell's nor Hertz's models were dependent on the ether's existence, however. This concept of an ether, though, remains with us in spirit today since the network technology known as Ethernet was named after the ether concept.

---

abbreviated FM), or by varying the phase (called phase modulation or phase shifting) of a wave. All three of these modulation techniques are discussed in Chapter 3.

Digital Communications

The term *digital* refers to any physical device or signal that is coded in a binary form. The term *digital communication* refers to any method of communication based on digital principles. A binary code is a system that uses the two symbols 0 and 1 to represent data. A single symbol, 0 or 1, is referred to as a binary digit, which is commonly called a bit (a contraction of the words *bi*nary and digi*t*). An example of digital data is binary coded text, which consists of letters of the alphabet and numerical data (collectively called alphanumeric data), as well as special character symbols such as $, @, <, and *. The assignment of a binary notation to these data is called a character code. One common code is the American Standard Code for Information Interchange (ASCII). For example, the ASCII representations of the digit 5, the lowercase letter c, and the special character @ are, respectively, 00110101, 01100011, and 01000000. Another example

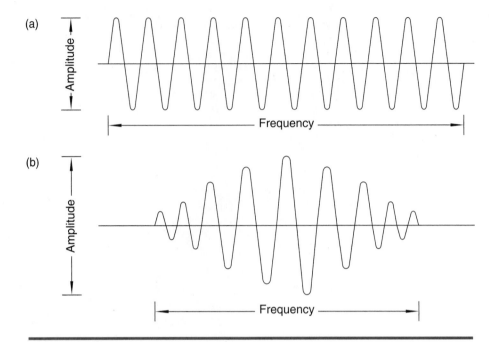

FIGURE 2.8 When represented in electrical form, sound waves produced by the human voice are continuous in nature. These waves vary in strength (called amplitude) and vary in the number of times they fluctuate over time (frequency). For example, the wave in (a) has less amplitude and greater frequency than the wave in (b). When we speak louder, amplitude increases. When we speak in a high-pitched voice, frequency increases.

NOTE OF INTEREST

Wavelength
Wavelength, as the name implies, is a measure of the length of a wave. It is the distance an electrical or light signal travels in one complete cycle. Radio signals are often described and classified according to their wavelength. For example, "the 40-meter ham band" is an explicit reference to radio waves that are approximately 40 meters long. In the RF spectrum (discussed in Chapter 6), "short-wave radio" and "microwave radar" are relative references to different wavelengths. For light signals, which are used in fiber-optic transmissions, wavelength and frequency are inversely related. That is, as one increases, the other decreases. This relationship is expressed using the formula, $\lambda = \dfrac{c}{f}$, where λ is the wavelength in meters, c is the speed of light (3×10^8 meters per second), and f is the frequency in hertz.

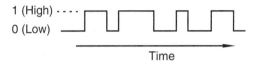

FIGURE 2.9 Example of a digital signal waveform.

of digital data is graphics, which are produced using specially designed software packages. Some packages transform numerical data into charts or graphs; other packages code the position of a point or points into standard *xy* or *xyz* coordinates for processing. A third example is digital photography in which photographs are captured and saved in digital format instead of using conventional analog methods. Today, nearly every type of signal can be converted into a digital format (i.e., as 0s and 1s), including traditional analog signals such as voice and video.

In digital communications, signals are *discrete* (i.e., off or on, 0 or 1). What makes a signal discrete is that there is no in-between. This is similar to a light bulb—either it is off or it is on. There is no "sort of on" or "sort of off" (although you could put a dimmer in the circuit, making the light bulb an analog device!). Therefore, we can conclude that a digital signal consists of two (and only two) states: electrical current applied or no current at all. On most systems, if power is applied, it is considered "on" and is usually interpreted as 1 by a computer. If there is no power, then we have an "off" state, and this is interpreted as 0. This is called *binary interpretation,* and the "on" and "off" states are interpreted as bits 1 and 0, respectively. Figure 2.9 shows a typical digital waveform as measured over some time interval. Thus, digital signals are created by the absence or presence of an electrical current.

Each type of digital circuit has a particular specification for which a range of currents represents a 0 and another represents a 1. This is necessary because of real-world factors such as electrical noise, cable resistance, and differences in ground potential between the transmitter and the receiver. We'll get deeper into some of these factors later, but for now, consider an example involving RS-232 (also called EIA-232), a standard serial interface that is discussed in Chapter 4. In RS-232, a 0 is represented by any voltage between -5 and -15 volts, and a 1 is represented by any voltage between $+5$ and $+15$ volts (Figure 2.10). Let's say that the transmitter sends a 1, for which it uses 12 volts. By the time it gets to the receiver, however, the potential might be reduced to 10 volts because of the electrical resistance of the wire. Nevertheless, the receiver interprets the signal as a 1 because it falls between +5 and +15 volts. A less technically oriented example is a game of darts. You get credit for a bull's-eye if your dart hits anywhere within the appropriate circle. If it were required to hit a single point for a bull's-eye, there would be far fewer bull's-eyes. The "engineers" who designed the game of darts took into account some real-world factors.

In our RS-232 example, you will note that there is a big "hole" from -5 to $+5$ volts. This gap provides for random electrical signals, called *noise,* which can create false signals in this range. (The concept of noise is discussed later in this chapter.) When engineers design communication circuits, they must take into account the possibility

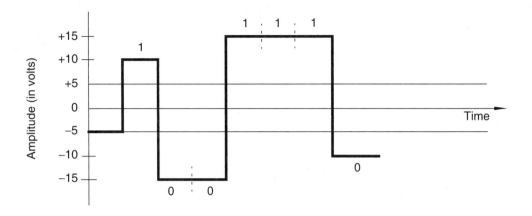

FIGURE 2.10 In RS-232, voltage that varies between −15 and −5 volts is interpreted as a binary 0, and voltage that varies between +5 and +15 volts is interpreted as a binary 1. Voltage that varies between −5 and +5 volts is ignored; that is, no interpretation is made.

of noise interfering with communications because in the real world of digital communication signaling, things are not quite as simple as "on" and "off." Thus, if a receiver detects, say, +3 volts, nothing happens. That is, the receiver "sees" neither a 0 nor a 1. On the other hand, if a receiver gets more than 15 volts, then both the transmitter and receiver will probably fail completely. At this point, all is lost, and 1s and 0s don't matter anymore. Such destructively high voltages might be the result of a nearby lightning strike, a component failure at either end, or a high-voltage power line short-circuiting to the communication cable.

2.5   Speed and Capacity of a Communications Channel

Any discussion about computer communications and networking inevitably involves the "speed" or capacity of a communications channel. From a most general perspective, speed implies data rate, that is, how fast data can be transmitted from one node to another; capacity implies the amount of data that can be carried by a communications channel. There is often some confusion about the concepts of speed and capacity and the terms used to describe them. Four frequently used and often misunderstood terms are bandwidth, data rate, throughput, and baud. A discussion of these terms follows.

Bandwidth and Data Rate

In analog communications, *bandwidth* refers to the total capacity of a communications channel. It is the difference between the highest and lowest frequencies capable of being carried over a channel. The greater the bandwidth, the more signals that can be carried over a given frequency range. For example, typical voice-grade lines transmit frequencies from 300 Hz to 3300 Hz. Thus, the bandwidth is 3300 Hz–300 Hz = 3000 Hz, or 3 kilohertz (kHz).

In digital communications, bandwidth refers to *data rate,* which is the amount of data that can be transferred over a communications medium in a given period. Data rate is measured in bits per second (bps) and can vary considerably from one type of channel to another. For example, LANs have data rates ranging from 4 million bits per second (referred to as megabits per second and abbreviated Mbps) to 1000 Mbps; the bandwidth of dialup connections using modems ranges from 300 bps to 33,600 bits per second (33.6 kbps) or 56 kbps; and WANs that use high-speed circuits can range anywhere from 1.5 Mbps to 45 Mbps to 622 Mbps and higher. Data rate should not be confused with *baud rate.* A baud is a unit of signaling speed, named after the French engineer Jean Maurice Emile Baudot (1845–1903). It is the number of discrete changes in a single period of a signal. For example, a communications channel transmitting at 300 baud means that the signaling rate of the channel is changing 300 times per second. Although baud represents a measurement of data transmission speed, it does not correspond to the number of bits being transmitted per second. Thus, baud rate is different from data rate. A more detailed discussion that explains this difference is reserved for Chapter 3, where the concepts related to baud are presented. For now, just realize that the two terms rarely are the same. Unless otherwise noted, we will always express bandwidth in terms of bits per second, or as a multiple of bits per second such as: kilobits per second (kbps), which is 1000 bps; megabits per second (Mbps), which is 1 million bps; and gigabits per second (Gbps), which is 1 billion bps.

Throughput

Another relatively misunderstood concept is *throughput.* We often hear bandwidth and throughput used interchangeably. However, there is, indeed, a difference. When applied to computer communications and networking, bandwidth represents the theoretical capacity of a communications channel expressed in bits per second. To understand the difference between bandwidth and throughput, let's assume the network we use is a Fast Ethernet LAN. (*Note:* We discuss Fast Ethernet in Chapter 9.) Fast Ethernet has a maximum transfer rate of 100 Mbps. Does this mean we can expect all data transfer rates to be at 100 Mbps? No. Extraneous factors such as a node's processing capability, input/output processor speed, operating system overhead, communications software overhead, and amount of traffic on the network at a given time all serve to reduce the actual data rate. Consequently, there is a difference between the maximum theoretical capacity of a communications channel and the actual data transmission rate realized. This "reality rate" is known as throughput, which refers to the amount of data transmitted between two nodes in a given period. It is a function of hardware or software speed, CPU power, overhead, and many other items. Summarizing, bandwidth is a measure of a channel's theoretical capacity; it describes the amount of data a channel is capable of supporting. Throughput, on the other hand, informs us of what the channel really achieves. Just because a medium or LAN architecture is specified to operate at a certain data rate, it is not valid to assume that this rate will be the actual throughput achieved on any given node or group of nodes.

Noise

Before we leave this section, there is one more concept we should discuss: noise, or more precisely, *electrical noise.* In the context of computer communications and networking, noise is any undesirable, extraneous signal in a transmission medium. It occurs in two forms— *ambient noise* and *impulse noise.* Ambient noise, also called *thermal noise,* is always present and is generated primarily by transmission equipment such as transmitters, receivers, and repeaters. Ambient noise also can be induced by external sources such as fluorescent light transformers, electrical facilities, heat, and in fact, the background radiation from the Big Bang. If ambient noise is present, receiving equipment can have problems in distinguishing between incoming signals. Impulse noise consists of intermittent, undesirable signals induced by external sources such as lightning, switching equipment, and heavy electrically operated machinery such as elevator motors and photocopy machines. Impulse noise increases or decreases a circuit's signal level; this causes the receiving equipment to misinterpret the signal. Whichever the type or source, noise degrades the quality and performance of a communications channel and is one of the most common causes of transmission errors in computer networks. Although some noise is always present, much of it can be avoided through proper cable installation.

There's one more type of noise we'll touch on briefly: *intermodulation noise.* Frequency division multiplexing, a concept we will discuss later, mixes multiple frequencies of data transmission on a single transmission medium. Intermodulation noise occurs when two of the frequencies interact to produce a phantom signal at a different frequency, which can be either the sum or the difference of the two original frequencies. For example, let us assume for simplicity that, in a frequency division multiplexing environment, a coaxial cable carries three different signals, at frequencies f_1, f_2, and f_3. Intermodulation noise can occur if f_3 is equal to the sum or difference of f_1 and f_2. Either way, the spurious signal at frequency f_3 can interfere with the transmission of valid data at that frequency.

Related to the concept of noise is Shannon's limit, which is a mathematical theorem named for the mathematician who derived it, Claude Shannon. Shannon's limit describes a model for determining the maximum data rate of a noisy analog communications channel. (A second theorem, Nyquist's theorem, determines the maximum data rate of a channel for noiseless environments. Nyquist's theorem is presented in Chapter 3.) Shannon's limit is given by the following formula:

$$\text{Maximum Data Rate } (MDR) = H \log_2\left(1 + \frac{S}{N}\right)$$

- *MDR* is given in bits per second (bps)
- *H* = bandwidth in Hertz (Hz)
- $\left(\dfrac{S}{N}\right)$ = a measure of the signal-to-noise ratio (often measured in decibels)

The signal-to-noise ratio (abbreviated SNR) is a measure of signal quality expressed in decibels (dB), which is a measurement that quantifies the strength of a signal. (A decibel is one-tenth of a *bel,* which was named after Alexander Graham Bell and is used to compare electrical power levels and sound intensities.) SNR is the ratio of signal strength to background noise on a cable. More specifically, SNR is the ratio between the desired signal and the unwanted noise in a communications medium.

A good example of an application of Shannon's limit is modem speeds. During the mid- to late 1990s, modem speeds increased from 14,400 bps to 28,800 bps, but then topped out at 33,600 bps. Conventional analog modems achieved a peak rate of 33,600 bps (or in some cases, 38,400 bps) because this was the maximum data rate possible for existing analog communications channels based on the channel's frequency and signal-to-noise ratio. An example of how this is calculated using Shannon's limit is shown in Box 2.1. To get around

BOX 2.1 Example of Shannon's Limit

Given dB $= 10 \left[\log_{10} \left(\frac{s}{n} \right) \right]$:

- If $\left(\frac{s}{n} \right) = 10$, then $10 \left[\log_{10} \left(\frac{s}{n} \right) \right] = 10[\log_{10}(10)] = 10(1) = 10$. Thus, SNR = 10 dB.

- If $\left(\frac{s}{n} \right) = 100$, then $10 \left[\log_{10} \left(\frac{s}{n} \right) \right] = 10[\log_{10}(100)] = 10(2) = 20$. Thus, SNR = 20 dB.

- If $\left(\frac{s}{n} \right) = 1000$, then $10 \left[\log_{10} \left(\frac{s}{n} \right) \right] = 10[\log_{10}(1000)] = 10(3) = 30$. Thus, SNR = 30 dB

and so on.

Example: If H = 3000 Hz and the signal-to-noise ratio (SNR) is 30 dB, what is the MDR?

Solution: Note from above that 30 dB implies $\left(\frac{s}{n} \right) = 1000$. Using Shannon's limit we have

$$MDR = (H) \left[\log_2 \left(1 + \frac{s}{n} \right) \right]$$
$$= (3000)[\log_2(1 + 1000)]$$
$$= (3000)[\log_2(1001)]$$

At this stage, we must now solve for $\log_2(1001)$. There are several ways in which this can be done. We can use a calculator that is capable of solving logarithms in base 2, we can use natural logarithms, or we can estimate the value. We will demonstrate the last two methods since we do not have a calculator capable of solving log functions in base 2.

Using Natural Logarithms

$$\log_2 1001 = x$$
$$2^x = 1001$$
$$\ln 2^x = \ln 1001$$
$$x \ln 2 = \ln 1001$$
$$x = \frac{\ln 1001}{\ln 2}$$
$$x \approx \frac{6.909}{0.6931}$$
$$x \approx 9.967$$

Substituting 9.967 into the equation:

$MDR = (3000)(9.967) = 29,902$ bps

Using Estimation

$$\log_2 1001 = x$$
$$2^x = 1001$$

$2^1 = 2$	$2^6 = 64$
$2^2 = 4$	$2^7 = 128$
$2^3 = 8$	$2^8 = 256$
$2^4 = 16$	$2^9 = 512$
$2^5 = 32$	$2^{10} = 1024$

Note that $\log_2(1001)$ must be between 9 and 10 since the logarithm's argument (1001) is between $2^9 = 512$ and $2^{10} = 1024$. Since it is closer to 10, we estimate it to be 9.9. Substituting 9.9 into the equation:
$MDR = (3000)(9.9) = 29,700$ bps

As a result, the maximum data rate of a communications channel with these parameters is approximately 30,000 bps (30 kbps). Note that this is the upper limit and in practice will rarely be achieved on a consistent basis.

Claude Elwood Shannon (1916–)

Born in Gaylord, Michigan, Claude Shannon graduated from Michigan University with degrees in mathematics and engineering and, in 1940, from the Massachusetts Institute of Technology (MIT) with master's and doctoral degrees in mathematics. In 1938, as a student at MIT, Shannon published the paper, "A Symbolic Analysis of Relay and Switching Circuits," which was based on his master's thesis. This paper is noteworthy because it was the first published work to describe a relationship between George Boole's logic theories of the mid-1800s and current-day relay circuits. Shannon theorized that the on–off states of electronic relay circuits could be represented respectively as a series of 1s and 0s, which could lead to information being electronically processed via on–off switches. Shannon's theories effectively provided the mathematical foundation for designing digital electronic circuits, which form the basis of modern-day information processing.

After graduating from MIT, Shannon served as a National Research Fellow at the Institute for Advanced Study at Princeton University and, in 1941, joined Bell Telephone Laboratories as a research mathematician. While at Bell Labs, Shannon applied his information-processing theories as part of his research for improving the transmission and reliability of information across long-distance telephone and telegraph lines. He described his research in the article, "Mathematical Theory of Communication," which was published in the *Bell System Technical Journal* in 1948. This paper, which quickly became known as "Information Theory" (or IT for short), contained the first published account of the term *bit* to denote the abbreviation of "binary digit" as a representation of the individual information units a computer processes. The paper also extended Nyquist's theory and the effect noise has on a communications channel. Information theory served as the basis for which the theoretical limit of any channel's capacity could be determined and eventually led to the design of efficient, error-free transmission over noisy channels. Shannon continued working for Bell Labs until 1972. The IEEE Information Theory Society's Claude E. Shannon Award has since been instituted to honor exemplary contributions to the field of information theory. A copy of Shannon's "Mathematical Theory of Communication" is available in Adobe PDF format from `http://cm.bell-labs.com/cm/ms/what/shannonday/shannon1948.pdf`.

Shannon's limit, hybrid analog–digital connections were established that consisted of both analog and digital channels. (Shannon's limit applies only to analog channels.) This enabled modem designers to increase modem speeds to 56,000 bps. However, even this strategy could not circumvent the physical limitations of analog circuitry, and hence, 56K modems became the fastest type of conventional dialup modems available that involve analog channels. (See Chapters 3 and 16 for additional information about modems and modem data rates.)

2.6   Multiplexing and Switching

Two other concepts related to computer communications and networking are multiplexing and switching. *Multiplexing* is a technique used to place multiple signals on a single communications channel. This is performed by a device called a multiplexer (mux for short). *Switching* is a process that involves establishing an appropriate path, which a data message will follow as it travels throughout a network en route between a sending source and a destination node. Switching is performed by switches, which use specific predetermined criteria as the basis of path determination. Multiplexing and switching are the two basic techniques used for transmitting data within a communications network. They make it possible for transmission facilities to be shared among users in an efficient and economical manner. A separate examination of these two concepts follows.

Multiplexing

Multiplexing is a process that enables data from multiple transmission channels to share a common link. In its simplest form, multiplexing involves combining data from several relatively low-speed input channels and transmitting these data across a single high-speed circuit. At the receiving end, this multiplexed data stream is then separated (a process called demultiplexing) relative to the data's respective channels and delivered to the corresponding output facilities. This is depicted in Figure 2.11. Through multiplexing, many different transmissions are possible using a single medium. For example, a communication medium can be divided into separate channels with one channel transmitting data, another transmitting voice, and a third transmitting video. Each of these separate, independent transmissions can occur simultaneously. Several multiplexing strategies abound, including frequency division multiplexing (FDM), time division multiplexing (TDM), statistical multiplexing, demand access multiplexing (DAM), wavelength division multiplexing (WDM), code division multiple access (CDMA), and inverse multiplexing. A brief overview and description of these strategies follow. (CDMA is a multiplexing scheme used in wireless communication, which is described in Chapter 4.)

Frequency Division Multiplexing (FDM)   This technique partitions the available transmission frequency range into narrower bands, each of which is a separate channel. The idea behind FDM is to divide the main frequency into appropriate subfrequencies with each subfrequency customized to the bandwidth of data that it must carry. This makes FDM very efficient and cost-effective. An example of FDM is the broadcast

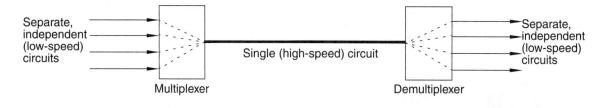

FIGURE 2.11   Multiplexing involves combining several separate (relatively low-speed) transmission facilities into a single (high-speed) communications channel for data transmission purposes. At the receiving side, this single channel is then demultiplexed into the corresponding channels. Multiplexing is performed via a multiplexer, or mux for short; demultiplexing is performed via a demultiplexer, or demux for short.

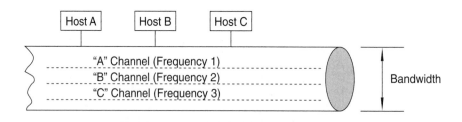

FIGURE 2.12   In frequency division multiplexing, the frequency of a communications medium is divided into subfrequencies, which are assigned to connected nodes, resulting in parallel transmissions.

method used by television stations. The FCC allocates a range of frequencies called a channel for a station to use, and the station subdivides this band into various subchannels. One subchannel carries engineering information for the station's technical staff, a second carries the analog signal for audio reception at the television set, and a third subchannel carries the video signal. What a remote unit can receive depends on the frequency for which the unit has been configured. FDM-based transmissions are parallel in nature (Figure 2.12).

Time Division Multiplexing (TDM)   This technique enables more than one signal to be transmitted over the same channel but at different time intervals. Time division multiplexing (TDM) assigns to each node connected to a channel an identification number and a small amount of time (i.e., a time slot) in which to transmit (Figure 2.13). Unlike FDM-based transmissions, which are parallel in nature, TDM-based transmissions are serially sequenced. Thus, nodes take turns transmitting over the channel, with each time slot permanently assigned to a specific channel. The amount of time a node gets for data transmission is a function of the number of nodes competing for the channel, the order in which nodes are requested for information (called the polling order), and the *clocking interval* of the TDM device.

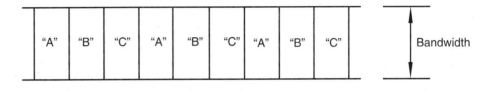

FIGURE 2.13   In time division multiplexing, the channel is partitioned into a sequence of time slots and each node is assigned a specific time slot in which to transmit.

Statistical Multiplexing   This method of multiplexing allocates part of a channel's capacity only to those nodes that require it (i.e., have data to transmit). This strategy permits a greater number of devices to be connected to a channel because not all devices necessarily require a portion of the channel at exactly the same time. A statistical multiplexer "senses" which input channels are active and then dynamically allocates bandwidth to these channels. Contrasting FDM and TDM with statistical multiplexing, note that in FDM and TDM a communications channel is partitioned into separate, fixed rate channels, which are not necessarily used all of the time. In statistical multiplexing, however, the channel is allocated to a device only when that device has data to transmit.

Demand Access Multiplexing (DAM)   In demand access multiplexing, a pool of frequencies is managed by a "traffic coordinator." The traffic coordinator assigns pairs of communications frequencies to a requesting station—one pair for transmission, a second pair for reception. This is the "demand" part—you demand a pair of frequencies, and if available, the traffic coordinator assigns them to you. The traffic coordinator then connects the two pairs of frequencies to another set of frequencies. This is the "access" part. When one or both stations are finished communicating, the allocated frequencies are deallocated and returned to the frequency pool, where they are made available for other incoming requests. This is the multiplexing part. DAM is similar to virtual memory allocation on computers. A "pool" of memory exists for all running processes. When a new process is started, memory is allocated from the pool. When the process is completed, the associated memory returns to the pool for use by another process. A major use of DAM exists in cellular communications.

Wavelength Division Multiplexing (WDM)   Wavelength division multiplexing is used with fiber-optic cables. In fiber-optic technology, electrical signals originating from a sending computer are converted into optical signals using a light source such as a laser or a light-emitting diode (LED), which is a semiconductor device that converts electrical energy into light. (Fiber-optic issues are discussed in Chapter 5.) WDM involves the simultaneous transmission of these light sources over a single fiber-optic channel. The light sources, which are of different wavelengths, are combined by a WDM multiplexer and transmitted over a single line. En route to their destination, the wavelengths are amplified simultaneously by optical amplifiers. When the signals arrive, a WDM demultiplexer separates them and transmits them to their respective destination receivers. We give an illustration of WDM in Figure 2.14. WDM can be

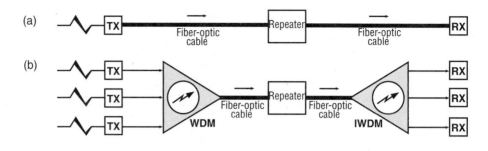

FIGURE 2.14 In a typical fiber-optic installation (a), a fiber-optic transmitter converts an electronic signal into light, which is sent through the fiber-optic cable to its destination. Repeaters, which are optical amplifiers, regenerate the light signal at appropriate points along the way. With wavelength division multiplexing (b), electronic signals originating from multiple data sources, each operating at different wavelengths, are combined into a wavelength multiplexer (WDM) and output onto a single fiber-optic cable. A demultiplexer (IWDM) is employed at the receiving end to split the signals. Source: adapted from Clark, 1997.

beneficial from both cost and performance perspectives. On the cost side, WDM saves money because it increases bandwidth without requiring the installation of additional fiber. The idea of minimizing or completely eliminating new fiber installations is attractive because installing new fiber can be expensive. On the performance side, WDM consolidates data from separate channels onto a single line. WDM also can reduce the number of optical-to-electrical conversions—required by today's fiber-optic networks—by implementing a strictly optical transmission method.

Inverse Multiplexing   Inverse multiplexing is the reverse of multiplexing. Instead of partitioning a single communication medium into several channels, an inverse multiplexer combines several "smaller" channels (i.e., low-speed circuits) into a single high-speed circuit. For example, through inverse multiplexing, two T1 circuits (1.544 Mbps) can be combined to form a 3-Mbps channel. Several Internet service providers use this strategy to offer their customers a larger "pipe" to the Internet. This technique is also sometimes generically called *line aggregation.*

Switching

As we stated earlier, switching involves the process of linking a sending source to an appropriate destination. Two basic switching strategies used in computer communications networks are *circuit-switching* and *packet-switching.* Networks based on the former are called circuit-switched networks, and those based on the latter are called packet-switched networks.

Circuit-Switching   In a *circuit-switched network,* a dedicated physical circuit must be established between the source and destination nodes before any data transmission can take place. Furthermore, this circuit must remain in place for the duration of a transmission. The public telephone system, known formally as the public switched telephone network (PSTN), is a good example of a circuit-switched network. When we dial a telephone number, a switch that resides at the telephone company's central office establishes a logical connection to a set of wires based on the number we dialed. This set of wires will either connect to a wire center (also called a frame) that services a particular area, or it will connect to another central office that contains yet another switch. Ultimately, a circuit will be established that connects the caller's and receiver's telephones. One feature of circuit-switching is that it promotes link sharing. Circuit-switching enables different data transmissions (i.e., different sender–receiver pairs) to use the same communications channels. There is one caveat, though. Sharing cannot occur at the same time because, during a particular transmission, the communications channel is reserved exclusively for that specific sender–receiver pair.

Packet-Switching   In a *packet-switched network,* instead of using a dedicated physical circuit for every node-to-node communication, nodes share a communications channel via a *virtual circuit.* A virtual circuit is a nondedicated connection through a shared medium that gives the high-level user the appearance of a dedicated, direct connection from the source node to the destination node. A virtual circuit is created by multiplexing a physical link so that the physical link can be shared by multiple network programs or data transmissions. This concept is extremely valuable for providing low-cost communications capabilities because it is very expensive to provide dedicated links for every data transmission, as in circuit-switched networks. A definition of *virtual* has been memorably coined in this way: "If you can see it and touch it, it's *physical;* if you can see it but can't touch it, it's *virtual;* if you can't see it and can't touch it, it's *gone.*"

In a packet-switched network, messages are partitioned into smaller messages called *packets,* which may contain only a few hundred bytes of data, accompanied by addressing information and sequence numbers. A packet represents the smallest unit of data that can be transferred via a given network. Packets are sent to the destination node one at a time, at any time, and not necessarily in a specific order. The network hardware delivers the packets through the virtual circuit to the specified destination node, which is responsible for reassembling them in the correct order. Unlike circuit-switched networks, where a dedicated link is established a priori, every packet in a packet-switched network must carry the destination node's address. In a circuit-switched network, only the first data message carries the destination address, which is needed to initially set up the link. Most data communications networks are packet-switched.

As mentioned in Chapter 1, packet-switching can be implemented using either a virtual circuit or a datagram service. The difference between these two transport schemes is that with virtual circuit packet-switching all the packets are transported along the same virtual path as if the path were a dedicated circuit. Furthermore, virtual-circuit packet-switching employs a store-and-forward transmission in which complete packets are stored first and then forwarded. In datagram packet-switching. however, packets are transmitted independently of each other. This implies that packets can travel along separate paths, which requires separate routes to be established for each packet transmission. Moreover, packets can arrive out of order, which requires the destination node to reassemble them in the correct order.

Circuit-Switching versus Packet-Switching   The main difference between circuit- and packet-switched networks is the use of *bandwidth,* which is the maximum capacity of a communications channel (see Chapter 3). In a circuit-switched network, a circuit's performance is predetermined and fixed. This means that bandwidth is allocated in advance and guaranteed for the entire transmission. Once a circuit is established, the full capacity of the circuit is available and the capacity of the circuit will never be reduced due to other network activity. This advantage of circuit-switched networks also gives rise to a disadvantage. Specifically, circuit costs are independent of the amount of data being transmitted; therefore, any unused bandwidth is wasted. On the other hand, packet-switched networks acquire and release bandwidth dynamically as needed. One major advantage is that several communications can occur between nodes concurrently using the same channel. Again, this advantage becomes a disadvantage when, as packet-switched networks become overloaded with more traffic, delays and congestion are introduced. Nevertheless, packet-switched networks are cheaper and offer better performance than circuit-switched networks. Furthermore, given recent developments in high-speed switching hardware, the channel capacity issue has eased a bit. Table 2.1 provides a summary of the differences between circuit- and packet-switching.

Hybrid Switching   A third strategy is *hybrid switching,* which combines the principles of circuit- and packet-switching. This technique first partitions a message into packets (packet-switching) and transmits each packet via a dedicated circuit (circuit-switching). As soon as a packet is ready for transmission, a circuit meeting appropriate bandwidth requirements is established between the sending and receiving nodes. When the packet reaches its destination, the circuit is broken down so that it can be used again. This scenario has many advantages, but it requires extremely fast circuit-switching equipment.

TABLE 2.1   Circuit-Switching versus Packet-Switching

Circuit-Switched	Packet-Switched
1. Bandwidth is allocated in advance and is guaranteed for the entire transmission.	1. Bandwidth is acquired and released dynamically on an as-needed basis.
2. Once circuit is established, the full capacity of the circuit is available for use, and the capacity of the circuit will never be reduced due to other network activity.	2. Several communications can occur between nodes concurrently using the virtual links over the same physical channel.
3. Circuit costs are independent of the amount of data being transmitted and hence any unused bandwidth is wasted.	3. As packet-switched networks become overloaded with more traffic, delays and congestion are introduced.
	4. Packet-switched networks are more cost-effective and offer better performance than circuit-switched networks.

2.7   Network Architecture and the OSI Reference Model

Network architecture is a formal, logical structure that defines how network devices and software interact and function. It defines communication protocols, message formats, and standards required for interoperability. New hardware or software products created within a specific architecture are generally compatible with other products created within the same architecture. Network architectures are designed by standards organizations and manufacturers. For example, IBM designed the Systems Network Architecture (SNA), Digital Equipment Corporation designed the Digital Network Architecture (DNA), and the International Organization for Standardization (ISO) designed the Open Systems Interconnect (OSI) architecture.

The OSI Model

In the early days of networking, as new networks were being developed, interoperability and design issues began to emerge. To address these issues, and to accommodate the interconnection of various proprietary and heterogeneous networks, ISO developed in 1974 an architecture and reference model intended to serve as the foundation for future network standards activities. The resulting model was formally called the *reference model for open systems interconnection,* or OSI for short. The OSI model provides a detailed set of standards for describing a network; it is a framework for the development of network protocol standards.

One of OSI's most redeeming features is that it formally defines and codifies the concept of *layered* network architecture. It uses well-defined operationally descriptive layers that describe what happens at each stage in the processing of data for transmission. This layering concept is extremely important because networks are nontrivial systems. Given a network's complex nature, it is extremely difficult to design an architecture that (a) has a high degree of connectivity, (b) is reliable, and (c) is easy to implement, use, and modify. Layers help reduce this complexity. By organizing a network's functions into a series of hierarchical layers, the design of a network is greatly simplified. For example, a layered approach enables the functions and services of one layer to be completely independent of and isolated from other layers. This allows us to change a layer's capabilities without significantly modifying the entire architecture. So as new technologies become available for one layer, they can be implemented without affecting the other layers. In theory, a layer can be completely removed, dramatically changed, and reinserted without affecting the other layers above or below it. Network layering is analogous to modular programming. Just as large computer programs are partitioned into separate, independent program modules, layers partition a network architecture into separate, independent components. Each layer is responsible for performing a specific set of functions and for providing a specific set of services. Specific protocols define both the services and the manner in which these services are provided.

The layers of the OSI model are (from top to bottom, starting at layer 7, the highest, and going to layer 1, the lowest): application, presentation, session, transport, network, data link, and physical. Each layer consists of two parts: a *service definition,* which defines the type of service a layer provides, and a *protocol specification,* which details the rules governing the implementation of a particular service. Lower layers provide services to upper layers. Collectively, these layers define the communication capabilities needed to effect communication between any two devices. Figures 2.15, 2.16, 2.17, and 2.18

Application (7)
• Consists of protocols that define specific user-oriented applications such as e-mail, file transfers, and virtual terminal.
• Examples include FTAM (File Transfer, Access, and Management) for remote file handling, X.400 (for e-mail), and CMIP (Common Management Information Protocol) for network management.

Presentation (6)
• Provides for data formats, translations, and code conversions.
• Concerned with syntax and semantics of data being transmitted.
• Encodes messages in a format that is suitable for electronic transmission.
• Data compression and encryption done at this layer.
• Receives message from application layer, formats it, and passes it to the session layer.
• In practice, this layer is usually incorporated within the application layer.

Session (5)
• Provides for coordination between communicating processes between nodes.
• Responsible for enforcing the rules of dialog (e.g., Does a connection permit half-duplex or full-duplex communication?), synchronizing the flow of data, and reestablishing a connection in the event a failure occurs.
• Examples include AppleTalk Data Stream Protocol for reliable data transfer between two nodes, NetBEUI (an extension of NetBIOS), and Printer Access Protocol for accessing a PostScript printer in an AppleTalk network.
• Uses the presentation layer above it and the transport layer below it.

Transport (4)
• Provides for error-free delivery of data.
• Accepts data from the session layer, partitions data into smaller packets if necessary, passes these packets to the network layer, and ensures that packets arrive completely and correctly at their destination.
• Examples involve varying classes of the OSI Transfer Protocol—TPx, where $x = \{0, 1, 2, 3, 4\}$. Each class describes a specific level of service quality such as whether a transmission provides for error detection or correction, or if the service is connection-oriented or connectionless.

Network (3)
• Responsible for the end-to-end routing or switching of data to establish a connection for the transparent delivery of data.
• Addresses and resolves all inherent problems related to the transmission of data between heterogeneous networks.
• Uses the transport layer above it and the data link layer below it.
• Formatted messages are referred to as packets.

Data Link (2)
• Responsible for the transfer of data between the ends of a physical link.
• Provides for error detection, "framing," and flow control.
• Resolves problems due to damaged, lost, or duplicate frames.
• Formatted messages are referred to as frames rather than packets.

Physical (1)
• Responsible for transmitting raw bits over a link; it moves energy.
• Accepts frames from the data link layer and translates the bit stream into signals on the physical medium, which lies below it.
• Concerned with issues such as the type of wire being used, the type of connector (i.e., interface) used to connect a device to the medium, and signaling scheme.

FIGURE 2.15 Summary of the OSI layers and functions.

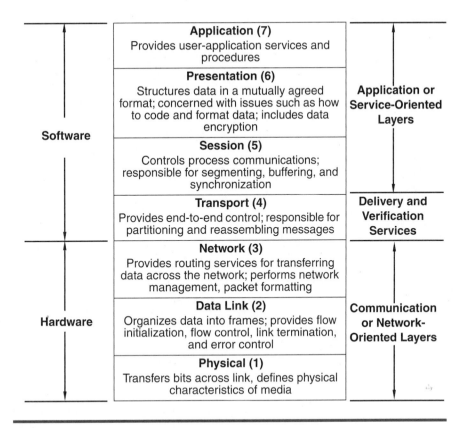

FIGURE 2.16 Another view of the OSI layers. Source: adapted from Conrad, 1988b.

provide additional information about OSI layers. (For readers who want to compare the OSI model to the TCP/IP model, see Figures 8.8, 8.9, and 8.10.)

OSI Service Types

In UNIX, an SAP is called a *socket,* and an SAP address is a *socket number.*

There are two different types of services OSI layers provide: *connection-oriented* and *connectionless.* Some layers also include multiplexing as an additional service, but this does not necessarily transcend all layers of the architecture. Services are available at *service access points* (SAPs), with each SAP having a corresponding address.

Connection-Oriented Service   This type of service implies that prior to the transfer of data a physical (and virtual) link is established between the sending and receiving nodes. This link remains in effect for the duration of the session. After the session is completed, the link is removed. Characteristics of a connection-oriented service include: wasted bandwidth, because the link must remain established even during idle periods of a transmission; a high potential for a hung network, since there is always a possibility that a link will not be terminated; and (on the bright side) guaranteed sequential

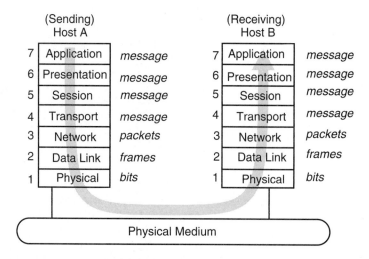

FIGURE 2.17 The OSI layering process begins at the application layer of the source machine where a message is created by an application program. This message moves down through the layers until it reaches layer 1. Underlying layer 1 is the actual physical medium. Data are then transmitted across this medium to the receiving host, where the information works its way up through the layers. As messages move down the layers, they are encapsulated with headers that are germane to a specific layer. These headers are removed as the data are passed upward through corresponding layers at the receiving host.

arrival of packets at the destination node. The telephone system is an example of connection-oriented service. You establish a connection (you dial a number); you transfer data over this circuit when the connection is made (you begin talking when the receiver is picked up); communication occurs in the proper sequence (words and sentences are received in the correct order); and you release the connection at the conclusion of the transfer (you hang up the phone, which frees the circuit). Note also the issues of wasted bandwidth and a hung network. If a telephone connection has been made but no one is talking, bandwidth is wasted because the circuit is established but not being used. Anyone trying to contact your house during this period of silence would be greeted by a busy signal—a "hung" connection.

Addressing on an information packet is not necessary for connection-oriented service because a physical, dedicated link is established between sending and receiving nodes before transmitting the information packets.

Connectionless Service This type of service differs from connection-oriented service in that no physical link is established between sending and receiving nodes prior to data transmission. Instead, a message is partitioned into packets and routed through the network. Each packet is independent of the other packets that carry parts of the message and hence must carry a destination address.

Packets also can arrive out of order. Think of the post office as providing connectionless service. If you send someone five separate letters numbered one through five, you must place the recipient's address on each letter. Once mailed, the letters do not necessarily follow exactly the same delivery route, and it is possible for the recipient to receive the letters out of sequence (e.g., letter three is received before letter two). Connectionless service is also either *reliable* or *unreliable*. Unreliable service requires no

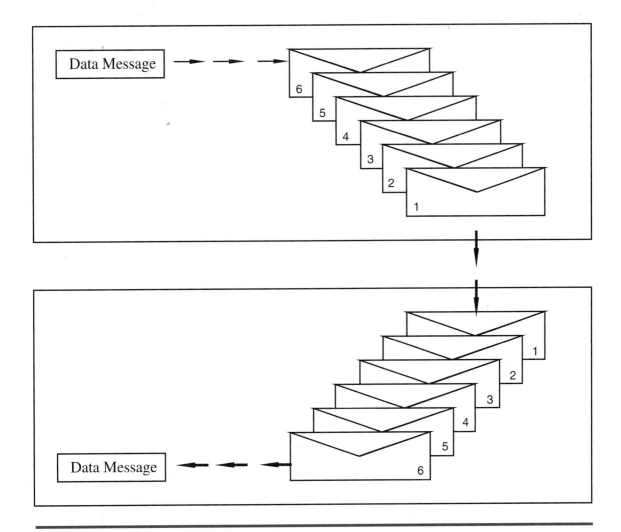

FIGURE 2.18 How layers work. Each layer "envelops" the data with its protocol. Each layer has a corresponding layer on the remote (destination) node, which is called a peer.

acknowledgment of receipt of data from the receiving node to the sending node. This is called a *datagram service.* Reliable service requires an acknowledgment. This is called an *acknowledged datagram service.* Using our post office metaphor, these services compare with mailing a "regular" letter versus mailing a registered letter with a return receipt request.

One of the best and most practical examples of these services is the Internet. We will illustrate the two services by sending a message across the Internet. Prior to doing so, though, we need to provide a little addressing methodology.[2] To send a message from

_____

[2] If any or all of the information that follows is unclear, don't worry about it for now. Many of these issues will be discussed in more detail in subsequent chapters. For the present, though, just try to concentrate on the concepts.

one node to another within the Internet, three different addresses are needed. The first address is the *hardware address,* which uniquely identifies each node. Hardware addresses are provided by the data link layer, which is discussed in Chapter 5. The second address is the *network address,* which identifies the network to which a node is connected. In TCP/IP, this is called an *Internet address* or an *IP* (for Internet Protocol) *address.* Network addresses operate at the network layer. Each network node that is part of the Internet has a unique IP address. (IP addresses do more than simply identify the network. See Chapter 8 for additional information about IP.) The third address is called the *port address,* which uniquely identifies a specific user application such as e-mail. All network applications have corresponding identifiers called *port numbers.*

To send a message from one node to another, a message is first created at the application layer. It undergoes whatever formatting is required as it works its way down through the layers. When the message reaches the network layer, a network address is assigned to the message. This network address identifies the specific network to which the destination host is connected. Depending on the protocol, this service is either connectionless or connection-oriented. For example, Telnet and SMTP are connection-oriented services. The network layer determines the path the message must follow to reach the destination node. It also encapsulates packets into IP datagrams and passes them to the data link layer. At the data link layer, the destination node's hardware address is added to the packet. This address uniquely identifies the location of the destination node within the destination network. The data link layer, among other tasks, also formats the packet into *frames,* which are like packets but exist at a lower level, and checks the integrity of each frame (see Chapter 5). Frames are then passed to the physical layer, which places them on the medium for transmission.

OSI Today

In the early to mid-1990s, the networking literature was replete with articles that extolled various advantages and virtues of OSI. Many network administrators, in fact, developed strategies to eventually migrate their networks to OSI, and some administrators went as far as professing that everyone's network should only support a single protocol: OSI. Even the U.S. government jumped onto the OSI bandwagon when it established GOSIP (Government OSI Profile), which mandated that all government organizations purchase OSI-compliant networking products beginning in 1992. In spite of all the hoopla and hyperbole, OSI never emerged as *the* network protocol, particularly in the United States. It seems that OSI got railroaded by TCP/IP, which serves as the protocol suite of the Internet (see Chapter 8). For example, in 1995, GOSIP was modified to include TCP/IP as an acceptable protocol suite for GOSIP compliance, and today, although OSI protocols are in use, their presence pales in comparison to that of their TCP/IP counterparts. Today, the most notable uses of OSI as a protocol suite implementation are in the upcoming worldwide Air Transport Network and in many power company power grid interoperation networks between companies. Several reasons (all speculative, of course) why OSI never materialized as *the* networking protocol follow.

- *Standards Development:* TCP/IP and OSI differ in the way their standards are developed and tested. As a formal international standards organization, ISO possesses considerable inertia, and the process of developing standards is painstaking. From its initial development, OSI was designed to do everything at once, and from the top down. In stark contrast to this approach, TCP/IP supports an open process for standards-making participation by its end users. The development of new or modification of existing TCP/IP protocols is also done on an as-needed basis. Furthermore, research, development, and testing of new or modified protocols can be performed on a production network, the procedure is in the open via Request for Comments (RFC) documents, and distribution of TCP/IP standards is free. (See Chapter 8 for more information about TCP/IP's standards process.) In contrast, OSI protocols are copyrighted and carry a nominal purchasing fee.

- *Snob Factor:* The underlying policy of TCP/IP was directed at connecting hosts primarily within the United States—specifically academic, research, government, and military organizations. OSI, on the other hand, was the product of an international standards body (ISO). Consequently, many European users perceived TCP/IP as a parochial de facto standard specific to the United States and wanted to embrace OSI. In the United States, though, users did not want to accept anything "different" and stayed true to TCP/IP.

- *Versatility and Robustness:* Compared to OSI, TCP/IP is simple and dependable, it has a proven track history (more than 25 years), it is nonproprietary, its developers have a pragmatic approach to its enhancement, and it meets the networking needs of a diverse population, including researchers, educators, and business personnel. Some people—including Vint Cerf, who is regarded as one of the Fathers of the Internet and who professes "IP over everything"—think of TCP/IP as the universal language of networking.

- *The Internet:* TCP/IP is inextricably linked to the Internet.

Nonetheless, the OSI model has had a lasting impact on networks, including TCP/IP. Although its acceptance has diminished considerably during the last half of the 1990s, the OSI model continues to provide a detailed standard for describing a network. It is from this perspective that the network design community continues to regard the OSI model as a theoretical framework for the development of networks and their architecture.

End-of-Chapter Commentary

The terms and concepts discussed in this chapter serve as the basis for understanding many of the concepts presented in the remaining chapters of the book. These terms will be further expanded, and additional terms will be defined as new concepts are introduced. For example, analog and digital communications concepts are discussed in more detail in Chapter 3, and we give a detailed presentation about the Internet and TCP/IP protocols in Chapter 8. The concept of the OSI layers is also examined in more detail in later chapters: Chapter 4 is dedicated to the physical layer; Chapter 5 presents a discussion on the data link layer; network hardware components that operate at either layer 1 or 2 are presented in Chapter 6; and Chapter 7 addresses concepts related to the network layer. Other chapters also expand on specific layer-2 and layer-3 protocols. Finally, in the event that you need a quick review of any of the terms or concepts presented here (or elsewhere in the book), see the Glossary.

CHAPTER REVIEW MATERIALS

SUMMARY

• Every network application such as e-mail has an underlying network application protocol (e.g., POP) that describes the manner in which the application is to be implemented across a network.

• Decentralized systems are characterized by autonomous control by non-MIS personnel, centralized systems place control of all operations and management under a single department (e.g., MIS), and distributed systems are a hybrid of centralized and decentralized systems.

• Distributed systems represent a special case of computer networks.

• The client/server paradigm represents a specific model that describes the interaction between the network services available via a network and the programs used by the user to access these services. The peer-to-peer model requires every host of a network to support both the client and server parts of an application. A third model, Web-based communications, although based on the client/server paradigm, has strong overtones of centralized computing. Its basic premise is that the network is the computer and that all resources can be acquired from the network via a Web-based application.

• Types of communication service methods include serial and parallel and synchronous, asynchronous, and isochronous communications. Serial communication is a data transmission method characterized by the sequential transmission of bits over a single channel; parallel communication refers to the simultaneous transmission of all bits of which a character is comprised. Synchronous transmissions are characterized by the absence of start–stop bits in the transmission of data; asynchronous transmissions include start–stop bits to designate the beginning and ending of a transmitted character; isochronous communications refers to the delivery of time-sensitive data such as voice or video transmissions. Networks capable of delivering isochronous service preallocate a specific amount of bandwidth over regular intervals to ensure that the transmission is not interrupted.

• Three data transmission modes include simplex, half-duplex, and full-duplex. In simplex communications, data flow in only one direction; in half-duplex, data flow in either direction but not simultaneously; and in full-duplex, data simultaneously flow in either direction.

• Analog data are continuous in nature and vary in strength and quantity over time. Digital data, however, are discrete in nature and are represented as binary digits, 0 and 1.

• All data sent from one point to another are transmitted as analog or digital signals (although frequently it is a little of both). Analog signals are continuously varying waveforms represented by a sine wave, and they have characteristics of amplitude, frequency, and phase. Digital signals are discrete and consist of one of two states: electrical current applied or no current at all. (This is expanded on in Chapter 3.)

• Bandwidth refers to the total capacity of a communications channel. In an analog context, bandwidth is the difference between the highest and lowest frequencies of a signal that the channel can transmit without a large attenuation of the signal and is measured in Hertz. In a digital context, bandwidth implies the maximum data rate of a channel and is measured in bits per second (bps).

• Throughput is another measure of a channel's capacity and is measured in bps. Compared to bandwidth, which provides a theoretical measure of the channel's data rate, throughput implies the data rate the channel actually achieves in a particular situation.

• A surface-level distinction between data rate and baud rate was also made. The former is a measurement of data throughput and the latter is a measurement of signal change. (This concept is discussed in greater detail in Chapter 3.)

• Electrical noise is an inherent part of all communications channels. Noise is any undesirable signal and is found in two forms: ambient, which is always present and generated by transmission equipment, and impulse, which is intermittent and induced by external sources such as lights or machinery. Shannon's limit can be used to calculate the maximum data rate of a noisy channel.

• Multiplexing is a technique used to place multiple signals on a single communications channel. Multiplexing strategies include: frequency division, which involves partitioning a channel's frequency into smaller, narrower frequencies; time division, which involves providing nodes with a specific time slot in which to transmit; demand access, which involves allocating pairs of frequencies—one for transmitting and one for receiving—to requesting nodes; statistical multiplexing, in which part of a channel's capacity is allocated only to nodes with data to transmit; wavelength division multiplexing, which involves combining and transmitting different wavelengths of a fiber-optic light source across a single channel; and inverse multiplexing, which combines several smaller (lower-speed) channels into a single higher-speed channel.

• Switching is a process that involves correctly connecting an input to its corresponding output. Circuit-switching uses a dedicated, physical circuit for every node-to-node communication. Packet-switching enables nodes to share a communications channel using a virtual circuit, which is a nondedicated connection that appears as if it were a dedicated, direct connection between the communicating nodes.

• Network architecture defines communication protocols, message formats, and standards required for interoperability. The OSI model is a seven-layered structure that provides a detailed set of standards for describing a network. The layered approach is important in a network architecture because each layer can be treated as independent modules, with lower layers providing service to upper layers. Two types of OSI services are available: connection-oriented, which is analogous to conventional telephone service, and connectionless, which is similar to the type of service provided by the post office. Although OSI protocols are not widely implemented, the OSI model continues to serve as a framework for the development of network protocol standards.

VOCABULARY CHECK

ambient noise
amplitude
analog communications
analog data
analog signal
application program
application protocol
asynchronous communications
bandwidth
baud
centralized system
circuit-switching
client/server model
connectionless service
connection-oriented service
content service provider (CSP)
data rate
decentralized system
demand access multiplexing (DAM)

digital communications
digital data
digital signal
distributed system
full-duplex communications
frequency
frequency division multiplexing (FDM)
half-duplex communications
hertz
Internet Protocol (IP)
inverse multiplexing
isochronous communications
multiplexing
network appliance
network architecture
network computer (NC)
network operating system (NOS)
noise

OSI model
packet-switching
parallel communications
peer-to-peer model
serial communications
servant
service access points (SAPs)
Shannon's limit
simplex communications
statistical multiplexing
synchronous communications
throughput
time division multiplexing (TDM)
virtual circuit
wavelength division multiplexing (WDM)
Web-based networking

REVIEW EXERCISES

1. Explain the difference between a network application and its corresponding protocol. Give a specific example (other than that described in the book) as part of your response.
2. Construct a protocol hierarchy, similar to the one given in Figure 1.1, for Windows NT.
3. List some of the advantages and disadvantages of decentralized, centralized, and distributed systems.
4. In your opinion, do you think network administration should be decentralized, centralized, or distributed? Why?
5. Explain why a terminal network does not satisfy our definition of a computer network, which was given in Chapter 1.
6. What is the difference between a distributed system and a computer network?
7. What is a network operating system (NOS) and how is it different from a computer operating system such as Windows or Mac OS?
8. Describe the client/server networking model.
9. Determine if your desktop computer is a terminal, server, or client.
10. Explain the difference between client/server and peer-to-peer networks.
11. Explain the concept of the Web-based networking model.
12. Give a nonnetworking example that describes the difference between serial and parallel communication. (*Hint:* Consider the transportation industry.)
13. Contrast synchronous, asynchronous, and isochronous communications.
14. In the section on synchronous and asynchronous communications, we stated that synchronous communication can eliminate up to 20% of associated overhead inherent in asynchronous communication. How did we come up with this percentage?
15. In problem 4 of Chapter 1, you were asked to describe the communications protocol being observed during a U.S. presidential press conference or during a military briefing. Would you characterize this protocol as simplex, half-duplex, or full-duplex? Why?
16. Explain the differences between analog and digital communications.
17. What is simple harmonic motion and what does it have to do with analog communications?
18. In terms of frequency and amplitude changes, compare male and female voice patterns.
19. In the United States, common household electrical supply is rated at 60 hertz. Explain what this means.
20. Explain the difference between bandwidth and throughput.
21. A 2-gigabyte (GB) Iomega® Jaz drive has a maximum data transfer rate of 8 Mbps. If you have to transfer 1.6 GB of data from a Jaz disk to your computer's hard disk, what is the least amount of time it will take to complete this transfer? What factors might contribute to a slower transmission rate?
22. What is electrical noise and where does it come from?
23. A communications channel must support up to a 10-kbps data rate. The channel has a signal-to-noise ratio of 50 decibels. What is the maximum bandwidth in hertz for the channel?
24. Explain the concept of multiplexing.
25. Describe and contrast time division multiplexing and frequency division multiplexing.
26. Which do you think is more efficient for irregular data flow and why: FDM, TDM, or statistical multiplexing?
27. What is switching and how does it differ from multiplexing?
28. What is the OSI model and what is its role relative to network architecture?
29. Identify and describe the layers of the OSI reference model.
30. What is the difference between a connection-oriented service and a connectionless service? Describe one situation each where you think connection-oriented service is desirable over connectionless, and vice versa.

SUGGESTED READINGS AND REFERENCES

ABRAMS, M. D. 1982a. *Computer Networking Tutorial.* Rockville, MD: Computer Network Associates.

———. 1982b. *Data Communications Tutorial.* Rockville, MD: Computer Network Associates.

AMBORT, D. 1990. Standards from Where? *LANtimes,* July, 61–64.

CLARK, E. 1997. WDM Expands Fiber's Horizons. *LAN Magazine,* March, 67-71.

CONRAD, J. W. 1988a. Open Systems Interconnection. In *Handbook of Communication Systems Management,* ed. J. W. Conrad. 237-251. Boston: Auerbach Publishers.

———. 1988b. Application of Data Communications Protocol Standards. In *Handbook of Communication Systems Management,* ed. J. W. Conrad. 253-266. Boston: Auerbach Publishers.

———. 1988c. Standards and Architecture for Local Area Networks. In *Handbook of Communication Systems Management,* ed. J. W. Conrad. 291-297. Boston: Auerbach Publishers.

DYSON, P. 1995. *The Network Press Dictionary of Networking.* 2nd ed. San Francisco: Sybex.

FEIBEL, W. 1995. *The Network Press Encyclopedia of Networking.* 2nd ed. San Francisco: Sybex.

FISHER, S. 1990. OSI Across the Water. *LANtimes,* July, 70.

GALLO, M., and W. HANCOCK. 1999. *Networking Explained.* Boston: Digital Press.

HANCOCK, B. 1989. *Network Concepts and Architectures.* Wellesley, MA: QED Information Sciences.

HIGGINS, K. J. 1994. How Evolution of TCP/IP Eclipsed OSI. *Open Systems Today,* 9 May, 54.

KAUFMAN, F. 1977. *Distributed Processing.* Newark, NJ: Coopers & Lybrand.

MALAMUD, C. 1991. TCP/IP—A Dependable Networking Infrastructure. *Networking Computing,* April, 84-86.

MARTIN, J., and K. CHAPMAN. 1989. *Local Area Networks: Architectures and Implementations.* Upper Saddle River, NJ: Prentice-Hall.

MCCLOGHRIE, K., and M. T. ROSE. 1994. Back to Basics: The Internet Transport Layer. *Connexions: The Interoperability Report,* June, 2-9.

MILLER, M. A., 1992. *Troubleshooting TCP/IP: Analyzing the Protocols of the Internet.* San Mateo, CA: M&T Books.

NOOR, A. I. 1988. Comparisons of Internetworking Architectures. In *Handbook of Communication Systems Management,* ed. J. W. Conrad. 267-276. Boston: Auerbach Publishers.

POSTEL, J. 1981a. Internet Protocol. *RFC 791,* September.

———. 1981b. Transmission Control Protocol. *RFC 793,* September.

QUARTERMAN, J. S., and J. C. Hoskins. 1986. Notable Computer Networks. *Communications of the ACM,* 10, 932-971.

SCHAEFFER, H. 1987. *Data Center Operations: A Guide to Effective Planning, Processing, & Performance.* 2nd ed. Upper Saddle River, NJ: Prentice-Hall.

SPENCER, L. T. 1990. Defining the OSI Model. *LANtimes,* September, 59.

TANENBAUM, A. S. 1996. *Computer Networks.* 3rd ed. Upper Saddle River, NJ: Prentice-Hall.

3 | Analog and Digital Communications Concepts

After studying this chapter, you will be able to do the following:

1. Distinguish between analog and digital signals.
2. Identify the amplitude, frequency, and phase of a given sine curve.
3. Determine if a given analog signal represents amplitude modulation, frequency modulation, phase modulation, or quadrature amplitude modulation.
4. Describe the operation of a modem and codec.
5. Describe the digital-to-analog conversion process.
6. Describe the analog-to-digital conversion process.
7. Construct the waveform based on Manchester encoding for a given bit stream and identify the bit stream of a given Manchester encoded waveform.
8. Construct the waveform based on differential Manchester encoding for a given bit stream and identify the bit stream of a given differential Manchester encoded waveform.
9. Construct the waveform based on nonreturn to zero, invert on ones (NRZI) encoding for a given bit stream and identify the bit stream of a given NRZI encoded waveform.
10. Understand the difference between data rate and baud rate.
11. Determine a modem's data rate given its baud rate.
12. Understand how the data rates of T1, DS-1, E-1, OC-1, and STS-1 circuits are constructed.
13. Understand the difference between T1 and SONET.

CHAPTER OUTLINE

In Section 2.4, we presented an overview of the basic concepts related to analog and digital communications. As part of the discussion, we learned that data are transmitted across a medium in the form of analog or digital signals. In this chapter, we extend the discussion by examining the various processes involved in taking analog or digital data, converting them into either analog or digital signals, and then transmitting these signals via an appropriate transmission facility. In Sections 3.1 and 3.2, we detail specific analog-to-digital, digital-to-analog, and digital-to-digital conversion schemes. Then, in Section 3.3, using the fundamental concepts related to some of these schemes, we revisit data rate and baud rate to provide a better understanding of why these two terms are not necessarily the same and should not be considered synonymous. We conclude the chapter with a discussion of the T1-carrier system and SONET, both of which serve as excellent applications of many of the terms and concepts presented in this and the previous two chapters.

3.1   Representing Data as Analog Signals

Referring to Figure 3.1, we see that regardless of the data type being transmitted (analog or digital), either type can be transmitted as analog or digital signals. In this section, we examine the various ways in which analog and digital data are converted to analog signals suitable for transmission. In the next section, we present a discussion of the manner in which analog and digital data are represented as digital signals. A summary of the most common analog-to-digital and digital-to-analog conversion methods is shown in Figure 3.2.

Converting Analog Data to Analog Signals

In the world of computer communications and networking, analog and voice communications are considered analogous. As a result, we will focus our discussion of converting analog data to analog signals from this perspective. During the early development

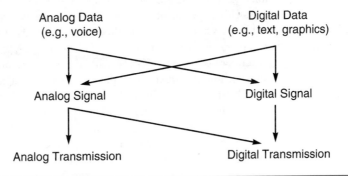

FIGURE 3.1   Analog data are transmitted as either analog or digital signals using either analog or digital transmission facilities. Digital data are transmitted as either analog or digital signals using digital transmission facilities only.

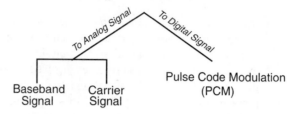

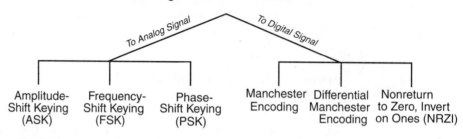

FIGURE 3.2 Various conversions schemes for representing analog or digital data as analog or digital signals.

stages of copper-based analog telephone networks, it was discovered that voice conversations can be transmitted adequately from 300 Hz to 3330 Hz. As a result, the telephone networks were originally designed to transmit voice conversations within a 3000 Hz range. Voice signals that generate frequencies less than 300 Hz or greater than 3300 Hz are discarded. This was not considered a problem because the human ear is not sensitive enough to hear subtle changes in frequency. Furthermore, even if someone's conversation was unintelligible, we can always ask the person at the other end of the line to repeat what he or she said. Transmitting voice messages via an analog communications system, then, involves re-creating human speech in the form of sound waves. This is performed by the telephone set. Without going into too much detail, a telephone set converts sound into electrical signals at the sender's end and then reconverts these electrical signals into sound at the receiver's end.

There are two basic ways in which analog data are represented as analog signals: at their original frequency—called a *baseband signal*—or at a different frequency. As an illustration of each, consider a standard (analog) telephone conversation. When we pick up a telephone and speak into it, the telephone network accepts (i.e., transmits) our analog voice signal at face value (but somewhere within the 300 Hz to 3330 Hz range). This face value acceptance is an example of a baseband signal. Alternatively, the telephone network can combine our signal into another signal (called a *carrier*) and then transmit these combined signals at a different frequency. A carrier is a continuous signal that operates at a predefined frequency. Changing a carrier so that it can represent data in a form suitable for transmission is called *mod-*

ulation. In analog modulation, an analog signal that represents the data is converted into another analog signal, which is the carrier. Recall from our earlier discussion of analog and digital communications in Chapter 2 that data represented as analog signals imply the data must be in the form of a sinusoidal wave. Further recall that this waveform has three defining attributes: amplitude, frequency, and phase. Thus, characteristics of a carrier that can be modified include the signal's amplitude, frequency, and phase. Modifying the amplitude of a wave (i.e., the signal's strength) is called *amplitude modulation* (AM), modifying a wave's frequency (i.e., its pitch) is called *frequency modulation* (FM), and modifying the phase of a wave (i.e., temporarily delaying the natural flow of the waveform) is called *phase modulation* (PM). All three modulation techniques are used in conventional radio and television broadcasting; FM and PM are also used in satellite communications. A discussion of these (and other) modulation techniques is provided in the next subsection.

Converting Digital Data to Analog Signals

Transmitting digital data (e.g., output from a computer) across an analog-based communications network (e.g., the plain old telephone system, POTS) requires representing the digital data in analog form. This is done by modifying (i.e., modulating) a continuous analog signal (i.e., a carrier) at the sender so that the signal conforms to the digital data being transmitted and then converting the signal back into digital form at the receiver. Thus, the modulation process involves coding and decoding data for transmission. The device that performs these functions is called a *modem,* which is a contraction of the words *modulator* and *demodulator.* Two modems are required—one at each end of a transmission line—and both modems must use the same modulation technique. A sending modem first produces a continuous carrier signal and then modifies the signal using a specific modulation technique. When the modified signal is received by the receiving modem, the signal is then converted back into digital form. When used in the context of converting digital data (or signals) into analog signals, the modulation techniques of AM, FM, and PM discussed earlier are respectively called *amplitude-shift keying* (ASK), *frequency-shift keying* (FSK), and *phase-shift keying* (PSK). A brief discussion of each modulation technique follows.

Amplitude-Shift Keying   Amplitude-shift keying (ASK) alters the amplitude of a signal (i.e., the signal's strength) so that it conforms to the digital data (0s and 1s). The process of ASK involves varying the signal's voltage while keeping the frequency constant. One amplitude is used to represent a binary 0 and a second amplitude is used to represent a binary 1. The concept of ASK is shown in Figure 3.3 where the graph of the standard sine curve, $y = \sin x$, is superimposed on the graph of $y = 3\sin x$, which has an amplitude three times that of the standard sine curve. In this illustration, a binary 0 could be represented by the curve with amplitude 1 and a binary 1 could be represented by the curve with amplitude 3, or vice versa. In more practical terms, a sending ASK modem generates a continuous carrier and uses this unmodulated signal to represent a binary 0; the modem also modulates this signal (using ASK) to represent a binary 1. A receiving ASK modem then interprets the unmodified carrier as 0 and the modulated signal as 1.

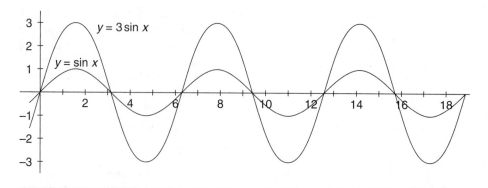

FIGURE 3.3   Concept of amplitude-shift keying. In this illustration, a binary 0 could be represented by $y = \sin x$ (amplitude of 1), and a binary 1 could be represented by $y = 3 \sin x$ (amplitude of 3).

Frequency-Shift Keying   Frequency-shift keying (FSK) alters the frequency (i.e., cycles per second) of a signal so that it conforms to the digital data (0s and 1s). Amplitude is kept constant. One frequency is used to represent a binary 0 and a second frequency is used to represent a binary 1. The concept of FSK is shown in Figure 3.4 where the graph of the standard sine curve, $y = \sin x$, is superimposed on the graph of $y = \sin 3x$, which has a frequency three times that of the standard sine curve. (Recall that frequency in this context is cycles per second.) Note that $y = \sin 3x$ has three complete cycles within the same time frame in which $y = \sin x$ completes one cycle. In this illustration, a binary 0 could be represented by the curve with frequency 1 and a binary 1 could be represented by the curve with frequency 3, or vice versa. Different frequencies (and hence different sine waves) are created using different tones. Once again, in practical terms, a sending FSK modem generates a continuous carrier and lets the signal's "standard" frequency represent 0. Whenever a 1 needs to be converted, the modem can either reduce or increase the frequency. The receiving FSK modem then interprets the "standard" frequency as 0 and the modulated frequency as 1.

Phase-Shift Keying   Phase-shift keying (PSK) modifies the phase angle of the carrier wave based on the digital data being transmitted. The changes in phase angle are what convey the data in a phase modulated signal. In its simplest implementation, one phase represents a binary 0 and a second phase represents a binary 1. The concept of PSK is shown in Figure 3.5 where the graph of the standard sine curve, $y = \sin x$, which has no phase shift, is superimposed on the graph of $y = \sin\left(x + \dfrac{\pi}{2}\right)$, which has a phase shift of $-90°$. In this example, a binary 0 could be represented by the curve with no phase shift and a binary 1 could be represented by the curve with a phase shift, or vice versa.

The general form of a sine curve is $y = A \sin (bx + c)$, where A = amplitude, b = frequency, and the phase shift is $-c/b$.

Changing the phase of a wave at different angles enables us to encode the data with more than one bit of information at a time. For example, if a phase shift occurs at each of the four angles 0°, 90°, 180°, and 270°, then two bits of information (called dibits) can be transmitted for each signal change. These dibit pairs are 00, 01, 10, and 11, respectively. Similarly, if a phase shift occurs at eight different angles

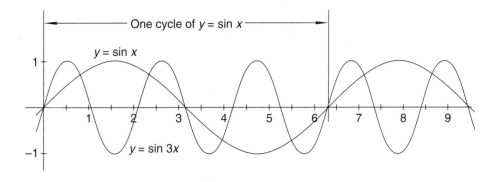

FIGURE 3.4 Concept of frequency-shift keying. In this illustration, a binary 0 could be represented by $y = \sin x$ (frequency of 1), and a binary 1 could be represented by $y = \sin 3x$ (frequency of 3).

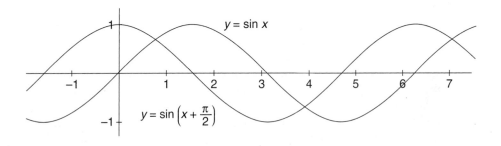

FIGURE 3.5 Concept of phase-shift keying. Note that when compared to the graph of $y = \sin x$, the graph of $y = \sin\left(x + \dfrac{\pi}{2}\right)$ is shifted left 90°. In this example, a binary 0 could be represented by $y = \sin x$ (no phase shift), and a binary 1 could be represented by $y = \sin\left(x + \dfrac{\pi}{2}\right)$ (phase shift).

(e.g., 0°, 45°, 90°, 135°, 180°, 225°, 270°, and 315°), then these eight signals can represent three bits of information (called tribits) per signal change. These tribits are 000, 001, 010, 011, 100, 101, 110, and 111, respectively. As a result, PSK can encode up to three bits per baud.

Quadrature Amplitude Modulation   Phase-shift modulation can also be combined with amplitude modulation. One common strategy is called *quadrature amplitude modulation* (QAM), which uses eight phase changes and two amplitudes to create 16 different signal changes. A constellation diagram that depicts this arrangement is shown in Figure 3.6. QAM can encode between four and seven bits per baud. A modified version of QAM called *trellis-coded modulation* (TCM) incorporates extra bits for error correction. Both QAM and TCM provide high data transfer rates because they are able to incorporate several bits per signal change.

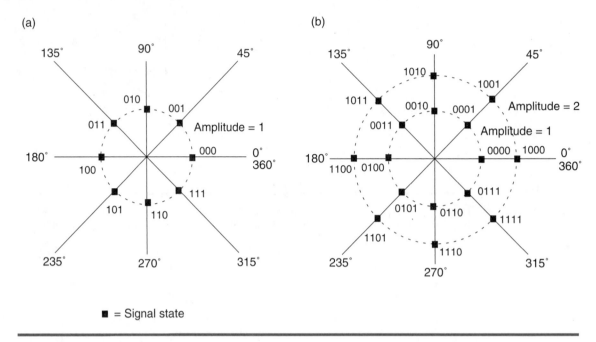

 = Signal state

FIGURE 3.6 Phase-shift keying involves changing the phase of a wave at different angles. This enables data to be encoded with more than one bit of information at a time. In part (a), a phase shift is shown occurring at eight different angles, with each angle representing a different signal. Each angle is used to encode three data bits (tribits) per signal change. In this illustration, the amplitude remains constant. In (b), a modified version of phase modulation called quadrature amplitude modulation is shown. Here, eight phases at two different amplitudes are being generated, resulting in 16 different signal changes. Each angle is used to encode four data bits (quadbits) per signal change.

A good example of digital-to-analog conversions is a conventional analog dialup network connection. Conventional analog dialup connections require standard analog modems (e.g., a 28.8-kbps modem) because during the 1970s, the telephone industry modernized its central offices with digital switching equipment. This new equipment replaced the analog-based public switched telephone network (PSTN) that was originally designed for voice transmission with one predicated on digital signaling and circuitry. Although the telephone network infrastructure is now digital, the entire network is not completely digital from end to end. The circuit between the end user and the telephone company's central office is still analog. This circuit is called the *local loop,* or more formally, the digital subscriber loop (DSL). It is also commonly referred to as "the last mile," although it is often much longer than a mile between terminus points. The local loop is predominately copper-based and represents the bottleneck to high-speed, home-based dialup networking. Thus, it has become the focus of a tremendous amount of attention, ranging from cable modem service by cable operators to *x*DSL modem service by telephone carriers. Many of these topics and is-

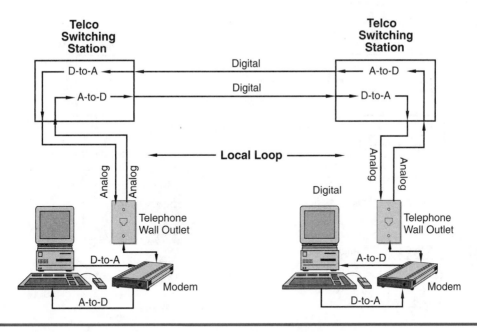

FIGURE 3.7 A typical analog dialup connection between two nodes involves four analog–digital conversions in each direction. (A-to-D = analog-to-digital conversion; D-to-A = digital-to-analog conversion.)

sues are discussed in later chapters. As a result, an analog dialup connection requires four analog-digital conversions in each direction. At the sending side, a modem converts digital data from a PC to analog form for transmission over the phone line to the telephone company's nearest switching station. Once there, the signal is then converted back to digital form where it is transmitted across the telephone company's digital network. When the signal reaches the switching station that serves the destination site, it is reconverted back to analog form and carried to the destination site. Finally, the modem at the destination site demodulates the signal from analog to digital form before it is passed to the receiving computer. This conversion process is shown in Figure 3.7.

An alternative to a standard analog modem dialup connection is a 56K modem connection, which requires only two analog-digital conversions in each direction. The two conversions required occur at the local site. A digital-to-analog conversion converts digital data from the PC to analog form for local loop transmission. Once the signal arrives at the telephone company's switch, the signal is converted from analog to digital form. The remaining part of the journey, however, is digital. Thus, a 56K modem involves a hybrid analog-digital path. The path is analog from the client site to the central office switching station, but the path from the switching station to the server site is completely digital. This is depicted in Figure 3.8.

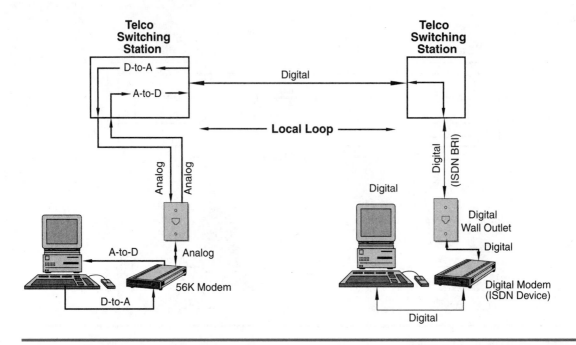

FIGURE 3.8 A 56K modem connection involves a hybrid analog–digital path. Unlike traditional analog modems, a 56K modem requires only two analog–digital conversions in each direction.

NOTE OF INTEREST

Fourier Analysis

In any computer communications network, we want the signal received by an end node to be identical to the signal transmitted by the sender. Unfortunately, this scenario can only occur when the length of the communications link is very short and the data transmission rate is relatively slow. This is obviously not practical in most networking applications. Consequently, when cable lengths are long or data rates fast, a received signal is not exactly the same as the corresponding signal that was transmitted. This is known as signal distortion. Fourier analysis is a systematic method for predicting signal distortion.

Fourier analysis was developed by the French mathematician Jean Fourier, who proved that any periodic wave can be represented as the sum of an aggregation of sine waves. A good approximation requires a finite number of waves; a perfect representation requires an infinite number of waves. Using Fourier analysis, we can predict how a transmitted signal will be received. Fourier analysis is based on two observations. First, any signal used in computer communications systems can be written as a sum of sine waves, and second, a signal represented as a sine wave is preserved (i.e., not distorted) when it is transmitted across a medium. (The signal is still subject to delay and attenuation, however.) One

NOTE OF INTEREST

Fourier Analysis (continued)

implication of Fourier analysis applied to computer communications and net-working is that only sine waves are guaranteed not to be distorted during trans-mission. This means that square waves such as those produced by digital signaling will become distorted during transmission. A second implication of Fourier analysis is that a square wave can be decomposed into a sum of sine waves. From a mathematical perspective, this is similar to approximating contin-uous functions using polynomials, known as Taylor polynomials. It is also similar to the Taylor or MacLaurin series expansion for functions in which a given func-tion is represented as an infinite series. For example, just as it can be shown that the function, $f(x) = \sin x$ can be expressed by the infinite MacLaurin series,

$$\sum_{k=0}^{\infty} \frac{(-1)^k x^{2k+1}}{(2k+1)!} = x - \frac{x^3}{3!} + \frac{x^5}{5!} - \frac{x^7}{7!} + \cdots,$$ it can be shown that the following

square wave given can be decomposed (i.e., represented) by the Fourier series ex-

pansion, $\dfrac{c}{T} + \dfrac{2}{\pi} \displaystyle\sum_{n=1}^{\infty} \dfrac{(-1)^n}{n} \sin\dfrac{n\pi c}{T} \cos\dfrac{n\pi x}{T}$.

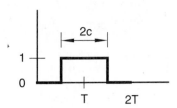

To use Fourier analysis to predict what a received signal will be, the following is done:

1. Determine the attenuation of the communications channel (called the gain) and the phase shift being used. These values are typically provided by the manufacturer of the medium.
2. Determine the function of the decomposition (i.e., the corresponding Fourier anal-ysis). This can be done by consulting a standard mathematics tables handbook.
3. Enter the gain and phase-shift values into the decomposed function and evalu-ate it. This yields a response function, which represents the output of an input signal after it has been transmitted across the communications channel.

Fourier analysis provides us with a tool to predict signal distortion, which enables us to determine the appropriate length of a transmission line given its frequency and data rate. This is one of the reasons cable length restrictions for conventional Ethernet (10 Mbps), Fast Ethernet (100 Mbps), and Gigabit Ethernet (1000 Mbps) are different depending on which data rate is being used and the cable's frequency rating.

Jean Baptiste Joseph Fourier (1768–1830)

Jean Baptiste Joseph Fourier was born in Auxerre, Bourgogne, France, in 1768. During his youth, Fourier studied Latin and French and, by the time he was 13, acquired a strong passion for mathematics. Fourier also had a keen interest in religion and began training for the priesthood in 1787. Ultimately, though, his love of mathematics, coupled with his strong desire to make a significant contribution to the mathematics field, led Fourier in 1789 to abandon his religious studies to pursue mathematical research. In 1790, Fourier began teaching at the Benedictine College, and in 1795, he continued his studies at the Ecole Normal in Paris where Lagrange and Laplace were among his instructors.

In 1798, Fourier left the academic world and joined Napoleon's army as a scientific advisor. Later that same year, he was with Napoleon on Napoleon's ill-fated expedition into Egypt in which the French fleet was destroyed in the Battle of the Nile. The fleet's destruction also destroyed the invading army's return passage to France, which resulted in the army living in French-occupied Egypt for nearly 3 years. While in Egypt, Fourier helped establish educational facilities and helped found the Cairo Institute, where he became a member of the mathematics division. He returned to France in 1801, where Napoleon, who left his army in Egypt to return to Paris in 1799, now held absolute power.

Shortly after his return, Fourier accepted Napoleon's request to serve as prefect in the city of Grenoble. It was here where Fourier wrote his seminal work, *Memoire sur la Chaleur* (i.e., *On the Propagation of Heat in Solid Bodies*), which expounded upon his ideas of heat transfer and outlined his new method of mathematical analysis that we now call Fourier analysis. The basic thesis of Fourier's theory was that if one had a complete set of functions, then any arbitrary function could be accurately described by a linear combination of the various members of this complete set of functions. Fourier formally reported his work in 1807, but it was not warmly received by the review committee for two reasons. First, the review committee did not feel that Fourier adequately explained his proofs, and second, key members of the committee were upset that Fourier did not cite their earlier work, which Fourier believed was flawed.

Three years later, Fourier submitted his 1807 *Memoire* along with additional work to the Paris Institute's mathematics prize competition on propagation of heat in solid bodies. There was only one other submission, and the judges, who consisted of Lagrange and Laplace, among others, awarded the prize to Fourier. Fourier's work was not published, however, because the judges argued that although his work proved that a complete set of functions would accurately describe many functions, he did not sufficiently prove that they could describe *any* function. Although the judges were correct in their assessment, Fourier was also correct when many years later others were able to complete his proof. Fourier analysis is extremely important in modern mathematics, and the ideas are the basis on which the wave function of complex systems is described.

3.2 Representing Data as Digital Signals

As digital technology and computer data applications emerged, analog technology was unable to separate data from noise in a satisfactory manner. This led to the introduction of digital signaling, which requires converting analog signals to digital signals. A discussion of the manner in which this conversion process is done is the focus of this section.

Converting Analog Data to Digital Signals

Representing analog data as digital signals requires converting the data's corresponding analog signal, which is in the form of a sine wave, into a digital signal, which is represented as 0s and 1s. Several methods are available for performing this analog-to-digital conversion. The most common approach is a process known as *pulse-code modulation* (PCM), and it involves two steps: sampling and coding.

Digitizing an analog signal requires taking regular samples of the amplitude of the signal's waveform over time so that the generated digital signal matches its corresponding analog signal. According to a sampling theorem known as Nyquist's theorem (see Box 3.1), if an analog signal is sampled at regular intervals and at twice the highest frequency on the line, then the sample will be an exact representation of the original signal. In voice communications, the normal range of frequencies generated by the human voice is from 300 Hz to 3300 Hz. This implies that 3300 x 2 = 6600 samples per second are required. However, in practice, telephone companies actually allocate 4000-Hz channels and install filters at 300 Hz and 3300 Hz instead of allocating 3000-Hz channels. Thus, 8000 samples per second are actually taken when converting voice to digital form. This higher sampling rate also provides support for higher voice frequencies. Doing the mathematics, this equates to 125 µsec per sample (1 divided by 8000).

Once a sample has been taken, it must then be converted into a binary digit, where 0 and 1 represent the absence and presence of voltage, respectively. Determining whether a sample gets coded 0 or 1 depends on where along the wave the sample is taken. If an eight-bit sample is used, then the sound wave can be partitioned into 256 (i.e., 2^8) possible points, any of which can be used as a sample. The first 128 points (i.e., 0 to 127) get coded 00000000, and the last 128 points (i.e., 128 to 255) get coded 00000001 (Figure 3.9). After the sampling and coding steps are complete, the resulting digital codes are transmitted as a digital signal waveform. The PCM process is summarized in Figure 3.10. Digitizing an analog signal via PCM is done using a device called a codec (coder-decoder), which can be thought of as the opposite of a modem. A codec converts analog data into a digital signal; a modem, on the other hand, converts digital data into an analog signal. An example of the PCM process is the construction of a T1 circuit and is given later in this chapter.

BOX 3.1 Nyquist's Theorem

In the early to mid-1920s, Henry Nyquist discovered that the maximum signaling rate of a noiseless channel was twice the number of samples. This discovery can be seen by observing the following standard sine wave carrier.

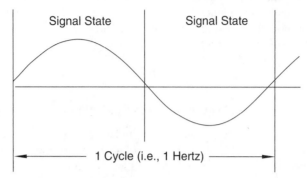

Observe that the natural form of a sine wave makes it possible for every half cycle to represent one signal state since the two half cycles are mirror images of each other. This leads to the logical conclusion that the sampling rate must be twice the highest frequency because each cycle of the waveform corresponds to two values—one for the positive amplitude level and one for the negative amplitude level. Thus, if we have w cycles per second (i.e., hertz), then we can have $2w$ signal states. Generalizing this concept, if a noiseless communications channel uses N values per signaling state, then the channel's maximum data transmission capacity in bits per second is given as

$$\text{Maximum Data Rate} = 2w\text{Log}_2N \text{ bps}$$

where w = the number of cycles expressed in Hertz and

N = the number of discrete signaling states used

This relationship is known as Nyquist's theorem and provides us with the maximum data rate of a noiseless communications channel. For example, if we have a 4000-Hz channel transmitting binary signals—and thus, two signaling states—then the maximum channel capacity is:

$$C = 2w\text{Log}_2N$$
$$= 2(4000)(\text{Log}_22)$$
$$= 8000(1)$$
$$= 8000 \text{ bps}$$

Note that Nyquist's theorem is the basis for pulse-code modulation (PCM), which specifies that an analog signal be sampled at regular intervals and at twice the highest frequency on the line to get a sample that is an exact representation of the original signal. Nyquist's theorem (and PCM) also has applications in CDs and digital audio tapes. For example, the upper limit of audio frequencies that can be reproduced digitally is a function of the sampling frequency. Thus, to capture a 20-kHz audio bandwidth, a sampling rate of 40 kHz is required. This is the sampling rate on which CD-quality audio is based.

   In addition to remembering that Nyquist's theorem applies to noiseless channels, it is equally important to remember that the theorem applies only to the signaling rate. Thus, if we increase the amount of data a signal carries via a modulation technique (as is discussed in this chapter), then the data transmission rate also increases without violating the theorem. For a demonstration of Nyquist's theorem see http://www.cs.brown.edu/people/dlg/gfxnotes/signal/nyquist.

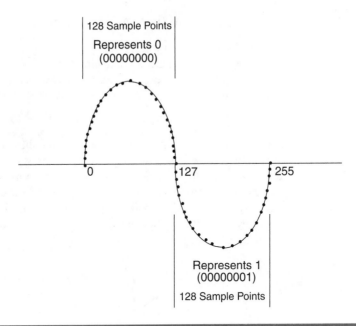

FIGURE 3.9 By using an eight-bit code to convert an analog signal into a digital signal via pulse-code modulation, an analog signal can be partitioned into $2^8 = 256$ possible sample points: 128 points represent 0, and 128 points represent 1. Source: adapted from Bates & Gregory, 1998.

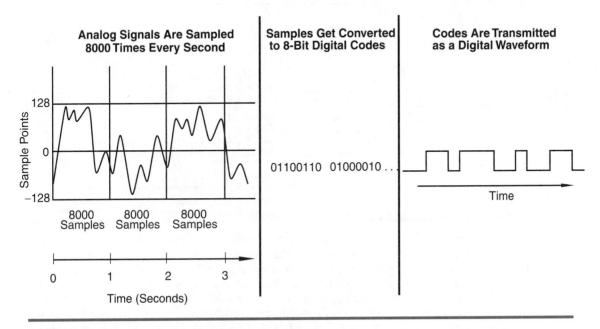

FIGURE 3.10 Example of the pulse-code modulation (PCM) process. Source: adapted from Parkinson, 1988.

Converting Digital Data to Digital Signals

Transmitting digital data (e.g., output from a computer) across a digital network (e.g., an Ethernet LAN) requires representing the digital data as a digital signal. Three common coding techniques used for this task are *Manchester coding, differential Manchester coding,* and *nonreturn to zero, invert on ones* (NRZI). A brief discussion of these coding techniques follows.

Manchester Encoding   Manchester encoding differs from standard digital transmission in two ways. First, instead of "high" equaling 1 and "low" equaling 0, a timing interval is used to measure high-to-low transitions. Second, instead of the timed transmission period being "all high" or "all low" for either 1 or 0, a state transition is encoded into the transformation. Specifically, a 1 is sent as a half-time-period low followed by a half-time-period high, and a 0 is sent as a half-time-period high followed by a half-time-period low (Figure 3.11). Consequently, the end of the last transmitted bit is

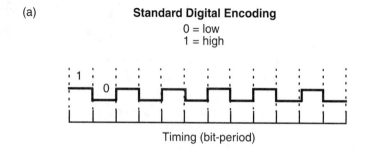

(a)   **Standard Digital Encoding**
0 = low
1 = high

Timing (bit-period)

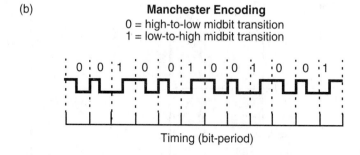

(b)   **Manchester Encoding**
0 = high-to-low midbit transition
1 = low-to-high midbit transition

Timing (bit-period)

FIGURE 3.11   Part (a) shows a typical digital transmission. When an electrical pulse is "on," the line is at a high level; when there is no pulse during a transmission ("off" state), the line is at a low state. For each bit-period, there is either a pulse or no pulse. Part (b) shows a Manchester encoded digital transmission. Here, each bit-period has two intervals. A 1 is sent as a half-time-period "low" followed by a half-time- period "high," (i.e., a low-to-high midbit transition), and a 0 is sent as a half-time-period "high" followed by a half-time-period "low" (i.e., a high-to-low midbit transition). Instances where no transition occurs at the midpoint of a bit interval are used for control purposes.

easily determined immediately following the transmission of the last bit. Manchester coding is used in Ethernet/802.3 networks. The main benefit of this approach is error recovery; part of the signal transition from high to low and from low to high can be clipped or distorted, and there is still "intelligence" in the timing interval to determine if the signal was rising or falling. This allows on-the-fly signal recovery and minimizes single bit errors.

Differential Manchester Encoding   Differential Manchester encoding is similar to Manchester encoding in that each bit-period is partitioned into two intervals, and a transition between "high" and "low" occurs during each bit-period. The difference between the two techniques is the interpretation of this transition. As stated previously, in Manchester encoding, a 1-bit represents a low-to-high midbit transition, and a 0-bit represents a high-to-low midbit transition. In differential Manchester encoding, the interpretation of these low-to-high and high-to-low midbit transitions is not as simple—they are a function of the previous bit-period. A low-to-high transition could be a 0 or a 1 depending on the value of the previous bit-period. More specifically, the presence of a transition at the beginning of a bit-period is coded 0, and the absence of a transition at the beginning of a bit-period is coded 1.

NRZI   NRZI is part of the nonreturn to zero (NRZ) family of codes in which positive and negative voltages are used for encoding 0s and 1s. In one form of NRZ, called *nonreturn to zero level* (NRZL), a constant positive voltage is used to represent a 0-bit and a constant negative voltage is used to represent a 1-bit. NRZI is a variation of NRZL. Instead of using level voltages to encode the data, though, encoding is based on transitions from one voltage state to another (i.e., from a low-to-high state or from a high-to-low state). Specifically, in NRZI, data are coded 0 if no transitions occur, but are coded 1 at the beginning of a transition.

An application of NRZI can be found in several LAN systems, which use as their signaling method a group encoding strategy known as the 4B/5B (four bits to five bits) method. The 4B/5B encoding scheme takes data in four-bit codes and maps them to corresponding five-bit codes (Table 3.1). These five-bit codes are then transmitted using NRZI. By transmitting five-bit codes using NRZI, a logical 1-bit is transmitted at least once every five sequential data bits, resulting in a signal transition. The 4B/5B-NRZI scheme makes it possible for LANs such as Fast Ethernet and FDDI to operate at 125 MHz and provides a data rate of 100 megabits per second. Note that the use of one extra bit for every five bits translates to only 20% overhead for every clock encoding. In contrast, Manchester coding requires 50% bandwidth overhead for clock encoding because it guarantees at least one signal transition for every bit transmitted. The 4B/5B-NRZI scheme allows LANS such as Fast Ethernet and FDDI to provide high-speed capability over less optimal media and data symmetry that allows for simpler implementation of analog capture circuitry for receiving nodes. As a point of interest, copper-based Gigabit Ethernet (see Chapter 9) also uses an NRZI scheme on the copper version of the technology.

TABLE 3.1   Fast Ethernet and FDDI 4B/5B Codes

Four-Bit Data	Five-Bit Encoding
0000 (0)	1 1 1 1 0
0001 (1)	0 1 0 0 1
0002 (2)	1 0 1 0 0
0003 (3)	1 0 1 0 1
0004 (4)	0 1 0 1 0
0005 (5)	0 1 0 1 1
0006 (6)	0 1 1 1 0
0007 (7)	0 1 1 1 1
0008 (8)	1 0 0 1 0
0009 (9)	1 0 0 1 1
1010 (A)	1 0 1 1 0
1011 (B)	1 0 1 1 1
1100 (C)	1 1 0 1 0
1101 (D)	1 1 0 1 1
1110 (E)	1 1 1 0 0
1111 (F)	1 1 1 0 1
S (Set)	1 1 0 0 1
R (Reset)	0 0 1 1 1
Q (Quiet)	0 0 0 0 0
I (Idle)	1 1 1 1 1
H (Halt)	0 0 1 0 0
T (Terminate)	0 1 1 0 1
J (Start 1)	1 1 0 0 0
K (Start 2)	1 0 0 0 1

3.3   Data Rate and Baud Rate Redux

In Chapter 2, we stated that *baud rate* is not necessarily the same as *data rate,* and hence, the two terms should not be considered synonymous. At that time, we did not go into any detail explaining why this is so. We simply asked you to accept this difference on our word. Now that we have developed an understanding of the concept of signaling, we are better prepared to explain baud rate versus data rate.

As noted in Chapter 2, both data rate and baud rate can be used to express the capacity of a communications channel. During the early days of computer communications and networking, when data transmission rates were very slow (e.g., less than 300 bps), baud was commonly accepted as an accurate measure of a channel's speed. Named after the French engineer Jean Maurice Emile Baudot, baud was first used to measure the speed of telegraph transmissions and is equal to the number of times the line condition (i.e., frequency, amplitude, or phase) changes each second. At low speeds (under 300 bps), data rate and baud rate are the same because signaling methods are relatively simple. As speed increases, however, signaling methods become more complex because several bits are frequently encoded per baud, which enables each signal to represent more than one bit of information. As an example, consider a communications channel transmitting at 2400 baud. This means that the signaling rate of the channel is changing 2400 times per second. If each signal is used to represent one bit, then the baud rate is equal to the data rate. In this instance, then, 2400 baud = 2400 bps. However, if each signal represents four bits, as is the case with quadrature amplitude modulation, then the baud rate remains at 2400, but now the data rate is 4 bits x 2400 signal changes per second, which is 9600 bps. As a result, the channel's baud rate stays at 2400, but its bandwidth is 9600 bps. Relating these concepts to a modem, if every bit that enters a modem is represented by a single signal change, then 1 bps = 1 baud. If, on the other hand, a phase modulation modem is being used where one signal change is being used to represent three bits, then 3 bps = 1 baud. Since it is rarely the case in data communications where 1 bps = 1 baud, baud rate and data rate are not considered the same, especially today where high-speed communications rule. Hence, data rate is the more accurate measure.

3.4   Digital Carrier Systems

We conclude this chapter with a discussion of various digital carrier systems, including T1 and DS circuits, as well as SONET and OC circuits. Collectively, these circuits embody many of the concepts presented in the chapter.

T1 and DS Circuits

One characteristic of electrical transmissions is *attenuation,* which is a decrease in signal strength. Attenuation occurs as the signal travels through a circuit or along a cable. The longer the cable, the greater the attenuation. Also, the higher the frequency of the signal, the greater the attenuation. Analog transmission facilities account for this signal loss by using analog amplifiers to boost the signal. Amplifiers are usually placed along a circuit every 18,000 to 20,000 feet. Although these amplifiers boost the signal, they also amplify noise, which as previously mentioned, is an inherent part of any communications systems. In some cases, amplified noise can distort a signal considerably to the point that it is unrecognizable. This is especially true for digital data, which have a low tolerance for signal distortion. To address this issue, digital signaling and the *T-carrier* system were introduced (circa 1962). In digital transmission facilities, attenuation is resolved by repeaters that regenerate digital signals to their exact form. This enables the new, regenerated signal to be compared to the previous signal, thus reducing the chances of propagating errors during a transmission. The T-carrier system, which uses time division multiplexing to support multiple channels in a single digital signal, was the first system designed to implement digitized voice transmissions.

The T1 terminology, which is a product of the T-carrier system, was originally defined by AT&T and describes the multiplexing of 24 separate voice channels into a single wideband digital signal. A T1 frame consists of 193 bits—eight bits per channel plus one bit for framing. (The concept of framing is discussed in Chapter 5.) Bits 1 through 8 are dedicated to channel 1, bits 9 through 16 are dedicated to channel 2, and so forth. Each voice channel is digitized using pulse code modulation and has a data rate of 64 kbps. When multiplexed into a digital signal, a voice channel is referred to as a *digital signal at level 0* (DS-0). Thus, DS-0 represents a single digital voice channel rated at 64 kbps. A T1 circuit carries a DS-1 signal, which consists of 24 DS-0 channels plus one 8-kbps channel reserved for framing. This results in an aggregate bandwidth of 1.544 Mbps.

The T1 concept eventually evolved to what is now known as the North American Digital Hierarchy (NADH), which consists of multiplexed T1 lines. For example, two T1 lines are combined to form a T1C circuit rated at 3.152 Mbps. (In DS terminology, T1C is known as DS-1C.) This is more than twice 1.544 Mbps because NADH uses bit-stuffing (see Chapter 5), which increases the aggregate bandwidth. A T2 circuit (DS-2) consists of 4 multiplexed T1 circuits and has an aggregate bandwidth of 6.312 Mbps; a T3 link (DS-3) consists of 28 multiplexed T1 circuits with an aggregate bandwidth of 44.736 Mbps; and a T4 channel (DS-4), rated at 274.176 Mbps, consists of 168 multiplexed T1 circuits. Table 3.2 provides a summary of this hierarchy. In practical terms and everyday usage, the terms T1 and DS-1 are considered synonymous.

T1 service has the same meaning in Australia and Japan as it does in the United States and Canada. However, in Europe, South America, Africa, parts of Asia, and Mexico, T1 is meaningless. Instead, an analogous service called E-1 (the E is for European) is used in these locations. An E-1 carrier supports thirty 64-kbps clear channels (i.e., no "in-band" overhead) plus two 64-kbps signaling and control channels. This results in an aggregate bandwidth of 2.048 Mbps. An E-1 carrier is normally supplied as a 30B + 2D ISDN circuit (see Chapter 12). As with T1 service, E-1 links can be multiplexed into higher-capacity lines. Table 3.3 summarizes this hierarchy.

The reason 64 kbps was selected as the basic building block of T1/DS-1 circuits is grounded in the early development of analog-to-digital conversions. Recall that telephone companies partitioned their circuits into channels of 4000 Hz, and hence, 8000 samples per second are used for the conversions. This equates to 125 μsec per sample (1 divided by 8000). Each sample is then converted into an eight-bit digital code with 00000000 representing the absence of voltage and 00000001 representing the presence of voltage. By using eight bits, 256 (2^8) possible points can be used to partition the wave for sampling, and the coding process used is PCM. Multiplying 8000 samples per second by eight bits per sample yields 64,000 bps. Thus, the digital representation of a single analog voice call requires 64,000 bits.

TABLE 3.2 Summary of NADH Line Rates

Digital Signal	T-Carrier	Data Transmission Rate (Mbps)	Number of Multiplexed DS-0 Channels	Number of Multiplexed DS-1 Channels
DS-0	—	0.064	1	—
DS-1	T1	1.544	24	1
DS-1C	T1C	3.152	48	2
DS-2	T2	6.312	96	4
DS-3	T3	44.736	672	28
DS-4	T4	274.176	4032	168

TABLE 3.3 Summary of European E-Carrier Line Rates

E-Carrier	Data Transmission Rate (Mbps)	Number of 64-kps Channels	Number of E-1 Channels	Number of E-2 Channels	Number of E-3 Channels	Number of E-4 Channels
—	0.064	1	—	—	—	—
E-1	2.048	30	1	—	—	—
E-2	8.448	120	4	—	—	—
E-3	34.368	480	16	4	—	—
E-4	139.264	1920	64	16	4	—
E-5	565.148	7680	256	64	16	4

It is instructive to note the construction of a T1's line rate. As stated earlier, each channel is sampled at a rate of 8000 times per second. This produces an eight-bit number for each sample. Seven of these bits represent data and one bit is used for control. This yields per channel transmission rates of 56,000 bps for data and 8000 bps for control. Since a T1 channel can support 24 simultaneous voice channels via TDM, we have 1,344,000 bps for data and 192,000 bps for control. Added to this is a separate 8000 bps channel for frame synchronization. This is summarized here.

Data: 56,000 bps per channel at 24 channels = 1,344,000 bps
Control: 8000 bps per channel at 24 channels = 192,000 bps
Framing: 8000 bps for frame synchronization = 8000 bps

The European standard is based on a 256-bit frame that consists of thirty-two 8-bit time slots. Similar calculations can be done using these values. E-1 circuits are also controlled out-of-band.

This line rate can be further confirmed by observing that a T1 frame contains 193 bits—168 for data, 24 for control, and 1 for synchronization; 193 bits at 8000 samples per second yields 1.544 Mbps. A T1 service is sometimes referred to as a "bit-robbing" service because circuit control is in-band; T1 steals a proportion of the available bandwidth for control purposes.

Fractional T1

Some U.S. carriers provide 256-kbps channels as part of their ISDN services, but these are being dropped in favor of 64-kbps channel services.

Fractional T1 service (FT1), as its name implies, provides a fraction of a T1's capacity. This is achieved by combining multiple DS-0 (i.e., 64-kbps) channels. For example, 128 kbps is two DS-0 channels, 256 kbps consists of four DS-0 channels, and 512 kbps consists of eight DS-0 channels. When ordering FT1 service from a telecommunications (telco) provider, you actually receive a full T1 channel but only pay for the number of DS-0 channels you order.

A 64-kbps FT1 line is less efficient than a 64-kbps ISDN channel in terms of the amount of bandwidth available for data communication. This is because T1 control frames are in-band. Thus, you only get 56 kbps for data with every channel; the remaining 8 kbps are for control. ISDN, on the other hand, uses a separate channel for control and thereby provides a full 64 kbps for data. Similarly, a 128-kbps FT1 line only provides 112 kbps for data, but a 128-kbps ISDN channel provides a full 128-kbps. FT1 service is attractive to customers who do not require full T1 service but need more capacity than an ISDN 64/128-kbps line.

A PBX stands for *private branch exchange* and is a telephone exchange used within an organization to provide internal telephone extensions and access to the public telephone network—the modern-day equivalent of what used to be called a *switchboard.*

T1 service costs vary widely and are based on a customer's location relative to the telco provider and the type of circuit desired. Consideration also must be given to end equipment purchases and monthly service charges, which include the cost of the circuit itself and any *local loop* charges. The local loop is essentially the cable that connects the telephone central office (or exchange) with the customer's location. Local loop charges usually vary directly with the distance of the customer's location from the central office. For example, to interconnect PBXs, a *channelized* circuit is used, which requires no special equipment. The trade-off is that you cannot partition the T1 link. If, on the other hand, you need to partition the link, then a nonchannelized circuit is needed, requiring two T1 multiplexers—one at each end of the circuit.

A T1 circuit also requires special termination equipment called a *CSU/DSU*. A *channel service unit* (CSU) performs many functions. It regenerates the signal, monitors the line for electrical anomalies, provides proper electrical termination, performs framing, and provides remote loop-back testing for diagnosing line problems. Some CSUs also support the Internet's Simple Network Management Protocol (SNMP). A *data service unit* (DSU), which is also referred to as *digital service unit,* provides the interface (usually V.35, a type of serial interface) for connecting a remote bridge, router, or switch to a T1 circuit. The DSU also provides flow control between the network and the CSU. Flow control is a feedback implementation method a receiver uses to inform the sender how much data it should send. Flow control provides the receiver with a way to prevent the sender from transmitting more data than the receiver can process. A CSU and DSU are usually combined to form a single unit—a CSU/DSU or DSU/CSU—which is sometimes described as the digital equivalent of a modem (i.e., a "digital modem") for a T1 line. Although the functions of a CSU/DSU and modem are similar, describing a CSU/DSU as a digital modem is misleading because a CSU/DSU does not perform any type of modulation or demodulation. Instead, a CSU/DSU works exclusively with digital signals; it provides an interface between a digital computing device and a digital transmission medium. Figure 3.12 shows a typical T1-based WAN link.

An E-1 circuit is terminated using a network termination unit (NTU), which provides broadly similar CSU/DSU functionality. Unlike the U.S. market, where the provision of a CSU/DSU is normally the responsibility of the end user, NTUs are always supplied by the telco in Europe. You should also note that line coding is different between T1 and E-1 circuits. In the United States, a technique called *bipolar with 8 zeros substitution* (B8ZS) is used, and in Europe, a technique called *high-density bipolar— 3 zeros* (HDB3) is used. Both B8ZS and HDB3 are variants of an encoding scheme known as *bipolar-AMI* (alternate mark inversion). In bipolar-AMI, a 0-bit represents no signal, and a 1-bit represents either a positive or negative signal where the first 1-bit is positive, the second 1-bit is negative, and all subsequent 1-bits alternate between positive and negative. One of the problems with bipolar-AMI is that a long string of 0s can lead to synchronization problems. The B8ZS encoding scheme resolves this problem by inserting 1-bits in the fourth and fifth 0 places as well as in the seventh and eighth 0 places. The placement of these 1-bits, however, violates the alternation rule. Specifically, the first inserted 1-bit, which replaces the fourth 0, matches the previous 1-bit. Thus, if a previous 1-bit represented a positive voltage, then the first inserted 1-bit will also represent a positive voltage. Furthermore, the third inserted 1-bit, which replaces

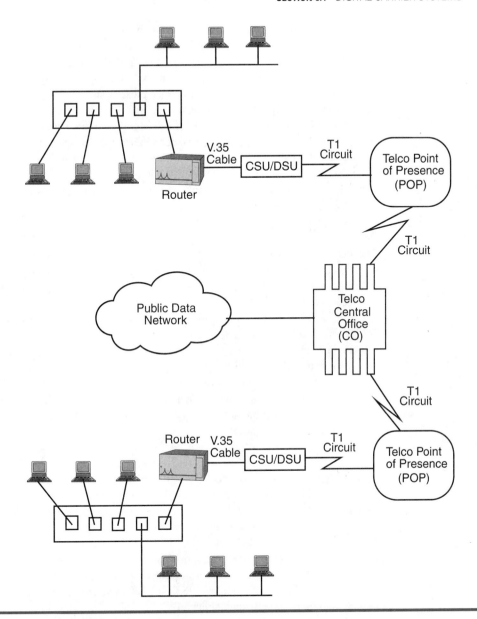

FIGURE 3.12   A typical configuration scheme of a leased T1 WAN connection between two sites involves a V.35 link between a router's V.35 port and a CSU/DSU. The CSU/DSU provides the interface to the T1 circuit. This circuit terminates at the telco's CO either directly or via a POP located near the customer's premises. The CO then provides connectivity to the network.

the seventh 0, will match the second inserted 1-bit that replaced the fifth 0. By replacing a string of eight 0s with two code violations, B8ZS guarantees that there will not be a sequence of more than seven successive no-signal bit times. Similarly, the HDB3 encoding scheme is the same as bipolar-AMI except that any string of four consecutive 0s is replaced with one code violation. Bipolar-AMI and B8ZS encoding methods are shown in Figure 3.13.

Prices for T1 multiplexers range from a few thousand dollars to as much as $100,000 or more depending on configuration (e.g., number of ports, bandwidth capacity). CSU/DSU units cost between $200 and $1000. Routers are priced from around $1000 to more than $50,000 depending on configuration needs. As we indicated earlier, circuit costs fluctuate. Factors that influence these costs include: geographical location; the telco provider (e.g., MCI WorldCom, AT&T, British Telecom, BellSouth); whether a local loop fee is required, which varies depending on the distance a customer's site is from the telco's nearest point of presence (POP); the service contract; whether or not you commit to a short-term (1 year) or long-term (2 to 5 years) subscription; the manner in which the circuit is routed; and many others. Given the many parameters on which circuit costs are based, we opt not to provide any estimates of these costs.

You may have noticed that POP was previously defined in Chapters 1 and 2 as Post Office Protocol. In the networking business, some identical abbreviations are used for completely different technologies and concepts. In the context of network topologies and telecommunications technologies, POP means point of presence. In the context of e-mail, POP means Post Office Protocol. This is an unfortunate but periodically encountered problem in the computer communications and network technology world. So, be careful which POP you are talking about when conversing with the phone guys versus the e-mail server manager—and, when you are referring to your father behind his back.

SONET and OC Circuits

The development and deployment of NADH led telco carriers to develop their own methods of providing T-carrier service based on NADH. This acceptance of NADH established it as a de facto standard. There was one problem, though. The telcos' T-carrier services were incompatible, which made it difficult for customers to exchange data between different carriers. As a result, subscribers became locked into one solution, and NADH eventually became a de facto proprietary standard. (See Chapter 1 for additional information about standards.) In addition to proprietary intercarrier circuits, NADH was also incompatible with the way Europeans multiplexed their signals. In the early days of networking, when proprietary standards ruled and communications were usually restricted to within a country's own borders, these issues were not significant. In an era of open systems, standards, and global telecommunications, however, these issues are of paramount importance.

To address the difficulties inherent in intercarrier circuits globally, two transmission technology standards were developed: *Synchronous Optical Network* (SONET) and the *Synchronous Digital Hierarchy* (SDH). SONET is an ANSI standard; SDH is an ITU-T standard. SDH was drafted after SONET and incorporates it. SONET and SDH (frequently written as SONET/SDH) are international physical layer standards that provide a specification for high-speed digital transmission via optical fiber. At the source interface, signals are converted from electrical to optical form. They are then converted back to electrical form at the destination interface.

In the ANSI world, SONET's terminology includes Optical Carrier level (OC-*n*) and Synchronous Transport Signal level (STS-*n*). STS rates represent electrical signals over copper, and their optical equivalents are expressed as OC rates. In the ITU-T world, the official term used is Synchronous Transport Module (STM-*n*). Table 3.4 contains a summary of OC-*n*, STS-*n*, and STM-*n* line rates.

The designation OC-*nc* indicates that multiple smaller circuits are concatenated to form a circuit. For example, OC-3 denotes a single 155.52-Mbps circuit, but OC-3c denotes three OC-1 circuits are concatenated to provide this bandwidth.

You might note that OC data rates are extremely fast. The recent advances in LAN technologies (e.g., 100-Mbps and Gigabit Ethernet) rendered WAN links as the bottleneck of an internetwork. Consider, for example, a WAN that interconnects two Gigabit Ethernet LANs by a T1 circuit. Although data transmission locally is occurring at a rate of 1000 Mbps, the transfer rate between LANs is a mere 1.544 Mbps, nearly 650 times slower. SONET resolves this bottleneck. Note also that OC-3 is the rate used by ATM

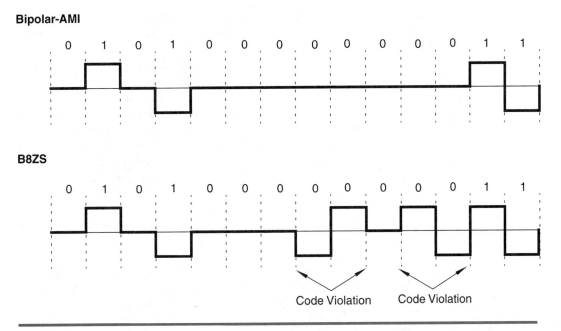

Bipolar-AMI

B8ZS

Code Violation   Code Violation

FIGURE 3.13 Encoding schemes for bipolar-AMI and B8ZS.

			Data Transmission	Number of DS-0	Number of DS-1	Number of DS-3
OC-*n*	**STS-*n***	**STM-*n***	**Rate (Mbps)**	**Channels**	**Channels**	**Channels**
OC-1	STS-1	—	51.84	672	28	1
OC-3	STS-3	STM-1	155.52	2,016	84	3
OC-9	STS-9	STM-3	466.56	6,048	252	9
OC-12	STS-12	STM-4	622.08	8,064	336	12
OC-18	STS-18	STM-6	933.12	12,096	504	18
OC-24	STS-24	STM-8	1,244.16	16,128	672	24
OC-36	STS-36	STM-12	1,866.24	24,192	1,008	36
OC-48	STS-48	STM-16	2,488.32	32,256	1,344	48
OC-96	STS-96	STM-32	4,976.64	64,512	2,688	96
OC-192	STS-192	STM-64	9,953.28	129,024	5,376	192

TABLE 3.4   Comparison of SONET and DS Line Rates

networks, which are discussed in Chapter 15. In fact, 155-Mbps (OC-3) ATM and 622-Mbps (OC-12) ATM were designed specifically to use SONET as their carrier service. Also, higher rate ATM can run only over SONET as of this writing.

As we indicated earlier, SONET was developed by the telcos to address the need for a fiber-optic based standard for broadband transmissions within the telecommunications industry. Its roots are from synchronous transfer mode (STM), which is used in

U.S. digital telephone networks. The basic building block of the SONET signal hierarchy is STS-1 (51.84 Mbps). This line rate is derived from the STS-1 frame and consists of 810 eight-bit bytes transmitted at 8000 Hz.

As a fiber-based medium, SONET offers several advantages over the copper-based T1 hierarchy. First, hundreds of thousands of simultaneous voice and data transmissions are possible using fiber. This is not feasible with copper cable. Second, fiber is immune to EMI (see Chapter 4). Third, fiber is available in either single or multimode and thus can be used for LAN connections or as the backbone of a WAN. As a synchronous transmission facility, SONET again offers several advantages over its asynchronous T1 counterpart. Bandwidth can be allocated on an as-needed basis and routes can be dynamically reconfigured. As a carrier service, SONET can serve as the transport facility for any type network technology or service, including ATM, FDDI, SMDS, and ISDN. Finally, SONET can support various topologies including point-to-point, star, and ring.

The word *plesiochronous* means "partially synchronized."

SDH has its roots in an early transport mechanism called *plesiochronous digital hierarchy* (PDH). PDH is similar to STM in that both use time division multiplexing. The difference is STM is applied to T-carrier circuits (e.g., T1 and T3), and PDH is applied to E-carrier circuits (e.g., E-1 and E-3). Aside from some minor differences, SDH is essentially the same as SONET, and at OC-3 rates and higher, the two are virtually identical.

End-of-Chapter Commentary

Several key concepts presented in this chapter will be revisited in later chapters within a specific context. For example, the digital signaling methods of Manchester, differential Manchester, and NRZI are discussed in Chapters 9 (Ethernet), 10 (Token Ring), and 11 (FDDI). Digital carrier systems are also reviewed and elaborated in Chapter 12 (ISDN). Finally, in Chapter 16 (Dialup Networking), we reexamine modems and the analog-to-digital/digital-to-analog conversion concepts.

CHAPTER REVIEW MATERIALS

SUMMARY

• The process of transmitting data involves converting data into appropriate signals suitable for transmission. Data transmitted using analog transmission facilities are converted into analog signals, which are electromagnetic waves that resemble a sine curve. Data transmitted using digital transmission facilities are converted into digital signals, which are created by applying a current (voltage present) or turning it off (voltage absent). Several techniques for converting data into signals are available. The focus of these techniques concentrates primarily on digital-to-analog, analog-to-digital, and digital-to-digital conversions.

• Digital-to-analog conversions (D-A) are needed because data produced by computers frequently must be transmitted via analog transmission facilities. A typical example of this is dialup network communications. D-A conversions are performed by modems, which modulate various characteristics of the sine curve, including amplitude, frequency, and phase. In all cases, a modem generates an unmodulated carrier signal and uses this signal to represent 0. It then modulates this signal using a specific modulation scheme, and the modulated signal is used to represent 1. In amplitude modulation (also called amplitude-shift keying), the strength of the carrier is changed by altering voltage; in frequency modulation (also called frequency-shift keying), a tone different from the carrier's tone is generated; and in phase modulation (also called phase-shift keying), the phase angle of the carrier is modified. A method that combines amplitude and phase modulation is quadrature amplitude modulation, which uses multiple phase and amplitude changes to generate different multiple signals. One common scheme uses eight phase changes and two amplitude changes to create 16 different signal changes. These signal changes in turn are used to represent multiple bits. Quadrature amplitude modulation and a modified version called trellis-coded modulation are used by high-speed modems which provide high data transfer rates.

• Analog-to-digital (A-D) conversions enable typical analog data such as voice communications to be transmitted via digital transmission facilities. A-D conversions are performed by a codec and use a process known as pulse code modulation, which takes 8000 samples per second of a sine wave. By using eight-bit samples, this wave is partitioned into 256 possible sample points. The first 128 points (i.e., 0 to 127) get coded 00000000, and the last 128 points (i.e., 128 to 255) get coded 00000001.

• Digital-to-digital (D-D) conversions are generally used in local area networks. Three methods for D-D conversions include: Manchester coding, which is used in Ethernet/802.3 networks, encodes a 1-bit as a low-to-high transition and a 0-bit as a high-to-low transition; differential Manchester coding, which is used in token ring networks, is similar to Manchester encoding with the following exception: The presence of a transition at the beginning of a bit-period is coded 0, and the absence of a transition at the beginning of a bit-period is coded 1; and nonreturn to zero, invert on ones, which is used in Fast Ethernet and FDDI networks, encoding is based on transitions from one voltage state to another (i.e., from a low-to-high state or from a high-to-low state): Data are coded 0 if no transitions occur, but are coded 1 at the beginning of a transition (see Figure 3.14 and Table 3.5).

• Data rate is a measurement of data throughput in bps, and baud rate is a measurement of signal change. If one signal change is used to represent n bits, then n bps is equal to one baud. Since this is rarely the case in high-speed data communications, data rate is the correct and more accurate measurement of a channel's capacity.

• The T-carrier system incorporates many of the concepts and issues presented in this and the preceding chapters. A T1 circuit comprises 24 separate voice channels that are time division multiplexed into a single digital signal using PCM. Thus, a T1 circuit implements digitized voice transmissions. Each digitized

TABLE 3.5 Summary of Digital Signal Encoding Strategies

Bit	Manchester	Differential Manchester	NRZI
0	High-to-low transition in middle of interval (i.e., half-time-period high followed by half-time-period low).	Presence of high-to-low or low-to-high transition at the beginning of a bit-period	No high-to-low or low-to-high transitions.
1	Low-to-high transition in middle of interval (i.e., half-time-period low followed by half-time-period high).	Absence of high-to-low or low-to-high transition at the beginning of a bit-period	High-to-low or low-to-high transition at the start of transition.

(a) A telephone converts analog data (sound waves) into analog signals.

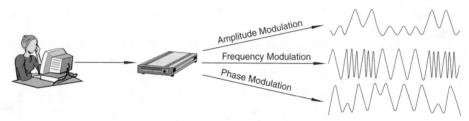

(b) A modem converts digital data into modulated analog signals (and reconverts the modulated analog signals back into digital data).

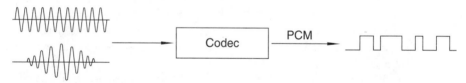

(c) A codec converts analog signals into digital signals.

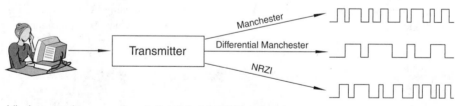

(d) A transmitter encodes digital data into digital signals.

FIGURE 3.14 A summary of the various analog and digital data-signal conversion schemes.

voice channel, called a DS-0, has a data rate of 64 kbps. A T1 circuit carries a DS-1 signal, which consists of 24 DS-0 channels plus one 8-kbps channel reserved for framing and has an aggregate bandwidth of 1.544 Mbps. A similar circuit, called E-1 carrier, is used in Europe and is rated at 2.048 Mbps.

• Adjunct to the T-carrier discussion are two other transmission technologies, SONET and SDH, both of which are international standards that provide a specification for high-speed digital transmission via optical fiber. This involves converting signals in electrical to optical form at the source and an optical-to-electrical conversion at the destination.

VOCABULARY CHECK

amplitude
amplitude modulation (AM)
amplitude-shift keying (ASK)
analog signal
analog-to-digital conversion
baud rate
carrier signal
channel service unit (CSU)
codec
data rate
data service unit (DSU)
differential Manchester
  coding
DS-0

digital signal
digital-to-analog conversion
digital-to-digital conversion
E-1
fractional T1
frequency modulation (FM)
frequency-shift keying (FSK)
Manchester coding
modem
modulation
nonreturn to zero, invert on ones
  (NRZI)
Nyquist's theorem
optical carrier (OC)

phase modulation (PM)
phase-shift keying (PSK)
pulse-code modulation (PCM)
quadrature amplitude modulation
  (QAM)
SONET
synchronous transport signal
  (STS)
T1

REVIEW EXERCISES

1. Explain the difference between a standard analog 28.8K modem connection and a 56K modem connection.

2. Explain the difference between data rate and baud rate.

3. Describe and contrast how modems and codecs work. Include in your description both the modulation and demodulation process of modems and the coding and decoding process of codecs.

4. Given the constellation diagram shown in Figure 3.15, determine and explain how many signal states are produced.

5. If a modem is designed with the constellation pattern shown in Figure 3.15, what is the modem's data rate if it is transmitting at 4800 baud?

6. If ASK and PSK can encode only one bit per baud, what is the maximum data transmission rate possible using modems based on these modulation techniques?

7. Note that a standard (unmodulated) sine wave represents two signal states: One signal state can be coded every half cycle. If we have H cycles (expressed in hertz), then we can code 2H signal states. Using the seven-bit ASCII character set as an example, note that the number of characters that can be represented can be expressed as $2^7 =$

128. Thus, with n bits, we can represent 2^n characters. Express this relationship in logarithmic form.

8. Using the logarithmic equation from problem 7, if we let n represent the number of signaling states of a communications channel, derive an expression that represents the channel's maximum capacity for transmitting data. (*Note:* This result is known as Nyquist's theorem and provides us with the maximum data rate of a noiseless communications channel.)

9. Determine the percentage of overhead in a T1 circuit and an E-1 circuit.

10. Given the bit stream 00110100, which is the ASCII representation of the numeral 4, sketch the waveforms for Manchester and differential Manchester encoding.

11. Using the 4B/5B codes from Table 3.1 for "c," "idle," and "halt," sketch the corresponding NRZI waveforms.

12. Given the Manchester waveform shown in Figure 3.16, identify the corresponding data bits.

13. If an OC-3 circuit (see Table 3.4) is going to be carried by a 100-MHz line, what signal-to-noise ratio is needed to support this circuit?

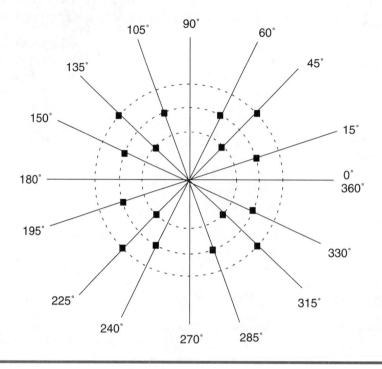

FIGURE 3.15

14. Explain what you believe the primary differences are between T-carrier circuits and optical circuits (OC).
15. Show how an E-1 circuit has a data rate of 2.048 Mbps.
16. Show how an STS-1 circuit has a data rate of 51.84 Mbps.
17. What is a local loop and why is it considered a bottleneck to high-speed home-based dialup networking?
18. What is meant by the terms "sampling" and "coding" relative to pulse-code modulation?

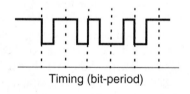

Timing (bit-period)

FIGURE 3.16

SUGGESTED READINGS AND REFERENCES

BATES, R. J., and D. GREGORY. 1998. *Voice and Data Communications Handbook.* New York: McGraw-Hill.

DYSON, P. 1995. *The Network Press Dictionary of Networking.* 2nd ed. San Francisco: Sybex.

FEIBEL, W. 1995. *The Network Press Encyclopedia of Networking.* 2nd ed. San Francisco: Sybex.

GALLO, M., and W. HANCOCK. 1999. *Networking Explained.* Boston: Digital Press.

———, and R. NENNO. 1985. *Computers and Society with BASIC and Pascal.* Boston: PWS.

HANCOCK, B. 1989. *Network Concepts and Architectures.* Wellesley, MA: QED Information Sciences.

———. 1996. *Advanced Ethernet/802.3 Management and Performance.* Boston: Digital Press.

HELD, G. 1988. Modem Modulation: Techniques and Compatibility Issues. In *Handbook of Communication Systems Management,* ed. J. W. Conrad, 419–431. Boston: Auerbach Publishers.

MORGAN, J. B. 1988. Data Communications Facilities. In *Handbook of Communication Systems Management,* ed. J. W. Conrad, 301–317. Boston: Auerbach Publishers.

PARKINSON, R. 1988. Digital Voice Trends. In *Handbook of Communication Systems Management,* ed. J. W. Conrad, 927–941. Boston: Auerbach Publishers.

STALLINGS, W. 1997. *Local and Metropolitan Area Networks.* 5th ed. Upper Saddle River, NJ: Prentice-Hall.

———. 2000. *Data and Computer Communications.* 6th ed. Upper Saddle River, NJ: Prentice-Hall.

STAMPER, D. A. 1991. *Business Data Communications.* 3rd ed. Redwood City, CA: Benjamin/Cummings.

TANENBAUM, A. S. 1996. *Computer Networks.* 3rd ed. Upper Saddle River, NJ: Prentice-Hall.

PHYSICAL, DATA LINK, AND NETWORK LAYER CONCEPTS

4 Physical Layer Concepts

In this chapter, we present an overview of the first layer of the OSI reference model, namely, the physical layer. This is the "touch-and-feel" layer. It provides for the physical transmission of data. We begin the chapter with an overview of physical layer issues. This discussion is then followed by an examination of the common physical and electrical characteristics of wire. Section 4.3 contains information about various copper-based transmission media, and Section 4.4 provides a similar discussion for fiber-optic cables. Section 4.5 is devoted to wireless communications, including radio and infrared transmissions, and includes information about the latest wireless LAN standards. Section 4.6 discusses satellite communications systems, including various satellite-based networking projects. The last section of the chapter provides information about structured cabling systems, which address the design and installation of a cable plant.

4.1   What Is the Physical Layer?

The physical layer is the lowest layer (layer 1) of the OSI model, which was discussed in Chapter 2. Before sending data on the network, the physical layer on the local node must process the raw data stream, translating *frames* received from the data link layer (layer 2) into electrical, optical, or electromagnetic signals representing 0 and 1 values, or bits. Frames, which are discussed in Chapter 5, are specially formatted bit sequences that incorporate both data and control information. The local physical layer is responsible for transmitting these bit sequences through the network medium to the physical layer of the remote node, where frames are reconstructed and passed to the remote node's data link layer.

From the most general perspective, the physical layer can be described by one word: wire. (If you are from the state of Texas, as is one of the authors, it's called "wharr.") Actually, it's a little more than just wire, but wire gives us an idea of what we are dealing with when we speak about the physical layer. You see, all aspects related to a transmission medium used for data communications, including both wired and wireless environments, are defined by physical layer protocols and specifications. These include the type of cable and connectors used, the electrical signals associated with each pin and connector—called *pinouts* or *pin assignments*—and the manner in which bit values are converted into physical signals.

Two examples are presented for your consideration. For the first example, consider a local area network. The physical layer of this network (abbreviated PHY in the documentation) defines, among other things, the type of cable permitted, the type of connectors we can use to attach the network cable to hardware devices, cable length restrictions, and the type and level of termination. A second example of a physical layer specification is the EIA RS-232C standard, which defines the electrical and physical characteristics used in serial communications. RS-232C specifies a 25-pin data bus (DB) connector that serves as an interface between a computer, referred to as the data terminal equipment, or DTE, and a peripheral device such as a modem or printer, referred to as the data communications equipment, or DCE. A later version of the RS-232C standard is RS-423, which defines a 9-pin DB connector. DB-9 connectors implement some of the signals from DB-25 and are used on IBM-PC or compatible microcomputers as a rear panel space-saving measure. The pinouts for the DB-25 and DB-9 connectors are shown in Figure 4.1.

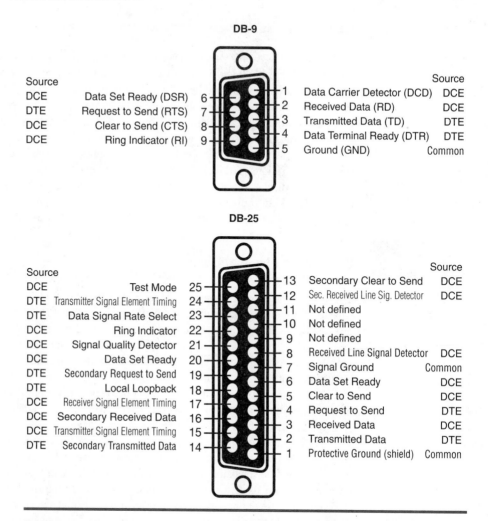

FIGURE 4.1 Pinouts of connectors used in RS-232-C serial communications. The DB-9 connector is frequently used for the low-speed serial port(s) on personal computers. The DB-25 connector is frequently encountered in modems. The numbers correspond to the pins of the connector; the accompanying text describes the signals associated with each pin. The column labeled Source refers to the signal source, either the data terminal equipment (DTE) unit (i.e., the computer) or the data communications equipment (DCE) unit (i.e., a peripheral device such as a modem).

4.2 The Physical and Electrical Characteristics of Wire

With the exception of wireless media, all network media have several common attributes, which can be placed into two broad categories: physical and electrical. In this section, we examine these common characteristics.

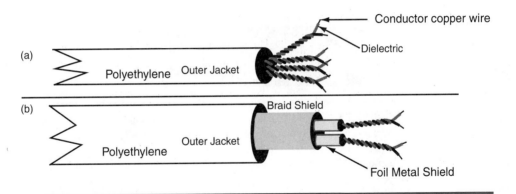

FIGURE 4.2   A UTP cable (a) and an STP cable (b). Pairs of wires are twisted around each other. One pair is used to transmit data; a second pair is used to receive data. Note the extra shielding in the STP cable.

Physical Characteristics

All physical media, regardless of their type, share three common physical elements. First, a *conductor* serves as a medium for the physical signal. This conductor is composed of either copper wire or glass or plastic fiber. In the case of copper, the wire can be stranded (i.e., composed of several thin wires) or solid, which can be thought of as a single "thick" strand. Stranded wire is usually stronger and more flexible. Furthermore, the thickness of a wire is given in terms of gauge, which represents the conductor's diameter. The lower the gauge, the thicker the wire. Thus, 22-gauge wire is thicker than 24-gauge. Most often, wire gauges are expressed in terms of AWG—American Wire Gauge— which is a classification system for copper wire based on a wire's cross-section diameter. For example, AWG 24 means that the conductor's diameter is 0.51 mm. The smaller the AWG number, the larger the diameter. Second, there is usually some sort of *insulation* material surrounding the conductor. The insulation serves as a protective "barrier" to the conductor by preventing the signal from "escaping" and preventing electrical interference from "entering." Finally, the conductor and insulation are encased in an outer sheath or "jacket." This jacket is composed of any of a number of materials, such as polyvinyl chloride (PVC) for nonplenum cable or Teflon for plenum cable. Plenum cable is used for cable "runs" through a return air system. The Teflon coating provides a low-flame spread and does not release toxic fumes as quickly as PVC does in case the cable burns during a fire. Both PVC and Teflon give off nasty toxic gases when burning. Teflon, however, is fire retardant (which is not the same as "fire resistant," where fire would not start) and takes much longer to get to a burning point. This decreases the chance of toxic fumes to affect people in a burning structure at the beginning of the fire.

Figure 4.2 shows the physical composition of two commonly used network cables: *unshielded twisted-pair* (UTP) and *shielded twisted-pair* (STP) cables. Twisted-pair cable consists of at least two insulated copper wires that have been twisted together. Examining both twisted-pair cable types relative to their physical attributes, we find that each consists of an inner core called a *conductor wire*, which is made of copper (or is comprised of copper and other metals such as tin or silver). The conductor wire is insulated

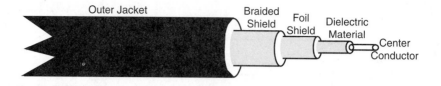

FIGURE 4.3 A coaxial cable typical of the types used in computer networks. Two layers of shielding provide protection against external noise and interference. The outer jacket protects the cable from the elements and may either be polyvinyl chloride (PVC) or Teflon; the latter is appropriate for cable runs in air plenums. Source: adapted from Leeds & Chorey, 1991a.

FIGURE 4.4 A fiber-optic cable. Source: adapted from Codenoll Technology Corporation, 1993.

by a dielectric material such as polyethylene. In UTP cable, this ensemble is housed within an outer jacket. In STP cable, each conductor wire pair is wrapped in a foil metal shield, and cable pairs are encased within a copper or tinned copper braid shield. The foil and braid shields make the wires less susceptible to electrical interference and noise.

A second type of network cable is *coaxial cable* (or simply, coax, pronounced *co*-axe). Coax consists of a single-wire copper conductor surrounded by a dielectric material and two types of shielding, a foil shield and a braided shield, arranged concentrically and encased in a PVC or Teflon outer jacket (Figure 4.3). This design heavily resists interference and has a high bandwidth. It is not totally impervious to noise, but it offers much more protection against the hazards that afflict UTP. The internal single-wire conductor can be stranded or solid; the former is preferred for hostile environments. Technically, coaxial cables exist in many, many cross-sectional diameters, ranging from several millimeters to several centimeters.

Another example of a commonly used network cable is *fiber-optic cable*. A sketch of its physical composition is shown in Figure 4.4. Fiber-optic cable consists of a glass fiber covered by a plastic buffer coating and surrounded by Kevlar fibers. The Kevlar fibers give the cable its strength. It is the same material used to make bulletproof vests and combat helmets. The Kevlar fibers are surrounded by a protective outer sheath. Notice once again the three primary physical attributes of cable: conductor, insulation, and outer sheath. The outer sheath (i.e., jacket) keeps the fiber safe and must meet any local electrical and cabling codes. Typically, fiber is enclosed in a fiber jacket called a buffer that is used to separate the fiber itself from any external contact and to protect the fiber from damage. Buffers range from standard dielectric, foam, or in the case of fibers that may be submerged in water or other liquids, gel-packed fiber. In such environments, gel-pack is useful because water that invades a cable can expand or contract (based upon pressure and temperature) and damage the fiber(s). Tight buffered cables allow

Stephanie Kwolek (1923–)

Stephanie Kwolek was born in New Kensington, Pennsylvania, in 1923. She earned a BS in chemistry in 1946 from Carnegie Institute of Technology (now Carnegie-Mellon University). Kwolek endeavored to attend medical school but was unable to afford the tuition and instead accepted a research position as a chemist with DuPont's Textile Fibers Laboratory in Buffalo, New York, after graduation. Although she regarded her employment as a "temporary measure," she found her work interesting and decided to make it her career. In 1950, Kwolek transferred to DuPont's Pioneering Research Laboratory in Wilmington, Delaware, where she stayed until her retirement as a research chemist in 1986.

While at DuPont, Kwolek's research focused on searching for new and better polymers, which are organic compounds (mainly synthetic) used for developing materials such as plastics, resins, and rubber. Her research resulted in the discovery of extremely rigid and strong petroleum-based synthetic fibers, which led to the development of DuPont's Kapton® polyimide film and Nomex® aramid fiber. During the 1960s, Kwolek also discovered a new branch of synthetics called liquid crystalline polymers, which resulted in a fiber that was five times stronger than steel, but only about half the density of fiberglass. DuPont marketed this material commercially beginning in 1971 and called it Kevlar®. Early Kevlar applications included bulletproof vests, radial tires, suspension bridge cables, and fiber-optic cable. Today, Kevlar is used to make, among others, skis, safety helmets, outdoor recreational equipment for hiking and camping, and puncture-resistant bicycle tires.

Although retired from full-time employment, Kwolek remains active by consulting for DuPont part-time and by doing committee work for the National Research Council and the National Academy of Sciences. She also enjoys mentoring young scientists, especially women. Kwolek is the recipient of the Kilby Award, the National Medal of Technology, and the 1999 Lemelson-MIT Lifetime Achievement Award. She also is recipient or corecipient of 17 U.S. patents, issued between 1961 and 1986, including five for the prototype from which Kevlar was created.

maximum protection for the fiber; loose buffered cables are useful in locations where the fiber (or tube) around the fiber will expand and contract (usually outdoors). A loose buffer (tube) around the fiber allows the buffer to expand and contract independently of the fiber itself.

Cables are jacketed with a variety of materials ranging from aluminum and Kevlar to PVC. Which jacket is used depends on local fire and electrical codes as well as where the cable is to be placed in the structure. As mentioned earlier, some materials such as PVC give off noxious fumes when burned and are therefore not allowed in areas where there is a return air plenum. Each jacket type has a variety of cable "stiffeners" inserted between the fibers to give the cable some rigidity and to afford the cable some strength when pulled or suspended. The number and type of stiffeners used (e.g., aluminum rods inserted in the jacket) vary from vendor to vendor.

Electrical Characteristics

The performance of a "wired" network is greatly dependent on the electrical characteristics of the cable used. Since bits ultimately become physical signals at the physical layer, signal quality is an important consideration when selecting a specific medium. Three very important electrical characteristics directly associated with signal quality are *capacitance, impedance,* and *attenuation.*

Capacitance   Capacitance is the property of a circuit that permits it to store an electrical charge. The capacitance of a cable determines its ability to carry a signal without distortion, which is the "rounding" of a waveform (Figure 4.5) due to a stored charge between the conductors of the cable. The more distorted a signal becomes, the more likely a receiving node will be unable to distinguish between 0s and 1s. High-quality cable has low capacitance—the lower the capacitance, the longer the distance a signal can travel before signal distortion becomes unacceptable. We must make an important point about capacitance and network data cabling. While network cable can have low characteristic capacitance per meter, the overall capacitance of the cable increases as the cable gets longer. Because of noise and other problems in transmission, a maximum cable length of about 100 meters exists for unshielded twisted-pair (UTP) network cable. This is true for even low-capacitance, high-quality UTP cable, which is used in a great preponderance of LANs. If the UTP cable is replaced with shielded twisted-pair (STP), which is very popular in token ring networks, there is still a maximum limitation under perfect conditions of about 100 meters. The reason for this limitation, however, is completely different than that for UTP cable. As STP cable gets longer, the capacitance builds up. This

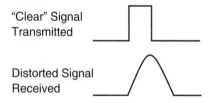

FIGURE 4.5 Capacitance eventually will distort a transmitted signal. Source: adapted from Leeds & Chorey, 1991a.

results in enough signal degradation to require some sort of signal amplification or regeneration for a signal to travel a greater distance. That's part of the reason there's a 100-meter length restriction on the UTP cable we use for our Ethernet LAN. There are other reasons as well, which we will address in our discussion of Ethernet/802.3 LANs in Chapter 9. (Also see the Note of Interest on Fourier Analysis in Chapter 3.)

Impedance   Impedance is a measure of the opposition to the flow of electrical current in an alternating current circuit. Measured in ohms (abbreviated by the Greek symbol omega, Ω), impedance is a function of capacitance, resistance, and inductance. Impedance mismatches, caused by mixing cables of different types with different characteristic impedances, can result in signal distortion. Cable manufacturers always list a cable's impedance, and you should pay close attention to these measurements. Also, different network hardware types may require different impedance values and may not work with values that are out of the range of performance for the hardware. For instance, most token ring equipment requires 150 Ω of impedance. On the other hand, Ethernet/802.3 twisted-pair networks want 85–111 Ω and don't appreciate 150 Ω at all.

Inductance is a property of an electrical circuit that opposes any change in the amount of current flowing within the circuit. Inductance in a circuit is analogous to inertia in mechanics and, in fact, is sometimes called electromagnetic inertia.

Attenuation   Attenuation is the decrease in signal strength, which occurs as the signal travels through a circuit or along a cable. The longer the cable, the greater the attenuation. Also, the higher the frequency of the signal, the greater the attenuation. Different types of cables are also subject to different amounts of attenuation. For example, in twisted-pair cable, the attenuation rises sharply as the signal frequency increases, whereas with coaxial cable, it rises less sharply as frequency increases. Fiber-optic cable, which is tuned for a specific wavelength, exhibits very low attenuation per unit of distance at that wavelength. Attenuation is measured in decibels (dB) of signal loss. When selecting cable, you should choose a type that has a low measure of attenuation for the network speeds and distances involved. Signal quality is affected most by the combination of attenuation and capacitance. This is illustrated in Figure 4.6.

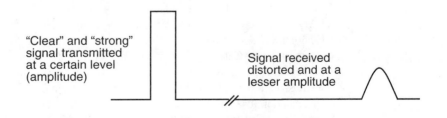

"Clear" and "strong" signal transmitted at a certain level (amplitude)

Signal received distorted and at a lesser amplitude

FIGURE 4.6   The combined effects of capacitance and attenuation result in a signal that is received distorted and weaker than what it was when transmitted. This can severely impact the performance of a network. Source: adapted from Leeds & Chorey, 1991a.

4.3

Copper Media

Copper cable comprises many different types of media, including unshielded twisted-pair (UTP), shielded twisted-pair (STP), IBM cable, and coaxial cable. Although all share common physical and electrical characteristics as noted earlier, the engineering of the cable and application distinguishes one from another. Let's examine these separately.

Unshielded and Shielded Twisted-Pair Cable

Twisted-pair cable is probably the most popular type of cable used in networks today. It works with all different types of networks. The name, twisted-pair, comes from how the cable is constructed. Twisted-pair cable consists of at least two insulated copper wires that have been twisted together. Data transmission requires four wires (two pairs): one pair to transmit data and one pair to receive data.

As noted in the previous section, twisted-pair cable is available in two varieties: unshielded and shielded. Standards for UTP and STP are provided by the Electronic Industries Association and the Telecommunications Industry Association (EIA/TIA). These organizations jointly developed the EIA/TIA-568 standard, which is a North American standard used worldwide. EIA/TIA-568 specifies the type of cable that is permitted for a given speed, the type of connectors that can be used for a given cable, and the network topology that is permitted when installing cables. The standard also defines the performance specifications that cables and connectors must meet. In short, EIA/TIA-568 represents a comprehensive standard for premises wiring that addresses network design and performance characteristics for physical media. Within the EIA/TIA-568 standard, there is an A version (568A) and B version (568B) that are used for industrial and nonindustrial networks, respectively.

The EIA/TIA-568 standard for UTP cable classifies the cable into the following categories: Categories 1, 2, 3, 4, 5, and 5E (Enhanced Category 5). Several other categories also exist, but they have not been standardized by EIA/TIA. They include Category 6, Category 7, Category 6/Class E, and Category 7/Class F. There's also a category for STP. Table 4.1 contains a summary of the various twisted-pair categories.

Of the various UTP cable types, Categories 3 and 5 receive the most attention in LAN circles today. However, with higher-speed LANs such as 100-Mbps and 1-Gbps Ethernet/802.3 becoming more commonplace, Category 5E as well as nonstandard Category 6 and Category 7 are receiving considerable attention. Category 3 is popular because it is the most common wire used for voice transmission in telephone systems in most commercial buildings. Furthermore, recent IEEE LAN protocols include a specification for Category 3 cable as a LAN medium for 100-Mbps networking. By using its existing cabling plant for local area networking, an organization does not have to modify its wiring infrastructure, thus saving a considerable amount of money. Categories 5, 5E, and the other higher-category copper UTP cables are popular because they are data-grade (not voice-grade, as is Category 3 cable). Category 5 is quite plentiful and has emerged as the cable of choice for 100-Mbps LANs. Organizations retrofitting their wiring infrastructure, or those engaged in new installations, are typically installing either Category 5 or Category 5E cable. Data-grade cable is usable for voice or

For more information about TIA, check out its Web site at http://www.tiaonline.org.

TABLE 4.1 Descriptions of Twisted-Pair Cable Categories

Category	Description
Category 1*	Used for voice transmission; not suitable for data transmission.
Category 2*	Low-performance cable; used for voice and low-speed data transmission; has capacity of up to 4 Mbps.
Category 3*	Used for data and voice transmission; rated at 10 MHz; voice-grade; can be used for Ethernet, Fast Ethernet, and token ring.
Category 4*	Used for data and voice transmission; rated at 20 MHz; can be used for Ethernet, Fast Ethernet, and token ring.
Category 5*	Used for data and voice transmission; rated at 100 MHz; suitable for Ethernet, Fast Ethernet, Gigabit Ethernet, token ring, and 155-Mbps ATM.
Enhanced Category 5*	Same as Cat 5 but manufacturing process is refined; higher-grade cable than Cat 5; rated at 200 MHz; suitable for Ethernet, Fast Ethernet, Gigabit Ethernet, token ring, and 155-Mbps ATM. Also known as Category 5E. Became a TIA standard in late 1999.
Category 6	Not yet a TIA standard, but general specifications are expected to include: 250-MHz rating; suitable for Ethernet, Fast Ethernet, Gigabit Ethernet, token ring, and 155-Mbps ATM. Should also be able to handle 550-MHz broadband video and 622-Mbps, 1.2-Gbps, and 2.4-Gbps ATM.
Category 6 (Class E)	Similar to Category 6 but is a proposed international standard to be included in ISO/IEC 11801.
Category 6 (STP)	Shielded twisted-pair cable; rated at 600 MHz; used for data transmission; suitable for Ethernet, Fast Ethernet, Gigabit Ethernet, token ring, and high-speed ATM.
Category 7	Not yet a TIA standard, but general specifications are expected to include: 600-MHz rating; capable of achieving higher speeds than Category 6. Will probably require new connectors instead of current RJ-45 connectors.
Category 7 (Class F)	Similar to Category 7 but is a proposed international standard to be included in ISO/IEC 11801.

* EIA/TIA-568 Standard

data. Voice-grade cable is usable for voice and for some types of data connections depending on the transmission speed and technique used.

Although UTP cable is a popular LAN medium, these cables pose problems in data transmission at the higher frequencies required by higher-speed networks. Two major factors are attenuation, which we discussed earlier, and crosstalk. Attenuation, as you might recall, occurs when the strength of a signal degrades as it travels along the cable. *Crosstalk* is electrical interference—it's another example of noise, which we discussed in Chapter 2. Crosstalk occurs when energy radiated from one wire pair is "picked up" on another pair. In one type of crosstalk, called *near-end crosstalk* (abbreviated NEXT), a signal on the transmit pair is so strong that it radiates to the receive pair. A direct consequence of this "spilled-over" radiation is that the receiving device cannot decipher the real signal. The combined effects of distortion and crosstalk result in an irregular variation in the shape or timing of a signal. This irregular variation is called *jitter* (kind of like a nervous person). Jitter is primarily caused by mixing unshielded and shielded cable.

Several factors, including the closeness of the wire pairs, the quality of the wire, and the number of twists per foot, cause crosstalk. Twisting wire pairs reduces crosstalk between a specific signaling pair. NEXT increases significantly for the first 60 feet (approximately 18 m). Higher-quality cable (read: more expensive) contains higher-quality wire compositions, better insulation, and improved twist per foot ratios between cable pairs, all of which will reduce NEXT.

In contrast to UTP, STP cable can dramatically reduce the hazards of crosstalk and noise because individual wire pairs are shielded. STP is still susceptible to the same kinds of interference that can wreak havoc over UTP, however. The difference is that STP can withstand more noise abuse than UTP and therefore can provide a more reliable transmission medium. STP cable, however, typically has a much higher impedance, which can cause signal reflections on transmission systems that require a lower-impedance cable—and that means data errors.

IBM Cable

IBM has its own classification of cable—the IBM Cable System (ICS)—which specifies nine cable types. Of the nine "types" defined, specifications are available for only seven; types 4 and 7 have no specifications. Table 4.2 contains a summary of ICS. Be very careful not to confuse ICS cable types with the categories of cable specified by EIA/TIA-568. A *type* is a grouping of categories and fiber-optic cables in a bundle based upon which type is being selected. A *category* is an EIA specification for a cable's construction.

Twisted-pair IBM cable is similar to non-IBM twisted-pair cable with one exception: The IBM version has more stringent specifications. This is why IBM adopted its own classification; it wanted to make certain that cable used in proprietary IBM environments satisfied IBM's high standards. IBM is not the only company to develop its own standards. Lucent Technologies, which used to be a major component of AT&T, and Anixter both have their own versions of cable bundles and specifications for installation.

TABLE 4.2 IBM Cable System

Type	Description
Type 1	2-pair STP, 22-gauge solid wire; used for token ring networks.
Type 2	Contains UTP and STP; 4-pair UTP, 22-gauge solid wire used for voice.
Type 3	2-pair UTP, 22-gauge solid wire used for data; 2-, 3-, or 4-pair UTP cable with 22- or 24-gauge solid wire; pairs must have a minimum of 2 twists/foot; voice-grade only.
Type 4	Not defined.
Type 5	Fiber-optic; 2 glass fiber cores at 100/140 micron; 62.5/125 micron fiber also allowed and is recommended by IBM; used as main ring of a token ring network.
Type 6	2-pair STP, 26-gauge stranded wire; used mostly as a patch cable to connect a node to a network.
Type 7	Not defined.
Type 8	2-pair STP, 26-gauge flat solid wire; designed for under-carpet installations.
Type 9	2-pair STP, 26-gauge solid or stranded wire; contains a plenum outer jacket; used for between-floor runs.

Coaxial Cable

Another type of copper cable is *coaxial cable*, which was described in the previous section. In computer networking, coax is described as either thick or thin. *Thick coax* is used as the medium for "Thick Ethernet," which is known as IEEE 802.3 10BASE5. Depending on the manufacturer, the cable's outer diameter ranges from 0.375 inch to 0.405 inch (0.96 cm to 1.04 cm). Thick coax resembles a garden hose and is known as "Etherhose" in slang terms in the industry. It has a designation of RG-8 with 50 Ω impedance. This medium is expensive and outdated; networks based on it today are usually inherited, not installed. *Thin coax* is used as the medium for "Thin Ethernet," which is known as IEEE 802.3 10BASE2. Its outer diameter ranges from 0.175 inch to 0.195 inch (0.448 cm to 0.5 cm). Thin coax is designated RG-58 and it too has 50 Ω impedance. Although quite popular in the 1980s and early 1990s, thin coax has fallen out of favor for UTP, and as is the case with Thick Ethernet, a Thin Ethernet is more likely to be inherited and not installed today.

In analog coaxial networks, such as residential cable television networks, cable such as RG-9 may be used, which typically has a greater impedance factor (62 Ω to 76 Ω) and differing electrical characteristics from those of RG-8. Similarly, RG-59 with an impedance of 75 Ω is used for home TV cable, but it looks almost the same as RG-58. It is easy to become confused because the cables within each genre look practically the same. In fact, use of the wrong type of cable is one of the most frequent causes of insidious network failure. Therefore, because not all coaxial cables are electrically the same, you must be careful to select the right one for the types of network equipment being considered for use. Reiterating what we just said (the distinction is very important): Although, outwardly, the cable used for cable TV resembles thin or thick coax, it is not the same electrically. Thin cable used for cable television is designated RG-59 and has 75 Ω impedance. This is quite different from thin network coax, which has 50 Ω impedance. As discussed earlier, impedance mismatches—caused by mixing cables with different impedances—can result in signal distortion.

While we're on the subject, the term BASE, which was mentioned in the first paragraph of this section on coaxial cable, is an abbreviation for *baseband.* A baseband network transmits digital signals directly without modulating their transmission. Thus, a baseband network is capable of transmitting only a single stream of data. This means that the transmission medium uses its entire bandwidth to carry a single signal. It does not mean, however, that the channel cannot be shared. Using multiplexing techniques such as time division multiplexing (TDM), nodes connected to a baseband network can share the medium, but they can only transmit when the channel is not busy. The transmission media of a baseband network can include twisted-pair cable, coaxial cable, and fiber-optic cable. Various topologies are also available, including star, ring, and bus. Baseband networks traditionally have been characterized by their limitations on transmission speed, maximum allowable distance, and maximum number of nodes. These limitations vary considerably, however, depending on the technology used. Three examples of baseband networks include thick coaxial Ethernet, thin coaxial Ethernet, and unshielded twisted-pair Ethernet. These three LANs are respectively designated by IEEE as 10BASE5, 10BASE2, and 10BASE-T. Note that the BASE designation implies that these are baseband LANs. The 10 designation refers to the LANs' transmission speed limitation, which in each of these cases is 10 Mbps. The last designations—5, 2, and

T—identify each LAN's maximum cable length or cable type. In the case of the first two, the cable type is presumed to be coaxial and the number represents the maximum cable length (5 = 500 meters; 2 = 200 meters). In 10BASE-T, however, the T represents cable type, specifically, unshielded twisted-pair. (See Chapter 9 for additional information about these LANs.)

In contrast to a baseband network is a *broadband network.* A broadband network typically uses frequency division multiplexing (FDM) to divide a channel's bandwidth into smaller, distinct channels, which can be used concurrently to transmit different signals. Thus, a broadband network is capable of transmitting voice, data, and video signals simultaneously over the same cable. Cable television, for example, uses broadband transmission with each channel occupying a bandwidth of approximately 6 MHz. The transmission media of a broadband network include coaxial and fiber-optic cables. Broadband networks are generally based on an analog design. Hence, when digital data are transmitted, modems are needed at each end to modulate and demodulate the signals. Besides channel separation, two additional defining characteristics of broadband networks include their ability to transmit data over long distances and their high bandwidth. Consequently, the term broadband is commonly used today in networking circles to refer to high-bandwidth access. Comparing the two, baseband is relatively simple and inexpensive to install, requires inexpensive interfaces, and is ideally suited for digital transmission. Broadband equipment is much more expensive, is based on analog signaling, and requires expensive amplifiers to strengthen its signal and personnel to maintain it.

Twin Axial Cable

We'll mention one more type of copper cable for completeness, because it exists in some computer networks, albeit proprietary ones that are a vestige of the mainframe days. It's called *twin axial* cable (twinax for short). It is much like coaxial cable except that there are *two* inner conductors instead of one. Because it is not used in the networks we discuss in this book, we'll stop right here.

4.4 Fiber-Optic Media

Fiber-optic cable, which was described in Section 4.2, is used in LANs as an alternative to copper cable. It carries data signals in the form of modulated light beams. The electrical signals from the sending computer are converted into optical signals by a light source—a light-emitting diode (LED) or a laser. (Recall from Chapter 2 that an LED is a semiconductor device that converts electrical energy into light.) With an LED source, the presence of light represents a 1, and the absence of light (i.e., no light pulse) represents a 0; with a laser source, which emits a continuous low level of light, a 0 is represented by the low level and a 1 is represented by a high-intensity pulse. This modulation technique is called intensity modulation. The light pulses enter one end of the fiber, travel through the fiber, and exit at the other end. The received light pulse is then converted back to electrical signals via a photo detector, which is a tiny solar cell.

Fibers, after a time, can develop microfractures (cracks) or strain fractures in suspended fibers. Fiber that has been physically pulled may have stress fractures. Many other nasty things can happen to perfectly good fiber. Glass fiber has very high tensile strength. The problem is that if a crack develops on the surface of the fiber, it may eventually cause the fiber to break or will cause optical dispersion problems in the meantime. This structural problem is similar to that of a pane of glass. Glass is fairly strong, but when scribed, the glass is easily broken. Further, when the pane is scribed and placed under strain, the scribed line will lengthen and weaken the pane, eventually causing breakage. Fiber cable can succumb to this problem. Another problem is *bend radius*. While fiber is much more flexible than copper cable and can be bent in much smaller radii than equivalent copper, microbends may appear in fiber that has been bent too tightly or "kinked." Microbends can cause light path disruption and increase the loss of the cable. Areas subject to chemical exposure, radical temperature changes, nuclear radiation, and other disruptive effects require special consideration in cable jacketing and type of fiber used. Check with the local installation specialist to find out which fiber type is best for your environment.

Fiber-optic cable is specified by the size of the glass fiber, which consists of two parts: an inner glass cylindrical core and an outer concentric glass cladding that has different optical characteristics than the core. The core and overall outside diameters are measured in microns (a *micron* is one micrometer, which is 1-millionth of a meter) and abbreviated by the symbol *μm*. A standard size is 62.5/125 μm—62.5 μm specifies the diameter of the inner glass core and 125 μm specifies the diameter of the outer concentric glass cladding. In Europe, 80/100 μm fiber is common. The inner glass core and outer glass cladding are the key elements of fiber-optic cable. The outer cladding of the glass is reflective; the inner core of the glass is transparent. Light goes through the transparent core, but remains in the core by bouncing off the reflective cladding, which is like a cylindrical mirror around the core. Thus, light stays in the fiber core as if it were a "light pipe" the same way water stays in the hollow core of a metal clad pipe. In addition to core size, fiber-optic cable is classified by the manner in which light rays travel through the medium. There are two general classifications: *multimode* and *single mode*.

Multimode Fiber   In multimode fiber, the core diameter ranges from 50 μm to 100 μm (i.e., from about 1/500th of an inch to about 1/250th of an inch). Also, in multimode fiber, different rays of light bounce along the fiber at different angles as they travel through the core (Figure 4.7). Therefore, the light rays actually travel different total distances as they go from one end of a long fiber-optic cable to the other end. Some light rays travel longer distances and some travel shorter distances, while the speed of light is a constant; therefore, some of the rays will arrive at the other end of the cable later than others. A consequence is that a pulse of light that enters one end of the cable might exit the other end with a little more spread (or dispersion) because some of the light rays get to the other end sooner than others. Thus, there is some amount of signal distortion at the receiving end of a transmission.

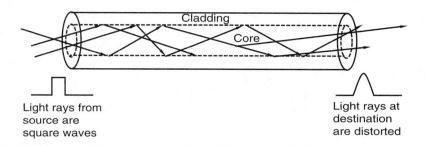

Light rays from
source are
square waves

Light rays at
destination
are distorted

FIGURE 4.7   In multimode fiber, the distance light rays travel through a cable varies. Some rays travel longer distances from sending and receiving nodes; others travel shorter distances. The cladding layer reflects any stray light waves, causing signal distortion at the receiving end. Source: adapted from Codenoll Technology Corporation, 1993.

Single-Mode Fiber   In single-mode fiber, the core diameter is 7 μm to 9 μm, which is about one-3000th of an inch. Therefore, it is considerably thinner than multimode fiber. When the diameter of the core is reduced to the order of a wavelength, the light cannot bounce off the walls of the core, allowing only a single ray of light, called the *axial ray,* to pass. (Single mode implies a single ray on a given frequency of light.) In single-mode systems, a light wave entering the fiber exits with very little distortion, even at very long distances and high data rates (Figure 4.8). In advanced systems (e.g., synchronous optical network, or SONET, which was discussed in Chapter 3), single-mode fiber transmission systems may allow multiple light sources in different light spectrums to interoperate over the same fiber (very similar in concept to multiple channels of TV on a cable system in a neighborhood). In this manner, the same fiber can increase its carrying capacity by changing out the electronics on both ends of a fiber link as additional speed is required through the fiber medium.

In a typical building or campus network, we usually do not have to worry about single mode versus multimode. Either can be used for almost any application. However, if we are connecting cities across a country (such as telephone and cable companies are currently doing), then single-mode fiber is used for these long distances. If either will do, it boils down to cost. Multimode fiber cable is much less expensive than single-mode fiber cable.

Fiber-optic cable is *the* ideal network medium when cable is involved. It is immune to electromagnetic interference (EMI) and other types of externally induced noise, including lightning. It is unaffected by most physical factors such as vibration. Its size is smaller and its weight lighter than copper. It has much lower attenuation per unit of length than copper. It can support very high bandwidth. With copper cable, we speak of bandwidth on the order of Mbps or Gbps with Gigabit Ethernet. With fiber-optic cable, we can speak of bandwidth in terms of Mbps, Gbps, terabits per second (Tbps), and beyond. In short, fiber is the most effective medium available in terms of bandwidth and reliability. Fiber-optic cable does have its drawbacks, however. First of all, glass fiber (the most common type of fiber) is more expensive than copper. Second, the signal strength of fiber degrades when there is any light loss. Third, if used as the medium for a LAN, it is limited to either a point-to-point or star configuration.

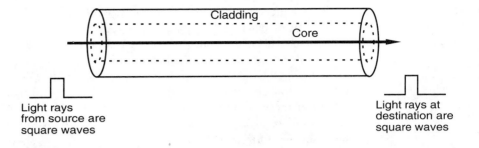

FIGURE 4.8 In single-mode fiber, all light rays travel the same distance from sending to receiving node. A direct consequence of this is no signal distortion at the receiving end, which results in higher bandwidth and lower attenuation per kilometer than multimode fiber. Single-mode fiber is the ultimate medium for long-distance connectivity. Source: adapted from Codenoll Technology Corporation, 1993.

An alternative to glass fiber is *plastic fiber,* which is constructed of plastic rather than glass and is more flexible than glass fiber. It also can be used in areas where it might be subjected to pressure that would crush a glass fiber. For example, if an office chair rolls over plastic fiber, the fiber springs back to its originally cast shape; glass fiber, on the other hand, breaks and, hence, must be cut and spliced. Plastic fiber, although available today, is not yet as popular as glass fiber. There are several reasons, including vendor availability, vendor expertise, manufacturing-related problems, and a very young set of standards for plastic fiber (it is known in IEEE circles as GRINPOF—graded index plastic optical fiber). Plastic fiber is also very easy to terminate and install. Glass fiber requires cutting and painstakingly careful polishing to ensure that signal loss is minimal at a splice or connection point. Plastic fiber is cut with a knife and heated in a special hand-held device that looks like a hair dryer. Through heat, the fiber is terminated and automatically polished, and it is available for use about 60 seconds later. Over time, plastic fiber will become the medium of choice for high-speed to-the-desktop connections due to its bandwidth, ease of installation, relative cheapness, and flexibility. At this writing, however, it is still pretty new in the industry and will require time to become popular.

Before we end this section, there is one more piece of information we need to impart. If you are planning a fiber-optic installation today, then you should keep in mind the following phrase:

multimode, graded-index, dual window fiber with a median frequency of 1300 nm

The multimode mode part of this expression was explained earlier. To understand the concept of graded-index, we first need to explain some properties of light. If a light ray travels within a medium of constant optical density, then the ray travels in a straight line. If, however, a light ray enters a medium of different optical density, and the ray enters the medium at an oblique angle, then the direction of the ray changes. This change of direction is called *refraction* and involves the bending of light. A common example of refraction is the "broken" appearance a stick has when it is immersed in water and viewed from an oblique perspective. The concept of "index" refers to a fiber-optic cable's *index of refraction,* which is a measure of the amount of bending a light ray undergoes as it travels within the cable. In a *graded-index* fiber, the core's refractive index is modified from its center to its edges to decrease the amount of modal dispersion. If you look at Figure 4.7, you will note that the light pulses are reflected off the cladding—this is what guides the light rays from source to destination. In multimode graded-index, variations in the density of the core medium change its index of refraction such that light is refracted (i.e., bends) toward the center of the fiber. So instead of light rays "bouncing" back and forth in a "V" and inverted "V" pattern as shown in Figure 4.7, we have more of a "rounded" pattern   . Thus, light rays within a graded-index fiber propagate along an oscillatory path, which decreases the amount of modal dispersion. This change in the fiber's refractive index reduces the amount light "bounces," which enables the signal to travel faster through the cable. In contrast to graded-index, there is *step-index* fiber. Unlike the gradual change of a graded-index fiber core's refractive index, the index of refraction of a step-index fiber's core is uniform. It should be clear that the graded-index concept is appropriate for multimode fiber, and step-index is appropriate for single-mode fiber.

The last part, *dual window, 1300 nm* refers to the fiber's ability to operate at more than one frequency. Specifically, dual window 1300 nm means that data can be transmitted at a wavelength of 1300 nanometers (a nanometer, abbreviated nm, is 1-billionth of a meter) with a corresponding frequency of 625 Mbps, one standard frequency step higher at 1550 nm (corresponding frequency of 2.4 Gbps), or one standard frequency step lower at 850 nm (155 Mbps). This is important if you want to use fiber for existing networks such as Ethernet/802.3 (which is perfectly happy with 850 nm) and later upgrade to ATM (which requires 1300 nm and 1550 nm for higher speed connections).

4.5 Wireless Communications

In wireless communications, signals travel through space instead of through a physical cable. There are two general types of wireless communication: *radio transmission* and *infrared transmission.*

Radio Transmission

Radio transmission refers to any wireless technique that uses *radio frequencies* (RF) to transmit information. RF transmissions are very popular today for wireless data services. Radio frequencies typically used for data communications are in the 800 MHz to 900 MHz range of the electromagnetic spectrum (Figure 4.9). In the United States, the Federal Communications Commission (FCC) has approved additional frequencies for wireless data services to operate in the 1.85-GHz to 2.20-GHz range. This slice of the RF spectrum is used for, among others, pagers, personal digital assistants (PDAs), laptops with PC cards (formerly known as PCMCIA cards), and cellular telephones. As a comparison, consider some of the more common frequencies and their applications. Cellular communications, for example, generally operate in the 824–849 MHz range

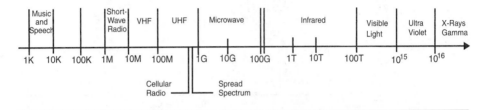

FIGURE 4.9 The electromagnetic spectrum (in Hz). Higher frequencies support greater bandwidth. Source: adapted from Breidenbach, 1990.

and the 869–894 MHz range; cordless phones and unlicensed wireless LANs (WLANs) operate in the 902–928 MHz range; pagers and beepers operate in the 931–932 MHz range; and general unlicensed commercial use operates in the 2.4–2.5 GHz range or 5.8–5.9 GHz range. Frequencies in the 902–928 MHz range are quite popular for data communications equipment. Furthermore, the three frequency ranges of 902–928 MHz, 2.4–2.5 MHz, and 5.8–5.9 MHz are generally used for various industrial, scientific, and medical applications and, hence, are commonly known as the ISM bands. Since these bands are not regulated by the FCC in the United States, unlicensed spread spectrum devices generally operate within these bands. The airwaves at these frequencies, however, are also crowded. Higher frequencies in the GHz range are less crowded, but access is controlled by the FCC. If licensing is to be avoided, then one must accept the attendant consequence, namely, low power, which cannot penetrate obstructions such as walls. This greatly reduces the range of a wireless network.

In a data communications network, signals from laptop wireless machines are transmitted via built-in antennas to the nearest wireless access point, which serves as a wireless repeater. These access points are connected to a backbone cable system (Figure 4.10). Radio waves typically are used to enhance existing cable systems rather than replace them. They are still susceptible to electromagnetic interference (EMI), however, and cannot penetrate interior drywalls or concrete bearing walls, particularly walls in buildings with steel frameworks, unless at a high enough frequency, which shortens the range of effective signal reach.

Microwave   One type of RF transmission method is *microwave,* which uses high-frequency waves and operates at a higher frequency in the electromagnetic spectrum (Figure 4.9). The microwave spectrum encompasses frequencies between 2 and 40 GHz. Access to these frequencies is strictly controlled by the FCC in the United States; therefore, users of microwave transmitters must be licensed. The FCC also monitors these frequencies for compliance. Microwave transmissions are considered a *line-of-sight* medium. Since microwave signals travel in a straight line, the transmitter and receiver must be in each other's line of sight. If not, because of their very short wavelength, microwave signals degrade once they encounter an obstruction. Even water droplets in the atmosphere attenuate microwave signals. Consequently, it is necessary to "spec out" the environment to ensure that a microwave transmitter and receiver will have a clear line of sight, sufficient power to offset attenuation, and a small enough distance between stations before installing them. A microwave medium uses parabolic

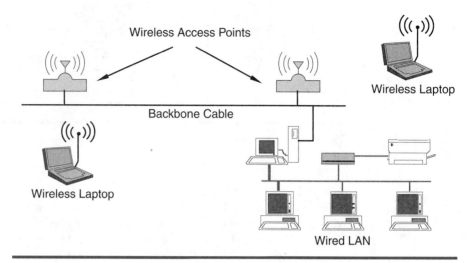

FIGURE 4.10 One example of a hybrid wireless environment. The "wireless access points" are directly connected to a backbone cable and serve as wireless repeaters for the wireless laptop computers. Completely wireless LANs also are possible. Source: adapted from Karvé, 1997a.

Sharpen your pencil and try to calculate how tall the towers would have to be to transmit a line-of-sight signal from, for example, Miami to Lisbon, a distance of about 6700 km.

antennas mounted on towers up to 30 miles apart. Because of the impact of the curvature of the earth on the line of sight, the higher the tower, the greater the range. Microwave data transmissions rates typically range up to 45 Mbps.

Line-of-sight media such as microwave are less expensive to install than cable for moderate distances in most situations. Microwave also offers a relatively high data rate (for a wireless medium). It also requires little or no maintenance, is fairly easy to implement, and has no recurring monthly or yearly costs, as is the case with leased circuits. On the other hand, line-of-sight transmissions are subject to environmental and atmospheric conditions (rain, fog, high humidity), as well as electromagnetic interference from many sources, including solar flares and sunspots. Furthermore, if units are placed too close to each other, overloading and signal interference can result. Because of these environmental and atmospheric drawbacks, you should not rely on microwave communication completely for mission critical operations. However, if an application can endure an occasional failure, then such media are acceptable.

Spread Spectrum Another radio technology is *spread spectrum,* which involves varying the frequency of a transmitted signal. This results in greater bandwidth than an unvaried signal. Spread spectrum has been around since World War II and was used to camouflage radio signals. Without it, a signal's frequency will remain constant, which makes the signal more easily susceptible to interference or interception. Spread spectrum transmission camouflages data by mixing signals with a pseudonoise (PN) pattern and transmitting the real signal with the PN pattern. The transmitted signal is spread over a range of the frequencies in the radio spectrum. Thus, to intercept a signal, the intercepting receiver must have two specific pieces of information: the mathematical function the transmitter is using to generate the PN pattern and the exact point in time the function is generated. Today, spread spectrum typically is employed in devices that

Hedy Lamarr (1914–2000)

Silver screen actress Hedy Lamarr was a Hollywood legend. She starred in approximately 25 films, sharing the spotlight with well-known screen icons such as Clark Gable, Spencer Tracy, and Judy Garland. Lamarr, who was raised in Austria and made her film debut at the age of 16, achieved film notoriety in the 1933 Austrian art film *Ecstacy,* where she appeared briefly in the nude. She also starred as Delilah in Cecil B. DeMille's 1949 film, *Samson and Delilah,* which costarred Victor Mature as Samson. Known more for her looks than her acting skills, Lamarr was featured in many scenes in which she simply stood around silently and looked beautiful. At one point in her career, Lamarr was regarded as The Most Beautiful Girl in the World, which she casually dismissed by stating, "Any girl can be glamorous. All she has to do is stand still and look stupid."

Although she was best known for her Hollywood career, Lamarr was also credited with developing the concept of spread spectrum. In 1941, Lamarr and composer George Antheil received a patent for a *secret communications system,* which enabled a transmission between sending and receiving devices to be scattered across different frequencies in the radio spectrum. (Lamarr's name was listed on the patent as Hedy Keisler Markey.) This frequency "scattering" made it more difficult for signals to be detected, jammed, or intercepted. The secret communications systems patent, which expired in 1965, served as the basis on which the concept of spread spectrum was developed. Today, spread spectrum is used extensively in wireless communications systems, including cordless and cellular telephones. In early 1997, Lamarr and Antheil were awarded the Electronic Frontier Foundation (EFF) Pioneer Award for their invention.

operate within the 902–928 MHz range, and many people equate the term "spread spectrum" with these devices. In reality, though, spread spectrum refers to a security technique and not a specific frequency. This is also why devices that employ spread spectrum technology are less prone to interference or unauthorized electronic eavesdropping than devices without it.

Infrared Transmission

Infrared (IR) transmission is another line-of-sight medium. It uses electromagnetic radiation of wavelengths between radio waves and visible light, operating between 100 GHz and 100 THz (terahertz). IR is generally restricted to LANs within or between buildings. IR transmission can occur in one of two ways: directed and diffused.

Directed IR requires an unobstructed line-of-sight connection between transmitter and receiver. It is basically a "point and beam" medium. In a *diffused IR* environment, a transmitter "floods" a specific area with a strong infrared signal. The light emitted from the transmitter is spread over a wide angle. The IR signal is transmitted by reflecting off ceilings, walls, and other surfaces. This is how a TV remote control device works. Thus, diffused IR can be thought of as a broadcast medium, whereas directed IR is point-to-point. Note that as a line-of-sight medium, IR is susceptible to some of the same kinds of problems as microwave, although it is less susceptible to electromagnetic interference than microwave.

Another wireless technology is *lightwave wireless.* In countries without a wire-based network infrastructure, it is much easier to implement a wireless connection topology than a physical cable topology. Lightwave connectivity refers to the use of line-of-sight laser-based connection facilities that allow long-distance light-based wireless networking without the need to install cable. Through the use of lightwave, a highly sophisticated transmission network is installed much more quickly than running fiber and yet provides a high-bandwidth solution for the installer. Lightwave is an ideal solution for many African countries and even for China, where a cable infrastructure is almost nonexistent.

Wireless LAN Standards

The future of wireless looks promising. After 8 years of existence, a standard was finally developed for wireless LANs (WLANs). It is called IEEE 802.11, and it was approved in 1997. This standard defines three different physical layer signaling methods and a common data link layer for wireless communication. (We discuss the IEEE 802.11 data link layer in Chapter 5.) Of the three physical layer signaling methods, two are RF-based, and one is infrared. The two RF-based physical layers are called *direct sequence spread spectrum* (DSSS) and *frequency hopping spread spectrum* (FHSS). Both operate at the 2.4-GHz to 2.4835-GHz ISM band. Data transmission rates for DSSS and FHSS initially were defined at either 1 Mbps or 2 Mbps. DSSS operates by spreading a signal over a wide range of the 2.4-GHz band. FHSS operates by transmitting short bursts of data on different frequencies. One burst is transmitted on one frequency, a second burst is transmitted on a second and different frequency, and so forth. Since each uses a different transmission method, the two RF physical layers cannot interoperate. The third physical layer defined in 802.11 is diffused infrared. WLANs based on diffused IR are not popular, however, and hence, most wireless media products currently support one of the RF physical layers. Although IEEE 802.11 specifies three different physical layers, only a single MAC method is used regardless of the physical layer selected (see Chapter 5).

Around the same time IEEE approved the 802.11 specification, the FCC opened up three new segments of the spectrum for wireless LANs: 5.15 GHz–5.25 GHz, 5.25 GHz–5.35 GHz, and 5.75 GHz–5.85 GHz. These bands have nearly no wireless congestion, and the higher frequencies are conducive to the development of products that operate at Ethernet speeds.

Shortly after the 802.11 standard was approved, the IEEE began a new standards effort for a higher rate WLAN technology called "802.11 High Rate." This endeavor led to the approval of IEEE 802.11b in mid-1998. IEEE 802.11b, which was jointly developed by Lucent Technologies and Harris Semiconductor, supports data rates of 5 Mbps and 11 Mbps for 802.11-compliant LANs that employ a DSSS physical layer. FHSS and IR WLANs are still limited to 802.11's original 1-Mbps or 2-Mbps data rates. The new higher-rate standard still relies on the same 2.4-GHz ISM band, however, and does not take advantage of the higher frequencies opened up by the FCC. The next evolution of WLANs appears to be IEEE 802.11a (yes, the letters are going in reverse), which will use a 5-GHz frequency and support a 50-Mbps transmission rate. Products based on 802.11a most likely will have a smaller signal range than products based on 802.11b because of higher electromagnetic radiation, which is attendant with higher frequencies.

Although the future of WLANs looks promising, especially in light of the recent activity surrounding the development and enhancement of WLAN standards, there are several barriers to the success of WLANs. Although prices are dropping, equipment costs still are relatively expensive. Furthermore, at 11 Mbps or even at 50 Mbps, WLAN data rates also are relatively slow in comparison with their wired counterparts, Fast Ethernet and Gigabit Ethernet. Finally, in recent years, many companies have spent millions of dollars upgrading their wire plants with either fiber, Category 5, or Enhanced Category 5 cable so they can support Fast Ethernet, Gigabit Ethernet, or ATM. Most of these companies probably do not want to scrap their cable plants and invest in WLANs. For the short term, it looks like WLANs will most likely carve out a niche market for themselves, and one such market is the residential home market. As families begin to install home-based networks, WLANs start to look very attractive from price, configuration, and performance perspectives. For example, an 11-Mbps home-based WLAN, coupled with a single broadband Internet connection such as xDSL or cable modem, will enable several family members to access the Internet without any pronounced performance degradation. For additional information about WLANs, see the Wireless LAN Alliance Web site at http://www.wlana.com.

4.6 Satellite Communications

Satellite communications are based on RF transmissions. Satellite communication systems consist of ground-based (also called terrestrial) stations made up of a parabolic antenna (transmitter/receiver) and orbiting transponders. The transponder receives a microwave signal from the ground unit (this transmission is called an uplink), amplifies it, and then transmits it back to earth (the return signal is called a downlink). The higher the altitude of a transponder, the longer it takes to traverse its orbit around the earth. An object located approximately 22,000 miles (36,000 km) above the equator is said to be in a *geosynchronous orbit* or a *geostationary earth orbit* (GEO). A satellite placed at this altitude (called a GEO satellite) traverses its orbit at approximately the same rate as the earth rotates. Thus, the satellite appears stationary with respect to the earth's rotation (Figure 4.11).

A geostationary earth orbit is also known as the Clarke orbit, named after author Arthur C. Clarke.

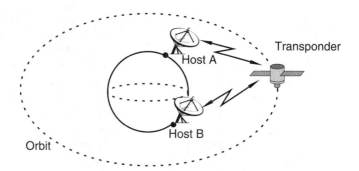

FIGURE 4.11 A satellite communication system. The transponder, a type of repeater, listens to some part of the spectrum. When it hears an incoming signal, it amplifies the signal and then rebroadcasts it at a different frequency. The downward signals can cover a large or narrow area.

Although signals travel at the speed of light, GEO satellite systems have high latency. After all, it takes time for a signal to travel 22,000 miles up and 22,000 miles down. Consider, for example, a typical satellite transmission involving two remote nodes. The sending node transmits a message to the satellite (sender-satellite uplink), the satellite transmits this message to the destination node (satellite-destination downlink), the destination node sends an acknowledgment to the satellite (destination-satellite uplink), and the satellite transmits the acknowledgment to the sender (satellite-sender downlink). The total distance involved in this transmission is four times 22,000 miles, or 88,000 miles. Dividing by the speed of light (186,000 miles per second), this transmission incurs a total *propagation delay* of nearly one-half second (470 milliseconds). GEO satellites can incur propagation delay anywhere from 274 milliseconds to as much as 1050 milliseconds. If you happen to have a home-based satellite system and cable TV, with each system connected to a different television, you probably know what we mean by propagation delay. If both televisions are set to receive the same program, the cable TV will receive its broadcast slightly ahead of the satellite-based TV. A direct consequence of this latency is that the longer it is, the less bandwidth the system can support. In contrast, microwave transmissions have a 3-ms/km delay, and coax has a 5-ms/km delay.

The bandwidth capability of satellite systems varies and is a function of the frequency at which the satellites transmit. Four common frequencies are C-band, Ka-band, Ku-band, and V-band. C-band is 6-GHz uplink and 4-GHz downlink. Ka-band is 28-GHz uplink and 18-GHz downlink. Ku-band is 14-GHz uplink and 12-GHz downlink. V-band is above 30 GHz and is still being researched and developed. Since satellites can operate at different frequencies, to prevent frequency interference, satellites cannot be placed any closer than 4° apart at the same altitude. A quick calculation reveals that only 90 satellites can be placed at the same altitude. A constellation of only eight GEO satellites, however, is needed to provide worldwide coverage.

In addition to propagation delay and the limited number of satellites, there are other disadvantages of satellite communications. First, satellite communications is expensive. It costs a lot of money to build and then deliver a satellite to its correct orbit. For example, we would probably not want to contract with NASA to launch a satellite into geosynchronous orbit to network two geographically dispersed sites. Well, we might want to, but our chief financial officer or budget manager might blow a gasket. Second, satellites have a limited operating life, and required maintenance or service can get very expensive. Again, we really should check with our boss before launching one. Signals from satellite communications can also be interfered with or blocked by buildings, foliage, or various atmospheric conditions. Finally, satellite transmissions are easily susceptible to eavesdropping (i.e., they can be monitored by unauthorized personnel). Thus, implementing appropriate security precautions is important.

Satellite communications does have its advantages over land-based links, though. Probably the biggest advantage of satellite communication is that satellites can reach geographically remote areas. This includes countries that have no or little communications or wiring infrastructures. Another advantage if you own the satellite system (e.g., NASA) is that there are no recurring leased line charges. If you do not own your own satellite, then there are recurring transponder fees or charges for leasing satellite time.

Several commercial satellite communications projects have recently been proposed or deployed. One project is the Teledesic Network project, which has Bill Gates as one of its partners. The Teledesic project comprises 840 interlinked *low-earth orbit* (LEO) satellites that are to provide global access to voice, data, and video communications beginning in the year 2002. It is supposed to support 1 million full-duplex E1 (2.048 Mbps) connections and have a capacity that will support millions of simultaneous users. Compared to GEO satellites, which orbit at approximately 22,000 miles, LEO satellites orbit anywhere from 300 miles to 1200 miles. Comparing velocities, the velocity of LEO satellites is greater than that of GEOs, which approximates the earth's orbit rate. Also, only eight GEO satellites are needed to provide global communications. Depending on their orbit, a constellation of up to 48 LEOs is needed for global coverage. Because GEO satellites' orbit matches the earth's, they are always in communication with an earth-based antenna. LEO satellites are only in sight of a terrestrial antenna for at most 15 minutes. Consequently, a LEO-based satellite communication must be transferred from one satellite to another within the constellation. LEO satellite systems also do not suffer from the type of propagation delay found with GEO satellite systems. The propagation delay of LEO satellites ranges from 40 milliseconds to 450 milliseconds, making them better candidates to support interactive applications such as videoconferencing. Besides LEO satellite systems, there are also *medium-earth orbit* (MEO) satellite systems, which usually orbit from 6000 miles to 12,000 miles and have a latency of approximately 250 milliseconds; MEOs need a constellation of 20 satellites for global coverage.

Another commercial satellite communications project is Iridium, which began providing hand-held global satellite-based telephone and paging services on November 1, 1998. Iridium operates under the parent company, Iridium LLC, which is an international consortium headquartered in Washington, DC, and comprising several key telecommunications companies, including Motorola and Sprint. The Iridium system consists of 66 LEO satellites orbiting 485 miles above the earth. Twelve ground station gateways link the Iridium satellite constellation to terrestrial wireless and landline public telephone networks. The satellites, which effectively serve as sky-based cellular towers, enable wireless signals to be transmitted overhead instead of through ground-based cells. Furthermore, the low-earth orbit makes the satellites close enough to the ground station gateways that they can receive signals of hand-held devices. Thus, regardless of location—from the middle of the Atlantic Ocean, to the top of Mt. Everest, to the jungles of Africa—subscribers of the Iridium system can make and receive telephone calls using their Iridium phones via a single telephone number. Furthermore, subscribers can use their Iridium phones in satellite mode when landline wireless cellular service is unavailable, but still operate them in normal cell mode when terrestrial wireless services are available. Finally, if subscribers' phones are turned off, they can still be contacted via their Iridium pager, 24 hours a day, 7 days a week.

As the world's first global satellite phone and paging company, Iridium LLC set lofty goals for itself. Although the company was able to achieve most of its technical goals, it fell far short of its subscriber base goal. One reason for this was the price of service. An Iridium telephone, for example, cost $3000, and a satellite call cost $3 per minute. Ultimately, on August 13, 1999, the company filed for bankruptcy. Unable to secure additional financial support or sell its assets, Iridium LLC was ordered to deorbit (i.e., crash back to earth) its satellites in March 2000. As of this writing, however, no deorbiting has occurred. Instead, Motorola is still providing service to Iridium subscribers. Although Iridium LLC has received interest from several potential buyers, no outside purchase of the Iridium system has taken place to date.

A third satellite communications project is Globalstar, which is led by founding partner, Loral Space & Communications and consists of a consortium of international telecommunications companies. The Globalstar system comprises a constellation of 48 LEO satellites orbiting at an altitude of 876 miles above the earth. Four additional satellites are also in orbit as spares. The 48-satellite constellation was completed in November 1999, and the four backup satellites were launched in January 2000. The constellation's design involves eight orbital planes of six satellites each, inclined at 52°. This configuration enables Globalstar to provide earth-based service from 70° north latitude to 70° south latitude. (Consult an atlas to identify areas that are and are not covered.) Furthermore, unlike other satellite communication systems, Globalstar software resides on the ground, not on the satellites. The Globalstar system delivers satellite telephony services through a network of exclusive service providers. Subscribers include cellular users who roam outside their coverage areas, people who work in remote areas where terrestrial systems do not exist, residents of underserved markets, and international travelers who need to keep in constant touch. Globalstar enables subscribers to use a single phone for both cellular and satellite calls and provides an array of services via a Globalstar phone, including traditional voice calls, short messaging service, global roaming, facsimile, and data transmission. Additional information about Globalstar can be found at http://www.globalstar.com.

A fourth and final project we will mention is a "metro-area satellite" project by Angel Technologies, a privately held St. Louis-based company. Using piloted FAA-certified High Altitude Long Operation (HALO) aircraft flying above 52,000 feet over cities, Angel Technologies intends to deploy wireless broadband "super-metropolitan area" networks on a city-by-city basis that will interconnect subscribers at multimegabit per second data rates. Equipped with a telecommunications payload, a HALO aircraft serves as the centralized hub of a wireless, line-of-sight, star-based topology network. Thus, connectivity between two hosts connected to the HALO network is via a single hop. Connectivity between HALO hosts and non-HALO hosts will be provided via dedicated HALO gateways connected to public switched networks. Compared to conventional high-speed wireless networks, the deployment of a HALO network within a metropolitan region does not require attention to matters such as roof rights negotiations for tower placement, compliance with local zoning laws, or tower construction. A HALO network can begin providing service to its subscribers almost immediately to anyone within its coverage area, which ranges from 50 miles to 75 miles in diameter. Scheduled to begin commercial service in 2001, the HALO network is expected to provide businesses with broadband services at data rates ranging from 5 Mbps to 25 Mbps and higher. Individual consumers can also subscribe to the HALO network for Internet access and network-based entertainment services at data rates ranging initially from 1 Mbps to 5 Mbps, with higher data rates available as the broadband market grows. Additional information about the HALO network can be found at `http://www.angelcorp.com`.

4.7 Structured Cabling Systems

Associated with a network's physical layer is the design and installation of the network's media. In any new cable installation or wiring retrofit project, a cable plan that specifies the type of cable to use and the manner in which the cables will be configured should be devised prior to any installation. The concept of cable planning is the focus of EIA/TIA-568, which we first introduced in Section 4.3. EIA/TIA-568 represents comprehensive *structured cabling systems standards* for premises wiring that address network design and performance characteristics for physical media. The standards are generic in nature (i.e., free of any specific vendor equipment) but still provide network administrators with enough information to design a robust cable plant that can accommodate different forms of transmissions (e.g., voice, data, video, multimedia) and support a multiproduct, multivendor environment.

A structured cabling system comprises six subsystems: building entrance, equipment room, backbone cabling, telecommunications closet, horizontal cabling, and work area (Figure 4.12). The *building entrance* provides interbuilding connectivity. This is where an organization's overall main network trunk line interconnects with a building's communications facilities so that LANs within the building have connectivity throughout the enterprise. The *equipment room* is the heart and soul of the building's network infrastructure. It contains equipment that provides connectivity to other buildings as well as to the telecommunications closets located on each floor of the building. Thus, a building's equipment room can support all of the functions of a telecommunications equipment but generally contains equipment that is more complex than what is located within a telecommunications closet. A building's *backbone cabling* interconnects the building's telecommunications closets, equipment rooms, and entrance. Thus, a backbone cable serves as the main trunk line for network connectivity. The specified backbone cabling topology is a hierarchical star.

A *telecommunications closet* (commonly called a wiring closet) houses a building's telecommunications equipment and is where cable is terminated or where cross-connects are made. Most buildings have one telecommunications closet per floor, and they are interconnected by a backbone cable. In other cases, a building entrance doubles as a telecommunications closet and provides connectivity to each floor of a building as well as

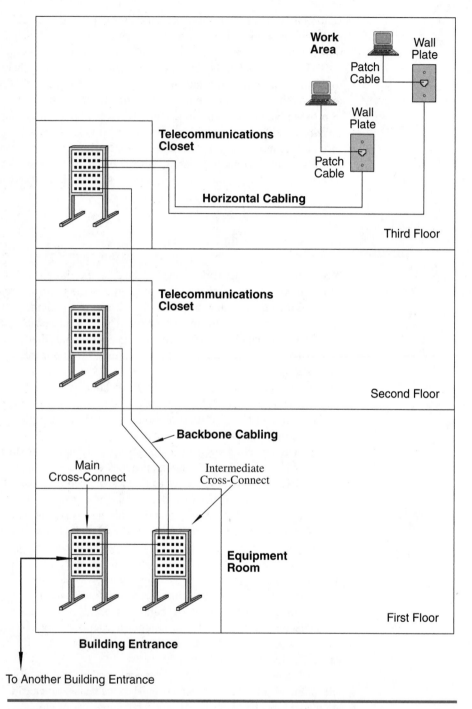

FIGURE 4.12 Main components (subsystems) of a structured cabling system.

interbuilding connectivity. In this latter case, there is no backbone cable. The *horizontal cabling* extends from the work area to the telecommunications closet and is based on a star topology. The horizontal cabling consists of the cable itself, the wall outlet (formally called the telecommunications outlet), cable terminations, and cross-connections. The *work area* extends from the wall outlet to the network station (formally called the station equipment). The work area consists of the station equipment, patch cables, and adapters.

Cable plants installed properly and according to standards should provide an organization with a wiring infrastructure that will accommodate current and future growth for at least 10 years. In the event an infrastructure requires frequent reconfigurations, one innovative approach is to install Sumitomo Electric Lightwave's FutureFLEX Air-Blown Fiber Optic (ABF) Cabling System. The ABF system consists of a flexible tube infrastructure that contains up to 19 small individual tubes housed within an outer jacket. Using a stream of nitrogen gas, bundles of fiber-optic cable are blown through the tubes and terminated in an equipment room, within a telecommunications closet, or even at the desktop (i.e., work area). Consequently, once the tube infrastructure is in place, fiber-optic cable can be provided anywhere to the network at any time.

End-of-Chapter Commentary

You should now have a good understanding of the fundamental concepts and terms related to the physical layer and the different types of transmission media (both wired and wireless) used at the physical layer. Many of these concepts are discussed in later chapters in specific contexts. For example, Chapters 7, 9, 10, 11, and 15 contain discussions of the various copper and fiber-optic cables presented here but from the perspective of their specific LAN applications. In Chapter 6, key physical layer concepts are applied to specific physical layer hardware components. In Chapter 9, we embellish our discussion of post-Category 5 cable when we introduce Gigabit Ethernet and the latest "gigabit copper" cabling designed to support gigabit speeds. Finally, Appendix C contains guidelines for installing UTP cable. Our next order of business is the data link layer, which is the subject of Chapter 5.

CHAPTER REVIEW MATERIALS

SUMMARY

• The physical layer is the lowest layer of the OSI model. Anything associated with connecting, maintaining, and disconnecting a physical circuit for data transmission occurs at this layer. These include the types of cable and connectors used, the electrical signals associated with each pin and connector, and the manner in which bits (the protocol data unit of the physical layer) are converted into physical signals.

• All physical media consist of a conductor that serves as the medium for a signal, insulation material that protects the conductor, and an outer jacket that surrounds the insulation material and conductor.

• Common electrical characteristics include the concepts of: capacitance, which is the ability of a cable to carry a signal without distortion; impedance, which is a measure of the opposition to the flow of electrical current in a cable; and attenuation, which is the degradation of a signal as it travels along a cable.

• Specific types of network media include UTP and STP cable, thin and thick coaxial cable, IBM cable, and glass and plastic-based fiber-optic cable (single-mode and multimode). EIA/TIA 568 has established specific categories for UTP and STP cable.

• Near-end crosstalk (NEXT) is a type of electrical interference common among various UTP and STP cable types.

• A discussion of wireless communications was restricted to information about specific radio transmission technologies, including microwave and spread spectrum. Microwave is a line-of-sight transmission, which implies signal degradation whenever an obstruction occurs between sending and receiving stations. Spread spectrum is a security technique used to camouflage radio signals. A second type of wireless communications is infrared (IR) transmission. Two types of IR transmissions include: directed IR, which is a "point-and-beam" technology, and diffused IR, which floods a specific area with a transmitted signal. Wireless LANs (WLANs) and corresponding IEEE standards are based on these wireless strategies.

• Satellite communications involves placing various communication satellites in orbit around the earth. Satellites can be placed in a geosynchronous orbit (22,000 miles above the equator), medium-earth orbit (6000 to 12,000 miles in space), or low-earth orbit (300 to 1200 miles in space). Although a geosynchronous orbit is the best (e.g., only eight satellites are needed for global coverage, and the satellites appear stationary to the earth), it also introduces propagation delays of approximately one-quarter of a second. Several high-profile satellite-based communications projects are currently underway.

• A structured cabling system involves standards related to the design and installation of a building's telecommunications wiring infrastructure. One standard, developed by EIA/TIA, specifies the minimum requirements for a cable plant within an office environment. This includes recommended topologies and cable lengths, specific media parameters based on expected LAN and cable performance, and connectors and pin assignments to ensure interoperability. An EIA/TIA-compliant cable plant has a useful life expectancy of more than 10 years.

VOCABULARY CHECK

attenuation	data communications	jitter
baseband cable	equipment (DCE)	near-end crosstalk (NEXT)
broadband cable	data terminal equipment (DTE)	pinouts
capacitance	frames	shielded twisted-pair (STP)
coaxial cable	IBM cable	unshielded twisted-pair (UTP)
conductor	impedance	
crosstalk	insulation	

REVIEW EXERCISES

1. Describe the function of the physical layer.
2. What is the purpose of a conductor wire?
3. Do you think attenuation is higher in solid conductor cables or stranded conductor cables? Why?
4. Why is stranded wire considered to be stronger than solid wire?
5. Explain the difference(s) between plenum and nonplenum cable.
6. Describe and contrast capacitance, impedance, and attenuation.
7. What impact does higher-quality cable have on capacitance and attenuation?

	Cable A	Cable B	Cable C
AWG/Stranding	24/solid	22/stranded	24/solid
Capacitance (per ft)	20	17	14
Attenuation (dB/1000 ft)	6.7–33	6.7–27	6.7–25
Impedance (ohms) at 1 MHz	105	85–120	130
NEXT (dB/1000 ft)	44	53	32
Number of pairs	4	4	4

8. The chart above contains specific electrical characteristics about three different UTP cables manufactured by the same vendor. Of the three cables, which would you select to use as the cable plant for your LAN? Why?

9. What is EIA/TIA-568?

10. Describe and contrast the various UTP category types.

11. What is crosstalk and what impact can it have on data transmissions?

12. Describe the differences between copper-based media and fiber-optic cable.

13. Why does fiber-optic cable have greater capacity than copper-based media?

14. Compare and contrast single-mode and multi-mode fiber-optic cable.

15. Compare and contrast graded-index and step-index fiber-optic cable.

16. Explain the concept of dual window as applied to fiber-optic cable.

17. What is the electromagnetic spectrum?

18. What is a line-of-sight medium?

19. Give an example of an appliance or equipment (other than what was given in the chapter) that uses direct IR and one that uses diffused IR.

20. Compare and contrast GEO, MEO, and LEO satellite communications systems.

21. The following two alternatives are available for transferring data between two points:
    a. a GEO-based communications satellite with a 10-Mbps transmission rate
    b. a terrestrial-based network comprised of T1 links (1.544 Mbps)

    Assume that the satellite can transfer any size packet (thus, at most only one packet is needed for any data transmission) and has a 270-ms propagation delay. Further assume that the T1-based network has a maximum packet size of 1000 bits, and four hops are required from source to destination. How many bits must be transmitted in a message to make the satellite network have a lower delivery time?

22. What is a structured cabling system? Include a brief description of the various subsystems associated with a structured cabling system.

23. Your supervisor has informed you that she is considering installing a wireless network because she is convinced that this is the future of networking. She has asked for your opinion and will use it as a basis for her decision. What would you say to her?

24. Defend or refute the following position statement: "Category 5 UTP is the best cable to use for a network wire plant."

SUGGESTED READINGS AND REFERENCES

BREIDENBACH, S. 1990. Motorola Develops Wireless Network. *LANtimes,* 5 November, 15–16.

CHIQUOINE, W. A. 1997. Enterprise Cable Management. *Network Magazine,* July, 114–119.

CLARK, E. 1998. Network Cabling's New High-Wire Act. *Network Magazine,* March, 74–79.

CODENOLL TECHNOLOGY CORPORATION. 1993. *The Fiber Optic LAN Handbook.* 5th ed. Yonkers, NY: Codenoll Technology Corporation.

CRAY, A. 1997. Wiring for Speed, Playing for Time. *Data Communications,* April, 75–80.

DYSON, P. 1995. *The Network Press Dictionary of Networking.* 2nd ed. San Francisco: Sybex.

FEIBEL, W. 1995. *The Network Press Encyclopedia of Networking.* 2nd ed. San Francisco: Sybex.

FRANK, A. 1994. Fiber Optics for Networks. *LAN Magazine,* November, 25–26.

GALLO, M., and W. HANCOCK. 1999. *Networking Explained.* Boston: Digital Press.

GRIER, J. 1995. The LAN Unleashed. *LAN Magazine,* September, 107–112.

HANCOCK, B. 1996. *Advanced Ethernet/802.3 Management and Performance.* Boston: Digital Press.

HENDERSON, T. 1995. Railroading the Category 5 Spec. *LAN Magazine,* October, 119–124.

HUDGINS-BONAFIELD, C. 1998. Networking in the 21st Century: The Sky's the Limit. *Network Computing,* 15 March, 70–94.

HUME, B., and C. OGDEN. 1993. Taming the Wire. *LAN Magazine,* September, 91–100.

JOHNSON, J. T. 1994. Wireless Data: Welcome to the Enterprise. *Data Communications,* 21 March, 42–55.

JONES, J. 1995. Cable Ready. *LAN Magazine,* September, 87–93.

KARVÉ, A. 1997a. Lesson 112: 802.11 and Spread Spectrum. *Network Magazine,* December, 25–26.

———. 1997b. The Wide World of Wireless. *Network Magazine,* December, 42–48.

KEOUGH, L. 1992. Premises Wiring: The Quiet Revolution. *Data Communications,* November, 103–115.

KILARSKI, D. 1997. Satellite Networks: Data Takes to the Skies. *Network Magazine,* December, 52–58.

KIM, D. 1994. Cable Ready. *LAN Magazine,* January, 83–90.

LAN TECHNOLOGY. 1990. Wireless Networking Gains Momentum: Vendors Exploit Different Technologies. *LAN Technology,* December, 25–28.

LEEDS, F., and J. CHOREY. 1991a. Cutting Cable Confusion: The Facts About Coax. *LAN Technology,* July, 31–49.

———. 1991b. Round Up Your Cable Woes. *LAN Technology,* October, 39–56.

———. 1991c. Twisted-Pair Wiring Made Simple. *LAN Technology,* April, 49–61.

MAKRIS, J. 1998. The Copper Stopper? *Data Communications,* March, 63–71.

MARA, F. 1996. Rewiring the Workplace. *LAN,* May, 101–107.

———. 1997. Testing High-Performance Copper Cabling. *Network Magazine,* July, 127–131.

MCMULLEN, M. 1995. Making Light of Data. *LAN Magazine,* September, 99–106.

MILLER, K. 1994. Cellular Essentials for Wireless Data Transmission. *Data Communications,* 21 March, 61–67.

MOLTA, D. 1996. How Far Is It to 802.11 Wireless LANs? *Network Computing,* 1 June, 126–129.

———, and J. Linder. 1995. The High Wireless Act. *Network Computing,* 1 July, 82–100.

MORSE, S. 1991. Sorting Out the Spaghetti: Ethernet Wiring Made Simple. *Network Computing,* October, 88–93.

MYERS, T. 1997. Ensuring Proper Cable Installation. *Network Magazine,* July, 121–125.

RICHARDSON, R. 1997. Home-Style Wiring. *Network,* June, 95–99.

SANDERS, R. 1992. Mapping the Wiring Maze. *LAN Technology,* 15 October, 27–36.

SAUNDERS, S. 1992. Premises Wiring Gets the Standard Treatment. *Data Communications,* November, 105.

———. 1994. Bad Vibrations Beset Category 5 UTP Users. *Data Communications,* June, 49–53.

SCHNAIDT, P. 1994. Cellular Hero. *LAN Magazine,* April, 38–44.

STALLINGS, W. 2000. *Data and Computer Communications.* 6th ed. Upper Saddle River, NJ: Prentice-Hall.

STRIZICH, M. 1993. Networks Unplugged. *LAN Magazine,* December, 53–64.

TANENBAUM, A. S. 1996. *Computer Networks.* 3rd ed. Upper Saddle River, NJ: Prentice-Hall.

TOLLY, K., and D. NEWMAN. 1993. Wireless Internetworking. *Data Communications,* 21 November, 60–72.

WITTMAN, A. 1994. Will Wireless Win the War? *Networking Computing,* 1 June, 58–70.

———. 1997. Earthquake or a New IEEE Standard? *Network Computing,* 15 August, 37.

5 Data Link Layer Concepts and IEEE LAN Standards

CHAPTER OBJECTIVES

After studying this chapter, you will be able to do the following:

1. Describe the operation of the data link layer relative to the OSI reference model.
2. Give examples of specific data link layer services.
3. Explain the difference between IEEE's and OSI's versions of the data link layer.
4. Identify the LAN standards that are part of IEEE's Project 802.
5. Explain the differences between the logical link control (LLC) and media access control (MAC) data link sublayers.
6. Describe the concepts of framing, flow control, and error control.
7. Understand the various fields of an IEEE 802.3 frame.
8. Distinguish between a MAC sublayer address and an Internet address.
9. Distinguish between error correction and error detection.
10. Understand how parity can be used to correct single-bit errors.
11. Understand the concept of cyclic redundancy checksums.
12. Calculate the CRC checksum, given a generator polynomial and a bit stream.
13. Distinguish among common invalid Ethernet/802.3 frames.
14. Distinguish between random access and token passing media access control protocols.
15. Describe the differences among the various carrier sense protocols.
16. Explain the concepts of data prioritization and quality of service.

CHAPTER OUTLINE

- **5.1** What Is the Data Link Layer?
- **5.2** The Logical Link Control (LLC) Sublayer
- **5.3** The Media Access Control (MAC) Sublayer
- **5.4** Data Prioritization and Quality of Service
- End-of-Chapter Commentary

- Chapter Review Materials
  - *Summary*
  - *Vocabulary Check*
  - *Review Exercises*
  - *Suggested Readings and References*

In this chapter, we discuss the second layer of the OSI model, namely, the data link layer. This layer handles the transfer of data between the ends of a physical link—it is responsible for transferring data from the network layer on the source machine to the network layer on the destination machine. We begin the chapter with an overview of the data link layer and provide information about IEEE, which developed data link layer protocols that serve as the basis for various LAN technologies such as Ethernet and token ring. In the remaining part of the chapter, we examine the data link layer from IEEE's perspective. Section 5.2 contains a discussion of the functions of the logical link control (LLC) sublayer, which is responsible for framing, flow control, and error control. In this section, we examine specific framing techniques, introduce two flow-control protocols, and learn various error-control schemes. The media access control (MAC) sublayer is the topic of Section 5.3, which describes two general access control protocols: random access methods and token passing methods. The last section, Section 5.4, contains information about the concepts of data prioritization and quality of service (QoS), which are integral to the delivery of time-sensitive data such as real-time voice and video traffic.

5.1   What Is the Data Link Layer?

Overview

As the second layer of the OSI reference model, the *data link layer* provides a service to the network layer (layer 3) using the services of the physical layer (layer 1). Some of the services the data link layer provides to the network layer include:

- provisioning links between network entities (generally these are adjacent nodes within a subnetwork);
- framing, which involves partitioning data into frames and exchanging these frames over the link;
- frame sequencing (if required), which involves maintaining the correct ordering of frames as they are being exchanged;
- establishing and maintaining an acceptable level of flow control as frames are being exchanged across a link;
- detecting (and possibly correcting) errors in the physical layer, which includes error notification when errors are detected but not corrected;
- selecting quality of services (QoS) parameters associated with a specific transmission, including ensuring that sufficient bandwidth is available and that transmission delays (i.e., latency) are predictable and guaranteed.

In short, and from a network architecture perspective, the data link layer regulates and formats transmission of data from software on a node to the network cabling facilities.

The data link layer is typically implemented on a node as a *device driver*. A device driver is a software component that is specific to both a piece of hardware, such as an Ethernet/802.3 network interface controller card (NIC), and the operating system of the computer in which it is installed. For instance, the data link layer of Ethernet/ 802.3 could be represented by the network card you purchased from a vendor such as SMC, 3Com, or Intel. The vendor includes a device driver with the card to enable the operating system on your computer (e.g., Windows, MacOS, NT, or UNIX) to recognize the card and allow the software protocol(s) to "talk" to the card when they are accessed. More simply, the data link layer is the "glue" between the wire and the software on a node. Without it, the particular network connection will not operate at all. The data link layer creates the network environment for the wire and dictates data formats, timing, bit sequencing, and many other activities for each particular type of network.

The IEEE and the Data Link Layer

In the early days of local area network development, there were no standards for LANs. Chaos and instability were the order of the day. Proprietary vendor standards ruled, customers became customers for life, and companies got fat. The dearth of industrywide standards effectively prevented customers from using "outside" products for fear of incompatibility. In February 1980, the IEEE (pronounced "eye triple E") assumed responsibility for setting LAN standards, primarily for the physical and data link layers, using the OSI reference model as a framework. IEEE, which stands for the Institute of Electrical and Electronics Engineers, is a professional society founded in 1963. IEEE members include engineers, scientists, and students. One of its many activities is to act as a coordinating body for computing and communication standards. Many international standards from the International Organization for Standardization (ISO) and the International Electrotechnical Commission (IEC) are based on IEEE networking standards.

For additional information about these organizations, see http://www.ieee.org; http://www.iso.ch; and http://www.iec.ch.

IEEE conducted its LAN standards development under the auspices of the IEEE Computer Society. A list of these standards is provided in Table 5.1, with corresponding

TABLE 5.1 Summary of IEEE Project 802 LAN Standards

IEEE 802.1 Defines an architectural overview of LANs.

IEEE 802.2 Defines the logical link control, which describes services for the transmission of data between two nodes. (ISO/IEC 8802-2)

IEEE 802.3 Defines the carrier sense multiple access/collision detection (CSMA/CD) access method commonly referred to as Ethernet. Supplements include 802.3c (10-Mbps Ethernet), 802.3u (100-Mbps Ethernet known as *Fast Ethernet*), 802.3z and 802.3ab (1000-Mbps Ethernet known as *Gigabit Ethernet*), and 802.3ae (*10-Gigabit Ethernet*). (ISO/IEC 8802-3)

IEEE 802.4 Defines the token bus network access method.

IEEE 802.5 Defines the logical ring LAN that uses a token passing access method; known also as token ring. (ISO/IEC 8802-5)

IEEE 802.6 Defines metropolitan area networks (MANs).

IEEE 802.7 Defines broadband LANs (capable of delivering video, data, and voice traffic).

IEEE 802.9 Defines integrated digital and video networking—Integrated Services LANs (ISLANs). (ISO/IEC 8802-9)

IEEE 802.10 Defines standards for interoperable LAN/MAN security services.

IEEE 802.11 Defines standards for wireless media access control and physical layer specifications.

IEEE 802.12 Defines the "demand priority" access method for 100-Mbps LANs, known also as 100BASE-VG or 100VG-AnyLAN.

IEEE 802.13 (Defines nothing—IEEE was concerned about the superstitious overtones associated with 13.)

IEEE 802.14 Defines a standard for cable TV-based broadband communication.

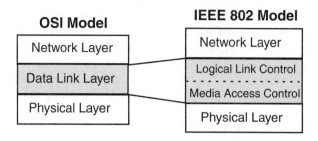

FIGURE 5.1 The IEEE's perspective of the data link layer.

ISO/IEC standards given in parentheses. Since IEEE's development of LAN standards was assigned the project number 802, for February 1980, the committee's collective body of work has become known as Project 802. Hence, the standards that have resulted are identified as IEEE 802.*x*.

IEEE initiated its development of LAN standards with an architectural model, defined in IEEE 802.1. This architectural model corresponds to the two lowest layers of the OSI model. The difference between IEEE and OSI models, though, is that IEEE divides OSI's data link layer into two parts: the *logical link control sublayer* (LLC) and the *media access control sublayer* (MAC) (Figure 5.1). Note that MAC has nothing to do with Apple Computer's Macintosh. The LLC sublayer, defined in IEEE 802.2, is the upper half of the data link layer. It encompasses several functions, including framing, flow control, and error control. The MAC sublayer is the lower half of the data link layer. It provides media access management protocols for accessing a shared medium.

5.2   The Logical Link Control (LLC) Sublayer

As stated in the previous section, the logical link control layer is responsible for framing, flow control, and error control. Let's examine these separately.

Framing

Framing refers to the process of partitioning a bit stream into discrete units or blocks of data called *frames*. Thus, it is the manner in which a specific network type formats the bits sent to the cable. Specific formats and timing sequences exist for each LAN type. By partitioning a bit stream into frames, framing enables sending and receiving machines to synchronize the transmission and reception of data because frames have detectable boundaries. Framing also facilitates error detection and correction. Once a bit stream is partitioned into frames, specific information about the contents of a frame is computed and transmitted within the frame. Using this information, a receiving node can determine the integrity of a received frame.

One common framing procedure involves inserting flag characters before and after the transmitted data message. For example, if we use the bit pattern 01111110 (six con-

Data set to be transmitted: 1 1 1 1 1 1 0 0 1 1 1 1 1 0 1 1

Data set after bit-stuffing: 1 1 1 1 1 0 1 0 0 1 1 1 1 1 0 0 1 1

Data set after bit-stuffing and
start–stop bits have been inserted: **0 1 1 1 1 1 1 0 1 1 1 1 1 0 1 0 0 1 1 1 1 1 0 0 1 1 0 1 1 1 1 1 1 0**

Thus, the frame to be transmitted is:

> 0 1 1 1 1 1 1 0   1 1 1 1 1 0 1 0 0 1 1 1 1 1 0 0 1 1   0 1 1 1 1 1 1 0
>
> *Start of Frame*   *User Data with Bit-Stuffing*   *End of Frame*

The data link layer on the receiving machine removes the start and stop bits and unstuffs the data set by removing the 0-bits that follow each set of five consecutive 1-bits.

FIGURE 5.2 An example of bit-stuffing, which is used for framing when the data set contains the start–stop bits pattern.

secutive 1-bits) as our start–stop flag, and if the data set (i.e., the message being transmitted) consists of 11101111, then the frame is 0111111011101111101111110. Thus, the data set has been "framed" by distinct boundaries consisting of start–stop flags. Note that the framing protocol associated with each type of network specifies the actual bit pattern used for start–stop flags.

By introducing a start–stop bit sequence into the data stream, a concern that emerges is how a receiving node is able to distinguish between real user data and the start–stop bits if a data message has the same pattern as the start–stop bits. If a data message contains a sequence of bits identical to the start–stop flag, then we must alter the data set to guarantee the uniqueness of the start–stop bit patterns. One way to do this employs a process known as *bit-stuffing*. For example, suppose a data set consists of the bit string 0111111001111101, and our start–stop flag is 01111110. Note that the data message includes one instance of our start–stop flag. We implement bit-stuffing by "stuffing" a 0-bit immediately after every fifth consecutive 1-bit in the data stream. The receiving node "unstuffs" these 0-bits by deleting every 0-bit that follows five consecutive 1-bits. This procedure is illustrated in Figure 5.2.

To illustrate the concept of a frame a little more concretely, let's examine an Ethernet frame. Before doing so, though, we need to make a distinction between Ethernet and IEEE 802.3, which many people call Ethernet. The reason we need to make this distinction is because Ethernet and IEEE 802.3 frame formats are different. Rather than get into a detailed discussion about these differences (we save that for Chapter 9), just be aware that Ethernet and IEEE 802.3 are not really the same. IEEE 802.3 is broadly deployed, but old habits die hard, and people continue to call it Ethernet. To avoid confusion, or to create more if you're so inclined, we use the nomenclature Ethernet/802.3 in this book when we want to refer to what people commonly call Ethernet.

With that said, let's look at the general format of an IEEE 802.3 frame, shown in Figure 5.3. Note that an IEEE 802.3 frame consists of eight fields: preamble, start frame delimiter, destination address, source address, length count, data, pad, and CRC checksum (discussed later). The preamble, used for synchronization, consists of seven identical bytes (56 bits). Each byte (8 bits or octet) has the bit pattern 10101010. The

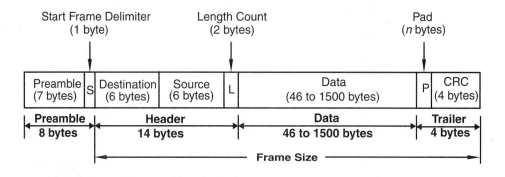

FIGURE 5.3   The contents and structure of an IEEE 802.3 frame.

start frame delimiter (S), which indicates the start of a frame of data, consists of the bit pattern 10101011. This is the start–stop flag used in IEEE 802.3. The destination address is the hardware address of the receiving station—normally 48 bits (the standard provides for a 16-bit value, but no one uses it). The source address is the hardware address of the sending station, also 48 bits in length. Both of these addresses are MAC sublayer addresses, which we will discuss shortly (also see Appendix A). The length count (L) is a two-byte field that indicates the length of the data field that follows. The data field contains the actual user data (i.e., the transmitted message). The data field is subject to minimum and maximum sizes, which are 46 and 1500 bytes, respectively. The pad field (P) contains dummy data that "pad" the data field up to its minimum length of 46 bytes, if necessary. Its size ranges from 0 to n bytes, where n is the number of bytes needed. Finally, the checksum field (CRC) contains the information needed for error detection, which is yet another task performed by the LLC sublayer in the data link layer. It is also called the frame check sequence (FCS) and it is four bytes long. (CRC stands for cyclic redundancy check and is discussed later in the chapter.)

For those readers who have used a network protocol analyzer, you might have seen Ethernet/802.3 frames displayed with only four fields instead of eight. You obviously bought a cheap protocol analyzer. (Just kidding.) Seriously, though, this is because the eight individual fields of an Ethernet/ 802.3 frame can be grouped into four main fields: *preamble* (preamble plus start frame delimiter), *header* (source and destination addresses plus length count), *payload* (user data plus padding), and *trailer* (the CRC checksum). We even showed this broader partitioning in Figure 5.3. If we ignore the preamble, the aggregate of the header, data, and trailer fields ranges from a minimum of 64 bytes to a maximum of 1518 bytes. These represent the minimum and maximum sizes of an IEEE 802.3 frame.

One further point of information about this frame is warranted at this stage of our lesson. Note that we referred to the source and destination addresses of this frame as "MAC sublayer addresses" and as "hardware addresses." Although the MAC sublayer is discussed in Section 5.3, it is important to note now that a *MAC sublayer address* is not the same as an *Internet address*. The MAC sublayer address is simply the hardware address of a particular node. If the node is connected to an Ethernet/802.3 network, then we refer to the hardware address as the Ethernet/802.3 address. If the node is connected to a token ring network, then the hardware address is called the token ring address. It all depends on the MAC sublayer protocol. You also should not confuse a MAC address

BOX 5.1   IEEE 802.3 MAC Sublayer Addresses

Ethernet addresses, also known as hardware or MAC addresses, are installed in ROM by the manufacturers of Ethernet controllers (i.e., the Ethernet network cards). The custodian of these addresses is the IEEE, which assigns addresses on a group basis to vendors who manufacture Ethernet hardware devices used in a heterogeneous network environment.

Ethernet addresses consist of 48 bits, represented as 12 hexadecimal digits (0–9, A–F), and partitioned into six groups of two. An example of an Ethernet address is 08:00:20:01:D6:2A. Dashes are sometimes used in place of colons, and sometimes no delimiter is used to separate the byte-pairs. Also, the letters A–F are used to represent the numbers 10–15, respectively. These letters are usually written in uppercase.

The higher-order three bytes (i.e., the left-most six hexadecimal digits) correspond to the manufacturer of the Ethernet device, and the lower-order three bytes correspond to the serial number of the device. For example, the address 08:00:20:01:D6:2A corresponds to an Ethernet controller manufactured by Sun Microsystems because the leftmost three bytes, 08:00:20, have been assigned to Sun; the remaining three bytes specify a unique serial number assigned by Sun to the device. Other examples of vendor prefixes include 00:00:0c (Cisco), 00:00:1D (Cabletron), and 08:00:07 (Apple). (See Appendix A for more information about Ethernet vendor prefixes.)

There are three different types of destination addresses. The first is called a *unicast address*, which essentially means that data are being transmitted to only a single network interface (i.e., device). Unicast destination addresses are denoted by either a 0 or an even number (2, 4, 6, 8, A, C, E) in the second hexadecimal digit of the vendor prefix. A *multicast* or *broadcast address* enables data to be transmitted to more than one destination node at the same time. A multicast address specifies a vendor-specific group of nodes. For example, the multicast address 09-00-87-90-FF-FF is for Xyplex terminal servers. Ethernet frames that have their destination fields set to this address will be received by all Xyplex terminal servers connected to the network. If a node wants to send data to *all* network-connected devices, then a broadcast address is used. This address is given as FF:FF:FF:FF:FF:FF. Multicast and broadcast Ethernet addresses are denoted by using an odd number (1, 3, 5, 7, 9, B, D, F) as the second hexadecimal digit.

Ethernet addresses should not be confused with Internet addresses. The former are six-byte addresses that have been "burned" into the controller card; the latter are logical addresses that correspond to a specific network protocol and are assigned by a network administrator and configured through software. If a device is connected to an Ethernet network, which in turn is connected to the Internet, then the device will have both Ethernet and IP addresses assigned to it. The Address Resolution Protocol (ARP), which is part of the TCP/IP protocol suite (see Chapter 8), is used to resolve IP addresses to Ethernet addresses. An ARP request is a network broadcast that announces the target node's IP address and requests the node to return its MAC address. On UNIX and Windows NT systems, this protocol can be invoked on the command line by the *arp* application program. Using the a extension (arp -a) displays the contents of the current ARP table maintained by the local host.

with the address of a Macintosh computer. Box 5.1 provides some detailed information about MAC sublayer addresses, and Appendix A contains a list of Ethernet/802.3 vendor prefixes, which are discussed in this sidebar. Finally, you might also want to revisit our discussion in Section 2.5, where we presented an example of sending a message across the Internet. In this example, we distinguish between a hardware address and an Internet address.

Flow Control

Flow control, which is another function of the LLC sublayer, refers to a process that controls the rate at which data are exchanged between two nodes. Flow control involves a feedback mechanism that informs the source machine of the destination machine's ability to keep up with the current flow of data transmission. Usually, a source node may not transmit frames until it receives permission from the destination machine.

Flow control is necessary because it is possible for a sending node to transmit frames at a rate faster than the destination node can receive and process them. This can happen if the source node is lightly loaded and the destination node is heavily loaded or if the source node has a faster processor than that of the destination node. Thus, flow control provides a mechanism to ensure that a sending node does not overwhelm a receiving node during data transmission. For example, consider a network that consists of several 80486 PC clients and a Pentium PC file server. Clearly, the processing speed of the server is much greater than that of the clients. In this scenario, the server is able to transmit frames to a client faster than the client can process them. Without flow control, the client's buffers will eventually fill with "backlogged" frames sent by the server. With its buffers full, the client will discard any subsequent data it receives. This can result in retransmissions by the sending node, which can exacerbate network congestion.

Stop-and-Wait Flow-Control Protocol

An example of a very simple flow-control protocol is the *stop-and-wait protocol*. As inferred by its name, stop-and-wait requires the sender to transmit one frame and then wait for the receiver to acknowledge receipt of this frame. The acknowledgment sent by the receiver is a basic frame (i.e., it does not have to carry any user data) that simply informs the sender that the receiver is now ready to accept another data frame. As a result, a receiver effects flow control via acknowledgments. A sender must wait until it receives an acknowledgment from the receiver for the frame it transmitted before it is permitted to transmit another frame. If a receiver withholds an acknowledgment, then the flow of data between sender and receiver stops. Although stop-and-wait is very effective, it is also very impractical for modern networking environments. First, as described, stop-and-wait uses a simplex transmission; data frames flow in only one direction. In most data communication environments, data transmission is full-duplex. Second, the protocol is ideal when transmitting large frames. Unfortunately, large frames are generally partitioned into smaller data units to accommodate a receiver's limited buffer size. Small frame sizes also facilitate faster error detection and reduce the amount of data that requires retransmission in the event that an error is detected. (Error-control concepts are discussed later in this section.)

Sliding Window Flow-Control Protocol

An enhancement to the stop-and-wait protocol is the *sliding window* concept, which improves data flow by having the receiver inform the sender of its available buffer space. Doing so enables the sender to transmit frames continuously without having to wait for acknowledgments to these frames as long as the number of frames sent does not overflow the receiver's buffers. The sliding window concept is implemented by requiring the sender to sequentially number each data frame it sends and by having the sender and receiver maintain information about the number of frames they can respectively send or receive. Flow-control protocols based on this concept are called *sliding window protocols.*

When numbering frames, a modulo numbering system is used based on the size of the protocol's window field. A modulo system is a mathematical system that cyclically repeats itself. For example, the set {0, 1, 2, 3} is a finite set that contains only the four given elements, namely, 0, 1, 2, and 3. This means that if we were to work with these set elements in sequence, after using the element 3, we must cycle back and start with 0. In general, a mathematical system that consists of the set of elements {0, 1, 2, 3, . . . , $m - 1$} is called a *modulo* or *mod m system.* Most sliding window protocols support either a three-bit or seven-bit window field. A three-bit field specifies a mod 8 system since $2^3 = 8$, and a seven-bit field specifies a mod 128 system. In a sliding window protocol with a three-bit window field, sequence numbers range from 0 to 7 and hence frames are numbered modulo 8. Thus, after a frame is assigned sequence number 7, the next frame is numbered 0. Similarly, in a protocol that uses a seven-bit window field, frames are numbered modulo 128 and use sequence numbers ranging from 0 to 127.

A general example of how the sliding window concept is used for flow control is provided in Figure 5.4, which shows a simplex data transmission from host *A* (the sender) to host *B* (the receiver). We assume a three-bit window field. An explanation of how this concept is implemented follows:

- In part 1, an initialization process takes place in which host *A* learns of host *B*'s buffer size. In this illustration, *B*'s receive buffer space is fixed at five, which means that *B* can store at most five frames at any one time before it runs out of storage space. To prevent *A* from overrunning *B*'s buffer space, *A* maintains a list of consecutive sequence numbers that correspond to the frames it may send. Since *B* cannot receive more than five frames at a time, *A*'s initial *send window* is of size five and consists of the frame sequence numbers 0 through 4, which respectively correspond to the five frames it may send.
- In part 2, *A* transmits frames 0 through 4 without acknowledgments.
- In part 3, *B* receives frames 0 and 1 and sends an acknowledgment for each of them. These acknowledgments also contain information about *B*'s buffer size. Here, *B* informs *A* that its *receive window* is now four. Note that *A*'s transmission is effectively throttled by its send window. *A* has already transmitted all the frames it was permitted to send. Since no acknowledgments have been received yet, *A* cannot send any more data.
- In part 4, *A* receives an acknowledgment for frame 0. As a result, *A* may advance the left side of its send window by one. However, *A* cannot advance the right side of this window because *B*'s new receive window size is four, which was indicated by frame 0's ACK. In the meanwhile, *B* receives and acknowledges frames 2 and 3 but, once again, reduces its receive window size to three.
- In part 5, *A* receives frame 1's acknowledgment and advances the left side of its send window one unit to the right to indicate that frame 1 was received by *B*. When *A* does this, notice that its send window is now at three. Since *B*'s receive window is currently at four, *A* is permitted to advance the right side of its send window one unit, which enables it to now transmit frame 5. At the other end of the link, *B* receives and acknowledges frame 4. *B* also, once again, changes its receive window—this time back to five.

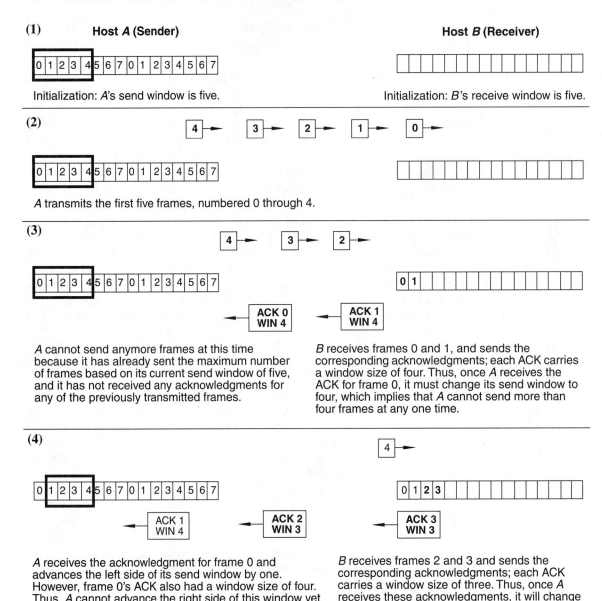

(1)

Host A (Sender)   **Host B (Receiver)**

Initialization: A's send window is five.   Initialization: B's receive window is five.

(2)

A transmits the first five frames, numbered 0 through 4.

(3)

A cannot send anymore frames at this time because it has already sent the maximum number of frames based on its current send window of five, and it has not received any acknowledgments for any of the previously transmitted frames.

B receives frames 0 and 1, and sends the corresponding acknowledgments; each ACK carries a window size of four. Thus, once A receives the ACK for frame 0, it must change its send window to four, which implies that A cannot send more than four frames at any one time.

(4)

A receives the acknowledgment for frame 0 and advances the left side of its send window by one. However, frame 0's ACK also had a window size of four. Thus, A cannot advance the right side of this window yet because it can only send at most four frames. Since A has not received any acknowledgments for frames 1–4, it is not permitted to transmit any more frames at this time.

B receives frames 2 and 3 and sends the corresponding acknowledgments; each ACK carries a window size of three. Thus, once A receives these acknowledgments, it will change its send window to three.

FIGURE 5.4   The sliding window concept used for flow control.

(5)

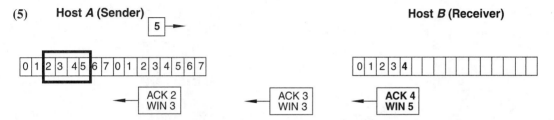

A receives the acknowledgment for frame 1 and advances the left side of its send window by one. Since this ACK carried a WIN of four, A may now advance the right side of its send window by one to maintain a send window size of four. In doing so, A is now permitted to transfer one more frame, namely, frame 5.

B receives frame 4 and sends its corresponding acknowledgment with a window size of five. Thus, once A receives this acknowledgment, it will change its send window to five, which will permit it to transfer five frames.

(6)

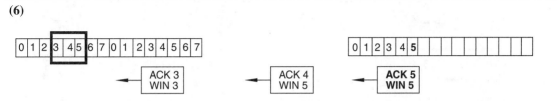

A receives the acknowledgment for frame 2 and advances the left side of its send window by one. However, since this ACK carried a WIN of three, A must now maintain a send window size of three and hence is not permitted to advance the right side of its send window or transmit any more frames.

B receives frame 5 and sends its corresponding acknowledgment with a window size of five.

(7)

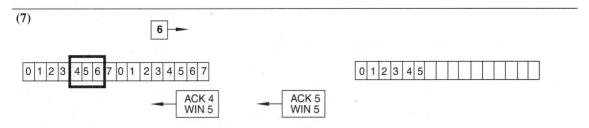

A receives the acknowledgment for frame 3 and advances both the left and right sides of its send window by one. This enables A to maintain a send window size of three and also transmit one more frame, namely, frame 6.

B has not received any frames at this stage and hence sends no acknowledgments.

FIGURE 5.4 (continued). The sliding window concept used for flow control.

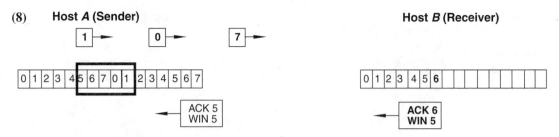

(8)   Host *A* (Sender)   **Host *B* (Receiver)**

A receives the acknowledgment for frame 4 and advances the left side of its send window by one. Since this ACK carried a WIN of 5, *A* can now maintain a send window size of five and hence advances the right side of its send window by three. This now permits *A* to transmit three more frames, namely, frames 7, 0, and 1.

B receives frame 6 and sends its corresponding acknowledgment with a window size of five.

(9)

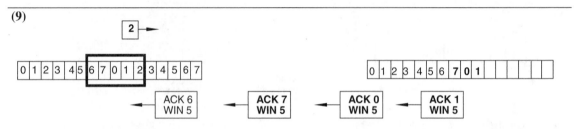

A receives the acknowledgment for frame 5, which has a WIN of five. Thus, *A* advances the left and right side of its send window by one and transmits frame 2.

B receives frames 7, 0, and 1 and sends their corresponding acknowledgments, which maintain *B*'s window size of five.

(10)

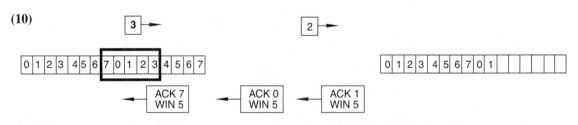

A receives the acknowledgment for frame 6, maintains its window size of five, and transmits frame 3.

B has not received any frames at this stage and hence sends no acknowledgments.

FIGURE 5.4 (continued). The sliding window concept used for flow control.

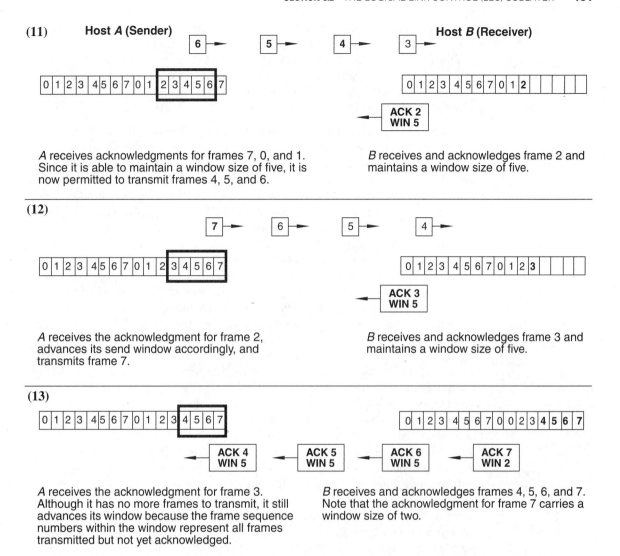

FIGURE 5.4 (continued). The sliding window concept used for flow control.

- In part 6, *A* receives frame 2's acknowledgment and advances the left side of its send window accordingly. However, since this ACK carried a receive window of three, *A* must now maintain a send window of three and hence is not permitted to transmit any more data. *B* receives and acknowledges frame 5 and maintains a receive window of five.

- In part 7, *A* receives frame 3's acknowledgment and advances the left side of its send window accordingly. *A* can also slide the right side of its window one unit to the right and still maintain a window size of three. This enables *A* to transmit frame 6.

- In part 8, *A* receives frame 4's acknowledgment, which carries a receive window size of five. *B*'s throttling of *A* has now been loosened, and *A* may slide its window to the right to reflect the acknowledgment it received and to maintain a send window of five. Thus, *A* is permitted to transmit frames 7, 0, and 1. (Recall that we are assuming a three-bit window field, which indicates a modulo 8 numbering system.) *B* receives and acknowledges frame 6 and continues to maintain a receive window of five.

- In parts 9 through 13, the sliding window concept continues to play out until *A* has completed transmitting all 16 frames.

As can be seen from this simple example, the sliding window concept effectively enables a receiver to control the sender's data flow. Note that when the sender advances the left side of its send window by one after it receives the corresponding acknowledgment, the send window represents a list of frame numbers that correspond to all transmitted but unacknowledged frames. Further note that if the maximum window size is one, then we have the stop-and-wait protocol since the sender cannot send a succeeding frame until the previous frame is acknowledged.

In our illustration of the sliding window concept, we took some liberties to facilitate its understanding. In reality, protocols based on this concept are not quite as straightforward. First, although not shown in our demonstration, a receiver's window size can be fixed. That is, it remains at its initial size. Second, some sliding window protocols do not send an acknowledgment for each frame received. Instead, one acknowledgment is sent that contains the next expected sequence number. For example, in Figure 5.4, part 6, instead of sending separate ACKs for frames 0–5, *B* would send one ACK that contains sequence number 6. This implies that *B* has correctly received all frames up to and including 5 and is expecting frame 6. Third, our illustration does not accommodate for lost frames or frames received out of order, which are two common occurrences in any data transmission facility. Thus, the sender must always maintain sufficient buffer space to store all transmitted frames until they are acknowledged in the event a frame has to be retransmitted. Similarly, a receiver must maintain sufficient buffer space to store frames that arrive out of order. Fourth, our illustration in Figure 5.4 depicts a simplex transmission. In most situations, a full-duplex operation is common. This enables both ends of a communications link to send and receive data frames at the same time. Full-duplex data transmission is implemented by having nodes attach acknowledgments to their data frames, a concept called *piggybacking*. Thus, instead of sending a separate acknowledgment frame, a host waits until it has data to send and includes this acknowledgment with its outgoing data frame. Full-duplex data transmission requires each host to maintain both send and receive windows since a host can simultaneously be both a sender and a receiver. Finally, sliding window protocols can also be designed to facilitate reliable data transfers and ordered frame delivery in addition to flow control.

A protocol called *go-back-n* is used when the initial transmission of a frame that must now be retransmitted was succeeded by *n* subsequent frame transmissions.

Error Control

The term *error control* refers to the process of guaranteeing reliable data delivery. That is, the data received are identical to the data transmitted. Two basic strategies exist for dealing with errors. The first method, *error correction through retransmission,* involves providing just enough information in the data stream so the receiving node can detect an error occurred during transmission. Once an error is detected, the receiving node can then request the sender to retransmit that unit of data. The second method, *autonomous error correction,* involves providing redundant information in the data stream so the destination node can both detect and correct any errors autonomously. Both methods are forms of *error correction.*

Error control using retransmission involves the use of acknowledgments—the receiving node provides the sending node with feedback about the frames it has received. A positive acknowledgment means a frame was received correctly; a negative acknowledgment (or no acknowledgment) implies a frame was not received correctly. Negative acknowledgments imply that the sending node needs to retransmit the frame. To guard against the possibility of lost or destroyed frames (due to hardware failure), the data link layer also supports timers. If a frame or acknowledgment is lost, the sending node's time limit eventually expires, alerting it to retransmit the frame. To guard against a destination node accepting duplicate frames, outgoing frames are assigned sequence numbers, which enable a destination node to distinguish between a frame that has been retransmitted from an original one. The management of timers and sequence numbers is an important function of the data link layer because it ensures that each frame is received by the network layer exactly once and in the correct order. It is important to note that not all LAN types implement sequence numbering at the frame level. In fact, very few do. In most LANs, the software above the data link layer must determine that something is missing and negotiate retransmission of the information. Just because the feature might exist in a specification does not mean that it is necessarily implemented in practice.

The concepts of error detection, acknowledgment, and retransmission are collectively referred to as *automatic repeat request* (ARQ). This term might be familiar to some readers who use modems because most modems have an ARQ indicator. ARQ is a general term for error-control protocols that feature error detection and automatic retransmission of "bad" frames. Commonly used ARQ standards are based on some of the flow-control protocols discussed earlier. Two in particular are stop-and-wait ARQ and go-back-n ARQ. Both protocols are patterned after their flow-control namesakes and involve retransmitting frames that either time out or are not positively acknowledged. A third protocol, selective-reject ARQ, involves a receiver sending only negative acknowledgments to indicate that an error was detected in a received frame. (This is in contrast to the previous two protocols in which an acknowledgment is sent for every frame received correctly.) Thus, only frames that time out or have a corresponding negative acknowledgment are retransmitted.

As previously stated, error correction can be performed in one of two ways. The first strategy, error correction through retransmission, is straightforward. If a destination node detects that a frame of data it received is not identical to the frame sent, then it requests the sending node to retransmit the original frame. The second strategy, autonomous error correction, is a little more complex and does not rely on retransmissions. Instead, the destination node, upon detecting a bad data frame, corrects the error(s) itself. Autonomous error correction requires that a transmitted frame contains redundant information to enable the destination node to correct any detected errors without requesting a retransmission. Note that error correction implies error detection.

The reason error control is necessary is because networks are fallible, complex systems, and errors occurring during data transmission are an inherent part of these systems. Network errors are caused by a wide variety of conditions. For example, errors can be caused by interference on the wire, hardware problems, software bugs, protocol-

- Bit string of "A":   1 0 0 0 0 0 1
- For even parity, parity bit is 0:   1 0 0 0 0 0 1 **0**
  (even number of 1-bits)
- For odd parity, parity bit is 1:   1 0 0 0 0 0 1 **1**
  (odd number of 1-bits)

FIGURE 5.5 Examples of parity bits.

related problems (e.g., incompatible protocols at either end), and buffer overflow. Some errors are intermittent—they come and go. These are the most difficult to detect. Others are "hard" errors that are easily identified. In a properly functioning network, however, errors usually are a function of line synchronization failures, crosstalk, defective hardware, and protocol-related problems (e.g., "collisions" in Ethernet/802.3).

One example of error control is a single-bit error-detection strategy that is based on the concept of parity. *Parity* refers to the use of an extra bit (called a *parity bit* or a *redundancy bit*) to detect single-bit errors in data transmissions. Parity can be specified as even, odd, or none. Even parity means that there must be an even number of 1-bits in each bit string; odd parity means that there must be an odd number of 1-bits in each bit string; and no parity means that parity is ignored. The extra bit (i.e., the parity bit) is forced to either 0 or 1 to make the total number of bits either even or odd. For example, consider the character *A*. Its ASCII representation is 1000001. Note this has two 1-bits, and two is an even number. If we require even parity, then we must append a 0 to this bit string because we need to maintain an even number of 1s. If we require odd parity, then we need to append a 1 because we need an odd number of 1s (Figure 5.5). When a single-bit error occurs, the receiver interprets the bit string as a different character than the one sent. Parity checking with one additional parity bit can *detect* this type of error. Unfortunately, however, a single-parity bit does not provide enough information to *correct* the error.

Parity can also be used for autonomous error correction. To do so, however, requires that additional information be included in a transmitted frame to enable the receiving node to correct any detected errors on its own, thus avoiding the need for retransmission. *Redundancy bits* (also called *check bits*) provide this information. A data set composed of both user data and redundancy bits is called a *codeword*. Using parity, we can construct codewords to correct single-bit errors only. An example of how this is effected is provided in Appendix B.

Upon reviewing Appendix B, you might note that autonomous error correction is expensive to implement. Several extra bits are required to convey redundant information so that the receiving node can locate an error. In the example given in Appendix B, we needed four extra bits just to be able to detect the location of a single-bit error. Once the position of such an error is located, correction is easy—simply flip the bit (i.e., complement the bit at that position). Consequently, autonomous error correction is usually implemented in simplex channels, where retransmissions cannot be requested, or in those instances where retransmission is more costly than implementing an autonomous error-correction scheme. For most situations, though, using retransmissions is the preferred method of error correction. To correct multibit errors, the price goes up. What we mean by this is we must increase the codeword's size to enable us to correct additional bits, adding a significant amount of overhead to the transmission. If the physical layer is operating so poorly that we expect many multibit errors, we probably ought to consider reengineering or replacing the equipment.

Richard Wesley Hamming (1915–1998)

Richard Wesley Hamming was born in Chicago in 1915. He received a BS in mathematics from the University of Chicago in 1937, an MA from the University of Nebraska in 1939, and a PhD in mathematics from the University of Illinois in 1942. In 1945, Hamming worked briefly at Los Alamos on IBM machines that were running calculations for the U.S. government's Manhattan Project, which was designed to produce an atomic bomb. After working at Los Alamos for 6 months, Hamming joined Bell Telephone Laboratories in 1946. Among his colleagues was Claude Shannon. (See separate biographical profile on Shannon in Chapter 2.) Between 1960 and 1976, when he retired from Bell Labs, Hamming was also a visiting or adjunct professor for City College of New York (CCNY), Stanford University, University of California at Irvine, and Princeton University. After retiring from Bell Labs, Hamming taught computer science at the Naval Postgraduate School in Monterey, California, and in 1997, became distinguished professor emeritus.

Hamming is best known for his work on error-correcting codes. He described his research in the article, "Error Detecting and Error Correcting Codes," which was published in the *Bell System Technical Journal* in 1950. As part of this research, he invented Hamming error-correcting codes and the concept of *Hamming distance,* which represents the number of corresponding bit positions in which two codewords differ. (A codeword consists of data bits plus redundant bits, which are used for error control.) For example, the Hamming distance of the two codewords 10100100 and 11100010 is three, since three corresponding bits differ, namely, those in bit positions, 2, 6, and 7 (working from left to right). Hamming called the minimum Hamming distance between pairs of distinct codewords in a code the *Hamming distance of the code* and then proved that a code whose minimum Hamming distance is d can correct t errors, where t is equal to the greatest integer of $(d-1)/2$. Thus, given a t-error correcting code, $d \geq 2t + 1$. The concept of Hamming distance is an integral component of coding theory.

Besides his work on error-correcting codes, Hamming contributed to the field of numerical analysis where he developed predictor-corrector methods for numerical integration. He also worked on digital filters, where he developed the Hamming spectral window. As an author, Hamming had a talent for imparting technical information in an accessible manner. Many of his books were well-received and continuously revised into new editions. Among them are *Numerical Methods for Scientists and Engineers* (1962, 1973), *Calculus and the Computer Revolution* (1968), *Introduction to Applied Numerical Analysis* (1971), *Computers and Society* (1972), *Digital Filters* (1977, 1983, 1989), *Coding and Information Theory* (1980, 1986), *Methods of Mathematics Applied to Calculus, Probability and Statistics* (1985), *The Art of Probability for Scientists and Engineers* (1991), and *The Art of Doing Science and Engineering: Learning to Learn* (1997). Hamming also wrote 75 technical articles and held three patents. Hamming received many awards for his technical contributions. Key among them were: the Association for Computing Machinery's Turing Award (1968), which is ACM's most prestigious technical award given to individuals selected for their technical contributions to the computing community; the Institute of Electrical and Electronics Engineers (IEEE) Emanuel R. Piore Award (1979); and the IEEE Richard W. Hamming Medal (1988), which was named after him (he was the first recipient) "For exceptional contributions to information sciences and systems." An excellent biography and obituary of Hamming, written by Samuel P. Morgan, is available in PostScript form at http://www.kohala.com/start/papers.others/hammingbio.ps

The location of a checksum within a frame is a function of the protocol being used.

To illustrate the concept of error control a little more concretely, let's revisit Figure 5.3, which shows the general format of an IEEE 802.3 frame. Ethernet/802.3 LANs use error correction with retransmission as their error-control strategy. This is done using a *checksum,* which is carried in the last field of the frame. Checksums are calculated using a procedure called *cyclic redundancy check* (CRC), which is an extremely powerful and robust error-detection method. To check a series of bits, CRC first constructs an algebraic polynomial whose terms' coefficients are the values of each of the bits. Thus, a data set with n bits corresponds to an $n - 1$ degree polynomial; the leftmost bit is the coefficient of the x^{n-1} term. For example, the eight-bit data set 10111101 is equal to the seventh-degree polynomial $1x^7 + 0x^6 + 1x^5 + 1x^4 + 1x^3 + 1x^2 + 0x^1 + 1$ or, equivalently, $x^7 + x^5 + x^4 + x^3 + x^2 + 1$. In the next step, the polynomial is divided by a predetermined *generator polynomial.* Thus, the data set is the dividend and the generator polynomial is the divisor. The remainder of this division is the CRC checksum, which is included with the frame. The receiving node performs an analogous procedure on a received frame, using the same generator polynomial. If the CRC checksum calculated by the receiving node is equal to what was sent, then a remainder of 0 results from the division, and the frame is interpreted as correct. If the two CRC checksums do not match, then the sending node is notified of this, and the entire frame is retransmitted. Three standard generator polynomials are:

- **CRC-16,** a 16-bit checksum used for various file transfer protocols. Its generator polynomial is $x^{16} + x^{15} + x^2 + 1$.
- **CRC-CCITT,** a 16-bit checksum that serves as an international standard. Its generator polynomial is $x^{16} + x^{12} + x^5 + 1$.
- **CRC-32,** a 32-bit checksum used in most LAN protocols. Its generator polynomial is $x^{32} + x^{26} + x^{23} + x^{22} + x^{16} + x^{12} + x^{11} + x^{10} + x^8 + x^7 + x^5 + x^4 + x^2 + x$. CRC-32 is used in Ethernet/802.3 and token ring LANs.

A simple example of CRC is shown in Box 5.2.

The efficiency of CRC is a function of the generator polynomial used. CRC-16 and CRC-CCITT will detect 100% of all single and double errors, all errors with an odd number of bits, all bursts of 16 bits or less, 99.997% of 17-bit error bursts, and 99.998% of 18-bit and longer error bursts. With CRC-32, however, the chances of bad data being received and not detected are approximately 1 in 4.3 billion (2^{32-1}). Although CRC-32 guarantees that there is little chance data transmission errors will go undetected, this does not mean we should be negligent in our responsibility as network managers or administrators. We should always strive to minimize network errors, and the best way to do this is to ensure that our network and all of its components are standards-compliant.

Before proceeding to the next section on the MAC sublayer, we conclude this section with a brief description of some common invalid Ethernet/802.3 frames that result from data transmission errors on an Ethernet/802.3 LAN. We will discuss causes of some of these errors in Chapter 9, but for now, we give a summary of them:

Oversized Frames. Oversized frames have more than 1518 bytes but also have a valid CRC checksum. Oversized frames usually indicate a software problem such as a faulty network driver. The industry slang term for this condition is a "long" frame.

BOX 5.2 CRC Checksums

The cyclic redundancy code (CRC) is an error-detection scheme that uses an algebraic polynomial to represent a bit stream. The sending node divides a data frame, T_b, which is interpreted as a single bit stream, by a specific divisor, D, called a generator polynomial. The remainder, R, of the division is then included in the frame's checksum field, and this frame, T_a, is transmitted as part of the frame. T_b represents the frame *before* a CRC checksum is calculated, and T_a represents the frame *after* the checksum is calculated. Thus, T_a is the frame that is actually transmitted by the sending node.

When the destination node receives the frame, it divides T_a by D. This implies that the destination node does exactly the same division using the same generator polynomial as the sender. If the transmitted frame is error free, then the remainder of the destination node's division is 0, and the destination node assumes the frame is valid. If the remainder is not 0, then an error occurred during transmission, and the destination node requests a retransmission of the frame. Following is an illustration of the CRC procedure. For this example, let's assume that the generator polynomial is $x^5 + x^4 + x^2 + x + 1$. This implies that the divisor, D, is 110111. Note that the x^3 term is represented as 0 in our divisor. Let's further assume that the data frame to be transmitted, T_b, is 111000111000.

Step 1
Since the generator polynomial is a fifth-degree polynomial, we first append five 0s to T_b.

$$111000111000 \rightarrow 11100011100000000$$

Step 2
Now divide the modified bit string from step 1 by D. Before doing this, it is important to note that binary polynomial arithmetic uses mod 2 arithmetic; that is, there are no carries or borrows. Addition and subtraction correspond to XOR. For example:

```
  101101
- 110011
  ------
  011110
```

With this in mind, we now perform the polynomial division.

```
              101011101000     = Quotient
110111 | 11100011100000000     = Tb
         110111
         ------
         111111
         110111
         ------
         100010
         110111
         ------
         101010
         110111
         ------
         111010
         110111
         ------
         110100
         110111
         ------
          11000    = Remainder
```

Step 3
Append the remainder to the initial bit string. The resulting string T_a is now transmitted. 11100011100**11000**

Step 4
The destination node receives the transmitted frame from step 3 and performs the same division.

```
              101011101000
110111 | 11100011100011000
         110111
         ------
         111111
         110111
         ------
         100010
         110111
         ------
         101010
         110111
         ------
         111010
         110111
         ------
         110111
         110111
         ------
         00000    = Remainder
```

Since the remainder is 0, the destination node assumes the frame is valid. If the remainder was not 0, the destination node requests a retransmission of the frame from the sender.

Runt Frames. Runt frames are short frames. They are at least 8 bytes but less than 64 bytes long and have a valid CRC checksum. Runts usually indicate a software problem such as a faulty network driver.

Jabbers. Jabbers are oversized frames that have an invalid CRC checksum. Jabbering is caused when a station has transmitted for too long. This normally causes an invalid CRC. Jabbers usually indicate a hardware problem, typically a faulty transceiver.

Alignment or Frame Errors. These are frames that do not end on a "byte-boundary." A frame error is detected when the total number of bits is not a multiple of eight (i.e., they cannot be grouped into an exact number of eight-bit bytes).

CRC Errors. Frames with CRC errors are of the proper size and alignment but have an invalid CRC checksum. CRC errors are caused by noise, bad connections, and faulty network hardware.

5.3 The Media Access Control (MAC) Sublayer

LANs employ a broadcast topology, meaning the nodes of a LAN share a single communications channel and must all contend for the same medium to transmit data. This is analogous to a large group of military personnel contending for the only working telephone on base during their first week of basic training—it can be a long wait when things are busy. Because of the potential chaos associated with such contention, LANs must employ protocols that define the who, the how, the when, and the for how long of channel allocation. Enter the medium access control sublayer! The MAC sublayer provides the protocols that define the manner in which nodes share the single physical transmission medium. The name says it all: Media, Access, Control. Two broad categories of access methods are most suitable for LANs: *random access* (sometimes called *stochastic* or *statistical*) and *token passing* (referred to as *deterministic*).

Random Access Protocols

Random access protocols define how a node can access a communications channel. These protocols employ the philosophy that a node can transmit whenever it has data to transmit. Random access protocols imply contention; in fact, sometimes we call them *contention protocols*. Contention is a phenomenon in which more than one entity competes to do something at the same time. For example, consider a classroom in which students and teacher are engaged in an open discussion—anyone can begin speaking without needing acknowledgment. In such a setting, anyone who wants to speak must contend with others who also want to speak simultaneously.

Note that contention creates chaos. In our classroom example, not everyone will be able to hear what one person is saying. For meaningful communication to take place, speakers must follow a rule that both ensures they can speak when they have something to say and resolves the problem when more than one person begins speaking at the same time. For example, one rule might be: "If more than one person begins speaking at the same time, everyone is to stop talking for just a split second, and then one person should take the lead and begin talking." Another rule might be to have a facilitator who calls on individuals to speak. Have you ever seen a presidential press conference? Reporters are always shouting to get their question asked. Regardless of how many reporters attempt to ask a question, only one person at a time speaks. In some cases, it is the reporter who shouts the loudest; in other cases, the president identifies the person who is permitted to speak.

Placing this in the context of a LAN, just as when more than one person attempts to talk at the same time, when two or more nodes try to communicate at approximately the same time, their transmissions "collide." In LAN terminology, we refer to this as a *collision.* Collisions are detected by nodes through the physical characteristics of the medium. More specifically, when a collision occurs, a channel's energy level changes (e.g., the voltage level on copper-based media is usually at least twice as high as expected). During such times, the nodes' signals become garbled. By monitoring the transmission line, nodes on the network are equipped to detect this condition.

What a node does when it detects a collision depends on the node's MAC sublayer protocol. Similar to the way people might observe different protocols when contending to speak, nodes employ various protocols to transmit data in a shared media environment. For example, to minimize the occurrence of collisions, nodes might follow a protocol that requires them first to "listen" for another node's transmission (somewhat incorrectly called a carrier, a term borrowed from radio terminology) before they begin transmitting data. We call these types of protocols *carrier sense protocols.* Carrier sense protocols require that before a node begins transmitting it must first listen to the wire to determine whether another node is transmitting data. Carrier sense transmission systems also employ circuitry that requires the system to "listen" to every bit transmission going out and compare that to what is actually heard on the transmission medium. If they match, wonderful. If they don't, something caused the bit to get hammered, and this means the transmission is garbled. How it is handled from there depends on the transmission framing method being used. There are four carrier sense protocols: *1-persistent CSMA* (carrier sense multiple access), *nonpersistent CSMA, CSMA with collision detection* (CSMA/CD), and *CSMA with collision avoidance* (CSMA/CA). We'll describe these one at a time.

1-persistent CSMA   When a node has data to transmit, it first senses the channel to determine if another node is transmitting. If the channel is not busy, then the node begins transmitting. If the channel is busy, then the node continuously monitors the channel until it senses an idle channel. Once it detects an idle channel, the node seizes the channel and begins transmitting its data. With this protocol, nodes with data to transmit enter a "sense and seize" mode—they continuously listen for a clear channel and, once detected, begin transmitting data. This protocol is similar to a telephone with a multiple redial feature. If it detects a busy signal when the call is first attempted, the telephone repeatedly dials the number until a connection is finally established. The "1" in 1-persistent CSMA represents the probability that a single waiting node will be able to transmit data once it detects an idle channel ($p = 1$). However, collisions can and do occur if more than a single node desires to transmit data at approximately the same time.

Nonpersistent CSMA   This protocol is similar to 1-persistent CSMA, except a node does not continuously monitor the channel when it has data to transmit. Instead, if a node

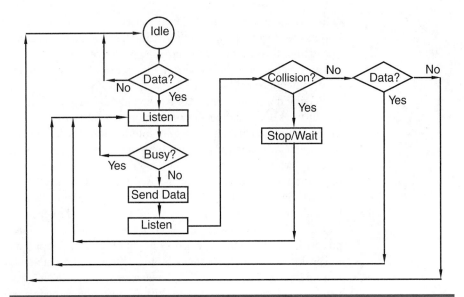

FIGURE 5.6 Flowchart depicting the CSMA/CD protocol.

detects a busy channel, it waits a random period and rechecks the channel. If the channel is idle, the node acquires the channel and begins transmitting its data. If, however, the channel is still busy, the node waits another random period before it checks the channel again. Both 1-persistent CSMA and nonpersistent CSMA protocols eliminate almost all collisions except for those that occur when two nodes begin transmitting data nearly simultaneously. For example, node *A* begins transmitting data on a clear channel. A few microseconds later (which is not enough time for node *B*'s sensing circuit to detect node *A*'s transmission), node *B* erroneously declares the channel clear and begins transmitting its own data. Eventually, the two transmissions collide. 1-persistent CSMA involves a significant amount of waiting and unfairness in determining which node gets the medium. It is "selfish" because nodes can grab the channel whenever they feel like it. Nonpersistent CSMA seems better because in its randomness there is fairness. In either case, though, there still remains the nagging problem of what to do about collisions. The next two CSMA protocols incorporate *collision detection* to provide a solution to the collision problem.

CSMA with Collision Detection (CSMA/CD) In this variant of either 1-persistent or nonpersistent CSMA, when a collision occurs the nodes (a) stop transmitting data, (b) send out a jamming signal, which ensures that all other nodes on the network detect the collision, (c) wait a random period of time, and then, (d) if the channel is free, attempt to retransmit their message. We illustrate the CSMA/CD algorithm in Figure 5.6. 1-persistent CSMA/CD is the MAC sublayer protocol used in Ethernet and IEEE 802.3 networks. We discuss this further in Chapter 9.

One question that frequently emerges when describing CSMA is the length of a random period. Well, it can be a long time, a short time, a moderate amount of time—it's random, but it is also extremely critical. If the wait time is too short, collisions will occur repeatedly. If the wait time is too long, the medium could be in a constant idle state.

Propagation delay also has an important effect on the performance of these protocols. Consider the example given for nonpersistent CSMA: Node A senses an idle channel and begins transmitting. Shortly after node A has begun transmitting, node *B* is ready to transmit data and senses the channel. If node *A*'s signal has not yet reached node *B*, then node *B* will sense an idle channel and begin transmitting. This will ultimately result in a collision. Consequently, the longer the propagation delay, the worse the performance of this protocol. Even if the propagation delay is zero, it is still possible to have collisions. For example, assume both nodes *A* and *B* are ready to transmit data, but they each sense a busy channel (a third node is transmitting at the time). If the protocol is 1-persistent CSMA, then both nodes would begin transmitting at the same time resulting in a collision. The specific amount of wait time is a function of the protocol. For quick explanation purposes, though, Ethernet/802.3's "random" amount of time is between 1 and 512 *slot-times* on the cable. We will expand on this concept when we discuss Ethernet/IEEE 802.3 later (so please don't ask what a slot-time is at this point).

CSMA with Collision Avoidance (CSMA/CA)   This protocol is similar to CSMA/CD except that it implements *collision avoidance* instead of collision detection. As with straight CSMA, hosts that support this protocol first sense the channel to see if it is busy. If the host detects that the channel is not busy, then it is free to send data. What if every host connected to a LAN is not always able to sense each other host's transmission? In such instances, collision detection will not work because collision detection is predicated on nodes being able to hear each other's transmissions. This is the case with wireless LANs (WLANs). We cannot always assume that each station connected to a WLAN will hear each other station's transmissions. One direct consequence of this is that a sending node will not be able to detect if a receiving node is busy or idle. To address this issue, we replace CD with CA and use something called *positive acknowledgment*. It works like this:

> The receiving host, upon receiving a transmission, issues an acknowledgment to the sending host. This informs the sending host that a collision did not occur. If the sending host does not receive this acknowledgment, it will assume that the receiving node did not receive the frame and it will retransmit it.

CSMA/CA also defines special frames called *request to send* (RTS) and *clear to send* (CTS), which further help minimize collisions. A sending node issues an RTS frame to the receiving node. If the channel is free, the receiving node then issues a CTS frame to the sending node. CSMA/CA is used in IEEE 802.11 (WLANs) and with Apple Computer's LocalTalk, a low-speed, peer-to-peer network schema that remains very popular for small sites with Apple Macintoshes.

Token Passing Protocols

Unlike random access protocols, token passing protocols do not involve collision detection but instead rely on granting nodes permission to transmit. Permission is provided in the form of a special control frame called a *token*. The underlying principle of token passing protocols is simple: The node that possesses the token may access the medium. Since possession of the token controls access to the medium, the possibility of contention is eliminated. The absence of contention also implies an absence of collisions. Thus, token passing schemes are both contention-free and collision-free protocols. The IEEE has defined two LAN protocols based on token passing. They are IEEE 802.4 (token bus) and IEEE 802.5 (token ring). While not defined by an IEEE standard, Fiber Distributed Data Interface (FDDI) also uses a token passing technology. Token ring and token bus are discussed in Chapter 10; FDDI is discussed in Chapter 11.

Random Access versus Token Passing Protocols

As previously mentioned, random access protocols are stochastic in nature. They are predicated on the principle that the probability two computers will transmit simultaneously (i.e., within a few microseconds of each other) is near zero. Given such a low probability, these protocols permit simultaneous transmissions. They are engineered to enable nodes to detect and resolve collisions resulting from such transmissions. Token passing protocols, in contrast, are deterministic in nature. They are predicated on the principle that no two nodes should be permitted to transmit at the same time. Thus, these protocols effectively eliminate contention and are viewed as collision-free or collision-avoidance protocols. A direct consequence of determinism is that it is possible to determine accurately the worst-case performance of a LAN.

Each access method has its own advantages and disadvantages. For example, contention protocols yield high performance for lightly loaded LANs, but when LAN traffic increases, protocol performance decreases. Performance of collision-free protocols is very predictable when a LAN is heavily loaded. However, this same feature also invokes a fixed delay even when a LAN is lightly loaded. To better understand these advantages and disadvantages, let's consider two example scenarios involving automobiles and street intersections.

In scenario A, we have an intersection that has no traffic control device (i.e., no stop or yield signs, no flashing yellow or red lights, no traffic signal, etc.). In scenario B, we have the same intersection, now controlled by a standard traffic signal light operated by a timer. The protocol for passing through the intersection in scenario A is as follows: As you approach the intersection, beep your horn. If you do not hear a horn in return, you may proceed without slowing down. If you hear another horn in response to yours, slow down and proceed with caution. The protocol for scenario B is simple: Obey the traffic signal. If it's green, you may proceed through the intersection; if it's red, you must stop and wait for a green light. Clearly, in scenario A, vehicles can pass through the intersection quite easily when traffic is light or nonexistent. On the other hand, once traffic increases, delays become more frequent and longer lasting, creating a greater likelihood of collisions. Scenario A is analogous to the schemes used for contention protocols. In scenario B, traffic is controlled via a traffic signal. Consequently, during heavy traffic loads you can predict approximately when you will be able to negotiate the intersection by counting the number of vehicles passing through while the signal is green. At the same time, however, what happens if you are stuck at this red light in very light traffic? You must still wait until the light turns green, whether the intersection is clear or not. This is a very inefficient use of time. Scenario B is analogous to collision-free protocols. Table 5.2 contains a summary of these advantages and disadvantages. Box 5.3 also provides a summary of statistical and deterministic LANs.

TABLE 5.2   Advantages and Disadvantages of Contention and Collision-free Protocols

Protocol	Advantage	Disadvantage
Contention	Faster access on lightly loaded systems	Poor performance at heavy loads
Collision-free	Very predictable at high loads	Fixed delay required at low loads

BOX 5.3   Statistical (Stochastic) versus Deterministic LANs

Statistical LANs
- can only estimate when the network will be available for use by a specific node
- are load-metric-based and not node-metric-based
- are difficult to predict performance
- produce burst-oriented traffic
- match more closely how network applications use the network

Deterministic LANs
- can determine exactly when a node will get to access the network
- are node-metric-based (i.e., number of nodes determines round-trip time)
- can determine exact round-trip time
- can determine overall performance in advance of using the network
- can determine the impact of additional stations and load prior to network connection

5.4   Data Prioritization and Quality of Service

Tagging data with a priority level is also called *class of service*, or CoS.

Two other concepts related to the data link layer are *data prioritization* and *quality of service* (QoS). Data prioritization involves assigning a priority level to data frames, and QoS involves establishing certain parameters for a specific transmission. Both data prioritization and QoS are required to deliver real-time voice and video traffic. Let's discuss both of these concepts from the perspective of an Ethernet/802.3 LAN. Once again, Chapter 9 is devoted to Ethernet/802.3. So you might want to review Chapter 9 first if you find some of the following information unclear.

Ethernet/802.3 is a shared-media standard based on contention. Thus, congestion is an inherent feature of Ethernet/802.3 networks, and it is normal for frames to be dropped. Two questions emerge from this: (a) How much congestion is acceptable? (b) Does it matter which frames are dropped? If congestion levels are too excessive and unacceptable, or if we do not want to lose any frames, then increasing bandwidth will help resolve these problems; data prioritization will not. An Ethernet/802.3 network will continue to experience congestion and lose frames regardless of whether a data prioritization scheme is implemented. The function data prioritization adds is control over which frames get lost. For example, if e-mail is the highest priority application on our network, then e-mail frames will be tagged as such and their transmission will take precedence over all other traffic. If Web-based applications are the highest priority, then they can be tagged as such using a data prioritization scheme. Tagging data frames with a specific priority level is important for real-time transmissions because during periods of congestion we do not want voice or video data sets to be dropped by switches. A high-priority assignment to these data sets ensures their delivery.

Data prioritization is only part of the equation, though. The delivery of time-sensitive data also requires that sufficient bandwidth be available and that transmission delays (i.e., latency) be predictable and guaranteed. This is the essence of QoS. A properly implemented QoS strategy ensures that all transmissions, regardless of their type (data, voice, or video), receive the necessary bandwidth, delivery times, and appropriate priority based on the importance of data delivery.

To address CoS and QoS, the IEEE introduced two data link layer protocols: IEEE 802.1p and IEEE 802.1q. IEEE 802.1p is an extension to IEEE 802.1d, which specifies how MAC-level bridges are to interoperate regardless of the IEEE LAN standard being used. (Bridges are discussed in Chapter 6.) What 802.1p adds to the 802.1d standard is a specification for implementing prioritization in 802.1d-compliant bridges. IEEE 802.1p defines a three-bit priority scheme, which provides eight different levels of priority. This new standard can be used on LANs that support prioritization, including 802.4 (token bus), 802.5 (token ring), 802.6 (DQDB), and 802.12 (100VG-AnyLAN). (Token bus and ring LANs are discussed in Chapter 10, 100VG-AnyLAN is discussed in Chapter 9, and DQDB is discussed in Chapter 14.) Data prioritization can also be incorporated into an FDDI network (Chapter 11). However, it cannot be used with current Ethernet/802.3 networks because Ethernet was never designed with data prioritization.

To resolve this, the IEEE developed 802.1q, which provides a data prioritization scheme to Ethernet/802.3. There is one small problem, though—in order to do so, the 802.3 frame had to be altered. Specifically, a four-byte 802.1q header is inserted between the source address and length fields (Figure 5.7). Thus, an 802.3 frame that includes an 802.1q header is incompatible with a standard 802.3 frame. This also makes an 802.1q-compliant device incompatible with an 802.3 device. Instead of seeing the length field, an 802.3 device will be greeted with 802.1q header information. One workaround to this device incompatibility issue is for vendors to manufacture 802.1q devices with a switch that disables 802.1q. Although disabling 802.1q also disables data prioritization, it enables 802.1q-compliant products to be purchased and installed in anticipation of migrating to a data prioritization scheme.

The frame-length difference, however, is not as easily addressed. At issue is the frame size. Ignoring the preamble, the maximum size of a standard 802.3 frame is 1518 bytes. The maximum size of an 802.3 frame that includes the 802.1q header is 1522 bytes. Two possible solutions abound: (a) Increase the size of 802.3 frames by four bytes or (b) reduce the length of the payload (i.e., the user data field) of 802.3 frames by four bytes so they can accommodate 802.1q header information. Rather than making a decision, the IEEE put the onus on the vendors. That is, the IEEE 802.1q specification allows for either solution to be incorporated. This means that it

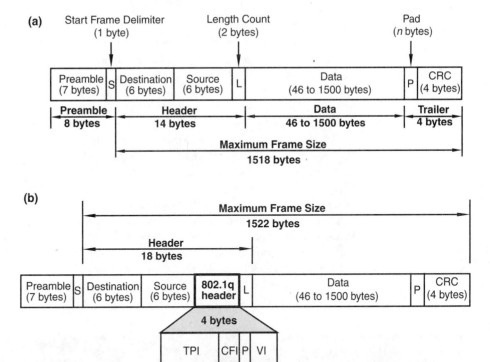

FIGURE 5.7 An IEEE 802.3 frame (a) with an IEEE 802.1q header (b) adds 4 bytes to the 802.3 frame. This changes the size of the frame's header from 14 bytes to 18 bytes, which increases the maximum frame size from 1518 bytes to 1522 bytes. The 3-bit priority (P) field of the 802.1q header provides for seven different priority levels.

is up to the vendors to decide which method they want to implement. It also raises the question of interoperability.

As is the case with any networking decisions, a thorough network analysis should be undertaken before implementing CoS and QoS. For example, if a network is transmitting only data (no voice or video) and we do not care about what frames are being discarded, then we probably do not need to be concerned with data prioritization. However, if a network is currently supporting, or if we are planning to implement on the network bandwidth intensive applications such as videoconferencing, distance education applications, or those electronic whiteboards that enable people to collaborate on-line, then we might want to consider a data prioritization scheme. If we are unsure whether we need a prioritization scheme, then we can always play it safe by ensuring that the Ethernet controller cards and switches we purchase support IEEE 802.1p and 802.1q. We should also confirm that all layer-3 devices (e.g., routers, switching routers) support multiple levels of queuing so that, if data prioritization is implemented, queues will not get overloaded.

End-of-Chapter Commentary

On this note, we conclude our discussion of the data link layer. Many of the concepts we discussed here will be expanded in subsequent chapters. For example, in our discussion of TCP in Chapter 8, we revisit the sliding window protocol concept. Our examination of Ethernet/802.3 LANs in Chapter 9 includes a discussion of the layer-2 differences among conventional Ethernet (10 Mbps), Fast Ethernet (100 Mbps), 100VG-AnyLAN (another 100-Mbps "Ethernet"), and Gigabit Ethernet (1000 Mbps). We also examine 802.3 performance issues and address the concept of collision management, both of which are part of the data link layer. Similarly, our discussions in Chapters 10 and 11 on token ring and FDDI, respectively, include matters related to the data link layer. In Chapter 13, we examine frame relay, which is a synchronous data link layer protocol based on the concept of packet-switching. Frame relay is designed with a variable-length frame size. Chapter 14 contains information about another interesting data link layer protocol: IEEE 802.6, distributed queue dual bus (DQDB). DQDB is used as the data link layer of a packet-switched, broadband MAN called switched multimegabit data service (SMDS). Finally, the concepts of data prioritization and quality of service are revisited in the chapters on Ethernet, token ring, SMDS, and ATM.

CHAPTER REVIEW MATERIALS

SUMMARY

• The data link layer, which corresponds to the second layer of the OSI model, is responsible for transferring data from the network layer on the source machine to the network layer on the destination machine.

• When viewed from the perspective of the IEEE LAN architecture, the data link layer is composed of two sublayers: the logical link control (LLC) and the medium access control (MAC). The LLC sublayer performs several functions, including framing and error control. Framing involves the use of start–stop bits to subdivide a bit stream into discrete blocks of data. This partitioning of a raw bit stream enables sending and receiving machines to synchronize their data transmission. Framing also promotes error control. Through the use of various error-detection methods, a receiving node can determine whether or not a received frame is accurate. If it isn't, then the receiving node can request a retransmission of the frame from the sending node.

• Two flow-control protocols are stop-and-wait and sliding window. Stop-and-wait requires the sending node to transmit one data frame and wait for an acknowledgment from the receiver before transmitting another frame. Sliding window involves the sender and receiver maintaining send and receive windows. The send window identifies all transmitted frames that have not been acknowledged, and the receive window represents the number of frames a receiver is able to accept based on its buffer size. Data flow is controlled by the sender adjusting its send window based on the receiver's receive window.

• Two methods of error detection include parity check and cyclic redundancy check (CRC). Parity check involves the use of a parity bit, which is set to 0 or 1 to ensure that the total number of 1-bits in a data set is even or odd. Depending on the desired parity (even or odd), if a frame arrives with the wrong parity (e.g., it has an even number of 1-bits when odd parity is being used, or vice versa), then a transmission error is detected by the destination machine. In CRC, the data integrity of a received frame is determined using a binary polynomial arithmetic algorithm. A CRC checksum based on the contents of a frame is first computed by the sending machine. This checksum is transmitted with the frame and then matched with the result obtained by the receiving machine, which performs the same calculation. If the checksums are not equal (i.e., the remainder of the destination node's division is not 0), then an error is detected. CRC-32, a 32-bit checksum, is used in most LAN protocols today and is capable of detecting nearly 100% of all transmission errors.

• Complementing the LLC sublayer is the MAC sublayer, which provides media access management protocols for accessing a shared medium. Two general methods are used by most LANs today: random access and token passing.

• Random access protocols are contentious in nature and involve collisions. These protocols are based on the principle that nodes can access the channel whenever they have data to transmit. Four such protocols, called carrier sense multiple access (CSMA) protocols, were described in the chapter: 1-persistent CSMA, nonpersistent CSMA, CSMA with collision detection (CSMA/CD), and CSMA with collision avoidance (CSMA/CA). Nodes following a 1-persistent CSMA scheme will constantly sense the channel whenever they have data to transmit and seize the channel as soon as they detect it is free. Nonpersistent CSMA is similar to 1-persistent CSMA, but nodes do not constantly monitor the channel when they have data to transmit. Instead, if a node detects a busy channel, it will wait a random period of time before it senses the channel again.

CSMA/CD adds to the previous two protocols the concept of collision detection, which provides some order when two nodes initiate a transmission at approximately the same time. After a node transmits data, it will sense the channel to detect if its transmission collided with that of another node's. If so, both nodes stop transmitting, send out a jamming signal to alert everyone that a collision occurred, and wait a random period of time before attempting another transmission. The last carrier sense protocol, CSMA/CA, is similar to CSMA/CD, but it is implemented in wireless LAN environments where all nodes cannot necessarily hear each other's transmissions.

• Token passing protocols provide a more simple concept of media access. Access to the medium is controlled via a special data frame called a token. The node that possesses the token is permitted to transmit data.

• Two additional concepts presented were data prioritization and quality of service (QoS), both of which are needed for transmitting real-time video and voice traffic. Data priority provides a mechanism for specifying the priority level of data frames. This way, during periods of congestion, frames tagged with higher priority levels take precedence over lower priority frames. Complementing data prioritization is QoS, which ensures that sufficient bandwidth is available and that transmission delays (i.e., latency) are predictable and guaranteed.

VOCABULARY CHECK

alignment errors	cyclic redundancy check (CRC)	nonpersistent CSMA
bit-stuffing	data link layer	1-persistent CSMA
carrier sense protocol	error control	oversized frame
check bits	error correction	parity
checksum	error detection	quality of service (QoS)
class of service (CoS)	flow control	random access protocols
codeword	frame	redundancy bits
collision	framing	runt frame
contention protocol	IEEE	sliding window protocol
CRC error	jabber	stop-and-wait protocol
CSMA with collision avoidance (CSMA/CA)	logical link control (LLC) sublayer	token
CSMA with collision detection (CSMA/CD)	media access control (MAC) sublayer	token passing protocol

REVIEW EXERCISES

1. Define the data link layer and explain how IEEE's version of the data link layer varies from that of OSI.

2. In our overview of the data link layer in Section 5.1, we said that it provides services to the network layer. Briefly describe each of the following service types from the data link layer perspective: unacknowledged connectionless service, acknowledged connectionless service, connection-oriented service. Which of the three service types is appropriate for situations in which error rates are low and recovery is provided by the upper layers?

3. Compare and contrast the LLC and MAC sublayers.

4. Explain the purpose of framing.

5. What effect do you think the absence of flow control would have on a network?

6. Both error-correcting and error-detecting codes involve adding redundancy to a frame. The type of redundant information that is included, however, is different. What is this difference?

7. Give an example of when autonomous error correction is appropriate.

8. What is parity and how can parity be used for error control?

9. By exclusive ORing (XOR) two codewords, we can determine how many corresponding bits differ by examining the number of 1-bits that result. For example,

```
101101 codeword 1
110011 codeword 2
──────
011110 XOR (4 bits differ)
```

The number of bit positions in which two codewords differ is called the *Hamming distance*. Thus, in our example, the Hamming distance is equal to four. If two codewords are a Hamming distance,

d, apart, then d single-bit errors are needed to convert one codeword into another. The Hamming distance of a complete code is that which yields a minimum distance. For example, if we have three codewords, C_1, C_2, and C_3, then we must perform three XORs—$(C_1 - C_2)$, $(C_1 - C_3)$, and $(C_2 - C_3)$—and the Hamming distance will be the minimum distance among these three XORs. In general, a Hamming distance of $(d + 1)$ can detect d errors, and a Hamming distance of $(2d + 1)$ can correct d errors. Assume that the following codewords are used to transmit the four symbols, S_1, S_2, S_3, and S_4. Determine the number of bit errors that can be detected and corrected.

$$S_1 = 00000000$$
$$S_1 = 11111111$$
$$S_1 = 01010101$$
$$S_1 = 11001100$$

10. Assume the CRC generator polynomial of $x^5 + x^4 + x^2 + 1$ is used to provide error checking. Use the algorithm demonstrated in Box 5.2 to compute the bit stream that will be transmitted if a message 111000111000 is sent.

11. Explain the various fields of an IEEE 802.3 frame.

12. Compare and contrast random access and token passing protocols.

13. Describe the difference between 1-persistent and nonpersistent CSMA.

14. Describe CSMA/CD.

15. Give a nonnetwork example, different from that given in the book, of contention.

16. What is a collision?

17. Explain the concept of data prioritization.

18. What is the difference between CoS and QoS?

SUGGESTED READINGS AND REFERENCES

CAMPBELL, R. 1994. The Last Word on Thick Ethernet. *LAN Technology*, January, 26–27.

CODENOLL TECHNOLOGY CORPORATION. 1993. *The Fiber Optic LAN Handbook*. 5th ed. Yonkers, NY: Codenoll Technology Corporation.

DYSON, P. 1995. *The Network Press Dictionary of Networking*. 2nd ed. San Francisco: Sybex.

FEIBEL, W. 1995. *The Network Press Encyclopedia of Networking*. 2nd ed. San Francisco: Sybex.

GALLO, M., and W. HANCOCK. 1999. *Networking Explained.* Boston: Digital Press.

HANCOCK, B. 1988. *Designing and Implementing Ethernet Networks.* Wellesley, MA: QED Information Sciences, Inc.

———. 1996. *Advanced Ethernet/802.3 Management and Performance.* Boston: Digital Press.

HUNT, C. 1995. *Networking Personal Computers.* Sebastopol, CA: O'Reilly & Associates.

MARTIN, J. 1989. *Local Area Networks: Architectures and Implementations.* Upper Saddle River, NJ: Prentice-Hall.

METCALFE, R., and D. BOGGS. 1976. Ethernet: Distributed Packet Switching for Local Computer Networks. *Communications of the ACM,* 19(7), 395–404.

PETERSON, L., and B. DAVIE. 1996. *Computer Networks: A Systems Approach.* San Francisco: Morgan Kaufmann.

STALLINGS, W. 1997. *Local and Metropolitan Area Networks.* 5th ed. Upper Saddle River, NJ: Prentice-Hall.

———. 2000. *Data and Computer Communications.* 6th ed. Upper Saddle River, NJ: Prentice-Hall.

TANENBAUM, A. S. 1996. *Computer Networks.* 3rd ed. Upper Saddle River, NJ: Prentice-Hall.

THE AG GROUP. 1993. *Etherpeek Network Analysis Software User Manual Version 2.0.* Walnut Creek, CA: The AG Group.

6 Network Hardware Components (Layers 1 and 2)

CHAPTER OBJECTIVES

After studying this chapter, you will be able to do the following:

1. Distinguish between layer-1 and layer-2 hardware components.
2. Identify the connector types used for UTP, coaxial, and fiber-optic cables.
3. Describe the operation and function of transceivers.
4. Describe the operation and function of repeaters.
5. Describe the operation and function of network bridges.
6. Describe the operation and function of network switches.
7. Explain the primary differences among repeaters, bridges, and switches.
8. Describe the operation and function of network interface cards.
9. Distinguish among the various types of PC cards.
10. Understand the concept of a spanning tree.
11. Explain the differences between store-and-forward switches and cut-through switches.
12. Understand the concept of propagation delay and latency relative to repeaters, bridges, and switches.
13. Describe the differences between a crossbar switch design and a backplane switch design.

CHAPTER OUTLINE

In Chapter 4, we focused mostly on media and the physical layer (layer 1 of the OSI model) and did not include any formal discussion about specific network components. Similarly, Chapter 5, which examined the data link layer (layer 2 of the OSI model), did not contain any information about network devices. In this chapter, we examine various network hardware devices that operate at either layer 1 or 2. These include connectors (Section 6.1), transceivers and media converters (Section 6.2), repeaters (Section 6.3), network interface cards and PC cards (Section 6.4), bridges (Section 6.5), and switches (Section 6.6).

6.1 What Are Connectors?

Overview

Connectors attach components together. Several types of connectors are available, serving various purposes. For example, connectors are used to: (a) connect network interface cards, such as an Ethernet card, to a cable; (b) connect cable segments (e.g., thin coax to thin coax); and (c) terminate a segment. In this last category, connectors actually connect the cable to a terminating resistor or an array of resistors and are consequently known as *terminators*. The type of connector used is usually a function of cable type. Connectors are also classified by their gender, and they do indeed "mate." You can use your imagination about how a connector's gender is derived, but a "plug" is usually "male" and a "jack" is usually "female." This universally understood terminology enables a clear specification of exactly which of a mating pair of connectors should be used in the particular application.

Connectors are also frequently labeled by their type. Three common types are DB-type, centronics, and DIN. *DB* (data bus) connectors serve as an interface between a computer and a peripheral device such as a printer or external modem; they are distinguished as a rectangular row of "pins" (for male connectors) or "holes" (for female connectors). Several types of DB connectors exist and are distinguished by the number of pins they contain. Common types include DB-9 (a 9-pin serial or video interface), DB-15 (a 15-pin video interface), DB-25 (a 25-pin serial interface—RS-232—or parallel printer interface), and DB-37 (a 37-pin serial interface based on RS-422). (Illustrations of DB-9 and DB-25 connectors are shown in Figure 4.1.) *DIN* (Deutsche Industrie Norm, a German industrial standard) and *centronics* connectors are similar to DB-type connectors except DIN connectors are circular instead of rectangular, and centronics connectors contain "teeth" instead of pins. DIN connectors are typically used to connect a keyboard to a computer; centronics connectors are used in similar applications as DB-type connectors. Other connector types include coax, v-type, fiber, video, SCSI, and modular. A brief description of these connectors based on cable type follows.

UTP Cable Connectors

Connectors used for unshielded twisted-pair cable are formally called *eight-pin modular connectors* (Figure 6.1). Eight-pin modular connectors resemble standard

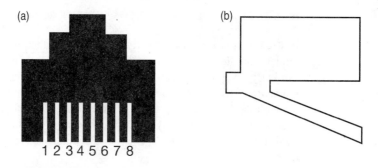

FIGURE 6.1 Top (a) and side (b) views of an RJ-45 connector. Formally known as eight-pin modular connectors, RJ-45s resemble standard telephone jacks and are used with UTP cable.

modular telephone connectors used in the United States. UTP connectors are commonly (and really, incorrectly) called *RJ-45 connectors*. In the strictest sense, the RJ designation refers to a specific series of connectors defined in the Universal Service Order Code (USOC) definitions of telephone circuits. RJ is telephone lingo for "registered jack." For example, RJ-11 refers to a four-wire connection used for standard home telephone lines in the United States. Hence, the correct term for UTP connectors used in LANs is eight-pin modular and not RJ-45. In some networking circles, though, the RJ designator has become a generic designation and implies any modular connector.

Coaxial Cable Connectors

There are several interpretations of BNC, including *bayonet Neill-Concelman* (named after its developers), *bayonet nut connector,* and *barrel nut connector.* We have also seen *British national connector.*

Connectors used with thin coax are known as *BNC connectors*. Several different types of BNC connectors are available and used for specific purposes. For example, *barrel connectors* are cylindrical and connect two segments of cable; *T connectors* are shaped like the letter T and connect a device to a cable—the horizontal part of the T connects two segments of cable (like a barrel connector) and the vertical part connects the device (Figure 6.2); *end connectors* are attached to the ends of a cable segment and mate the cable to either a barrel or T connector; and BNC *terminators* are attached to each end of a thin coaxial trunk cable to prevent signal reflections, which can interfere with other signals. Terminators provide electrical resistance at the end of a cable and "absorb" signals to keep them from bouncing back and being heard again by the devices connected to the cable.

For the thick coaxial cable used in early Ethernet applications, a *Type N* connector was employed to connect cable segments to each other (via barrel connectors) and to end terminators. N connectors are large threaded connectors that accommodate the half-inch (12.5 mm) size of the coaxial cable. In "ThickWire" Ethernet networks, transceivers were attached to the medium either by "intrusive tap," which required the cable to be cut and female N connectors installed on both the cut ends, in turn connecting to the male N connectors on the transceiver, or by "vampire tap," which penetrated the cable. These methods are discussed in Chapter 9.

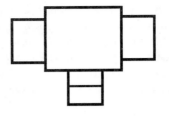

FIGURE 6.2 Example of a BNC T connector.

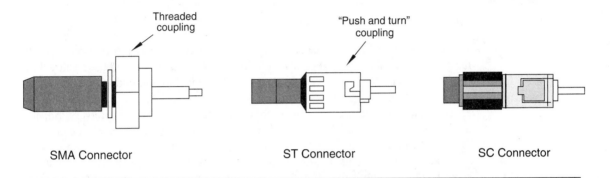

FIGURE 6.3 Examples of different types of fiber-optic cable connectors.

Fiber-Optic Cable Connectors

Several different types of fiber-optic connectors exist. Before the issuance of the EIA/TIA-568A standard, the most popular were *ST connectors,* which are similar to BNC connectors in that you push and turn the connectors to mate them to a device. *SC connectors* are those approved by the EIA/TIA-568A standard, by virtue of which they are destined to eclipse the popularity of the ST type. SC connectors, which are also called 568SC, are available in single and dual varieties, the latter designed to aid differentiation between transmit and receive fibers. *SMA connectors* use a threaded coupling mechanism—you attach them by screwing one end onto another. SMA connectors are designed to meet stringent military specifications. Another type of fiber-optic connector is the MIC (medium interface connector) used in FDDI networks (Figure 6.3).

Other Connectors

Two other examples of connectors found in computer communications and networking environments include v.35 and SCSI connectors. *V.35 connectors* are high-speed serial interfaces typically found on routers, switches, high-speed modems, and CSU/DSUs. One common application is connecting routers to CSU/DSUs. *SCSI* (small computer systems interface; pronounced "scuzzy") *connectors* are high-speed parallel interfaces that enable computer peripheral devices such as scanners, CD-ROM drives, tape drives, and hard disk drives to connect directly to a computer. In most applications, up to seven different SCSI devices can be *daisy-chained* using a single SCSI adapter. In this type of configuration, the devices are serially linked with the first device connected to the second device, the second device connected to the third device, the third device connected to the fourth device, and so forth. The last component of a daisy-chained configuration terminates the electrical connection. This is done either internally, or externally using a SCSI terminator.

6.2 Transceivers and Media Converters

Transceivers

Transceivers are layer-1 devices used in Ethernet/802.3 networks to connect nodes to the physical medium. They serve as both the physical connection and the electrical interface between a node and the physical medium, enabling the node to communicate with the medium.

The function of transceivers is described by the term itself—transceivers *trans*mit and re*ceive* signals simultaneously. When a node sends data, the transmitting circuitry of the transceiver places the data bits on the medium. Simultaneously, the transceiver's receiving circuitry listens to the transmission. If what is heard is the same as what was sent, then everything is fine. If not, the transceiver presumes that an error has occurred and notifies the node of this condition. (This error is called a "collision," which is discussed in Chapter 9.) In a nutshell, a transceiver essentially performs three functions: It sends data, it receives data, and it notifies its host node if an error condition has occurred during a transmission.

> In Ethernet V2.0, a transceiver performs a fourth function: It asserts signal quality error, or SQE. This is discussed in Chapter 9.

Today, transceivers are usually integrated into *network interface cards*, which are discussed later. This integration allows a node to be connected directly to the medium via a cable without the need for an external transceiver. A network interface card's on-board transceivers support UTP, ThinWire, and fiber-optic cable connections. Many network interface cards also can be purchased with a "universal" connector, called a 15-pin *attachment unit interface* (AUI), which allows a device to be connected to UTP, thick or thin coax, or fiber-optic cable via an external transceiver (Figure 6.4). Ethernet/802.3 network interface cards (Figure 6.5) can be purchased with any three connector types. AUI connectors and cables, which are rapidly fading into Ethernet history, are 15-pin D-shell type connectors (Figure 6.6). On the computer side, the AUI is female; on the transceiver side, it is male. Many readers might be familiar with AUI connectors; they're the ones with those weird slide-lock things that never seem to work. Don't despair; we were not able to get the slide lock to work correctly all of the time either. AUI connectors are also available with screw-in retainers. Many older Ethernet/802.3 devices such as bridges or switches (discussed later) could be purchased with AUI connector ports so that users could connect any of the three media types to any port using one of the external transceivers shown in Figure 6.4. As we have stated, however, the use of AUI became less and less prevalent in the late 1990s.

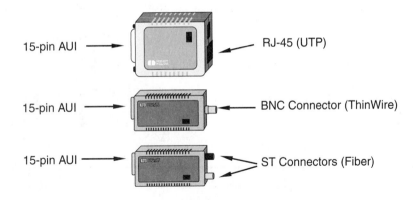

FIGURE 6.4   Three types of Ethernet/802.3 transceivers that serve as media converters. When connected to a network interface card's 15-pin AUI connector, the card is able to support twisted-pair, ThinWire, or fiber-optic cable.

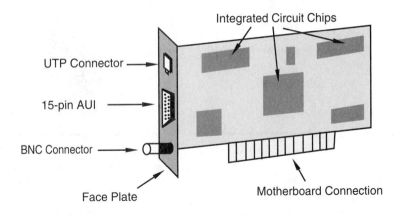

FIGURE 6.5   Sample Ethernet network interface card. This NIC can support any one of three media types: UTP, transceiver cable via an AUI, and ThinWire. NICs are installed into a node by inserting them into an expansion slot on the motherboard.

ThickWire Ethernet networks also use external transceivers with AUI connectors to connect a node to the cable. In this setting, the transceiver was a bulky stand-alone device that required special transceiver cable to connect the node to the transceiver. The transceiver cable carried signals between the network cable and the node (Figure 6.7). There were also multiport transceiver units such as the Digital Equipment Corporation DELNI, which contained eight AUI ports providing a total of eight independent transceiver cable connections. This technology is archaic, having been replaced by miniature external transceivers such as those shown in Figure 6.4. There is no longer a need

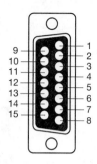

FIGURE 6.6   Standard 15-pin attachment unit interface (AUI).

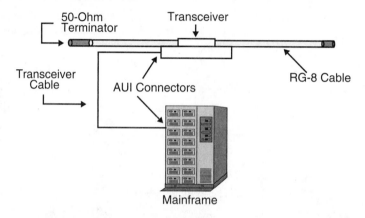

FIGURE 6.7   An external transceiver used in ThickWire Ethernet LANs. Special transceiver cable is used to interconnect the node to the transceiver. The connector on the computer side is a 15-pin female AUI, and the connector on the transceiver is a 15-pin AUI male.

for transceiver cable because network cards provide a direct interface for different network media.

Associated with AUI connectors are the terms AAUI and MAU. *AAUI* stands for Apple attachment unit interface, which was Apple's proprietary AUI. Older model Macintosh computers such as the Centris 650 and Power Macintosh 7100 have built-in AAUI ports, as evidenced by yet another variety of subminiature 15-pin connector on their rear panels. To connect these machines to an Ethernet/802.3 LAN, you must first purchase an AAUI-to-AUI adapter to change the proprietary interface to AUI, BNC, or RJ-45. Why Apple chose to do this is anyone's guess. Later model Macintoshes have built-in standard connectors, mainly RJ-45. As for *MAU*, this stands for media attachment unit; it is another term for a transceiver.

Media Converters

Media converters are also layer-1 devices, and they enable different network media to be connected to one another. For example, using a media converter, you can connect a coaxial cable to UTP cable, a coaxial cable to fiber-optic cable, a 100-Mbps Ethernet UTP segment to 100-Mbps Ethernet fiber-optic segment, and half- or full-duplex UTP segments to 10-Mbps Ethernet fiber-optic segments. (See Chapter 9 for a discussion of 100-Mbps Ethernet and full-duplex Ethernet.) Some people like to think of transceivers as media converters because transceivers support various types of media via a standard AUI connection. Nevertheless, media converters operate at the physical layer and provide a simple mechanism for extending the distance between two devices by mixing copper and fiber cable.

Media converters are nonstandard devices and are not covered under the IEEE 802.3 standard.

6.3   Repeaters

Repeaters, like transceivers, provide both physical and electrical connections. Their function is to regenerate and propagate a signal. Repeaters, which are also called *concentrators*, are used in Ethernet/802.3 LANs to extend the length of the LAN. You see, depending on the type of medium, the length of an Ethernet/802.3 LAN segment has specific length restrictions. For example, a 10-Mbps Ethernet/802.3 LAN that uses UTP cable (10BASE-T) has a maximum length restriction of 100 meters, and a ThinWire (coax) Ethernet/802.3 segment (10BASE2) cannot exceed 185 meters. The reason for these restrictions is signal quality. As a segment exceeds its maximum length, the signal quality begins to deteriorate. (Recall the concept of attenuation from Chapter 4.) In many instances, these length restrictions are not always practical, so network managers have to extend their LANs by interconnecting individual segments. A repeater makes this possible. It receives signals from one cable segment, regenerates, retimes, and amplifies them, and then transmits these "revitalized" signals to another cable segment. We discuss the application of repeaters in Ethernet/802.3 LANs in more detail in Chapter 9. Repeaters are a source of *propagation delay* in a network. Propagation delay is the amount of time a signal spends getting from one point in a circuit to another. It is affected by the speed and efficiency of the components between the two points.

Repeaters versus Hubs

Frequently, the term *hub* is used to describe a repeater. We must exercise caution when doing so, though. Some people think of a hub as a repeater, whereas others view a hub generically as any device that connects two or more network segments. In this latter case, we then need to qualify the device (e.g., repeater hub, switching hub, bridging hub, etc.). A hub can also be a device that supports several different media (Figure 6.8). Still another type of repeater hub is a stackable repeater hub. *Stackable repeater hubs* consist of individual repeater units "stacked" one on top of another. Instead of a common shared backplane that is part of a chassis-based repeater, stackable hubs use a "pseudobackplane" based on a common connector interface. An external cable interconnects the individual hubs in a daisy-chained manner. Once interconnected, the entire chain of hubs becomes a single logical unit that functions as a single repeater. Stackable hubs are less expensive than chassis-based devices. An illustration of a stackable hub is shown in Figure 6.9.

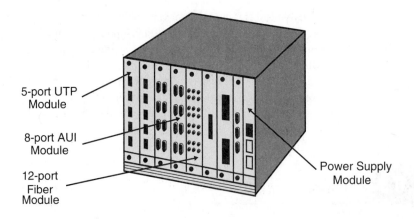

5-port UTP Module

8-port AUI Module

12-port Fiber Module

Power Supply Module

FIGURE 6.8 This multislot chassis-based repeater hub (also called a concentrator) can accommodate several different media types, including UTP, coax, and fiber. Since each interface module shares the same backplane as the repeater module, the Ethernet ports on each module use the same repeater. Thus, repeater hubs are capable of supporting many Ethernet connections using only a single repeater. For example, if one of the modules is a 12-port ThinWire board, then this one board can support 12 separate 185-meter ThinWire segments. Since 30 devices can be connected to one ThinWire segment, this board can support $12 \times 30 = 360$ nodes.

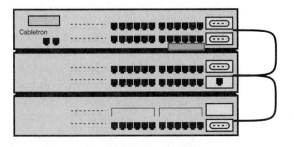

FIGURE 6.9 Stackable hubs are daisy-chained together using an external cable, which enables them to function as a single hub.

In Ethernet circles, the term *Ethernet hub* can also take on different meanings. Once again, we need qualification. At one point several years ago, an Ethernet hub was a repeater. Today, however, *switches* have replaced repeaters in many Ethernet/802.3 LANs, and the term *hub* now commonly refers to a switch instead of a repeater. Physically, repeater and switch hubs look the same. For example, consider the illustration in Figure 6.10. Without any type of qualification, this four-port device could be a repeater hub or it could be a switch. We don't know. Functionally, repeater and switch hubs are not the same. A repeater hub takes an incoming signal, amplifies it, and then repeats (i.e., broadcasts) it to all of the hub's ports regardless of the destination port. A switch, on the other hand, only transmits data between the hub's sending and receiving ports (Figure 6.11). We will talk more about switches later in this chapter.

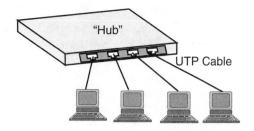

FIGURE 6.10 A four-port "hub." Without any type of qualification, we do not know if this is a repeater hub or a switch hub.

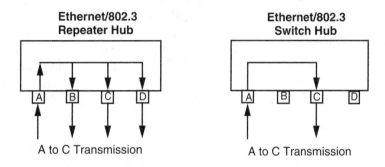

FIGURE 6.11 In a repeater hub, if data on port A are destined to port C, all ports receive the data. In a switch hub, if data on port A are destined to port C, only port C receives the data.

There are two more pieces of information we should mention. Although repeaters are layer-1 devices, several vendors incorporate some intelligence into them. For example, many Ethernet/802.3 repeater hubs are capable of detecting Ethernet "collisions" (discussed in Chapter 9) and temporarily shutting down any segment that exhibits an excessive number of collisions. You should also know that, in an Ethernet/802.3 LAN, Ethernet rules restrict the number of repeaters allowed. We discuss this in more detail in Chapter 9. For now, though, just realize that repeaters are layer-1 devices that regenerate signals.

6.4 Network Interface Cards and PC Cards

Network Interface Cards

Network interface cards operate at the data link layer (layer 2 of the OSI model). Many people think of network interface cards as Ethernet cards, but this is not entirely correct. An *Ethernet card* is a network interface card used in Ethernet/802.3 networks. Not all network interface cards are Ethernet cards, though. A network interface card is known by many names. Some of the more common ones are *LAN adapter, network adapter, network card*, and *network board*. Generally, we prefer to call them *NIC* (pronounced "nick"). A

NIC can support different types of networks and media. For example, an Ethernet/802.3 NIC is designed specifically for Ethernet/802.3 networks and can be purchased with connectors supporting UTP, BNC, AUI, and fiber (see Figure 6.5). An Ethernet NIC is often called an Ethernet card or *Ethernet adapter*. Similarly, a token ring NIC is designed specifically for token ring networks, can support various media, and is called a *token ring card* or *token ring adapter*. So you see, it's a semantic thing. We have the generic name (i.e., network adapter) and the specific name (i.e., Ethernet card).

In a generic sense, all NICs are functionally equivalent because they are layer-2 devices. As layer-2 devices, NICs perform typical layer-2 functions, including organizing data into frames, transferring frames between the ends of a communication channel, and managing the link by providing error control, initialization, control termination, and flow control (see Chapters 2 and 4). However, it is the network's architecture (Chapter 2) that determines the manner in which these functions are implemented. As an example, consider the function of framing. The format of Ethernet frames is not the same as that of token ring frames (see Chapters 9 and 10). Hence, an Ethernet NIC does not frame data in exactly the same manner as a token ring NIC. A token ring NIC is also responsible for token passing and includes chips for monitoring and reporting network errors.

NICs also have layer-1 components as part of their construction and hence perform layer-1 activities in addition to layer-2 activities. For example, on a sending node, the NIC performs framing (layer 2) and converts bit values into electrical signals using an appropriate coding scheme (layer-1). At the receiving node, the NIC monitors the medium for transmissions, captures data from the medium if the frame's destination address matches the NIC's address (or if it is a broadcast or multicast), and then passes the data to the node for processing. The NIC also checks the integrity of a captured frame (error control). Thus, a NIC can be regarded as a combination layer-1/layer-2 device.

Some NICs are built-in as an integral part of the computer's design. However, many desktop PCs, including Intel-based and Macintosh units, are not always manufactured with built-in network support. In such computers, a network adapter is needed to connect the PC to a LAN. Add-in NICs exist for nearly all expansion slot types used in computers manufactured today. Installation of a NIC is relatively straightforward: Insert the card into an existing expansion slot, install special network "driver" software to enable the NIC to communicate with the networking software, reboot the machine, and test the card. On Intel-based (or compatible) machines, a NIC also must be assigned an I/O address and an interrupt request (IRQ). These assignments must be made to prevent the NIC from conflicting with other installed boards. (This is not necessary for Macintosh computers.) Many of the reputable NIC manufacturers do this via software; others require you to set DIP switches on the card. Many NICs support Plug-n-Play (PnP)—that is, they comply with the PnP specifications—which enables them to be configured automatically without user intervention.

As a network device that must communicate with its host's network operating system, NICs employ special communications software called a *LAN driver*. A driver is critical to the operation of a NIC and must be written so the card supports the appropriate network protocols and operating system. Incorrect LAN drivers are invariably the source of network performance problems. Normally, a NIC requires a separate driver for each combination of network protocol and operating system. However, two specification standards—the network driver interface specification (NDIS) and the open data-link interface (ODI)—provide generic interfaces that reduce the number of drivers required. Thus, a NIC that supports either NDIS or ODI only needs a single driver and can support multiple network protocols including TCP/IP, IPX/SPX, and NetBIOS. Similarly, standard driver specifications exist for MacOS's Open Transport networking.

Although most NICs, regardless of vendor, have a high degree of interoperability (e.g., an Ethernet/802.3 card from one manufacturer most likely will communicate with an Ethernet/802.3 card from a different manufacturer), all NICs are not the same. Consequently, several considerations are in order when purchasing one. First of all, we need to make sure the NIC's data bus is appropriate for the host system. For example, we don't want to use an 8-bit NIC in a Pentium server. At the same time, we don't want to use a 32-bit NIC in a 386 workstation. Second, some NICs include an on-board processor, on-board RAM, or both. A NIC with an on-board processor is able to do more work than one without this feature and, consequently, relieves the host system's processor from performing certain functions. The on-board RAM provides a NIC with additional buffer space, which improves communication between the host system and the network. Assuming all things are equal and we can afford it, a 32-bit NIC with on-board processing and RAM will perform faster than a NIC without these features. Third, some NICs include on-board LEDs. For example, a UTP-based Ethernet card might contain LEDs for link status, collisions, and activity. These LEDs can provide valuable diagnostic information about the card's state or network activity. Another consideration is whether the card supports *autosensing* for 10/100-Mbps Ethernet/802.3 LANs or if the card supports full-duplex networking. We should also make sure that the card we purchase is compatible with the host system's bus architecture. Thus, if our PC is an ISA bus machine or a PCI bus machine, we need to make sure that the NIC we purchase is ISA- or PCI-compatible. Finally, the drivers that come with the card must support our network and operating system. Ideally, the drivers should be either ODI- or NDIS-compliant, or both, for Intel/Windows systems.

PC Cards

Another network device that serves the same purpose as a NIC (i.e., to effect communication between a node and the network) is a *PC card* (Figure 6.12). Once known as *PCMCIA* (Personal Computer Memory Card International Association) *cards,* PC cards were originally designed to serve as memory cards (and thus, their initial name). They have since evolved into multipurpose plug-in devices and are today called PC cards. These devices are small (about the size of a credit card, only thicker) plug-in adapters used in portable or laptop computers. Three different types are available. *Type 1 cards,* the earliest, are only 3.3 millimeters thick and enhance the memory capabilities of a device. Memory support includes ROM (read-only memory) and flash memory (a special form of ROM that can be reprogrammed). Some manufacturers use Type I cards for software upgrades. *Type II cards* are 5 mm thick and are used for modems and network adapters for both Ethernet and token ring. These devices are similar to NICs and support various media types including RJ-11 for a modem connection and RJ-45 for UTP-based LANs. Both Ethernet/802.3 and token ring adapters are supported. *Type III cards* are 10.5 mm thick and are generally either miniature hard disks or wireless NICs. As of

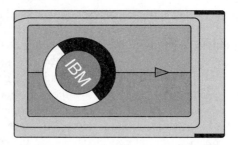

FIGURE 6.12 PC cards are multipurpose plug-in devices for portable computers and can be used as memory devices, modem and network adapters, or hard disk drives.

this writing, a *Type IV card* is being considered that will be approximately 16 mm thick and support hard disk drives that have a capacity greater than what is currently available from Type III cards. PC cards are installed into an appropriate PCMCIA slot within a portable computing device. Type III slots also accept Type I or Type II cards, and Type II slots also accept Type I cards. Most laptops manufactured today contain at least one Type III or Type II slot.

6.5   Bridges

Overview

A network *bridge* interconnects two or more individual LANs or LAN segments. Unlike repeaters, which are layer-1 devices, bridges connect networks that have different physical layers. This is what makes them layer-2 devices—the physical layer is transparent to bridges. Bridges also can connect networks using either the same or different type of architectures (e.g., Ethernet to Ethernet, token ring to token ring, or Ethernet to token ring) (Figure 6.13).

As layer-2 devices, bridges are transparent to protocols operating at higher layers. This means that regardless of the network protocol being used, bridges will pass or discard frames independent of the protocol. Thus, two networks based on different protocols connected to the same bridge are viewed as a single logical network. Bridges also force the repeater count in an Ethernet/802.3 network (see Chapter 9) to return to 1. Bridges, however, are highly susceptible to *broadcast storms* since they will pass broadcast frames from one network to another. A broadcast storm occurs when several broadcasts are transmitted at the same time. Broadcast storms can use up a substantial amount of network bandwidth and, in many cases, can cause a network to crash or shut down. Bridges are also *store-and-forward* devices. This means they capture an entire frame before deciding whether to filter or forward the frame. This provides a high level of error detection because a frame's CRC checksum can be computed by the bridge and matched to that of the frame. If the CRC checksum is not correct, the frame is dropped. This prevents the propagation of corrupt frames.

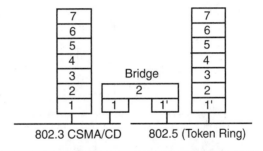

FIGURE 6.13 OSI representation of a bridge. Bridges can connect networks using different architectures such as Ethernet and token ring.

Bridge Standards

Two bridge standards have been defined by IEEE. The first is a *transparent bridge* and is used in IEEE 802.3 ("Ethernet") and 802.5 (token ring) networks. The second is a *source routing bridge,* which was introduced by IBM and is used exclusively in token ring networks. Bridges pass frames between LANs and provide filtering. They allow frames from a node on one network to be forwarded to a node on another network but discard any frames destined for the same network from which the frames originated. Thus, bridges keep local traffic local but forward traffic destined for a remote network. Since bridges operate at the data link layer, they check the hardware (i.e., the MAC-level) address of a particular network interface card to determine whether to forward or discard a frame.

Transparent Bridges   A transparent bridge is a "plug and play" unit—you connect it to your network and power it on. Operating in *promiscuous mode,* a transparent bridge captures every frame that is transmitted on all the networks to which the bridge is connected. The bridge examines every frame it receives and extracts each frame's source address, which is then added to a "learned address" table maintained by the bridge. Eventually, this table contains an entry for each unique source address and the port on which the frame was received. For example, in Figure 6.14, when node 1 (with a hardware source address of 1) transmits a frame, the bridge "learns" that node 1 is on channel A (i.e., port A) and adds a corresponding entry to its address table. The bridge also examines the destination address of the frame to determine if the frame should be forwarded or filtered. All broadcast and multicast frames always get forwarded. If the destination address is not a broadcast or multicast address, and it is not found in the bridge's address table, the frame is forwarded by default. This is what the bridge does when it is first powered on and its address table is empty. This procedure is referred to as *flooding.* The only condition under which a frame does not get forwarded (i.e., is discarded or filtered) occurs when the frame's destination address is found in the address table and corresponds to the same channel on which the frame was received. So if node 1 transmits a frame to node 3 in Figure 6.14, the bridge does not forward the frame to channel B; the destination address (3) is a source address on the same channel on

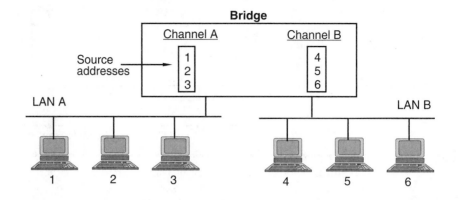

FIGURE 6.14 Bridges interconnect separate networks, making them appear as a single network. Operating at the data link layer, a bridge builds a table of hardware addresses that identifies the address of each node and the segment to which a node is attached. Using this table, a bridge either forwards a frame from one network to the other or discards the frame depending on whether the destination node is local or remote. For example, a frame from node 3 to node 1 does not get forwarded to channel B. Thus, none of the nodes on LAN B "sees" node 3's transmission. However, a frame from node 3 to node 5 is forwarded from channel A to channel B. A bridge will, however, forward any broadcast frames from LAN A to LAN B, and vice versa.

which the frame originated. On the other hand, if the destination is node 5, or if the frame is a broadcast or multicast, then the bridge forwards the frame.

Source Routing Bridges   Source routing bridges were introduced by IBM for use in token ring networks. With source routing, the sending machine is responsible for determining whether a frame is destined for a node on the same network or on a different network. If the frame is destined for a different network, the source machine designates this by setting the high-order bit of the group address bit of the source address to 1. It also includes in the frame's header the path the frame is to follow from source to destination. Source routing bridges are based on the assumption that a sending machine will provide routing information for messages destined for different networks. By making the sending machine responsible for this task, a source routing bridge can ignore frames that have not been "marked" and forward only those frames with their high-order destination bit set to 1. An illustration of source routing bridges is given in Figure 6.15.

Spanning Tree   For reliability, some networks contain more than one bridge, which increases the likelihood of *networking loops*. A networking loop occurs when frames are passed from bridge to bridge in a circular manner, never reaching their destination. To prevent networking loops when multiple bridges are used, the bridges communicate with each other and establish a map of the network to derive what is called a *spanning tree* for all the networks. A spanning tree consists of a single path between source and destination nodes that does not include any loops. Thus, a spanning tree can be considered a loop-free subset of a network's topology. The spanning tree algorithm, specified in IEEE 802.1d, describes how bridges (and switches) can communicate to avoid network loops.

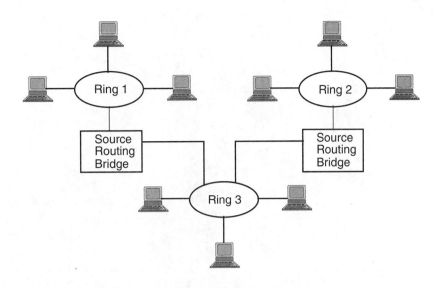

FIGURE 6.15 Bridges used to interconnect separate token ring networks are called source routing bridges. As is the case with transparent bridges used in Ethernet/802.3 networks, source routing bridges copy frames from one ring to another. They also retransmit frames to the next station on the same ring. Unlike transparent bridges, source routing bridges depend on the sending station to provide routing information for frames destined for a different network.

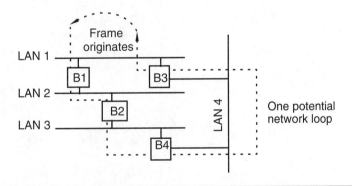

FIGURE 6.16 A possible network loop.

To illustrate the concepts of a network loop and the spanning tree, look at Figure 6.16, which has four network segments interconnected by four bridges. LAN 1 is connected to LAN 2 by B1; LAN 2 is connected to LAN 3 by B2; and LAN 3 is connected to LAN 4 by B4. Note also that LAN 1 is connected to LAN 4 by B3. Thus, multiple bridges are being used on LAN 1. Let's assume that a frame originates on LAN 1 and none of the bridges (B1–B4) has an entry for the frame's destination. Here is an example of how a network loop can develop:

Radia Perlman (1951–)

Radia Perlman's work has had a profound impact on the field of networking, and she is considered a specialist in the areas of bridging and routing, as well as sabotage-proof networks. Best known as the inventor of the spanning tree algorithm used in bridges and switches, Perlman is also the inventor of many of the algorithms that make modern link-state routing protocols robust and efficient, including self-stabilizing flooding of routing updates and designated routers. This technology is the core of all modern link-state protocols, including IS-IS, OSPF, and PNNI. As a tribute to her accomplishments, Perlman was featured in the 25th anniversary edition of *Data Communications Magazine* (October 21, 1997) as one of the 25 people whose work has most influenced the networking industry. She is also the author of the book, *Interconnections: Bridges, Routers, Switches, and Internetworking Protocols* (published by Addison-Wesley), as well as the coauthor of *Network Security: Private Communication in a Public World* (published by Prentice-Hall). Both books were included in *Network Magazine's* top-ten list of most useful networking reference books. Perlman's undergraduate and graduate work was done at Massachusetts Institute of Technology, where she earned SB and SM degrees in mathematics and a PhD in computer science. She is currently a distinguished engineer at Sun Microsystems, Inc., and holds about 50 patents.

After writing the spanning tree algorithm, Perlman also wrote a spanning tree-based poem, "Algorhyme," which was a parody of Joyce Kilmer's poem, "Trees." It is reprinted here with her permission.

> *I think that I shall never see a graph more lovely than a tree.*
> *A tree whose crucial property is loop-free connectivity.*
> *A tree that must be sure to span, so packets can reach every LAN.*
> *First the root must be selected, by ID it is elected.*
> *Least-cost paths from root are traced.*
> *In the tree these paths are placed.*
> *A mesh is made for folks by me, then bridges find a spanning tree.*

1. A frame originates on LAN 1; neither B1 nor B3 has the destination address as an entry, so neither knows on what network the destination node resides. Hence, B1 and B3 must forward the frame to their respective LANs. That is:
   - B1 forwards the frame to LAN 2.
   - B3 forwards the frame to LAN 4.
2. The frame is now on LAN 2 and LAN 4. Once again, neither B2 nor B4 knows on what LAN the destination node is located since they do not have the destination address in their tables:

- B2 forwards the frame to LAN 3.
- B4 forwards the frame to LAN 3.
3. The frame is now on LAN 3, having come from different LANs, and B2 still does not have the destination address as an entry in its table:
- B2 forwards the frame to LAN 2.
- B4 forwards the frame to LAN 4.
4. The frame is now on LAN 2 and LAN 4, and neither B1 nor B3 knows the location of the destination node's LAN:
- B1 forwards the frame to LAN 1. (We have a network loop.)
- B3 forwards the frame to LAN 1. (We have a network loop.)

The spanning tree algorithm would disable the port on B3 that connects LAN 4 with LAN 1. If B4 were to fail, the algorithm would then automatically enable the LAN 1 to LAN 4 connection via B3.

Bridges versus Repeaters

If we had to choose between using a repeater or a bridge, we would select neither. Instead, we would use a switch (see the discussion that follows). In the rare instance where we do need to select between a repeater or bridge, though, then we need to compare several options. The purpose of a repeater is to extend a network. The purpose of a bridge is to segment network traffic. In choosing between a repeater and a bridge, we need to determine the manner in which the device will be used. Repeaters and bridges also provide electrical isolation. That is, if the device fails, then nodes on the same physical segment can still communicate with each other, but nodes on different segments cannot. So, if the purpose is to electrically isolate segments, then either device will do the job.

Bridges, unlike repeaters, also can connect networks in different geographical locations that require a telecommunications link for connectivity. Wireless bridges are also available for limited-distance remote connections. Remote bridges that use radio waves can be placed up to 25–30 miles (40–48 km) apart, provided the terrain and weather allow for it and if the bridges have directional antennas. Remote bridges using laser communication techniques can be spaced approximately 3500 feet (1050 m) apart.

In an Ethernet/802.3 environment, replacing a repeater with a bridge does not necessarily improve Ethernet LAN performance. The performance of a bridge is measured by the number of frames per second it can forward (the *forwarding rate*) and the amount of delay that is introduced due to forwarding (the *forwarding delay*). In an ideal setting, a 10-Mbps Ethernet/802.3 bridge forwards 14,880 64-byte frames per second. This is referred to as *wire speed* (see Chapter 9). Furthermore, an ideal 10-Mbps Ethernet/802.3 bridge has a 60-μs forwarding delay for 64-byte frames. The propagation delay of a repeater is less than 3 μs. Also keep in mind that a repeater propagates errors, but a bridge does not.

Before replacing a repeater with a bridge, we must design the network properly based on traffic patterns. For example, in a repeater-based LAN, it does not matter where a server is located. However, in a bridge-based LAN, if a server is placed on one physical segment, and all nodes that must communicate with the server are on a different segment, then performance will be worse than the repeater-based configuration. The concept of network segmentation and partitioning is discussed in further detail in Chapter 9.

6.6 Switches

A network *switch* is a device that performs switching. This was defined in Chapter 2 as a process that involves establishing an appropriate link a data message will follow as it travels throughout a network en route from a sending source and destination node. The concept of switching has broad applications in computer communications and networking, as well as in telecommunications. Switches are available in various LAN and WAN environments, including Ethernet/802.3, token ring, FDDI, frame relay, SMDS, and ATM. Switches have also been designed to operate at different layers of the OSI model, including layers 2, 3 and 4. What distinguishes these switches from one another is their application and the criteria they use on which to make path determinations. In this section, our discussion of switches is provided from an Ethernet/802.3 perspective. Other types of switches will be presented in subsequent chapters.

Layers 2 and 3 of the OSI model are merging, and it is becoming difficult to distinguish between traditional layer-2 devices such as LAN switches and layer-3 devices such as routers. This is addressed in Chapter 7.

Ethernet switches are layer-2 devices that are essentially modified multiport bridges. Like bridges, each port on an Ethernet switch supports a separate LAN segment, and each port can accommodate different media, including ThinWire, UTP, and fiber-optic cable. Furthermore, each switch port filters traffic sent over its attached segment. Thus, traffic destined for a node on the same segment does not cross the switch's port boundary; it remains local to that segment. Furthermore, if a node on one segment sends frames to a node connected to a different segment (i.e., a different switch port), the frames are forwarded across the port boundary and through the switch to the appropriate destination port without any other port seeing the transmission.

What makes switches different from bridges is their architecture. Repeaters and bridges are designed for shared media LANs; the architecture of switches, however, permits multiple, simultaneous data transmission paths between ports. Each switch port is assigned a specific MAC address, with data paths between ports being hardwired and part of the switch's internal circuitry (called the *switch fabric* or *switch matrix*). When a data frame enters a switch port, the port's network adapter translates the MAC destination address of the frame to a specific switch port address and then transfers the frame to that MAC-specified destination port. Thus, the data transmission in a switch is based on a static port-to-MAC address association. Some switches support only one MAC address per port; others support more than one. The bottom line is that nodes connected to bridges share bandwidth; nodes connected to switches do not share bandwidth—they have "private" connections. Ethernet switches have three basic design architectures: *store-and-forward, cut-through,* and *hybrid.*

Store-and-Forward Switch

A store-and-forward switch is similar to a store-and-forward bridge. A switch that incorporates the store-and-forward design (sometimes referred to as a *buffering switch*) operates exactly like an Ethernet bridge—it waits until it receives an entire data frame before forwarding it. When the switch receives a frame, it first performs an integrity check to ensure that the frame does not contain any errors. As a result, data reliability is excellent in this type of switch since "bad" frames (e.g., incorrect CRC checksums) are never forwarded. After checking for errors, the switch extracts the destination address

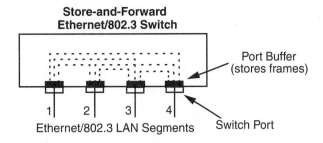

FIGURE 6.17 A store-and-forward Ethernet switch has buffers at each port. When a frame enters a port from a segment, the switch stores the frame in that port's buffer until the entire frame is received and checked for errors. If the frame is error-free, the destination address is identified and the frame is placed at the destination segment's port without any other port seeing the transmission. Source: adapted from Majkiewicz, 1993, and Sharer, 1995.

from the frame's address field, performs an address table lookup to identify the destination port to which the frame should be sent, and forwards the frame to the destination port if it is different from the port at which the frame arrived. (If the port is the same, the switch discards the frame.) An illustration of a store-and-forward switch that contains individual port buffers is given in Figure 6.17.

Cut-Through Switch

The cut-through architecture is what really separates switches from traditional store-and-forward bridges. A *cut-through switch* operates in the following way: If a frame arriving at one port in the switch is to be transmitted to a different port, the switch begins this transmission as soon as it reads the destination address of the frame. This technology improves Ethernet performance considerably by reducing delays. Cut-through switches can be implemented using either a crossbar or backplane design.

Crossbar Design A *crossbar design* identifies the frame's destination address and the path within the switch that the frame must follow to get to the destination port. Once these have been determined, the switch transfers the part of the frame it has already received (the preamble, start frame delimiter, and destination address) to the destination port. All remaining parts of the frame (source address, length count, data, pad, and checksum) are immediately transferred as they are received by the switch via this same data path. An illustration of a crossbar switch is shown in Figure 6.18. Note that this design can introduce delay if the data path is not clear for transmission. For example, suppose a frame arrives from segment 2 destined for segment 3. If the path to segment 3 is busy (e.g., a transfer might be occurring from segment 1 to 3), then the frame must remain in segment 2's buffer until the path is clear. This can "back up" traffic on segment 2.

Backplane Design In contrast to the crossbar approach, the *backplane design* places frames on a high-speed backplane, which interconnects all ports. If the destination port is free, frames are immediately transferred. If the destination port is busy, frames are buffered onto the backplane until the port is clear. This eliminates the potential congestion

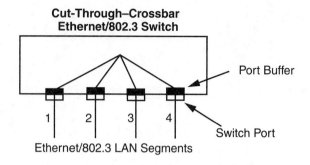

FIGURE 6.18 Cut-through Ethernet switches transmit frames as soon as the destination address is known. In the crossbar design, the data paths connecting the ports are all interconnected. If this path is busy with a current transmission, delays will occur. Source: adapted from Majkiewicz, 1993, and Sharer, 1995.

problem of the crossbar approach. The key to this design is the switch's backplane, which requires a data rate greater than the aggregate throughput of the switch. For example, an eight-port 10-Mbps Ethernet switch has a total throughput of 80 Mbps. Given that a transmission involves at least two nodes, it is possible to have as many as four simultaneous transmissions occurring in parallel. To avoid bottlenecks, a 10-Mbps switch must be able to handle at least 40 Mbps of aggregate data flow. Typically, a cut-through switch based on the backplane design has a backplane that is at least equal to the total aggregate throughput of the segments. In our illustration, this would be 80 Mbps. Some switches have gigabit per second backplanes. Viewed from this perspective, switches do not actually increase the speed of a 10-Mbps segment. Rather, they increase the aggregate throughput capability of a network. Thus, switches simply are high-throughput devices that provide the capacity for multiple segments to operate concurrently. An illustration of the backplane design is shown in Figure 6.19. Cut-through switches generally are more expensive than store-and-forward switches because of their more sophisticated circuitry.

Ethernet cut-through switches, which are discussed in Chapter 9, neither check CRC checksum values nor minimum frame lengths. Thus, a cut-through switch will propagate "bad" frames throughout an Ethernet/802.3 network.

Hybrid Switch

A *hybrid switch* integrates the best features of store-and-forward (reliable frame transmission) and cut-through (low latency) designs. A hybrid switch can be configured on a per port basis to change automatically from cut-through switching to store-and-forward switching if error rates exceed a user-defined threshold. When error rates fall below this threshold, the switch reverts to cut-through switching. An additional capability is a "runt-free" mode in which the switch discards frames smaller than the mandated 64 bytes minimum size for Ethernet. This ensures the filtering of collision fragments while maintaining the low-latency characteristics of cut-through switching.

Switch Performance

Switches provide high throughput with low or fixed *latency*. Used in this context, latency is the amount of delay a network device introduces when data frames pass through it. Thus, latency is the amount of time a frame spends inside a network device

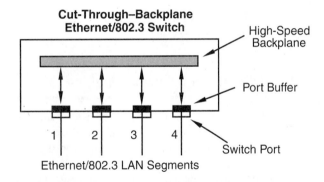

FIGURE 6.19 Backplane-based cut-through Ethernet switches also transmit frames as soon as the destination address is known. In the backplane design, though, data frames are placed on a high-speed backplane for transmission. The speed of this backplane is greater than the aggregate throughput of the switch. If a destination port is busy, the frame remains on the backplane; this eliminates the kind of delays inherent in the crossbar design. Source: adapted from Majkiewicz, 1993, and Sharer, 1995.

such as a bridge or switch. Switch latency is usually measured from the instant the first bit of a frame enters the device to the time this bit leaves the outbound (i.e., destination) port. Depending on a switch's architecture, its latency is usually less than 100 μs. In comparison, bridge latency of 400 μs is common, and routers have latency as high as 1500 μs (i.e., 1.5 ms). Low latency is good because the lower it is, the faster a device processes a data frame. If latency is too high, then time-sensitive network protocols such as SNA or IPX can time out. Latency also is an issue for time-sensitive applications such as full-motion video.

Store-and-forward switches provide both traffic isolation and error immunity to any destination port. The trade-off for error immunity, though, is high latency, which can be in milliseconds rather than microseconds. Since store-and-forward switches wait until an entire frame has arrived before forwarding it, latency, which is dependent on frame size, can range from 61 μs to 1200 μs over a 10-Mbps channel. This could be a serious concern for some applications.

Cut-through switches have extremely low latency, usually on the order of 20 to 40 μs. Furthermore, since cut-through switches begin forwarding frames the moment the destination address is known, latency is independent of frame size. Thus, a maximum-size Ethernet/802.3 frame (1518 bytes) has the same latency as a minimum-size Ethernet/802.3 frame (64 bytes). This is not the case with store-and-forward switches, where latency varies directly with frame size. Considering that the total round-trip bit propagation speed of a standard 10-Mbps Ethernet/802.3 network is approximately 51.2 microseconds, the speed of a cut-through switch approximates cable or wire speed, which is 14,880 packets per second using 64-byte packets (see Box 9.3 in Chapter 9). The trade-off, though, is there is no opportunity for the switch to check the integrity of a frame before it is forwarded to its destination port. Thus, if corrupt data messages are contained in the fields that follow the destination and source address fields of a data frame, the frame is still forwarded to the destination port. Errors on a specific port are propagated to other ports on the switch or throughout the network. This reduces bandwidth and can delay forwarding error-free frames.

End-of-Chapter Commentary

This concludes our discussion of layer-1 and layer-2 network components. In subsequent chapters, some of the concepts discussed in this chapter are extended. For example, in Chapter 7, we discuss internetworking and network layer (layer-3) concepts and components. Two additional topics that are discussed in Chapter 7 that were referenced in the current chapter are routers and switches. Another topic of this chapter, Ethernet switches, is expanded in Chapter 9. The topic of switching is also extended in later chapters. For example, token ring switching is discussed in Chapter 10, FDDI switching is discussed in Chapter 11, frame relay switching is discussed in Chapter 13, and ATM switching is discussed in Chapter 15. Finally, for a review of layer-1 and layer-2 concepts, refer to Chapters 4 and 5, respectively.

CHAPTER REVIEW MATERIALS

SUMMARY

- Layer-1 components include connectors, transceivers, media converters, and repeaters.
- Connectors are used to attach components together. They attach peripheral devices to a computer (e.g., DB, DIN, and centronics connectors), connect network interface cards to a cable, connect cable segments, and terminate segments (e.g., terminators). Several different types of connectors are available, and all are a function of cable type. For example, eight-pin modular (RJ-45) connectors are used for UTP cable, the various flavors of BNC connectors are used for coaxial cable, and fiber-optic cable uses ST, SC, or SMA connectors. Other connectors that were discussed include v.35 and SCSI connectors. V.35 connectors are used for high-speed serial connections, and SCSI connectors are used for high-speed parallel interfaces for computer peripheral devices such as scanners and CD-ROM drives.
- Transceivers provide an interface between a network node and the physical medium. As described by their name, transceivers enable a node to place data onto a medium for transmission and remove received data from the medium for processing. A transceiver can also notify a node of an error condition resulting from a transmission. Transceivers are used in Ethernet/802.3 LANs and are generally integrated into Ethernet NICs. Transceivers are also available as separate stand-alone devices and include different connector types to support different media.
- Media converters are special devices that enable two different cable types such as UTP and fiber-optic cables to be interconnected.
- Repeaters provide both physical and electrical connections. The role of a repeater is simply to refresh a signal—it takes a transmitted signal, regenerates it to full strength, and then propagates it. As an electrical device, repeaters introduce propagation delay into a network. In short, propagation delay is the amount of time a signal remains "inside the box."
- Layer-2 devices include network interface cards (NICs), PC cards, bridges, and switches.
- NICs are adapters used to connect devices to a network. They perform framing, monitor the medium for transmissions, capture data from the medium and pass them to their hosts' nodes for processing, check for errors, and are responsible for token passing. NICs also perform a layer-1 function, namely, they convert bits to physical signals.

- PC cards are special plug-in modules used in portable computing devices. Various types of PC cards are available, including Type I (used as memory cards), Type II (used for modems and network adapters), and Type III (used for hard disks). Type II PC cards can be thought of as NICs for laptop computers.
- Bridges interconnect LANs by passing frames from one network to another. Bridges also serve as filtering devices by preventing local traffic (data frames in which both the source and destination addresses are on the same network) from being passed to another network. Bridges can connect networks based on the same architecture (e.g., Ethernet to Ethernet) or interconnect networks of different architectures (e.g., Ethernet to token ring).
- Two types of bridges are common. Transparent bridges, which are used in Ethernet/802.3 networks, operate in promiscuous mode and capture every transmitted frame. Source routing bridges are used in token ring networks. To prevent networking loops from occurring when multiple bridge units (or switches) are installed on a network, bridges (and switches) employ the spanning tree algorithm, which is specified in IEEE 802.1d. As is the case with repeaters, bridges also introduce propagation delay.

- Two broad switch types available are store-and-forward and cut-through. Store-and-forward switches are similar to bridges in that complete frames are first stored inside the device and examined for errors. If no errors are detected, then the frame is forwarded to the destination node. Unlike a bridge, however, only the source and destination nodes see a switch's transmission. Cut-through switches begin transmitting a frame to the destination node as soon as the switch identifies the destination node's address. Although delay is less than that of store-and-forward switches, cut-through switches can propagate errors since no integrity checks are done on the frame prior to sending it to the destination node. A hybrid switch is also available that combines the best features of store-and-forward and cut-through switches.
- Cut-through switches employ different design architectures. A crossbar design establishes a link between the source and destination switch ports as soon as the frame's destination address is determined. A backplane design, however, places all data frames onto a high-speed backplane that interconnects all switch ports. Thus, all frames are buffered on the backplane until the destination port is free. This eliminates the potential of congestion, which is inherent in the crossbar design.

VOCABULARY CHECK

AAUI
attachment unit interface (AUI)
barrel connector
BNC connector
bridge
broadcast storm
buffering switch
connector
cut-through switch
DB connector
DIN connector

hub
latency
media access unit (MAU)
media converter
network interface card (NIC)
PC card
PCMCIA card
promiscuous mode
propagation delay
repeater
RJ-45 connector

SC connector
SCSI connector
SMA connector
spanning tree
ST connector
store-and-forward switch
switch
terminator
transceiver
wire speed

REVIEW EXERCISES

1. Compare and contrast DB, DIN, and centronics connectors.
2. Explain the difference between standard telephone and UTP cable connectors.

3. What is the purpose of a BNC terminator?
4. What effect do you think connectors have on data transmissions?

5. Explain how a transceiver can be used as a media converter for Ethernet/802.3 networks.

6. What is the purpose of a repeater?

7. Do you think a repeater's latency is less than or more than that of a bridge or switch? Why?

8. What distinguishes a network component as a being labeled a layer-1 or layer-2 device?

9. Explain the purpose and operation of a NIC.

10. What do you think some of the advantages and disadvantages are of having a NIC built into the motherboard of a computing device instead of as an add-on component?

11. Some on-line computer vendors sell computer packages that include only one type of network interface card. Furthermore, most vendors do not reveal the card's specifications. If you were purchasing a new computer and wanted to include an Ethernet card as part of the package, what specific features would you want the card to have and why?

12. Give an example of where you can use each type of PC card.

13. Explain how bridges can be used to filter traffic.

14. When do you think a bridge is more appropriate to use than a repeater?

15. Describe the concept of store-and-forward.

SUGGESTED READINGS AND REFERENCES

BAKER, F. 1995. Switching Gears. *LAN Interoperability: A Quarterly Supplement to LAN Magazine,* May, 45–52.

BAY NETWORKS. 1996. *Fundamentals of Switching: A Guide to Workgroup Networking.* Santa Clara, CA: Bay Networks.

BOARDMAN, B. 1996. Good Things Come in Small Packages: Combo PC Cards. *Network Computing,* 1 April, 108–116.

BREYER, R., and S. RILEY. 1996. *Switched and Fast Ethernet.* 2nd ed. Emeryville, CA: Ziff-Davis.

CHIPCOM. 1993. *Network Switching Solutions.* Southborough, MA: Chipcom.

DYSON, P. 1995. *The Network Press Dictionary of Networking.* 2nd ed. San Francisco: Sybex.

FEIBEL, W. 1995. *The Network Press Encyclopedia of Networking.* 2nd ed. San Francisco: Sybex.

FELTMAN, C. 1994. Sizzling Switches. *LAN Magazine,* February, 115–128.

GALLO, M., and W. HANCOCK. 1999. *Networking Explained.* Boston: Digital Press.

GERBER, B. 1994. More PCMCIA Slots, Please. *Network Computing,* 1 August, 161–162.

HIGGINS, K. J. 1994. Switching Hubs: Rising Network Stars. *Open Systems Today,* 20 June, 50–58.

KOHLHEPP, R. J. 1996. Stacking Managed Hubs in Your Favor. *Network Computing,* October, 112–115.

KRIVDA, C. 1995. Another Swipe at Switching. *LAN,* October, 129–134.

MAGIDSON, S. 1994. PCMCIA: Finally, Standards Bring Compatible Products. *Network Computing,* 15 February, 124–127.

MAJKIEWICZ, J. 1993. Switching—Everybody's Doing It. *SunExpert,* September, 48–63.

MCMULLEN, M. 1993. Using PCMCIA Cards and Wireless Connectivity, PDAs May Become Handy. *LAN Magazine,* December, 40–48.

SCHNAIDT, P. 1994. Switch Hunt. *LAN Magazine,* June, 75–84.

SHARER, R. 1995. A Switch in Time. *LAN Magazine,* May, 109–114.

STEINKE, S. 1995. Ethernet Switching. *LAN Magazine,* March, 25–26.

TRISTRAM, C. 1994. PCMCIA on the Desktop. *Open Computing,* December, 81–82.

UNGERMANN-BASS NETWORKS. 1995. *LAN Switching Buyer's Guide.* Santa Clara, CA: Ungermann-Bass Networks.

WITTMAN, A. 1994. The Switch. *Network Computing,* 1 September, 62–72.

WOBUS, J. 1993. When to Avoid Adding Ethernet Hubs. *Network Computing,* January, 154–157.

WONG, H. H. 1996. Increase Ethernet Performance with Switched Technology. *Technical Support,* June, 37–43.

7 Internetworking and Network Layer Concepts and Components

After studying this chapter, you will be able to do the following:

1. Describe the OSI representation of an internetwork.
2. Describe the difference between an internet and the Internet.
3. Describe the operation of the network layer.
4. Understand the concept of a routing protocol.
5. Describe the difference between a routing protocol and a routing algorithm.
6. Explain the difference between distance-vector and link-state routing algorithms.
7. Compare and contrast the routing protocols RIP, OSPF, IGP, and BGP.
8. Explain the differences between routers and layer-3 switches.
9. Understand the concept behind layer-4 (and higher) switching.
10. Explain the concept of a virtual private network (VPN).
11. Describe the various strategies and benefits of virtual private networks.

CHAPTER OUTLINE

In Chapters 4, 5, and 6, we introduced many of the concepts and hardware components related to layers 1 and 2 of the OSI model. Our discussion in these chapters also was relative to local area networks. In this chapter, we extend our previous discussions to wide area links. We begin the chapter by introducing the concept of internetworking from a WAN perspective. This section is then followed by a discussion of the third layer of the OSI model, namely, the network layer. As part of this discussion, we provide information about key network layer-related concepts, including routing protocols and routing algorithms. Examples of two different routing algorithms—Bellman-Ford and Dijkstra's shortest path first—are also provided. In Section 7.3, we embellish our earlier discussion of routing protocols by examining several specific protocols, including RIP and OSPF. A comparison between routers, which are traditional layer 3 devices, and upper-layer switch devices is the subject of Section 7.4. Finally, in Section 7.5, we introduce virtual private networks (VPNs) and include a brief case study that illustrates various VPN strategies and benefits.

7.1   Internetworking Concepts

In Chapter 1, we defined a computer network as a collection of computers and other devices that use a common network protocol to share resources with each other over a network medium. Just as computers (and other devices) can be connected to one another, so too can computer networks. If a collection of computer networks are connected to one another, then we have what is known as a network of networks, which is formally called an *internetwork.* Thus, an internetwork refers to a collection of interconnected networks that function as a single network. The individual networks comprising an internetwork are called *subnetworks,* the devices connected to a subnetwork are called *end nodes* (or end systems), and the devices that interconnect subnetworks are called *intermediate nodes* (or intermediate systems).

An internetwork can involve local networks (e.g., LAN-to-LAN or LAN-to-mainframe connections), long-distance connections between networks requiring WAN connections (e.g., LAN-to-WAN connections), and WAN-to-WAN connections. (See Chapter 1 for additional information about LANs and WANs.) For example, a network located in an office on one floor of a building can be connected to another network located on a different floor of the same building. Collectively, these two interconnected networks represent an internetwork. Figure 7.1 shows a simple internetwork involving a LAN-to-LAN connection. A good illustration of an internetwork is a college campus network, which typically consists of several autonomous departmental LANs interconnected via a campuswide backbone. In this configuration, the departmental LANs are considered subnetworks, and the overall college network is considered an internetwork.

The term internetwork is often used in its abbreviated form, *internet.* So, in the most generic sense, an internet is nothing more than a collection of interconnected networks. When used as a proper noun and spelled with an uppercase *I,* the term *Internet* refers to the world's largest internetwork, which consists of hundreds of thousands of interconnected networks worldwide and has associated with it a certain culture. In fact, we can think of the Internet as a *wide area internetwork* (WAI). The

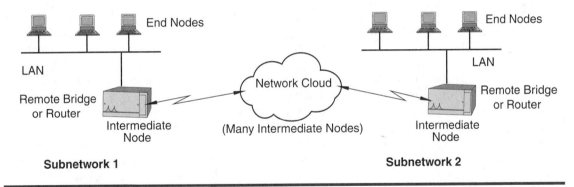

FIGURE 7.1 A wide area network interconnects geographically separated LANs using a point-to-point topology. A WAN transmission facility consists of remote bridges or routers and a data communication circuit. What happens inside the WAN cloud is a function of the network protocol and technology used.

Internet (proper noun form) also implies a set of networks that support the same network protocol, namely, TCP/IP. Thus, the Internet is a collection of computer networks based on a specific set of network standards (TCP/IP), which describe how the computers of each individual network are to communicate with each other. The Internet allows individual, autonomous networks to function and appear as a single large network. The Internet and TCP/IP are discussed in more detail in Chapter 8. Note that although it might appear so, the Internet is not a computer network because it does not satisfy our definition of a computer network. The Internet does not consist of a collection of computers and other devices. Instead, it consists of a collection of computer networks.

While we're on the subject, we might as well introduce some more terminology spawned by the Internet craze: intranet and extranet. An *intranet* is the internal network implementation of traditional Internet applications within a company or an institution. Examples of applications that run on corporate or institutional internets are Web server and e-mail. There are many others. It is, in the strictest sense, still an internet (notice the lack of an uppercase *I*), but it is easier to understand that the speaker is referring to the internal corporate network by calling it an intranet. To make things even more confusing, a popular networking term for an interconnection from the internal intranet to a customer or noncompany network that is not the Internet connection is called an *extranet* connection. This may involve a leased-line connection or some other network type of connection; it may also involve the use of a secure protocol to "tunnel" through the Internet. In summary, an intranet is an internal company network that implements traditional Internet services; an extranet is a network connection to noncompany entities that are not being accessed via an Internet connection; an internet represents any collection of interconnected networks, and *the* Internet is a series of worldwide network services available from an Internet service provider (ISP), which is discussed in more detail in Chapter 8.

With all of this vocabulary out of the way, let's now get back to the topic at hand, namely, the concept of internetworking. The manner in which networks are connected to one another depends on the type of networks involved. To help guide us in determining which method to use, networks are usually classified in one of three ways relative to the concept of internetworking: identical, similar, and dissimilar. *Identical networks* employ exactly the same architecture and cabling; *similar networks* have different architecture or different cabling; and *dissimilar networks* employ different hardware, software, protocols, and often support different functions or applications. Dissimilar networks are sometimes referred to as *heterogeneous networks*. It should be obvious that the internetworking strategy for interconnecting identical networks is different from interconnecting similar or dissimilar networks.

There are three general ways in which internetworks are formed, and each method is closely aligned with the bottom three layers of the OSI model. More specifically, identical networks can be interconnected at the physical layer (layer 1), similar networks can be interconnected at the data link layer (layer 2), and dissimilar networks can be interconnected at the network layer (layer 3). This implies that the hardware devices used to link these networks also operate at the respective layer. For example, in Chapter 6, we learned that repeaters can be used to extend the length of a LAN. Since repeaters operate at the physical layer, the LANs that are interconnected must be exactly the same. Thus, a repeater provides connections at the physical layer and works with only a specific LAN architecture, as shown in Figure 7.2(a).We also learned in Chapter 6 that a bridge and a layer-2 switch provide connections at the data link layer. These devices support different physical layers and can interconnect different LAN architectures, as in Figure 7.2(b). Bridges and layer-2 switches also are network-protocol independent, which enable them to interconnect networks using different network protocols (e.g., TCP/IP and IPX). Unlike routers (discussed below), which operate at layer 3 and do protocol translations, though, bridges and layer-2 switches ignore layer-3 information. Interconnectivity is achieved by forwarding frames between networks by using hardware addresses, not network addresses. In this context, an internetwork consisting of two dissimilar networks connected by a bridge or switch can be viewed as a single logical network.

This leads us to layer-3. Internetworks that use layer-3 devices can have different physical and data link layers, as in Figure 7.2(c). Layer 3 devices also can support different network protocols (e.g., IP, IPX, AppleTalk). Interconnectivity is achieved by forwarding packets from one network to another using network layer information (e.g., network addresses). In a heterogeneous networking environment in which dissimilar networks are interconnected, layer-3 devices perform *network protocol translation*. One device that provides connections at the network layer is called a *router*. Thus, a router's job is to interconnect physically different networks and route packets from one network to another. It determines a path to a destination node and then starts the packet on its way. Routers that support more than one network layer protocol are called multiprotocol routers. So if a packet originating from an IP network is passed to an AppleTalk network, a multiprotocol router rebuilds (or reformats) the packet to the proper form so it can be interpreted by a node on the AppleTalk network. Since routers operate at the third layer of the OSI model, they do not forward broadcast packets unless they are configured to do so. Routers also employ routing protocols that determine the least-cost path a packet is to travel from source to destination nodes.

As an example, consider a simple WAN that interconnects two LANs. A typical scenario involves two remote bridges or routers (one at each end) interconnected via a WAN data communications circuit similar to that shown in Figure 7.1. WANs use ei-

Different LAN architectures require different bridging techniques. For example, there is transparent bridging for Ethernet/802.3, source routing bridging for token ring or FDDI, and transparent/source routing bridging for mixed environments. See Chapter 6 for more information about these different bridging methods.

Another device that operates at the network layer is a layer-3 switch. We will discuss layer-3 switches in Section 7.4.

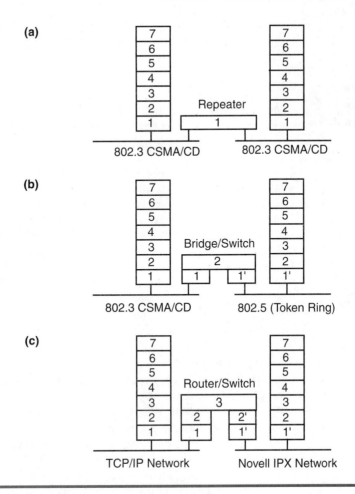

FIGURE 7.2 An OSI representation of internetworking. In a repeater-based internetwork (a), the LAN architecture must be the same. A bridge- or switch-based internetwork (b) has different physical layers and connects different types of LAN architectures. (*Note:* MAC-based bridges can only interconnect similar LAN architectures.) Bridges and layer-2 switches are also network protocol independent. A router- or layer-3 switch-based internetwork (c) operates at layer 3 of the OSI model and interconnects networks using different network protocols. These devices perform protocol translations.

ther circuit-switching or packet-switching techniques. (See Chapter 2 and Table 2.1 for more information about packet- and circuit-switching.) In a circuit-switched WAN, a fixed connection is established between source and destination nodes prior to transmission, each packet takes the same path, and all packets arrive in sequence. ISDN (see Chapter 12) is one example of a circuit-switched WAN. In a packet-switched WAN, connections are established during the transmission process. Thus, packets do not necessarily travel the same route, and they might arrive out of sequence at the destination node. Examples of a packet-switched WAN include frame relay, SMDS, and ATM. As a result, what happens inside the network cloud shown in Figure 7.1 depends on the technology used. In later chapters, we will peak inside this cloud and examine exactly what is taking place when we discuss some of these technologies

<table>
<tr><td>**7.2**</td><td></td></tr>
</table>

7.2 The Network Layer and Routing Concepts

Network Layer Overview

When constructing an internetwork, attention must be given to several critical issues such as addressing, flow control, error control, routing, access control, and the size of the message that is permitted on the network. When dealing with identical or similar networks, the first two layers of the OSI model are in control, and these issues are addressed by these lower two layers. However, when an internetwork comprises dissimilar networks, then the third layer of the OSI model, namely, the network layer, must enter the picture. The network layer performs several functions, including providing services to the transport layer (layer 4), performing congestion control, and formatting data messages so they are recognized by the destination network (called packet formatting). The network layer is also responsible for the end-to-end routing or switching of data from source network to destination network.

To illustrate how the network layer works, we will use the TCP/IP model instead of the OSI model. (See Chapter 8 for a comparison of the TCP/IP and OSI models.) The TCP/IP layer that functions similar to OSI's network layer is the Internet layer, which also is called the network layer. The heart and soul of this layer is the Internet Protocol (IP)—the IP of TCP/IP. IP is a connectionless datagram service and is responsible for routing packets between nodes. (A *datagram* is an IP network layer packet. See also Chapter 2 for information about connectionless service.) In short, IP receives data bits from the upper layer, assembles the bits into packets (i.e., IP datagrams), and then selects the "best" route based on some criterion, called a *metric* (e.g., distance, number of router "hops," bandwidth), which the packets should take to reach their destination. Since IP is connectionless, every packet must contain the address of the destination node. This address, called an Internet or IP address, is assigned to an Internet node by a network administrator or by an automated protocol (e.g., DHCP) as part of the node's initial network configuration. An IP address uniquely identifies a host similar to the way a street address uniquely identifies a residence or the way a social security number, driver's license number, or student ID number uniquely identifies a person. It is used by the network layer as a road map to locate a host within the Internet by determining what path a packet is to follow en route to its final destination.

Packets destined for a host connected to the same LAN as the sending host are generally delivered directly by the sending host. To transfer packets destined for a host connected to a remote network, however, dedicated routers are usually used. Routers are also referred to as *gateways*. For example, consider Figure 7.3, which contains four interconnected networks (N1 through N4), five hosts (H0 through H4), and five routers (R1 through R5). If H0 sends a packet to H1, no special router is needed to route the packet. H0 effectively serves as its own gateway for locally destined packets. However, if H0 sends a packet to H2, then at least one router is involved in the transfer. The

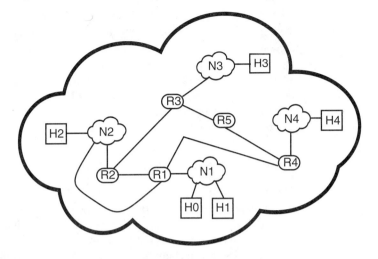

FIGURE 7.3 A network and associated subnetworks (subnets) are typically pictured as clouds. Shown in this figure are four interconnected subnets (N1 through N4), five hosts (H0 through H4), and five routers (R1 through R5). As an example of routing, note that data packets originating on H1 and destined for H2 can take several paths through the network. One path is through R1 only. A second path is R1-R2. Still a third path is via R1-R4-R5-R3-R2. If the network layer is IP-based, which provides connectionless datagram service, all of these routes are possible.

packet could go through any of the following router paths: R1 only, R1-R2, or R1-R4-R5-R3-R2.

Although routers are used to deliver packets from one network to another, IP does not guarantee that a packet will indeed be delivered to its destination. If an intermediate router, for example, contains incorrect or stale routing information, packets might get lost. IP does not take any action to retransmit undelivered packets. This is done by higher-level protocols, specifically TCP. Additionally, IP fragments and reassembles packets when necessary so they do not exceed the maximum packet length (called the *maximum transmission unit,* or MTU) a physical network is capable of supporting. If a packet's size is greater than a network's MTU, the packet is partitioned into smaller units (called *fragmenting*) and sent to the destination in the form of several separate packets. The complete packet is then reassembled at the destination node before it is passed to the higher levels. Reassembly of an IP datagram can only occur at the destination node and not at any of the intermediary nodes the packet traverses. This is because IP is a connectionless datagram service—datagrams can take different paths en route to their destination, and hence, an intermediary node might not receive all of the fragmented datagrams.

When too many packets are present in a subnet, performance degrades. This situation is called *congestion.* Congestion occurs when routers are too slow, causing queues to lengthen. Additionally, if routers are too fast, queues will build up whenever input traffic is greater than the capacity of output lines (e.g., three input lines delivering packets at top speed and all need to go out on the same line). The ultimate level of congestion is known as *deadlock,* a concept with which you might be familiar if you have studied multitasking operating systems. Deadlock occurs in this context when one router cannot proceed until a second router does something, and the second router cannot proceed because it is waiting for the first router to do something. The network layer is responsible for providing congestion control, which deals with making certain that a subnet can carry the offered traffic. It is global in scope and involves all hosts, routers, and other factors. Note that congestion control is not the same as flow control, which applies to point-to-point traffic between a sender node and a receiver node.

Routing Protocol Concepts

The path a packet takes through a network from source to destination is a function of routing protocols. Examples include the Routing Information Protocol (RIP), RIP Version 2 (RIP-2), Open Shortest Path First (OSPF), and Intermediate System to Intermediate System (IS-IS). The first three are part of the TCP/IP suite and can only route IP packets. IS-IS can route both IP and OSI Connectionless Network Layer Protocol (CNLP) packets.

Closely related to routing protocols is the concept of router protocols. The term *router protocol* formally specifies three different types of router-related protocols: those that provide a service, those that greet neighbors, and those that do routing. For example, since IP provides a service to the transport layer, it is considered a network layer *service protocol* for TCP/IP. *Neighbor-greeting protocols* are those that enable nodes and routers to find each other so they know which nodes and routers are accessible. These protocols also provide address-translation capabilities. One example is the Address Resolution Protocol (ARP), which is part of the TCP/IP suite (Chapter 8). Finally, examples of routing protocols include RIP and OSPF, both of which are discussed later in this section.

Routing protocols are a function of network protocols. For example, if our network protocol is TCP/IP, then several routing protocol options are available including RIP, RIP-2, and OSPF. If our network protocol is OSI's CNLP, then our routing protocol is IS-IS. Most network protocols, however, can be encapsulated in TCP/IP and routed using TCP/IP-based routing protocols. *Protocol encapsulation,* also called *tunneling,* "wraps" packets from one network protocol in a packet for another protocol. This wrapped packet can then be routed through a network using a routing protocol that is supported by the "wrapper" network protocol. AppleTalk packets, for instance, can be routed through the Internet by wrapping them into TCP/IP packets. Tunneling also is used for transporting nonroutable protocols across a WAN. For example, DEC's LAT and Microsoft's NetBEUI protocols do not provide network layer service and hence cannot be routed. These protocols can be sent across a WAN, though, by encapsulating them within a routable protocol such as IP. Thus, IP tunneling is commonly used within the Internet. Tunneling effectively removes network protocol restrictions inherent in a particular network. Routing protocols perform two primary functions. First, they determine the "best" path a packet should take when it travels through a network from source to destination, and second, they maintain routing tables that contain information about the network's topology. In the Internet world, IP is used to transport packets through the Internet based on the information contained in routing tables.

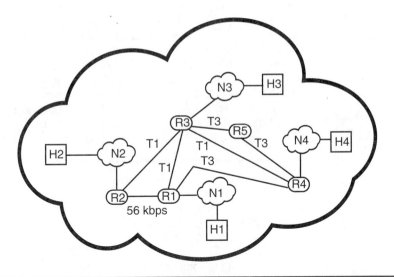

FIGURE 7.4 The determination of the "best" path a packet should take is based on metrics. One metric is number of hops. Another is bandwidth. If the best path is determined by number of hops, then the route a packet takes from H1 to H2 is through routers R1-R2 because this represents the least number of hops: two. On the other hand, if a bandwidth metric is used, then the best path is either R1-R3-R2 or R1-R4-R5-R3-R2.

Routing protocols rely on *routing algorithms* (discussed in the next subsection) to calculate the least-cost path from source to destination. A routing algorithm is that part of the network layer software responsible for deciding on which output line an incoming packet should be placed. If the subnet is packet-switched, then this decision is made for every incoming packet. If the subnet is circuit-switched, then routing decisions are only made when the virtual circuit is being set up. Routing algorithms use a "least-cost metric" to determine the best path. Common cost metrics include hops (the number of router-to-router connections a packet passes through en route to its destination), propagation delay, bandwidth, time, channel utilization, and esoteric metrics such as error rates. As an example, consider the network and associated subnets shown in Figure 7.4. The number of hops between H1 and H2 is two if the packet travels via the path R1-R2. Similarly, if the packet takes the path R1-R3-R2 or R1-R4-R5-R3-R2, then the number of hops is three and five, respectively. Given these various paths, the best or least-cost path is R1-R2 since its hop count is the smallest. Hop count metrics ignore line speeds or delays. Thus, in Figure 7.4, packets will always take the path R1-R2 (assuming the links are "up") even though it might be a "slower" path than either R1-R3-R2 or R1-R4-R5-R3-R2. A UNIX program that displays the path a packet traverses is called *traceroute*. The output of a trace made between two Web servers—from www.fit.edu to www.ucf.edu—is shown in Figure 7.5. The numbers within parentheses are the Internet addresses of the nodes, and the numbers at the end represent the round-trip time (in milliseconds) it takes a packet to reach a gateway. Three separate probes are sent between each intermediate node. Note that the source node is five hops away from the destination node.

The Windows 2000 equivalent is called *tracert.*

traceroute -s www.fit.edu www.ucf.edu
traceroute to www.ucf.edu (132.170.240.131) from www.fit.edu, 30 hops max, 40 byte packets
1 bsport.fit.edu (163.118.2.1) 4 ms 3 ms 2 ms
2 172.17.16.53 (172.17.16.53) 8 ms 8 ms 8 ms
3 172.17.16.30 (172.17.16.30) 86 ms 77 ms 61 ms
4 campusgw3.cc.ucf.edu (132.170.60.1) 67 ms 33 ms 16 ms
5 132.170.12.2 (132.170.12.2) 60 ms 15 ms 22 ms
6 www.ucf.edu (132.170.240.131) 13 ms * *

FIGURE 7.5 The UNIX traceroute program traces the route an IP packet follows from a source node to a destination node. In this figure, we show the path of a packet from www.fit.edu to www.ucf.edu. The number of router hops is five (the last entry is the destination node, not a router). Each line shows the logical name of the router, its IP address, and the round-trip time in milliseconds of three separate 40-byte packets (called probes) sent between intermediate routers.

Routers also maintain routing tables that contain, among others, the destination address of a node or network, known router addresses, and the network interface associated with a particular router address. When a router receives a packet, it looks at the packet's destination address to identify the destination network, searches its routing table for an entry corresponding to this destination, and then forwards the packet to the next router via the appropriate interface. For example, Table 7.1 shows sample routing table information generated on a UNIX system with IP address 187.96.25.2. The command used to generate this table is *netstat -r.*

Similar output can be generated on a Windows 2000 system using the command *route print.*

First note the table's last entry, which illustrates local-host routing. This entry indicates that any packets destined for the local network (187.96.25.0) will be forwarded via gateway 187.96.25.2, which is the IP address of the host. In this context, the local host acts as a simple router. Now look at the second entry of the table. This entry indicates that all packets with destination address 215.103.16.227 are forwarded to the router whose address is 187.96.25.13 via interface *le0*. This router in turn will have information on where to forward the packet so that it will ultimately reach its destination. Similarly, the third entry indicates that packets with destination address 215.103.16.141 are be forwarded to the gateway whose address is 187.96.25.35, which is accessible via interface *le1*. Finally, the second to last entry of the table references a *default route,* which is a special route that contains the address of a default router. When a router receives a packet that contains an unknown destination address (i.e., there is no entry for the address in the routing table), the router forwards the packet to the default router. As a result, if the host system receives a packet with the destination address 212.133.65.3, the host will forward the packet to the router whose destination address is 187.96.25.1 since there is no entry in the host's routing table (Table 7.1) for 212.133.65.3. Routers exchange routing table information with neighbor routers periodically. The type of information exchanged and the frequency of routing table updates are a function of the routing protocol used.

A special type of route is called a *static route,* which is a fixed route that is entered into a router's routing table either manually or via a software configuration program. The selection of the route is determined by a network manager. Although static routes can be beneficial in some instances, they cannot be changed dynamically to compensate for changes in a network's topology.

TABLE 7.1   Sample Routing Table Information

Destination	Gateway	Flags[a]	Ref[b]	Use[c]	Interface
localhost	localhost	UH	0	33106	lo0
215.103.16.227	187.96.25.13	UGHD	29	102	le0
215.103.16.141	187.96.25.35	UGHD	116	16128	le1
default	187.96.25.1	UG	0	2888304	
187.96.25.0	187.96.25.2	U	210	29024	le0

[a] U = Route is up and operational; G = Packet must pass through at least one router;
   H = Route is to a specific host and not a network; D = Route was created dynamically
[b] Current number of routes that share the same link layer address
[c] Number of packets sent using this route

Routing Algorithms

Two general algorithms are available for computing metric information: *distance-vector* and *link-state*. The goal of both types of algorithms is to route a packet from one point in the network to another point in the network through some set of intermediate routers without "looping," a situation in which a packet is forwarded across the same link several times. The primary difference between distance-vector and link-state algorithms is the manner in which they collect and propagate routing information throughout the network. Let's examine these two algorithms separately.

Distance-Vector Algorithms   A *distance-vector routing algorithm* determines the distance (hence the name) between source and destination nodes by calculating the number of router hops a packet traverses en route from the source network to the destination network. An example of a distance-vector algorithm is the Bellman-Ford algorithm, which is described in Box 7.1. Two distance-vector-based routing protocols are RIP and RIP-2, which exchange routing tables with their neighbors every 30 seconds. RIP and RIP-2 also support a maximum of 15 hops. Thus, if the number of router-to-router hops between source and destination nodes is greater than 15, then the network to which the destination node is connected is considered "unreachable." This limitation restricts the size of an internetwork to 15 consecutively connected networks.

Link-State Algorithms   In a *link-state routing algorithm* every router of a network does not send every other router its routing table. Instead, routers send each other information about the links they have established to other routers. This information is sent via a *link-state advertisement* (LSA), which contains the names and various cost metrics of a router's neighbors. LSAs are flooded throughout an entire router's domain. (An example of how this is done is described later in our discussion of OSPF.) Routers also store the most recent LSA they receive, and destination routes are calculated using LSA information. Thus, rather than storing actual paths, which is the case with distance-vector algorithms, link-state algorithms store the information needed to generate such paths. An example of a link-state algorithm is Dijkstra's shortest path algorithm, which iterates on length of path to determine a shortest route. Link-state-based routing protocols include OSPF, OSI's IS-IS, and Netware's Link Services Protocol (NLSP). Box 7.2 illustrates Dijkstra's shortest path algorithm.

BOX 7.1 Bellman-Ford Algorithm

The Bellman-Ford routing algorithm is distance-vector-based and iterates on the number of hops a source node is from a destination node. To illustrate this algorithm, consider the following undirected graph, which depicts a sample network. The vertices *A, B, C, D, E,* and *F* may be thought of as routers, and the edges connecting the vertices are communication links. Edge labels represent an arbitrary cost. Our goal is to find the shortest path from *A* to *D* using the number of hops as the basis for our path selection.

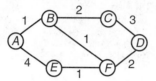

We examine the costs of all paths leading from *A* to each node on a hop-by-hop basis.

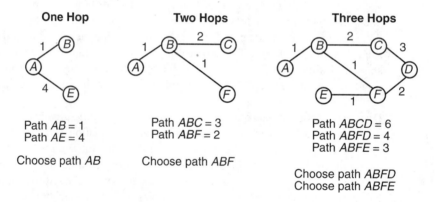

One Hop	**Two Hops**	**Three Hops**
Path *AB* = 1	Path *ABC* = 3	Path *ABCD* = 6
Path *AE* = 4	Path *ABF* = 2	Path *ABFD* = 4
		Path *ABFE* = 3
Choose path *AB*	Choose path *ABF*	
		Choose path *ABFD*
		Choose path *ABFE*

In the last step (three hops), two paths are selected. The first path, *ABFD,* represents the least-cost path from *A* to *D* based on the hops metric. The second path, *ABFE,* is selected because it represents the least-cost path from *A* to *E.*

The final result of the Bellman-Ford algorithm yields a tree that represents the least cost incurred from the source node to every node of the network. Similar trees can be generated for every node of the network. Node *A*'s least-cost tree for our example is as follows:

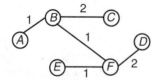

From Node *A*:
- the least-cost path to *B* is *AB* = 1
- the least-cost path to *C* is *ABC* = 3
- the least-cost path to *D* is *ABFD* = 4
- the least-cost path to *E* is *ABFE* = 3
- the least-cost path to *F* is *ABF* = 2

BOX 7.2 Dijkstra's Shortest Path First (SPF) Algorithm

Dijkstra's SPF routing algorithm is link-state-based and iterates on the distance metric. The algorithm uses a "closest nodes" concept and is based on the following principle:

Given a source node, n, *the shortest path from* n *to the next closest note,* s, *either (a) is a path that directly connects* n *to* s *or (b) includes a path containing* n *and any of the previously found intermediate closest nodes plus a direct link from the last intermediate closest node of this path to* s.

Consider the following undirected graph, which depicts a sample network. The vertices *A, B, C, D, E,* and *F* may be thought of as routers, and the edges connecting the vertices are communication links. Edge labels represent an arbitrary cost metric. Our goal is to find the shortest path from *A* to *D* based on distance.

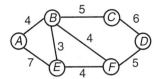

To implement this algorithm, it is helpful to maintain a running record of the successive closest nodes to the source node. We will let *k* represent the *n*th closest node. Thus, node *A* corresponds to *k* = 0. That is, the zero closest node to *A* is itself. This is the initialization step of the algorithm. We now begin our search for the successive closest nodes to *A*.

First Closest Node (*k* = 1)

The first closest node to *A* is either *B* or *E* since they are both directly connected to *A*. Since the *AB* path has a smaller cost, we select it. Thus, *B* is the first closest node to *A*.

k	Node	Path
0	A	—
1	B	AB

Second Closest Node (*k* = 2)

The second closest node to *A* must either be (a) a direct link from *A* or (b) via a path that includes the first closest node. The possible paths and related costs are: *ABC* = 9, *ABF* = 8, *ABE* = 7, or *AE* = 7. There are two shortest paths: *ABE* and *AE*. Thus, *E* is the second closest node to *A*.

k	Node	Path
0	A	—
1	B	AB
2	E	ABE
		AE

Third Closest Node (*k* = 3)

The third closest node to *A* must be via a path that includes nodes *B* or *E*. (There are no more direct links to *A*.) The possible paths and related costs are: *ABC* = 9, *ABF* = 8, *ABEF* = 11, or *AEF* = 11. The shortest path is *ABF*. Thus, *F* is the third closest node to *A*.

k	Node	Path
0	A	—
1	B	AB
2	E	ABE
		AE
3	F	AEF

Fourth Closest Node (*k* = 4)

The fourth closest node to *A* is via a path that includes nodes *B, E,* or *F*. The possible paths and related costs are: *ABC* = 9 or *ABFD* = 13. The shortest path is *ABC*. Thus, *C* is the fourth closest node to *A*. Note that neither *ABEF* nor *AEF* is considered at this stage of the algorithm because *F* was previously found to be the third closest node.

k	Node	Path
0	A	—
1	B	AB
2	E	ABE
		AE
3	F	AEF
4	C	ABC

Fifth Closest Node (*k* = 5)

The fifth closest node to *A* is via a path that includes nodes *B, E, F,* or *C*. The possible paths and related costs are: *ABCD* = 15, *ABFD* = 13, *ABEFD* = 16, and *AEFD* = 16. The shortest path is *ABFD*. Thus, *D* is the fifth closest node to *A*.

k	Node	Path
0	A	—
1	B	AB
2	E	ABE
		AE
3	F	AEF
4	C	ABC
5	D	ABFD

Since *D* is the destination node, the shortest path from *A* to *D* is *ABFD*.

7.3 Sample Routing Protocols

Autonomous Systems and Interior and Border Gateway Protocols

Adjunct to the various routing protocols like RIP and OSPF is something known as *protocol areas,* which are also called *routing domains.* In the Internet, routing domains are referred to as *autonomous systems* (AS), which are a collection of networks controlled by a single administrative authority. The networks within an AS also share a common routing strategy. That is, the routers connecting the networks within an AS trust each other and exchange routing information using a mutually agreed upon routing protocol. The network and associated subnets shown in Figure 7.3 can be regarded as an AS if all the routers employ the same protocols.

An *Interior Gateway Protocol* (IGP) is an Internet protocol used to exchange routing information within an AS. Examples of these *intra*domain protocols include RIP, RIP-2, OSPF, IGRP, and Enhanced IGRP. Each AS must also support a router that can exchange routing information with other autonomous systems. Routing protocols used for this purpose are known as exterior gateway protocols. Examples of these *inter*domain protocols include EGP, the Exterior Gateway Protocol, defined in RFC 904, and BGP, the *Border Gateway Protocol,* defined in RFC 1105 and RFC 1771. Both EGP and BGP are part of the TCP/IP protocol suite. Of the two, however, BGP has evolved into a robust Internet routing protocol and the term "border gateway protocol" is used in favor of the term "exterior gateway protocol."

AS, IGP, and BGP are fundamental to the way in which the Internet is designed. As a global internetwork, the Internet is partitioned into autonomous systems, which enable different areas of the Internet to be administered separately from one another. Within an AS, routers run the same interior gateway protocol. By keeping an AS administratively separate, different autonomous systems can also run different IGPs within their respective areas. For example, one AS might run RIP, another might run OSPF, and a third AS might support IGRP. These separate autonomous systems can then be interconnected via routers that run a border gateway protocol. Thus, routers within an AS communicate via an IGP, and "border" routers—those between autonomous systems—communicate via a BGP. This concept is expanded later in the chapter during our discussion of OSPF.

> IGRP and Enhanced IGRP are Cisco Systems' Interior Gateway Routing Protocols.

RIP

The Routing Information Protocol Version 1 was derived from the Xerox Network System's (XNS) routing protocol, which was also called RIP. RIP was bundled with BSD UNIX in 1982 as part of the TCP/IP protocol suite and became the de facto standard for IP routing. As mentioned earlier, RIP uses a distance-vector algorithm that determines the best route by using a hops metric. When used in small homogeneous networks, RIP is a very efficient protocol and its operation is fairly simple. RIP keeps all routing tables within a network updated by transmitting routing table update messages every 30 seconds. After a RIP-enabled device receives an update, it compares its current information with the information contained in the update message. Current routing table entries are replaced with updated information when the update message contains any of the following entries: (a) a route and corresponding metric to a previously unknown destination (this information is added to the existing table), (b) a new route to an existing destination with a smaller metric (the old route is replaced by the new route), and (c) a new metric for the same route to an existing destination (the old metric is replaced by the new one).

RIP uses timers to handle link or neighbor router failures. If a router does not hear from any of its neighbors within 180 seconds, the protocol assumes the node or link is dead. Once this determination is made, the router sends out a special message to its responding neighbors about this failure. Routing table entries that include routes via the dead link or node are then altered accordingly. RIP also imposes a 15-hop maximum—if a destination network is more than 15 hops away, RIP classifies the network "unreachable." In router jargon, the destination network's cost goes to infinity. Thus, the network becomes too expensive to reach and hence is unavailable.

Routers implementing RIP occasionally misinterpret old routing information as new, which can then cause routing loops. To resolve this situation, RIP employs several strategies. These include *split-horizon, split-horizon with poisoned reverse,* and *hold-down.*

Split-Horizon The split-horizon strategy ensures that a router never sends routing information back in the direction from which it came. For example, let's assume router *A* receives a routing table update from router *B.* Once *A* receives this information, *A* updates its routing table to reflect the routes listed in *B*'s routing table. Now, when *A* is ready to send its own routing table update to *B,* split-horizon prevents *A* from sending any updates back to *B* that were made based on the information *B* sent to *A.* Generalizing, with split-horizon, routing information provided by a neighbor is eliminated in any updates sent back to that neighbor.

Split-Horizon with Poisoned Reverse This strategy is similar to split-horizon with one exception: Routing information provided by a neighbor is included in any updates sent back to that neighbor. Such routes, however, are assigned a cost factor (i.e., metric) of infinity. This means that a network is unreachable. For example, consider the network shown in Figure 7.4. Note that R2 and R3 are neighbor routers, and each can claim a route to R4 through each other (e.g., R2-R3-R4, R2-R3-R5-R4, R2-R1-R3-R4, and R3-R2-R1-R4). Assume R2 receives a routing table update from R3 that includes the R3-R2-R1-R4 path. With poisoned reverse, R2's update to R3 indicates that R4 is unreachable (i.e., its metric is infinity). This prevents R3 from claiming that a path to R4 exists through R2. Thus, any path to R4 from R3 must either be a directly connected link (R3-R4) or through other routers (e.g., R3-R5-R4 or R3-R1-R4). The poisoned reverse update is also very effective in eliminating routing loops because when two routers have routes pointing at each other (as was the case in our illustration), the update will immediately make that link unreachable.

Hold-Down The hold-down strategy requires routers not to update their routing tables with any new information they receive for a prescribed period of time called the *hold-down time.* To illustrate this, let's assume that a link within a network fails. Let's further assume that two routers, *A* and *B,* exchange routing table updates and that *B* has

(a) RIP Packet Format

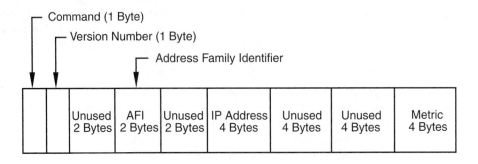

(b) RIP-2 Packet Format

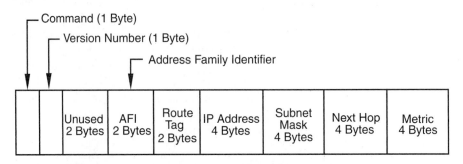

FIGURE 7.6 RIP Version 1 packets (a) contain several unused fields. These fields are defined in RIP-2 (b), thereby extending the usefulness of the RIP protocol. RIP-2 is completely compatible with RIP. The command, version number, AFI, and metric fields have exactly the same meaning in both versions. The version number field for RIP-2 will have a 2 for any RIP message that carries information in any of the unused fields from Version 1. The content of the 2-byte unused field in both versions is ignored. (*Note:* RIP updates can be up to 520 bytes long. Thus, multiple entries, from the AFI, can be placed in the datagram.) Source: adapted from RFC 1058 and RFC 1723.

been informed of the link failure from one of its other neighbors but *A* has not. If *A* does not receive information about the failed link before it sends *B* a routing table update, *B* will receive *A*'s update, see that the "failed" link is active, and incorrectly reinstate it. With hold-down implemented, though, *A* will receive information about the failed link before it sends an update to *B*. Thus, hold-down enables routing table updates to be propagated to all routers in a timely manner, thereby ensuring that new routes are indeed new and not old ones. By making the hold-down time longer than it takes to "count to infinity," routing loops can be avoided.

Hold-down is not standardized and hence should be considered implementation specific.

The format of a RIP packet is shown in Figure 7.6(a). The command field identifies the packet as either a request (a router asks its neighbor to send its routing table) or a response (a routing table update). The version number field contains the version of RIP being used. The AFI field identifies the protocol family of the address contained in the address field. Thus, if the address is an Internet address, the AFI field is coded to represent IP. The address field is the destination address of the network being advertised. The metric field contains the hop count to the address listed in the address field. Using only half of its 24 bytes, RIP carries the least amount of information necessary for routers to route messages through a network. Thus, overhead is minimal. RIP is defined in RFC 1058.

RIP-2

As originally designed, RIP does not support the concepts of autonomous systems, subnetting, or authentication. RIP also cannot interpret BGP or EGP routes. To address some of these issues, several extensions to the original protocol were incorporated to extend its usefulness. This protocol, RIP Version 2, which is shown in Figure 7.6(b), maintains RIP's command, version number, AFI, IP address, and metric fields. RIP-2 messages that carry information in any of the unused fields from Version 1 will have a 2 in the version number field. The content of the two-byte unused field in both versions is ignored. Thus, a RIP-2 packet does not alter the contents of RIP. The new features of RIP-2 include the following:

- **Authentication.** If the AFI field of the first entry in a message is FFFF, then this signifies that the message is an authentication packet. Presently, RIP-2 only supports simple passwords for authentication.
- **Interpretation of IGP and BGP Routes.** The route tag field enables RIP to distinguish between intradomain RIP routes and interdomain RIP routes, which are usually imported from an exterior gateway protocol such as BGP or another interior gateway protocol such as OSPF or IGRP.
- **Subnet Masks.** The original version of RIP assumed that all networked devices used the same subnet mask and hence did not carry subnet mask information. RIP-2 removes this assumption by supporting variable-length subnet masks. This is an extremely important feature because today's network addresses are partitioned into subnets, and routers need a subnet mask to determine routes. The subnet mask field contains the subnet mask, which is applied to the IP address to yield the network address. If this field is 0, then no subnet mask is included for a particular entry. (See the discussion on subnet masks and Box 8.1 in Chapter 8 for additional information about subnet masks.)
- **Next Hop Field.** This field contains the IP address of the immediate next hop to which packets are to be forwarded based on the packet's destination address. This field eliminates packets being routed through extra hops in a system.
- **Multicasting.** Another advantage is that, instead of broadcasting updates, RIP-2 supports multicasting. This reduces the load on hosts that are not listening to RIP-2 packets.

RIP-2 is specified in RFC 1723.

Although RIP-2 improves RIP's capabilities, it still has several deficiencies. The biggest problem with RIP is that it was never designed for large heterogeneous networks. As a network grows, destinations that are more than 15 hops away are classified unreachable in RIP. Furthermore, RIP's hops routing metric is not always the

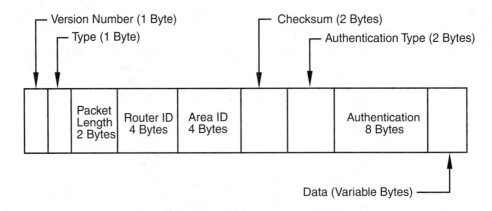

FIGURE 7.7 Contents of an OSPF packet header. The version number field contains the version of OSPF that is being implemented. The type field specifies the type of OSPF packet that is being transmitted. Several types are possible: Hello messages, database descriptions, request and response messages, and acknowledgments. The packet length field specifies the length of the packet. The router ID field identifies the packet source. The area ID field indicates the OSPF "area" associated with the packet. The checksum field is a standard CRC checksum. The authentication type field specifies the type of authentication required. The authentication field contains the authentication. Source: adapted from RFC 2328.

most efficient one to use. Unfortunately, the hops metric cannot be changed to any other metric. Finally, RIP is not as resistant to network changes (e.g., handling link failures), and it requires a greater amount of bandwidth for routing updates than other routing protocols because the entire routing table is sent. Many organizations still use RIP, but the major routing Internet protocol today is OSPF.

OSPF

As noted earlier, the Open Shortest Path First protocol is an interior gateway protocol based on a link-state algorithm; RIP is distance-vector-based. Many of RIP's limitations are resolved with OSPF. For example, OSPF is specifically designed for large heterogeneous IP networks. OSPF supports a 16-bit routing metric, which enables network managers to design least-cost routing schemes based on traffic load, propagation delays, line speed, and bandwidth, instead of relying solely on hops. Routing updates with OSPF are also very efficient and can be authenticated via passwords, digital signatures, and the like. As a link-state-based protocol, OSPF updates routes only when the status of a link changes. Furthermore, OSPF does not broadcast entire routing tables to update neighbor routers. Instead, small link-state packets called link-state advertisements containing specific information about a router's network links are transmitted. OSPF also employs the concept of *areas*. Thus, updates are not bandwidth intensive because, except for area summary updates, they only occur within a prescribed area. "Area routing" also insulates intradomain routing from external routing problems. Other features of OSPF include quick recovery after changes are made in a network's topology, resistance to routing loops, and the capability to interpret and redistribute EGP and IGP routes independently. The contents of an OSPF packet header are shown in Figure 7.7, and the protocol is specified in RFC 2328.

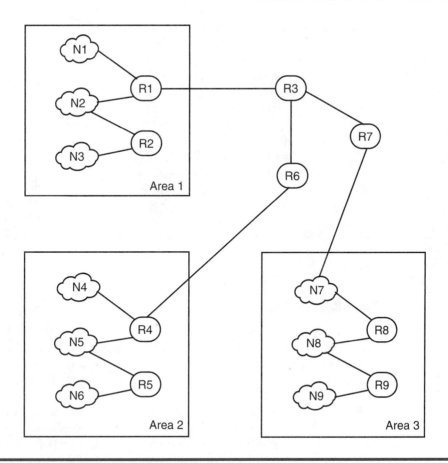

FIGURE 7.8 A sample OSPF routing environment. Source: adapted from Moy, 1990.

In an OSPF environment, a collection of networks and hosts (i.e., an internetwork) is grouped together to form an area. Routers within an area, called intraarea routers, route packets among the networks of that area. Intraarea routers maintain identical topological data. OSPF areas are interconnected via area border routers, which keep separate topological data about the areas to which they are connected. These areas can then be interconnected to form an autonomous system (AS). Thus, in an OSPF environment, routers are connected together to form networks. These networks can in turn, be connected to form areas. Autonomous systems are then formed by interconnecting areas. To illustrate this concept, consider Figure 7.8, which shows an OSPF environment that consists of three areas. Routers R1 and R2, R4 and R5, and R8 and R9 are intraarea routers for areas 1, 2, and 3, respectively. Furthermore, R1 is an area border router for area 1, R4 acts as an area border router for area 2, and R7 is the area border router for area 3. Each area is a separate autonomous system, and the intraarea routers only carry information about the networks within their areas. For example, packets originating on network N1 and destined for N3 are routed internally via R1 and R2. Packets originating on N1 and destined for N7, though, must be directed to area border router R1. These packets are then forwarded to R3 and R7.

Note that with areas in place, OSPF routing occurs at two different levels. The lower level is intraarea routing. The higher level is interarea routing, which consists of traffic that traverses the backbone. The backbone in Figure 7.8 is comprised of routers R3, R6, and R7. To minimize the amount of routing updates on the backbone, each area has a designated router and a backup designated router. Within an area, each router exchanges link-state information with the designated router. This router, or its backup if the designated router fails, is then responsible for generating link-state advertisements (LSAs) on behalf of that network.

When a new router is first added to a network, it sends a "hello" message to each of its neighbors. Hello messages are also sent periodically by all routers to inform their neighbors that they are still alive. Using a link-state algorithm such as Dijkstra's shortest path algorithm (see Box 7.2), OSPF routers build a topological database consisting of their view of the network. This information is then transmitted via link-state advertisements to neighbor routers. For intradomain routers, LSAs are exchanged only with routers within their area. Area border routers exchange LSAs with other area border routers.

OSPF was recently modified to accommodate IPv6. For additional information, see RFC 2740.

Other Routing Protocols

Three other routing protocols of interest are IGRP, EIGRP, and IS-IS. All three are interior gateway protocols and, like OSPF, are alternatives to RIP. IGRP and EIGRP are proprietary Cisco Systems protocols and hence are appropriate for Cisco environments. IS-IS is an OSI routing protocol. A brief description of each follows.

IGRP   The Interior Gateway Routing Protocol was developed by Cisco to address some of the problems associated with routing in large heterogeneous networks. The key difference between IGRP and RIP is the routing metric. In IGRP, a mathematical formula that takes into consideration factors such as bandwidth and delay is used to calculate a metric value. The path with the smallest calculated metric is determined as the least-cost (i.e., "best") path. Another difference between the two protocols is that IGRP employs the concept of "trusted neighbor," which is a neighbor router from whom a router will only accept routing updates. Trusted neighbors are defined as part of the configuration process. IGRP addresses issues related to routing loops by implementing the concepts of split-horizon and hold-downs similar to RIP's implementations.

EIGRP   Enhanced IGRP is another routing protocol designed by Cisco. It combines the best features of distance-vector and link-state routing protocols. For example, EIGRP uses "hello" messages to learn of neighbor routers. It also uses a specially designed protocol, the Reliable Transport Protocol, to transmit routing updates instead of using broadcasts. Subnet masking is also supported by EIGRP. Routing metrics are distance-vector-based and are calculated via Cisco's diffusing-update algorithm (DUAL).

IS-IS   The formal title of this protocol is "Intermediate System to Intermediate System Intra-Domain Routing Exchange Protocol." It is an OSI protocol designed to run within an AS, which is called a "routing domain" in the OSI world. IS-IS uses a link-state routing algorithm to calculate least-cost paths. Overall, its operation is similar to OSPF.

Classless Interdomain Routing

Another concept related to routing and the Internet is *classless inter-domain routing* (CIDR), which allows sites to advertise multiple Class C networks by using a single prefix. A Class C network is one that has been assigned a Class C Internet address. These addresses begin with a decimal number ranging from 192 to 223 (e.g., 198.69.25.54). Class C networks support up to 254 unique host IDs. (See Chapter 8 for information about Class C IP networks.) CIDR was developed as a solution to the routing table explosion caused by the rapid growth of the Internet. As the Internet grew, the folks in charge of assigning Internet address began issuing multiple Class C addresses to organizations that had more than 254 hosts to connect to the Internet. This meant that more individual networks needed to be announced for routing purposes and maintained by routers. With more networks needing to be announced, coupled with RIP's "feature" of updating routing tables every 30 seconds, most of the available Internet bandwidth was being used for routing table updates rather than user data. CIDR alleviated this problem by summarizing Class C network prefixes and using them as routing entries instead of the actual network addresses. For example, in a CIDR-less environment, an organization that is issued 96 Class C network addresses must have an entry for each address in its router's routing table. With CIDR, though, a special prefix is assigned to these 96 networks that indicates they all belong to the organization's routing domain. Thus, only one routing entry is needed instead of 96. OSPF, BGP, and RIP support CIDR.

7.4 Routers and Switches

Overview (Review) of Switches and Switching

Before we examine the differences between routers and switches, let's briefly review the history of switches and switching. The concept of switching in the telecommunications industry has its roots in circuit-switching. Recall from Chapter 2 that a circuit-switched network employs connection-oriented links. In a circuit-switched network, a dedicated hardware switch first establishes a physical circuit between the source and destination nodes before communication takes place. The switch also keeps this circuit in place for the duration of the transmission. Furthermore, the switch is responsible for managing the link and addressing all related end-to-end connection issues (e.g., flow control, circuit path).

In a packet-switched network, instead of using a dedicated physical circuit for every node-to-node communication, nodes share a communications channel via a virtual circuit. Bandwidth in a packet-switched network is dynamically established and released on an as-needed basis. Thus, a packet-switched network uses bandwidth more efficiently than a circuit-switched network. Furthermore, if the link is connectionless, then messages are partitioned into packets and sent to the destination one at a time and not necessarily in the correct order. By doing so, the switch does not have to concern itself with end-to-end communication issues.

One of the key differences between a connection-oriented and a connectionless link is that the former requires knowledge of the state of the network, whereas the latter does not. Prior to the development of local and wide area data networks, switching was always connection-oriented. In the data network world, however, switching became connectionless. For example, when a router routes a packet through a network, no advance path is established, there is no concern about flow control, and heck, the router doesn't even care if the packets are arriving in the correct order. All of these issues are left for the upper layers. Thus, a router acts like a connectionless switch. So, the primary difference between a switch and a router is really one of semantics. Switches historically infer connection-oriented links; routers use connectionless links.

Layer-2 and Layer-3 Switches versus Routers

In the strictest sense, LAN switches are layer-2 devices that examine and use layer-2 data (e.g., MAC addresses) to forward or filter traffic. Since they operate at the data link layer, these devices are supposed to be transparent to protocols operating at higher layers. This implies that regardless of the network protocol being used, switches pass or discard frames independent of network protocols and cannot filter broadcasts. Similarly, and again *in the strictest sense*, routers are layer-3 devices that use layer-3 data (e.g., network addresses) to forward or filter traffic. Routers filter packets based on network protocols, and they can filter broadcasts. Most routers also incorporate some sort of bridging capability. Hence, they can operate at either layer 2 or layer 3.

In the real world, though, LAN switches have encroached on the router's territory. Many LAN switch vendors now incorporate traditional router functionality into their products. For example, some Ethernet switches are capable of examining layer-3 header information, which is then used to filter network protocols or broadcasts. Some switches also are capable of creating virtual LANS (see Chapter 9) using either MAC sublayer addresses (layer 2) or network addresses (layer 3) as the basis for forwarding/ filtering frames or packets. As a result, switches have begun replacing routers at the local area network level.

The replacement of routers with switches in LAN configurations did not go unnoticed by router manufacturers. Cognizant of the LAN switch's encroachment, router manufacturers began modifying their products to incorporate a switch's primary feature—wire speed operations. To provide routers with this capability, router manufacturers designed and implemented *application-specific integrated circuit* (ASIC) chips that perform traditional router table lookups and packet forwarding at hardware speeds. ASIC-based routers still examine every packet and calculate network routes as traditional routers do; they just do it much faster. Thus, physically, this new breed of routers provides switchlike performance. Logically, however, they perform the same operations. Furthermore, unlike layer-2 switches, which establish connection-oriented links between source and destination nodes, routers still route packets on a connectionless basis. Nevertheless, ASIC-based routers are referred to as layer-3 switches or routing switches. Along this same line, because LAN switches have layer-3 functionality, they are referred to as layer-3 devices. Regardless of what you call them (is a router a switch or is a switch a layer-3 device?), the bottom line is this: Layers 2 and 3 of the OSI model are merging, and it is becoming difficult to distinguish between switches and routers.

Layer-4 Switching

The concept of *layer-4 switching* is based on using information from the upper layers (layers 4, 5, 6, or 7) to make routing decisions. For example, Web-based packets might be routed in one direction and e-mail packets in another even if both packets have the same destination address. The Web-based packets might take a route that has higher bandwidth capability; the e-mail packets' route might have more delays. Another illustration is Web-browsing traffic, which might take a different path than an electronic commerce-based packet.

The idea behind layer-4 switching is to examine each packet and use its upper-layer information to make routing decisions. Routers that have this capability are being touted as layer-4 switches. This terminology is a malapropism, however, because switches are connection-oriented and routers are connectionless. Switching implies establishing a connection between source and destination ports, which does not occur at layer 4. Regardless of the type of information being used to determine a path or the layer that is providing this information, packets are still being forwarded on a connectionless basis. It is more appropriate to refer to layer-4 switches as either layer-2 or layer-3 *application switches* because application information from upper layers is being used for routing decisions.

IP Switching

IP Switching initially was the name a network vendor (Ipsilon Networks) coined to describe its proprietary layer-3 switching strategy. Ipsilon has since been acquired by Nokia, and the term now refers to different strategies for speeding up the processing of IP traffic. The focus of each of these strategies is to apply layer-2 switching technology to layer-3 routing. The primary reason for doing this is to improve the packet forwarding performance of routers and to enable routers to provide sufficient network guarantees to support a specific quality of service (QoS) level. Several strategies follow without explanation. The reader is encouraged to consult Suggested Readings and References for additional information about these strategies. (See also Chapters 5, 8, and 15 for additional information about QoS and class of service, CoS.)

One strategy is to run IP over ATM. (See Chapter 15 for more information about ATM.) This strategy itself has several approaches. These include ATM LAN Emulation (LANE), Classical IP Over ATM (IPOA), Next Hop Resolution Protocol (NHRP), and Multiprotocol Over ATM (MPOA), which is an extension of LANE and uses NHRP. Of these approaches, MPOA is receiving considerable attention. A second strategy is Ipsilon's IP Switching technology, which employs a specially designed IP switch that can distinguish between "flow-oriented" traffic (e.g., ftp, http, multimedia) and "short-lived" traffic (e.g., e-mail, name server lookups). The IP switch processes all short-lived packets just like traditional routers. Flow-oriented packets, however, get switched to their destinations at hardware speeds. A third IP switching strategy is the IETF's Multiprotocol Label Switching (MPLS) standard, which combines Cisco Systems' Tag Switching approach with IBM's ARIS (Aggregate Route-based IP Switching) strategy. Other strategies include extremely fast routers that process several million IP packets per second and layer-3 switches as discussed earlier.

Brouter versus Router

For completeness, a *brouter* combines the features of a bridge and router. Its name comes from "bridging router." It has the forwarding capabilities of a router and the network protocol independence of a bridge. Brouters can process packets at either the data link or network layers. When used as a bridge, brouters forward frames and can be used to filter local traffic. When used as a router, brouters transfer packets across networks. Brouters had their 15 minutes of fame in the early 1990s. They have since been replaced by switches.

7.5   Virtual Private Networks (VPNs)

A practical illustration of the network layer is a *virtual private network* (VPN), which involves using the Internet as a private WAN. A VPN is an IP connection between two sites over a public IP network. Examining this concept further, a VPN is first and foremost a virtual network (this is the V and N of VPN), which implies that the paths data travel between a source and destination are being shared by other transmissions. Second, it is a private network (this is the P and N in VPN), which implies that the data transmitted between a source and destination are not accessible to unauthorized users. Thus, a VPN involves using a public network infrastructure, such as the Internet, as a private WAN where data are transported between source and destination nodes. Furthermore, data transported across a VPN are encrypted so that only the source and destination nodes can decrypt them. (See Chapter 17 for additional information about encryption and decryption.) In this manner, a publicly accessible network like the Internet can be used for moving highly confidential information in a secure manner. The VPN exploitation of the last couple of years is centered mainly on IP-based networks such as the Internet.

VPN Strategies

One of the major problems of VPN technologies is the great variety of implementation styles and methods, which causes much confusion when trying to develop a strategy for their use in a company. A brief description of several VPN implementations follows. (The reader is encouraged to review the various VPN security strategies, which are provided in Chapter 17.)

Router-to-Router VPN-on-Demand Tunnel Connections Between Sites   In this implementation, a VPN-capable router is set up to know that when a connection is made to a specific IP address on the connected network, it should set up an encrypted linkage for all traffic between the two routers. This is often also called an encrypted "tunnel" facility, as the connection does not individually encipher the sessions as much as it creates a master session between the two routers and channels all user traffic inside the master session (like moving cars through a tunnel). The tunnels are created with the first user connection between the site(s) and are persistent until the last user disconnects from the site pair, which causes the routers to stop the tunnel session. This type of VPN relies on router compatibility. Among others, routers must have compatible VPN capabilities, key exchange, and cryptographic support. This method is also highly vendor specific—usually, two different vendors of routers will not interoperate in a tunneled manner. VPNs via a tunnel implementation may or may not be encrypted depending on vendor offering. A good example of this is Cisco's Layer Two Forwarding (L2F) protocol.

Router-to-Router VPN-on-Demand Multiprotocol Tunnel Connections Between Sites over an IP Network   Similar to the previous definition, this type of VPN implementation allows the customer to use an IP network between two sites to carry tunneled packets for other protocols besides IP. An IP-based VPN is established between two sites over the public IP network. The routers know that when another protocol, such as Netware's IPX or Apple's AppleTalk, issues a connection request to a specific node on the other side of the IP network, a "transparent" connection needs to be established and the non-IP protocol tunneled to the remote site. This type of connectivity is extremely useful in companies that have small to medium remote sites and want the benefits and cost savings of connectivity to a shared IP network, but are not running IP as the only protocol between sites. It's also a big cost savings method for international network connections. The cost of a public IP network with multiprotocol VPN tunneling is considerably less than a 56-kbps private network connection.

Router-to-Router VPN-on-Demand Encrypted Session Connections Between Sites   Like a tunnel, specific routers are defined with each other as to whether they support VPN, encryption, or other security. Unlike a tunnel, each session is encrypted and match-paired with its partner on the other side of the public network. While this is simpler to manage session-wise than a tunnel, it can have a greater amount of overhead for highly connected applications between the same two site pairs in a network.

Firewall-to-Firewall VPN-on-Demand Tunnel Connections Between Sites   (See Chapter 17 for more information about firewalls.) Like the equivalent router facilities, this provides an equivalent service. The major difference is the ability to impose security rule restrictions and traffic management, auditing, authentication, data encryption, and other security features that firewalls offer but routers do not. This provides additional security and accounting information useful for management of the facilities. An example of an emerging standard for this is *IP security* (IPSec) from the Internet Engineering Task Force (IETF). IPSec is a suite of protocols that includes an authentication header (AH) and an encapsulating security payload (ESP). AH provides address authentication for IP traffic, and ESP defines IP data encryption. (See Chapter 17 for additional information about IPSec.) IPSec enables the same or dissimilar firewall vendors to negotiate a protocol methodology that provides the described VPN facilities or subsets thereof. Be careful: Some vendors' offering of IPSec does not interoperate with other vendors and only supports their own firewall implementations.

Firewall-to-Firewall VPN-on-Demand Multiprotocol Tunnel Connections Between Sites over an IP Network   This strategy is similar to the router approach but with all the firewall facilities as well. For this type of VPN to work with multiple protocol tunneling, the firewall must be capable of handling multiple protocol filtering and security.

Client-to-Firewall IP Tunnel VPN Facilities   In some recent implementations, a client VPN tunnel manager and encryption software package is installed on a client system, such as a laptop. The firewall implements a proxy facility that knows how to deal with the client. The client, upon connecting to the site via the IP network, negotiates a VPN tunnel with the site firewall via the client VPN software. Once the session tunnel is activated, the firewall and client system provide a secure connection over the public IP network. In this approach, VPN client facilities are usually required for a variety of operating system environments to satisfy the remote connectivity facilities. This type of service, although it is becoming more common, is usually not seen implemented on a router-based VPN solution. This is jointly due to the need to maintain database information on the client side and the complexity of key distribution and management, which usually require a disk-based system to deal with the items involved (most routers are diskless). An example of this is the V-One implementation called SmartGate, which implements a proxy on the firewall side of the connection and either a soft-token or hard-token software package on the client side to connect to the proxy on the firewall for the VPN facility. Another is the proxy suite from Aventail that provides many equivalent services for NT.

Client-to-Server IP Tunnel VPN Facilities   Companies such as Microsoft are implementing a VPN tunneling facility that allows the software on a client to initiate and connect a VPN tunnel between itself and either a local or remote server on a network. This provides the ability for end-to-end VPN services and, with encryption, the opportunity to provide secure VPN facilities from the source of information to the destination of information. Microsoft provides this capability with their Point-to-Point Tunneling Protocol (PPTP) currently available in Windows NT and very soon for other operating system offerings (e.g., Windows 98). PPTP works hand-in-hand with IP.

Client and Server Firewall Implementation with Full VPN Capabilities   This approach provides the greatest level of complexity and the greatest level of security by implementing a full firewall facility on every system on the network. This provides the VPN facilities previously described but also the ability to support full network security policy management and control on both sides of the connection (client-only VPN facilities do not provide client network access control services). An example of this type of approach is the server and client versions of Network-1 Security Solutions' FireWall/Plus, where the server and desktop machines have full firewall facilities to provide full network access control between the systems and network in addition to VPN facilities.

Dedicated VPN Box   Some vendors have come up with dedicated systems that can connect either in front of or behind a router facility to implement VPN facilities between a company and a public IP network such as the Internet. These boxes are simple to implement and usually provide much higher performance than software-based solutions implemented in firewalls or via other schemes. Normally, however, they do not provide an adequate client-level security facility for VPNs and are mostly dedicated for site-to-site access. They also can be expensive for highly connected sites. As you can see, there is a bewildering array of VPN choices and solutions depending on need and fiscal resources.

VPN Benefits

All costs are given in U.S. dollars.

To illustrate the benefits that can be derived from a VPN, consider the following illustration. The organization described has more than 60 sites located in the United States, Europe, and Asia. This should give you an idea of the costs and benefits associated with VPNs. This illustration brings into a practical context several networking terms and concepts developed in earlier chapters. It also introduces some concepts that are provided in subsequent chapters. In this latter case, appropriate chapters are referenced.

The current network used to interconnect the sites is an extensive one composed of frame relay (see Chapter 13), leased line, dialup (see Chapter 16), and X.25 packet-switching. In this network, the average connection speed is 56 kbps with an average connection cost of approximately $176,000 per month. This amount is for communications costs only and does not include any provision for the required modem pools and other types of interconnection hardware. By using frame relay and upgrading only 20 of the 60 sites to T1 circuits (1.544 Mbps), the monthly communications costs are expected to exceed $510,000 per month, $360,000 of which is for the 20 T1 sites alone because of their overseas locations. The other 40 sites require the same services, but not necessarily the entire range of connection speeds required at other larger sites. In the major sites, the need to upgrade from 56 kbps to T1, and in a couple of cases, T3 (45 Mbps), is forthcoming due to a major change in corporate use of network resources to move large amounts of data. Other needs include:

- allowing customers to access specific applications on in-house systems (there may be up to 20,000 customers doing this daily in the future);
- providing extranet connectivity to customer sites using the SNA, AppleTalk, and IPX protocols in addition to IP;
- enabling remote, secure, corporate user access via modems (there could be as many as 2000 users accessing internal resources daily);
- expanding small business sites and office presence worldwide so that a small office in a remote city consisting of two to four users and associated equipment can rapidly interconnect newly acquired companies;
- enabling rapid implementation of high-speed connections due to seasonal changes or promotional issues at offices worldwide;
- managing network resources with minimal or no human utilization from internal resources;
- adding modem, ISDN, and other remote low-speed connections without affecting specific in-place network resources from a configuration perspective;
- adding customer and vendor connections quickly for multiple protocol suites with minimal or no internal resource expenditure to add connection capability;
- providing intranet server capabilities to all employees domestically and internationally regardless of network protocol access type used in a user's local area;
- developing consistent configuration rules and conformance criteria;

- implementing internationalized methods of standards and performance criteria for all sites so that consistent performance and access reliability are achieved;
- allowing network performance to scale from very small (single system) to millions of session accesses per day at a given site with the same connection methodology for simplicity;
- implementing expandable network architecture that can handle not only multiple protocols and their interconnection, but multiple versions of the protocols at the same time;
- supporting audited and logged network access via secured facilities at each site;
- implementing very stringent security controls for highly critical systems and network interconnects to ensure that only properly authorized users gain access to critical components; and
- providing a redundant and resilient network environment in the case of performance adversity or network outage by one or more vendors to critical locations.

To solve these problems, a network was designed with the following components:

1. The same public IP provider at all sites will be used whenever possible. For this implementation, UUNET and CompuServe were selected as network vendors for interconnection of sites because they possess high-speed access facilities at all of the customer's site locations. Further, both vendors have substantial dialup and ISDN facilities that allow remote location interconnection at very low or fixed price configurations. Selecting two vendors also allows for diversity and support of user sites that may not have connection facilities to the preferred vendor of the two but does have access to the other.
2. A multiprotocol firewall was selected to provide site-to-site multiprotocol VPN for all protocols, five-layer network security (frame, packet, application, stateful, and proxy in the same product at the same time), scaling (Intel 80486 through Alpha SMP systems), client VPN proxy facilities for remote single system and laptop users, strong authentication for specific systems personnel, remote management of the firewall, and many other facilities that are essential in providing secure networking connectivity. An additional reason for this selection is the ability of the product to be used on Internet connections, intranet (there is a server and desktop version), and extranets when connecting to customer or known third-party sites.
3. A common network vendor for all interconnection WAN routers and hubs was selected to ensure proper network interconnectivity, management, and minimization of human resources and technical expertise requirements.

With this approach, the 20 main sites—which had an average upgrade fee of $18,000 per site per month and required specific routing topologies to one or two centralized sites—can be upgraded for an average per site cost of $7000 per month.[1] This per month communications fee is normal for a public IP connection. This means that flat-rate costs per month for the 20 sites are approximately $140,000. This is 39% of the original cost estimate for the upgrade at the same speed, but it also includes all the other ancillary network connectivity requirements.

---

[1] This figure is higher in some countries, but substantially lower in others, for a T1 connection.

Additional costs for this implementation include 20 full-functionality firewall facilities (an average of $20,000 per site for an Alpha-based Windows NT system, including firewall software and support). Since the new connectivity method provides a $13,000 per month savings, the firewall and all facilities for its interconnection are paid for in less than 2 months per site. Additional expected per user costs for client VPN are approximately $250 per system, which will grow slowly. Costs for modem and ISDN pools are eliminated, as are the maintenance, operations, and network management costs and efforts.

For completeness, the customer examined the potential use of a router-only solution with VPN capabilities, but the solution could not solve the remote laptop and small site VPN problem nor the filtering and security management issues that only a firewall can solve. While a router is required for this type of connection to be feasible, so is the right type of firewall so that all the ancillary controls, audit trail, logging, security services, and multiple protocol session control and management are available regardless of how the customer needs to connect to the facility. While this solution is still implemented at this writing, initial results are very positive and the cost savings described in this example are real.

End-of-Chapter Commentary

In this chapter, we examined many aspects related to layer 3 of the OSI model. Several of the topics or concepts developed here are further explored in other chapters. For example, much of the Internet-related information, including a more detailed discussion of TCP/IP, is given in Chapter 8. Telephone circuits are revisited in Chapter 16 as part of a discussion on modems, and VPNs are examined from a network security perspective in Chapter 17. Several WAN technologies and services are also discussed in subsequent chapters. These include ISDN (Chapter 12), frame relay (Chapter 13), SMDS, (Chapter 14), and ATM (Chapter 15).

CHAPTER REVIEW MATERIALS

SUMMARY

- An internetwork is a collection of interconnected computer networks, including LANs and WANS, which operates as a single network.
- The terms internet and Internet are both abbreviations for internetwork. When used as a noun and spelled with a lowercase i, internet is any internetwork; when used as a proper noun and spelled with an uppercase I, Internet refers to the world's largest internetwork, which is based on the TCP/IP protocol suite.
- Internetworks can be created at layers 1, 2, or 3 of the OSI model. Internetworks that operate at the physical layer must maintain exactly the same architecture and cabling; internetworks that operate at the data link

layer may have different architecture or cabling; and internetworks that operate at the network layer are heterogeneous networks that may use different hardware, software, protocols, and applications.
- Heterogeneous networks require network protocol translation. Traditionally, this service has been provided by routers, which are layer-3 devices responsible for determining the appropriate path a packet takes as it traverses the internetwork between source and destination nodes.
- Routers determine source–destination paths using routing protocols, which are network protocol dependent. In a heterogeneous network environment, a process known as tunneling is used to encapsulate one

protocol into another for transporting data across the network.

• Routing protocols employ specific routing algorithms to determine appropriate source–destination paths, and path determination is based on a least-cost metric. Common routing metrics include the number of hops between source and destination nodes, the amount of propagation delay that might exist, the amount of bandwidth available, the length of time it will take, and error rates.

• Routes can be either dynamic or static. A dynamic route is one that is established at the time a packet is ready for transport. This route can change for every new packet depending on network conditions. A static route is a fixed route that is manually configured. Once in place, every packet will follow this fixed path regardless of changes in a network's topology or conditions.

• Two general types of routing algorithms are distance-vector and link-state. Distance-vector algorithms determine source–destination paths by calculating the number of hops a packet encounters; routers within an internetwork inform their neighbor routers of these paths by exchanging their routing tables periodically. In contrast to this, routing protocols based on link-state algorithms only exchange specific information about the links they have established instead of their complete routing tables. Furthermore, the information these routers use to determine source–destination paths can include metrics other than distance. The Bellman-Ford algorithm is an example of a distance-vector algorithm; Dijkstra's shortest path first algorithm is an example of a link-state algorithm.

• Within the Internet, routing protocols are classified as either intradomain or interdomain. Intradomain protocols permit the exchange of routing information among routers within a specific area governed by a single administrative authority (called an autonomous system in the Internet world and routing domain in the OSI world). Examples include the Routing Information Protocol (RIP) and Open Shortest Path First (OSPF). Collectively, these protocols are known as Interior Gateway Protocols (IGP). RIP is a distance-vector protocol; OSPF is a link-state protocol. Interdomain routing protocols permit the exchange of routing information across autonomous system borders. An example of an interdomain protocol is the Border Gateway Protocol (BGP).

• Two versions of RIP are available. Both determine the best route by using a hops metric. The first version of RIP was at one time the de facto standard for IP routing. The second version of RIP, known as RIP-2, adds additional functionality to the original version without modifying the contents. RIP-2 features include authentication for security measures, the ability to interpret IGP and BGP routes, support for multiple-length subnet masks, a next hop field that eliminates packets from being routed through extra hops, and multicasting support.

• OSPF is designed for large heterogeneous IP networks. It supports several routing metrics in addition to hops, is extremely efficient in propagating routing table updates, and supports authentication by passwords or digital signatures.

• Routers traditionally have performed router table lookups and packet forwarding in software. Current routers, however, now perform these functions in hardware via application-specific integrated circuit (ASIC) chips. Given the speed at which these functions are now executed, ASIC-based routers are commonly known as layer-3 switches or routing switches because they provide switchlike performance.

• Layer-4 switching involves determining source–destination paths based on the information provided by the upper layers. Although devices designed to make routing decisions based on application information are being called layer-4 switches, packets nevertheless are being forwarded on a connectionless basis. Since switches operate on a connection-oriented basis, these layer-4 devices should be called layer-2 or layer-3 application switches.

• The concept of IP switching involves various strategies for increasing the rate at which IP traffic is processed. This concept warrants attention because faster IP processing is necessary for quality of service (QoS) support within the Internet.

• A virtual private network (VPN) refers to an IP connection between two sites over a public IP network that has its payload traffic encrypted so that only source and destination nodes can decrypt the traffic packets. A VPN enables a publicly accessible network to be used for highly confidential, dynamic, and secure data transmissions.

VOCABULARY CHECK ▰▰▰▰▰▰▰▰▰▰▰▰▰▰▰▰▰▰▰▰▰▰▰▰

autonomous system	hold-down	Routing Information Protocol
brouter	Interior Gateway Protocol (IGP)	(RIP)
classless interdomain routing	Internet vs. internet	routing protocol
(CIDR)	internetwork	split-horizon
congestion	intranet	split-horizon with poisoned
datagram	IP Security (IPSec)	reverse
deadlock	layer-4 switching	static route
distance-vector algorithm	link-state algorithm	subnetwork
extranet	Open Shortest Path First (OSPF)	tunneling
fragmenting	router	virtual private network (VPN)
gateway		

REVIEW EXERCISES ▰▰▰▰▰▰▰▰▰▰▰▰▰▰▰▰▰▰▰▰▰▰▰▰

1. In this chapter, we defined an internetwork as a collection of interconnected networks that function as a single network. We also stated that an internetworking strategy for interconnecting identical networks is different from interconnecting similar or dissimilar networks. What do you think some of these differences are and why?

2. In addition to differences in strategy between homogeneous and heterogeneous networks (problem 1), another issue that must be addressed when designing internetworks is the size of the networks that are being connected as well as the overall size of the internetwork itself. What key factors do you think need to be considered relative to the problem of scaling?

3. Explain the manner in which internetworking is accomplished at each of the bottom three layers of the OSI model.

Use the following scenario to answer questions 4 –9:
   A local high school has an internal network backbone that interconnects three separate LANs. One LAN is located in the media center, a second is in the mathematics lab, and the third is in the faculty resource room. LAN users are able to exchange e-mail, files, and printing services. The school, however, is not connected to the Internet.

4. Is the school network considered an internetwork? Why or why not?

5. Is the school network considered an intranet? Why or why not?

6. Are the individual LANs considered subnetworks? Why or why not?

7. In what way(s) do you think these individual LANs are connected?

8. Let us assume that the school receives a grant to enhance its current networking environment and uses the money to wire every classroom and connect every teacher's classroom computer to the network. What internetworking-related issues do you think must now be addressed that did not have to be considered initially?

9. Let us further assume that the school connects its network to the Internet. What internetworking-related issues do you think must now be considered?

10. Briefly describe the function of the network layer.

11. One function of a routing protocol is to determine the "best" path between sending and receiving nodes. What is considered a "best" path?

Use the following description to answer questions 12–14:
   Assume we have three separate point-to-point packet-switching networks. The designs of the networks are star (see Figure 1.2), a partially meshed loop (Figure 1.3a), and a fully meshed loop (Figure 1.4a). Further assume that each network has N nodes and that the centralized hub in the star design is a network switch and any transmission to the switch is considered a hop.

12. In a best-case scenario (i.e., all communication lines are up and running), what is the minimum

number of hops needed to transmit data between any two nodes on each network?

13. In a worst-case scenario (i.e., critical communication lines are down), what is the minimum number of hops needed to transmit data between any two nodes on each network?

14. What is the average number of hops needed to transmit data between any two nodes on each network?

15. Use the UNIX program traceroute or the Windows program tracert to determine the number of hops between your node and another Internet node. Interpret the output.

16. Use the UNIX program netstat with the -r option or the Windows program route with the print option to generate the routing table of your host. Interpret the output.

17. What do you think some of the advantages and disadvantages are between static routes and dynamically configured routes?

18. Use Figure 7.9 to determine the best path (i.e., cheapest way) and the worst path (i.e., most expensive) from A to O. The cost factors for the links are as follows: Ethernet: Cost = 5; T1: Cost = 10; 64K: Cost = 15; 56K: Cost = 20; 19.2K: Cost = 25. (*Note:* Least cost is always first. If there is more than one least cost, then the path with the least number of hops is first.)

19. Consider a county road map that shows all possible routes from town A to N different towns located within the same county. Let's assume that at each town's map marking there is a single information box that lists the distance from each town to all other towns via each route. For example, if there are five roads leading from town A to town B, then the information box at town A would contain the distances between the two towns for each route. Similarly, if there are three roads leading from town B to town C, then

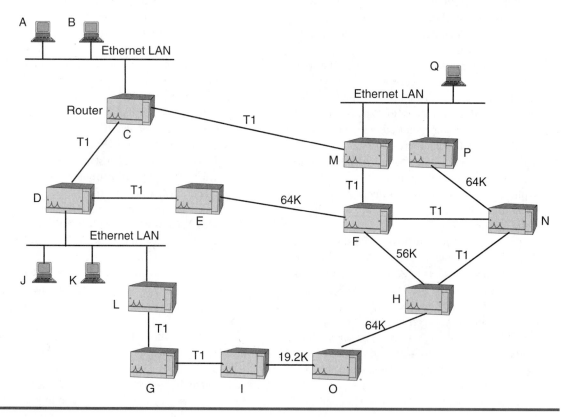

FIGURE 7.9

town B's information box would contain the distances between B and C for each route. Thus, anyone reading the map can automatically identify the shortest path between towns. Which routing algorithm, distance-vector or link-state, do you think this illustration mimics and why?

Use the following modification to problem 19 to answer questions 20–24:

Instead of having a road map, assume that at the beginning of each road leading from one town to another a sign is posted that contains specific information about each route. Further assume that this routing information is updated periodically to provide accurate information about that road's condition.

20. What type of information do you think needs to be placed on these signs?
21. How often does this information need to be updated?
22. Given a choice between distance-vector routing and link-state routing, which do you think is the better way for neighboring towns to update road information and why?
23. What possible problems will arise if the information is not updated in a timely manner?
24. Given the different types of information that can now be made available, how would you determine the shortest distance between towns?
25. One of the major problems with RIP (and any distance-vector-based routing protocol) is its inability to respond to network changes in a timely manner. Discuss some of the strategies RIP employs that address these problems.
26. Apply the Bellman-Ford's, and Dijkstra's algorithms to find the shortest path from A to F in the network shown in Figure 7.10.
27. Apply the Bellman-Ford's and Dijkstra's algorithms to find the shortest path from A to H in the network shown in Figure 7.11.
28. Suppose in Figure 7.10 that the BC path was −3. What happens if we apply Dijkstra's algorithm to this modified network? Will it find the shortest path from A to F? Why or why not?
29. RIP and OSPF are considered distributed routing protocols since routers periodically exchange information with each of their neigh-

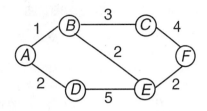

FIGURE 7.10

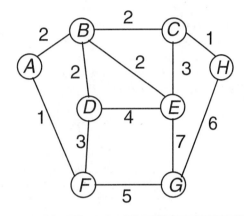

FIGURE 7.11

bors. Is it possible to have routing protocols that are centralized in nature? How do you think centralized routing would work? What do you think would be some of the inherent problems of centralized routing?
30. Following the same line of thought as in problem 29, consider the concept of decentralized routing. How do you think this would work and what inherent problems do you think exist?
31. What advantages do autonomous systems (ASs) bring to routing? What major problem does AS fail to eliminate and how does CIDR help address this problem?
32. Explain the differences between routing and switching.
33. Explain the differences among layer-2, layer-3, and layer-4 switching.
34. Briefly summarize and compare the various VPN strategies discussed in the book.

SUGGESTED READINGS AND REFERENCES

ANDERSON, P., and G. James. 1998. Switching at Layer-4. *Network World,* 20 July.

ASCEND COMMUNICATIONS, INC. 1998. *Virtual Private Networks for the Enterprise: A Resource Guide for Information Technology and Network Managers Worldwide.* Alameda, CA: Ascend Communications.

BAKER, F. 1994. OSPF Fundamentals. *LAN Magazine,* December, 71–78.

BAKER, S. 1994. Attaining Gigabit Speed. *UNIX Review,* 17–26.

CALLON, R., V. HAIMO, and M. LEPP. 1989. Routing in an Internetwork Environment. *Connexions: The Interoperability Report,* 3(8): 2–7.

COLTUN, R. 1989. OSPF: An Internet Routing Protocol. *Connexions: The Interoperability Report,* 3(8): 19–25.

CONOVER, J. 1998. Slicing Through IP Switching. *Network Computing,* 15 March, 50–67.

DAVIE, B., P. DOOLAN, and Y. REKHTER. 1998. *Switching in IP Networks: IP Switching, Tag Switching, and Related Technologies.* San Francisco: Morgan Kaufmann.

DERN, D. P. 1990. Standards for Interior Gateway Routing Protocols. *Connexions: The Interoperability Report,* 4(7): 2–10.

ENGER, B. 1989. Adopting a Gateway. *Connexions: The Interoperability Report,* 3(8): 32–37.

FITZGERALD, S., and L. BICKNELL. 1998. Troubleshooting High-Speed WANs. *Network Magazine,* 15 January, 87–91.

———, and E. GREENBERG. 1994. Ready for Takeoff. *LAN Magazine,* May, 97–104.

GALLO, M., and W. Hancock. 1999. *Networking Explained.* Boston: Digital Press.

GARCIA-LUNA-ACEVES, J. J. 1989. Loop-free Internet Routing and Related Issues. *Connexions: The Interoperability Report,* 3(8): 8–18.

GAW, S. 1998. Building the Universal Backbone. *Network Magazine,* 15 January, 74–79.

GEIER, J. 1996. Choose Your Own Route. *LAN,* September, 103–108.

HAGENS, R. 1989. Components of OSI: ES-IS Routing. *Connexions: The Interoperability Report,* 3(8): 46–51.

HALL, E. 1998. Implementing Prioritization on IP Networks. *Network Computing,* 15 August, 76–79.

HEYWOOD, P. 1998. A Switch in Plans. *Data Communications,* July, 25–26.

KARVÉ, A. 1997. IP Switching Gets Focused. *Network Magazine,* June, 81–85.

LEPP, M. 1989. The IETF Open Routing Working Group. *Connexions: The Interoperability Report,* 3(8): 26–31.

LEWIS, C. 1996a. Alternatives to RIP in a Large Internetwork. *Network Computing,* 1 October, 126–131.

———. 1996b. Should RIP Finally Rest in Peace? *Network Computing,* 1 September, 124–128.

MCQUILLAN, J. 1997. Routers and Switches Converge. *Data Communications,* 21 October, 120–124.

MOY, J. 1990. OSPF: Next Generation Routing Comes to TCP/IP Networks. *LAN Technology,* April, 71–79.

NEWMAN, D., T. GIORGIA, and F. YAVARI-ISSALOU. 1998. VPNs: Safety First, but What About Speed? *Data Communications,* July, 59–67.

PETERSON, L., and B. DAVIE. 1996. *Computer Networks: A Systems Approach.* San Francisco: Morgan Kaufmann.

Roberts, E. 1997. IP on Speed. *Data Communications,* March, 84–96.

SCHOLL, F. 1997. Upgrading Your Backbone. *Network Magazine,* May, 95–99.

STALLINGS, W. 1996. Make Way for the Hot WANs. *LAN,* January, 48–54.

———. 2000. *Data and Computer Communications.* 6th ed. Upper Saddle River, NJ: Prentice-Hall.

STEINKE, S. 1996a. Getting Data over the Telephone Line: Lesson 92: CSUs and DSUs. *LAN,* April, 27–28.

———. 1996b. The Internet as Your WAN. *LAN,* October, 47–52.

———. 1997. Lesson 105: Switching vs. Routing. *Network Magazine,* May, 27–28.

———. 1998. What Is a Switch Today? *Network Magazine,* January, 136.

TANENBAUM, A. S. 1996. *Computer Networks.* 3rd ed. Upper Saddle River, NJ: Prentice-Hall.

TSUCHIYA, P. 1989. Components of OSI: Routing (An Overview).*Connexions: The Interoperability Report,* 3(8): 38–45.

8

The Internet and TCP/IP

CHAPTER OBJECTIVES

After studying this chapter, you will be able to do the following:

1. Discuss the history and development of the Internet.
2. Provide examples of Internet resources and the ways in which the Internet is used.
3. Compare and contrast a commercially and publicly accessible Internet and one that is the exclusive domain of the computer network research community.
4. Describe current high-speed Internet backbone initiatives.
5. Outline the organization and structure of Internet governance.
6. Explain the Internet standards process.
7. Understand current Internet-based security strategies.
8. Discuss the history and development of the TCP/IP protocol suite.
9. Compare and contrast the OSI and TCP/IP models.
10. Compare and contrast TCP/IP's transport layer protocols, TCP and UDP.
11. Describe TCP/IP's network layer protocol, IP.
12. Explain the concept of IP addressing, including subnetting, address resolution, and address assignments.
13. Compare and contrast IPv4 and IPv6.
14. Understand the basic operations of various TCP/IP application protocols, including SMTP, MIME, POP, TELNET, FTP, and HTTP.

CHAPTER OUTLINE

Ihe Internet and TCP/IP were discussed briefly in several earlier chapters. For example, we examined the general concept of an internet (lowercase *i*), contrasted it with the Internet, and introduced Internet-related terms such as intranet and extranet. We also introduced several TCP/IP-based application protocols such as the Simple Mail Transfer Protocol (SMTP) and the Post Office Protocol (POP) for e-mail, the File Transfer Protocol (FTP) for file transfers, and the Hypertext Transfer Protocol (HTTP) for Web applications. In this chapter, we expand our discussion of the Internet and some of the protocols of the TCP/IP suite. We begin the chapter with an overview of the Internet itself. This is followed by sections on the Internet's history, its administration, and its security. Our discussion on the Internet's protocol suite, TCP/IP, begins in Section 8.4 where we provide a brief history of TCP/IP's development and contrast it with the OSI model. Section 8.5 discusses the Internet's transport and network layer protocols. Section 8.6 provides information about IP Version 4 addresses. This discussion includes the concept of subnetting, address resolutions, and IP address assignments. This section is then followed up with a discussion of IP Version 6 addresses, where we compare IPv4 and IPv6 addresses. We conclude the chapter with a discussion of several TCP/IP application protocols, including SMTP, POP, TELNET, FTP, and HTTP.

8.1 What Is the Internet?

Defining the Internet today is a bit more problematic than it was several years ago. Its definition varies from person to person. For example, in Chapter 7, we said that the Internet is a collection of computer networks based on a specific set of network standards—TCP/IP. Other users, whose focus might be on the information they have acquired or the people with whom they have communicated, might define the Internet as a global collection of diverse resources or as an electronic community of people. Still others, whose only experience with the Internet is using the World Wide Web, might say the Internet and World Wide Web are synonymous, and hence, the Internet is the World Wide Web. Consequently, defining the Internet is a function of perspective. Regardless of the definition or perspective, the Internet interconnects individual, autonomous, heterogeneous computer networks and enables them to function and appear as a single global network.

One of the main attractions of the Internet is the services and resources that are available from it. Some of the services include e-mail, remote logins, file transfers, network news—an electronic forum that consists of special interest groups and discussions (there are currently over 15,000 network news groups that cover a very wide and diverse number of topics)—search tools or "engines" that allow a user to locate specific information based on user input, communication resources such as Internet relay chat (IRC), interactive games, and Web browsers that enable you to view resources that have been formatted as hypertext files. There is streaming audio and video, which enable users to listen to audio recordings or view videos in real time. There are also programs that enable two-way interactive videoconferencing to take place via the Internet. Through these services, users can acquire information about nearly anything.

There are also several high-profile Internet services or resources available. These include electronic commerce (e-commerce), voice over IP (VOIP), and virtual private networks (VPNs). E-commerce involves using the Internet for credit card purchases of items such as automobiles, airline tickets, computer-related products, and books; VOIP enables users to place telephone calls across the Internet (see Chapter 18); and VPNs enable organizations to establish private interconnected corporate LANs using the Internet (see Chapter 17).

8.2 Internet History

ARPANET

The Internet's roots can be traced back to 1957 when the United States formed the Advanced Research Projects Agency (ARPA) within the Department of Defense (DoD). The formation of ARPA was the United States' response to the former Soviet Union's launch of Sputnik, the first artificial earth satellite. ARPA's mission was to establish the United States as the world's leading country in defense- and military-applicable science and technology. ARPA, which later became known as Defense ARPA (DARPA), established in 1969 an early internetwork called ARPANET, the Advanced Research Projects Agency Network. The builder of ARPANET was a company named Bolt, Baranek, and Newman, which later became known as BBN Communications. Originally, the Internet meant ARPANET, and access to ARPANET was restricted to the military, defense contractors, and university personnel involved in defense research. ARPANET technology was based on packet-switching, and in 1969, with the connection of its first four nodes—Stanford Research Institute (SRI), University of California at Santa Barbara (UCSB), University of California at Los Angeles (UCLA), and University of Utah— ARPANET heralded the era of packet-switching networking.

BITNET, CSNET, and UUCP

In the late 1970s and early 1980s, independent of the Internet, cooperative decentralized computer networks started to form. The majority of these networks began on college and university campuses and served the academic community. Three of the more notable ones were BITNET, CSNET, and UUCP.

BITNET   The *Because It's Time Network* (BITNET) was a low-speed and inexpensive academic network consisting of interconnected IBM mainframes. Using a proprietary IBM-based network protocol, BITNET connectivity was via 9600-bps leased circuits and was based on the store-and-forward principle. Networking services available via BITNET included file transfer, e-mail, and an IBM application called *remote job entry* (RJE). In an RJE environment, small processors located at remote sites were used to transfer "jobs" to and from a main computer that served as the "master" to these smaller processors. This scheme is based on a paradigm known as *master/slave*.

CSNET   BITNET eventually merged with another early academic network called the *Computer Science Network* (CSNET) to form the Corporation for Research and Educational Networking (CREN). CSNET was similar to the ARPANET. It was a large internetwork developed to provide connectivity to the nation's computer science community. The development of CSNET was grounded in the restricted use of the ARPANET. Owned by the Department of Defense, ARPANET's use was prohibited by anyone outside the defense community. In an effort to increase collaboration among the nation's computer scientists, the National Science Foundation (NSF) funded CSNET. Recognizing that the most popular ARPANET service was e-mail, the developers of CSNET initially thought an e-mail-only-based network could be developed to connect academic and research institutions that did not have access to ARPANET. CSNET eventually evolved into a *metanetwork*—it consisted of several different physical networks logically designed to serve one community. Connectivity to CSNET was via a centralized machine called CSNET-RELAY, and connectivity to CSNET-RELAY was via other networks. These included a public packet-switching network called X.25NET, a dialup network called Phonenet, and the ARPANET. CSNET provided its users with Internet-type services such as e-mail, member registry, and domain name service (DNS). Other services such as file transfer and remote logins were also available on some parts of CSNET. CSNET, BITNET, and CREN have since disbanded now that Internet access is easily attainable.

UUCP The UUCP network is a global network of interconnected UNIX machines. Standard telephone lines serve as the medium for connectivity, and the network is based on the store-and-forward principle (Figure 8.1). Using a suite of programs known as UUCP (UNIX-to-UNIX Copy), users can exchange e-mail and network news (also called Usenet news). Given its minimal requirements (UNIX machine, modem, and telephone connection) and relatively inexpensive nature, the UUCP network grew quickly throughout the world and is still in existence today.

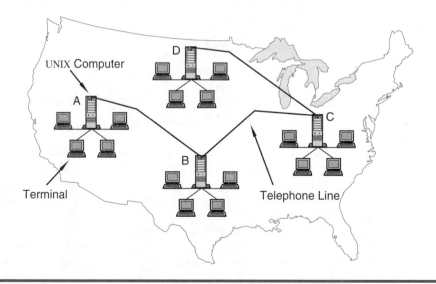

FIGURE 8.1 An example of a nationwide UUCP network. A message from host A to host D would first be transferred to host B, then to host C, and finally to host D.

NSFNET

Around 1983, the academic and research science community convinced Congress that the United States had to meet the Japanese supercomputing challenge. This challenge was a product of the Japanese government, which committed itself to a national goal of developing a computer capable of displaying common sense, possessing a general knowledge about how the world works, having insight into human nature, having a vocabulary of 10,000 words, and speaking and understanding English and Japanese, all by the end of the 1980s. In the United States, Japan's national goal was perceived as analogous to the United States' national goal of the 1960s of putting a man on the moon and returning him safely to earth by the end of that decade. Suffice it to say, the Japanese supercomputing challenge was taken very seriously in the United States.

In responding to the Japanese challenge, Congress authorized the National Science Foundation to fund the construction and operation of U.S. supercomputer centers. By the end of 1985, six such centers were established throughout the country. These centers also were connected to the ARPANET, which had by then (1984) split into two separate networks: ARPANET, for nonmilitary and research purposes, and MILNET, an unclassified military network. The supercomputer center network and the ARPANET were interconnected at Carnegie-Mellon University (CMU) in Pittsburgh, Pennsylvania. Thus, network traffic originating at any of the supercomputer centers and destined for the ARPANET (or vice versa) was first sent to CMU and then transferred to the local ARPANET node (Figure 8.2).

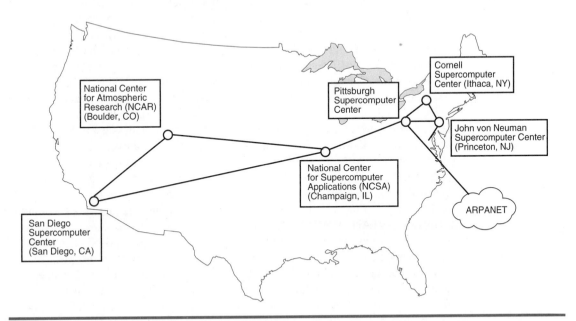

FIGURE 8.2 The National Science Foundation's supercomputer network. This network interconnected the six NSF-funded supercomputer centers. The network also was interconnected to the ARPANET through a node at Carnegie-Mellon University in Pittsburgh.

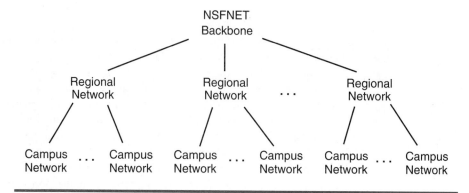

FIGURE 8.3 The NSFNET hierarchy.

With a supercomputer center network in place, the next issue was to provide researchers with direct and convenient electronic access to these centers from researchers' home institutions. To meet this challenge, NSF began funding in 1986 the development of a national "backbone" network. Eventually, a three-level or tiered network evolved consisting of a backbone network, several regional or midlevel networks, and local area networks of colleges and universities (Figure 8.3). The regional networks were organized geographically either by state or region. For example, NYSERnet—New York State Educational Research Network—serviced New York State, and SURAnet—Southeastern Universities Research Association Network—serviced the southeastern part of the country. Thus, the backbone provided connectivity to the regional networks, which in turn provided connectivity to campus LANs (Figure 8.4). The first two levels of this network (the national backbone and the regional networks) became known as the *National Science Foundation Network* (NSFNET) and was a model for interconnecting independent and autonomous networks. Initially, the NSFNET backbone was based on 56-kbps leased circuits. From 1989 to 1992, the backbone was reconfigured twice to handle increasing traffic loads. This reconfiguration included adding new circuits, deleting others, and increasing the backbone's bandwidth—first to T1 (1.5 Mbps) and then to T3 (45 Mbps). The T3 backbone is shown in Figure 8.5.

During the 1980s, other government organizations such as the Department of Energy (DoE) and the National Aeronautics and Space Administration (NASA) also began developing their own private networks. These networks interconnected the NSFNET. Eventually, all of these government-sponsored networks, including NSFNET, ARPANET, MILNET, and SPAN (the Space Physics Analysis Network), became known as the Internet. Although the Internet was comprised of many different networks, the NSFNET was perceived as *the* Internet by many people. This perception was grounded in the NSFNET's national presence and by its open-door policy to any research or educational organization. In fact, through its networking infrastructure program, the National Science Foundation provided funding to any college or university that wanted to connect its LAN to the NSFNET. Funds were used to purchase hardware and pay for high-speed line charges related to a school's NSFNET connection.

A modified version of this program exists today and extends to K-12 schools.

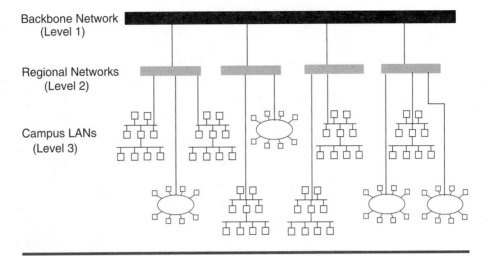

FIGURE 8.4 Example of the three levels of networks that evolved from the National Science Foundation's networking initiative. The first two levels made up NSFNET.

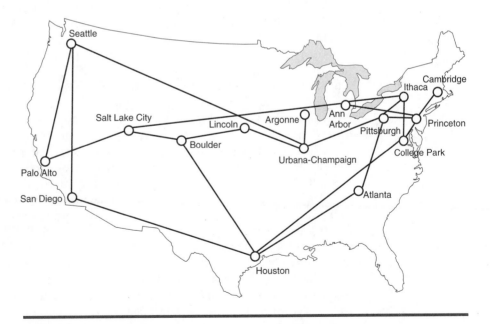

FIGURE 8.5 The T3 NSFNET backbone, circa 1992–1993.

A Commercial Internet

As NSFNET became more popular, the business community quickly took notice and re-alized there was money to be made from it. Connectivity to the NSFNET backbone, however, was governed by NSF's Acceptable Use Policy, which—although usually ig-nored and often broadly interpreted—restricted the use of the NSFNET backbone to ed-ucational or research activities. This meant that the NSFNET could not be used for commercial purposes. In response to this policy, the *Commercial Internet Exchange* (CIX) was born in the early 1990s to meet the emerging connectivity needs of the com-mercial market. CIX was a subscription organization that consisted of a consortium of commercial and nonprofit regional network providers that started offering Internet ser-vice independent of the NSFNET backbone and without NSF's restriction on traffic type. It established a national backbone comprised of different telephone carriers (e.g., Sprint, MCI) and interconnected the NSFNET backbone at selected points. Thus, com-mercial Internet traffic might start at a local organization, travel through various re-gional providers, get routed to a CIX node, and then get transferred to another CIX provider without ever crossing the NSFNET backbone.

During the early to mid-1990s, a commercial Internet began to take shape consist-ing of "20% bottom-line" people instead of research or educational visionaries. Dur-ing this period, private Internet service provider (ISP) businesses were started by entrepreneurs who recognized the growing demand for Internet access by both the general public and the business community. ISPs ranged from small "mom and pop" operations that provided connectivity to a specific locale to regional or state provid-ers to national and international providers. The source of connectivity for these ISPs was the backbones developed by the major long-distance telephone carriers—Sprint, AT&T, and MCI—which all operated their own private national networks indepen-dent of NSF access restrictions.

In 1990, ARPANET was decommissioned, and the level of commercialization of the Internet led the National Science Foundation to remove the NSFNET backbone from active service on April 30, 1995. This latter action, however, did not occur without con-siderable forethought. For example, in May 1993, two years prior to NSFNET's retire-ment, NSF solicited proposals to design a new infrastructure capable of serving the needs of not only government, research, and educational organizations, but also those of the commercial user and general public. Furthermore, NSF maintained its commit-ment to the educational and research communities that comprised NSFNET by subsi-dizing the regional network providers' connections to a commercial network service provider. This support ended in 1999. Most of the regional providers selected MCI as their primary carrier; the remaining few chose Sprint or ANS, which was purchased by America Online in 1995. Today, network traffic such as e-mail, Web browsing, and file transfers is carried by commercial providers; the former regional NSFNET networks now receive connectivity through commercial network service providers; and NSF-NET's three-tiered hierarchical national backbone has been supplanted with several in-dependent backbones that interconnect at specially designated exchange points (more on this later) where ISPs meet and distribute traffic (Figure 8.6).

Summarizing its history, over the past 30 years, the Internet has evolved from a U.S. Department of Defense network research project (ARPANET) to an NSF-subsidized educational and research data communications medium for university, government, and

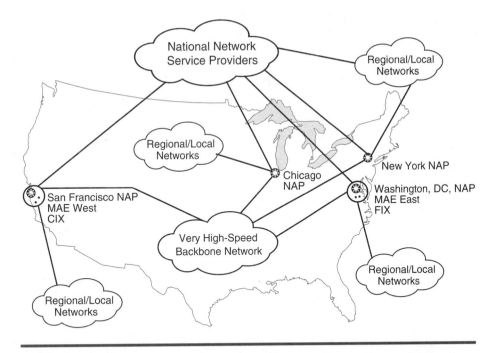

FIGURE 8.6 The new national network infrastructure consists of a "private" very high-speed backbone network service funded by NSF, several independent commercial backbones operated by network service providers such as Sprint, MCI WorldCom, and AT&T, and various interconnection centers where traffic from network providers is exchanged. Network service providers also interconnect the former NSFNET regional networks and thousands of smaller networks operated by independent Internet service providers (ISPs), which provide businesses, schools, and individual users access to the Internet.

Various network connectivity maps are available from ftp://ftp.cs. wisc.edu/ connectivity_ table/

research personnel (NSFNET) to a commercial, global network linking tens of millions of consumers, businesses, schools, and other organizations. Today, nearly every country in the world has some form of Internet connection. Initially, the ARPANET was the Internet. NSF then entered the picture, and the Internet was perceived as a collection of various networks anchored by NSFNET. Today, both ARPANET and NSFNET have given way to a commercially flavored Internet that is transforming the Internet from its roots as a collection of networks to a global network of communities.

The Current Public Internet

As noted earlier and illustrated in Figure 8.6, the Internet's infrastructure comprises numerous backbones operated by national, regional, and local Internet service providers. The major national backbones are high-speed networks owned by telecommunications organizations such as Sprint, AT&T, and WorldCom. Regional backbones are generally owned by regional Bell operating companies (RBOCs) such as BellSouth and Verizon (formerly Bell Atlantic) or by newly formed competitive local exchange carriers (CLECs). (See Chapter 1 for additional information about RBOCs and CLECs.) Local backbones are typically operated by small, independent Internet service providers (ISPs) or by CLECs. The major backbone providers (sometimes called Tier 1 ISPs) provide access to regional and local ISPs; many regional providers also provide access to local ISPs.

Given the multitude of independent backbones, the Internet relies on network access points (NAPs) and a routing arbiter for interregional connectivity. *Network access points* are special high-speed Internet exchange points (IXPs) or "switching stations" where different network backbone providers meet and exchange traffic on each other's backbone. This is where the individual networks comprising the Internet join together. NAPs conceptually represent the "Inter" part of the Internet. For example, if you have an Internet account from an ISP whose network connects to AT&T's backbone and your next-door neighbor receives Internet service from an ISP whose network connects to BellSouth's backbone, then an e-mail message sent from you to your neighbor (or vice versa) is exchanged at a NAP. To facilitate this traffic exchange, a *routing arbiter* maintains special servers that contain routing information databases of network routes (i.e., electronic road maps). Thus, the routing arbiter enables traffic entering a NAP from one backbone to be routed to the correct destination backbone.

Initially, the National Science Foundation funded four NAPs in the United States, one each in New York, Chicago, Washington, DC, and San Francisco. These NAPs are operated respectively by Sprint, Ameritech Advanced Data Services (AADS), Metropolitan Fiber Systems (MFS), and Pacific Bell. Augmenting the four official NAPS are additional de facto NAPs, IXPs, and private and public exchange points. These include seven *metropolitan area exchange* (MAE) points, which are located in Vienna, VA (MAE-East), San Jose, CA (MAE-West), Dallas (MAE-Dallas), Houston (MAE-Houston), Los Angeles (MAE-LA), Chicago (MAE-Chicago), and New York (MAE-NY). There is also the commercial Internet exchange (CIX) in Santa Clara, CA, as well as two federal IXPs, FIX-East in College Park, MD, and FIX-West in Ames Research Center in Mountain View, CA. Finally, another NAP, the Florida MIX (Multimedia Internet Exchange), will be established in south Florida and operated by BellSouth by the end of 2000 or early 2001. Most national service providers maintain connections to the four official NAPs and to most of the MAEs. Unlike the NSF-funded NAPs, where traffic exchanges flow freely among all connected backbones, however, other IXPs usually require peering agreements among the ISPs that connect to their sites. Thus, two backbones that connect to MAE-LA, for example, do not exchange traffic with each other unless they have a peering arrangement. Establishing a peering agreement generally involves negotiation and technical cooperation to enable the two ISP networks to exchange traffic. Finally, outside the United States, NAPs are located in several parts of the world, including London, Amsterdam, Paris, Tokyo, and Hong Kong.

Additional information about Internet exchange points is available at http://www.mfst.com/MAE/doc/MAE.doc and http://www.ispworld.com Another excellent site is Mapnet, which provides an interactive tool for visualizing the Internet's infrastructure of multiple backbones simultaneously. It is located at http://www.caida.org/tools/visualization/mapnet/backbones Once at this site, you can view the Internet's backbone infrastructure from the world, USA, Asian, and European perspectives. You can also select the type of backbone to view—commercial or research.

Other Internet Backbone Initiatives

In addition to the current public Internet, several additional Internet backbone initiatives have been developed. These include the very high performance Backbone Network Service + (vBNS+), Internet2, the Next Generation Internet (NGI), and the National Information Infrastructure (NII).

vBNS+   The *very high performance Backbone Network Service* + originated as another NSF-funded research and educational network. The contract to develop and operate this network was awarded by NSF to MCI WorldCom in 1995. When initially developed, the network was called the very high performance Backbone Network Service (without the +) and provided researchers with an appropriate testbed-research environment for deploying and evaluating new high-speed internetworking technologies. The original vBNS also maintained a strict usage policy: Access to the vBNS was restricted to only those organizations that received NSF awards under NSF's High Performance Computing and Communications (HPCC) program. This enabled researchers to develop and test new network technologies on a national scale without the frequent congestion and other inherent problems of the public Internet.

On April 1, 2000, vBNS officially became vBNS+. The transition from vBNS to vBNS+ was more than a name change, though. vBNS+ represents a new network. Unlike the original vBNS OC-12 (622 Mbps) ATM backbone, the vBNS+ backbone technology is packet over SONET. Furthermore, vBNS+ is comprised of multiple links running at OC-48 (2.4 Gbps) speed. For an average size packet of 300 bytes, the throughput rate of these links (i.e., the available bandwidth for the packet's payload) is 2072 Mbps. vBNS+ also provides access to the public Internet—something its predecessor did not—and does not have a restricted access policy. Today, vBNS+ service is open to the entire U.S. higher education community, which enables university faculty and researchers across the country to have access to many of the high-performance networking applications that were only available to NSF HPCC program awardees through vBNS. Some of the services available from vBNS+ include native IP multicasting, quality of service (QoS), virtual private network (VPN) services, IPv6 native service, and (the obvious) high-bandwidth throughput with negligible loss. Ongoing research and testing activities supported by vBNS+ include IPv6-enabled wireless networking, IP telephony, high-bandwidth multicast, and wire speed security filtering. Finally, vBNS+ is a support service for Internet2 and Next Generation Internet (NGI) initiatives (see below). See `http://www.vbnsplus.net` for additional information about vBNS+.

Internet2 *Internet2* is a not-for-profit consortium led by the University Corporation for Advanced Internet Development (UCAID). It comprises over 170 U.S. universities, government organizations, and private sector firms. Internet2's mission is to develop and deploy advanced network technologies and applications that support the research endeavors of colleges and universities. Internet2 members use vBNS+ to test and advance their research. Although implicit in its name, Internet2 is not a separate network and will not replace the current Internet. It is simply a collaborative project involving academia, industry, and government. Additional information about Internet2 can be found at `http://www.internet2.edu`

NGI The *Next Generation Internet* initiative, announced by President Bill Clinton in 1996, is a research and development (R&D) program for designing and testing advanced network technologies and applications. This initiative's mission is also to forge collaborative partnerships between the private and public sectors. As stated earlier, the vBNS+ serves as the medium for NGI. Unlike Internet2, which is university led, NGI is federally led. Nevertheless, the two initiatives are engaged in parallel and complementary work. Additional information about NGI can be found at `http://www.ngi.gov`

NII   The *National Information Infrastructure* is a federal policy initiative to facilitate and accelerate the development and utilization of the nation's information infrastructure. The perception of the NII is one of a "seamless web" of telecommunications networks consisting of computers, specialized databases, radios, telephones, televisions, and satellites. The NII is expected to provide consumers with convenient and instantaneous access to nearly any kind of information ranging from research results to medical and educational material to entertainment.

8.3   Internet Administration

Governance and Organization

The governance and administration of the Internet are overseen by various organizations composed mostly of volunteers from the global Internet community. These organizations consist of the Internet Society (ISOC), the Internet Architecture Board, the Internet Engineering Task Force, and the Internet Research Task Force. The administrative organizational structure of the Internet is shown in Figure 8.7.

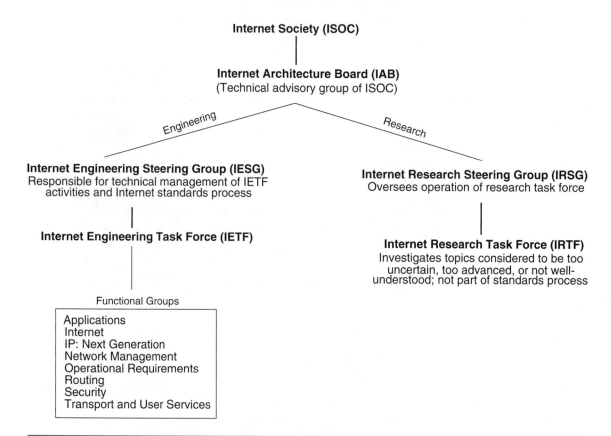

FIGURE 8.7   The administrative organizational structure of the Internet.

The *Internet Architecture Board* (IAB), formerly known as the Internet Activities Board, is responsible for the overall planning and designing of the Internet. Some of its responsibilities include setting Internet standards, managing the publication of RFC documents (discussed later), and resolving technical issues. Assigned to the IAB are the *Internet Engineering Task Force* (IETF) and the *Internet Research Task Force* (IRTF). IETF is primarily concerned with addressing short- or medium-term Internet engineering issues. For example, IETF was responsible for examining the design and implementation of a new Internet Protocol, IPv6 (discussed later), the Open Shortest Path First (OSPF) routing scheme (see Chapter 7), and other initiatives such as enabling TCP/IP to support multimedia more efficiently. IRTF works on long-term research projects. An example of its work is the e-mail privacy issue. Both task forces also have steering committees that prioritize and coordinate their respective activities. IETF's steering committee is the Internet Engineering Steering Group (IESG), and IRTF's steering committee is the Internet Research Steering Group (IRSG). The ultimate authority of the Internet is the *Internet Society* (ISOC), an international organization comprised of volunteers who promote the Internet as a medium for global communication and collaboration. ISOC publishes a newsletter called *Internet Society News,* which provides its readers with information surrounding the administration and evolution of the Internet. More information about these organizations can be obtained from their Web sites: ISOC (`http://www.isoc.org`); IAB (`http://www.iab.org/iab`); IETF (`http://www.ietf.org`); and IRTF (`www.irtf.org`)

Standards Development

Internet standards are initially developed by IETF, reviewed by IESG, and ultimately approved by the IAB. Throughout the standards development process, *Request for Comments* (RFCs) are prepared by the RFC editor. RFCs, which address various aspects of a particular protocol under consideration, generally contain technical information about a protocol, but they can provide nontechnical information as well. Although the International Organization for Standardization (ISO; see Chapter 2) promotes approved Internet standards internationally and may also take information from RFCs in developing their own ISO approved standards, RFCs never become international standards.

Nearly all of the information about the Internet's history and its protocols is contained in RFCs. They are the working notes of the Internet research and development community. They provide network researchers and designers with a medium for documenting and sharing new ideas, network protocol concepts, and other technically related information. They contain meeting notes from Internet organizations, describe various Internet protocols and experiments, and detail standards specifications.

RFCs presently comprise two subseries: for your information (FYI) documents and standards (STDs) documents. FYIs provide information about Internet-related topics but in a less technical manner; STDs identify RFCs that specify Internet standards. Consequently, all Internet standards are published as RFCs, but not all RFCs are Internet standards. In addition to RFCs are Internet drafts, which are working documents of the IETF. Internet drafts enable the Internet community to read and comment on proposed Internet-related documents before they are officially published as an RFC. Internet drafts are considered temporary documents and have a shelf life of only 6 months. To facilitate the dissemination process, and to maintain a spirit of openness, RFCs and FYIs are available on-line at `http://www.rfceditor.org`. There are presently nearly 3000 RFCs ranging from the serious to the not so serious. Two less serious RFCs written during the Christmas season are RFC 968, "'Twas the Night Before Start-up," written by Vint Cerf in 1985 (Cerf is widely known as the Father of the Internet) and RFC 1882, "The 12 Days of Technology Before Christmas," written in 1995 by Bill Hancock, one of the authors of this book. For more information about the Internet standards process, see RFC 2026, "The Internet Standards Process—Revision 3."

Internet Security

(The subject of network security, including types of attacks, hardware strategies for dealing with these attacks, and security-related protocols such as IP Security, or IP-Sec, is discussed in Chapter 17.) Given the different Internet services and resources available today, Internet security is undoubtedly of paramount concern for users. Unfortunately, the TCP/IP protocol suite was not initially designed with security in mind. This was not an oversight on the part of the original designers of TCP/IP. Remember that TCP/IP was initially developed to serve the research and academic communities to facilitate the exchange of research and scholarly activities. Inherent in this academic endeavor was a presumption of trust and honesty. Also, many of the compromises of TCP/IP protocols today were not anticipated by the TCP/IP designers 25 years ago. The first major security breach of the Internet occurred on November 2–3, 1988, when a student exploited a security "hole" in the Simple Mail Transfer Protocol (SMTP). Now known as the "Worm incident," many of the computers connected to NSFNET at that time were affected and rendered useless. Since then, there have been many attempts (some successful, some not) to exploit known weaknesses in other TCP/IP protocols. There also is no shortage to the number of individuals who have nothing better to do than search for creative ways to compromise a system.

In response to these attacks, several approaches are available. The easiest thing to do is not connect a system or network containing critical data to the Internet. A second strategy is to encrypt sensitive data prior to transmission across the network. A third approach is to install filters on routers that either deny or permit certain traffic to enter your network. Alternatively, special purpose firewall devices that serve as buffers can also be installed between your network and the outside world. On the protocol front, there is Secure HTTP (https) for protecting Web transactions, e-mail security is available via Secure MIME (S/MIME) and Pretty Good Privacy (PGP), and several protocols have been developed to help secure VPNs, including the Point-to-Point Tunneling Protocol (PPTP), Layer 2 Forwarding (L2F), Layer 2 Tunneling Protocol (L2TP), and IP Security (IPSec). All are discussed in Chapter 17. It should also be noted that all the hardware or protocol software-based protection in the world can easily be undermined by irresponsible users. As a result, it is important that organizations establish and enforce network security and acceptable use policies, educate users about network security issues, and employ common-sense practices such as not giving unauthorized people your password. (See Box 17.3 for additional suggestions.) Finally, several resources are available on-line that are specifically geared to

Internet security. The best place to begin is the Computer Emergency Response Team (CERT), located at `http://www.cert.org`. Another location is the SANS (System Administration, Networking, and Security) Institute Web site at `www.sans.org`. Especially noteworthy is SANS' "Consensus List of the Top Internet Security Threats" (`www.sans.org/topten.htm`).

8.4   What Is TCP/IP?

A Brief History

TCP/IP, which stands for *Transmission Control Protocol/Internet Protocol,* is a formal protocol suite that is primarily based on two subprotocols: TCP, an OSI layer-4 protocol, and IP, an OSI layer-3 protocol. TCP/IP's history is tied to the development of the ARPANET, which initially was based on a protocol called the *Network Control Protocol* (NCP). The ARPANET's original design was grounded in two fundamental principles: The physical network was assumed not to be completely reliable, and network protocols could not be dependent on any proprietary hardware or software. The presumption of a completely unreliable network might seem a little odd at first. However, the ARPANET was a Department of Defense project and, thus, accepted the reality that the physical network could be disrupted by a catastrophic event. This spurred TCP/IP's development. The nonproprietary principle, coupled with the success of the early ARPANET, led to TCP/IP becoming available on a wide variety of hardware and software platforms.

Helping in the development of TCP/IP were Vint Cerf and Robert Kahn. In the early 1970s, both Cerf and Kahn, as part of an ARPA internetworking research program, developed the idea of gateways and wrote the first specification for the basic TCP/IP protocols now used in the Internet. The idea behind the development of TCP/IP was to enable different packet networks to be interconnected so the host computers did not have to know anything about the intermediate networks linking them together. By 1982, ARPA established TCP/IP as the protocol suite for ARPANET, and the Department of Defense declared them standards for military use. This led to one of the first definitions of an internet as a connected set of networks, specifically those using TCP/IP, and "Internet" as connected TCP/IP internets. The idea behind the Internet was the seamless linking of many different kinds of packet-switched networks. This was facilitated by the robustness of TCP/IP, which enabled data communications across analog lines, packet radios, satellite links, Ethernet networks, and others.

As the ARPANET grew in the 1980s, so did computer networking. The popularity of computer networks was helped in part by the proliferation of individual computers and workstations—users wanted to connect their systems together. Recognizing the potential of a large marketplace, networking's popularity quickly led to the development of several proprietary networking protocols. This in turn also led to problems of interoperability. Within a closed, homogeneous networking environment (e.g., DECnet or SNA), interoperability was not an issue because all networked devices spoke the same language. This was not the case, however, in a heterogeneous or mixed-vendor environment.

Vinton G. Cerf

Vinton G. Cerf is widely known as a Father of the Internet. Cerf initially became involved with the development of the Internet when, as a graduate student at UCLA from 1967–1972, he was part of a team that worked on one component of the U.S. Department of Defense Advanced Research Projects Agency's (DARPA) packet-switching network project, ARPANET. After completing his doctorate in 1972, Cerf became an assistant professor in computer science and electrical engineering at Stanford University.

While at Stanford in 1973, Cerf reestablished his earlier collaborative relationship with Robert Kahn, the primary architect of the ARPANET. Kahn, who was employed by Stanford Research Institute (SRI) at the time, was working together with personnel from Bolt, Baranek, and Newman and Collins Radio on another DARPA research endeavor. Called the "Internetting project," this new research program was designed to interconnect different types of packet networks. These included a packet radio network for mobile networking, a global packet satellite system that was based on the earlier work of Norman Abramson and the University of Hawaii's ALOHA network, and the ARPANET. Critical to the project's success was making the underlying network technology transparent to the host computers that were communicating across the multiple packet networks. Cerf and Kahn ultimately developed the idea of gateways and co-wrote the first specification of the Transmission Control Protocol in 1974. Cerf and Kahn's original TCP design did not distinguish between TCP and IP, however, and after various trials, the two protocols became separate. The collection of networks that emerged from this project became known as the Internet, and the set of communication protocols developed as part of the project was denoted the TCP/IP protocol suite, named after the project's two primary protocols.

Cerf eventually left his teaching position at Stanford and joined DARPA in 1976, where he stayed until 1982. During his tenure at DARPA, Cerf played a key role leading the development of Internet and Internet-related data packet and security technologies. From 1982 to 1986, he was vice president of MCI Corporations' (now MCI WorldCom) Digital Information Services, where he was the chief engineer of MCI Mail, which was one of the first commercial electronic mail services. Later, Cerf served as vice president of the Corporation for National Research Initiatives (CNRI), but then rejoined MCI in 1994. He was also the founder of the Internet Society and served as the society's president from 1992–1995. Cerf is currently WorldCom's senior vice president for Internet architecture and technology and is responsible for the design and development of the network architecture to support WorldCom's advanced Internet frameworks for delivering

Vinton G. Cerf (continued)

a combination of data, information, voice, and video services for business and consumer use. He is also a distinguished visiting scientist at the Jet Propulsion Laboratory, where he is working on the design of an interplanetary Internet.

Cerf has a BS in mathematics from Stanford University and an MS and PhD in computer science from UCLA. He is a fellow of the Institute of Electrical and Electronic Engineers (IEEE), the Association for Computing (ACM), the American Association for Advancement of Science (AAAS), and the American Academy of Arts and Sciences. Cerf is also the recipient of numerous awards and commendations, including the Marconi Fellowship, the Alexander Graham Bell Award presented by the Alexander Graham Bell Association for the Deaf, the NEC Computer and Communications Prize, the Silver Medal of the International Telecommunications Union (ITU), the IEEE Alexander Graham Bell Medal, the IEEE Koji Kobayashi Award, the ACM Software and Systems Award, the ACM SIGCOMM Award, the Computer and Communications Industries Association Industry Legend Award, the Yuri Rubinsky Web Award, the Kilby Award, the Yankee Group/Interop/Network World Lifetime Achievement Award, the George R. Stibitz Award, the Werner Wolter Award, and the Library of Congress Bicentennial Living Legend medal.

Around this same time, the University of California at Berkeley's Computer Science Department was enhancing the original version of the UNIX operating system. Called BSD UNIX, one of its new features was the incorporation of the TCP/IP protocol suite. This software was freely available and soon became quite popular at universities throughout the country. Given that TCP/IP was bundled with UNIX, and that TCP/IP was being used successfully in a real-time network (ARPANET), the National Science Foundation mandated that all NSF-funded supercomputer centers and computer networks that comprised NSFNET use TCP/IP as their network communications protocol. NSF's mandate essentially established TCP/IP as a de facto standard.

The TCP/IP Model versus the OSI Model

TCP/IP's development preceded the OSI model (see Chapter 2) by several years. Both had similar design goals, however: to fill a need for interoperability among heterogeneous computer systems. Unlike OSI, TCP/IP was never intended to be an international standard. It was developed to satisfy the need to interconnect various U.S. Department of Defense projects, including computer networks, and to allow for the addition of dissimilar machines to the networks in a systematic, standardized manner. As a pre-OSI protocol architecture, TCP/IP was not designed specifically with layers the way the OSI model was designed, and it does not fit neatly into the seven layers of the OSI model. However, we can conceptualize TCP/IP's layers as being similar to the OSI layers because many of TCP/IP's functions are similar to those of

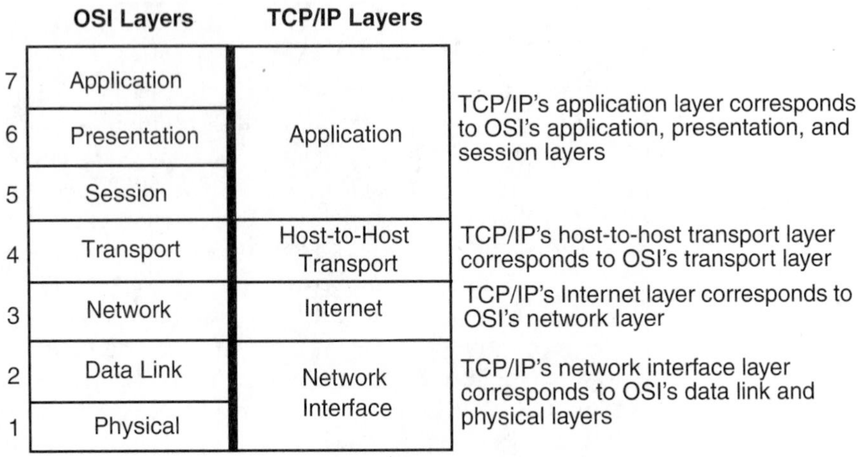

OSI Layers		TCP/IP Layers	
7	Application	Application	TCP/IP's application layer corresponds to OSI's application, presentation, and session layers
6	Presentation		
5	Session		
4	Transport	Host-to-Host Transport	TCP/IP's host-to-host transport layer corresponds to OSI's transport layer
3	Network	Internet	TCP/IP's Internet layer corresponds to OSI's network layer
2	Data Link	Network Interface	TCP/IP's network interface layer corresponds to OSI's data link and physical layers
1	Physical		

FIGURE 8.8 A comparison of the OSI and TCP/IP layers.

A five-layered TCP/IP model maintains OSI's physical and data link layers as separate levels instead of combining them into a single layer as shown in Figure 8.8. In this scenario, TCP/IP's first layer is called the physical layer and its second layer is called the network access layer.

the OSI model. Although there is no universal agreement on the description of TCP/IP as a layered model, it is usually described as either a four- or five-layered model depending on an author's perspective. For our purposes, we elect to describe TCP/IP as a four-layered architecture, as shown in Figure 8.8.

TCP/IP's layers are similar to OSI's layers in terms of the functions and services they provide. The TCP/IP *application layer* serves as the communication interface for users by providing specific application services to the user such as remote terminal login (i.e., virtual terminal), file transfer, and e-mail. Corresponding application protocols include Telnet, FTP, and SMTP. The TCP/IP *host-to-host transport layer* (known simply as the *transport layer*) is responsible for end-to-end data delivery. This layer is defined by two protocols: the *Transmission Control Protocol* (TCP) and *User Datagram Protocol* (UDP). Both protocols are described in the next section. The TCP/IP *Internet layer* (also called the *network layer*) transfers user messages from a source host to a destination host. The heart and soul of this layer is the *Internet Protocol,* which is the IP of TCP/IP. IP is a connectionless datagram service responsible for routing packets between nodes. In short, IP receives data bits from the lower layer, assembles the bits into packets (IP datagrams), and selects the "best" route based on some *metric.* (Recall from Chapter 1 that a metric is a description of the "cost" of a route used by routing hardware and software to select the best possible route.) The TCP/IP *network interface layer* connects a host to the local network hardware. Its functions include making a connection to the physical medium, using a specific protocol for accessing the medium, and segmenting data into frames. It effectively performs all of the functions of the first two layers of the OSI model. A summary description of the TCP/IP model is given in Figures 8.9 and 8.10.

Application (4)
- Similar to OSI application layer.
- Serves as communication interface by providing specific application services.
- Examples include e-mail, virtual terminal, file transfer, WWW.

Transport (3)
- Defined by two protocols:

User Datagram Protocol (UDP)
- Is a connectionless protocol.
- Provides unreliable datagram service (no end-to-end error detection or correction).
- Does not retransmit any unreceived data.
- Requires little overhead.
- Application protocols include Trivial File Transfer Protocol (TFTP), NFS, Simple Network Management Protocol (SNMP), Bootstrap Protocol (BOOTP), and Domain Name Service (DNS).

Transmission Control Protocol (TCP)
- This is the TCP of TCP/IP.
- Is a connection-oriented protocol.
- Provides reliable data transmission via end-to-end error detection and correction.
- Guarantees data are transferred across a network accurately and in proper order.
- Retransmits any data not received by destination node.
- Guarantees against data duplication between sending and receiving nodes.
- Application protocols include Telnet, FTP, SMTP, and POP.

Internet (2)
- Heart and soul is Internet Protocol (IP)—the IP of TCP/IP.
- Transfers user messages from source host to destination host.
- Is a connectionless datagram service.
- Route selection is based on some metric.
- Uses Internet or IP addresses as a road map to locate a host within the Internet.
- Relies on routers or switches (dedicated nodes that connect two or more dissimilar networks).
- Integral part is Internet Control Message Protocol (ICMP), which uses an IP datagram to carry messages about state of communications environment.

Network Interface (1)
- Connects a host to the local network hardware.
- Makes a connection to the physical medium.
- Uses a specific protocol for accessing the medium.
- Places data into frames.
- Effectively performs all functions of the first two layers of the OSI model.

FIGURE 8.9 Summary of the TCP/IP layers and functions.

OSI Layers		Included Protocols		TCP/IP Layers
7	Application	SNMP TFTP	FTP Telnet	Application
6	Presentation	NFS DNS	Finger SMTP	
5	Session	BOOTP	POP	
4	Transport	UDP	TCP	Host-to-Host Transport
3	Network	IP		Internet
2	Data Link	Network Interface Cards		Network Interface
1	Physical	Transmission Media		

FIGURE 8.10 A third comparison of the OSI and TCP/IP layers. Source: adapted from Miller, 1992.

8.5 TCP/IP's Transport and Network Layer Protocols

As can be seen from Figures 8.9 and 8.10, the TCP/IP protocol suite defines two different transport layer protocols: the *User Datagram Protocol* (UDP) and the *Transport Control Protocol* (TCP), and one network layer protocol, namely, the *Internet Protocol* (IP). Prior to discussing UDP, TCP, and IP, we first provide an overview of how TCP/IP's four layers interoperate relative to these three protocols. This overview, which was initially introduced in Chapter 2 as part of our discussion on connectionless and connection-oriented services, is presented from the perspective of transferring a data message from one node to another across the Internet. It is repeated here with greater emphasis on the concepts of port numbers and data encapsulation among TCP/IP's layers.

Additional information about UDP and TCP can be found in the RFCs at http:// www.rfceditor. org

Overview of Internet-Based Communications and the Role of UDP, TCP, IP, and Port Numbers

To send a message from one node to another across the Internet, three different addresses are needed: the MAC sublayer address (also know as the hardware address), the network address (in this case, the IP address), and the port address. The hardware address uniquely identifies a node on a network, the IP address specifies the network the node is connected to, and the port address uniquely identifies the specific application protocol or process (e.g., e-mail) that produced the data message. (Hardware and network addresses were discussed in Chapters 5 and 7, respectively. IP addresses are also discussed in greater detail later in this chapter.) This leaves port addresses. Port addresses, which are also known as *well-known port numbers* or *well-known services,* identify the specific process or application a user accesses on a host. Port numbers are two bytes long and are standardized according to the application protocol. For example, the two popular e-mail protocols, the Simple Mail Transfer Protocol (SMTP) and the Post Office Protocol, Version 3 (POP3), are assigned port numbers 25 and 110, respectively. Other examples include telnet (port 23), domain name server (port 53), finger (port 79), and http (port 80).

RFC 1700 also contains a listing of registered port numbers, which are not controlled by IANA. These numbers, which are in the range of 1024–65535, are available for use by the general user.

Well-known port numbers are controlled by the Internet Assigned Numbers Authority (IANA). Furthermore, RFC 1700, "Assigned Numbers," contains a complete listing of all well-known ports used in the Internet, and the /etc/services file on UNIX systems contains a list of well-known ports as well. Whenever possible, the same port assignments are used with both UDP and TCP. Standardized port numbers originally ranged from 0–255, but were expanded to 0–1023 in 1994. A sample of well-known port numbers is provided in Table 8.1.

Port numbers are contained within the UDP or TCP header, which is generated at TCP/IP's transport layer and corresponds to layer 4 of the OSI model (see Figure 8.10). Thus, a data message is first created on the sending machine at TCP/IP's application layer (OSI layers 5–7) by a specific application protocol. This data message is passed to TCP/IP's transport layer (OSI layer 4) and encapsulated into either a UDP or TCP header, which includes the port address that identifies the application or process that created the message. (Note that the application determines whether UDP or TCP will be used.) The resulting UDP or TCP data structure is then passed to TCP/IP's Internet layer (OSI layer 3) and encapsulated into an IP header, which contains the network address that identifies the network and host running the specified application or process. Finally, the IP datagram is passed to TCP/IP's network interface layer (OSI layers 1–2), encapsulated into a data frame that contains the hardware address of the destination machine on the remote network (recall from Chapters 5 and 6 that hardware addresses are "burned" into NICs), and then placed on the medium for transmission. A summary of this process is shown in Figure 8.11. UDP's and TCP's role in this transfer process is a function of the type of transport service being provided. UDP provides connectionless service; TCP provides connection-oriented service. With this overview in mind, let's now focus our attention on the three primary protocols involved in this data encapsulation description. We begin with UDP and TCP.

The User Datagram Protocol (UDP)

UDP is a connectionless protocol that provides an unreliable datagram service. It does not furnish any end-to-end error detection or correction, it does not retransmit any data it did not receive, and it has no ability to perform error or flow control. This implies that all UDP-based application programs must bear the onus of providing a mechanism for error and flow control and for recovering from lost packets. In short, all data reliability and integrity issues fall to the application programs that use UDP. This makes UDP faster than TCP in performance when the network is not congested because it carries less overhead than TCP. However, when the network is congested, UDP-based applications will most likely result in session time outs and poor performance. Application protocols based on UDP include the Trivial File Transfer Protocol (TFTP), Network File

TABLE 8.1 A Sample of Well-Known Port Numbers (Extracted from RFC 1700)

Decimal/Protocol	Keyword	Description
0/TCP		Reserved
0/UDP		Reserved
5/TCP	RJE	Remote Job Entry
5/UDP	RJE	Remote Job Entry
7/TCP	ECHO	Echo
7/UDP	ECHO	Echo
9/TCP	DISCARD	Discard
9/UDP	DISCARD	Discard
11/TCP	DAYTIME	Daytime
11/UDP	DAYTIME	Daytime
17/TCP	QOTD	Quote of the Day
17/UDP	QOTD	Quote of the Day
20/TCP	FTP-DATA	File Transfer (Default Data)
20/UDP	FTP-DATA	File Transfer (Default Data)
21/TCP	FTP	File Transfer (Control)
21/UDP	FTP	File Transfer (Control)
23/TCP	TELNET	Telnet
23/UDP	TELNET	Telnet
25/TCP	SMTP	Simple Mail Transfer
25/UDP	SMTP	Simple Mail Transfer
42/TCP	NAMESERVER	Host Name Server
42/UDP	NAMESERVER	Host Name Server
49/TCP	LOGIN	Login Host Protocol
49/UDP	LOGIN	Login Host Protocol
53/TCP	DOMAIN	Domain Name Server
53/UDP	DOMAIN	Domain Name Server
58/TCP	XNS-MAIL	XNS Mail
58/UDP	XNS-MAIL	XNS Mail
67/TCP	BOOTPS	Bootstrap Protocol Server
67/UDP	BOOTPS	Bootstrap Protocol Server
68/TCP	BOOTPC	Bootstrap Protocol Client
68/UDP	BOOTPC	Bootstrap Protocol Client
69/TCP	TFTP	Trivial File Transfer
69/UDP	TFTP	Trivial File Transfer
79/TCP	FINGER	Finger
79/UDP	FINGER	Finger
80/TCP	WWW-HTTP	World Wide Web HTTP
80/UDP	WWW-HTTP	World Wide Web HTTP
88/TCP	KERBEROS	Kerberos
88/UDP	KERBEROS	Kerberos
110/TCP	POP3	Post Office Protocol—Version 3
110/UDP	POP3	Post Office Protocol—Version 3
119/TCP	NNTP	Network News Transfer Protocol
119/UDP	NNTP	Network News Transfer Protocol
531/TCP	CONFERENCE	Chat
531/UDP	CONFERENCE	Chat

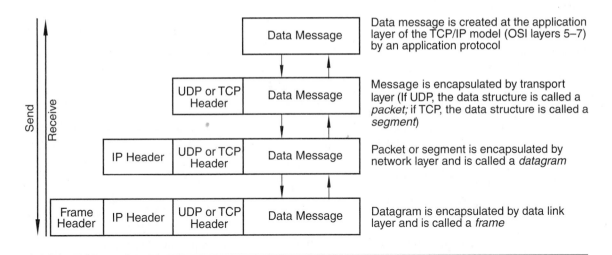

FIGURE 8.11 A conceptual view of data encapsulation. Each layer encapsulates (or deencapsulates) the data structure from the previous layer into its own independent data structure. The four layers shown here correspond to TCP/IP's four layers as shown in Figure 8.10. A data message is first created on the sending machine at TCP/IP's application layer. It is then passed to the transport layer where it is encapsulated with either a UDP or TCP header. If the application protocol is connectionless, then a UDP header is prepended and the new data structure is called a *packet*. If the application is connection-oriented, then a TCP header is prepended and the new data structure is called a *segment*. This transport layer header includes the source and destination port numbers corresponding to the application protocol. The transport layer data structure is then passed to the network layer where an IP header is prepended. The IP header includes the source and destination network addresses. This new data structure is now called a *datagram*. Finally, the datagram is passed to TCP/IP's network interface layer where a frame header is prepended. Included with this header are the source and destination hardware addresses. The resulting data frame is then passed to the physical layer for transmission. On the receiving machine, each layer's header is stripped off as the data structure works its way up the layers.

System (NFS), the Simple Network Management Protocol (SNMP), the Bootstrap Protocol (BOOTP), and Domain Name Service (DNS). Figure 8.12 contains a diagram of the UDP header format.

Note from Figure 8.12 that the UDP source and destination ports refer to a well-known port number. As we discussed earlier, these well-known port numbers correspond to a specific application. Port numbers are important because they enable the sending node to identify on which port the destination machine is running the application program that created the data message. For example, if a user on a sending node uses TFTP to transfer a file from a destination node, the sending machine "knows" that the destination machine will be running the TFTP application process on port 69. Further note that UDP (as does TCP) uses IP to send and receive datagrams, as shown in Figure 8.11. This is why UDP (and TCP) is layered above IP. It ensures that a UDP-based message gets encapsulated into an IP datagram for delivery to a destination node across the Internet.

(a)

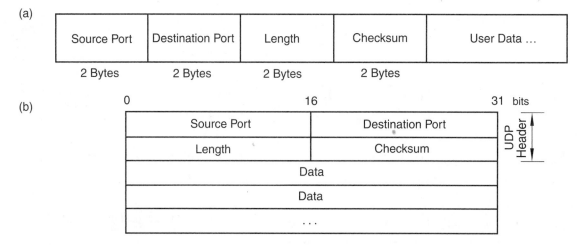

(b)

Source Port: 16 bits in length and contains the well-known port number corresponding to the application protocol that created the data message. This field is optional and is filed with 0s if not used.

Destination Port: 16 bits in length and contains the well-known port number corresponding to the application protocol that created the data message.

Length: This 16-bit field corresponds to the length of the UDP datagram. The minimum length of a UDP datagram is 8 bytes.

Checksum: This optional 16-bit field contains the checksum of the datagram. The calculation of the checksum includes the source and destination addresses and the protocol field from the IP header, which is shown in Figure 8.20. (This combination of UDP and IP header fields is called the UDP pseudoheader.) These fields are included in the checksum so that the datagram is delivered to the correct destination network and host. If the checksum field is not used, then it is filled with 0s.

User Data: This field contains actual user data created by an application protocol such as SMTP or POP3 for e-mail.

FIGURE 8.12   Format and contents of a UDP header. Part (b) is a block diagram frequently shown in the RFCs.

The Transport Control Protocol (TCP)

The Transport Control Protocol is the TCP of TCP/IP. It is a full-duplex, connection-oriented protocol that performs several functions, including providing for reliable data transmission by furnishing end-to-end error detection and correction, guaranteeing that data are transferred across a network accurately and in the proper sequence, retransmitting any data not received by the destination node, and guaranteeing against data duplication between sending and receiving nodes. Application protocols that generally use TCP include Telnet, File Transfer Protocol (FTP), Simple Mail Transport Protocol (SMTP), and Post Office Protocol (POP).

The format and contents of the TCP header are shown in Figure 8.13. You will note that when compared to UDP's header (see Figure 8.12), TCP's header contains similar

(a)

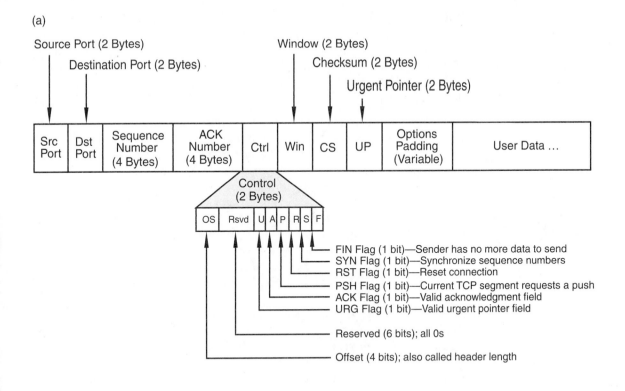

(b)

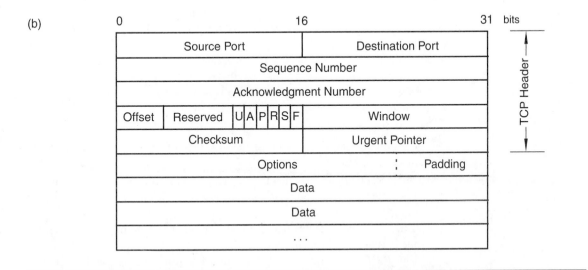

FIGURE 8.13 Format and contents of a TCP header. Part (b) is a block diagram view frequently shown in the RFCs.

information carried by UDP. For example, the first four bytes of the header specify the source and destination ports. Thus, like UDP, TCP uses port numbers to identify and deliver data to the correct application. The TCP header also carries a considerable amount of additional information, however. This additional overhead is needed because TCP guarantees reliable host-to-host data transfers. This guaranteed reliability is manifest in the following fields:

Sequence Number: This field carries the sequence number assigned to the first byte of data being transmitted. It is used so that the TCP process at the receiving host can keep the data segments it receives in the correct order. When a connection is first established between sending and receiving hosts, the SYN bit in the two-byte control field is set to inform the receiving host that the number given in the sequence number field is the initial sequence number for synchronization purposes. The next byte of data sent will then increment this number by 1. Generally, the initial sequence number is 0, and the first data byte is 1. Sequence numbers are needed because TCP was not designed to deliver data as independent packets. Instead, TCP delivers data as a continuous byte stream. Thus, sequence numbers keep track of the order in which byte streams are sent and received.

Acknowledgment Number: This field is used to verify the receipt of data. Acknowledgments are only provided by the receiving host when it receives a data segment with a valid checksum. This strategy is known as positive acknowledgment with retransmission (PAR). Thus, if the sender does not receive a positive acknowledgment from the receiver within a certain time frame, then it will assume the data segment did not arrive, or it arrived damaged, and retransmit the data. The number given in the acknowledgment number field by the receiving host is the sequence number of the next byte of data the host expects to receive. When the acknowledgment number field is used, the ACK bit in the two-byte control field is also set.

Control: This two-byte field provides control information.

—The four-bit *offset* specifies the length, measured in 32-bit multiples, of the current TCP segment header. This field is needed because TCP headers are of variable length (although they must be at least 20 bytes in length).

—The six-bit *reserved* field is set to all 0s and is reserved for future use.

—The six one-bit flags are used to specify the type of segment being transferred. For example, when set:

• The *URG* flag indicates that the segment contains urgent data and should be processed by the receiver as soon as possible. (See the urgent pointer field description that follows.)

• The *ACK* flag indicates that the segment contains data in the acknowledgment number field as discussed earlier.

• The *PSH* flag indicates that the current segment being "built" contains data that must be delivered immediately. A "push" event is initiated by an upper-layer process and is interpreted as, "Transfer all queued data to receiver immediately."

- The *RST* flag is used when an event arises that causes an ungraceful disconnect. In such instances, a host sends a TCP segment with the RST bit. The receiving host interprets this segment as an immediate termination alert and responds by aborting the segment. TCP will also inform the corresponding application of this event.
- The *SYN* flag indicates that the segment contains data in the sequence number field as discussed earlier.
- The *FIN* flag is used to terminate a TCP connection. When the host that initiates a termination segment receives a positive acknowledgment, the TCP connection is closed.

Window: The two-byte *window* specifies the maximum number of bytes the receiving host is capable of accepting. In short, it provides end-to-end flow control; the window field enables the receiver to control the flow of bytes from the sender. Thus, the amount of data the sender transmits can never exceed the window size established by the receiver. The receiver can change the window size anytime during an established connection as additional buffer space becomes available. A window size of 0 informs the sender to stop transmission until it receives a non-0 window size. Since TCP supports full-duplex, both sender and receiver may provide flow-control information via the window field.

Checksum: This two-byte field is used to verify that the transmitted segment is valid. TCP uses a pseudoheader similar to UDP to provide error control on the IP header, the TCP header, and user data. Like UDP, TCP prepends the pseudoheader to the segment, and the checksum calculation is performed over the entire data structure (pseudoheader plus TCP segment).

Urgent Pointer: This two-byte field is used in tandem with the one-bit URG flag as a signal to the receiving node that it needs to inform the corresponding application program that urgent data are being transmitted and need to be processed. An example of an urgent data instance is a hung Telnet session. To abort this session, the user on the local host would press the escape character, which is then transmitted to the remote host as urgent data. The urgent pointer field specifies where within the segment the urgent data end and the regular (i.e., nonurgent) data begin.

Options and Padding: This variable-byte field specifies any options a particular TCP process requires. A common option used is maximum segment size, which is used to restrict the size of a TCP segment. Padding is then used to fill the remaining bits of the field with 0s so that it ends on a 32-bit boundary.

Establishing a TCP Connection

TCP is a connection-oriented protocol, which implies that a logical connection must first be established (i.e., "nailed up") between two nodes before any data are transferred. (Recall from Chapter 2 that this logical connection is called a virtual circuit.) To do this, TCP uses a process known as a *three-way handshake,* which involves an initiating host (i.e., a client) requesting that a link be established between it and a server. In its simplest form, this handshake consists of two nodes exchanging three TCP segments. This is illustrated in the first three steps of Figure 8.14 and can be described in the following general terms:

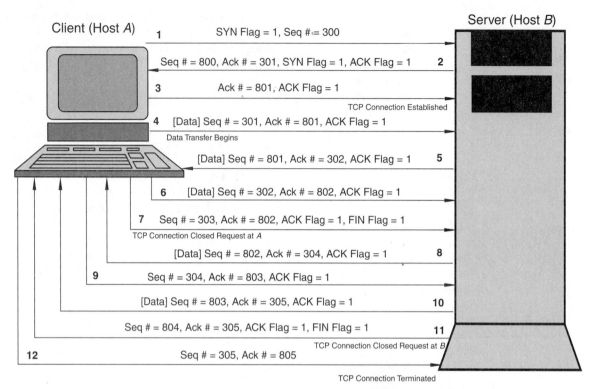

1 A sends a synchronization segment to B indicating its desire to establish a connection and that its initial sequence number is 300. This means that the first data segment A sends will be numbered 301.

2 B receives A's synchronization segment and sends A a synchronization and acknowledgment segment. Note that B's initial sequence number is 800, which means that B's first data segment will be numbered 801.

3 A receives B's synchronization and acknowledgment segment and sends an acknowledgment segment. At this stage, a TCP connection is established between A and B.

4 A transmits data segment 301 to B and informs B that it is expecting segment number 801.

5 B receives A's segment and sends A data segment 801. This segment also acknowledges receipt of A's segment by informing A that it expects to receive segment 302.

6 A receives B's segment and sends B data segment 302, which also acknowledges receipt of B's segment.

7 A sends B a finish segment, which informs B that A is closing its side of the TCP connection.

8 B receives A's last two segments and sends A data segment 802. Note that this segment also acknowledges receipt of A's previous transmissions by setting the acknowledgment number to 304. At this stage, A cannot transmit any new data segments but continues to transmit acknowledgment segments.

9 A acknowledges B's latest transmission.

10 B receives A's acknowledgment segment and sends A data segment 803.

11 B sends A a finish segment, which informs A that B is closing its side of the TCP connection.

12 A receives B's latest transmissions and acknowledges them. At this stage, the link is terminated since neither A nor B has any more data to transmit.

FIGURE 8.14 Pictorial description of a TCP connection. TCP's three-way handshaking process, which is used to establish a TCP connection, is illustrated in steps 1–3, and link termination is illustrated in steps 7–12.

- The client (node A in Figure 8.14) generates and transmits a TCP segment that has the one-bit synchronize (SYN) flag set to 1 and the four-byte sequence number field set to the initial sequence number (x) it intends to use for the current connection. The SYN bit, which is part of the TCP header's control field (see Figure 8.13), notifies the server that the client wants to establish a connection; the sequence number informs the server of the initial sequence number on which data segments transmitted by the client will be based. (Recall that sequence numbers enable a node to keep data segments in the correct order.)

- Upon receipt of this first segment, the server records the sequence number and then responds to the client by generating and transmitting an acknowledgment segment, which has the SYN and acknowledgment (ACK) bits of the control field set to 1. Additionally, this segment's four-byte ACK number field is set to one more than the client's initial sequence number $(x + 1)$, and the four-byte sequence number field is set to the server's initial sequence number (y). Note that the one-bit SYN flag = 1 because the synchronization process (i.e., the handshaking) is still ongoing and that the one-bit ACK flag = 1 because the ACK number field contains data. Further note that the ACK number $(x + 1)$ informs the client that the server expects the next segment to be numbered $(x + 1)$ and that the server's initial sequence number (y) informs the client of the initial sequence number on which data segments transmitted by the server will be based.

- Lastly, the client acknowledges receipt of the server's segment, and at this stage, a link is established.

The client and server's initial sequence numbers do not have to be the same since these numbers are administered locally.

As an illustration of this three-way handshaking process, consider the first three steps shown in Figure 8.14. In this example, host A initiates a TCP connection to host B by sending a synchronization segment with an initial sequence number of 300. Host B responds to this segment by sending a synchronization/acknowledgment segment. The acknowledgment number it uses is 301, which confirms receipt of A's segment and indicates that B expects the next segment it receives from A to be numbered 301. This segment also contains B's initial sequence number, 800. A now responds to B by sending an acknowledgment segment using an acknowledgment number of 801, which confirms receipt of B's segment by indicating that A expects the next segment it receives from B to be numbered 801. At this stage, the TCP connection is established and data segments can now be exchanged between the two hosts. From this illustration, note the implicit understanding acknowledgment numbers provide the two nodes in their exchange of segments: By sending an acknowledgment number of $n + 1$, a node is not only informing its mate at the other end of the connection that it expects the next segment to be numbered $n + 1$, but it is also stating implicitly that it has successfully received all previous segments numbered n or less. This is the heart of TCP's reliability feature.

Closing a TCP Connection

A TCP connection is closed when a host has no more data to transmit. Since TCP is a full-duplex protocol, a TCP connection can be closed in one direction but remain open in the other direction. Thus, in Figure 8.14, host A can close its side of the connection but continue to receive data from B, host B can close its side of the connection but continue to receive data from A, or both A and B can close the connection simultaneously.

Regardless of which host initiates the close request, the procedure is the same and is similar to the three-way handshaking process used for establishing the connection except the one-bit finish (FIN) flag is set to 1 instead of the SYN flag.

As an illustration of how this is done, examine steps 7–12 in Figure 8.14. At steps 6 and 7, the client transmits its last data segment (302) and then initiates a close request by sending a finish segment (303) that has FIN = 1. The server acknowledges these transmissions at step 8, and the client side of the connection is now terminated. Although *A* will no longer be sending *B* any more data segments, it still may continue receiving data from *B* and is capable of acknowledging receipt of these data segments. This is shown in steps 8–10. In step 11, *B* sends *A* a finish segment, which indicates that it no longer has any more data to transmit. Finally, in step 12, *A* acknowledges receipt of *B*'s finish segment, and the overall link is terminated. Note that the overall connection is not closed until the second FIN segment is acknowledged.

The entire process of establishing, transferring data between both ends of, and closing a TCP connection is readily apparent when using a TCP-based Web browser application such as Netscape. The user on the client machine (host *A* in Figure 8.14) requests data from a Web server (host *B*). The client application makes a call to the TCP software to establish a link to the server (steps 1–3 in Figure 8.14). Once the link is established, the client submits its request(s) and the server responds accordingly (steps 4–6). When the client and server have no more data to transfer, the application program informs the TCP software of this state and directs the link to be terminated (steps 7–12).

TCP Reliability and Flow Control

TCP's reliability feature is a function of its sequence and acknowledgment numbers. This was discussed earlier and illustrated in Figure 8.14. Each time a host receives a valid TCP segment, it sends an acknowledgment as part of each outgoing segment. If, on the other hand, a valid segment was not received, then no acknowledgment is sent. Thus, if the transmitting node fails to receive an acknowledgment for a previously transmitted segment within a specified time period, it will retransmit the segment. This is why TCP is regarded as a *positive acknowledgment with retransmission* (PAR) protocol. The use of sequence numbers also enables the receiving host to reassemble data segments in the correct order in the event that they were to arrive out of sequence.

In addition to reliability, TCP also provides end-to-end flow control. This is done using the two-byte window field (see Figure 8.13). At each end of a link, TCP maintains send and receive buffers. The send buffer contains two sets of data: data waiting to be transmitted and data that have been transmitted but not yet acknowledged. This second data set represents data generated by the application program and ready for transmission. The receive buffer also contains two data sets: correctly ordered data that have been received but not yet processed by the application and data that arrived out of sequence, which require TCP to reorder in the correct sequence. Using the window field, a receiver advertises a window size that is less than or equal to the size of its available buffer space. Thus, on the receive side, the available buffer space must take into account the amount of data currently occupying the buffer at any given time.

On the send side, two things must be done. First, the sending entity must calculate a window size that will limit the amount of data it can send. This calculation, which is a function of the receiver's advertised window size and the difference between the amount of data sent and the amount of data acknowledged, is necessary because without it a sender can overrun a receiver's buffer space. For example, assume the receiver's advertised window is 1000 bytes. If the sender, at this moment in time, has currently transmitted 700 bytes of which 500 bytes have been acknowledged, then the sender's window size is 1000 − (700 − 500) = 800 bytes. This means that at this particular moment, the sender can continue sending segments as long as the total number of bytes it sends does not exceed 800 bytes of data. In addition to computing this value, the sending node must also ensure that its own buffer space does not get overrun by the application process writing data that are ready for transmission. Thus, the difference between the amount of data waiting to be transmitted and the amount of transmitted data that has been acknowledged must be less than or equal to the maximum size of the send buffer.

Note that the manner in which TCP uses the window field to provide flow control represents a modified version of the simple sliding window protocol we discussed in Chapter 5. In TCP's version, the window size is dynamic, namely, it varies over time with each transmitted segment. As a receiver's buffer fills, it advertises a smaller window size; as more space becomes available, it advertises a larger window size. All the while, the sender is also calculating the maximum amount of data it can transmit. A variable size window field not only improves flow control, but it also facilitates reliability. Further observe that if a sending node receives an advertised window size of 0, then it is prohibited from transmitting any more data. This will eventually lead to a full send buffer because the application process will continue to generate data ready for transmission. At this stage, TCP will block the application process, which will effectively stop the application from generating any more data. Only until a non-0 window size is advertised will the sender be able to resume data transmissions.

TCP has a built-in mechanism that permits the sending node to probe the receiver periodically with one-byte segments if it receives a 0-sized window. One of these segments will eventually evoke from the receiver a response that contains a non-0-sized window.

TCP Enhancements

Although TCP continues to function admirably with little change since its development (which is nearing 30 years), this does not mean that it does not require any modifications. TCP is still inadequate in certain situations. Fortunately, TCP was designed so that enhancements to the protocol can be made without major ramifications.

One of TCP's inadequacies is its window size. As we discussed earlier, TCP's window field specifies the maximum number of bytes a sender can transmit without stopping and waiting for an acknowledgment from the receiver. The original protocol was designed with a 16-bit window field, which implies that the maximum buffer size a receiver can advertise is $2^{16} - 1 = 65,535$ bytes. Note that this 16-bit restriction is not an issue when TCP is implemented on today's high-speed switched Ethernet LANs because latency is low, and hence, data are transmitted, received, and acknowledged with little delay. This is not the case, however, for WAN-based TCP implementations. Compared to LANs, WANs typically exhibit high latency. As a result, a 16-bit window size can adversely restrict data flow between two nodes. This restriction was removed by the introduction of the TCP option, *window scale*, which was initially defined in RFC 1072 and then later redefined in RFC 1323. The window scale option takes advantage of TCP's options field (see Figure 8.13). It enables a receiver to advertise a window size of up to 30 bits by specifying a 14-bit value in the options field. This 14-bit value specifies the number of bits the original window field should be "moved to the left."

For example, if the original window field contains sixteen 1-bits, and the window scale option consists of the 14-bit field 00000000011111, then the receiver's maximum window size is interpreted as $2^{16+5} - 1 = 2^{21} - 1 = 2,097,151$ bytes. This option, which enables a receiver to increase its maximum buffer size up to one gigabyte, is negotiated as part of the three-way handshaking process. Current implementations of this option include Microsoft's Windows 98/2000 and Sun Microsystems' Solaris 7 and Solaris 8 operating systems.

A second TCP embellishment focuses on its time-stamp function. As noted earlier, TCP's PAR requires a sender to retransmit all unacknowledged data segments if it does not receive an acknowledgment from the receiver within a specified time frame. Once again, the LAN/WAN difference becomes apparent. On LANs, this time threshold can be short. On WANs, however, a short time threshold can result in an "early" time expiration; that is, the sender is given a "time's up" alert and retransmits a segment before the original segment actually arrives at its destination. Standardized algorithms for establishing appropriate time stamps are now specified in RFC 1323.

A third enhancement to the TCP protocol improves its use of sequence numbers. Recall from our earlier discussion that TCP identifies all segments by sequentially numbering them and that acknowledgments carry the sequence number of the segment the receiver next expects to receive. So if a receiver receives segments 23–89, it will send an acknowledgment with sequence number 90, which implies that it has correctly received all segments up to and including segment 89. The inadequacy in this scheme is the sequential nature in which segments are acknowledged. For example, assume a receiver receives segments 23–89 and 112–200. It must submit an acknowledgment with a sequence identifier of 90 since it did not receive segments 90–111. The original version of the protocol does not accommodate for segment "gaps." This inadequacy is resolved by the *selective acknowledgment* option, which is specified in RFC 2018. If a gap exists in the receiver's buffers, it sends an acknowledgment that identifies the last cumulative data byte it received (e.g., 89) and then uses TCP's options field to specify all additional data segments it received after the missing segments (e.g., 112–200). The selective acknowledgment option is negotiated during the three-way handshaking process via the selective acknowledgments permitted function, which is also defined in RFC 2018.

The Internet Protocol (IP)

(Most of the information presented here is linked to Chapter 7, which deals specifically with network layer issues. The reader is encouraged to reference the appropriate figures and tables of that chapter.)

The network layer transfers user messages from a source host to a destination host. In TCP/IP, the heart and soul of this layer is the Internet Protocol, which is the IP of TCP/IP. IP receives data bits from the lower layer, assembles the bits into packets (called *IP datagrams*), and selects the "best" route based on some metric to route the packets between nodes.

IP is connectionless, which implies that every datagram must contain the address of the destination node. This address, called an Internet or *IP address* (see Section 8.6), is assigned to a node's network interface as part of the node's initial network configura-

A metric is a description of the "cost" of a route used by routing hardware and software to select the best possible route. See Chapter 7 for more information.

tion. An IP address uniquely identifies a host similar to the way a social security number uniquely identifies a person. It is used by the network layer as a road map to locate a host within the Internet by determining what path a datagram is to follow en route to its final destination.

Datagrams destined for a host connected to the same local network as the sending host are delivered directly by the sending host. To transfer datagrams destined for a host connected to a remote network, however, IP relies on routers or switches (see Chapter 7), which connect two (or more) dissimilar networks to each other. In the context of the network layer, routers and switches are frequently referred to as *gateways*. Thus, an IP gateway routes packets between the networks to which it is connected. As datagrams are routed through the Internet, each intermediate gateway maintains a routing table that contains entries of the location of the next gateway to which a datagram should be transferred based on the destination address of the datagram. A UNIX and Microsoft NT command line utility that displays IP routing information for a local host is *netstat*. (An example of this command's output is shown in Table 7.1.)

When a datagram passes through an intermediate gateway en route to another network, it is called a hop. IP routing is usually accomplished via a simple hop-by-hop algorithm. If a packet doesn't incur a route through a router, then it hasn't incurred a hop. If, on the other hand, a packet transverses through two gateways in reaching its final destination, then we say the destination is two hops away. (See Figure 7.4 for an example of hops and Table 7.1, which contains a traceroute output that shows the number of hops a packet takes as it traverses a network.)

An important concept in routing a packet is that of "cost." Each link to another gateway has a pseudocost assigned to it by the network manager of the link. This pseudocost is used to compute the maximum cost allowed by a system to reach another system. Most routing algorithms used for IP routing use a least-cost/least-hops methodology. This means that the primary path a datagram takes is determined by the least cost to transfer the packet from source to destination. If something on that path fails, then the next least cost is used. If there are two or more paths with the same cost, then the least hops are computed and the shortest hop path with the least cost is taken. A side-effect of this type of routing is used by the routing algorithm to determine that a system is not reachable. What happens in a gateway is the destination node's cost goes to infinity. Thus, by definition, the node is simply too expensive to reach and hence is unavailable to the network. (See the discussion of RIP in Chapter 7.)

Although gateways are used to deliver packets from one network to another, IP does not guarantee that a packet will indeed be delivered to its destination. If an intermediate gateway, for example, contains incorrect or stale routing information, packets might get lost. IP does not take any action to retransmit undelivered packets. This is done by higher-level protocols, specifically TCP. Additionally, IP fragments and reassembles datagrams when necessary so they do not exceed the maximum packet length (called the maximum transmission unit, or MTU) a physical network is capable of supporting. If a packet's size is greater than a network's MTU, the packet is divided into smaller units (called fragmenting) and sent to the destination in the form of several separate datagrams. The complete packet is then reassembled at the destination node before it is passed to the higher levels. Reassembly of an IP datagram can only occur at the destination node and not at any of the intermediary nodes the datagrams transverse. This is because IP is a connectionless datagram service—datagrams can take different paths en route to their destination, and hence, an intermediary node might not receive all of the fragmented datagrams.

An integral part of IP is the *Internet Control Message Protocol* (ICMP), which uses an IP datagram to carry messages about the communications environment of the Internet. Although ICMP is layered above IP, it is generally discussed and shown with IP (as it is in Figure 8.9) because of its relationship to IP. ICMP allows interconnected nodes to exchange messages to report flow-control problems, to report that a destination node is unreachable, to notify a host to use a different gateway to route packets, and to test the status of a link to a remote host. For example, if a gateway receives a datagram destined for a host that is unreachable, the gateway will send an ICMP "host unreachable" message to the originator. This message is triggered when the local router sends an Address Resolution Protocol (ARP) request to the target node requesting the node's MAC sublayer address. On an Ethernet network, the MAC address is the node's Ethernet address (see Chapter 5). The ARP request is a network broadcast that announces the target node's IP address and requests the node to return its MAC address. If the node does not reply within a specified period of time, then a "host unreachable" message is sent by the router to the source node. A "host unreachable" message signifies that the target host is not connected to the local network, the target host is a valid local node but is currently off-line, or the local network is congested and the router's ARP request is timing out before it reaches the target host.

Another example of an ICMP message is "network unreachable." This message is sent by a router when it cannot reach the target network. This can be due to a downed link (e.g., a cable cut or disconnected port), an incorrectly configured network address mask (discussed later), or an incorrectly entered network address. An example of an ICMP-based application is the UNIX and Microsoft NT command *ping,* which allows one node to test the communication path between it and a destination node. The output of this command in verbose mode is shown in Figure 8.15. Normally, ping simply reports whether a destination node is "alive." In verbose mode, ping reports the round-trip time of a packet between source and destination. Note how ping gives specific information about the con-

```
gallo@bb> ping -s zeno.fit.edu
PING zeno.fit.edu: 56 data bytes
64 bytes from zeno.fit.edu (163.118.5.4): icmp_seq=0. time=128. ms
64 bytes from zeno.fit.edu (163.118.5.4): icmp_seq=1. time=127. ms
64 bytes from zeno.fit.edu (163.118.5.4): icmp_seq=2. time=128. ms
64 bytes from zeno.fit.edu (163.118.5.4): icmp_seq=3. time=120. ms
64 bytes from zeno.fit.edu (163.118.5.4): icmp_seq=4. time=130. ms
^C
----4.5.118.163.in-addr.arpa PING Statistics----
5 packets transmitted, 5 packets received, 0% packet loss
round-trip (ms) min/avg/max = 120/126/130
```

FIGURE 8.15 Output of the *ping* program using the *s* option.

dition of the network environment. For example, lengthy round-trip times would indicate some sort of problem between the source and destination nodes, and the percentage of packet loss is also beneficial in assessing the condition of a link.

Another protocol that operates at TCP/IP's network layer is the *Resource Reservation Protocol* (RSVP), which was recently developed by the Internet Engineering Task Force (IETF). RSVP can be thought of as an IP-based quality of service (QoS) protocol that provides a mechanism to control network latency for specific applications. (See Chapter 5 for additional information about QoS.) This is done by prioritizing data and allocating sufficient bandwidth for data transmission. QoS is inherent in technologies such as token ring and ATM, but is absent in Ethernet/802.3 and IP. With RSVP, though, Ethernet/802.3 or IP end nodes can reserve a specific amount of bandwidth from the network for a particular transmission. This feature is critical for transmitting data from time-sensitive applications such as real-time voice and video. For example, a videoconferencing application might receive a high-priority tag that requires a certain amount of bandwidth, a specific transmission rate, and maximum latency.

For RSVP to be effected across a WAN, every router that is along the path an RSVP data packet traverses must support RSVP. If not, then the application fails. Furthermore, if the WAN cannot support an RSVP request (e.g., there is insufficient bandwidth available), then the application will not run. These two issues pose serious challenges to running an RSVP application across the Internet. The IETF, however, is working diligently to address these issues. For example, IETF working groups have been established to integrate RSVP into the OSPF and BGP routing protocols. On another front, the IETF's Integrated Services Working Group is considering modifying the type of information contained in an IP packet header's type of service field to identify the level of service a packet should receive. Finally, IPv6, the next generation of IP that is discussed later in the chapter, has provisions for QoS via the 24-bit flow label field (see Figure 8.21). ATM's QoS offers a more elegant approach to transmitting time-sensitive data across a WAN than RSVP. However, the current level of work and attention IETF is giving to the issue of QoS makes the concept of IP QoS more of a reality than a contradiction in terms.

8.6   IP Addresses

Internet addresses (called IP addresses for short) are node addresses that identify their location within the Internet. IP addresses play an important role in the successful delivery of data across the Internet. If a node cannot be located, then data cannot be delivered to it. Currently, two versions of IP addresses are available: Version 4 (IPv4) and Version 6 (IPv6). IPv4 is discussed in this section; IPv6 is discussed in the next section.

IPv4

IP Version 4 addresses (IPv4) consist of 32 bits (0 through 31) partitioned into four groups of eight bits each (called *octets*). Since it is difficult for us to read addresses in binary notation, IP addresses are expressed in decimal form; a decimal point (read as "dot") separates the octets. An example of an Internet address is 204.163.25.37. Each octet of an IP

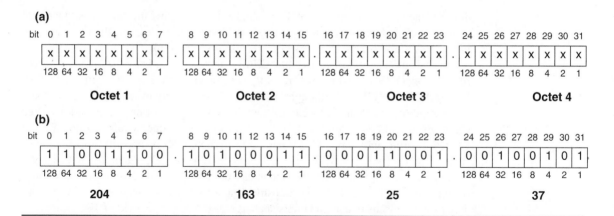

FIGURE 8.16 IP Version 4 addresses are 32 bit-length addresses partitioned into four octets. These octets are shown in (a) using the letter x to represent bits. In (b), the binary and decimal equivalents of the IP address 204.163.25.37 are shown.

address is treated as an independent unit. Since octets comprise eight bits, the contents of each octet can contain anywhere from eight 0-bits to eight 1-bits. The decimal equivalent of an all 0-bit octet is 0, and the decimal equivalent of an all 1-bit octet is $(2^8 - 1) = 255$. This is illustrated in Figure 8.16(a) with the letter x being used in a general manner to represent bits. The bit pattern for the IP address 204.163.25.37 is shown in Figure 8.16(b).

IPv4 addresses are organized into one of five classes: A, B, C, D, or E. Classification is determined by the value of the first four bits (bits 0 through 3).

Class A Addresses. If bit 0 is 0, then the address is a Class A address and begins with a decimal number ranging from 0 to 127. (0 and 127 are reserved.) Thus, the bit pattern of the first octet ranges from 00000000 to 01111111. An example of a Class A address is 13.123.17.8.

Class B Addresses. If the first two bits are 10, then the address is a Class B address and begins with a decimal number ranging from 128 to 191. Thus, the bit pattern of the first octet ranges from 10000000 to 10111111. An example of a Class B address is 163.118.5.4.

Class C Addresses. If the first three bits are 110, then the address is a Class C address and begins with a decimal number ranging from 192 to 223. Thus, the bit pattern of the first octet ranges from 11000000 to 11011111. An example of a Class C address is 198.42.239.17.

Class D Addresses. If the first four bits are 1110, then the address is a Class D address and begins with a decimal number ranging from 224 to 239. Thus, the bit pattern of the first octet ranges from 11100000 to 11101111. Class D addresses are used for multicast addresses.

Class E Addresses. If the first four bits are 1111, then the address is a Class E address and begins with a decimal number ranging from 240 to 255. All Class E addresses are reserved for future use.

In addition to address classes, IPv4 addresses also distinguish between the address of a network (called the *network identifier*) and the address of a host (called the *host identifier*) connected to a specific network. This is similar to a telephone number—an area code identifies the region, and the phone number identifies a specific location in that re-

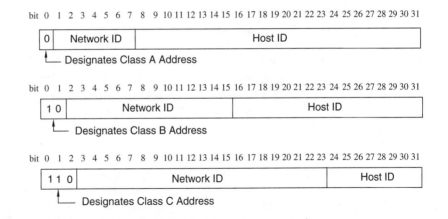

FIGURE 8.17 IPv4 addresses can also be interpreted from a network- and host-ID perspective. In a Class A address, bits 1–7 represent the network ID, and the remaining bits represent the host ID. In a Class B address, bits 2–15 stand for the network ID, and bits 16–31 represent the host ID. Finally, in a Class C address, bits 3–23 specify the network ID, and the last eight bits represent the host ID. In addition, the first three bits of an IPv4 address specify the address class. (Class D and Class E addresses are not shown but follow a similar pattern.)

gion. Class A addresses use bits 1 through 7 for the network ID and bits 8 through 31 for the host ID; Class B addresses use bits 2 through 15 for the network ID and bits 16 through 31 for the host ID; and Class C addresses use bits 3 through 23 for the network ID and bits 24 through 31 for the host ID. This is illustrated in Figure 8.17.

Finally, each address class allows a different maximum number of possible networks and hosts. These upper limits are based on the number of bits used for the network and host identifiers. For example, since Class A addresses use seven bits (bits 1 through 7) for the network identifier and 24 bits (bits 8 through 31) for the host identifier, there are a maximum of $2^7 = 128$ Class A networks, each capable of supporting $2^{24} = 16,777,216$ hosts. Similarly, Class B addresses have a maximum of $2^{14} = 16,384$ networks and $2^{16} = 65,536$ hosts; and Class C addresses support $2^{21} = 2,097,152$ networks, each capable of supporting $2^8 = 256$ hosts. Since IPv4 reserves the use of all 0s or all 1s for special addresses, each of the preceding calculations should be reduced by 2 to yield the true number of unique networks and hosts allowable for each network class. (See Box 8.1 for information about subnetting IPv4 addresses and Figure 8.21 for the format and structure of IPv6 addresses.)

Subnetting IPv4 Addresses

Subnetting refers to the partitioning of a network address space into separate autonomous subnetworks. To understand this concept, let's first set the stage by examining a "flat" Class C network, which does not use subnetting. A flat Class C address consists of 256 host IDs. As discussed earlier, IP reserves two of these IDs for special purposes. These are always the first and last host IDs. The first ID is used to identify the network itself (although historically this is the "all 0s" broadcast address); it represents the overall network address. The last ID specifies the network's broadcast address.

Thus, given the Class C network identifier 198.42.17, the address 198.42.17.0 is reserved for network identification; the address 198.42.17.255 is reserved for broadcasting; and the remaining 254 addresses, from 198.42.17.1 to 198.42.17.254, are used as host IDs. As a result, an unsubnetted Class C address consists of one network address, one broadcast address, and 254 unique host IDs.

When an IPv4 address is subnetted, the flat address space is partitioned into multiple subnetworks. Through subnetting, we can make efficient use of an IPv4 address because subnetting reduces wasted address space. For example, suppose an organization has been assigned the Class C network address 198.42.17.0 but only has 60 nodes to connect to the Internet. Without subnetting this address space, 194 host addresses are being unused. This is wasteful given the current state of IPv4 address depletion. A more efficient use of this network address space is to partition it into smaller sizes so that fewer host addresses are unused. In this case, we would partition the network into four subnetworks. So instead of having 256 possible host IDs, each subnetwork would have 256/4 = 64 host IDs. Since one host ID must be reserved for the subnetwork address and a second ID for the subnet's broadcast address, each subnetwork can only support a maximum of 62 host IDs. Nevertheless, for the given situation, this is quite adequate resulting in only 2 unused host IDs as opposed to 194. Subnetting is an efficient way of using the limited IPv4 address space.

Key to subnetting is a network's *subnet mask.* When used with subnetting, a subnet mask specifies which bits are part of the network ID and which bits are part of the host ID. To illustrate this concept, consider once again the Class C network address 198.42.17.0. Without subnetting, this address has the corresponding mask of 255.255.255.0. Note that a mask is expressed in dotted notation similar to a network address and is also 32 bits in length. Note further that the binary representation of this mask consists of 24 consecutive 1-bits followed by 8 consecutive 0-bits:

11111111   11111111   11111111   00000000
255   255   255   0

A network address and its corresponding mask are denoted by writing the network address and the number of 1-bits contained in the mask and delimiting the two expressions by a slash symbol. Thus, in this example, the expression 198.42.17.0/24 denotes that the network address has a corresponding mask of 24 consecutive 1-bits, which implies that the mask's remaining octet consists of 8 consecutive 0-bits.

The logical AND of two bits is equal to 1 only when the two bits being combined are 1. In all other cases, the result is 0. Thus, 0 AND 0 = 0, 0 AND 1 = 0, 1 AND 0 = 0, and 1 AND 1 = 1.

When a network address is combined with its corresponding subnet mask via a logical AND, the network ID part is preserved but the host ID becomes 0. In this way, the subnet mask is used to *mask* the network ID from the host ID. As an example, consider the Class C address 198.42.17.239. Given the subnet mask 255.255.255.0, we can extract the network ID by combining the two addresses via a logical AND, as is shown here:

198.42.17.239:	11000110	00101010	00010001	11101111
255.255.255.0:	11111111	11111111	11111111	00000000
Result of AND:	11000110	00101010	00010001	00000000
	198	**42**	**17**	**0**

As a result, the subnet mask is able to correctly determine the network number that the destination node is connected to (i.e., network 198.42.17). Furthermore, by adding the host ID part of the address (239) to the corresponding bits of the mask (i.e., 11101111 + 00000000), the correct destination node is also identified. Thus, the IPv4 address 198.42.17.239 is correctly identified as node 239 on network 198.42.17.0.

Of course, none of this was really necessary since the predefined structure of a Class C address designates this information. However, as indicated earlier, IPv4 addresses are wasteful by default and hence are partitioned into multiple subnetworks. This is done by "stealing" bits from the host ID part and joining them to the network ID part. When taking bits from the host ID, we always use the higher-order bits because they are adjacent to the network ID bits. For example, one subnetting scheme involves using one host ID bit as part of the network address. In this setting, the network ID part would contain 25 bits and the host ID part would contain 7 bits. This scheme results in two subnetworks, with each subnet having its own network and broadcast addresses. Furthermore, since only 7 bits remain in the host ID part, each subnetwork supports a maximum of $2^7 - 2 = 126$ host IDs. (Remember that one address is used to specify the subnetwork's address, and a second address is used as the subnetwork's broadcast address.) If the Class C address 198.42.17 were partitioned using this scheme, then the two subnetworks and corresponding subnet host addresses would be as follows:

Subnet	Subnet Address	Host ID Range	Broadcast Address
1	198.42.17.0	198.42.17.1 to 198.42.17.126	198.42.17.127
2	198.42.17.128	198.42.17.129 to 198.42.17.254	198.42.17.255

These subnets are denoted 198.42.17.0/25 and 198.42.17.128/25. Here, the /25 indicates that the given network address has a corresponding subnet mask of 25 consecutive bits, which implies that the mask's last octet is 10000000. The reason we need a mask with 25 consecutive 1-bits is because we used 1 bit from the host ID to create a 25-bit network ID. To extract the correct network ID, we have to AND it with the mask, which must have the correct number of consecutive 1-bits to correspond with the network ID's length.

Note that when subnetting is used, it is extremely critical to correctly identify the subnet to which a host is connected. As an example, consider once again the destination address 198.42.17.239 from our earlier discussion. Without specifying a corresponding subnet mask, the default mask is 255.255.255.0, and the address is interpreted as node 239 on network 198.42.17.0. However, this interpretation is incorrect in the current situation because the destination address really specifies node 111 on subnetwork 198.42.17.128. To make this correct interpretation, the address needs to be denoted as 198.42.17.239/25, which once again implies that a subnet mask consisting of 25 consecutive 1-bits followed by 7 consecutive 0-bits is used. The concept of subnetting and the use of subnet masks are demonstrated further in Box 8.1.

BOX 8.1 Subnet Masking

A subnet mask partitions an IPv4 address into two parts: the network ID and host IDs. The concept of subnet masking is as follows:

> *If a bit in an IPv4 address is used as part of the network ID, then the corresponding mask bit is set to 1. If a bit in an IP address is used as part of the host ID, then the corresponding mask is set to 0.*

For example, the Class C IPv4 address 192.203.97.0 with subnet mask 255.255.255.0 implies that the network address is 192.203.97, the host ID addresses correspond to this network range from 192.203.97.1 to 192.203.97.254, and the network broadcast address is 192.203.97.255.

To conserve the IPv4 address space, network addresses are subnetted by borrowing bits from the host ID portion of the network address. To illustrate this concept, consider the following Class C address, which has its last octet (the part that represents the host ID) expanded into its eight-bit equivalent with corresponding decimal values.

```
192.203.97. ┌ __  __   __   __   __  __  __  __ ┐
  Network   │ 128  64   32   16    8   4   2   1 │
  Address   └                                    ┘
                         Host ID Portion
```

If we "steal" the highest-order bit of the host ID portion of this address (i.e., 128) to use as part of the network address, then the subnet mask becomes 255.255.255.128.

```
192.203.97. ┌ _1_ ┊ __   __   __   __  __  __  __ ┐
            │ 128 ┊ 64   32   16    8   4   2   1 │
            └     ┊                               ┘
  Network Address ┊        Host ID Portion
```

Thus, one bit is for subnetting and seven bits are for host IDs. This yields $2^1 = 2$ subnets and $2^7 = 128$ host IDs. Since each network requires one address to name the network and one for broadcasting, the actual number of host IDs per subnet is $2^7 - 2 = 126$.

	Subnet 1	Subnet 2
Network Address:	192.203.97.0	192.203.97.128
Host IDs:	192.203.97.1 to 192.203.97.126	192.203.97.129 to 192.203.97.254
Broadcast Address:	192.203.97.127	192.203.97.255

(It should be observed that the "all 1s" subnet is not recommended in the RFCs and hence should be avoided. As a result, having a mask one-bit wide would allow only one subnet to be defined, subnet 0; subnet 128 would be illegal.)

BOX 8.1 Subnet Masking (continued)

Similarly, if the two leftmost bits of the host ID are used (128 + 64), the subnet mask is 255.255.255.192. This implies $2^2 = 4$ subnets, each with $2^6 - 2 = 62$ host IDs.

	Subnet 1	Subnet 2	Subnet 3	Subnet 4
Network Address:	192.203.97.0	192.203.97.64	192.203.97.128	192.203.97.192
Host IDs:	192.203.97.1 to 192.203.97.62	192.203.97.65 to 192.203.97.126	192.203.97.129 to 192.203.97.190	192.203.97.193 to 192.203.97.254
Broadcast Address:	192.203.97.63	192.203.97.127	192.203.97.191	192.203.97.255

Routing protocols need to support subnet masking to determine correct routing information. For example, consider the destination address 192.203.97.143 with the subnet mask 255.255.255.192. Let's examine an expanded view of these addresses.

Mask: 255.255.255.

1	1	0	0	0	0	0	0
128	64	32	16	8	4	2	1

Host ID: 192.203.97.

1	0	0	0	1	1	1	1
128	64	32	16	8	4	2	1

The correct subnet is determined by "masking" the bits in the host field from the 1-bits in the mask. This is done by combining these bits via a logical AND.

```
              Mask:  1 1 0 0 0 0 0 0
           Host ID:  1 0 0 0 1 1 1 1
Result of logical AND:  1 0 0 0 0 0 0 0
```

Since $10000000_2 = 128_{10}$, the correct subnet is 128. That is, the host with address 192.203.97.143 is attached to the subnetwork whose address is 192.203.97.128. Furthermore, when the six bits of the host ID (001111) are added to the corresponding bits of the mask, the result is 001111_2, which is equal to 15_{10}. Thus, the destination address 192.203.97.143 is correctly identified as host 15 on subnet 128 of network 192.203.97. If the routing protocol does not support subnet masking, then the destination address corresponds to host ID 143 on network 192.203.97.0, which is incorrect.

Although our subnetting discussion focused on Class C addresses, Class A and Class B addresses can also be subnetted following a similar scheme. For example, the Class B address 163.118.0.0 by default specifies a flat network address space with a 16-bit network ID and a 16-bit host ID. Thus, this unsubnetted network address comprises a single network with 65,536 host IDs with a subnet mask of 255.255.0.0. This same address can be subnetted into 256 autonomous subnets with each subnet supporting 256 host IDs by using 8 higher-order bits of the host ID as part of the network ID. By doing so, the network ID will consist of 24 bits, the host ID will consist of 8 bits, and the corresponding subnet mask will be 255.255.255.0. Hence, this scheme effectively subnets a Class B address into 256 Class C equivalent addresses. Once again, note how much more efficient this is than maintaining a single (flat) address space with 65,536 nodes.

Subnetted networks themselves can also be subnetted. For example, a Class C address could first be partitioned into two subnets via a /25 mask. One of these subnets could then be further partitioned into two subsubnets with a /26 mask, and the other subnetwork could be partitioned into three subsubnets with a /27 mask. Similarly, a Class B address could be subnetted into 256 Class C equivalent addresses with a /24 mask, and then any one of these subnets could be further subnetted using an appropriate mask of varying lengths. This concept of partitioning a network address into unevenly sized subnets is called *variable length subnet masking*.

IP Address Resolutions: DNS

Every host (well, almost every host) that is connected to the Internet has both an IP address and a corresponding logical name. This logical name, which is generically referred to as a domain name, is another type of addressing construct used for identifying Internet nodes. For example, the IP address that corresponds to www.att.com is 192.20.3.54. The translation from logical name to IP address, called name resolution, makes it easier for us to deal with Internet addresses. After all, we are mere humans and, as such, have a limited capacity for memorizing long strings of numbers, particularly when they are formatted as IP addresses, and especially if they are IPv6 addresses, which are 128 bits long. Without name resolution, Web site addresses or e-mail addresses could not employ names of organizations, descriptive titles, acronyms, and the like. They would all be numerically based. (Remember: You are nobody unless you are somebody@somewhere.com.)

Before we explain the translation process, it might be helpful first to understand the concept of domain names. Domain names are organized in a hierarchical treelike fashion. At the top of the tree are top-level domains. There are currently seven three-letter descriptive top-level domains that represent general entities, plus two-letter country codes assigned to different countries throughout the world. The top-level domains include com for commercial organizations (e.g., for-profit companies); edu for educational organizations (currently restricted to 4-year colleges and universities; all other schools are part of the us country domain); gov for government organizations

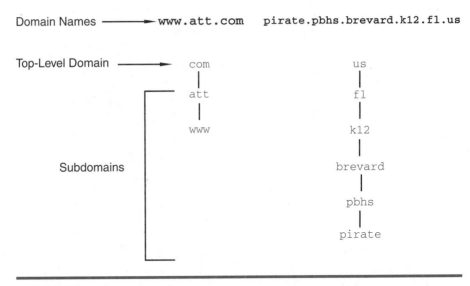

FIGURE 8.18 Domain names are structured in a right-to-left hierarchy. The top-level domain is the rightmost part of an address. All sublevels are subdomains of their immediately preceding higher-level domain. If a domain name includes the hostname as its lowest level, then the structure is called a fully qualified domain name.

Several new top-level domain names were approved in late 2000, including .info for general use, .biz for business, .name for individuals, .pro for professionals, .museum for museums, .coop for business cooperatives, and .aero for the aviation industry.

or agencies (currently restricted to U.S. federal government agencies); int for international treaty organizations; mil for U.S. military organizations; net for Internet service providers; and org for any miscellaneous organization including not-for-profit organizations. The two-letter country codes are those specified in the ISO-3166 document. Examples include us for United States, ca for Canada, and au for Australia. Under each top-level domain are sublevels, and each lower level is considered a subdomain of its immediately preceding higher level. There has been considerable discussion to create additional top-level domains to be more reflective of today's Internet.

When expressed as a logical Internet address, the domain name hierarchy is structured from right to left—the top level is at the right and the bottom level at the left—and consists of multiple levels separated by dots. For example, www.att.com is a three-level structure. Its top-level domain is com, att is a subdomain within com, and www is the name of a host within att. As another illustration, consider the six-level domain name, pirate.pbhs.brevard.k12.fl.us. Its top-level domain is us; fl is a subdomain in us (it's for the state of Florida); k12 is a subdomain within fl (it represents public schools from kindergarten through 12th grade); brevard is a subdomain of k12 (it's the name of a county school district); pbhs is a subdomain of brevard (it's the name of a specific school); and pirate is the name of a host within pbhs. This is another fully qualified domain name (Figure 8.18).

If the lowest level is the name of a host, then the entire structure is called a fully qualified domain name, or FQDN.

To translate domain names to IP addresses, a domain name service is used. The translation process involves configuring host machines as domain name system

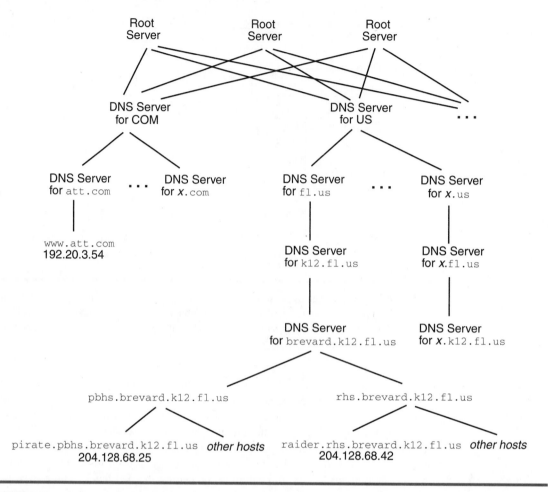

FIGURE 8.19 DNS servers provide name resolution service. Each subdomain has at least one name server that is authoritative for that domain. That is, it maintains complete and accurate information about all the hosts within its subdomain. Name servers also have the address of other servers they can contact in the event they cannot resolve a name locally. They also have the address of at least one root server, which provides interdomain name resolution capability.

(DNS) servers. DNS servers store specific address information about a particular domain or subdomain. They are located at each top-level domain and at various subdomains within a top-level domain. Special root servers are also used to process interdomain DNS requests. Each subdomain has at least one DNS server that is authoritative for that domain. This means that it contains accurate and complete domain name-IP address resolution records for all the connected hosts within that domain. For example, in Figure 8.19, let's assume that a user on host `pirate` wants to connect to the Web server `raider`, which is in the `rhs.brevard.k12.fl.us` domain. The Web browser on `pirate` places a DNS query to the DNS server for `brevard.k12.fl.us`, which is authoritative for the `brevard.k12.fl.us` domain. This DNS server looks up the information in its database and returns the address 204.128.64.2. Now suppose this same user wants to connect to the Web server `www.att.com`. A similar query is made to the `brevard.k12.fl.us` DNS server. This time, though, it does not have any information about the `att.com` domain and hence cannot resolve the name. This DNS server then initiates a process of trying to get the name resolved. Each DNS server has the address of other name servers, including at least one root server. If a DNS server cannot resolve a name, it replies by specifying the name server that should be contacted next. Eventually, a root server gets involved. Root servers maintain information about all the authoritative name servers for each top-level domain. Thus, if the `brevard` name server cannot get `www.att.com` resolved by the higher-level name servers within its domain, a root server will eventually provide it with the `att.com` DNS server's address. The `brevard` name server then contacts the `att.com` name server, which will return the address 192.20.3.54. The `brevard` name server then sends this information to the client process on `pirate`. The `brevard` server will also store this address locally in its cache along with other names it has resolved recently. This helps reduce the number of DNS lookups and makes the DNS process more efficient.

A UNIX and Microsoft NT program that is used to acquire the IP address of a domain name is *nslookup*. To find the IP address of a domain name, simply enter `nslookup` followed by the domain name. For example, `nslookup www.att.com` returns the address 192.20.3.54. This command can also be used for IP address resolution, which translates numerical IP addresses to corresponding domain names.

DNS is not the only method of name resolution. A simple but inefficient alternative is to maintain on every local machine a host file that contains the fully qualified domain names and their respective IP addresses of all the hosts you need to contact. Some operating systems enable you to use both DNS and host files. For example, a host might be configured to use host table lookup first and DNS second. This way, if a host cannot resolve a hostname via its local host file, it can then place a DNS query.

IP Address and Name Assignments

Control of IP addresses initially was governed by the federally funded Internet Assigned Numbers Authority (IANA). The IANA service had authority over all number spaces used in the Internet, including Internet addresses. IANA has long been a part of the University of Southern California's Information Science Institute and was under the direction of Internet pioneer Jon Postel until his death on October 16, 1998. In 1999, the Internet Corporation for Assigned Names and Numbers (ICANN), a private non-profit corporation with international representation, was expressly formed to assume IANA responsibilities as well as those of other government organizations that provided domain name service. The transition from a U.S. government-controlled service to a private organization governed by an international board of directors took approximately 1 year. Additional information about IANA and ICANN is available at `http://www.iana.org` and `http://www.icann.org`

IP address assignments are handled in a distributed fashion via an Internet registry (IR) system, which is hierarchical in structure and involves several organizations. Starting at the top, this hierarchy consists of ICANN (see preceding paragraph), regional Internet registries (RIR), and local Internet registries (LIR). RIRs are established under the authority of IANA and include the American Registry for Internet Numbers (ARIN), the Asian-Pacific Network Information Center (APNIC), and Réseaux IP Européens Network Coordination Centre (RIPE NCC). ARIN, which assumed registry responsibilities from InterNIC, is the RIR for North America, South America, the Caribbean, and sub-Saharan Africa; APNIC is the RIR for countries in the Asian Pacific region (e.g., Japan, China, Thailand); and RIPE NCC is the RIR for Europe and surrounding areas. LIRs are established by IANA and RIRs. In some cases, LIRs are also Internet service providers (ISPs). The way IP address assignments work is as follows: The IANA allocates blocks of IP address space to regional Internet registries. The RIRs allocate blocks of IP address space to their local Internet registries. LIRs then assign addresses to either end users or ISPs. The assignment of IP addresses using this structure enables routing information for end users to be aggregated once it leaves a provider's routing domain. This reduces the number of route announcements and state changes throughout the Internet. (See Chapter 7 for more information about routing.) There has been some discussion of establishing two more RIRs: one for South America and one for Africa.

8.7 IPv6

The Need for IPv6

IPv6 was developed for the same reason other new Internet protocols have been developed or existing ones modified: growth. Due to the tremendous growth of the Internet, the number of available IPv4 addresses is shrinking. Furthermore, with the deployment of more networks, routing tables are overflowing and unable to handle the demand of maintaining information about every network. This depletion of IP addresses and routing table overflow are analogous to the telephone company running out of area codes and old telephone switches unable to place calls to certain numbers. This is why we now have area codes with middle digits other than 0 or 1, a toll-free 888 exchange in addition to the traditional 800 exchange, and multiple area codes serving the same area. Although the original developers of TCP/IP in the early 1980s accounted admirably for the future growth of TCP/IP, no one could have predicted the exponential growth that is occurring within the Internet today.

Although the driving force behind this phenomenal growth can be linked to the computer market, this probably will not be the case in the near future. Indeed, the computer market will continue growing; there are still many schools and small businesses

For those of you who are wondering, Version 5 of IP, namely, IPv5, is an experimental Internet protocol designed for real-time parallel data transmissions. So although it appears that the Internet Engineering Steering Group (IESG) skipped a version number when it assigned the number 6 to the new protocol, in reality, this was not the case.

not yet connected to the Internet. However, the future growth of the Internet will probably be fueled by several new markets, including the following:

Personal Communication Devices. Fax machines, personal digital assistants (PDAs), telephones, and nomadic units that rely on wireless communications are very popular. These devices are network addressable and hence require a unique IP address. Furthermore, some of these devices must be capable of automatically configuring (and reconfiguring) themselves with correct addressing information when moved from one remote location to another.

Networked Entertainment. Video-on-demand, stereos, CDs, and interactive television will one day be network addressable. For example, in a world of networked television sets, every TV will effectively become an Internet host and require a unique IP address.

Networked Controlled Devices. A wide range of devices from simple appliances, such as lights and electronic security devices, to heavy motors, such as heating and air conditioning units, or any other equipment currently controlled by analog switches will be controlled via networked communications.

Each of these markets is huge, and they all have a common attendant characteristic: They all bring to the table a new set of requirements that IPv4 does not support. For example, there will be a need for (among others) large-scale routing, automatic configuration and reconfiguration of host addresses, and built-in authentication and encryption for security purposes. In addition to providing such functionality, it also is imperative that the new IP continues to support existing applications.

IPv6 versus IPv4

IPv6, which is sometimes called IPng (for next generation), provides a solution that resolves current addressing problems and is capable of delivering the necessary functionality for emerging markets. Designed as an evolutionary replacement, IPv6 maintains most IPv4 functions, relegates certain functions that either were not working or were rarely used in IPv4 as optional, and adds new functionality that is missing from IPv4.

Although the IPv4 header has 14 fields, it is unusual to see more than 12 in use. The options field is rarely used, and hence, the padding field, which is only used for alignment when options are used, is also rarely required.

Some of the specific differences between IPv4 and IPv6 are readily apparent when you examine the format and content of their headers, shown in Figures 8.20 and 8.21, respectively. Three obvious differences are (a) size—the IPv4 header length is variable because of its options and padding fields, but IPv6 is a fixed 320 bits; (b) the number of fields—IPv4 has 14 fields, but IPv6 has only 8; and (c) address field size—source and destination addresses are 32 bits each in IPv4, but 128 bits each in IPv6. The address fields make up 80% of the IPv6 header (256 bits). Without these two fields, the IPv6 header is only 64 bits in length, which makes it much smaller than the corresponding IPv4 header.

4	4	8	16	16	3	13	8	8	16	32	32	Variable	
V	HL	ST	TL	ID	F	FO	TTL	P	HC	SA	DA	OPT	PAD

V This 4-bit field specifies the protocol *version* number. For IPv4, it is 0100.

HL This 4-bit field specifies the *header length* in 32-bit words. It is needed because the OPT and PAD fields do not have fixed lengths. (The header length does not include the length of the user data field, which immediately follows the PAD field. The data field is not shown here because it is not part of the header.)

ST This 8-bit *service type* field specifies the manner in which a packet (i.e., datagram) is routed. It contains three subfields, as shown below:

Precedence (3 bits)	Type of Service (4 bits)	MBZ (1 bit)

- The *precedence* subfield specifies the priority of the datagram (from 000 = normal to 111 = network control).
- The *type of service* (TOS) field specifies transport control information relative to delay, throughput, reliability, and cost. For example, 1000 = minimize delay; 0100 = maximize throughput; 0010 = maximize reliability; 0001 = minimize monetary cost; and 0000 = normal service (default). (See RFC 1349 for more information about TOS.)
- The *MBZ* (must be zero) field is currently unused.

TL This 16-bit field specifies the *total length* of the packet. Given the field's 16-bits, the maximum size of an IPv4 packet is 2^{16} = 65,535 bytes.

ID This 16-bit field specifies the unique *identification* number that was assigned to the packet. This number is used to reassemble fragmented packets.

F This 3-bit *flag* field is used to control fragmentation.

FO This 13-bit *fragment offset* field provides reassembly information for fragmented packets.

TTL This 8-bit *time to live* field is a counter (often called a *hop count*) that specifies the number of seconds a packet is permitted to remain alive (i.e., active) on the Internet. This field gets decremented whenever it is processed by a router. When TTL = 0, the packet is discarded and an error message is sent to the source node that sent the packet.

P This 8-bit field specifies the layer-4 *protocol* used to create user data.

HC This 16-bit field contains *header checksum* information, which is used for maintaining packet integrity.

SA This is the 32-bit IP *source address*. (see Box 8.1).

DA This is the 32-bit IP *destination address*. (see Box 8.1).

OPT This variable-bit field is reserved mostly for control *options* (e.g., network testing or debugging). Eight options are available, and the length of this field varies depending on the option used.

PAD This variable-length *padding* field is used in conjunction with the option field. It pads the option field with enough 0 bits to ensure that the header length is a multiple of 32 bits.

FIGURE 8.20 Format and contents of an IPv4 header. The length of each field is given in bits.
Source: adapted from RFC 791, RFC 1702, and RFC 1349.

4	4	24	16	8	8	128	128
V	P	FL	PL	NH	HL	SA	DA

V   This 4-bit field specifies the protocol version number. For IPv6, it is 0110. This is the only field that has exactly the same meaning and position in both IPv4 and IPv6 headers.

P   This 4-bit field specifies the priority of the packet data. This field is new to the IP header; it was not part of IPv4. There are $2^4 = 16$ different priority levels, which are divided into two groups. The first group, which is specified by priority levels 0 through 7, designates packets that can respond to congestion control. For example, in an IP-based frame relay network, in the presence of congestion, the destination node can reset its transmission window value to 0, which effectively informs the sender to stop transmitting data to the receiver until a nonzero window size is received from the receiver (see Chapter 12). The second priority group is specified by priority levels 8 through 15 and designates packets that cannot respond to congestion control. This second priority group is used for critical data such as voice and video. These packets will not backoff in response to congestion control.

FL   This 24-bit flow label field designates packets that require special handling. One use of this field is to provide quality of service (QoS) via RSVP. This field is new to the IP header; it was not part of IPv4.

PL   This 16-bit field specifies the payload length of the user data that follows the header. IPv6's PL replaces IPv4's total length field, which specifies the length of the header and data.

NH   This 8-bit next header field replaces IPv4's protocol field. NH specifies the type of header that immediately follows the IPv6 header. NH enables extension headers to be inserted between the IP header and the TCP or UDP headers that precede user data. An example of this field is the use of IPSec's authentication and encryption headers for security. This field also effectively replaces IPv4's header length and option fields.

HL   This 8-bit hop limit field is used to specify the number of seconds a packet can remain active on the Internet. The value of this field is decremented by 1 second each time it passes through a router. HL replaces IPv4's TTL field.

SA   This field carries the 128-bit IP source address. Except for its length, SA has exactly the same meaning as IPv4's SA field. Its location within the packet is different, though.

DA   This field carries the 128-bit IP destination address. Except for its length, DA has exactly the same meaning as IPv4's DA field. Its location within the packet is different, though.

FIGURE 8.21   Format and contents of an IPv6 header. The length of each field is given in bits. Source: adapted from RFC 1752, RFC 1883, and RFC 2373.

Although IPv6 embodies a "less is more" philosophical structure, it still supports a wide variety of options. Consider, for example, the next header (NH) field, which specifies the type of header that immediately follows the IPv6 header. NH enables extension headers for optional layer-3 data to be inserted between the IP header and the upper-layer headers (e.g., TCP or UDP) that precede user data. An example of this field is the use of IPSec's authentication and encryption headers for security (see Chapter 17). NH effectively combines the functions of IPv4's protocol, header length, and option fields. IPv6 also provides support for prioritizing traffic via its 4-bit priority (P) field and for assigning special handling designations (e.g., QoS) to packets through its 24-bit flow label (FL) field. Both of these features were not available in IPv4. Additional information about IPv6 can be found in RFC 1883, which contains a complete set of specifications for the new protocol. The Internet draft "The Case for IPv6" also contains information about IPv6.

IPv6 Addresses

As we have stated, one of the most significant differences between IPv4 and IPv6 is IP address size, which was increased from 32 bits in IPv4 to 128 bits in IPv6. Thus, IPv6 addresses have four times as many bits as IPv4 addresses (128 vs. 32). This means there are 2^{128} IPv6 addresses versus 2^{32} IPv4 addresses. Evaluating 2^{128} with our outdated calculator, the result is displayed in scientific notation as $3.402823665 \times 10^{38}$. Hinden (1996), however, was able to calculate this value exactly: 340,282,366,920,938,463,463,374,607,431,768,211,456. When compared to IPv4's 4 billion addresses (i.e., 4,294,967,295), you start to get some feel for the size of IPv6's address space. Hinden also reported that there are enough 128-bit IPv6 addresses to, at worst, provide each square meter of the earth's surface with 1564 addresses and, at best, 3,911,873,538,269,506,102 addresses. The new address space also allows for more levels of addressing hierarchy, simpler autoconfiguration of addresses, and support for other network protocol addresses. Other notable features include:

- Support for three types of addresses: unicast, anycast, and multicast. Unicast addresses identify a single interface. Anycast addresses are assigned to a set of interfaces and routed to the nearest one assigned to that address. The determination of which node is nearest is based on the metric used by the routing protocol (see Chapter 7). Multicast addresses are assigned to a group of interfaces and delivered to all of the interfaces in the assigned group.

> IPv6 addresses are assigned to physical interfaces, not nodes.

- Support for auto-readdressing, which allows a packet to be automatically routed to a new address.
- Support for autoconfiguration of network addresses. IPv6 hosts can acquire their network address dynamically. This is done via a "plug and play" method or through full support for the Dynamic Host Configuration Protocol (DHCP).
- Support for data authentication, privacy, and confidentiality (see Chapter 17).
- Support for priority routing. This enables a source node to assign a delivery priority level to its outgoing packets. This enables "real-time" packets (e.g., packets carrying full-motion video data) to be sent at a constant rate without interruption of delivery.

An IPv6 address is quite different in appearance than an IPv4 address. IPv6 addresses, like IPv4 addresses, are still grouped into classes. The delimiter, however, is no longer the familiar "dot" notation. IPv6 addresses are expressed in hexadecimal form and written as eight 16-bit integers. Also, instead of IPv4's familiar dot notation, IPv6 uses a colon as its delimiter. An example of an IPv6 address is 2A01:0000:0000:0000:12FB:071C:04DE:689E. To reduce the complexity in writing these address, leading 0s in a hex group can be eliminated. Thus, the sample address can be expressed as 2A01:0:0:0:12FB:71C:4DE:689E. Frequently, many IPv6 addresses also contain contiguous strings of 0 bits. For example, IPv6 support of IPv4 address formats involves placing 0s in either the higher-order 80 or 96 bits of an IPv6 address. (More on this later.) In such cases, a double colon can be used to designate multiple 0 groupings. Thus, the sample IPv6 address just given can be expressed in a reduced form as 2A01::12FB:71C:4DE:689E. In this example, the double colon denotes three hex groupings of 0000. The double colon notation can only be used once in an address. It also can be used to designate leading or trailing 0s of an address.

As noted in the preceding paragraph, IPv6 provides support for IPv4 address formats. Such addresses are referred to as "IPv6 addresses with embedded IPv4 addresses." Two different formats are available. The first consists of 96 higher-order 0-bits followed by the 32-bit IPv4 address. A convenient format for expressing this is to mix the colon and dot delimiters. For example, the IPv4 address 206.43.152.78 is expressed in IPv6 form as 0:0:0:0:0:0:206.43.152.78. This address can be further reduced by using the double colon delimiter to represent the leading 0s of the address. Thus, an equivalent form is ::206.43.152.78. This address is formally called an IPv4-compatible IPv6 address and is used to represent nodes that support IPv6 but must route IPv4 packets over an IPv6 network. A second format consists of 80 higher-order 0-bits, followed by one hex grouping of Fs, followed by the IPv4 address. Thus, our sample IPv4 address is expressed in this form as ::FFFF:206.43.152.78. This address type is called an IPv4-mapped IPv6 address and is used to represent IPv4 nodes that do not support IPv6.

The first field of an IPv6 address is a variable-length format prefix, which specifies the various categories of addresses. Examples of some prefixes and their meanings follow:

- **010** designates an IPv6 provider-based unicast address, which is assigned to nodes connected directly to the Internet. The general structure of an IPv6 provider-based unicast address is shown in Figure 8.22.
- **1111 1110 10** designates a link-local address, which is assigned to isolated network sites. An isolated site is one in which nodes are connected to a network, but the network does not have a router and is not connected to the Internet.
- **1111 1110 11** designates a site-local address, which is assigned to sites that have a router connection but are not connected to the Internet.
- **1111 1111** designates a multicast address.
- **0000 0000 0000 0000 0000 0000** designates an embedded IPv4-compatible IPv6 address.

Additional information about the IPv6 addressing architecture can be found in RFC 1884, RFC 2073, RFC 2373, and RFC 2374.

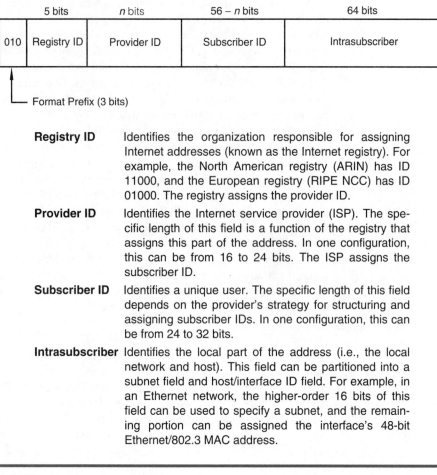

Registry ID   Identifies the organization responsible for assigning Internet addresses (known as the Internet registry). For example, the North American registry (ARIN) has ID 11000, and the European registry (RIPE NCC) has ID 01000. The registry assigns the provider ID.

Provider ID   Identifies the Internet service provider (ISP). The specific length of this field is a function of the registry that assigns this part of the address. In one configuration, this can be from 16 to 24 bits. The ISP assigns the subscriber ID.

Subscriber ID   Identifies a unique user. The specific length of this field depends on the provider's strategy for structuring and assigning subscriber IDs. In one configuration, this can be from 24 to 32 bits.

Intrasubscriber Identifies the local part of the address (i.e., the local network and host). This field can be partitioned into a subnet field and host/interface ID field. For example, in an Ethernet network, the higher-order 16 bits of this field can be used to specify a subnet, and the remaining portion can be assigned the interface's 48-bit Ethernet/802.3 MAC address.

FIGURE 8.22 General structure of an IPv6 provider-based unicast address. Source: adapted from RFC 2050, RFC 2073, and RFC 2374.

IPv6 Migration

IPv6 is more than an IPv4 upgrade; it's a completely new version of the Internet Protocol. Its addressing is different, its headers are more specialized, it provides for more options including flow control and security, and it supports host mobility autoconfiguration along with some other new features. Converting to IPv6 cannot occur overnight. It is unlikely that every Internet user will switch to IPv6 on a predetermined date and time. Can you image the entire Internet world being in sync and pressing the Return key at the same time? Hardly. Instead, the Internet must slowly and methodically migrate from IPv4 to IPv6 over several years.

Migrating to an IPv6 Internet without disrupting the current operation of the existing IPv4 network is a real issue. It is imperative that IPv6 and key functions of IPv4 interoperate during the transition period. The current IPv6 migration plan supports several types of transitions. First, incremental upgrades will be permitted. This means that any IPv4 device can be upgraded to IPv6 independent of any other networked device, with one exception—the DNS server must first be upgraded to handle IPv6 address records. Second, incremental deployment will be supported. This means that new IPv6 nodes can be installed at any time without any modifications necessary. Third, the transition must support current IP addresses. Thus, if an existing IPv4 node is upgraded to IPv6, it does not have to be assigned a new IPv6 address. Rather, it can continue using its existing IPv4 address. Finally, there should be little or no preparation work needed on the part of a network administrator to either upgrade a device from IPv4 to IPv6 or deploy a new IPv6 device. Overall, this transition is to be processed in two phases. At the end of Phase 1, both IPv4 and IPv6 devices will coexist on the Internet; at the end of Phase 2, only IPv6 devices will exist. During Phase 1, it is believed that IPv6 and IPv4 nodes will interoperate, new IPv6 devices will be deployed in an incremental fashion with few interdependencies, and end users, system administrators, and network operators will be capable of making the transition without too much difficulty.

To aid network administrators in their renumbering efforts, an organization called Procedures for Internet Enterprise Renumbering (PIER) is available. Information about PIER can be found at `http://www.ietf.org/proceedings/9bdec/charters/pier/charter.html` Additional information about IPv6 renumbering issues is also available from RFC 1916, RFC 2071, and RFC 2072.

8.8 TCP/IP Application Level Protocols

Some of the most frequently used TCP/IP-based application protocols include the Simple Mail Transfer Protocol (SMTP), the Multipurpose Internet Mail Extensions (MIME), and the Post Office Protocol (POP) for e-mail, the Telnet protocol (TELNET) for virtual terminal connections, the File Transfer Protocol (FTP) for file transfers, and the Hypertext Transfer Protocol (HTTP) for Web applications. A brief description of these protocols follows.

Electronic Mail: SMTP, MIME, and POP

Electronic mail (e-mail) refers to the concept of creating, sending, receiving, and storing messages or documents electronically. Nearly every computer system has a program that serves as an interface for e-mail service. This interface provides users with a utility to, among others, compose, read, save, forward, and print mail messages. In addition to providing a user interface, a local system's e-mail service also supports background processes that govern how incoming and outgoing e-mail messages are stored, how users are presented with incoming e-mail, and how often delivery of outgoing messages is attempted. A generic diagram of how local e-mail service operates is shown in Figure 8.23.

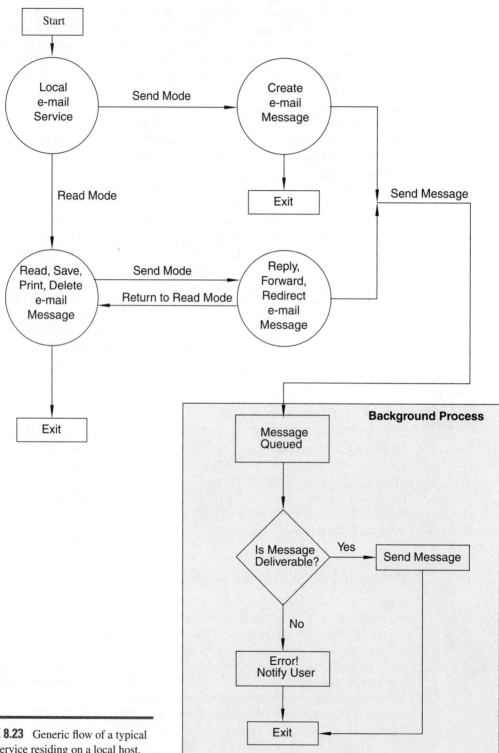

FIGURE 8.23 Generic flow of a typical e-mail service residing on a local host.

The Simple Mail Transport Protocol (SMTP)

Of all the activities depicted in Figure 8.23, the only one that is not performed by the local e-mail service is message delivery. The method by which e-mail messages are transferred from one host to another is defined by a mail protocol, and in the Internet, the standard mail protocol is the *Simple Mail Transfer Protocol* (SMTP), which is defined in RFC 821. SMTP delivers mail to port 25 of the receiving host and operates in the following manner:

> When a user sends an e-mail message, the sending host, through its mail service, places a copy of the message in a special location known as the mail queue. The sending host then attempts to establish a special mail connection to the receiving host as indicated by the mail address. A connection is established when the receiving host sends an acknowledgment to the sending host that it is ready to accept mail. Assuming a mail connection is successful, the sending host transfers a copy of the mail message to the receiving host's mail queue. When both sending and receiving hosts confirm the transfer was successful, the message is removed from the sending host's mail queue and the receiving host's mail service moves the message from the mail queue to the recipient's mailbox. If the local host has no additional messages to send, the protocol then allows for the two systems to interchange roles—that is, the sending host becomes the receiving host and the receiving host becomes the sending host. This allows mail to flow in the opposite direction. Thus, the host that was originally receiving mail can now send any mail stored in its queue destined for the host that was originally sending. Once all mail is delivered between the two systems, a command to terminate the connection is issued and if agreed by both hosts, the mail connection is closed.

Note that SMTP focuses only on transferring messages across a link from one host to another. The protocol has nothing to do with any other mail-related activities. These are provided by the local e-mail service. Further note that SMTP is TCP-based and hence provides a reliable mail delivery service since mail messages remain on the sending host until they are transferred successfully to the receiving host. For example, if the transfer of a mail message between hosts is not successful (e.g., a connection to the receiving host wasn't possible or a connection failed during the transfer of mail), then the message remains in the local mail queue. This local mail queue is periodically checked for undelivered mail by the system's mail program, and if any is found, a new mail connection is attempted. If mail is undelivered after a specified period of time (e.g., 5 days), it is ultimately returned to the sender with a note of explanation.

The UNIX command *mqueue* is used to list the contents of the local system's mail queue.

The transfer of mail between two hosts via SMTP is performed using a specified set of commands defined by the protocol. The actual operation of the protocol begins with the initiating host (i.e., the SMTP sender) establishing a TCP connection to the destination host (i.e., the SMTP receiver). Once a connection is established, the SMTP sender and receiver engage in a "conversation" that involves a succession of commands and responses exchanged between sender and receiver. For each command issued by the sender, exactly one reply is provided by the receiver. A description of SMTP commands is given in Table 8.2; a description of the reply codes issued by a receiver in response to a command is given in Table 8.3; and Figure 8.24 contains an example of a typical exchange.

An exchange similar to that shown in Figure 8.24 can be replicated by establishing a Telnet session to port 25 of a receiving host.

TABLE 8.2 SMTP Commands[a]

Name	Example of Use	Description
HELO	HELO `mailserver.bt.com` <CRLF>[a]	Identifies SMTP sender to SMTP receiver
MAIL	MAIL FROM:<`jb@bt.com`> <CRLF>	Begins mail exchange by identifying originator
RCPT	RCPT TO:<`mickie1@ba.org`<CRLF>	Identifies mail recipient
DATA	DATA<CRLF>	Signifies that what follows is mail message
SEND	SEND FROM:<`jb@bt.com`> <CRLF>	Send mail message to terminal
SOML	SOML FROM:<`jb@bt.com`> <CRLF>	"Send or Mail"; Send mail message to terminal *or* mailbox
SAML	SAML FROM:<`jb@bt.com`> <CRLF>	"Send and Mail"; Send mail message to terminal *and* mailbox
RSET	RSET <CRLF>	Specifies current mail transaction is to be aborted
VRFY	VRFY <user><CRLF>	Requests SMTP receiver to confirm that "user" is a valid user
EXPN	EXPN <mail-list><CRLF>	Requests SMTP receiver to expand given "mail-list" if valid
HELP	HELP [SMTP Command]<CRLF>	SMTP help command
NOOP	NOOP<CRLF>	No operation; generates OK from receiver
QUIT	QUIT<CRLF>	Ends current SMTP session by closing the TCP connection
TURN	TURN<CRLF>	Reverses role of SMTP receiver and sender

[a] <CRLF> means Carriage Return, Line Feed.

TABLE 8.3 SMTP Reply Codes (Extracted from RFC 821)

Code	Description
211	System Status, or system help reply
214	Help message (Information on how to use the receiver or the meaning of a particular nonstandard command; this reply is useful only to the human user)
220	<domain> Service ready
221	<domain> Service closing transmission channel
250	Requested mail action okay, completed
251	User not local; will forward to <forward-path>
354	Start mail input; end with <CRLF>.<CRLF>
421	<domain> Service not available, closing transmission channel (This may be a reply to any command if the service knows it must shut down)
450	Requested mail action not taken: mailbox unavailable (e.g., mailbox busy)
451	Requested action aborted: local error in processing
452	Requested action not taken: insufficient system storage
500	Syntax error, command unrecognized (This may include errors such as command line too long)
501	Syntax error in parameters or arguments
502	Command not implemented
503	Bad sequence of commands
504	Command parameter not implemented
550	Requested action not taken: mailbox unavailable (e.g., mailbox not found, no access)
551	User not local; please try <forward-path>
552	Requested mail action aborted: exceeded storage allocation
553	Requested action not taken: mailbox name not allowed (e.g., mailbox syntax incorrect)
554	Transaction failed

SMTP Sender (S): mailserver.bt.com
SMTP Receiver (R): ba.org

1

S: (mailserver.bt.com establishes a connection to ba.org)

R: 220 ba.org ESMTP Sendmail 8.9.3/8.9.1; Tue, 16 May 2000 12:51:49 -0400 (EDT)

2

S: **HELO mailserver.bt.com**

R: 250 ba.org Hello mailserver.bt.com, pleased to meet you

3

S: **MAIL FROM:<jb@mailserver.bt.com>**

R: 250 <jb@mailserver.bt.com>. . . Sender ok

4

S: **VRFY <mickie1>**

R: 252 Cannot VRFY user; try RCPT to attempt delivery (or try finger)

5

S: **RCPT TO:<mickie1>**

R: 250 <mickie1>. . . Recipient ok

6

S: **DATA**

R: 354 Enter mail, end with "." on a line by itself

7

S: **Hi,**

Just a quick message to demonstrate some of the SMTP commands.

.

R: 250 MAA25178 Message accepted for delivery

8

S: **QUIT**

R: 221 s1.cfe.fit.edu delivering mail

1 A connection to the receiving host is made by the sending host.
2 The sending host identifies itself to the receiving host.
3 The sending host indicates to the receiving host that it has mail from user jb.
4 The sending host attempts to verify that the recipient, mickie1, on the receiving host is a valid user, but the receiving host responds that it cannot execute a VRFY command.
5 The sending host identifies to the receiving host that its mail is intended for mickie1; the receiving host acknowledges that mickie1 is a valid recipient on its system.
6 The sending host issues a DATA command, which implies that all subsequent text is to be treated as a mail message. The receiving host responds accordingly and instructs the sending host to end the mail message by placing a period on a line by itself.
7 The sending host enters the mail message.
8 The sending host issues a QUIT command, which causes the receiving host to deliver the mail message and terminate the connection.

FIGURE 8.24 Sample SMTP command/response exchange between an SMTP sender and receiver.

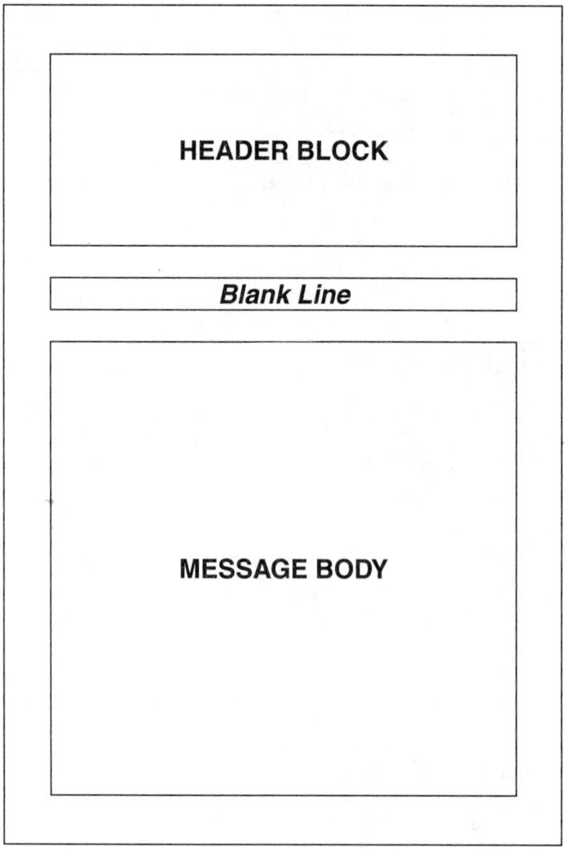

FIGURE 8.25 RFC 822 mail message format.

E-mail messages that are exchanged via SMTP all follow the same format, which is defined in RFC 822. This format consists of a header block, followed by a blank line, followed by the body of the mail message (Figure 8.25). The header block comprises individual lines that include a field name, followed by a colon, followed by specific information related to the field (called the field body). For example, the header line

```
Sender: jb@mailserver.bt.com
```

contains the field name, `Sender`, and the field body, `jb@mailserver.bt.com`, which is the e-mail address of the sender. The field name and body are delimited by a colon. A description of typical RFC 822 header fields is given in Table 8.4, and an example of an RFC 822-compliant message that uses some of these fields is shown in Figure 8.26.

TABLE 8.4 Frequently Used RFC 822 Header Fields

Field	Description
Date	The date the message was sent
From	The name and address of the sender
To	The name and address of the recipient
Subject	A statement that describes the content of the message
Return-Path	Identifies a path back to the originator of the message (added by mail transport service)
Reply-To	Identifies the address where replies should be sent if different than the *From* line address
In-Reply-To	Identifies the message to which the current message is replying
Cc	Address to which copy of the message is being sent
Message-ID	Message identification
Received from	The name of the SMTP sending host
Received by	The name of the SMTP receiving host
Received via	The physical path on which the message arrived
Received with	The mail protocol the message used for delivery
Received id	The receiver message id

Header

```
From: jb@mailserver.bt.com Thu Oct 25 08:54:10 1990

Return-Path: <jb@mailserver.bt.com>

Received: from mailserver.bt.com by ba.org (4.1/SMI-DDN) id AA07077; Thu,
25 Oct 90 08:54:07 EDT

Date: Thu, 25 Oct 90 09:12:25 EDT

From: jb@mailserver.bt.com (Janie Busch)

Message-Id: <9010251312.AA04733@mailserver.bt.com>

To: mickie1@ba.org

Subject: Re: E-mail Address
```

Blank Line

Body of Message

```
Mickie,
Thanks for sending me the address.
Ciao.


JB
```

FIGURE 8.26 Sample RFC 822 mail message.

RFC 822 was designed for sending messages containing lines of ASCII text only. This avoids the problems that are inherent in supporting other character sets. By restricting messages to consist of only ASCII text, it is not necessary, for example, to determine a binary representation for sending binary files or to have to translate between a standard character set and the character set of the local host. The combination of a standard header format and support for only ASCII text makes it relatively easy to process and send mail messages across heterogeneous systems.

The Multipurpose Internet Mail Extensions (MIME)

Unfortunately, RFC 822's simple formatting feature limits its functionality. In today's world of multimedia, users want to be able to exchange nontext files (e.g., graphic, video, or audio) in addition to plain-text files. To address this limitation, the *Multipurpose Internet Mail Extension* (MIME) was developed and is defined in RFC 1521. Note that MIME is an extension of the current SMTP-based mail system; it is not a replacement. Specifically, MIME extends the concept of what we call e-mail by providing support for different data types and for complex message bodies. The MIME specification includes new message header fields, definitions for new content formats, and definitions for transfer encodings. The new header fields provide information about the message body; the new content formats identify the type of content the message body contains (e.g., text, audio, video); and the transfer encodings enable data to be reencoded into a seven-bit short-line format so they can be delivered using a seven-bit mail transport protocol such as SMTP, which restricts mail messages to lines no longer than 1000 characters. Table 8.5 contains a description of MIME header fields, Table 8.6 contains a description of MIME content types, and Table 8.7 contains a description of MIME transfer encodings.

The Post Office Protocol (POP)

In the early days of the Internet, mail messages were stored in users' mailboxes, which were located on a centralized host. Typically, these hosts were running the UNIX operating system, and access to e-mail meant logging into the e-mail server—either directly via a hard-wired terminal or remotely via Telnet—and using the server's mail utility. Interacting with a server's mail utility was not a pleasant experience for many users because UNIX mail service was a text-based program that usually required special commands (called tilde commands) to facilitate the manipulation of mail messages. For example, in the AT&T System V mail program, ~v invoked the vi editor, ~p displayed the contents of the current mail message, and ~r *filename* inserted the contents of the file, *filename,* into the current mail message. Although programs like *pine* helped tame the interface problem, interacting with the system's mail service was still unpleasant for many.

In addition to the interface problem, there was the mail storage problem. As desktop computing grew, more and more users began accessing their local e-mail server from their desktop PCs using Telnet. This was not convenient on two fronts. First, users were unable to take advantage of their PC's native operating system features when interacting with the mail program—when it came to e-mail, users' PCs had to be employed as dumb terminals. Second, users' mail messages were stored on a remote server and not directly on their PCs. What users wanted was the ability to transfer the contents of their

TABLE 8.5 MIME Header Fields Defined in RFC 1521

Field	Description
MIME-Version	Provides a version number that declares a message to be MIME-compliant to a MIME specification. Version 1.0 implies conformity to RFC 1521 and RFC 1522.
Content-Type	Specifies the type and subtype of data contained in message body (see Table 8.6).
Content-Transfer-Encoding	Specifies the encoding used for data transport.
Content-ID	Identifies MIME entities in various contexts. (optional)
Content-Description	Text-based description of the data contained in the message body. (optional)

TABLE 8.6 MIME Content Types Defined in RFC 1521

Type	Subtype	Description
Text (Data composed of textual information using different character sets)	• Plain	• Plain unformatted text. This is the primary Content-Type for Internet e-mail.
Multipart (Data composed of multiple independent sections)	• Mixed	• Used when the body parts are independent (i.e., they may contain data of any content type) but need to be placed together in a specific order.
	• Alternative	• Indicates that the message body contains the same data represented in different formats. The formats are ordered by increasing faithfulness to original content.
	• Digest	• Indicates that the document data consist of Content Type = Message/RFC 822.
	• Parallel	• Similar to Mixed except there is no specific data order and hence may be viewed simultaneously.
Message (Data are an encapsulated mail message)	• rfc822	• Syntax of encapsulated message is RFC 822 compliant.
	• Partial	• Enables large messages to be fragmented for delivery.
	• External-Body	• Message body contains a pointer that points to an external source containing a large message.
Application (Data do not fit any other category)	• Octet-stream	• Indicates that message body contains binary data.
	• Postscript	• Indicates message body is Adobe PostScript data.
Image (Data composed of a still image)	• JPEG	• Indicates data in JPEG format using JFIF encoding.
	• GIF	• Indicates data in GIF format.
Audio (Message composed of voice data)	• Basic	• Message body is audio encoded using eight-bit ISDN mu-law [PCM]. Assumes a sample rate of 8000 Hz and a single channel.
Video (Data composed of moving graphic image)	• MPEG	• Indicates message body consists of video data coded according to the MPEG standard.

TABLE 8.7 MIME Transfer Encodings Defined in RFC 1521

Encoding	Description
7bit	Data represented as seven-bit U.S. ASCII; no encoding is done.
8bit	Data contain "short lines" but also might include non-ASCII characters, which contain octets with the high-order bit set; no encoding is done.
binary	Data contain non-ASCII characters and line size most likely not RFC 821 compliant; no encoding is done.
quoted-printable	Used to encode data that consist mostly of ASCII characters. Non-ASCII characters are encoded using one of several rules defined in RFC 1521. Since most of the data are being encoded in ASCII, the encoded representation is still recognizable by humans.
base64	Encoding scheme that represents three octets of data as four six-bit characters. This scheme is similar to the one used for Pretty Good Privacy (PGP).
x-token	Any proprietary encoding scheme developed by a software developer.

This two-way transfer could also be done using a file transfer protocol such as Kermit, but such protocols are terminal-based and not network-based.

mailboxes from the mail server to their desktop PC and to use the full features of their PC's native operating system to interact with e-mail. It should be noted that there was nothing stopping users from creating an e-mail message locally on a PC using a word processing program like Word. The problem was sending this message to the mail server for delivery to the message's recipient and to transfer the contents of the users' mailboxes back to the PC. The *Post Office Protocol* (POP) was designed to effect this two-way transfer in a simple and convenient manner.

The POP protocol is very similar to SMTP and uses an SMTP-like command set. Two versions of POP are available. POP2 is defined in RFC 937 and uses well-known port number 109; POP3 is defined in RFC 1939 and uses port 110. PC-based e-mail programs such as Eudora provide users with an interface that takes full advantage of a PC's native OS and uses the client version of the POP protocol for e-mail transfers between the PC and designated mail server, which runs the POP server version. Although the POP2 and POP3 command sets are different and incompatible, both protocols operate in a similar manner. Following is the basic operation of the POP3 protocol:

> The server invokes the POP3 service by listening on TCP port 110. When a client wants to use the service, it establishes a TCP connection with the server. When the connection is first established, the server sends a greeting that identifies the POP3 process. The current session then enters into an authorization state in which the client identifies itself to the server by sending the user's username and password for the mail account located on the server. Assuming valid authorization, the session then enters into a transaction state in which the client directs the server to manipulate the user's mailbox relative to the client e-mail program's configurations. These can include (among others) retrieving all unread mail, deleting messages, and sending queued messages.

As is the case with SMTP, each POP command issued by the client generates a response by the server. Thus, the client and POP server exchange commands and responses, respectively, until the connection is closed or aborted. In POP3, only two response types are defined: +OK and –ERR. The POP3 command set is shown in Table 8.8.

TABLE 8.8 POP3 Commands[a]

Name	Syntax	Description
USER	USER *username* <CRLF>[a]	Indicates the user's account name on the mail server.
PASS	PASS *password* <CRLF>	Indicates the user's password on the mail server.
STAT	STAT <CRLF>	Report of the number of unread messages.
LIST	LIST [*m*] <CRLF>	List the size of all messages or of only message number *m*.
RETR	RETR *m* <CRLF>	Retrieve message number *m*.
DELE	DELE *m* <CRLF>	Delete message number *m*.
NOOP	NOOP <CRLF>	No operation; generates +OK from receiver.
RSET	RSET <CRLF>	Unmark all messages marked as deleted.
TOP	TOP *m n* <CRLF>	Retrieve the first *n* lines of message *m* (e.g., TOP 6 10 retrieves the first 10 lines of message number 6).
UIDL	UIDL [*m*] <CRLF>	Provides unique id information about message *m*.
APOP	APOP *name digest* <CRLF>	Alternative POP authentication method that does not involve sending a clear password over the network during frequent, intermittent POP sessions.
QUIT	QUIT <CRLF>	• If entered from authorization state, current session terminates (TCP connection is closed). • If entered from the transaction state, current session enters update state and all messages marked for deletion are deleted; any mailbox locks are then released and the TCP connection is closed.

[a] <CRLF> means Carriage Return, Line Feed.

The TELNET Protocol

TELNET is a general purpose remote login protocol included in the TCP/IP protocol suite; it is defined in RFC 854. TELNET provides *virtual terminal service,* which enables a user who has a direct connection on a local host to log into a remote host and interact with this remote host as if the user were directly connected to it. Once a remote login session is established, the TELNET protocol provides the necessary mechanism for keystrokes entered on the local host to be passed directly to the remote host. TELNET uses TCP for reliable data transport and is accessible via the *telnet* application program, which is a built-in function on UNIX- and Windows-based (i.e., Windows 95/98/2000) machines. Third-party *telnet* application programs such as NCSA Telnet for Macintosh are also available. When used for remote terminal access, the TELNET server listens for client TELNET TCP connection requests on well-known port number 23.

The TELNET protocol defines an imaginary, bidirectional character device called a *network virtual terminal* (NVT), which is designed to maintain terminal characteristic information about the terminals located at each end of a TELNET connection. Through the NVT, a standard networkwide representation of a terminal is provided so that both client and server have an agreed upon convention for how a terminal appears over the network. When a TELNET connection is first established, each end is assumed to originate and terminate at the NVT, and both client and server map their local device characteristics and conventions to the NVT.

The TELNET protocol also permits the negotiation of additional services beyond the minimal terminal services provided by the NVT. Thus, if a client and server want to use a different set of conventions for a particular connection, then they can negotiate specific options to implement. For example, each end of a TELNET connection might consist of devices that support more sophisticated terminal characteristics. In this instance, the two terminals might want to change the character set they use for this connection. In another example, hosts might want to invoke a data format change from ASCII to binary. Regardless of what changes are made, TELNET's option negotiation service provides client and server with the ability to enhance their communications.

As a remote login protocol, TELNET is not as sophisticated as other protocols that provide similar capability. For example, the UNIX-based remote login facility, *rlogin,* exports most of a user's local environment to the remote host. This enables the remote terminal type to be equivalent to the local terminal environment (as defined by the environmental variable TERM), and if windows are being used, window size is also maintained. Given its simple nature, a TELNET session might not pass the local computing environment to the remote host. This means that when a remote connection is established, local terminal settings most likely will not be maintained at the other end of the connection. This can result in terminal emulation problems, which can lead to a high degree of user frustration, particularly during an editing session. Fortunately, most telnet application programs provide some form of keyboard mapping that minimizes this problem. Along this same line, the TELNET protocol also defines a standard representation of five control functions. These include: Interrupt Process, which suspends, interrupts, aborts, or terminates a process; Abort Output, which stops output being generated by a process from being sent to a user's terminal; Are You There, which enables a user to receive visible confirmation that the remote system is still "up"; Erase Character, which provides the equivalent of a delete key; and Erase Line, which erases the current line of input. Finally, some remote hosts are IBM-based devices that do not support ASCII terminal controllers. A virtual terminal connection to such sites requires special software that emulates an IBM 3270 terminal. An application called tn3270 is designed for such connections.

When using the TELNET protocol for virtual terminal service across the Internet, users should exercise patience. In the presence of network congestion or high remote system activity, it is not uncommon for response times to be in the tens of seconds. It is also common for TELNET connections to simply time out, which effectively closes the TCP connection. The "Are You There" control function is often helpful to confirm that a connection is still active. Frustrated TELNET users can probably appreciate the following adage:

> If you can see it and touch it, it's physical. (This represents a direct connection.)
> If you can see it but can't touch it, it's virtual. (This represents a TELNET connection.)
> If you can't see it and can't touch it, it's gone. (This is what happens when a TELNET connection times out.)

The File Transfer Protocol (FTP)

The *File Transfer Protocol* (FTP) is the standard application protocol of the TCP/IP protocol suite that is used for exchanging files between two systems. FTP uses TCP as its transport protocol and involves two separate connections. One connection is used to support the actual data transfer process; the second connection is used to handle various control processes relative to the actual FTP session. A conceptual model of these two processes and connections is shown in Figure 8.27. An FTP server process listens on well-known port 21 for an initial connection request from an FTP client. Once a connection is established, the control process creates a separate TCP connection for a particular data transfer. Since the same port number cannot be used, the server uses well-known port 20. The client reports the port number it will use for the data transfer connection to the server via the control connection.

A separate data transfer connection (and corresponding data transfer process) is established for each file transfer. There is only one control connection, however, for an FTP session. Thus, once the control connection is closed, the FTP session is terminated, and any data transfer processes that are active also get terminated by the respective hosts. To keep things simple, FTP uses TELNET's basic NVT to exchange data across the control connection. (No option negotiation is allowed.)

The user interface to the FTP protocol is provided by the ftp application program, which is available on UNIX- and Windows-based (i.e., Windows 95/98/2000) machines. Third-party ftp application programs such as Fetch for the Macintosh are also available. Since FTP uses TELNET for its control connection, a user must first establish a valid login (i.e., valid username and password) on the remote system before a file transfer can be effected.

> Client port numbers are randomly assigned.

> Many Internet servers, called *anonymous FTP servers,* run a restricted ftp program that permits access to their systems using the login name *anonymous* and the user's e-mail address or local login name as the password.

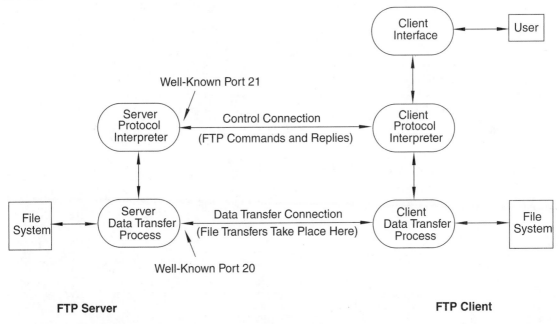

FIGURE 8.27 Conceptual model of the FTP process. Source: extracted from RFC 959.

Assuming valid authorization, the user is then placed in "command mode," from which all FTP commands and options are enabled or disabled. Commands and corresponding replies are transferred across the control connection. A list of FTP commands and options is generated by entering "help" or a question mark at the FTP command prompt. A list of commonly used FTP commands is given in Table 8.9, and a list of commonly used FTP options is given in Table 8.10. Unless otherwise specified, all transferred files are stored in the current working directory of the receiving host.

TABLE 8.9   Commonly Used FTP Commands

Command Syntax	Description
get *remotefile* [*localfile*]	Transfers one file from the remote host to the local host (i.e., we *get* a file). If used with the optional argument, *localfile*, then the file is stored on the receiving host with the name, *localfile*. If the optional argument is not specified, then the transferred file is given the same name on the receiving host as it has on the sending host.
mget *remotefile-1 . . . remotefile-n*	Transfers multiple files from the remote host to the local host.
put *localfile* [*remotefile*]	Transfers one file from the local host to the remote host (i.e., we *put* a file). If used with the optional argument, *remotefile*, then the file is stored on the receiving host with the name, *remotefile*. If the optional argument is not specified, then the transferred file is given the same name on the receiving host as it has on the sending host.
mput *localfile-1 . . . localfile-n*	Transfers multiple files from the local host to the remote host.
cd	The *change directory* command; used to change the remote directory from its current location to a new location.
lcd	The *local change directory* command; used to change the local directory from its current location to a new location.
dir	The *directory* command; used to list the contents of the current remote directory.
pwd	The *print working directory* command; used to display the current working directory of the remote host.
mkdir	The *make directory* command; used to create a new directory on the remote host.

TABLE 8.10   Commonly Used FTP Options

Option	Description
ascii	This option sets the *representation type* of subsequent transferred files to *network ASCII*. Use this option to transfer ASCII formatted files.
binary	This option sets the *representation type* of subsequent transferred files to *image*. Use this option to transfer binary formatted files.
case	By enabling this option, remote computer files whose names are in uppercase letters are written to the local directory using lowercase letters.
prompt	This option toggles interactive prompting, which occurs when multiple files are being transferred using *mget* or *mput*. If *prompt* is enabled when *mput* or *mget* is executed, then prior to transferring each file of a file list, users are prompted to confirm that they want to transfer file.

The Hypertext Transfer Protocol (HTTP)

The *Hypertext Transfer Protocol* (HTTP) is the protocol on which the World Wide Web (WWW) is based. First implemented in 1990, HTTP is considered a request–response protocol. An HTTP client program establishes a TCP connection to an HTTP server program and requests a specific service from the server; the server program in turn accepts this connection and responds to the client's request. Request messages are made through a *user agent,* which is a Web browser, editor, search engine, or any other end user tool, and response messages are provided by the server after it has received and interpreted the request message. Both request and response messages follow the generic format of RFC 822 (see Figure 8.25). They consist of a start line, a header field that comprises zero or more headers, a blank line to signify the end of the header field, and a message body that contains the resource content (called an *entity*). Request header fields are used by clients to pass additional information about themselves and about a particular request to a server. Table 8.11 contains a list and description of request header fields. Response header fields are used by servers to pass additional information about themselves to clients as well as information about further access to a requested resource. Table 8.12 contains a list and description of response header fields. In addition to request and response header fields, all request and response messages contain general header fields. These are listed and described in Table 8.13. If a message contains a message body, which is used to transfer a specific resource or entity, then entity header fields are used to define the contents. Entity header fields are listed and described in Table 8.14. Finally, response messages also contain a three-digit status code, which the server returns to provide information about its attempt to understand and satisfy a particular client request. Table 8.15 contains a list and description of these result codes.

TABLE 8.11   HTTP Request Header Fields: Used by Clients to Pass Additional Information About Themselves and About a Particular Request to a Server

Field	Description
Accept	Specifies the media types (e.g., audio, image, text) the client will accept as a response by the server. If this field is absent, then it is assumed that the client will accept all media types.
Accept-Charset	Specifies the character sets the client will accept as a response by the server.
Accept-Encoding	Similar to the accept field, but it restricts the content-codings (e.g., gzip, compress, deflate) the client will accept as a response by the server for the current request.
Accept-Language	Similar to the accept field, but it restricts the set of client-preferred natural languages.
Authorization	Used to authenticate a client to a server; consists of the user agent's *credentials* that are relative to the requested resource.
Expect	Identifies the specific behaviors the client requires from the server when it responds to the current request.
From	Provides the server with the user agent's human user's Internet e-mail address.
Host	Specifies the Internet host and port number of the resource being requested.
If-Match	A conditional list of entity tags that the server uses to verify which entities the client has already received. If the client's listed tag matches a server's entity tag, then the server responds with that entity. *(continued)*

TABLE 8.11   HTTP Request Header Fields: Used by Clients to Pass Additional Information About Themselves and About a Particular Request to a Server (continued)

If-Modified-Since	A conditional time clause that directs the server not to return the requested resource if the resource has not been modified since the specified time.
If-None-Match	A conditional list of entity tags that indicates to the server which entities the client presently has that are not current.
If-Range	Indicates to the server that if the specified entity is unchanged, then the server is to respond with only missing entities; otherwise, an entire new entity should be returned. Should be used with the range header.
If-Unmodified-Since	A conditional time clause that directs the server to perform the requested operation if the requested resource has not been modified since the specified time.
Max-Forwards	Limits the number of times a request can be forwarded en route to the origin server.
Proxy-Authorization	Used to identify a client to a proxy server that requires authentication.
Range	Byte ranges that specify the sequence of bytes that represent the length of an entity; enables a client to request specific parts of an entity as designated by the entity's byte range.
Referer	Allows a client to specify a resource's URI from which the Request-URI was obtained; enables a server to generate a list of resource back-links.
TE	Specifies the extension transfer-codings the client will accept as a response by the server and whether or not it is willing to accept trailer fields in a chunked transfer-coding.
User-Agent	Provides the server with information about the user agent originating the request.

TABLE 8.12   HTTP Response Header Fields: Used by Servers to Pass Additional Information About Themselves to Clients as Well as Information About Further Access to a Requested Resource

Field	Description
Accept-Ranges	Informs client of the server's acceptance of range requests for a resource. An accept-range of "none" indicates that the client is not to attempt a range request.
Age	Provides a time estimate in seconds of how long it has been since a particular response was generated at the origin server.
ETag	Provides the current value of the entity tag for the requested resource.
Location	Identifies the location where the current request must go either to be completed or to identify a new resource; used to redirect the recipient to the appropriate location if different from the Request-URI.
Proxy-Authenticate	Provides information about the authentication scheme and parameters applicable to the proxy for the current Request-URI; used with a proxy authentication required (status code 407) response to inform the requesting client that a proxy authentication is required.
Retry-After	Indicates how long service is expected to be unavailable to the requesting client; used with a service unavailable (status code 503) response.
Server	Provides information about the software the origin server used to address the request.
Vary	Identifies the request-header fields that determine whether or not a cache may use the response to reply to a subsequent request without revalidation.
WWW-Authenticate	Consists of at least one challenge that indicates the authentication scheme(s) and parameters applicable to the Request-URI; included in all unauthorized (status code 401) response messages.

TABLE 8.13   HTTP General Header Fields

Field	Description
Cache-Control	Provides specific directives that must be followed by all caching mechanisms throughout the length of a connection (called the request–response chain). The directives are designed to prevent caches from adversely interfering with a request or response.
Connection	Allows the sender to specify options that are desired for a given connection.
Date	Specifies the date and time the message was originated.
Pragma	Provides implementation-specific directives that might apply to any recipient along the request–response chain.
Trailer	Indicates that the given header fields are present in the trailer of a message encoded with chunked transfer-coding.
Transfer-Encoding	Indicates the type of transformation applied to the message body so the message can be transmitted safely between sender and recipient.
Upgrade	Specifies any additional protocols the client supports and would like to use; informs the server of the client's protocol capabilities and preferences in the event the server finds it appropriate to change protocols.
Via	Identifies the intermediate protocols and recipients a request or response is subjected to en route between the user agent and server or between the origin server and client; used by gateways and proxies and is analogous to a mail message's receive field defined in RFC 822.
Warning	Contains supplemental information about a message that might not be reflected in the message itself.

TABLE 8.14   Entity Header Fields: Used to Define the Contents of an HTTP Message Body

Field	Description
Allow	Specifies the "methods" supported by the resource identified in the Request-URI. Examples of methods include GET, which is a request to retrieve the resource and return it in the entity body; HEAD, which is identical to GET except the server returns only the response headers as it would with GET and not the message body; and DELETE, which requests that the origin server delete the specified resource.
Content-Encoding	Indicates any additional content codings that have been applied to the entity body as well as the decoding mechanisms necessary to obtain the media type referenced by the content-type header field. Content-encoding enables a document to be compressed without losing its underlying media type identity.
Content-Language	Describes the natural language(s) of the intended audience for the enclosed entity.
Content-Length	Specifies the size (in number of octets) of the entity body.
Content-Location	Identifies an entity's accessible location if different from the requested resource's URI.
Content-MD5	Used to provide an end-to-end message integrity check of the entity body; the content is an MD5 digest that has been applied to the entire entity body. Defined in RFC 1864.
Content-Range	Used to identify exactly where a partial entity is to be placed within a full entity body; provides the specific byte ranges of the partial entity relative to the full entity. (continued)

TABLE 8.14 Entity Header Fields: Used to Define the Contents of an HTTP Message Body (continued)

Content-Type	Specifies the media type of the entity body.
Expires	Specifies the expiration date and time of a response; used to determine when the response is considered stale. An expire value that is 1 year in the future from the time the response is sent is interpreted as a response that "never expires."
Last-Modified	Specifies the date and time at which the origin server believes the resource was last modified.

TABLE 8.15 HTTP Status Codes

1xx Codes: Informational: Request Received; Continuing Process	
100 Continue	An interim response used to inform the client that the initial part of the request was received and was not rejected by the server; the client should continue with its request.
101 Switching Protocols	Server acknowledges client's request (indicated in the upgrade general header field) to change application protocols for the current connection and will switch to the protocol(s) defined in the response's upgrade header field.
2xx Codes: Successful: Action Was Successfully Received, Understood, and Accepted	
200 OK	Request has succeeded.
201 Created	The request was completed and a new resource was created, which is referenced by the returned URI(s).
202 Accepted	The request was accepted for processing but processing has not been completed. (It is possible that the current request might be disallowed once processing occurs.)
203 Nonauthoritative Information	The returned information contained in the entity header fields is not authoritative; it was acquired from a local or third-party copy instead of from the origin server.
204 No Content	The server has completed the request but there is no information to return; hence, the response message does not contain an entity body.
205 Reset Content	The server has completed the request and the user agent should reset the document view that initiated the request.
206 Partial Content	The server has fulfilled the partial GET request for the resource.
3xx Codes: Redirection: Further Action is Required by User Agent to Complete the Current Request	
300 Multiple Choices	The requested resource is not uniquely represented; information about each resource representation, including specific locations, is being provided so the user agent can select its preferred representation.
301 Moved Permanently	The requested resource has been assigned a new permanent URI; future references to this resource should use the returned URI.
302 Found	The requested resource resides temporarily under a different URI; future references to this resource should continue to use the requested URI.
303 See Other	The response to the current request is available under a different URI and should be retrieved using a GET method on that resource.

TABLE 8.15 HTTP Status Codes (continued)

304 Not Modified	The client performed a conditional GET request, and although access was allowed, the document was not modified.
305 Use Proxy	The requested resource is only accessible via a proxy, identified by the URI in the response header's location field.
306 Unused	Used in a previous version of the specification; not currently used and is reserved.
307 Temporary Redirect	The requested resource resides temporarily under a different URI; future references to this resource should continue to use the requested URI.

4xx Codes: Client Error: Request Contains Bad Syntax or Cannot Be Completed

400 Bad Request	The request contained malformed syntax and could not be understood by the server.
401 Unauthorized	The request requires user authentication.
402 Payment Required	Reserved for future use.
403 Forbidden	The server understood the request but refuses to act on it.
404 Not Found	The server could not find anything matching the requested URI; commonly used when the server does not want to reveal why the request was refused or when no other response is available. (Sometimes referred to as *link rot* or *dead link*.)
405 Method Not Allowed	The specified method is not allowed for the requested resource.
406 Not Acceptable	The requested resource can only generate response entities with content characteristics that are different from those provided in the requested message's accept header field.
407 Proxy Authentication Required	The client must first authenticate itself with the proxy; similar to code 401.
408 Request Time Out	The client's request was not produced within the time the server was prepared to wait.
409 Conflict	The request was not completed due to a conflict with the current state of the resource.
410 Gone	The requested resource is not available at the server and no forwarding information is known.
411 Length Required	The server refuses to accept the request without a defined content length.
412 Precondition Failed	One or more of the preconditions specified in the requested message's header fields returned a false value when tested by the server.
413 Requested Entity Too Large	The server refuses to process a request because the requested entity is larger than the server is willing or able to process.
414 Requested URI Too Long	The server refuses to service the request because the requested URI is longer than the server is willing to interpret.
415 Unsupported Media Type	The server refuses to service the request because the requested entity is formatted using an unsupported format.
416 Requested Range Not Satisfiable	The request was not processed because it included an invalid range relative to the requested resource.
417 Expectation Failed	The request was not processed because the server could not satisfy the information given in the requested message's expect header field.

TABLE 8.15 HTTP Status Codes (continued)

5xx Codes: Server Error: Server Fails to Fulfill What Appears to Be a Valid Request	
500 Internal Server Error	The server had an unexpected condition that prevented it from fulfilling the request.
501 Not Implemented	The server does not support the functionality required to fulfill the request.
502 Bad Gateway	The server, while acting as a gateway or proxy, received an invalid response from the upstream server it accessed in attempting to fulfill the request.
503 Service Unavailable	The server presently cannot process the request; this is presumed to be a temporary condition caused by any number of factors, including a system overload or scheduled maintenance.
504 Gateway Time Out	The server, while acting as a gateway or proxy, did not receive a timely response from an upstream or auxiliary server it needed to access to fulfill the request.
505 HTTP Version Not Supported	The server does not support, or refuses to support, the HTTP protocol version specified in the requested message.

Uniform Resource Identifiers (URIs) and Uniform Resource Locators (URLs)

An origin server is any server that contains a given resource.

Most HTTP communication requests apply to a specific resource that resides on an *origin server.* When used in the context of WWW, a resource generically refers to any object that can be accessed via the Internet. Examples include text files, graphical images, photographs, audio files, e-mail messages, newsgroup articles, and video clips. In short, anything that can be represented digitally and stored on an Internet-connected device is considered a resource. Specific resources are identified throughout the WWW using a *uniform resource identifier* (URI), which contains the name, location, or any other defining attribute of the specified resource. URIs conceptually represent a universal set of names and addresses of all resources regardless of their location. The URI concept is important because it allows all object names, regardless of their locations or attributes, to be treated the same.

One example of a URI most readers are familiar with is the *universal resource locator* (URL). URLs are used to identify a resource's location by specifying the access method needed to acquire the resource. The general form of a URL consists of two parts delimited by a colon; that is:

scheme : scheme-specific data

The first part, called the *scheme,* consists of a specific protocol that is used to access the resource; the second part is a function of the particular scheme (i.e., protocol) selected. As an example, consider the HTTP URL, which uses the HTTP protocol to identify a resource's location. The general form of this URL is

`http://host:port/url-path`

where *host* is the fully qualified domain name of an Internet-connected node, *port* is the port number to which the TCP connection is made (the HTTP well-known port number is 80), and *url-path* provides the details of how the specified resource is accessed relative to the scheme being used. Thus, both the syntax and interpretation of *url-path* are a function of the scheme. Note that in the general form of the HTTP URL, the scheme is the access method, namely, the HTTP protocol, and the scheme-specific data begin with the double slash (//). Thus, the given URL

http://www.fit.edu

informs us that the resource we seek is accessible via the HTTP protocol. Since this protocol is the foundation of the WWW, we know that the resource is located at a Web site whose address is designated by the *host* portion of the URL, namely, www.fit.edu. Moreover, since *port* is not given, we also know that the user agent makes a connection to the origin server on port 80. Finally, since no paths are listed, we know that the object we seek is a top-level resource, most likely the home page for the designated site.

RFC 1738, which provides the primary specifications for URLs, lists several different IP-based access protocol methods, including FTP, http, gopher, nntp, and telnet. Table 8.16 provides a description of these URL schemes. It should be noted that the general concept of URI continues to evolve and that new URLs are expected to be introduced. For example, RFC 2806 provides information about URLs for telephone calls and describes the syntax for the schemes of telephone, fax, and modem. Additionally, RFC 2732 provides the conventions used for formatting IPv6 addresses within URLs.

An alternative to URLs is the Common Names Resolution Protocol (CNRP), approved by the Internet Engineering Task Force (IETF) in September, 2000. CNRP enables users to access Web sites and send e-mail using more human-friendly names instead of strings of characters, slashes, dashes, and dots. For additional information about CNRP, see http://www.ietf.org/html.charters/cnrp-charter.html

HTTP Connection Methods

There are two primary ways in which HTTP connections can be established. The first and simplest type involves a single connection between the client and server, enabling the user agent and server to communicate directly via an established virtual circuit. In this scenario, the user agent transmits its request messages directly to the server, and the server transmits its response messages directly to the user agent. Given that no intermediary connections exist, it is presumed that the requested resource also resides on the server. Thus, the server in this example is also the origin server since it contains the requested resource. The second type of connection involves the presence of intermediate devices in the request–response chain. HTTP defines three types of intermediate devices: *proxy, gateway,* and *tunnel.*

• A proxy is an intermediate application program that acts as both a client and server; it is used as a proxy to the actual application. In the HTTP specifications, a proxy is regarded as a forwarding agent. It receives requests for a URI, rewrites all or part of the original request message, and then forwards this reformatted message to the server specified in the URI. A common use of a proxy is when a client is behind a firewall. In this scenario, a connection is established between the client and proxy and the proxy and origin

TABLE 8.16   Universal Resource Locator (URL) Schemes as Defined in RFC 1738

Scheme	Description	General Form and Syntax
ftp	The FTP URL. Designates files and directories that reside on Internet hosts and are accessible via the FTP protocol.	*ftp:// user:password@host:port/url-path* • *user* is optional. If not specified, but one is requested by the FTP server, then "anonymous" is given. • *password* is optional. If not specified, but one is requested by the FTP server, then user's e-mail address is given. • The *url-path* is optional. If given, it is interpreted as a series of FTP commands and has the following general form: *cwd1/cwd2/. . ./cwdN/name ; type=typecode* — each *cwd* entity represents an argument to FTP's "change working directory" command. — possible typecodes are a, i, and d. — *; type=typecode* may be omitted. — *cwdx* and *name* may be empty. • *port* defaults to 21 if omitted.
http	The HTTP URL. Designates resources that reside on Internet hosts and are accessible by the HTTP protocol.	*http:// host:port/path?searchpart* • No username or password is permitted. • *path* is an HTTP selector. • *searchpart* is a query string. • *path* is optional and can be omitted. • *?searchpart* is optional and can be omitted. • *port* defaults to 80 if omitted.
gopher	The Gopher URL. Designates resources that reside on Internet hosts and are accessible by the Gopher protocol.	*gopher:// host:port/gopher-path* • *gopher-path* is any of the following: gophertype
mailto	The mailto URL. Designates an Internet e-mail address. Does not directly access any specific resource.	*mailto:rfc822-addr-spec* • *rfc822-addr-spec* refers to the address specification defined in RFC 822.
news	The news URL. Designates USENET newsgroups or articles as specified in RFC 1036.	*news:newsgroup-name* *news:message-id* • *newsgroup-name* is the name of a newsgroup (e.g., *alt.binaries.pictures*); * is used to access all newsgroups. • *message-id* is the ID number of a specific article.
nntp	The NNTP URL. An alternative protocol for accessing USENET news.	*nntp:// host:port/newsgroup-name/article-number* • *newsgroup-name* is the name of a newsgroup. • *article-number* is the ID number of a specific article. • *port* defaults to 119 if omitted.

TABLE 8.16 Universal Resource Locator (URL) Schemes as Defined in RFC 1738 (continued)

telnet	The TELNET URL. Designates an interactive service (not a resource) that is accessible by the TELNET protocol.	*telnet:// user:password@host:port/* • *port* defaults to 23 if omitted.
wais	The wais URL. Designates WAIS databases, searches, or individual documents available from a WAIS database. (The WAIS protocol is defined in RFC 1625.)	*wais:// host:port/database* *wais:// host:port/database?search* *wais:// host:port/database/wtype/wpath* • The first form designates a searchable WAIS database. • The second form designates a specific search. • The third form designates a specific document to be retrieved from a WAIS database. • *database* is the name of the database being queried. • *wtype* identifies the object type. • *wpath* specifies the WAIS document id. • *port* defaults to 210 if omitted.
file	The file URL. Designates a file that is accessible to a specific host and not universally accessible over the Internet.	*file:// host/path* • *path* is a hierarchical directory path of the form *directory/directory/. . ./name*
prospero	The prospero URL. Designates resources that are accessed via the Prospero Directory Service.	*prospero:// host:port/hsoname;field=value* • *hsoname* is a host-specific object name in the Prospero protocol. • *port* defaults to 1525 if omitted.

server. Now, client requests and corresponding server responses are submitted to the proxy, which in turn passes them to the server and client, respectively.

• A gateway is a server that acts as an intermediary to another server. A gateway operates differently than a proxy because a gateway receives client requests as if it were the origin server. A common application of a gateway is when an access protocol other than http is used. For example, when a user submits a Web request to retrieve an updated version of its Web browser software, the requested resource generally is located on an FTP server. Thus, transparent to the user, the initial request is made to a gateway server, which contacts the appropriate FTP server to acquire the requested resource. The gateway server then translates this resource back into HTTP form for delivery to the client.

• A tunnel is an intermediary program that acts as a relay point between two connections. Unlike a proxy or gateway, a tunnel does not operate on HTTP requests or responses. A tunnel is used when a client/server connection needs to pass through an intermediary. A common example is when a secure connection is needed for a specific HTTP transaction. In this scenario, the client and server first establish an authenticated connection to a tunnel, which is then maintained throughout the HTTP session. The tunnel process terminates when both ends of the relayed connections are closed. Tunneling is commonly used in virtual private networks (VPNs), which are discussed in Chapter 7, to encapsulate encrypted data into an IP packet so that data can be transported across the

Once a tunnel is active, it is not considered a party to the HTTP connection.

public Internet in a secure manner. Protocols designed to effect this include the Point-to-Point Tunneling Protocol (PPTP), the Layer 2 Tunneling Protocol (L2TP), and the Internet Security (IPSec) protocol. These protocols are discussed in Chapter 17.

When HTTP was initially designed, separate TCP connections were established to acquire each URL. This was extremely inefficient, resulting in increased server loads and overall network congestion. The current implementation of HTTP now uses the concept of *persistent connections*. With persistent HTTP connections, fewer TCP connections need to be opened and closed, clients can make multiple requests without waiting for each response (a procedure called *pipelining*), network congestion and latency are reduced, and new HTTP features or versions can be implemented more easily.

End-of-Chapter Commentary

In this chapter, we discussed various aspects of the Internet, as well as an overview and brief history of TCP/IP and its relationship to the Internet. Various TCP/IP concepts also were presented. These included network layer, transport layer, and application layer protocols such as IP, TCP, UDP, SMTP, MIME, POP, TELNET, FTP, and HTTP. We also discussed Internet addressing schemes, including IPv4 and IPv6, subnetting, and name resolution. Some of the information in this chapter is linked to other chapters, and many of the examples used throughout the book are presented from an Internet perspective. These include Chapters 1, 2, 7, 12, 13, 16, and 17. Chapter 7 contains a discussion of subnetting, routing, and virtual private networks that use the Internet. Security issues, including IPSec, are presented in Chapter 17. Finally, in Chapter 18, we examine various convergence technologies including voice over IP (VOIP). You are encouraged to review these chapters to gain additional information about the Internet and its related protocols.

CHAPTER REVIEW MATERIALS

SUMMARY

- The Internet represents a global collection of heterogeneous networks connecting hundreds of thousands of computer networks, millions of nodes, and tens of millions of users. The Internet enables us to access information from nearly anywhere in the world directly and conveniently. Through the Internet, we can communicate with people from around the world using services such as electronic mail or chat. We can engage in virtual tours of libraries, visit the White House, become our own travel agent, listen to music, and view video clips using the World Wide Web. Vendors throughout the world, including auto-

mobile dealers, bookstores, and gift-specialty shops now sell products directly to consumers via the Internet. The Internet and related technologies are also ushering in a world of entertainment and interactive services such as video-on-demand and two-way videoconferencing. In short, the Internet has spurred technological advances in our society that affect nearly all modes of communication.

- The Internet began in 1969 as a U.S. government-sponsored, restricted-access research network called ARPANET, which introduced the concept of packet-switching. During the 1970s and 1980s, other academic and research-oriented networks were formed that provided similar resources and services to ARPANET. Among the more notable ones were BITNET, CSNET, and UUCP. In the mid-1980s, a federally funded national backbone network, NSFNET, was developed that interconnected colleges, universities, and research communities throughout the United States. Access to NSFNET, which also connected to ARPANET, was restricted to the academic and research communities. In the early 1990s, a commercial Internet was formed that operated independently of NSFNET. This commercial Internet ultimately evolved into the current public Internet and led to the decommissioning of NSFNET in 1995.

• Several high-speed networking initiatives emerged in the wake of decommissioning NSFNET. Included among them are the very high performance Backbone Network Service +(vBNS+), Internet2, the Next Generation Internet (NGI), and the National Information Infrastructure (NII).

• No single organization governs the Internet. Instead, Internet governance and administration are under the auspices of several organizations located throughout the global Internet community. The Internet's organizational structure consists of the Internet Architecture Board (IAB), the Internet Engineering Task Force (IETF), and the Internet Research Task Force (IRTF), all of which are overseen by the Internet Society. Internet standards development is open and prepared as RFCs, which are made available to the Internet community and promoted internationally by the Internet Society.

• The Internet was not designed initially to be a secure medium. However, given the types of services and resources currently accessible via the Internet, many of the applications that deliver these services and resources are now designed with security capabilities. Many critical Internet-related protocols have also been redesigned or enhanced with security support, and new secure protocols such as IPSec have been developed.

• The network protocol of the Internet is TCP/IP, a nonproprietary and open protocol. As a pre-OSI protocol architecture, TCP/IP does not fit cleanly into the seven layers of the OSI model. From a functional perspective, TCP/IP can be viewed as a four-level model consisting of an application layer, a transport layer, a

network layer, and a network interface layer. Compared to OSI, the application layer of TCP/IP subsumes the top three layers of OSI, and the network interface layer includes the bottom two layers of OSI. The remaining two layers of TCP/IP, network and transport, are similar to their OSI counterparts.

• TCP/IP's transport layer consists of two primary protocols: the User Datagram Protocol (UDP) and the Transport Control Protocol (TCP). UDP is connectionless and provides unreliable datagram service; TCP is connection-oriented and provides reliable data transmission.

• Port addresses, also known as *well-known port numbers* or *well-known services,* identify the specific process or application a user accesses on a host. Examples of well-known port numbers include 23 (TELNET), 25 (SMTP), 80 (HTTP), and 110 (POP). Port numbers are contained within TCP or UDP headers.

• A TCP connection is established using a three-way handshake in which a client initiates a connection request to a server, the server acknowledges this request, and the client acknowledges the server's acknowledgment.

• A TCP connection can be closed separately by either host or by both hosts at the same time. If a host closes its end of a TCP connection, it can continue to receive data segments but cannot transmit anything except acknowledgments.

• TCP uses positive acknowledgment with retransmission (PAR) to confirm that it has received a valid data segment. If the transmitting node does not receive an acknowledgment within a certain time period, it will retransmit the data.

• TCP uses the concept of window size, which is a field within the TCP header, to effect flow control.

• The IP part of TCP/IP represents the protocol's Internet layer. IP is the heart of this layer and represents the foundation of TCP/IP. It provides an underlying mechanism for transferring packets, called IP datagrams, between different machines regardless of their locations. A key component of IP is ICMP, which provides status information about Internet connectivity. Other resources that are useful in assessing Internet connectivity include *netstat,* which provides a listing of a specific machine's routing table, and *ping,* which is used to determine certain conditions of a network.

- IP addresses are network addresses used to identify the location of Internet nodes. The most predominant IP address version used today is IPv4, which is a 32-bit address partitioned into four groups of eight bits each. IPv4 also is organized into five different classes (A–E), which are identified by at most the first four bits of an address. The two most widely assigned classes are Class B, which is designated by the leading bits 10 and provides for $2^{14} = 16,384$ unique networks, and Class C, which is designated by the leading bits 110 and provides for $2^{21} = 2,097,152$ unique networks. Each Class B network can support $2^{16} = 65,536$ unique hosts; each Class C network can support $2^8 = 256$ unique hosts. IP addresses are frequently partitioned into subnets for greater efficiency. All numerical IP addresses are assigned logical names for human use. These logical names are then resolved to their respective IP numerical equivalents, and vice versa. The most efficient domain name resolution process is performed by special domain name servers.

- IPv6, the replacement protocol to IPv4, resolves the address problems of IPv4 and provides the necessary functions to meet the needs of emerging markets such as nomadic personal computing devices, networked entertainment, and networked controlled devices. Using 128-bit addresses, IPv6 offers several types of addresses including unicast, anycast, and multicast, supports priority routing, provides for the automatic configuration and reconfiguration of addresses, supports data authentication, privacy, and confidentiality via encryption, and supports priority routing. Furthermore, IPv6 is designed to interoperate with IPv4. Transition from IPv4 to IPv6 is currently underway.

- The Simple Mail Transfer Protocol (SMTP) is responsible for the end-to-end delivery of electronic mail messages between two hosts. SMTP delivers mail to port 25 of the receiving host and uses TCP as its transport mechanism. Mail delivery is effected via a series of SMTP sender and receiver commands. All SMTP-based e-mail messages also have the same format and use header fields to communicate information about message delivery. SMTP is limited to transmitting seven-bit ASCII text messages.

- The Multipurpose Internet Mail Extension (MIME) is an extension to SMTP. MIME defines additional message header fields that provide new information about a message's body, several different content formats that support multimedia e-mail, and various transfer encodings that enable content to be formatted and converted into different forms.

- The Post Office Protocol (POP) enables users to transfer the contents of their mailboxes to their desktop PCs. POP is similar to SMTP and uses an SMTP-like command set. Two versions of POP are presently in use: POP2, which uses well-known port 109, and POP3, which uses well-known port 110.

- The TELNET protocol is a general purpose remote login protocol that provides virtual terminal service. Through TELNET, users are able to establish a login to a remote machine directly from their local machine as if they were physically connected to the remote node. TELNET uses TCP as its transport mechanism and provides default service on port 25.

- The File Transfer Protocol (FTP) is a TCP-based application used for exchanging files between two systems. An FTP session always involves two separate connections. The first connection is used for control purposes; the second is used for the actual data transfers. Port 21 is used for the control connection and port 20 is used for the data transfer process.

- The Hypertext Transfer Protocol (HTTP) is the basic protocol of the World Wide Web. It is a request–response protocol that uses TCP as its primary transport mechanism. Request messages are generated by a user agent (e.g., a Web browser), and response messages are generated by a server. As is the case with SMTP, clients and servers use header fields to pass additional request or response information to each other. Request and response messages also contain general header fields as well as entity header fields that provide information about a message and its contents. Response messages also contain a three-digit status code that the server uses to provide information about its attempt to understand and satisfy a particular client request.

- Specific resources are identified throughout the World Wide Web using a uniform resource identifier (URI). An example of a specific type of URI is the universal resource locator (URL), which identifies a resource's location via the access method needed to acquire it. Examples of URL schemes include ftp, http, gopher, mailto, nntp, telnet, and file.

- HTTP uses persistent connections and can include a direct connection between a user agent and origin server or a connection that involves one or more inter-mediaries between a user agent and origin server. Three types of intermediaries are proxy, gateway, and tunnel.

VOCABULARY CHECK

Commercial Internet Exchange
   (CIX)
File Transfer Protocol (FTP)
gateway
Hypertext Transfer Protocol
   (HTTP)
Internet Architecture Board (IAB)
Internet Control Message Protocol
   (ICMP)
Internet Engineering Task Force
   (IETF)
Internet Protocol (IP)
Internet Research Task Force (IRTF)
Internet Society (ISOC)
Internet2

IP address
metric
metropolitan area exchange (MAE)
Multipurpose Internet Mail Extensions (MIME)
National Information Infrastructure (NII)
netstat
network access point (NAP)
ping
positive acknowledgment with retransmission (PAR)
Post Office Protocol (POP)
quality of service (QoS)
Request for Comment (RFC)

Resource Reservation Protocol
   (RSVP)
routing arbiter (RA)
Simple Mail Transport Protocol
   (SMTP)
subnet mask
Transmission Control Protocol
   (TCP)
uniform resource identifier (URI)
uniform resource locator (URL)
User Datagram Protocol (UDP)
variable length subnet masking
very high performance Backbone
   Network Service + (vBNS+)
well-known port number

REVIEW EXERCISES

1. Based on your Internet-based experiences and interactions, how would you define the Internet?
2. Using a Web browser, do a search on the history of the Internet.
3. Using a Web browser, search for a copy of NSFNET's Acceptable Use Policy and discuss this policy in light of today's Internet use.
4. Go to `http://www.vbns.net` and review the current status of the vBNS+.
5. What is the National Information Infrastructure and in what ways do you think the NII will impact your life?
6. Go to the Internet Engineering Task Force Web site (`http://www.ietf.org/`) and review three current Internet drafts.
7. Go to the Internet Engineering Task Force Web site (`http://www.ietf.org/`) and review the RFC process, which is available via the RFC editor Web pages.
8. Go to `http://www.rfc-editor.org/isi.html` and review the various current, draft, and proposed Internet standards.

9. Compare and contrast the TCP/IP "stack" with the OSI model.
10. Why do you think the designers of UDP made the checksum field optional?
11. What advantages or disadvantages do you think there are to maintaining a standardized list of well-known port numbers?
12. If you have access to a UNIX host, examine its /etc/services file for port addresses.
13. Which TCP/IP transport protocol do you think should be used if you have no faith in hardware (i.e., "Hardware is not your friend.")? Why?
14. Which TCP/IP transport protocol do you think lends itself more to LANs? Why?
15. Look at Figure 8.20 (IPv4 header). Note that there is no checksum on the data portion of the datagram. What options do you have for ensuring that the data portion contained within an IP datagram is valid?
16. If a TCP header is 44 bytes in length, what four-bit offset should be used within the header's con-

trol field? What is the smallest number this field must have? Why?

17. In a TCP transfer, the sending host transmits 20 bytes of data with a sequence number of 142. Assume that the receiving host receives a valid segment. What number will the receiver place in the acknowledgment number field of the segment header it sends to the sender?

18. What factors do you think will affect setting an appropriate TCP time-out period before the sending host performs a retransmission?

19. In our discussion of TCP's *three-way handshaking* process, note that no data were transferred until the connection was established. (Why?) Do you think it is possible for a TCP connection to be established via a three-way handshaking in which the segments being exchanged between sender and receiver also carry data? Why?

20. Consider a network architecture that does not provide a reliable end-to-end communication protocol like TCP. What impact do you think the absence of such a protocol would have on the overall design and operation of a network?

21. When do you think it is appropriate for application programmers to use UDP as a data transport service and why?

22. Execute the *netstat* routine on your host and examine its output.

23. Use the *traceroute* (or *tracert*) utility on your system to determine how many hops away your system is from another site.

24. Use the *ping* utility on your system to determine if a node is "alive" and the round-trip time of packets sent between your host and the destination node.

25. Determine if your organization has migrated from IPv4 to IPv6. If not, inquire if and when this transition will occur.

26. IP reassembles datagrams at the destination host and not at the routers or switches. Why do you think this is so?

27. Examine the IP address of your host. What class is it? How can you tell?

28. Subnet the Class C network address 198.69.25.0 into eight subnets.

29. Use the utility *nslookup* to determine the IP address of a host you commonly connect to via a Web browser.

30. Determine if your host maintains a hosts file (e.g., /etc/hosts), and if so, review the contents of the file. Also determine if your host is configured to use this host's file as part of the host's domain name server process.

SUGGESTED READINGS AND REFERENCES

ALBITZ, P., and C. LIU. 1992. *DNS and BIND.* Sebastopol, CA: O'Reilly & Associates.

AUERBACH, K., and C. WELLENS. 1995. Internet Evolution or Revolution? *LAN,* October, 60–65.

BAKER, S. 1993a. The Evolving Internet Backbone. *UNIX Review,* September, 15–21.

———. 1993b. Joining the Internet Club. *UNIX Review,* October, 23–33.

BANTA, G. 1996. Internet Pipe Schemes. *Internet World,* October, 62–70.

BERNERS-LEE, T. 1994. Universal Resource Identifiers in WWW: A Unifying Syntax for the Expression of Names and Addresses of Objects on the Network as Used in the World-Wide Web. *RFC 1630,* June.

BERNERS-LEE, T., L. MASINTER, and M. MCCAHILL. 1994. Universal Resource Locators (URL). *RFC 1738,* December.

BERNERS-LEE, T., R. FIELDING, and L. MASINTER, 1998. Universal Resource Identifiers (URI): Generic Syntax. *RFC 2396,* August.

BORENSTEIN, N. and N. FREED. 1993. MIME (Multipurpose Internet Mail Extensions) Part One: Mechanisms for Specifying and Describing the Format of Internet Message Bodies. *RFC 1521,* September.

BRADNER, S. 1996. The Internet Standards Process— Revision 3. *RFC 2026,* October.

BRADNER, S., and A. MANKIN. 1995. The Recommendation for the IP Next Generation Protocol. *RFC 1752,* January.

BROWN, R. 1993. TCP/IP: Reliable Glue for Enterprise Networks. *Networking Management,* June, 76–80.

CALLON, R. 1987. A Proposal for a Next Generation Internet Protocol. *Proposal to X3S3,* December.

COLLINSON, P. 1993. IP. *SunExpert Magazine,* October, 34–40.

COMER, D. E. 1991. *Internetworking with TCP/IP. Volume 1: Principles, Protocols, and Architecture.* Upper Saddle River, NJ: Prentice-Hall.

COOPER, L. F. 1996. Controlled Chaos at Work—The Commercialization of the Internet. *Communications Week,* 1 April, issue 603.

CRAY, A. 1998. Voice over IP: Here's How. *Data Communications,* April, 44–58.

DUTCHER, W. 1997. IP Addressing: Playing the Numbers. *Data Communications,* 21 March, 69–74.

FARROW, R., and R. POWER. 1998. Internet Security: Trouble in the Stack. *Network Magazine,* May, 95–96.

FENTON, B. 1997. Death of the Internet. *Popular Mechanics,* January, 41–44.

FIELDING, R., J. GETTYS, J. MOGUL, H. FRYSTYK, L. MASINTER, P. LEACH, and T. BERNERS-LEE. 1999. Hypertext Transfer Protocol—HTTP/1.1. *RFC 2616,* June.

FREED, N., and N. BORENSTEIN. 1996. Multipurpose Internet Mail Extensions (MIME). Part One: Format of Internet Message Bodies. *RFC 2045,* November.

GALLO, M., and W. HANCOCK. 1999. *Networking Explained.* Boston: Digital Press.

GELLENS, R., C. NEWMAN, and L. LUNDBLADE. 1998. POP3 Extension Mechanism. *RFC 2449,* November.

HALL, E. 1999. Advanced TCP Options. *Networking Computing,* 8 February, 110–114.

———, and D. WILLIS. 1998. VOIP in the Enterprise. *Networking Computing,* 1 October, 41–62.

HELD, G. 1997. IP for the Next Generation. *Network,* July, 65–70.

HINDEN, R. M. 1996. IP Next Generation Overview. *Communications of the ACM,* 39(6): 61–71.

———, B. CARPENTER, and L. MASINTER. 1999. Format for Literal IPv6 Addresses in URLs. *RFC 2732,* December.

HOFFMAN, P., L. MASINTER, and J. ZAWINSKI. 1998. The mailto URL Scheme. *RFC 2368,* July.

HORAK, R. 2000. *Communications Systems & Networks.* Foster City, CA: M & T.

HUDGINS-BONAFIELD, C. 1995. How Will the Internet Grow? *Network Computing,* 1 March, 80–91.

———. 1996. The Prospect of IP Renumbering. *Network Computing,* 1 June, 84–92.

HUITEMA, C. 1994. The H Ratio for Address Assignment Efficiency. *RFC 1715,* November.

HUNT, C. 1992. *TCP/IP Network Administration.* Sebastopol, CA: O'Reilly & Associates.

HURLEY, H. 1998. Value-Added ISPs. *Network Magazine,* 15 January, 35–38.

KARVÉ, A. 1997. IP Multicast Streams to Life. *Network Magazine,* October, 53–58.

———. 1998. IP Telephony Finds Its Voice. *Network Magazine,* January, 57–61.

KLEINROCK, L. 1992. Technology Issues in the Design of the NREN. In *Building Information Infrastructure,* ed. B. Kahin. 174–198. New York: McGraw-Hill Primis.

KROL, E. 1993. FYI on "What Is the Internet?" *RFC 1462,* May.

LANGE, L. 1996a. Internet Inc.—Bandwidth Becomes Big Business. *CMP Media, Inc.,* 1 June, issue 48.

MANDELBAUM, R., and P. MANDELBAUM. 1992. The Strategic Future of the Mid-level Networks. In *Building Information Infrastructure,* ed. B. Kahin. 59–118. New York: McGraw-Hill Primis.

McCLOGHRIE, K., and M. T. ROSE. 1994. Back to Basics: The Internet Transport Layer. *Connexions: The Interoperability Report,* August, 2–9.

MEEHAN, T. 1997. Six Great Myths of IPv6. *Data Communications,* November, 140.

MILLER, M. A. 1992. *Troubleshooting TCP/IP: Analyzing the Protocols of the Internet.* San Mateo, CA: M&T.

MOSKOWITZ, R. G. 1995. Plan Now for the New Internet Protocol. *Network Computing,* 1 May, 144–150.

MYERS, J., and M. ROSE. 1996. Post Office Protocol—Version 3. *RFC 1939,* May.

PETERSON, L., and B. DAVIE. 1996. *Computer Networks: A Systems Approach.* San Francisco: Morgan Kaufman.

POSTEL, J. 1981a. Internet Protocol. *RFC 791,* September.

———. 1981b. Transmission Control Protocol. *RFC 793,* September.

———. 1982. Simple Mail Transfer Protocol. *RFC 821,* August.

———, and J. REYNOLDS. 1983. Telnet Protocol Specification. *RFC 854,* May.

POSTEL, J., and J. REYNOLDS. 1985. File Transfer Protocol (FTP). *RFC 959,* October.

REYNOLDS, J., and J. POSTEL. 1994. Assigned Numbers. *RFC 1700,* October.

SHIPLEY, G. 1997. Plumbing 101: Choosing the Right ISP. *Network Computing,* 1 March, 116–118.

STALLINGS, W. 2000. *Data and Computer Communications.* 6th ed. Upper Saddle River, NJ: Prentice-Hall.

STEVENS, W. R. 1990. *UNIX Network Programming.* Upper Saddle River, NJ: Prentice-Hall.

STONE, M. 1991. Guide to TCP/IP Network Addressing. *LAN Technology,* April, 41–45.

TANENBAUM, A. S. 1996. *Computer Networks.* 3rd ed. Upper Saddle River, NJ: Prentice-Hall.

"The National Information Infrastructure: Agenda for Action." 1993. 58 Federal Regulation 49,025, 21 September.

TRISTRAM, C. 1995. The Trouble with TCP/IP. *Open Computing,* February, 52–54.

VAHA-SIPILA, A. 2000. URLs for Telephone Calls. *RFC 2806,* April.

WILLIS, D. 1996. Interchange Carriers as ISPs: Long-Distance Runaround. *Network Computing,* 1 September, 104–115.

———, and J. MILNE. 1996. Domestic Internet Service Providers: Adapt or Perish. *Network Computing,* 1 June, 100–108.

LOCAL AND WIDE AREA NETWORKING TECHNOLOGIES

9

Ethernet and IEEE 802.3 Networks

CHAPTER OBJECTIVES

After studying this chapter, you will be able to do the following:

1. Discuss the history of Ethernet.
2. Describe the primary differences between Ethernet V2.0 and IEEE 802.3.
3. Describe the physical and data link layers of IEEE 802.3.
4. Explain the meaning of IEEE 802.3 LAN designations such as 100BASE-T.
5. Explain the difference between network diameter and collisions domain.
6. Describe and apply the 5-4-3 repeater placement rule.
7. Understand the issues involved in assessing an Ethernet/802.3 LAN performance.
8. Explain the fundamental principles of segmentation.
9. Compare and contrast the various switched Ethernet strategies.
10. Describe full-duplex Ethernet.
11. Explain the concept of virtual LANs.
12. Compare and contrast the various Fast Ethernet specifications.
13. Compare and contrast Fast Ethernet and 100VG-AnyLAN.
14. Compare and contrast CSMA/CD and demand priority.
15. Describe the two Gigabit Ethernet strategies and specifications.
16. Discuss Gigabit Ethernet relative to ATM.

In this chapter, we focus our attention on Ethernet networks. In previous chapters, we informally examined aspects of Ethernet technology to illustrate various network concepts. For example, in our discussions of the data link layer in Chapters 5 and 6, Ethernet was used as an example to demonstrate frame formats, MAC hardware addresses, and network switches. In this chapter, the subject of Ethernet is presented in a more formal and comprehensive manner. We begin the chapter with a review of Ethernet's history. This is followed by a presentation of the original IEEE 802.3 protocol, which operates at 10 Mbps. Beginning with the third section, the many evolutions of conventional Ethernet are presented: Switched and full-duplex Ethernet are discussed in Section 9.3 along with the concept of virtual LANs; Section 9.4 examines the two variations of 100-Mbps Ethernet, namely, Fast Ethernet and 100VG-AnyLAN; and Section 9.5 reviews Ethernet's most recent incarnation, Gigabit Ethernet. We end the chapter with an overview of other Ethernet-related projects.

9.1 The History of Ethernet

In the Beginning

Ethernet is a local area network protocol developed jointly by Xerox, Intel, and Digital Equipment Corporation (DEC) at the Xerox Palo Alto Research Center (PARC) in the mid-1970s. It was designed as a technology that would allow for the interconnection of office devices. The name Ethernet was derived from the old electromagnetic theoretical substance called *luminiferous ether*, which was formerly believed to be the invisible universal element that bound together the entire universe and all its associated parts. Thus, an "ether" net is a network that connects all components attached to the "net."

Although the concept of Ethernet was originally developed at PARC, Ethernet's genesis is with Norman Abramson of the University of Hawaii in the late 1960s to early 1970s. Abramson developed a network called ALOHA, which was used to connect the main campus site in Oahu to seven other campuses on four of the Hawaiian Islands. Using a technique called *contention,* Abramson demonstrated that multiple nodes on a network could use the same channel for communications and they could send data whenever they had data to send. The primary differences between the ALOHA network and Ethernet are that ALOHA permitted any node to transmit data at any time, made no provision to allow a node to detect if another node was sending data, and had no procedure for dealing with what would come to be known as *collisions.* Collisions occur when two or more nodes attempt to transmit data simultaneously. Without a mechanism for dealing with the eventuality of simultaneous transmissions, ALOHA required many retransmissions. Ethernet, on the other hand, was designed with both carrier sense capability and collision detection (see Chapter 5).

Through a consortium organized in the early 1980s, Xerox, Intel, and DEC published a vendor standard now known as the *Ethernet Blue Book.* This book described the methods in which Ethernet would be developed and implemented. It also described how Ethernet hardware and data link services would function. Work on this standard continued to evolve, culminating in the 1982 publication of a cooperative standard titled *Ethernet Version 2.0.*

Robert M. Metcalfe (1946–)

Robert (Bob) Metcalfe was born in 1946 in Brooklyn, New York, but grew up on Long Island. He graduated from Massachusetts Institute of Technology (MIT) in 1969 with BAs in electrical engineering and business management. He also earned an MA in applied mathematics from Harvard University in 1970, as well as a PhD in computer science in 1973. While working on his PhD, Metcalfe accepted a position in 1972 at Xerox's Palo Alto Research Center (PARC) in California. His research at PARC involved developing a method to interconnect prototypes of a new personal computer called the Alto, and in 1973, he and his colleague, D. R. Boggs, invented the local area networking technology Ethernet. Metcalfe and Boggs characterized Ethernet as "a system for local communications among computing stations." In essence, Ethernet technology transformed the PC from a data processing unit into a communications device. Metcalfe and Boggs' description of Ethernet, along with Ethernet's design principles, topology, implementation issues, expansion capabilities, performance issues, and protocol was presented in their paper, "Ethernet: Distributed Packet Switching for Local Computer Networks," which was published in the *Communications of the ACM* in 1976 (Volume 19, Number 7).

Although PARC had a stellar reputation for its staff of geniuses who developed innovative technologies, it was not a place that fostered the conversion of these technologies into commercial products or applications. Consequently, in 1979, Metcalfe left PARC and founded 3COM Corporation in Santa Clara, California, to advance the PC-based LAN concept and to make Ethernet the standard LAN technology. He named the company 3COM to denote a confluence of sorts of the three words *com*puters, *com*munication, and *com*patibility. In 1990, he retired from 3Com.

Metcalfe is the recipient of the Association for Computing Machinery (ACM) Grace Murray Hopper Award (1980), the Institute of Electrical and Electronics Engineers (IEEE) Alexander Graham Bell Medal (1988), and the IEEE Medal of Honor (1996). Presently, Metcalfe is vice president of technology for International Data Group (IDG), which publishes nearly 300 magazines—including *InfoWorld,* where he writes a weekly column on networking issues called "From the Ether"—in 90 countries. Copies of Metcalfe's columns are available on-line from *InfoWorld* at http://www.infoworld.com/opinions/morefromtheether_f.html

Ethernet versus IEEE 802.3

Although the Xerox-Intel-DEC consortium developed and produced an Ethernet standard (V2.0), it was not an acceptable domestic or international standard for LAN technology. Consequently, the IEEE formed subcommittee 802.3 and produced an IEEE standard for a technology very similar to the Ethernet V2.0 specification. Rumor has it that the IEEE wanted to make Ethernet V2.0 its standard, but the Xerox-Intel-DEC consortium wanted to maintain the patent. To avoid any type of patent infringement, the IEEE modified Ethernet V2.0 and produced the IEEE 802.3 specification. These patents have since been given to the IEEE, and anyone can now license Ethernet from IEEE for a flat fee of $1000. Due to its influence with U.S. and international standardization authorities, IEEE 802.3 eventually became ISO standard IS88023.

The two Ethernet specifications, V2.0 and IEEE 802.3, are similar because IEEE used the technological details of Ethernet V2.0 as a basis for the 802.3 standard. However, several serious technical differences were introduced in the IEEE version that make the two standards incompatible. These included differences in cable size, transceiver function, frame formats, and topology. A brief overview of these differences follows.

Cable Differences   In the V2.0 standard, the Ethernet cable (thick coax) is prescribed with a 0.395-inch diameter. In the IEEE specification, the cable's diameter was increased to 0.405 inch. The IEEE's rationale for increasing the cable diameter was that the larger diameter provided better electrical characteristics. The only problem a larger diameter cable presented was that V2.0 compliant transceivers could not be used on IEEE 802.3 compliant cable. This presently is not a serious issue because a "thick" Ethernet network is something you are more apt to inherit than install. Vendors also manufactured transceivers capable of connecting to both V2.0 and IEEE 802.3 cables.

Transceiver Function Differences   A second modification to the V2.0 standard is the manner in which transceivers function. Recall from Chapter 6 that a transceiver enables a node to communicate with the cable. Specifically, it transmits and receives simultaneously, and it notifies a node if a collision occurred. When a transceiver is connected to the cable, there is usually no way to determine if the transceiver is working unless there is a data transmission. In the V2.0 specification, a signal known as *signal quality error* (SQE) is periodically generated by the transceiver and read by the controller (i.e., the network card) of the host to which it is connected. Historically, this is called *heartbeat* and effectively informs the host's controller that the transceiver is "alive." In the IEEE 802.3 standard, transceivers do not generate a heartbeat unless a real signal quality error occurs. Thus, SQE effectively is used for network management. Given this difference in the operation of V2.0 and 802.3 transceivers, if a V2.0 controller is mated with an IEEE 802.3 transceiver, the controller interprets the absence of a heartbeat from the transceiver as a "dead" transceiver. To accommodate both standards, vendors incorporated a switch into their transceivers that can enable or disable SQE.

Frame Format Differences   A third difference between the two specifications entails how data frames are formatted at the data link layer. Although V2.0 and IEEE 802.3 frames range from a minimum of 64 bytes to a maximum of 1518 bytes (see Chapter 5), they do have one major difference: V2.0 frames contain a two-byte "type" field, which is used to identify the different higher-level protocol types used by DEC, Intel, and Xerox (e.g., IP, IPX). The IEEE 802.3 specification does not support a protocol type field. Instead, the V2.0 "type" field is replaced with a "length" field, which specifies the length in bytes of the bit string that represents user data (see Figure 5.3). The absence of a protocol type field in the IEEE 802.3 frame precludes the network layer from knowing the network protocol being used for the frame. This information is provided by the logical link control (LLC). Recall from Chapter 5 that the IEEE partitions the OSI data link layer into the MAC and LLC sublayers. In an 802.3 frame, an LLC header containing higher-level protocol information is provided at the beginning of the frame's data field. The combination of LLC header and data field is known as the LLC protocol data unit (LLCPDU). Ethernet V2.0 frames do not have an LLC component. The exclusion of a "type" field in the 802.3 standard, coupled with the way in which IEEE partitions the data link layer into two sublayers, render V2.0 and 802.3 frames completely incompatible at the data link layer. Unlike the previous two differences of cable diameter and SQE function, nothing can be done to compensate for these differences.

Other Differences Two other differences between V2.0 and 802.3 are topology and cable type. IEEE 802.3 supports both bus and star topologies, but Ethernet V2.0 supports only a bus topology. Finally, 802.3-compliant networks can be either baseband or broadband, but in V2.0, only baseband Ethernet networks are supported.

The bottom line is vendor support for IEEE 802.3 overshadows that for Ethernet V2.0; any new "Ethernet" network we install probably will be based on the IEEE 802.3 protocol. Nevertheless, there are still many "old" Ethernets in existence, and it is possible that we might inherit one that incorporates both V2.0- and 802.3-compliant products. IEEE 802.3's market dominance should not be interpreted as its being "superior" to V2.0. Rather than comment on whether one standard is better than another, we will say this: There is nothing intrinsically wrong with V2.0 other than it is a proprietary standard that does not comply with the prescribed ISO standard for Ethernet-like networks. Furthermore, although the two standards are similar—802.3 was designed after V2.0—they are different enough to be considered incompatible. This incompatibility resulted from political as well as technical issues and is best left to historians and analysts. One final word on notation: In casual usage, IEEE 802.3 is commonly referred to as Ethernet. What we need to realize, though, is that technically it is *not* Ethernet— only V2.0 is considered Ethernet. Consequently, in this book, to play it safe, we use the notation "Ethernet/802.3" when referring to Ethernet networks.

For completeness sake, the LLC sublayer also contains a source service access point (SSAP) and a destination service access point (DSAP). These SAPs provide the mechanism for source and destination nodes to communicate and are needed for protocol-type identification. See the Internet's Request for Comment, RFC 1340, for additional information.

9.2 10-Mbps Ethernet/802.3 LANs

Physical and Data Link Layer Information

At the physical layer (Chapters 4 and 6), the IEEE 802.3 standard addresses issues such as cable type, cable length, and connector types. Ethernet/802.3's physical layer also encodes data prior to transmission using Manchester encoding, which ensures that the end of a transmission (carrier sense failure) is properly detected. Recall from Chapter 3 that Manchester encoding differs from standard digital transmission in two ways. First, instead of "high" equaling 1 and "low" equaling 0, a timing interval is used to measure high-to-low transitions. Second, instead of the timed transmission period being "all high" or "all low" for either 1 or 0, a state transition is encoded into the transformation. Specifically, a 1 is sent as a half-time-period low followed by a half-time-period high,

FIGURE 9.1 IEEE 802.3 LANs are designated by bandwidth in Mbps, whether the LAN is baseband or broadband based, followed by either the type of cable it supports or its maximum length in meters.

and a 0 is sent as a half-time-period high followed by a half-time-period low. Consequently, the end of the last bit transmitted is easily determined immediately following the transmission of the last bit. (See Chapter 3 for additional information about digital encoding schemes.)

At the data link layer (Chapters 5 and 6), the standard is based on 1-persistent CSMA/CD and uses a binary exponential backoff algorithm to calculate the wait time. The average wait time for a new packet is set to an arbitrary initial value. This value is then doubled each time a collision results when a transmission is attempted with the same packet. The Ethernet/802.3 data link layer also specifies a minimum frame size of 64 bytes and a maximum frame size of 1518 bytes. The frame format consists of a 7-byte preamble, a 1-byte start frame delimiter, a 6-byte destination address, a 6-byte source address, a 2-byte length count, a data field that ranges between 46 and 1500 bytes, a pad field that ranges from 0 to as many bytes as are necessary to get the data field to a minimum 46 bytes, and a 4-byte CRC checksum field (see Figure 5.3 and Chapter 5).

An Ethernet/802.3 address consists of 48 bits, represented as 12 hexadecimal digits, and partitioned into six groups of two. The higher-order three bytes (the leftmost six hexadecimal digits) represent the manufacturer of the Ethernet device; the lower-order three bytes represent the serial number of the device. For example, the address 08:00:20:01:D6:2A corresponds to an Ethernet/802.3 device manufactured by Sun Microsystems (as indicated by Sun's code 08:00:20) that has the serial number 01:D6:2A. The IEEE is responsible for assigning Ethernet addresses. (See Appendix A for additional information about Ethernet address prefixes. See also Box 5.2 for additional information about Ethernet/802.3 addresses.)

IEEE 802.3 LANs are designated using the following general format (see also Figure 9.1):

Signaling Rate (Mbps)—Band (Base or Broad)—Length (Meters) or Cable Type

Thus, a 10-Mbps baseband LAN that uses UTP cable is designated as *10BASE-T* (the T is for twisted-pair), and a 10-Mbps ThickWire baseband LAN is designated as *10BASE5* (the 5 is for 500-m segment length). A brief description of the various IEEE 802.3 10-Mbps LAN specifications is given in Table 9.1. Examples of the various types are also provided in Figures 9.2 (ThickWire), 9.3 (ThinWire), 9.4 (UTP), and 9.5 (UTP). We suggest you study Table 9.1 and Figures 9.2 through 9.5 before proceeding further.

TABLE 9.1   Summary of IEEE 802.3 Specifications for 10-Mbps Ethernet

Type	Description[a]
10BASE5 ThickWire	**Cable:** Thick coax (RG-8); **Topology:** Bus; **Connectors:** Transceivers, transceiver cable, 15-pin AUI; uses "vampire" tap; **Max Segment Length:** 500 m; **Max Nodes per Segment:** 100—spaced in 2.5-m increments; **Max Diameter:** 2500 m; **Misc:** 50-ohm termination at each end of cable; one end grounded to building ground
10BASE2 ThinWire	**Cable:** Thin coax (RG-58); **Topology:** Bus; **Connectors:** BNC; **Max Segment Length:** 185 m; **Max Nodes per Segment:** 30—minimum 0.5 m between nodes; **Max Diameter:** 925 m; **Misc:** 50-ohm termination at each end of cable; one end grounded to building ground
10BASE-T UTP Ethernet	**Cable:** Category 3, 4, or 5 UTP; **Topology:** Star; **Connectors:** RJ-45, patch panels, repeaters; **Max Segment Length:** 100 m; **Max Nodes per Segment:** 2; **Max Diameter:** 500 m; **Misc:** Each node is connected directly or indirectly to a hub; indirect connections are via wallplates or patch panels
10BASE-FB[b] Fiber Backbone	**Cable:** Fiber; **Topology:** Point-to-point; **Connectors:** Fiber-optic transceivers, ST; **Max Segment Length:** 2000 m; **Max Nodes per Segment:** 2; **Max Diameter:** 2500 m; **Misc:** Backbone-only technology used to interconnect Ethernet repeaters; maximum of 15 repeaters permitted; uses synchronous signaling to retime the optical signals for data transmissions
10BASE-FL[b] Fiber Link	**Cable:** Fiber; **Topology:** Point-to-point or star; **Connectors:** Fiber-optic transceivers, ST; **Max Segment Length:** 2000 m; **Max Nodes per Segment:** 2; **Max Diameter:** 2500 m; **Misc:** Can be used to interconnect workstations or repeaters; maximum of five repeaters permitted; replaces fiber optic inter-repeater link (FOIRL); if 10BASE-FL is mixed with FOIRL, max segment length is 1000 m
10BASE-FP[b] Fiber Passive	**Cable:** Fiber; **Topology:** Star; **Connectors:** Fiber-optic transceivers, ST; **Max Segment Length:** 500 m; **Max Nodes per Segment:** 33; **Max Diameter:** 2500 m; **Misc:** Used for small installations such as workgroup LANs; specifies a passive hub, which means it uses no electronics (including power) and hence is immune to external noise

[a] All types subscribe to the 5-4-3 repeater placement rule.
[b] Part of the 10BASE-F Standard for fiber-optic Ethernet.

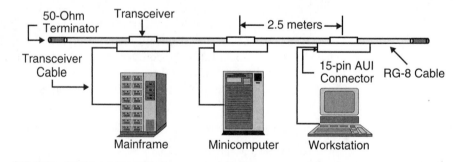

FIGURE 9.2 Example of a 10BASE5 (ThickWire Ethernet) LAN. The topology is a bus configuration, the maximum length of a single segment is 500, and a single segment supports up to 100 nodes. Nodes are connected to the cable via transceivers and transceiver cable; transceivers are spaced 2.5 m apart to prevent signal interference. The actual physical connection of a transceiver involves drilling into the cable using a "vampire tap." Each end of the cable is terminated with a 50-ohm resistor, and one end of the cable must be grounded.

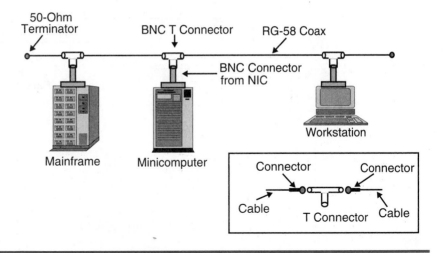

FIGURE 9.3 Example of a 10BASE2 (ThinWire Ethernet) LAN. The topology is a bus configuration, the maximum length of a single segment is 185 m, and a single segment supports up to 30
nodes. Nodes are connected to the cable via BNC T connectors, which must be spaced at least
0.5 m apart to prevent signal interference. Each end of the cable is terminated with a 50-ohm
resistor, and one end of the cable must be grounded. A segment is composed of several pieces of
cable, with each piece being connected via a T connector (see inset).

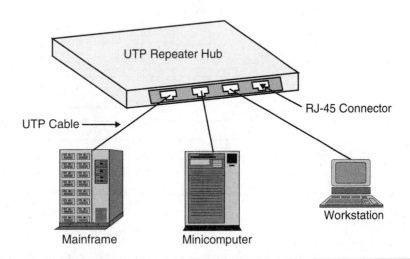

FIGURE 9.4 Example of a typical 10BASE-T (Twisted-Pair Ethernet) LAN. The topology is a
star configuration, and the maximum length of a segment is 100 m. Note that only two nodes can
be connected per segment—a workstation and a repeater. Both the hub and a device's network
interface card (NIC) contain eight-pin modular (RJ-45) connectors. Cable can be Category 3, 4,
or 5; higher grade cables provide better performance.

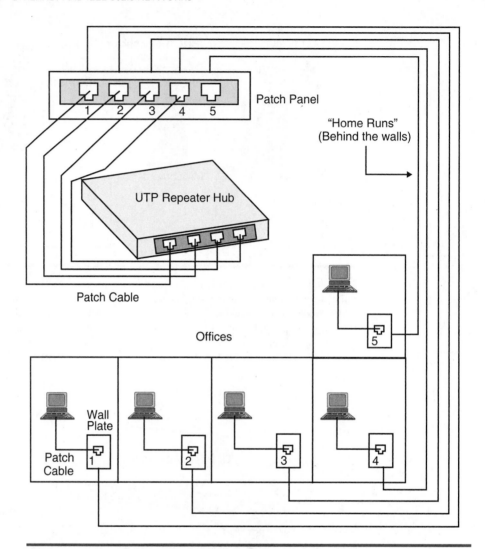

FIGURE 9.5 A typical 10BASE-T wiring scheme involves a centralized hub located in a wiring closet and cable installed between a patch panel and a wall plate located in an office or room. This length of cable is referred to as a "home run." Each end of these home runs is then "punched down" behind the patch panel and wall plates. Patch cable is used to connect ports on the patch panel to the hub and workstations to wall plates. The total length of all cable for one workstation (hub to patch panel, home run, and patch cable from wall plate to NIC) must be no more than 100 m.

Although patch panels provide a certain level of convenience, they also represent a potential source of additional noise. Nevertheless, patch panels are useful in many situations. For example, note that patch panel port 5 is wired to office 5, but the workstation in office 5 does not have a connection to the LAN because patch panel port 5 does not have a connection to the hub. Connectivity can be provided to office 5, though, simply by disconnecting a patch cable from one of the patch panel ports and reconnecting it to port 5.

Note from Table 9.1 the descriptions given for the various 10-Mbps 802.3 LAN types. The IEEE 802.3 specifications for the maximum number of nodes per segment and maximum segment length, coupled with minimum and maximum frame sizes of 64 and 1518 bytes, respectively, are necessary due to Ethernet's contentious nature. The maximum number of nodes per segment ensures that an Ethernet network does not get saturated; the minimum packet size and maximum cable-segment length enable Ethernet nodes to accurately detect collisions on the network, and the maximum frame size allows nodes to detect the completion of a transmission, which facilitates error detection. We will expand on these concepts later, but for now it is important to be cognizant of them.

The Concept of Network Diameter and Collision Domain

In Table 9.1, the term *max diameter* is used as part of a network's description. *Diameter* in this context is a term that emanates from the branch of mathematics called graph theory, which is frequently employed by theoretical and applied computer scientists in the study of network design. The diameter of a 10-Mbps Ethernet/802.3 network is the overall length between the network's two remotest nodes. For example, consider the 10BASE-T LANs shown in Figures 9.6 and 9.7. The first has a network diameter of 200 m; the second LAN's diameter is 300 m.

The maximum diameter of a 10-Mbps Ethernet/802.3 is the maximum distance possible for a *single* Ethernet/802.3 LAN. By *single,* we mean an Ethernet/802.3 LAN that consists of either one segment or multiple segments connected by repeaters. Maximum diameters vary among LAN types because they use different cable. For example, the network diameter of a 10BASE5 LAN, which uses RG-8 coaxial cable, ranges from a minimum of 500 m (for one segment) to a maximum of 2500 m (five segments connected by four repeaters). Similarly, a 10BASE-T LAN uses unshielded twisted-pair cable and has a network diameter that ranges from 200 m to 500 m (Figure 9.8).

In our definition of an Ethernet/802.3's maximum diameter, you might have noticed that we stated it as the maximum distance of a single LAN. (We purposely ital-

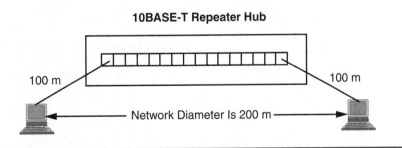

FIGURE 9.6   A network diameter is the distance between the two remotest nodes of a network. In this illustration, we have a 10BASE-T LAN that can connect up to 16 nodes via a UTP repeater hub. If each node is connected to the hub with the maximum segment length permitted (100 m), then the network diameter is 200 m—100 m from sending node to repeater port plus 100 m from repeater port to receiving node.

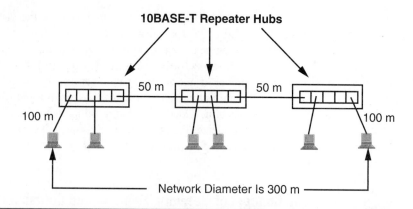

FIGURE 9.7 In this illustration, a 10BASE-T LAN consists of four segments interconnected by three repeaters. If the links between nodes and their respective ports are 100 m each, then the network diameter is 300 m—100 m from sending node to port, plus two 50-m hub links, plus 100 m from port to receiving node. Remember: The network diameter is always the distance between the farthest two nodes.

icized the word single to call your attention to it.) If you are thinking this implies that an Ethernet/802.3 LAN may be extended, you are correct, but it must be done very carefully. From our discussion in Chapter 6, we learned that several devices are available for extending LANs. These include repeaters, bridges, switches, and routers. Installing these devices, however, cannot be done in a cavalier manner. For a network to function properly, it must comply with its corresponding design rules. In the case of an Ethernet/802.3 LAN, maintaining the correct diameter is part of the design rules.

You see, Ethernet/802.3 LANs are based on CSMA/CD (see Chapter 5). Thus, collisions are an inherent part of these LANs, and every Ethernet/802.3 LAN has what is known as a *collision domain*. A collision domain consists of a single network where two nodes can cause a collision. In the case of a single-segmented Ethernet/802.3 LAN, the independent segment represents the collision domain; in a multisegmented Ethernet/802.3 LAN, however, the collective segments comprise the collision domain. For example, in Figures 9.2 and 9.3, the collision domain comprises the single ThickWire or ThinWire segment. In Figures 9.4, 9.5, and 9.6, the collision domain comprises the segments connected to the single repeater. In Figures 9.7 and 9.8, though, multiple segments are interconnected via multiple repeaters. This extends the network's diameter, which increases the distance between the two remotest nodes. Physically, the networks in Figures 9.7 and 9.8 appear to be separate. Electrically, though, these physically separate networks belong to one collision domain. The bottom line is that a single collision domain contains a maximum of 1024 end nodes, and its diameter cannot be more than 2500 m.

CSMA/CD design rules specify that if a node's transmission results in a collision, the node must be able to detect the collision before it stops transmitting. If not, the node will never know that the frame it transmitted was corrupted. For example, look at Figure 9.8

10BASE-T Repeater Hubs

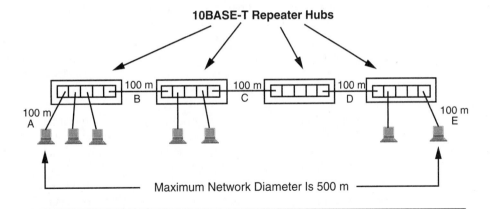

Maximum Network Diameter Is 500 m

FIGURE 9.8 The maximum diameter of a 10BASE-T LAN is 500 m. Note how this configuration complies with the 5-4-3 repeater placement rule. There are five segments (labeled A through E), four repeaters, and at most only three segments populated with end nodes.

and consider the following scenario involving the nodes at the opposite ends of the collision domain (i.e., the workstations attached to segments *A* and *E*, respectively):

- Node *A* transmits a frame.
- Around the same time, node *E* wants to transmit a frame. It senses the channel but does not "hear" anything because *A*'s transmission has not reached *E*. Sensing an idle channel, *E* transmits a frame.
- The two frames collide.
- *E* must now send a jamming signal to all the nodes connected to the network, including *A*. Furthermore, the jamming signal must reach *A* before *A* stops transmitting. If the collision occurred at *E*'s "front door" (i.e., just before A's frame reached *E*), the jamming signal must travel a considerable distance.

On an Ethernet/802.3 LAN, timing is everything. Although electrical signals on Ethernet media travel at nearly the speed of light, it still requires a specific amount of time for a signal to travel from one node to another across the network. In Ethernet/802.3 jargon, time is measured using the unit *bit-time,* which is equal to 0.1 μs. Thus, a one-bit transmission requires 0.1 μs. Recall that the smallest Ethernet/802.3 frame is 64 bytes long, which is 512 bits. This implies that to transmit a 64-byte frame requires 512 bit-times or 51.2 μs. This means that a 64-byte frame has a collision domain of 512 bit-times or 51.2 μs. Thus, any delay cannot be greater than 51.2 μs. Returning to our scenario, to maintain a round-trip delay of no more than 512 bit-times, node *E* has to send a jamming signal before *A* transmits more than 256 bits (i.e., 256 bit-times). This will then give *E* 256 bit-times for its jamming signal to reach *A*. If the LAN is up to spec, then the round-trip delay will not exceed 512 bit-times.

Since repeaters, bridges, switches, and routers all introduce and add to the overall delay of a network, we have to understand what impact this delay will have on the overall performance of our LAN. Delay, which is also called *latency,* is measured by the amount of time a signal remains "inside" a device. For example, in the case of repeaters, delay is how long it takes a repeater to transmit a regenerated signal after receiving it. Of the various devices available for extending an Ethernet/802.3 LAN, only repeaters need careful consideration because they are layer-1 devices that regenerate all incoming signals, including collisions, and propagate these regenerated signals to all the segments connected to its ports. Repeaters extend the diameter of a network but are considered to be part of the same collision domain of networks designed using only repeaters. Bridges, switches, and routers, however, are layer-2 or layer-3 devices. They perform filtering and frame translations (e.g., from an 802.3 format to an 802.5 format). They do not propagate collision signals from one segment to another. Hence, these devices effectively partition a network into multiple collision domains. For example, in Figure 9.8, if the third repeater from the left were a bridge, then there would be two separate collision domains. The first contains the first two repeaters, and the second contains the last repeater. (The network diameter remains the same.) Thus, if we intend to extend our network using repeaters, we have to limit how many repeaters are connected to the network so we can maintain that 512 bit-time upper limit.

The 5-4-3 Repeater Placement Rule

Since the amount of delay introduced by repeaters varies from one vendor to another, a general rule of thumb called the *5-4-3 repeater placement rule* can be followed if we do not want to calculate the total delay ourselves. The 5-4-3 rule requires no more than five segments of up to 500 m each, no more than four repeaters, and no more than three segments that have end nodes connected to them. This rule is also known as the 4-repeater rule or the 5-4-3-2-1 rule. In the latter, the 2 implies that two of the five segments are used as interrepeater links, and the 1 implies that a configuration using the maximum parameters permitted results into one collision domain. If a LAN consists of a single segment (Figures 9.1 and 9.2) or a single UTP repeater hub (Figures 9.4, 9.5, and 9.6), then the 5-4-3 repeater placement rule is of no practical concern. However, if a LAN's diameter is going to be extended using repeaters, then the 5-4-3 repeater placement rule becomes extremely critical.

In lieu of this general rule, we can always calculate the actual delay of our network. If we want to do this, then we must: (a) get the vendor latency specifications for all the repeaters, NICs, and cable used on our network; (b) add the delays; (c) multiply the sum by 2 (we want round-trip values); and (d) see if the product is less than or equal to 51.2 μs. If it isn't, then our network is not Ethernet/802.3 compliant. It is usually a lot easier just to follow the 5-4-3 repeater placement rule.

If we choose neither to follow the 4-repeater rule nor calculate the actual delay, then our network might be noncompliant and could possibly develop problems. Some problems manifest themselves as bad or invalid frames. These include oversized frames, runt frames, jabbers, alignment or frame errors, and CRC errors; all were discussed in Chapter 5. Timing errors can also lead to retransmissions. For example, a sending node that does not receive an acknowledgment from the receiving node within a prescribed time period assumes the frame was lost and retransmits it. Continual retransmissions can ultimately lead to degradation of network performance. Probably the biggest problem with Ethernet networks is collisions. Box 9.1 contains a description of some common causes of collisions, and Box 9.2 addresses Ethernet performance issues.

BOX 9.1 Common Causes of Collisions

Common causes of collisions in Ethernet/802.3 include the following:

Propagation Delay. Different types of media have different propagation delays, as do repeaters and bridges. If nodes are far apart on long segments, there is a greater chance of collisions due to propagation delay, especially in high-traffic environments. Add repeaters or bridges to the configuration and the probability increases. Thus, the length of certain types of Ethernet/802.3 media can have a dramatic effect on whether collisions occur.

Nodes Not Following the Rules. The IEEE specifications establish specific rules for collision detection and retransmission. Unfortunately, not all vendors follow these rules. When a vendor violates the rules on collision detection, it can affect the performance of the network. The 802.3 standard specifies that after a collision, retransmission of a packet should occur after generation of a random amount of timer delay not to exceed 1024 slot-times, which occurs on the tenth to fifteenth consecutive collision. (One slot-time is defined as 51.2 μs for 10-Mbps cable plants.) This means that if a collision occurs, a jamming signal is sent, a random number is generated, and the controller waits that long before retransmission. The controller then seizes the cable (after sensing it) and sends

the packet again (if the cable is idle). Although the wait interval is supposed to be between 1 and 1024, some vendors violate this rule and set a ceiling lower than 1024; doing so does not allow random numbers higher than a predetermined value, thus allowing a system to acquire the network quicker than those that generate a higher random number in accordance with the IEEE standard.

Noise. Noise is a pretty obvious source of collisions. Recall that noise is any type of undesirable signal. Noise can come from a variety of locations, including external sources or harmonic distortion. Various everyday office equipment such as copiers, laser printers, ballast transformers on fluorescent tube lighting, and HVAC motors also causes noise problems. Noise is more problematic with UTP cable.

Improper Segmentation of Cable. This reason is restricted to coaxial cables. ThickWire cable should be cut in accordance with the standard and at specific lengths (e.g., 23.4 m, 70.2 m, etc.); ThinWire networks should have at least 0.5 m distance between nodes. Improper segmentation can cause noise and harmonic distortion problems, thus increasing the likelihood of collisions.

Babbling Transceivers. When a transceiver fails, it begins to spew all kinds of trash on a cable; collisions inevitably occur.

Workarounds to the 5-4-3 Repeater Placement Rule

One way to increase the number of Ethernet ports and still comply with the 5-4-3 repeater placement rule is to use chassis-based repeater hubs (see Figure 6.8). These hubs have individual slots in which multiport Ethernet interface boards (also called *blades, cards,* or *modules*) are installed. The primary feature of a chassis hub is that each board is connected to the same backplane to which the repeater unit is connected. Since all boards share the same backplane with the repeater, all of the devices connected to the hub use only one repeater.

Another workaround is stackable repeater hubs (see Figure 6.9). These devices consist of individual hubs "stacked" one on top of another. Instead of a common chassis backplane, stackable hubs use a "pseudobackplane" based on a common connector interface. An external cable interconnects the individual hubs in a daisy-chain. Once interconnected, the entire

BOX 9.2 Ethernet/802.3 Performance Issues

Many Ethernet/802.3 performance-related problems stem from poorly designed and installed Ethernets, systems that are configured incorrectly, and standards violations (e.g., incorrect cable length, too many devices connected to a segment, etc.). Following are some additional problems that can adversely affect an Ethernet/802.3 LAN's performance:

Frame Deferrals. When a host is ready to transmit a frame but the network is busy, a frame deferral occurs. Thus, the transmitting node must defer or wait until the network is idle. If the average load is high (over 30%), then deferrals might be normal. If, on the other hand, network load is light, there are few errors, and frame deferrals are present, then a high burst rate contention most likely exists on the network. As a general rule, frame deferrals should never exceed 10% of the transmitted frames of a given system.

Collisions. High-traffic loads for short bursts of time on nodes that are close (electrically speaking for propagation delay) do not necessarily translate into collisions. However, high-traffic loads from bursty nodes that are electrically distant do tend to cause serious collision problems on the network.

Session Disconnects. Nodes that cannot communicate effectively with each other eventually time out. Such a disconnect might be due to network congestion (due to bursty traffic) or the inability of the network to send traffic back to the node in a prescribed time frame.

Congestion. Hardware controllers for Ethernet/802.3 devices have a finite amount of CPU power and a finite amount of memory on the cards. When a burst of traffic arrives, the controller must collect all data frames—regardless of whether the node is the correct recipient—before the controller logic can determine if the frames are valid for the node. A high burst rate of traffic can cause all buffers on a node to fill quickly and can cause the controller to lose data destined for that node while collecting data destined for other systems. When a node cannot receive data because its buffers are full, the frames are lost. Eventually, data retransmission occurs resulting in increases in both traffic load and bursting rates.

Retransmissions. As nodes lose data destined for them, the data must be retransmitted. This causes additional bursts of traffic and an artificially inflated traffic level on the network. The single most common problem that results in retransmissions is due to controller congestion—the Ethernet controller on the receiving host is not capable of reading the frames on the cable fast enough to capture all the frames offered by the sending node the first time.

chain of hubs becomes a single logical unit that counts as only one repeater hub on the network. Stackable hubs are less expensive than chassis-based devices and permit additional hubs to be added to the stack without any need for worrying about repeater hop counts. There is an upper limit, though, to the number of hubs that can be stacked. Known as the *stacking height,* this number is between 6 and 12 depending on the manufacturer.

Performance Issues

Given its design, Ethernet/802.3 LAN performance could degrade considerably as more nodes are connected. To determine whether an Ethernet/802.3 LAN is overloaded, two strategies are available. The first follows a basic management principle: Delegate the decision to others—in this case, the users. If user complaints become persistent, frequent, and loud enough, then the network probably is overloaded. The second strategy is to approach the task of analysis scientifically—get the proper tools and training and then systematically measure the LAN's performance. For those readers who want to delve into this second strategy, there are a couple of issues that need to be understood before doing so. First, you need to understand that it is very difficult to measure the true performance of any Ethernet/802.3 LAN because it does not use fixed frame sizes. For example, an Ethernet/802.3 LAN that transmits only maximum-sized frames (1518 bytes) has a theoretical maximum efficiency rate of more than 95%. This means 95% of the LAN's transmission time is being used to transmit real user data. At the other end of the scale, a LAN that transmits only minimum-sized frames (64 bytes), where user data are only 1 byte plus 45 bytes of padding, has a theoretical maximum efficiency rate of less than 2%. So, the efficiency of an Ethernet/802.3 LAN is a function of the frame sizes transmitted.

A second concept of performance is *utilization,* which is the amount of time the LAN spends successfully transmitting data. Many performance monitoring tools will provide a user with average and peak utilization times, which are reported as percentages. Both have different meanings. For example, an average utilization of 20% means that over some period of time (e.g., a 10-hour period), on average, 20% of the LAN's capacity is used for successfully transmitting data. On the other hand, a 20% peak utilization means that at a specific moment in time, 20% of the LAN's capacity was utilized. Associated with the concept of utilization is *throughput,* which is a measure of the amount of data transmitted between two nodes in a given time period (see Chapter 4). Throughput and utilization are the same except they use different units of measure. For example, if the average utilization of a 10-Mbps Ethernet/802.3 LAN is 20%, then this implies that 20% of the possible 10-Mbps bandwidth (2 Mbps) is being used on average to successfully transmit data.

This discussion of measuring performance issues inevitably leads to the question, "What are some acceptable parameters?" The subject of "acceptable" Ethernet/LAN performance parameters is an often debated topic. Rather than commit to specific parameters, we will give you some guidelines so you can decide what is acceptable. First, every LAN is different. For example, a 50% average utilization rate might be acceptable in one context but unacceptable in another. Some network managers believe that when average utilization exceeds 30% of a 10-Mbps Ethernet/802.3 LAN (3 Mbps), access times to the channel become unacceptable and overall network performance degrades. Hence, they set their thresholds accordingly and take action when they are reached. Second, don't get alarmed at high peak utilization rates. It is not uncommon, particularly during large downloads from a server, for an Ethernet/802.3 LAN to experience a peak utilization of 95% or higher. If this rate is sustained for a prolonged period of time (e.g., 5 or 10 minutes), then there probably is a problem. Third, be sensitive to response times. Increased response times could imply that the network is becoming saturated, which implies a sustained utilization rate of more than 80%. Note that the way CSMA/CD is designed, nodes even on a saturated LAN will eventually be serviced. However, the response time might not be acceptable. The bottom line is this: Although a 10-Mbps Ethernet/802.3 LAN has a theoretical capacity of 10 Mbps, actual utilization will always be less than this theoretical value. Furthermore, it is up to you to decide what parameters are acceptable for your LAN.

9.3   Switched Ethernet, Full-Duplex Ethernet, and Virtual LANs

The proliferation of client server computing and multimedia applications in the 1990s, coupled with the ever-increasing number of network users, has led to what someone in the industry once termed as "networking in slow motion" (NISM). For Ethernet/802.3 LANs, NISM is usually manifest by slow response times, low throughput, high rates of collisions, and increased complaints by users. With the exception of user complaints, these are all symptoms of network congestion. One witty response to the network congestion problem is to introduce more fiber into a network's diet because of fiber's nearly unlimited bandwidth potential. Increasing bandwidth, though, is not always the correct solution to solving congestion problems. This issue will be discussed later in the chapter. Fortunately, there are several viable strategies for relieving network congestion. These options are the product of evolutionary improvements made to conventional Ethernet/802.3 and are characterized by signaling rates greater than those of conventional Ethernet/802.3's 10 Mbps. In this section, three specific strategies are introduced: switched Ethernet, full-duplex Ethernet, and virtual LANs. In subsequent sections, 100-Mbps and 1000-Mbps Ethernets are examined. We begin this section by introducing the concept of segmentation to set the stage for our discussion of switched Ethernet.

The Concept of Segmentation

As noted earlier, collisions are an inherent part of the design and operation of an Ethernet/802.3 network, and given its contentious nature, as more nodes are added to the network, the likelihood of collisions increases. Adding more nodes to an Ethernet/802.3 LAN also increases bandwidth utilization, and a general guideline followed by many network managers is something called the 30% rule. This rule is based on the following observation: When the average utilization exceeds 30% of Ethernet's 10-Mbps channel capacity, access times to the channel become unacceptable and overall network performance degrades. A direct implication of this rule is that the throughput of a highly utilized 10-Mbps Ethernet segment will only be a fraction of the full 10 Mbps available. Although this is true, a 10-Mbps Ethernet LAN can support hundreds of nodes running various applications without ever reaching this level of average utilization. The 30% rule is a pretty good guideline to follow, but it should be used in concert with the ultimate goal of achieving consistently high end-to-end network throughput. One of the most efficient ways in which high bandwidth utilization averages can be resolved is through *segmentation,* which involves configuring a network so that it consists of several separate (but still interconnected) segments. Segmentation, which is also called *partitioning,* improves overall network performance, enhances security, and increases reliability.

One way to partition an Ethernet/802.3 network is to create separate segments with fewer users. This is illustrated in Figure 9.9. In part (a), a typical Ethernet/802.3 LAN consisting of nine hosts is shown. In part (b), this network is partitioned into three separate segments, each consisting of three hosts and a bridge. Segments are interconnected by a common backbone and isolated from each other using the bridges. An alternative to the configuration of (b) is shown in part (c). Once again, the original Ethernet/802.3 LAN of (a) is partitioned into three isolated segments, each consisting of three hosts. In this illustration, though, the segments are interconnected via a multiport bridge rather than a common backbone. Thus, the backbone of (b) has been "col-

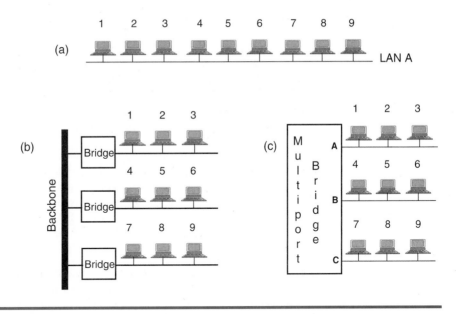

FIGURE 9.9 In (a), an unsegmented Ethernet LAN is shown. In (b), this LAN is partitioned into three separate segments using individual bridges connected to a backbone, and alternatively, in (c), a multiport bridge is used in which the backbone of (b) is "collapsed" into the multiport bridge. In a properly segmented network, at least 80% of the network traffic generated by the nodes on a LAN remains local to that LAN. Keeping remote access to a minimum (no more than 20%) minimizes backbone congestion and increases network performance.

lapsed" into the multiport bridge. Comparing the configurations of (b) and (c) to that of (a) in Figure 9.9, it can be seen that segmentation helps reduce network traffic loads by reducing the number of nodes having to contend for the same shared medium. In part (a), nine hosts are in contention, but in (b) and (c), only three hosts each contend for the same medium. This strategy works well as long as it follows the 80/20 rule—80% of the traffic between nodes remains on the same physical cable segment; the remaining 20% of traffic traverses a layer-2 or layer-3 device. If not, then this configuration can actually degrade a network. Another strategy is to partition a network by physically connecting all workstations and servers that need to communicate with each other to the same segment. One way this can be implemented is to place all servers at partition boundaries. This is illustrated in Figure 9.10. You can also partition a network in a similar manner using switches, firewalls, or routers.

The concept of segmentation is simple enough to understand, but it is not always easy to implement. Partitioning requires proper network analysis prior to implementation. If not properly configured, we can actually increase traffic loads rather than reduce them. For example, suppose in Figure 9.10 that a node on the C segment needs to communicate with the server on the A segment on a frequent basis. Now, instead of keeping this node's transmissions local to the C group, traffic must cross the backbone. This increases backbone traffic, which increases overall network congestion. Partitioning a network into separate physical segments is easy to do and maintain when dealing with static workgroups. However, in dynamic workgroup settings where employees are assigned to work on different projects for different periods of time, partitioning is difficult to implement. For example, suppose 50

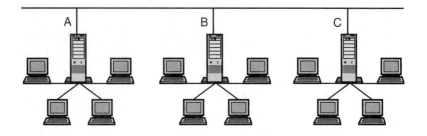

FIGURE 9.10 Another way to partition a network is to physically connect all nodes with their server and to place all servers at partition boundaries. In this illustration, there are three separate partitions—A, B, and C. Note that network traffic is reduced since the majority of communication occurs within a separate segment. At the same time, by having the servers on the partition boundaries, nodes from one segment are not locked out from communicating with a server located on another segment.

people located in three different buildings are assigned to a project that uses applications installed on a centrally located server. It is quite impractical to move these people and their workstations to the same physical location and segment that support the server. Consequently, 100% of this workgroup's network traffic will traverse the backbone.

Switched Ethernet

Improving the realistic constraints of segmentation led to the development of Ethernet switches and the concept of *switched Ethernet*. (In Chapter 6, we provided a general discussion about Ethernet switches and switch architecture. Now might be a good time to review this information.) The concept of switched Ethernet is based on the following principle: If the traffic a node receives is restricted to only the traffic destined for it, then network loads are reduced because every host would not need to examine every frame placed on the network. Thus, switched Ethernet transforms traditional Ethernet/802.3 from a broadcast technology to a point-to-point technology—it isolates network traffic between sending and receiving nodes from all other connected nodes. This is done using Ethernet switches, which are improved bridges that were first introduced in 1990. Today, Ethernet switches are a key element in Ethernet/802.3 LANs, and the switch concept is now a part of ATM, token ring, FDDI, and 100-Mbps and 1000-Mbps Ethernet networks. Ethernet switches are available in various varieties including *workgroup, private,* and *backbone*. These terms describe a switch's application in contrast to the terms store-and-forward and cut-through, which describe a switch's architecture or operation (see Chapter 6).

Workgroup Switch Workgroup switches (also called *segment switches*) are very fast multiport bridges because each port supports a shared medium. A workgroup switch partitions a single shared medium into multiple shared media. For example, in Figure 9.11(a), each node is contending for a piece of a 10-Mbps channel. In part (b), though, only ten nodes per segment now contend for the shared medium. Thus, each node in part (b) effectively receives one-tenth of the channel rather than one-hundredth as in (a), which improves overall network performance tenfold. Workgroup switches are capable of supporting up to 1024 MAC addresses per port. (Recall that 1024 is the maximum number of nodes permitted on an Ethernet/802.3 LAN.)

(a) 100 Nodes Share One 10-Mbps Channel

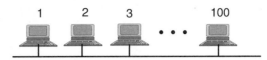

(b) Ten 10-Mbps Segments, Each with Ten Nodes

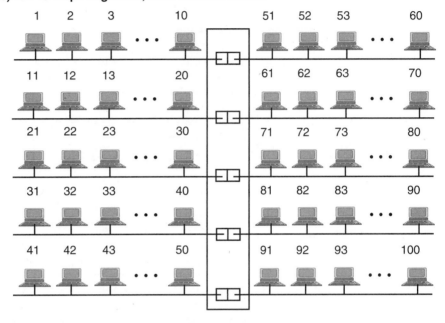

FIGURE 9.11 The 100-node unsegmented 10-Mbps Ethernet network in (a) implies each node occupies one-hundredth of the shared medium. In (b), a workgroup Ethernet switch is used to partition this network into multiple LAN segments with ten nodes each. Each node now receives one-tenth of a 10-Mbps channel, and overall network performance for all nodes increases by a factor of 10.

Private Switch Unlike workgroup switches, private switches support only one MAC address per port, providing each node with its own dedicated 10-Mbps segment. This eliminates contention for the cable, thereby liberating the end nodes from performing collision detection. Private switches are appropriate for workstations running applications requiring high bandwidth. An illustration of a private Ethernet switch is given in Figure 9.12.

Switches supporting 100 Mbps and 1000 Mbps are also available. These switches are particularly appropriate for client server applications. For example, in Figure 9.12, if node 8 were a server and nodes 1–7 were clients, all traffic would be to or from the server. Since each port supports a dedicated 10-Mbps link, a bottleneck could conceivably exist at the server port. This situation is resolved by using a 10/100 switch, which includes dedicated 10-Mbps and 100-Mbps ports. Clients are connected to the 10-Mbps ports, and servers are connected to the 100-Mbps ports. This is shown in Figure 9.13. Some switches accommodate both shared and dedicated segments. Thus, dedicated ports are assigned to users who require greater bandwidth (e.g., those who frequently transfer large graphical images to or

Private 10-Mbps Ethernet Switch

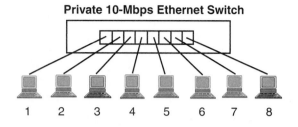

FIGURE 9.12 A private 10-Mbps Ethernet switch resembles a UTP repeater hub. Unlike a repeater hub, a private switch dedicates a full 10-Mbps channel to each port, which supports only one node (i.e., one MAC address). Since each node has its own dedicated segment, there is no need for a node to perform collision detection.

Private 10/100-Mbps Ethernet Switch

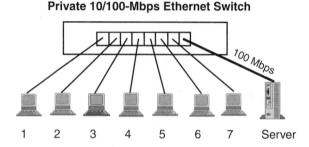

FIGURE 9.13 A 10/100-Mbps private Ethernet switch can be used in a client/server environment to assign dedicated 10-Mbps channels to each client and a full, dedicated 100-Mbps channel to the server. Since all traffic is to and from the server, the higher-bandwidth segment reduces the possibility of a bottleneck existing at the server port.

from a server), and shared LAN segments are used for low-bandwidth users (e.g., those whose applications include only e-mail). An illustration is provided in Figure 9.14.

Backbone Switch   A third and final application of Ethernet switches involves incorporating them into the network backbone. Within this context, switches are referred to as backbone switches, and the network topology is described as a *collapsed backbone*. Backbone switches can be employed either at the building level or for the entire enterprise. They usually are chassis-based devices and accommodate different media types. Backbone switches also are available with fault tolerance (e.g., multiple power supplies) and redundancy features. Deploying a building backbone switch can contribute to a gradual reduction of overall backbone traffic, and collapsing the entire backbone into a single hub centralizes the backbone, which can enable better management control over the network elements. An example of a backbone switch is given in Figure 9.15.

Associated with a vendor's switch specifications is the term *wire speed*. When used in this context, wire speed means that the device's filtering and forwarding rate is equal to the maximum (i.e., fastest) rate possible. In Ethernet/802.3, wire speed is equal to 14,880 frames per second. This is frequently reported as 14,880 packets per second (pps). Box 9.3 provides additional information about this concept.

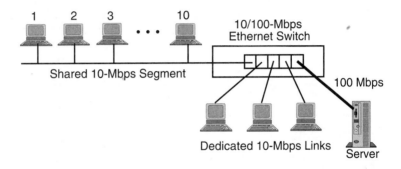

FIGURE 9.14 Some Ethernet switches are capable of supporting a mix of different segments. Here, ten nodes are connected to a shared 10-Mbps segment, three nodes have their own dedicated 10-Mbps segments, and a file server is connected to a dedicated 100-Mbps segment.

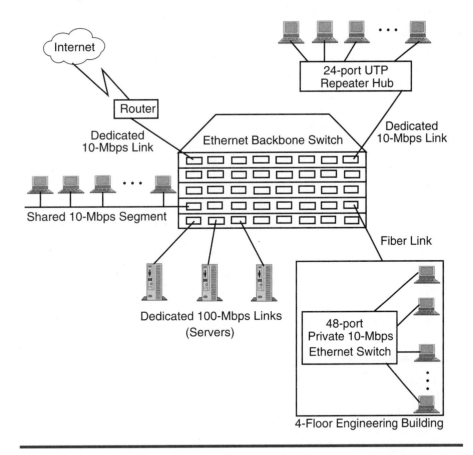

FIGURE 9.15 A backbone Ethernet switch enables an organization's entire network to be collapsed into the switch. These switches are chassis-based and have gigabit per second backplanes. They also support multiple media types, shared or dedicated segments, and both 10-Mbps and 100-Mbps segments. To compensate for a single source of failure, backbone switches have provisions for fault tolerance and redundancy.

BOX 9.3   Understanding Ethernet "Wire Speed" and Capacity

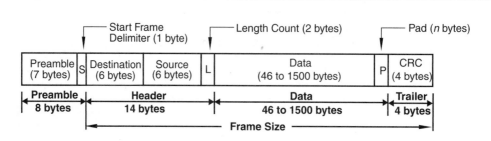

In a standard 10-Mbps IEEE 802.3 frame (pictured here), observe that the data field, also referred to as the frame's *payload,* is accompanied by the fields containing addressing, length, and error-control information. These header and trailer fields require 18 bytes. Ignoring the 8-byte preamble, which is not considered part of the frame because it contains no interpretable data, the size of an IEEE 802.3 frame varies from 64 bytes to 1518 bytes. Clearly, as the size of the data field increases, the ratio of fixed overhead to data increases. Thus, 64 bytes is not only the smallest, but also the most inefficient, IEEE 802.3 frame size. A worst-case scenario for network devices such as bridges, switches, and routers is constantly having to process 64-byte frames. Thus, various performance tests of networking devices are usually conducted using 64-byte frames. Let's calculate the frame rate for these minimum-sized IEEE 802.3 frames.

- A 64-byte frame is equal to $8 \times 64 = 512$ bits
- A 10-Mbps transmission rate is equal to 10 bits per microsecond (μs)
- Thus, at 10 Mbps, a 64-byte frame is transferred in $512/10 = 51.2$ μs

The 8-byte preamble requires another 6.4 μs, and between each two frames is an *interframe gap* requiring 9.6 μs. Summing all these times, we obtain a total of 67.2 μs per frame. If we divide 1 second by this sum, we get 0.0148809 μs. Thus, one frame occupies 0.0148809 μs. Since there are 1 million microseconds in 1 second, if we multiply 0.0148809 by 1,000,000, we get 14,880. Therefore, a 10-Mbps Ethernet network transmits a maximum of 14,880 64-byte frames in 1 second. This frame rate, 14,880 frames per second, is referred to as *wire speed* in the literature. Cut-through switches have wire speed filtering and forwarding rates. We further calculate that a maximum-size Ethernet frame (i.e., 1518 bytes) plus all its associated overhead is transmitted in 1230.4 μs, which yields a maximum frame rate of 812. In other words, given a transmission rate of 10 Mbps, 812 maximum-length Ethernet frames can be transmitted in 1 second. Using these calculations, we can now estimate the amount of payload that can be transferred each second on a 10-Mbps Ethernet/ 802.3 LAN. We multiply the frame rate by the size of the data field. As noted earlier, the data field ranges from 46 bytes to 1500 bytes, which, at frame rates of 14,880 and 812 per second, respectively, yields 5.476 Mbps and 9.861 Mbps. Clearly, a network dealing with only the largest possible frames would come closest to delivering the promise of 10-Mbps Ethernet; however, in reality, we can expect a transmission rate closer to the middle of the range we calculated.

Since the frame format for Fast Ethernet is the same as 10-Mbps Ethernet, the time parameters given for 10 Mbps hold except for the interframe gap, which is one-tenth as long, or 0.96 μs. Doing similar calculations, the wire speed for Fast Ethernet is 148,809 frames per second, and the maximum frame rate is 8120.

BOX 9.3 Understanding Ethernet "Wire Speed" and Capacity (continued)

We cannot, however, calculate the time parameters for Gigabit Ethernet, which operates at 1000 Mbps, by simply multiplying our 10-Mbps Ethernet results by 100. This is because a Gigabit Ethernet frame has a *carrier extension* that increases the minimum frame size to 512 bytes. Nevertheless, we still can calculate similar parameters for Gigabit Ethernet by following the same procedure we used for 10-Mbps Ethernet.

- A 512-byte frame is equal to $8 \times 512 = 4096$ bits
- A 1000-Mbps transmission rate is equal to 1000 bits per microsecond (μs)
- Thus, at 1000 Mbps, a 512-byte frame is transferred in $4096/1000 = 4.096$ μs

In Gigabit Ethernet, the interframe gap is one-hundredth of that for 10 Mbps, or 0.096 μs. Furthermore, the 8-byte preamble requires another 0.064 μs. Summing all these times, we obtain a total of 4.256 μs per frame. If we divide 1 second by this sum, we get 0.2349624 μs. Thus, one frame occupies 0.2349624 μs. Since there are 1 million microseconds in 1 second, if we multiply 0.2349624 by 1,000,000, we get 234,962. Therefore, a 1000-Mbps Ethernet network transmits a maximum of 234,962 512-byte frames in 1 second. Since Gigabit Ethernet's maximum frame size is still 1518 bytes, Gigabit Ethernet can transmit $812 \times 100 = 81,200$ maximum-sized frames per second. A technology currently being reviewed by IEEE increases Ethernet's 1500-byte data field to 9000 bytes, which results in what is called an Ethernet *jumbo frame*. Jumbo frame technology enables data transfer rates to approach gigabit speeds on a Gigabit Ethernet LAN, which is currently limited in performance due to the relatively small data field. For example, a 900,000-byte message requires 600 frames that support a 1500-byte data field, but only100 jumbo frames. Thus, the amount of processing overhead for Gigabit Ethernet is six times more than the jumbo frame Gigabit Ethernet's overhead for the same message.

Full-Duplex Ethernet

The introduction of private Ethernet switches effectively eliminates contention since each node connected to the switch has its own dedicated segment. As a direct consequence, it is possible for nodes to transmit and receive data simultaneously. That is, private Ethernet switches promote *full-duplex Ethernet.* This is significant because Ethernet was initially designed as a broadcast network based on a physical bus topology. This design limits Ethernet/802.3's operation to half-duplex because nodes have to listen for collisions while transmitting. In a UTP cable environment, this means that one pair of cables is used to transmit, and the receiving pair listens for collisions.

With collision detection disabled, full-duplex nodes can transmit and receive data at the same time. Thus, aggregate throughput per segment is doubled from 10 Mbps to 20 Mbps—10 Mbps on the transmit pair and 10 Mbps on the receive pair. Full-duplex Ethernet requires a private Ethernet switch that supports full-duplex ports, and hosts require full-duplex NICs. Full-duplex Ethernet cards are best suited for servers rather than clients because servers have considerably more bidirectional traffic than clients. The advantages of full-duplex Ethernet also cannot be realized unless end nodes are running a multi-threaded operating system such as UNIX or Windows NT. Nodes not running this type of OS will realize only a marginal performance increase from full-duplex hardware. Compared to other high-speed networking initiatives such as 100/1000-Mbps Ethernet or FDDI, full-duplex Ethernet is relatively inexpensive, easy to implement, and has no real price penalty. As with all networking initiatives, the issue of interoperability needs to be considered and addressed before a decision is made to upgrade a 10-Mbps Ethernet to full-duplex Ethernet.

Virtual Local Area Networks (VLANs)

Another strategy for addressing the constraints of segmentation is to establish *virtual local area networks* (VLANs). VLANs are created using Ethernet switches. Unlike nodes connected to a physical LAN, nodes that comprise a VLAN are not physically connected to the same medium. They are connected in a virtual sense using specially designed software that groups several ports in a switch into a single workgroup. Nodes connected to these ports are considered part of a virtual workgroup, and network traffic from any node/port is (usually) limited to only those nodes or ports assigned to the workgroup. Depending on the switch, traffic filtering is performed using either MAC addresses (layer 2) or network addresses (layer 3). In the case of the latter, a switch must operate at layer 3 (the network layer), and the switch must support the routing protocol used in the network. In an IP-based network, if the switch supports the Internet Protocol, then workgroups are created by using a node's IP address. The advantage of using layer-3 protocols on which to base a VLAN is that an individual node can be assigned to more than one virtual subnetwork at the same time. A server, for example, can be shared on a virtual basis by more than one workgroup. VLANs based on MAC addresses enable any node to be assigned transparently to a workgroup, but virtual subnets cannot share nodes. An illustration of a VLAN is shown in Figure 9.16.

A VLAN strategy fits very nicely into a dynamic work environment in which various workgroups are formed for short-lived projects. Personnel selection criteria for these projects are usually based on employee strengths and expertise, not employee location. Consequently, a workgroup might involve 25 people who are dispersed throughout an organization and who require access to equally dispersed servers. VLANs can resolve this problem because they permit users who are connected to different physical segments to be organized into logical workgroups independent of users' physical location. As users relocate within an organization by changing job assignments, offices, or computers, their node addresses (MAC or network) are deleted from one workgroup table and added to another. VLANs also can reduce congestion, problems of isolation, and improve network security.

Although Ethernet switches certainly help improve the overall performance of a heavily loaded LAN, they are not necessarily the cure for the limitations of the common Ethernet. If a network's architecture is poor to begin with, a switch will only mask the problems by increasing throughput without really identifying and resolving the true problems. Consequently, prior to installing a switch, it is prudent first to study how a network is being used. This includes performing a network analysis to determine traffic loads and patterns, user applications, location of users and servers, and type of data transmissions. In some cases, giving attention to specific network administration tasks might prove sufficient. For example, Ethernet/802.3 performance and efficiency can be improved through collision management, standards adherence, proper system configurations, software upgrades, and segmentation using bridges. Nevertheless, there are certain situations that lend themselves to switching. These include dynamic workgroup

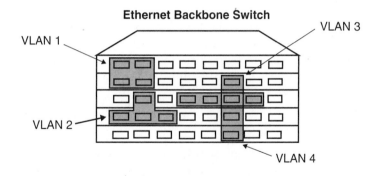

FIGURE 9.16 Some Ethernet switches support virtual LANs, which group together selected ports to form independent subnets. Traffic between ports of a VLAN is restricted to only those members of a "port group." Some switches also support routing protocols so that ports can belong to more than one VLAN, as is illustrated in VLANs 3 and 4.

settings, frequent data transmissions involving large data files such as graphical images, distributed network environments that employ several servers, and LANs that must support video or multimedia applications. If a decision to "switch" is made, remember that all switches are not alike. Switches have different architectures (as discussed in Chapter 6), are designed for different types of applications, and some switches also have routing capabilities (called layer-3 switches). Once again, it is important to understand how a network is being used before modifying it.

9.4 100-MBPS Ethernet LANs

Although switched and full-duplex Ethernet—and segmentation—improve overall network performance, these implementation strategies for enhancing 10-Mbps Ethernet/802.3 performance do not actually increase data transmission rates; that is, they do not speed up the network. There are several reasons we need to increase the speed of an Ethernet/802.3 LAN. First, the introduction of more sophisticated operating systems and applications, faster processors, and greater disk and memory capacities has led to a pronounced degradation in overall network and application performance. Second, many companies now use Internet technologies to build private corporate intranets that rely on standard Web browsers such as Netscape's Communicator and Microsoft's Internet Explorer to provide employees with access to critical corporate data. These Web browsers are capable of supporting bandwidth-intensive rich media data types, including high-resolution graphics, 3D imaging, audio, video, and voice. Third, the introduction of multimedia client/server applications, the deployment of network computers and Java-based servers, and an increasing number of network users are taxing first-generation Ethernet.

To address this issue of speeding up the network, IEEE increased Ethernet/802.3's 10-Mbps data transmission rate first to 100 Mbps and then to 1000 Mbps. This strategy is different from the 10-Mbps Ethernet strategies discussed earlier and can be best understood by viewing a network as a crowded highway. A strategy that employs segmentation, switched Ethernet, or full-duplex Ethernet adds more lanes to the highway. A 100-Mbps or 1000-Mbps technology, however, actually increases the speed limit of the highway by orders of magnitude from 10 Mbps to 100 Mbps to 1000 Mbps. The concept of 100-Mbps Ethernet was first introduced in 1992, and two 100-Mbps Ethernet standards were ultimately approved by IEEE 3 years later: Fast Ethernet (IEEE 802.3u) and 100VG-AnyLAN (IEEE 802.12).

Fast Ethernet

To entice the IEEE to adopt Fast Ethernet technology as a standard, an organization called the Fast Ethernet Alliance (FEA) was formed in August 1993. Within 2 years, FEA membership grew to more than 80 vendors, including 3Com, Cabletron, Intel, DEC, and Sun Microsystems. In June 1995, this new technology became the IEEE 802.3u standard and was given the specification 100BASE-T. With its goals accomplished, the FEA concluded its activities in September 1996.

The designation *100BASE-X* is sometimes used to represent 100BASE-TX and 100BASE-FX.

100BASE-T evolved from 10BASE-T, specifically, and conventional Ethernet, generally. At the physical layer, 100BASE-T employs a star topology and supports twisted-pair and fiber-optic cable. Unlike 10BASE-T, though, Fast Ethernet has three different media specifications: *100BASE-TX, 100BASE-T4,* and *100BASE-FX* (Table 9.2). The first two use twisted-pair cable; the third uses fiber-optic cable. Note the absence of co-axial cable, which was the mainstay of the original Ethernet specification. All three components of the standard are designed to interoperate with one another. Fast Ethernet also uses the same connector types as 10BASE-T and maintains a 512 bit-time collision domain. There is one obvious difference, though—speed. Fast Ethernet is ten times faster than conventional Ethernet—100 Mbps versus 10 Mbps. This tenfold increase in speed has two direct implications. First, it reduces the amount of time it takes to transmit one bit by a factor of 10. In Fast Ethernet, 512 bit-times are equal to 5.12 μs instead of 51.2 μs. Second, the network diameter is reduced by a factor of 10. These diameters are summarized in Table 9.2.

Many network fundamentalists equate Ethernet with CSMA/CD. It is their belief that if the MAC sublayer protocol of a LAN technology is not CSMA/CD-based, then the word "Ethernet" should not be used either to reference or to describe the technology.

At the data link layer, Fast Ethernet is unchanged from its 10-Mbps counterpart. The frame format, the minimum and maximum frame sizes (including the amount of user data a frame can transmit), and the MAC address format are all identical to conventional Ethernet. Perhaps most important, though, Fast Ethernet uses exactly the same media access method, namely, CSMA/CD, as conventional Ethernet. This provides a simple and seamless migration path for current users of 10-Mbps Ethernet/802.3, particularly shared or switched 10BASE-T users.

A description of the three Fast Ethernet specifications follows.

TP-PMD was once called CDDI—copper distributed data interface—which applied to running FDDI over UTP. FDDI is discussed in Chapter 11.

• **100BASE-TX** transmits and receives data over two pairs of EIA/TIA 568-compliant Category 5 UTP cable or two pairs of IBM Type 1 STP cable. It uses a full-duplex signaling system based on FDDI's twisted-pair physical medium dependent (TP-PMD) sublayer, which is an ANSI standard that defines the manner in which data are encoded/decoded and transmitted. Networks based on the 100BASE-TX standard must be Category 5-compliant throughout, including wire, connectors, patch panels, and punch-down blocks. Since many new network installations employ four-pair Category 5 UTP cable, a 100BASE-TX installation leaves managers with an "extra" two

TABLE 9.2 Summary of IEEE 802.3u (Fast Ethernet—100 Mbps) Specifications

Type	Description
100BASE-TX	**Medium:** 2-pair Category 5 UTP or IBM Type 1 STP; **Topology:** Star; **Max Segment Length:** 100 m; **Connectors:** Category 5 compliant 8-pin modular (RJ-45), patch panels, patch cables, punch-down blocks; **Media Access Control:** CSMA/CD; **Network Diameter:** 200 m when used with one Class I or one Class II repeater; 205 m when used with two Class II repeaters; 261 m when used with mix of UTP/Fiber cable and one Class I repeater; 289 m when used with mix of UTP/Fiber cable and one Class II repeater; 216 m when used with mix of UTP/Fiber cable and two Class II repeaters; **Misc:** Full-duplex operation
100BASE-T4	**Medium:** 4-pair Category 3, 4, or 5 UTP or IBM Type 1 STP; **Topology:** Star; **Max Segment Length:** 100 m; **Connectors:** 8-pin modular (RJ-45), patch panels, patch cables, punch-down blocks; **Media Access Control:** CSMA/CD; **Network Diameter:** 200 m when used with one Class I or one Class II repeater; 205 m when used with two Class II repeaters; 231 m when used with mix of UTP/Fiber cable and one Class I repeater; 304 m when used with mix of UTP/Fiber cable and one Class II repeater; 236 m when used with mix of UTP/Fiber cable and two Class II repeaters; **Misc:** Half-duplex operation
100BASE-FX	**Medium:** 2-strand 62.5/125 multimode fiber-optic; **Topology:** Star; **Max Segment Length:** 412 m (half-duplex) or 2 km (full-duplex); **Connectors:** ST, SC, or FDDI's media interface connector; **Media Access Control:** CSMA/CD; **Network Diameter:** 272 m when used with Class I repeaters; 320 m when used with one Class II repeater; 228 m when used with two Class II repeaters; **Misc:** Designed primarily to interconnect Fast Ethernet repeaters

pairs of wires that can be used for voice communication or be reserved for future network enhancements. Presently, these "extra" two pairs cannot be used to support another high-speed LAN.

• **100BASE-T4** uses a half-duplex signaling system to transmit and receive data over four pairs of Category 3, 4, or 5 UTP cable or four pairs of IBM Type 1 STP cable. One pair of wires is used exclusively for transmitting data, one pair is used exclusively for receiving data and collision detection, and the remaining two pairs are used either for transmitting or receiving. As a result, three pairs of wires can be used for data transmission or three pairs can be used for data reception. This scheme of using three wire pairs for transmitting or receiving data reduces overall cable frequency because the signal can be divided among these wires. A direct effect of this design is that lower-quality cable such as voice-grade Category 3 can be used to support a higher-speed technology such as Fast Ethernet. 100BASE-T4's advantage over 100BASE-TX is that the former can be used in Category 3 or 4 wiring installations. Thus, organizations can scale-up their 10-Mbps Ethernet networks to 100 Mbps without modifying their existing cable plants, or they can opt to install

Category 3 wire, which is less expensive than the superior grade Category 5 wire, and still benefit from 100-Mbps Ethernet. Although 100BASE-T4 supports inferior cable such as Category 3, it does not support 25-pair Category 3 wire for horizontal runs, which is commonly installed for voice transmission. 100BASE-T4 is not without its drawbacks, however. Unlike 100BASE-TX, which uses only two pairs of wire, 100BASE-T4 must use all four wire pairs. It also does not support full-duplex operation.

• **100BASE-FX** supports 100-Mbps Ethernet operation over two strands of 62.5/125 micron multimode fiber-optic cable (one strand for transmitting data and one pair for receiving data). It shares the same signaling system as that of 100BASE-TX except it uses FDDI's fiber physical media dependent sublayer. Unlike 100BASE-TX or 100BASE-T4, 100BASE-FX segments are known formally as *link segments,* which are designed to connect only two nodes in a point-to-point topology. Consequently, 100BASE-FX's primary application is at the backbone and is used to connect Fast Ethernet hubs.

Unlike Manchester coding, which conventional Ethernet is based on, 100BASE-T relies on two different encoding techniques. 100BASE-TX and 100BASE-FX use the 4B/5B encoding scheme, and 100BASE-T4 uses an encoding scheme known as 8B/6T. Originally defined for FDDI (Chapter 11), 4B/5B takes data in four-bit codes and maps them to corresponding five-bit codes that are transmitted using NRZI. The 4B/5B-NRZI scheme makes it possible for Fast Ethernet (and FDDI) to operate at 125 MHz and provides a data rate of 100 Mbps. (See Chapter 3 for more information about encoding techniques.) The 8B/6T method maps eight-bit data blocks to a specific code group consisting of six symbols. These code groups are then transmitted across three output channels. The effective data rate on each channel is 33 Mbps, with a signaling rate of 25 Mbaud.

IEEE 802.3u also defines two classes of repeaters. *Class I repeaters* support both of Fast Ethernet's signaling schemes (100BASE-T4 and 100BASE-TX/FX), and *Class II repeaters* support only one signaling scheme (100BASE-T4 or 100BASE-TX/FX, but not both). Class I repeaters have a latency of no more than 0.7 μs; the latency of Class II repeaters is less than or equal to 0.46 μs. The two signaling types are interoperable at both node and hub levels. When maximum cable lengths are used, only one Class I repeater or a maximum of two Class II repeaters—with a maximum interrepeater link of 5 m—can exist within any single collision domain. Furthermore, since Class II repeaters can only be used to connect segments that have the same signaling schemes, 100BASE-T4 segments cannot be connected to 100BASE-TX/FX segments using a Class II repeater. A direct consequence of these new classes of repeaters is that the 5-4-3 repeater placement rule for 10-Mbps Ethernet does not apply to Fast Ethernet. The network diameters for 100BASE-T also have different ranges depending on which repeater is used, the number of repeaters used, and the cable type (see Table 9.2).

From a technological perspective, the designers of 100BASE-T made it easy for network managers to deploy Fast Ethernet at their sites in a relatively seamless fashion. When viewed from an inexperienced or naive network administrator's perspective, converting or migrating to Fast Ethernet from conventional Ethernet might indeed appear "easy." For example, one can reasonably argue that if the physical layer satisfies Fast Ethernet specifications, all that is required to convert from 10-Mbps

Ethernet/802.3 to Fast Ethernet is to swap out a node's network interface card. From a practical perspective, though, *any* network migration or upgrade endeavor is usually problematic. Given this basic tenet, converting to Fast Ethernet is not necessarily easily accomplished. Consider the cable plant. Although 100BASE-T supports UTP, it requires four pairs of Category 3, 4, or 5 UTP cable (100BASE-T4). Four pairs of Category 3 cable mean that all eight wires of a standard Category 3 UTP bundle must be used to achieve a data rate of 100 Mbps. This is not feasible for sites using two pairs of Category 3 UTP for their 10BASE-T networks if the other two pairs of wire are being used for telephone connections (or for additional Ethernet connections). For 10BASE-T LANs using two pairs of Category 5 UTP, all is not well either. Cable installation requirements for 100BASE-TX are extremely stringent, requiring all components (from connectors to patch panels to number of twists per inch) to be certified Category 5 compliant. Many so-called Category 5 10BASE-T LANs do not meet these specifications and hence will have to be modified. Finally, coaxial cable-based LANs (ThinWire or ThickWire) also will require major changes to their cable plants since 100BASE-T does not support coaxial cable. In fact, none of the newer higher-speed LAN technologies supports coaxial cable, which is viewed by some as a diminishing technology without a future.

In addition to the cable plant, incorporating Fast Ethernet into an existing LAN or as a new LAN installation also has an impact on several network design issues. There are shorter cable lengths, and Fast Ethernet only permits two types of repeaters. This translates to pronounced limitations on network diameters and collision domains. These restrictions can have a dramatic effect on how a network is designed. For example, more wiring closets might be necessary for a 100BASE-T than for a 10BASE-T installation, and additional hardware (e.g., bridges or switches) will be required to extend a 100BASE-T LAN.

Finally, attention should be given to both topology and network nodes. Fast Ethernet must be configured as a star, not as a bus. Furthermore, Fast Ethernet was designed with switches in mind, not bridges. Deployment of 100BASE-T also presupposes the use of nodes capable of supporting the increase in speed. Hence, LANs consisting of ISA bus-based nodes will not benefit from Fast Ethernet, and workstations using anything less than a 32-bit operating system will not realize an increase in throughput either.

Here's the bottom line: Networks are nontrivial and Fast Ethernet is no exception. Network managers considering implementing Fast Ethernet as part of a new LAN installation, or integrating it into an existing 10-Mbps Ethernet LAN, need to give serious attention to the various physical limitations, restrictions, and design issues related to 100BASE-T. It is also prudent for managers to understand the IEEE specifications and their ramifications before getting involved with Fast Ethernet. There are, however, some things that can be done to ease the migration. For example, new 10BASE-T nodes can be accommodated for 100BASE-T migration by installing 10/100-Mbps NICs, which employ an autosensing/negotiation feature that enables them to operate at data rates of either 10 Mbps or 100 Mbps. Also, since many Ethernet switches incorporate both 10-Mbps and 100-Mbps ports, it is possible for 10BASE-T and 100BASE-T segments to be connected to the same switch. Specific strategies for migrating or upgrading to Fast Ethernet are provided in Box 9.4.

BOX 9.4   Migrating or upgrading to 100BASE-T

Following are several strategies to consider if you are planning to migrate or upgrade an existing 10-Mbps Ethernet/802.3 LAN to Fast Ethernet:

1. For organizations that are not yet ready to implement 100BASE-T but are still adding new users to their 10BASE-T LAN, the simplest and most cost-effective 10BASE-T to 100BASE-T migration strategy is to install 10/100-Mbps network interface cards in new nodes. These cards can automatically sense the correct data transmission rate based on the hub port to which they are connected. This strategy will also preserve an organization's current investment in its 10BASE-T LAN.

2. For organizations that want a "blended" 10/100-Mbps network, a paramount concern is how to interconnect the two networks. Several strategies are possible. One method is to use a bridge. This is probably the least expensive and easiest installation. A second method is to use a router. This can be cost prohibitive, though, and usually increases the complexity of a network. A third strategy is to use a switch that can support both 10-Mbps and 100-Mbps connections. Some switches permit shared 10-Mbps segments to be mixed with dedicated 10-Mbps and dedicated 100-Mbps segments. Although more costly than bridges, switches do provide a nice migration strategy for a mixed environment.

   In a mixed or blended environment, be careful with network diameters and collision domains. It is possible to maintain a 500-m network diameter in this type of environment. One configuration involves 100-m segments to

a Fast Ethernet Class II repeater. This repeater is then interconnected to a 10/100-Mbps switch that contains 10BASE-T connections. The switch interconnects to an unpopulated 10/100-Mbps switch, which then connects to a second Class II repeater. This second Class II repeater can support end nodes such as servers.

3. For organizations planning to upgrade to 100BASE-T:
   a. Confirm that you really need to upgrade. "Tuning" a network through network analysis, reengineering, segmentation, software upgrades, and collision management can provide tremendous improvements in network performance.
   b. Confirm that your cable plant meets the proper specifications.
   c. Confirm that all nodes have sufficient horsepower (e.g., PCI bus-based, 32-bit OS) and that all servers have sufficient buffering capacity.
   d. Confirm that all users require 100 Mbps. If not, list item 2 might be more appropriate; consider installing full-duplex 10-Mbps switches.
   e. Know, understand, and follow the various specifications related to 100BASE-T.
   f. Plan on installing only one repeater hub per collision domain.
   g. Use bridges or switches to connect to secondary wiring closets.
   h. Use two-port switches to extend network diameter.
   i. Invest in 100BASE-T-compliant diagnostic equipment.

100VG-AnyLAN

100VG-AnyLAN is a competing technology to Fast Ethernet. Formally specified as IEEE 802.12, 100VG-AnyLAN was approved as an IEEE standard in June 1995; it was designed to serve as an upgrade path for 10-Mbps Ethernet/802.3 and 4/16-Mbps token ring. There are relatively few 100VG-AnyLAN installations today compared to Fast Ethernet installations. The primary reason for this dearth is that 100VG-AnyLAN is not

TABLE 9.3 Summary of IEEE 802.12 (100VG-AnyLAN) Specifications

Category	Description
Media	4-pair Category 3 UTP (100 m); 4-pair Category 4 UTP (100 m); 4-pair Category 5 UTP (200 m); 2-pair Category 5 UTP (under investigation); 2-pair Type 1 STP (200 m); 25-pair UTP cable using 50-pin telco connectors; 2 strands 62.5/125 multimode fiber (2000 m)
Media Components	8-pin modular (RJ-45) connectors; patch panels; patch cables; punch-down blocks
Network Cards	100VG-AnyLAN compliant NICs
Hubs	100VG-AnyLAN compliant repeater hubs—all hubs have an uplink port to connect to another VG hub; all ports can be used as downlink ports to connect to end nodes or another VG hub; all ports can be configured in normal mode (only receives data destined for it) or monitor mode (receives all data)
Maximum Nodes	1024 on a single-shared (unbridged) LAN; no more than 250 is recommended, however
Collision Domain	N/A; However, the term priority domain is used to describe a 100VG-AnyLAN network that consists of a root hub and all of its connected nodes, including lower-level hubs and nodes
Network Diameter	8000 m
Topology	Hierarchical star with up to five levels of cascaded repeater hubs
MAC Sublayer	Demand priority—uses a priority-based round-robin arbitration scheme to determine network access; supports both Ethernet/ 802.3 and IEEE 802.5 frame formats
Transmission Mode	Half-duplex hubs cannot transmit and receive simultaneously because of crosstalk; this is due primarily to Category 3's lower electromagnetic characteristics
Future Enhancements	The following are currently under consideration as of this writing: (1) Data transmission rates of 1.063 Gbps and 1.25 Gbps for fiber-optic links and 500 Mbps for 4-pair Category 5 links; (2) Single-mode fiber permitted; (3) Fiber-optic links based on Fibre Channel 8B10B link protocol; (4) Use of VG switches and full-duplex operation for dedicated links; (5) 8-km maximum network diameter with up to five levels of cascaded repeaters

compatible with conventional Ethernet. Specifically, its MAC sublayer is not CSMA/ CD; it is a technology called *demand priority,* which is similar to that of token ring. Rather than provide a lengthy dialog about the differences between the two standards, Table 9.3 contains a summary of 100VG-AnyLAN, and Table 9.4 compares 100VG-AnyLAN to Fast Ethernet. We will, however, explain the concept of demand priority.

100VG-AnyLAN is designed to use cascaded repeater hubs in a hierarchical star topology. The demand priority protocol specifies the manner hubs poll their ports to identify

TABLE 9.4 Comparison Between 100BASE-T and 100VG-AnyLAN		
	100BASE-T (IEEE 802.3u)	**100VG-AnyLAN (IEEE 802.12)**
Media		
Category 3 UTP	4-pair (100 m)—100BASE-T4	4-pair (100 m)
Category 4 UTP	4-pair (100 m)—100BASE-T4	4-pair (100 m)
Category 5 UTP	2-pair (100 m)—100BASE-TX	2-pair (N/A)
	4-pair (100 m)—100BASE-T4	4-pair (200 m)
25-pair UTP	Not supported	Supported
IBM Type 1 STP	Yes (100m)—100BASE-T4/TX	Yes (100 m)
Fiber-optic (62.5/125)	412 m half-duplex—100BASE-FX	Yes (2000 m)
	2 km full-duplex—100BASE-FX	
Topology		
Network diameter	Varies from 200 m to 320 m depending on cable type and repeaters used	8 km
Cascading repeaters	Two levels	Five levels
MAC Sublayer		
Media access	CSMA/CD	Demand priority
IEEE 802.3 frames	Yes	Yes
IEEE 802.5 frames	No	Yes
Application Support		
Time-sensitive data	No	Yes
Performance		
100-m throughput	80%	95%
2500-m throughput	Not supported	80%

nodes with data to transmit and the order of these transmissions. The protocol works in the following general manner (an example of this polling strategy is given in Figure 9.17):

A 100VG-AnyLAN repeater hub polls each node connected to it for a transmission request. The hub performs this query by continuously scanning its ports sequentially, from lowest connected port to highest connected port. If a node needs to transmit data, a transmission request is conveyed to the hub at the time the node is polled. Only one data frame per node per polling cycle is transmitted, and data frames are identified by the hub as either normal- or high-priority. Frames designated high-priority (e.g., real-time video and audio) are processed (i.e., given access to the network) before normal-priority-designated frames (e.g., data files).

An Ethernet NIC set in promiscuous mode collects all messages placed on the medium regardless of their destination address.

Each hub has at least one uplink port, which connects to a higher-level hub; every port can be used as a downlink port to connect to an end node or a lower-level hub. Hub ports can be configured to operate in either *normal* or *monitor mode*. Ports operating in normal mode receive only those data frames destined for it as determined by a frame's destination address. Monitor mode, on the other hand, is similar to Ethernet's *promiscuous mode*—every data frame received by the hub is directed to all ports configured to operate in monitor mode.

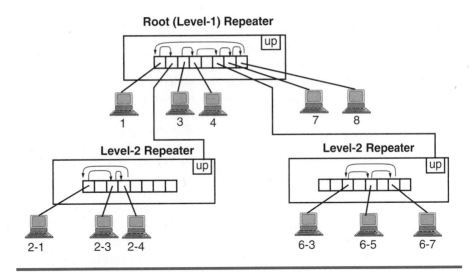

FIGURE 9.17 An example of a two-level 100VG-AnyLAN network. The hub's polling order in this illustration is 1, 2-1, 2-3, 2-4, 3, 4, 6-3, 6-5, 6-7, 7, 8. If during a polling cycle nodes 3, 2-4, 6-5, and 7 have high-priority requests pending, then the data transmission order is 2-4, 3, 6-5, 7, 1, 2-1, 2-3, 4, 6-3, 6-7, 8 for that cycle. If priority requests are the same (all normal or all high), then the data transmission order is the port order. However, if the priority requests are not the same, then the transmission order is determined by considering the priority of the node's pending request and the physical port order of the node. For example, if nodes 3 and 7 have normal-priority requests, but node 4 has a high-priority request, then the transmission order is 4, 3, 7. Source: adapted from Schnaidt, 1994a.

Using a round-robin scheme, repeaters continuously poll all their connected ports in sequence to determine which nodes have data transmission requests pending. A polling cycle begins when a hub polls the lowest-numbered port connected to it and ends when the highest-numbered connected port is polled. A polling cycle is repeated continuously in port order. Nodes are permitted to transmit only one frame of data per polling cycle. The process of polling and determining data transmission order is called *prioritized round-robin arbitration* and is the heart of the demand priority protocol. Theoretically, a maximum of five levels of cascading is permitted in a 100VG-AnyLAN network. However, in practice, a maximum of three is the general rule.

The type of priority assigned to a data frame is not part of the demand priority protocol and hence does not occur at the MAC sublayer. Instead, data priority assignment is performed by the upper-layer application software and passed to the MAC sublayer as part of a data frame. It is the demand priority protocol's design that enables it to identify the type of data transmission request and process high-priority data before normal-priority data. As a result, this media access method is highly suited for transmitting isochronous data, that is, time-sensitive data such as multimedia applications and real-time video and audio for videoconferencing. To guard against high-priority data transmissions from monopolizing a network, VG hubs are designed with a *watchdog protocol* that monitors the "wait time" of pending normal-priority requests. All normal-priority requests that have been waiting between 200 ms and 300 ms have their priority label changed automatically from normal to high. They are then placed on the hub's high-priority list and processed in port-order fashion. Thus, all normal-priority data are guaranteed access to the network.

100VG-AnyLAN's demand priority protocol is a very robust technology. It is deterministic, collision-free, supports a priority scheduling scheme, exhibits stable behavior during high load times, and uses bandwidth efficiently (demonstrated 95% throughput at 100 m). Demand priority also improves some of the shortcomings of token ring, including eliminating token rotation delays (see Chapter 10).

Although regarded by some as technically superior to Fast Ethernet, 100VG-AnyLAN was not warmly embraced by the Ethernet network community. One obvious clue to this is its IEEE designation: 802.12 versus a subset of 802.3. The reason for this is that many Ethernet purists do not consider 100VG-AnyLAN "Ethernet" because of its access method. They contend that Ethernet implies a contention-based MAC sublayer protocol, and since demand priority eliminates collisions and the concept of collision domains, 100VG-AnyLAN is therefore not Ethernet. The absence of CSMA/CD led the IEEE to prohibit the 100VG-AnyLAN working group from using the Ethernet designation. IEEE also believes that Ethernet is not Ethernet without CSMA/CD.

Comparing market share, the 100-Mbps turf war has already been won by Fast Ethernet. Regardless of IEEE's (and others') view about 100VG-AnyLAN not being Ethernet, 100VG-AnyLAN is still a compelling technology. It supports both Ethernet/802.3 and token ring frame formats, is an alternative to Fast Ethernet as an upgrade path for 10-Mbps Ethernet, and can serve as an upgrade path for 4/16-Mbps token ring LANs as well. Its lack of market share should not preclude you from considering 100VG-AnyLAN as part of your upgrade strategy or as a new installation. Any decisions about LAN upgrades or new installations should be driven by your organization's networking needs and the best technology available that satisfies those needs.

9.5   Gigabit Ethernet

Overview

Just as the dust was beginning to settle on the Fast Ethernet standard, the IEEE, in March 1996, commissioned the Higher Speed Study Group (HSSG) to investigate increasing Fast Ethernet's data transmission rate tenfold to 1000 Mbps. That's 1 *billion* bits per second. Now, some people might question the need for a 1 billion bits per second technology. However, in the world of networking, fast is never fast enough. The deployment of bandwidth-hungry multimedia applications, the integration of faster computer systems, and the migration of Fast Ethernet from the backbone to the desktop are creating bottlenecks at the server level or at interswitch connections. Gigabit Ethernet alleviates this congestion by providing a faster backbone technology. Remember, when Ethernet was first developed, the majority of the applications and computer systems of that era could not saturate a 10-Mbps channel. Today we have 64-bit servers, improved bus speeds, 100 Mbps desktop units, and applications such as real-time, two-way video conferencing. So yes, Gigabit Ethernet really is necessary for some network environments.

To support the IEEE's standards efforts in this endeavor, and to educate customers and the networking industry on this new technology, the Gigabit Ethernet Alliance (GEA) was formed in May 1996. Using the Fast Ethernet Alliance as its model, the Gigabit Ethernet Alliance sought to rally the same combination of suppliers and consumers of FEA to (a) support the extension of Fast Ethernet standards and (b) address customers' needs for interoperability among 10/100/1000-Mbps Ethernet products. GEA quickly grew in size to more than 100 vendor members within 6 months of its creation.

In July 1996, IEEE approved two separate task forces to define standards for *Gigabit Ethernet.* One task force, IEEE 802.3z, was created for Gigabit Ethernet over fiber; the second task force, IEEE 802.3ab, was created for Gigabit Ethernet over copper. The IEEE 802.3z standard was approved in June 1998; the IEEE 802.3ab standard was ratified October 1999. Two separate task forces were established because the development of each standard required different technology strategies. For example, Gigabit Ethernet over fiber's technology was predicated on an existing fiber-based protocol called Fibre Channel (discussed later). However, there was no similar existing protocol to run gigabit speeds over copper. By creating a separate task force to address the copper-based endeavor, the IEEE 802.3z task force was able to maintain a dedicated focus to establishing a fiber-based gigabit Ethernet standard.

It is also interesting to note that nearly a year before the fiber-based Gigabit Ethernet standard was ratified, Gigabit Ethernet products were available from vendors. The reason this was possible is because in January 1997, the 802.3z task force closed the specification to new features, thus enabling leading network vendors to develop Gigabit Ethernet products. By agreeing on a stable first draft of the specification, vendors were able to get a jump on product development. They also were able to demonstrate their products' interoperability at the October 1997 Networld+Interop show. Remember: The Gigabit Ethernet Alliance, which was comprised of network vendors, was formed for the express purpose of designing a Gigabit Ethernet specification. Thus, it was in their best interest to resolve any issues related to the specification as quickly as possible. In the end, Gigabit Ethernet was one of the fastest standards to be approved among the second-generation high-speed LAN standards. GEA was indeed a quick study of the Fast Ethernet Alliance. A similar early product rollout and Networld+Interop demonstration occurred in 1999 for copper-based Gigabit Ethernet.

Before we examine the two Gigabit Ethernet standards, we need to remind you once again that bigger is not necessarily always better. It is not prudent to increase bandwidth for the sake of increasing bandwidth. Bigger and faster backbones are no panacea for network congestion. Deploying Gigabit Ethernet undoubtedly will reduce overall network congestion, but without conducting an a priori network analysis to determine the source of the congestion, the deployment of Gigabit Ethernet will do nothing more than mask the problem. Some people call this strategy "bandwidth Band-Aid®." Before deploying any new high-speed backbone technology, including Gigabit Ethernet, network managers should examine all areas of potential bottleneck (e.g., desktop, servers, and backbone). This will help them assess exactly where increased bandwidth is to be deployed, when it needs to be deployed, and provide a sound rationale for deploying it. Okay. We are now stepping off of our soapbox, but only for a little while.

TABLE 9.5   Conventional Ethernet versus Fast Ethernet versus Gigabit Ethernet

	Conventional Ethernet	Fast Ethernet	Gigabit Ethernet
Data Rate	10 Mbps	100 Mbps	1000 Mbps
Max Segment Lengths:			
Category 5 UTP	100 m	100 m	100 m
IBM Type 1 (STP)	500 m	100 m	25 m
Multimode Fiber	2 km	412 m (half-duplex) 2 km (full-duplex)	260–550 m
Single-Mode Fiber	25 km	20 km	3 km

Source: 3Com (Adapted from Tolley, 1997a.)

TABLE 9.6   Media and Distance Comparisons of Gigabit Ethernet

	Media	Max Distance
1000BASE-SX	62.5-μm Multimode Fiber	220–275 m[a]
	50-μm Multimode Fiber	500–550 m[b]
1000BASE-LX	62.5-μm Multimode Fiber	550 m
	50-μm Multimode Fiber	550 m
	9-μm Single-Mode Fiber	5,000 m (5 km)
1000BASE-CX	Coaxial	25 m
1000BASE-T	Category 5 UTP	100 m

[a]200 m for TIA 568 fiber-optic wiring standard; 275 m for ISO/IEC 11801 building wiring standard
[b]550 m based on ANSI Fibre Channel specifications

Source: adapted from Conover, 1998; Henderson, 1998; and Tolley, 1997a.

IEEE 802.3z: Gigabit Ethernet over Fiber

At the physical layer, IEEE 802.3z supports three specifications: *1000BASE-SX* (short wavelength fiber), *1000BASE-LX* (long wavelength fiber), and *1000BASE-CX* (short-haul copper). Table 9.5 compares Gigabit Ethernet with conventional and Fast Ethernet, and Table 9.6 contains specific media and distance information for each Gigabit Ethernet specification. See also Figure 9.18, which summarizes the various IEEE 802.3 Ethernet specifications.

At the data link layer, Gigabit Ethernet uses the same 802.3 frame format, supports full-duplex and switched connections, maintains the same 96-bit interframe gap (see Box 9.3), and has a 64-byte minimum frame size. Gigabit Ethernet also supports the same CSMA/CD access method in full-duplex mode, but it uses a slightly modified version of CSMA/CD in half-duplex mode—the minimum CSMA/CD carrier and slot-times are 512 bytes instead of 64 bytes. Thus, the minimum-sized frame of Gigabit Ethernet is 512 bytes, not 64 bytes. This modification was necessary to maintain a 200 m collision diameter in half-duplex. If this was not done, then the maximum diameter would have been one-tenth the size of a Fast Ethernet LAN (25 m) because when you

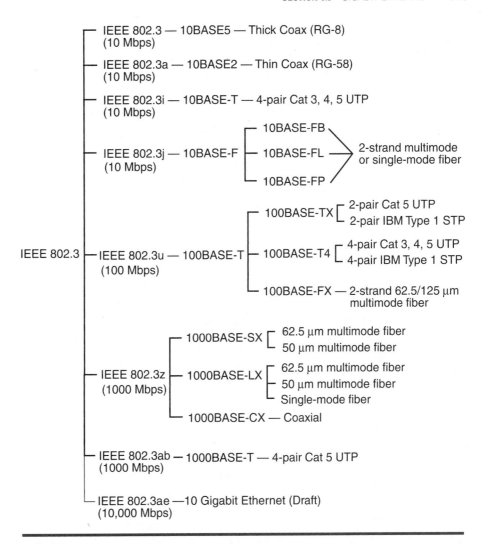

FIGURE 9.18 Various IEEE 802.3 specifications for the different variants of baseband Ethernet and their respective media.

increase the bit rate, the collision domain and overall network diameter decrease. A maximum network diameter of 25 m is not very practical.

As stated earlier, IEEE adopted the ANSI *Fibre Channel* signaling protocol and modified it for IEEE 802.3z. Fibre Channel (FC) is a family of ANSI (American National Standards Institute) standards that defines a specific communications interface for high-speed data transfers between different hardware systems. FC's applications include the medical profession, where large images (e.g., 100-MB+ X-rays) are transferred from a scanner to a computer to a screen, and the electronic publishing industry, where large files are transferred from an designer/creator's machine to a publisher's computer. It has also become the "backbone" of high-speed data storage systems used for storage area networks (SANs). FC is organized into a five-level hierarchy (FC-0

For additional sources of information about FC see the Fiber Channel Association Web site at http:// www.amdahl.com/ ext/carp/fca/ fca.htm or call the FCA at 1-800-272-4618.

through FC-4). IEEE 802.3z signaling is based on FC-0 and FC-1. FC-0 supports a variety of physical media and data rates; FC-1 defines the signaling encoding technique used for transmission and synchronization across a point-to-point link (8B/10B—eight bits of data are encoded into ten-bit characters and transmitted serially). IEEE 802.3z modified the link frequency from the 1.062-GHz ANSI standard to 1.25 GHz so that a full 1000-Mbps data rate is supported.

There are several possible scenarios for deploying Gigabit Ethernet over fiber. The primary application is to provide a faster backbone. As Fast Ethernet becomes more widespread and deployed at the desktop, the need for a higher-speed backbone becomes paramount. Thus, one scenario is to connect all interconnected Fast Ethernet switches directly into a Gigabit Ethernet switch. This effectively upgrades the 100-Mbps links between the Fast Ethernet switches to a gigabit link. Along this same line, Gigabit Ethernet switches can be used to replace any Fast Ethernet switch that functions as a collapsed backbone. Another method is to swap out all the Fast Ethernet switches that provide connectivity to servers and replace them with Gigabit Ethernet switches. The server NICs will also have to be upgraded to Gigabit Ethernet NICs if this strategy is implemented.

IEEE 802.3ab: Gigabit Ethernet over Copper

The IEEE 802.3ab standard has one physical layer specification: 1000BASE-T, which defines running Gigabit Ethernet over Category 5 cable at distances up to 100 m. This distance restriction is equivalent to that of Fast Ethernet. However, unlike Fast Ethernet, all four pairs of Category 5 UTP must be used. In a move to promote interoperability among all three IEEE 802.3 Ethernet standards, some vendors have designed their transceivers to be 802.3ab and 802.3u (Fast Ethernet) compliant.

The issue of how well Gigabit Ethernet will run over Category 5 UTP has been a nagging one, and defining the physical layer for 802.3ab has not been easy for the task force. Although it is possible to transmit data over Category 5 UTP at gigabit speed, success depends on a clear signal path. This means that if anything obstructs the signal as it travels from source to destination, then reflections can occur and reduce the reliability of network performance. "What objects can cause reflections?" you might ask. Oh, little things like eight-pin modular (RJ-45) connectors or punch-down blocks. It is important to note that this is not unique to Gigabit Ethernet. Reflections are always present in copper cable when used for radio frequency transmission in both 10-Mbps and 100-Mbps Ethernet links (see Chapter 4). The difference is that at these relatively lower speeds, reflections and related interference are not as serious. Furthermore, unlike 100BASE-TX (Fast Ethernet over Category 5 UTP), which uses only two pairs of wire (one pair to transmit and one pair to receive), 1000BASE-T requires four pairs and transmits signals bidirectionally on all four of them, that is, 250 Mbps per pair. Since Gigabit Ethernet uses all four pairs of copper simultaneously, the potential for electrical noise increases. This includes something called far-end crosstalk (FEXT), which is similar to NEXT (Chapter 4) except FEXT involves the occurrence of crosstalk at the end of the cable opposite from the transmitter. Another type of electrical noise that needs to be considered when running Gigabit Ethernet over copper is echo, which describes what happens when a signal is reflected back to the transmission source. Also called return loss, echo is usually a function of impedance mismatches caused by bad connectors or patch cables.

As you can see, implementing Gigabit Ethernet over copper involves considering parameters other than just cable length, attenuation, and NEXT. As of this writing, TIA is modifying its current cable testing standards document, TSB-67, to include these and other factors that have to be considered when all four pairs of copper cable are being used at the same time. This new document, TSB-95, will define the necessary testing parameters for certifying the copper cable plant for Gigabit Ethernet. For an update on these standards, see TIA's Web site at `http://tiaonline.org`

Although current Category 5 and Enhanced Category 5 cable will support Gigabit Ethernet, new high-speed copper cable designed specifically for gigabit speed is currently available from various vendors. Called *gigabit copper,* these new offerings include Category 6 UTP, Category 6 STP, and Category 7 UTP (see Table 4.1). Although gigabit copper has higher frequencies, this does not necessarily translate to higher speeds. Contrary to what some network managers might believe, there is not a 1:1 ratio between megahertz and megabits. From a design perspective, though, gigabit copper supports gigabit encoding schemes. One drawback to gigabit copper is a lack of standards. This means that parameter specs provided by vendors are subject to different interpretations. Case in point: One cable manufacturer uses the number 350 in the name of one of its products, giving the impression that the cable is rated at 350 MHz. Upon further investigation, the cable's spec sheet reveals that the cable cannot support data transfers beyond 200 MHz. It is so named, though, because it provides "stable electrical performance" up to 350 MHz. Another potential problem with gigabit copper is that standards committees like EIA/TIA are vendor-based consortia and therefore politically charged. Trying to assess what a final gigabit copper standard will look like is difficult enough without being influenced by politics.

As stated earlier, Gigabit Ethernet over copper was ratified in late 1999, and thus, its current deployment is not yet widespread. It is anticipated, though, that 802.3ab will most likely be used as an intrabuilding backbone and to interconnect servers. These areas are the most logical choices because they are currently based on Category 5 UTP in many organizations. From a cost consideration, it makes sense to deploy copper-based Gigabit Ethernet instead of replacing a building's cable plant or a server's connection cables with fiber for the sake of having a gigabit backbone or providing gigabit server connections. Why go through all of that when the same thing can be achieved using an existing Category 5 UTP infrastructure? Even if a cable retrofit is in order, it is anticipated that current Category 5 cable plants will most likely get upgraded to gigabit copper for horizontal installations. It is also interesting to note that as part of AT&T's Hero project in 1984, there was a 1-Gbps test of Category 3 UTP, as well as a test of 40-Mbps Fiber Network protocol over coaxial cable. It was determined that STP could handle, without any modification to the waveform, up to about 1 GHz. UTP, on the other hand, with modifications to the waveform, would permit transmission rates up to about 1 GHz. With phase encoding, compression, and other types of bit-level encoding, it was recently shown that Category 5 UTP can support transmission rates of 2.4 Gbps over a 20-m link and that 1 Tbps (terabits per second, which is 1 million million, or 1 million Mbps) is on the horizon.

Gigabit Ethernet versus Asynchronous Transfer Mode (ATM)

Since Gigabit Ethernet's current application is as a high-speed LAN backbone, a comparison to asynchronous transfer mode (ATM), which is another high-speed network technology that can be deployed as either a WAN or LAN backbone, is warranted. Although

ATM is formally discussed in Chapter 15, a few noteworthy comparisons are presented here for completeness. First, Gigabit Ethernet is a connectionless technology that transmits variable-length frames; ATM is a connection-oriented technology that transmits fixed-sized cells. (See Chapter 2 for information about connection-oriented vs. connectionless services.) Second, Gigabit Ethernet (any Ethernet for that matter) as originally specified is designed specifically as a local area network technology—it is optimized for transmitting data from one node to another on a LAN. It was never designed to support multimedia-type applications such as real-time voice and video. ATM, on the other hand, was designed specifically to transmit any type of data, including voice and video traffic. ATM also supports different class of service (CoS) for data prioritization and can guarantee a quality of service (QoS) needed for real-time voice and video traffic. (See Chapter 5 for additional information about QoS and CoS). In contrast, Gigabit Ethernet does not directly support CoS or QoS. However, the IEEE developed IEEE 802.1p, which specifies how data prioritization is handled within a MAC-layer device. Another protocol related to this concept is IEEE 802.3x full-duplex/flow control, which enables full-duplex switch ports to send flow-control commands to workstations that are connected to them. Both are deployed in silicon at the port level of Gigabit Ethernet switches. The IEEE also has introduced 802.1q, which adds prioritization to Ethernet/802.3 in general. Extending this concept to the upper layers, the Internet Engineering Task Force (IETF) has developed the Resource Reservation Protocol (RSVP), which operates at layer 3 and enables end nodes to reserve a specific amount of bandwidth throughout an IP network for a particular transmission. (See Chapter 8 for more information about RSVP.) ATM's CoS and QoS undoubtedly offer a more elegant approach to transmitting time-sensitive data than the combination of 802.1p, 802.3x, 802.1q, and RSVP. Nevertheless, many people believe that this combination provides Gigabit Ethernet with an acceptable level of CoS and QoS for the short term.

Although one can view Gigabit Ethernet and *local* ATM as competing LAN backbone technologies, the reality is that both have their pros and cons, both can fill specific LAN needs, and both can coexist. For example, if network traffic is primarily data based and cost is a consideration, Gigabit Ethernet is the logical choice. If explicit QoS is paramount for voice and video traffic support, or if a seamless LAN-to-WAN or WAN-to-LAN connection is desired, then ATM is the more appropriate technology. A third illustration has Gigabit Ethernet being deployed within buildings to provide a gigabit-speed building backbone and ATM being deployed as the enterprisewide backbone. In this example, both ATM and Gigabit Ethernet are used as complementary technologies instead of competing technologies.

Gigabit Ethernet's Bottom Line

On the positive side, Gigabit Ethernet:

- provides a tenfold increase in raw performance over Fast Ethernet;
- provides familiar technology so that existing investments in hardware, software, and personnel are maintained (and protected);
- represents a relatively small learning curve;
- offers tremendous scalability;
- is a natural extension to 10/100-Mbps Ethernet networks;

- supports all existing networking protocols;
- is complementary to ATM;
- is intended to run over Category 5 UTP;
- is an IEEE standard; and
- might support acceptable levels of CoS and QoS for real-time video and voice transmissions.

On the negative side, Gigabit Ethernet:

- requires new switches and NICs;
- might require workstation upgrades to take advantage of the increase in speed;
- is relatively expensive since it is still a new technology; and
- has no inherent CoS and QoS support.

Is Faster Better?

Fast Ethernet and Gigabit Ethernet as well as other high-speed, second-generation LANs offer three distinct advantages over their first-generation counterparts. First is the signaling rate itself. Higher signaling rates imply faster data transmissions—it takes less time for a node to transmit and receive a data frame. A second advantage is high-speed networks have higher bandwidth capacities. A direct consequence of this is more data can be transmitted over the same medium than by first-generation LANs. This eliminates the "workstation bottleneck," which occurs when nodes connected to first-generation LANs are capable of processing more data than what can be supported by these earlier LANs. Finally, high-speed networks can support more nodes without experiencing degradation. This is possible because each node requires a smaller percentage of the network's overall bandwidth. Given these advantages, then, is faster better? The answer to this question is, "It depends." The mere availability of high-speed LANs should not prompt network managers to scrap their existing first-generation LAN installations and replace them with second-generation technologies. In other cases, though, deployment of high-speed network technologies might be warranted. Consequently, it is prudent first to examine all aspects of the existing infrastructure before deciding if high-speed LANs are needed.

Ethernet as a WAN Protocol: IEEE 802.3ae—10-Gigabit Ethernet

Will 1-Gigabit Ethernet be Ethernet's upper limit? No way. As of this writing, the 10-Gbps Ethernet project is well underway with a target completion date of March 2002. The purpose of this project is to extend IEEE 802.3 to 10 Gbps. There is another purpose, however. The designers also endeavor to move Ethernet from the LAN to MAN/WAN environments. If we think about this for a moment, a single Ethernet throughout—from the desktop to the WAN—makes sense because it will keep the overall network simple. For example, data transported across an Ethernet-based LAN/MAN/WAN would not require any protocol translations. Thus, the inherent transmission latencies that are attendant to a multiprotocol world, as well as the management problems that often accompany working in a multiprotocol environment, are eliminated. Equally important is that an end-to-end Ethernet protocol will also ensure the highest level of compatibility with currently installed 802.3 LANs. However, unlike the rapid development of Fast and Gigabit Ethernets, which are respectively based on FDDI and fibre channel technologies, there are no current physical layer technologies from which multigigabit can borrow.

The present 10-Gigabit Ethernet discussion is focusing on defining 802.3 MAC parameters so that full-duplex data transmission rates can occur at 10 Gbps with minimal modifications to current 802.3 physical and data link layer protocols. The new standard most likely will support two data rates. The first is a 10-Gbps rate that will be compliant with the LAN. The second is an OC-192c rate that will support data transmissions across the WAN. (See Chapter 3 for more information about OC-*nc* rates.) A half-duplex 10-Gbps CSMA/CD will not be supported. An important distinction to note is that the proposed 10-Gbps Ethernet standard will be a supplement to the existing IEEE 802.3 standard, specifically, IEEE 802.3ae, and hence will not be a new standard. The physical layer specifications for the proposed 10-Gbps Ethernet include support for link distances of 100 m and 300 m over multimode fiber and 2 km, 10 km, and 40 km over single-mode fiber. (Note the absence of copper.) Furthermore, LAN, MAN, and WAN technologies will share the same MAC.

The initial application of 10-Gigabit Ethernet is expected to be in a service provider's WAN backbone and points of presence (POPs). It will also compete directly with SONET (see Chapter 3), which is currently emplaced within a carrier's WAN backbone and can achieve equivalent data rates. Although a final version of the standard is slated for March 2002, the word within networking circles is that a draft specification might be available before the end of 2000. If this is indeed the case, then 10-Gigabit Ethernet products could be available between the fourth quarter of 2000 and the first quarter of 2001. Stay tuned.

9.6   Other Ethernet-Related Projects

Besides those discussed, several noteworthy enhancements to the original IEEE 802.3 standard that have either been made or are being reviewed by the IEEE 802.3 working group warrant mentioning. First, there is *IEEE 802.3y 100BASE-T2,* which provides full-duplex 100-Mbps operation over two pairs of Category 3 UTP or better cable. A second enhancement is *IEEE 802.3w binary logarithmic access method* (BLAM), which serves as a fully compatible and interoperable alternative to Ethernet's current binary exponential backoff algorithm. Third, IEEE 802.12 (100VG-AnyLAN) is being modified to support both Ethernet and token ring frame formats at 531 Mbps and 850 Mbps. Finally, there is *IEEE 802.3ad,* which involves something called *link aggregation,* or *trunking.* Link aggregation enables multiple Gigabit Ethernet links to be combined so that their respective bandwidths can be aggregated into a single "trunk." This process effectively increases overall bandwidth between switches or between server-switch connections. See the IEEE Web site (http://www.ieee.org) for additional information about these and other IEEE standards.

> Link aggregation is currently being used for switch-switch and server-switch Fast Ethernet connections, and aggregated speeds ranging from 200 Mbps to 800 Mbps are being realized for these connections.

Before we end this chapter, we should mention one more Ethernet-related technology. It's called *IsoEthernet,* which is short for Isochronous Ethernet, and is an IEEE standard—IEEE 802.9a. The term *isochronous* means time-sensitive. Hence, in the context of networking, IsoEthernet is designed to support time-sensitive applications such as videoconferencing and telephony. It is also inextricably linked to ISDN technology—it runs both Ethernet and ISDN B channels over the same network. (See Chapter 12 for more information about ISDN.) The Ethernet channel is used for normal data networking needs; the ISDN B channels are used for time-sensitive applications. Thus, IsoEthernet is really two networks in one. It contains a 10-Mbps Ethernet channel for 10BASE-T traffic and a separate 6.144-Mbps channel for isochronous traffic. IsoEthernet requires IsoEthernet network adapters at all end nodes requiring isochronous capability and IsoEthernet hubs at wiring closets. IsoEthernet also has been overshadowed by Gigabit Ethernet and local ATM technologies and, therefore, has found little vendor support. Nevertheless, it is anticipated that the 802.9a standard will be modified to include support for 100BASE-T, switched 10BASE-T, and 16-Mbps ATM.

End-of-Chapter Commentary

In this chapter, we presented a formal discussion of Ethernet and the various IEEE "Ethernet" protocols. Several concepts discussed in this chapter are also presented in other chapters in an informal manner. These include network topologies and architectures (Chapter 2), physical layer concepts (Chapter 4), the concepts of framing, flow control, and MAC and LLC sublayer issues (Chapter 5), Ethernet switches (Chapter 6), CoS/QoS (Chapter 5), and ATM issues (Chapter 15). In the next chapter, we present some of these same concepts but apply them to token ring networks.

CHAPTER REVIEW MATERIALS

SUMMARY

• Ethernet's roots began in the late 1960s at the University of Hawaii with a networking project called ALOHA, which was used to interconnect the university's main and remote campuses located throughout the Hawaiian Islands. Ethernet evolved into a LAN protocol for interconnecting office devices and is now the dominant LAN technology, claiming more than 85% of all installed network connections.

• The two early Ethernet standards were Ethernet V2.0—a cooperative, proprietary standard by Xerox, Intel, and DEC—and the international standard first developed as IEEE 802.3, which has since overshadowed V2.0. Of the various technical differences between the two standards, their frame format differences render the two technologies incompatible.

• 10-Mbps Ethernet/802.3 has four different physical layer specifications: 10BASE5 (thick coaxial cable), 10BASE2 (thin coaxial cable), 10BASE-T (UTP cable), and 10BASE-F (fiber-optic cable).

• The overall length of an Ethernet/802.3 LAN is called its network diameter and is the distance between the LAN's two remotest nodes.

• An Ethernet/802.3 collision domain comprises a single network in which two nodes' transmissions can collide. In an Ethernet/802.3 LAN, time is measured by a unit known as bit-time, which is equal to one-tenth of a microsecond. This means that it takes 0.1 μs to transmit one bit of information and 51.2 μs to transmit a 64-byte frame, which is the minimum-sized Ethernet/802.3 frame. Thus, the collision domain of a minimum 10-Mbps Ethernet/802.3 frame is 512 bit-times or 51.2 μs.

• The 5-4-3 repeater placement rule is applicable to 10-Mbps Ethernet/802.3 LANs and specifies that an Ethernet/802.3 LAN should have at most five segments of up to 500 m each, four repeaters, and three segments with end nodes connected to them. The 5-4-3 repeater placement rule can be circumvented by using chassis-based repeater hubs or stackable repeater hubs.

• Segmentation is a network configuration strategy that involves dividing an Ethernet/802.3 LAN into several separate (but still interconnected) network segments. This strategy is effective if at least 80% of LAN traffic is confined to a local segment and does not have to cross the backbone to reach another segment.

• Switched Ethernet is another network configuration strategy that involves replacing repeater hubs or bridges with network switches. This effectively changes conventional Ethernet from a broadcast, half-duplex technology to a point-to-point, full-duplex technology.

• Switched Ethernet strategies include (a) using workgroup switches to partition a single shared medium into multiple shared media; (b) incorporating private switches, which provides users with a dedicated Ethernet segment and eliminates contention; and (c) collapsing the network backbone into a backbone switch.

• Ethernet Switches also can be configured to create virtual LANs, which enable users to be assigned to arbitrary administrative units.

• Fast Ethernet, 100BASE-T, increases conventional Ethernet's 10-Mbps data transmission rate to 100 Mbps. Fast Ethernet has three physical layer specifications: 100BASE-TX (two-pair Category 5 UTP or IBM Type 1 STP), 100BASE-T4 (four-pair Category 3, 4, or 5 UTP or four-pair IBM Type 1 STP), and 100BASE-FX (fiber-optic cable). 100BASE-TX and 100BASE-FX use a full-duplex signaling scheme based on FDDI; 100BASE-T4 uses a half-duplex signaling scheme. 100BASE-T employs exactly the same data link layer specification as 10BASE-T.

• The 5-4-3 repeater placement rule does not apply to Fast Ethernet. Instead, Fast Ethernet supports two types of repeaters. Class I repeaters support both Fast Ethernet signaling schemes; Class II repeaters only support one and hence can only be used to connect segments that use the same signaling method.

• A second 100-Mbps Ethernet strategy is known as 100VG-AnyLAN, which has a similar physical layer specification as 100BASE-T but employs a different data link layer specification called demand priority.

• Gigabit Ethernet increases conventional Ethernet's data transmission rate to 1000 Mbps. Two Gigabit Ethernet standards exist. IEEE 802.3z involves three physical layer specifications: 1000BASE-SX, 1000BASE-LX, and 1000BASE-CX. The first two are fiber-optic based; the third is coaxial based. The second standard is IEEE 802.3ab and comprises only one physical layer specification: 1000BASE-T, which supports four pairs of Category 5 UTP cable. IEEE 802.3z's signaling scheme is based on Fibre Channel.

• In full-duplex mode, Gigabit Ethernet's data link layer is the same as that of conventional and Fast Ethernet. In half-duplex mode, though, Gigabit Ethernet uses a modified version of CSMA/CD: The minimum-sized frame is 512 bytes, not 64 bytes.

• A proposal for 10-Gbps Ethernet that operates at both the LAN and WAN levels is currently being discussed, and a standard is expected to be completed by March 2002.

• IsoEthernet is a defunct technology that incorporates two networks: 10-Mbps Ethernet/802.3 for data transmissions and a 6.144-Mbps channel for time-sensitive (isochronous) data such as videoconferencing and telephony.

VOCABULARY CHECK

bit-time	Fibre Channel	segmentation
Class I repeater	5-4-3 repeater placement rule	signal quality error (SQE)
Class II repeater	full-duplex Ethernet	switched Ethernet
collapsed backbone	Gigabit Ethernet	throughput
collision domain	IsoEthernet	utilization
collisions	latency	virtual local area network
demand priority	network diameter	(VLAN)
Ethernet	partitioning	wire speed
Fast Ethernet	promiscuous mode	workgroup switch

REVIEW EXERCISES

1. Briefly explain the major differences between Ethernet V2.0 and IEEE 802.3.

Use the following information to answer questions 2-4:

The only difference between Ethernet V2.0 and IEEE 802.3 frame formats is that the former specifies a two-byte type field following the source address field, whereas IEEE 802.3 specifies a two-byte length field. Assume that an 802.3 sending node transmits a data frame that comprises a 1500-byte payload and that the destination node is running Ethernet V2.0.

2. What hexadecimal value does the sending node insert in its length field?

3. What does the destination node do upon receiving this frame?

4. Assume that the sending node is transmitting a TCP/IP packet. Can the receiving node still communicate with the sending node via TCP/IP? In other words, can a node still transmit and receive TCP/IP data if the lower layers can't communicate? Why or why not?

5. Ethernet/802.3 is based on 1-persistent CSMA/CD. Explain what this means.

6. Is a 0-byte data field legal in Ethernet/802.3? What problem do you think a 0-byte data field might pose and how is this resolved?

7. Ethernet/802.3 specifies a minimum length frame of 64 bytes. Suppose there was no minimum frame length and that Ethernet/802.3 nodes were permitted to transmit frames of much shorter length (e.g., 2-byte frames). What impact would this have on collisions and why?

8. What is the purpose of the preamble and start frame delimiter fields of Ethernet/802.3 frames?

9. An Ethernet/802.3 node can be in any one of three states. Identify and describe each state.

Use the following information to answer questions 10-13:

Ethernet/802.3 is based on 1-persistent CSMA/CD (see Chapter 5). If a collision occurs, all transmitting nodes detecting a collision generate a jamming signal to alert all other nodes that a collision occurred and then back off a random period of time before attempting to transmit again. The length of time a node waits is calculated using a binary exponential backoff algorithm. Specifically, each node randomly picks either 0 or 1 and then waits that number of slot-times before attempting a subsequent transmission. (Recall that 1 slot-time = 51.2 μs.) In general, for each subsequent transmission attempt that ends in a collision, the random number a node picks is between 0 and $2^n - 1$, where n = the total number of consecutive transmission attempts by a specific node that ended in a collision. Ultimately, if a node's transmission results in a collision after 10 consecutive attempts, the randomized interval reaches an upper limit of 1023. After 16 attempts, failure is reported by the sending node(s), and no additional transmission attempts are made.

10. Assume two nodes attempt to transmit at approximately the same time and their transmissions collide. What happens if both nodes pick the same random number? What is the probability of this happening?

11. Assume that the first two transmission attempts of the two nodes in problem 10 collide. What set of numbers is available to the nodes at this stage from which they will randomly select their wait time? What is the probability that both nodes will select the same number?

12. Assume that the two nodes of problem 10 eventually select different random numbers after four consecutive failed transmission attempts. Does this guarantee that their next transmission attempt will be collision-free? Why or why not?

13. What function does the binary backoff algorithm provide? Why not just make every node select a number from 0 to 1023? After all, the probability of two nodes selecting the same number from this set is less than one-thousandth of a percent.

14. Go to IEEE's Web site, `http://standards.ieee.org/regauth/oui/index.html`, and identify the vendor Ethernet address prefixes of the hardware devices connected to your LAN.

15. As mentioned in the text, work has already begun on designing a 10-Gigabit Ethernet standard. Given the IEEE's general format for

designating LANs, what designation do you think this new standard will be assigned?

16. Explain the difference between network diameter and collision domain relative to 10BASE-T. Why is the concept of collision domain not applicable to switched Ethernet LANs?

17. A high school has a schoolwide 10BASE-T LAN installed with network ports located in all classrooms, offices, laboratories, and the library. With the exception of the library, each network port has only one computer connected to it. The library, on the other hand, has a chassis-based repeater hub that interconnects 35 PCs. Several teachers, independent of one another, install small four- or eight-port repeater hubs in their respective classrooms so that more than one computer has network access. Discuss the ramifications of these teachers' actions relative to overall schoolwide network performance.

18. Will closer-spaced Ethernet/802.3 nodes take less or more time to resolve conflicts? Why?

19. Briefly explain the concept of segmentation relative to Ethernet/802.3 LAN topology and performance.

20. Compare and contrast the three different types of Ethernet/802.3 switches: workgroup, private, and backbone.

21. What is full-duplex Ethernet and what advantage does it have over conventional half-duplex Ethernet?

22. From a network management perspective, discuss some of the advantages and disadvantages of a switched Ethernet/802.3 environment.

23. Explain the advantage 4B/5B-NRZI encoding has over Manchester encoding relative to providing a 100-Mbps data transmission rate. (*Hint:* See Chapter 3.)

24. Explain why the 5-4-3 repeater placement rule does not apply to Fast Ethernet.

25. Discuss one advantage and one disadvantage of upgrading a 10-Mbps Ethernet LAN to Fast Ethernet.

26. Discuss one strategy that could be used to improve overall performance without having to upgrade a 10-Mbps Ethernet LAN to Fast Ethernet and explain how this strategy can actually improve performance.

27. Identify and briefly discuss two tasks you would need to do as the network administrator to determine if upgrading a 10-Mbps Ethernet LAN to Fast Ethernet was feasible or needed.

28. Do you think 100VG-AnyLAN's data link layer protocol, demand priority, is superior or inferior to Ethernet's CSMA/CD protocol? Why?

29. Consider Figure 9.17. Assume that nodes 2-4, 6-3, and 6-7 have normal-priority requests and all other nodes have high-priority requests. What is the polling order?

30. Given the assumptions of problem 29, let's further assume that all normal-priority nodes have been waiting to transmit their data for more than 200 ms and that the high-priority nodes continue to have high-priority data to transmit. What is the polling order now?

31. Beginning with conventional, half-duplex, 10-Mbps Ethernet, each subsequent evolution of Ethernet increased the data transmission rate tenfold. Accordingly, then, the maximum network diameter should decrease by a factor of one-tenth. This was indeed the case for Fast Ethernet, which has a maximum diameter of 250 m. However, this is not the case with Gigabit Ethernet, which has a 200-m network diameter instead of a 25-m diameter. What happened and where did IEEE get this 200-m length?

32. Compare and contrast Gigabit Ethernet with ATM.

33. Why do you think a half-duplex 10000-Mbps Ethernet will not be supported?

34. What are the trade-offs of addressing network congestion problems by simply increasing bandwidth?

35. Why is promiscuous mode both a dangerous feature and yet a very desirable one?

SUGGESTED READINGS AND REFERENCES

BALDWIN, C. 1994. *High Speed Networking Technologies: Options and Implications.* Southborough, MA: Chipcom Corporation.

BOLLES, G. 1991. A Guided Tour of 10BASE-T. *Network Computing* (fall): 16–22.

BREYER, R., and S. RILEY. 1996. *PC Week Switched and Fast Ethernet.* 2nd ed. Emeryville, CA: Ziff-Davis.

CHAE, L. 1995. Tutorial—Lesson 88: Fast Ethernet. *LAN Magazine,* December, 27–28.

CLARK, E. 1998a. Gigabit Ethernet Goes High Gear. *Network Magazine,* February, 61–65.

———. 1998b. The Gigabit Gambit. *Network Magazine,* September, 48–53.

COHEN, R. 1996a. A Comparison of the Performance of 100BASE-TX and 100VG Networks. *Connexions: The Interoperability Report,* 10(12): 16–24.

———. 1996b. 100VG and 100BASE-T Tutorial. *Connexions: The Interoperability Report,* 10(11): 25–27.

CONOVER, J. 1997. The Road to Fast Ethernet Networks. *Network Computing,* 15 February, 146–149.

———. 1998. Building a Better Ethernet Infrastructure. *Network Computing,* 1 October, 88–94.

COSTA, L. F. 1994. *Planning and Designing High Speed Networks Using 100VG-AnyLAN.* Upper Saddle River, NJ: Prentice-Hall.

FELTMAN, C. 1996a. Ethernet Earns Its Wings. *LAN Interoperability: Quarterly Supplement,* May, 14–20.

———. 1996b. Virtual LAN, Real Performance. *LAN,* January, 67–72.

FLYNN, D., and T. PERKINSON. 1994. Fast Ethernet vs. AnyLAN: Degrees of Separation. *Data Communications,* May, 158.

FOGLE, D. 1996. Tutorial—Lesson 90: Ethernet Frame Types. *LAN Magazine,* February, 27–28.

FRANK, A. 1995. Flocking to a Faster Network. *LAN Magazine,* August, 67–77.

———. 1996. Multimedia LANs and WANs. *LAN Magazine,* July, 81–86.

———, and D. FOGLE. 1996. 100VG-AnyLAN's High-Speed Hopes. *LAN Magazine,* January, 128–133.

FRATTO, M. 1997. Unlocking Virtual Private Networks. *Network Computing,* 1 November, 53–78.

GALLO, M., and W. HANCOCK. 1999. *Networking Explained.* Boston: Digital Press.

GEIER, J. 1996. Up Close and Personal. *LAN Interoperability: Quarterly Supplement,* May, 39–45.

GIGABIT ETHERNET ALLIANCE. 1996. *Gigabit Ethernet: White Paper,* August. Gigabit Ethernet Alliance.

GOHN, B. 1997a. Policy-Based Services for Ethernet Networks. In Special Supplement by 3Com Corporation. *LAN,* January, 8–9.

———. 1997b. Switching and Routing—And Everything in Between. In Special Supplement by 3Com Corporation. *LAN,* January, 10–12.

GORALSKI, W., and G. KESSLER. 1996. Changing Channels. *LAN Interoperability: Quarterly Supplement,* May, 6–12.

GREENSTEIN, I. 1990. Fiber-Optic LANs Improve in Price and Performance. *Network Management,* June, 84–89.

HALL, E. 1998. Bringing Prioritization Services to Ethernet. *Network Computing,* 1 August, 94–100.

HELD, G. 1996. The LAN Guessing Game. *LAN Magazine,* May, 93–100.

———. 1999. Avoiding High-Speed LAN Potholes. *Network Magazine,* January, 68–71.

HENDERSON, T. 1995. Flooring It with Ethernet. *LAN Magazine,* March, 55–62.

———. 1998. Gigabit Ethernet Blueprint. *Network Magazine,* September, 42–46.

HINDIN, E. 1998. Say What? QoS in English. *Network World,* 17 August.

JOHNSON, J. 1995. The Need for Speed. *InformationWeek,* 23 October, 36–48.

KARVÉ, A. 1996. Multimedia Takes the Stage. *LAN Magazine,* May, 123–127.

———. 1997. Ethernet's Next Frontier. *LAN,* January, 40–47.

———. 1998. Pushing Beyond Gigabit Ethernet. *Network Magazine,* September, 54–58.

———. 1999. Gigabit Ethernet Gets a New Look. *Network Magazine,* August, 36–42.

KESSLER, G. 1993. Changing Channels. *LAN Magazine,* December, 69-84.

KRIVDA, C. 1995. Another Swipe at Switching. *LAN,* October, 129–134.

LIPPIS, N. 1996. Gigabit Ethernet Starts to Sizzle. *Data Communications,* November, 31–32.

LOUNSBURY, A. 1997. Gigabit Ethernet: The Difference Is in the Details. *Data Communications,* May, 75–80.

MAKRIS, J. 1998. The Copper Stopper? *Data Communications,* March, 63–73.

MANDEVILLE, R., and D. NEWMAN. 1997. VLANs: Real Virtues. *Data Communications,* May, 83–91.

———, and D. SHAH. 1998. Gigabit Ethernet Gets It Done. *Data Communications,* February, 66–81.

METCALFE, R., and D. BOGGS. 1976. Ethernet: Distributed Packet Switching for Local Computer Networks. *Communications of the ACM,* 19(7): 395–404.

MINOLI, D. 1993. Isochronous Ethernet: Poised for Launch. *Network Computing,* August, 156–161.

MOLTA, D. 1996. The Ten Greatest Networking Myths. *Networking Computing,* 1 September, 121–122.

PIEPER, K., and R. Fowler. 1997. The Next Step in the Ethernet Evolution. In Special Supplement by 3Com Corporation. *LAN,* January, 1–2.

RICHARDSON, R. 1997. VPNs: Just Between Us. *LAN,* February, 99–103.

ROBERTS, E. 1996. Weighed Down by Doubts: Is the Proposed High-Speed Spec Too Good to Be True? *Data Communications,* November, 55–58.

———. 1997. Gigabit Ethernet: Fat Pipe or Pipe Bomb? *Data Communications,* May, 58–72.

SAUNDERS, S. 1994. Full-Duplex Ethernet: More Niche Than Necessity? *Data Communications,* March, 87–92.

SCHNAIDT, P. 1994a. Plug in at 100. *LAN Magazine,* March, 71–79.

———. 1994b. Tutorial—Lesson 73: Which Fast LAN? *LAN Magazine,* September, 25–26.

———. 1996. Is Gigabit Ethernet the Next Miracle Cure? *Network Computing,* 15 October, 33.

SCHOLL, F. 1993. 10BASE-F Stretches the Ethernet Backbone. *Data Communications,* October, 103–108.

SHIMADA, K. 1994. Fast Talk About Fast Ethernet. *Data Communications,* 21 March, 21–22.

SHIPLEY, B. 1996. Ethernet's Endurance Contest. *LAN Magazine,* May, 67–72.

SKORUPA, J., and G. PRODAN. 1997. Battle of the Backbones: ATM vs. Gigabit Ethernet. *Data Communications,* April, 87–89.

SNYDER, J. 1996. Ethernet in the Fast Lane. *MacWorld,* March, 128–133.

STALLINGS, W. 2000. *Data and Computer Communications.* 6th ed. Upper Saddle River, NJ: Prentice-Hall.

STEINKE, S. 1995a. Ethernet Switching. *LAN Magazine,* March, 25–26.

———. 1995b. The State of the Ethernet. *LAN Magazine,* March, 44–52.

TOLLEY, B. 1997a. Standards Emerging for Gigabit Ethernet. In Special Supplement by 3Com Corporation. *LAN,* January, 3–4.

———. 1997b. The Lowdown on High Speed: Gigabit Ethernet and ATM. In Special Supplement by 3Com Corporation. *LAN,* January, 5–7.

TOLLY, K. 1994. Full Speed Ahead for Full-Duplex Ethernet. *Data Communications,* March, 39–40.

UNGERMANN-BASS NETWORKS. 1995. *LAN Switching Buyer's Guide.* Santa Clara, CA: Ungermann-Bass Networks.

WITTMANN, A. 1993. Fast Ethernet—The Curtain Rises on a New Debate. *Network Computing,* May, 18–22.

———. 1994. Faster Anyone? HP's 100VG-AnyLAN. *Network Computing,* 1 October, 47–49.

WOBUS, J. 1993. When to Avoid Adding Ethernet Hubs. *Network Computing,* January, 154–157.

WONG, H. H. 1996. Increase Ethernet Performance with Switched Technology. *Technical Support,* June, 37–43.

ZEICHICK, A. 1997. Glossary: IEEE 802. *Network Magazine,* November, 28.

10 | Token Ring

In this chapter, we present an overview of token ring networks, IEEE 802.5. Unlike Ethernet/802.3 LANs in which nodes contend for media access, token ring LANs use a token passing scheme; that is, media access in token ring LANs is controlled by the possession of a token. We discussed general issues relating to token passing, including a comparison of random access and token passing protocols, in Chapter 5, which you might want to review before proceeding. We begin the chapter with an overview of token ring LANs, including their topology and operation. Section 10.2 discusses physical layer specifications. The next three sections present information about token ring's media access scheme: Section 10.3 examines token ring frame formats; Section 10.4 discusses priority scheduling; and Section 10.5 presents network monitoring. Section 10.6 features second-generation token ring LANs. These include switched, full-duplex, and high-speed token ring. We conclude the chapter with a brief overview of a second token passing protocol called token bus (IEEE 802.4). Although token bus use is uncommon, we compare token bus to token ring for completeness.

10.1   What Is Token Ring?

A *token ring network* is a local area network technology based on a token passing protocol for media access control. (See Chapter 5 for more information about token passing protocol concepts.) Data frames on a token ring network are transmitted from node to node, in either a clockwise or counterclockwise direction, over a point-to-point link. A token ring LAN is implemented either as a logical ring using a physical ring topology (Figure 10.1) or as a

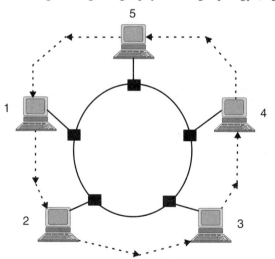

FIGURE 10.1   A token ring network consists of a logical ring implemented in a physical ring topology. A token, which is a special frame, and data are transmitted in a point-to-point manner from one node (called a lobe) to the next. The direction of circulation is fixed and either clockwise or counterclockwise (but not both). For example, on a counterclockwise rotating ring, if lobe 3 has a "free" token and wants to send data to lobe 2, data frames must circulate the ring in the order 3-4-5-1-2. On a clockwise rotating ring, though, the transmission order is 3-2.

logical ring structure arranged in a physical star configuration (Figure 10.2). It is also possible to extend the configuration in Figure 10.2 to include a ring consisting of several interconnected hubs. This is shown in Figure 10.3, which describes the arrangement in the special language of token rings. From Figure 10.3, note the following: Token ring hubs are called *multistation access units* (MAUs); nodes are called *lobes;* the distance between MAUs is called the *main ring length;* and the distance between an MAU and its lobes is called the *lobe length.*

In a typical token ring connection, lobes are physically connected to an MAU in a star configuration, but there is a logical ring topology within the MAU. Lobes are connected to the ring using an IBM Data Connector, which enables lobes to be removed without disrupting the ring. MAUs also can be interconnected using special "ring in/ring out" ports, which preserve the ring structure. Special relay switches (also called bypass switches) are used to maintain the integrity of the ring in the event of lobe failure. For example, in Figure 10.3, if lobe 12 stops working or if there is a break in the cable connecting lobe 12 to the ring, the ring is broken. In such instances, the relay switch closes, thus preserving the ring.

Token ring networks are defined by IEEE 802.5, which is based in part on IBM's set of token ring specifications. IBM is the primary vendor associated with token ring LANs. Although IBM's token ring specifications differ from the official IEEE specs, most people usually speak about the IBM specs when discussing token ring LANs. Some of token ring's advantages include its ability to run on many different media types, its efficient use of bandwidth (e.g., if packet size is 1000 bits, efficiency is 99%), its stable behavior during high load times, its deterministic nature (it has a known upper bound on channel access), and its priority scheme that enables nodes with high-priority data to reserve the network for data transmission. Disadvantages include the need for special recovery procedures when the network fails, difficulty in configuring new hosts to an established LAN, and in the case of priority scheduling, the susceptibility of low-priority nodes to increased delays in accessing the network. Many of these issues and concepts are discussed in the sections that follow.

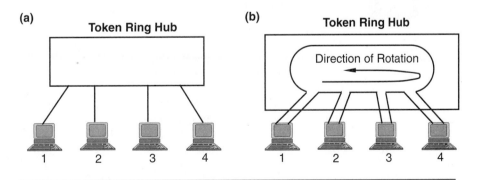

FIGURE 10.2 A typical token ring network consists of lobes connected to a hub in a physical star configuration (a). Internally, lobes are actually interconnected via a logical ring (b).

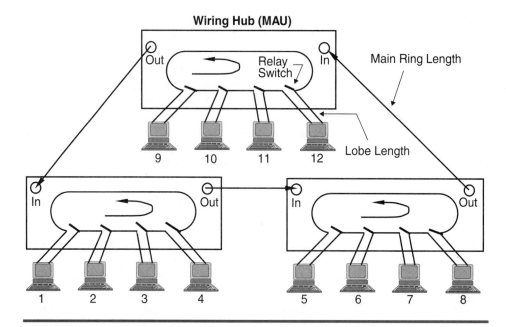

FIGURE 10.3 An example of a typical token ring network configuration. Token ring hubs are called multistation access units (MAUs), and nodes are called lobes. The main ring length is the distance between MAUs, and the lobe length is the distance between an MAU and its lobes. Physically, lobes are connected to an MAU in a star configuration. Within an MAU, however, a logical ring topology exists. Lobes are connected to the ring using an IBM Data Connector, which enables lobes to be removed without disrupting the ring. MAUs also can be interconnected using special "ring in/ring out" ports, which preserve the ring structure. Note the presence of relay switches within each hub. Relay switches (also called bypass switches) are used to maintain the integrity of the ring in the event of lobe failure. For example, if lobe 12 stops working or if there is a break in the cable connecting lobe 12 to the ring, the ring is broken. In such instances, the relay switch closes, thus preserving the ring.

10.2　Physical Layer Specifications

At the physical layer, IEEE 802.5 supports STP, UTP, coaxial, and fiber-optic cable. STP cable has a 150-ohm impedance; UTP cable has a 100-ohm impedance. The topology is usually star-based using token ring hubs (called wiring concentrators or multistation access units—MAUs), with hubs interconnected to form a main ring path (see Figure 10.3). Data rates include 4 and 16 Mbps, although some variations can include 20 and 40 Mbps. In a 4-Mbps token ring, lobes can transmit only one frame at a time during a single transmission. Lobes connected to token rings with higher data transmission rates, however, can transmit multiple frames during a single transmission.

Maximum cable lengths for lobe connections (i.e., lobe lengths) are 100 m if IBM Type 1 or 2 cable is used, 66 m for Types 6 and 9, and 45 m for UTP. (See Chapter 4 for an explanation of IBM Type cables.) Maximum cable lengths for hub interconnections depend on several factors, including the number of repeaters used, the number of hubs, and so forth. Some general guidelines are as follows: 200 m if using Type 1 or 2 cable; 120 m if using Type 3 cable; 45 m if using Type 6 cable; and 1 km if using fiber-optic cable. Type 1 and Type 3 networks can operate at 4 or 16 Mbps. Also, with STP cable, 260 devices can be connected to a single token ring network; with UTP cable (Category 3, 4, or 5), only 72 devices can be connected to the ring.

Token ring uses a form of Manchester encoding called *differential Manchester encoding*. Recall from Chapter 3 that Manchester and differential Manchester encoding are similar in that each bit-period is partitioned into two intervals and a transition between "high" and "low" occurs during each bit-period. The difference between the two techniques is the interpretation of this transition. In Manchester encoding (see Figure 3.1), a 1-bit represents a low-to-high mid-bit transition, and a 0-bit represents a high-to-low mid-bit transition. In differential Manchester encoding, the interpretation of these low-to-high and high-to-low mid-bit transitions is not as simple—they are a function of the previous bit-period. A low-to-high transition could be a 0 or a 1 depending on the value of the previous bit-period. More specifically, the presence of a transition at the beginning of a bit-period is coded 0, and the absence of a transition at the beginning of a bit-period is coded 1. Note also that for a token ring network to achieve its maximum bandwidth, its clock speed must be twice the transmission rate. Thus, a 16-Mbps token ring must have a clock speed of 32 MHz.

10.3   Frame Formats

The Token Frame

At the data link layer, access to the network is controlled by a special "token" frame, which circulates around the ring when all lobes are idle. A token frame comprises a one-byte start frame delimiter, a one-byte access control field, and a one-byte end frame delimiter. This is shown in Figure 10.4. The *starting delimiter* consists of the string JK0JK000; the *ending delimiter* string is JK1JK10E. J and K are nondata symbols known as *code violations;* E is the error-detection bit, which is assumed to be 0.

> The end delimiter also uses an I-bit to indicate that the current frame is an intermediate frame if a transmission contains more than one data frame.

A code violation occurs if there is no transition at the midpoint of a bit signal. If an absence of a transition is detected at both the start and midpoint of a bit-time, then a J violation occurs. If a transition is detected at the beginning of a bit-time but is absent at the midpoint of a bit-time, then a K violation occurs. The inclusion of J and K code violations in the starting and ending delimiters uniquely identifies these bit streams as delimiters and not user data.

The *access control* field consists of eight bits: three priority bits (P), a token bit (T), a monitor bit (M), and three reservation bits (R). *Priority bits* can be set from 0 (lowest) to 7 (highest). Thus, a token ring network has eight possible priorities (000 to 111) relative to data transmission. The use of these bits is discussed later in the chapter. The *token bit* identifies the frame as a token (T = 0) or data (T = 1). If the token bit is set to 0, the frame is considered a "free" or idle token. Only one free token is permitted on the ring, and the lobe that has the free token controls the ring and is permitted to transmit data. Thus, unlike Ethernet/802.3 networks, only one lobe at a time can transmit data on a token ring network. The *monitor bit* is used by one lobe, called the *monitor station*

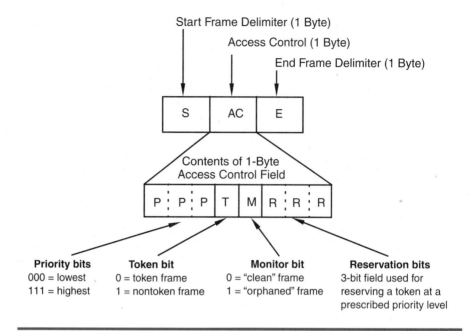

Start Frame Delimiter (1 Byte)

Access Control (1 Byte)

End Frame Delimiter (1 Byte)

| S | AC | E |

Contents of 1-Byte
Access Control Field

| P | P | P | T | M | R | R | R |

Priority bits
000 = lowest
111 = highest

Token bit
0 = token frame
1 = nontoken frame

Monitor bit
0 = "clean" frame
1 = "orphaned" frame

Reservation bits
3-bit field used for
reserving a token at a
prescribed priority level

FIGURE 10.4 Format and contents of an IEEE 802.5 token frame.

or active monitor, to oversee the status of the token. When a lobe transmits data, or when the token is idle, M is set to 0. When the monitor station receives a data frame, it sets M to 1. If the monitor station now receives a data frame that has M set to 1, it knows that the transmitting lobe did not strip the data off the frame after the frame completed a full pass around the ring. The monitor station then removes this "orphaned" frame from the ring and issues a new token. The monitor station is discussed later in the chapter. The *reservation bits* are used for reserving a token at a particular level of priority. These, too, are discussed later in the chapter.

The Data Frame

The contents of a token ring data frame are shown in Figure 10.5. Note that the first three fields of the data frame are equivalent to the token frame. A lobe that possesses the free token and has data to transmit changes the access control field's token bit to 1 and then augments the token frame by including a frame control field, destination and source addresses, user data, a CRC checksum, and a frame status field. In other words, the token frame is transformed into a data frame, which is then transmitted around the ring from lobe to lobe.

When a lobe receives a data frame, it will identify the frame as data and not a token because the token bit of the access control field is set to 1. The lobe will also check the frame's destination address. If the lobe is not the intended recipient, it then places the frame back on the ring. When the intended destination lobe receives the frame, it copies the frame into memory, sets the A and C bits of the frame status field to 1, and places the entire frame back on the ring where it will continue to be transmitted from lobe to

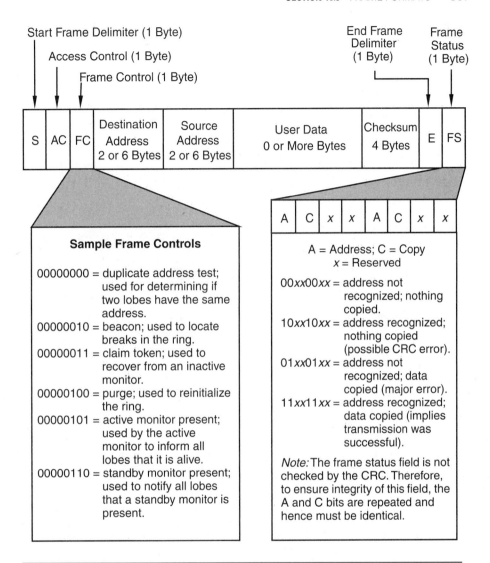

Start Frame Delimiter (1 Byte)

Access Control (1 Byte)

Frame Control (1 Byte)

End Frame Delimiter (1 Byte)

Frame Status (1 Byte)

| S | AC | FC | Destination Address 2 or 6 Bytes | Source Address 2 or 6 Bytes | User Data 0 or More Bytes | Checksum 4 Bytes | E | FS |

| A | C | x | x | A | C | x | x |

Sample Frame Controls

00000000 = duplicate address test; used for determining if two lobes have the same address.
00000010 = beacon; used to locate breaks in the ring.
00000011 = claim token; used to recover from an inactive monitor.
00000100 = purge; used to reinitialize the ring.
00000101 = active monitor present; used by the active monitor to inform all lobes that it is alive.
00000110 = standby monitor present; used to notify all lobes that a standby monitor is present.

A = Address; C = Copy
x = Reserved

00xx00xx = address not recognized; nothing copied.
10xx10xx = address recognized; nothing copied (possible CRC error).
01xx01xx = address not recognized; data copied (major error).
11xx11xx = address recognized; data copied (implies transmission was successful).

Note: The frame status field is not checked by the CRC. Therefore, to ensure integrity of this field, the A and C bits are repeated and hence must be identical.

FIGURE 10.5 Format and contents of an IEEE 802.5 frame. Note that the S, AC, and E fields comprise the token frame. Thus, an IEEE 802.5 data frame is really a modified token frame that includes the frame control, destination and source addresses, user data, checksum, and frame status fields.

lobe. When the sending lobe receives the frame after the frame's complete pass around the ring, it examines the frame status field. If the A and C bits are set to 1, then data transmission was successful. If not, then the frame is retransmitted. In the case of a successful transmission, the lobe removes the data from the frame and changes the token bit to 0. Thus, the data frame is transformed back to a token frame. This free token is then placed on the ring and sent to the next lobe in line. The lobe that has possession of the token is permitted to continue transmitting data until it has no more data to send or its time limit expires, whichever comes first. In IEEE 802.5, the length of time a lobe can possess a token—called the token holding time—is 10 ms.

To illustrate this operation, consider the sample LAN in Figure 10.1. Let's assume that lobe 2 has data to transmit to lobe 5, and lobe 4 has data to transmit to lobe 1. Let's further assume that lobe 2 has the free token. Lobe 2 modifies the free token to "busy," inserts its data, and sends the frame to lobe 3. Lobe 3 examines the frame, determines it is not the intended recipient, and returns the frame to the ring where it is transmitted to lobe 4. Lobe 4 grabs the frame off the ring and sees that it is data and not a token. Hence, it cannot transmit its data. Lobe 4 also determines that it is not the intended recipient, so it returns the frame to the ring where it is transmitted to lobe 5. Lobe 5 receives the frame and ascertains that its destination address matches that of the frame's. The lobe then makes a copy of the frame and stores it in memory. If the frame is valid and the data successfully copied, lobe 5 then sets the A and C bits to 1 and returns the frame to the ring. (It also processes the data it receives.) Lobe 1 receives the frame, examines it, and returns it to the ring. The frame, having completed a full pass around the ring, is now received by lobe 2. Seeing that the A and C bits were properly set, lobe 2 strips the data from the frame. If its token holding time has elapsed, it then resets the token bit to 0 and places the free token frame on the ring. Otherwise, it transmits another frame of data. When lobe 2 returns the free token to the ring, it is transmitted to lobe 3. Since lobe 3 does not have any data to transmit, it returns the token to the ring for transmission to lobe 4. Since lobe 4 has data to transmit, it transforms the token into a data frame, and the data transmission process begins again with lobe 1 being the intended recipient.

10.4   Priority and Reservation

As indicated earlier, a token can have several different priority levels, ranging from 0 (lowest) to 7 (highest). When a lobe receives a free token, it must first compare the priority value contained within the token to the priority of the data it has to transmit. If a lobe's data have a priority level equal to or greater than that of the token's, then the lobe may transmit its data. If the token's priority is higher than the lobe's data, then the lobe cannot transmit its data and must pass the token to its neighbor lobe. During a particular transmission, a lobe may reserve the token at a higher level than the token's current level. By doing so, it preempts the lobe that is currently transmitting data. To illustrate this, consider the token ring LAN in Figure 10.2(b). Let us make the following eight assumptions: (a) the ring rotates counterclockwise; (b) lobe 2 has data to transmit to lobe 1; (c) the priority level of lobe 2's data is 0 (e.g., an e-mail message); (d) lobe 2 has just received a free token with a priority level of 0; (e) lobe 3 has data to transmit to lobe 4; (f) lobe 3's data priority is 1; (g) lobe 4 needs to transmit a video frame to lobe 3; and (h) the priority level of lobe 4's data is 5. Given these assumptions, the operation of the ring is as follows:

1. Lobe 2 transforms the token frame into a data frame.
2. Lobe 2 transmits the data frame to lobe 3.
3. Lobe 3 examines the frame but takes no action because it is not the recipient. It also cannot transmit its data because the token is busy. Lobe 3 passes the frame to lobe 4.

4. Lobe 4 receives the frame. Because it has data with a priority of 5, lobe 4 makes a reservation at priority 5 by setting the three reservation bits of the token's access control field from binary 000 to 101 (i.e., 5). Lobe 4 passes the frame to lobe 1.

5. Lobe 1 receives the frame. Since it is the recipient, it saves the source address (lobe 2), computes the 32-bit checksum, changes the frame's frame status field to reflect that it received the data, and then transmits the frame to lobe 2.

6. Lobe 2, seeing that the transmission was successful, strips the data from the frame. Normally, lobe 2 would continue transmitting data until it has no more data to transmit or until its time limit expired. It would then issue a free token with a priority level of 0 to lobe 3. However, because the frame that was returned has a reservation priority of 5, lobe 2 cannot transmit any more data frames because their priority level is 0, which is less than the reserved priority of 5. As a result, lobe 2 must issue a new free token with a priority level of 5 and transmit it to lobe 3.

7. Lobe 3 receives the free token but is not permitted to transmit its data because the data's priority level is less than 5. It passes the token to lobe 4.

8. Lobe 4 receives the token, changes it to "busy," and transmits its data to lobe 1.

9. After the frame is returned to lobe 4, if there are no additional frames to transmit, or if the time limit expired, lobe 4 transmits a free token to lobe 1; the priority level remains at 5, though.

10. Lobe 1 passes the token to lobe 2.

11. Lobe 2 receives the token and notes that the token is "free" and the priority level is the same one it used when it last issued a new token. Lobe 2 reissues a new token at its previous priority level of 0. (The lobe that upgraded the priority level of the token is also responsible for reestablishing the previous level after all higher-priority data frames are transmitted.)

IEEE 802.5's priority scheduling is excellent for transmitting time-sensitive data such as real-time video or voice. Any lobe with data frames at a higher priority than that of the frame currently being transmitted can reserve the next token at this higher level when the current token and frame are passed to it. As demonstrated in our illustration, when the next token is issued, it will be at this higher level. Furthermore, no other lobe is permitted to transmit data unless its data frames have a priority level equal to or greater than the newly issued one. As beneficial as this scheme is, though, token ring priority makes it possible for lobes with high-priority data to prevent lobes with low-priority data from ever accessing the medium.

10.5 Monitor Stations

A token ring network employs a monitor station to oversee the ring and ensure that it is functioning properly. This monitoring lobe, called the *active monitor,* is usually a high-priority lobe. All other lobes, known as *standby monitors,* monitor the active monitor. If the active monitor becomes disabled, a contention protocol is invoked among the standby monitors to elect a new active monitor.

When a token ring network is first started, the active monitor generates the first token and begins the process that enables each lobe to learn the address of its neighbor that is next in line (called the "downstream" lobe). During the operation of the ring, the active monitor performs several tasks, including monitoring the ring for valid frame transmissions, maintaining the ring's master clock, and ensuring there are proper delays in the ring. The active monitor also is sensitive to two possible error conditions. The first is a lost token. If no token is detected after a predetermined amount of time expires, the active monitor assumes the token is lost and issues a new one. The second possible error is a persistently busy token. To check for this condition, a special bit within the token is set. If this bit is still set when the token is returned to the active monitor, it assumes the source station did not remove the data from the network. It then changes the token to "free" and passes it to the next lobe. One task an active monitor cannot do is detect breaks in the ring, which can occur if a lobe fails or the cable connecting the lobe to the ring is broken. To recover from either of these cases, special relay switches (also called bypass switches) are used. In case of a host failure, a bypass switch can be closed either manually or automatically, effectively removing the dead lobe from the ring. This is illustrated in Figure 10.3.

10.6   Second-Generation Token Ring

Although token ring LANs are not as popular as Ethernet/802.3 LANs, token ring has nevertheless benefited from some of the technological advances made for Ethernet/802.3. These include switched token ring, dedicated token ring, full-duplex token ring, and 100-Mbps token ring. A gigabit token ring specification is also in development. A brief examination of these technologies follows.

Switched Token Ring

The concept of a switched token ring probably seems like a misnomer to some readers. We can hear your reasoning: Switches benefit traditional Ethernet/802.3 LANs because they eliminate contention, which in turn makes the operation of Ethernet/802.3 collision-free. Token ring LANs, however, are collision-free by design. So how in the world can switch technology improve the operation of a token ring network? If this is your train of thought, then you are absolutely correct. Ethernet/802.3's MAC layer protocol (CSMA/CD) is contention-based and highly susceptible to performance problems during periods of high activity. Token ring's token passing protocol, however, is inherently deterministic and quite stable during peak load times. Token ring networks do not experience the same type of performance problems as are found in Ethernet/802.3 networks. A token ring network's performance, for example, does not begin to degrade until its utilization rate approaches 90% and in many cases can achieve a bandwidth utilization rate as high as 95%. So, yes, Ethernet/802.3 networks are a better candidate for switching technology than token ring networks because the former can benefit more from the type of performance boosts available from switches. With the introduction of client/server applications, imaging, multimedia, and the consolidation of servers, however, token ring networks—including 16-Mbps token ring, which has higher bandwidth than 10-Mbps Ethernet—are experiencing congestion and performance problems similar to those of Ethernet/802.3 networks. To help alleviate these problems, several vendors have ported the switched technology originally developed for Ethernet/802.3 to token ring.

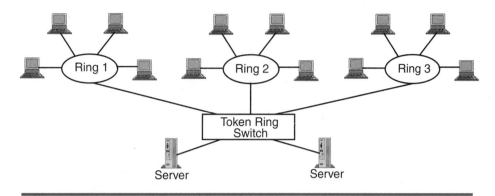

FIGURE 10.6 Incorporated within the backbone, a token ring switch acts as a multiport source routing bridge and enables large networks to be partitioned into smaller segments. The net effect is a collapsed backbone, which reduces both overall network traffic and traffic at the server ports. (Compare this configuration to the one shown in Figure 6.15.)

Token ring switches are similar to Ethernet switches in that they are capable of supporting workgroups, desktop, or backbone connections, and they use either store-and-forward or cut-through technology to forward frames from one network to another. In a workgroup environment, individual token ring networks are interconnected via the switch. In this capacity, the token ring switch acts like a multiport source routing bridge that is connected to multiple ring numbers. (See Chapter 6 for information about the concept of source routing and source routing bridges.) With private connections, individual stations have a full, dedicated 16-Mbps link to the switch; lobes do not share a 16-Mbps channel with other lobes. Finally, as a backbone switch, an organization's entire network backbone is incorporated into the switch, which resembles the collapsed backbone concept discussed earlier for Ethernet/802.3 networks.

In large token ring networks, workgroups usually feed into the backbone. This configuration promotes congestion, particularly if the workgroups are 16-Mbps networks and the backbone also is operating at 16-Mbps. Although source routing bridges or routers are used to segment the network into smaller components, this introduces additional delay into the network. Consequently, one of the primary applications of token ring switches is at the backbone where they replace source routing bridges. This application enables organizations to consolidate local servers into centrally located "super" servers because the backbone is now the switch itself. An illustration is shown in Figure 10.6.

Some token ring switches also provide support for *virtual rings* and source route transparent bridging. With virtual rings, several individual token ring networks are collectively viewed as a single (virtual) ring. Although these individual networks are indeed separate and connected to different switch ports, source routing between lobes connected to two separate networks is now transparent since the networks appear to be on the same (virtual) ring. Virtual ring support also eliminates the need to configure new ring numbers when connecting new token ring networks to a switch because the new rings appear to the network as part of the original ring. An illustration of the virtual ring concept is given in Figure 10.7.

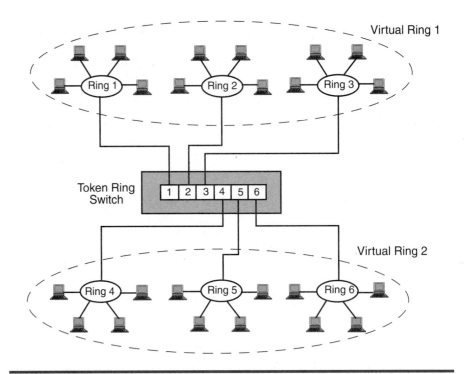

FIGURE 10.7 Token ring switches that support virtual rings enable multiple independent rings to be viewed as a single ring. For example, rings 1, 2, and 3 are viewed by the switch as a single ring, namely, virtual ring 1. Support for virtual rings eliminates the need to configure new ring numbers when a new ring is added to the switch. Additionally, since the networks comprising a virtual ring are considered a single ring, transparent bridging is in effect. Thus, transparent bridging exists for the rings connected to switch ports 1, 2, and 3 and for the rings connected to switch ports 4, 5, and 6. Source routing bridging, however, is necessary for exchanging data between virtual rings 1 and 2.

Dedicated Token Ring

As is the case with switched Ethernet, a token ring switching environment advances the concept of dedicated token ring, which enables lobes to have access to a full 16-Mbps channel instead of sharing the segment with other lobes. Dedicated token ring does not require any new hardware or software either—all you do is connect a lobe (via its NIC) to a port on the switch. In a dedicated switched environment, only two lobes are involved in the transmission and receipt of data. Consequently, dedicated lobes can transmit data whenever they have data to send. A new method for dedicated token ring, called Transmit Immediate (TXI), also is defined by IEEE 802.5. In TXI, dedicated lobes are not permitted to begin transmitting data until they possess a token. Assigning lobes, especially those that transmit and receive a high volume of traffic, to dedicated links can improve overall network performance since this further segments a network.

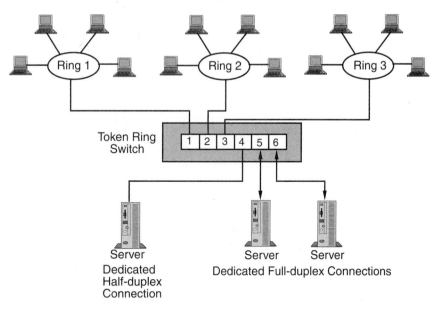

Shared Half-duplex Connections

FIGURE 10.8 Dedicated token ring connections provide lobes with private network segments instead of shared segments. Incorporating support for full-duplex token ring into a dedicated lobe's NIC, bandwidth to the lobe is doubled to 32 Mbps since the lobe can simultaneously transmit and receive data. A token ring switch, in combination with dedicated and full-duplex support, dramatically increases overall network performance.

Full-Duplex Token Ring

Although dedicated switched ports enable lobes to have their own private network segments, they are still operating in half-duplex. By installing additional software drivers or upgrading the firmware of NICs, lobes can support full-duplex token ring, which provides 16 Mbps of bandwidth in both directions. This enables stations to transmit and receive data at the same time. Stations such as "super" servers, which are the source of high-volume traffic, are excellent candidates for full-duplex token ring. The combination of full-duplex token ring with a dedicated switched environment can dramatically boost the performance of a token ring network (Figure 10.8).

High-Speed Token Ring

The IEEE 802.5 working group has created three separate initiatives for high-speed token ring (HSTR): IEEE 802.5t, which is HSTR over Category 5 UTP cable; IEEE 802.5u, which is HSTR over fiber-optic cable; and IEEE 802.5v, which is gigabit token ring. The first two specifications were completed in 1999. The third specification was ratified in 2000. HSTR is a switched-only 100-Mbps technology. Deployment is restricted to the backbone, interswitch links, and server connections. There are no shared links as with classic token ring. HSTR uses the same MAC sublayer as 4/16-Mbps token ring and incorporates autonegotiation into its NICs for 4/16/100-Mbps autosensing.

Compared with Ethernet, the installed base of token ring networks and the market for token ring products are indeed relatively insignificant. Nevertheless, the vendors that comprise the High-Speed Token Ring Alliance (HSTRA) feel an obligation to protect the existing market and established users by advancing token ring technology to be on a par with that of Ethernet. At the very least, HSTR gives users and managers of token ring technology hope that token ring is not being ignored. Unfortunately, all is not well with the political and marketing sides of HSTR. Cisco, Cabletron, and Texas Instruments—all charter members of HSTRA—withdrew from the organization. Furthermore, Cisco reported that it will not develop any products that are IEEE 802.5 compliant, but instead will develop and market its own proprietary HSTR products. Many token ring managers also have indicated via surveys that they intend to migrate to Fast Ethernet or ATM and hence will not purchase HSTR products. So, although HSTR appears to be a promising IEEE technology standard that will serve as a smooth migration from 4/16-Mbps token ring, vendor support is problematic at best. Additional information about HSTR can be found at `http://www.hstra.com`, the High-Speed Token Ring Alliance's home page.

10.7 Token Ring versus Token Bus

Another token passing protocol LAN is *token bus,* which is defined in IEEE 802.4. A token bus network is characterized as a logical ring on a physical bus. Physically, the network resembles a bus topology, but logically, it is arranged as a ring with respect to passing the token from lobe to lobe. An illustration of a token bus network is shown in Figure 10.9. Although token passing is point-to-point (i.e., from lobe to lobe), data transmission is based on broadcasting. For example, in Figure 10.9, if

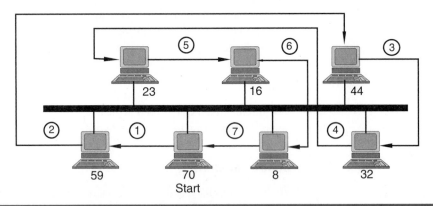

FIGURE 10.9 A token bus network physically resembles a bus topology; logically, however, it is a ring. A token is transmitted from lobe to lobe using network addresses and occurs in descending order. The lobe that possesses the token is permitted to transmit data. The lobe order in the figure is 70-59-44-32-23-16-8.

lobe 44 has the token and wants to send data to lobe 70, it simply places data frames on the bus. The broadcast nature of the bus topology causes all lobes to hear the transmission, but only lobe 70 reads and processes the data. After lobe 44 has completed its transmission, it then passes the token to lobe 32. Thus, from the perspective of actual data transmission, IEEE 802.4 is similar to that of IEEE 802.3—it is based on broadcasting. However, medium access control is similar to IEEE 802.5.

At the physical layer, IEEE 802.4 uses 75-ohm coaxial cable or fiber-optic cable. If coax is used, data rates include 1, 5, and 10 Mbps. If fiber-optic cable is used, data rates are 5, 10, and 20 Mbps. IEEE 802.4 also supports priority scheduling and can be configured to operate in one of four priority modes, 0 (lowest), 2, 4, and 6 (highest). As is the case with IEEE 802.5, this priority scheme makes it possible to allocate network bandwidth to high-priority (level-6) data such as video, digitized voice, and multimedia applications. Lower-priority data are transmitted if sufficient bandwidth is available.

IEEE 802.4 is not a popular LAN protocol; it is primarily used for control of industrial and factory automation processes. It also is the basis of the General Motors Manufacturing Automation Protocol (MAP), which supports real-time applications.

End-of-Chapter Commentary

This chapter presented an overview of token ring networks. Two related chapters are Chapter 11, FDDI, which uses a token ring technique similar to the IEEE 802.5 specification, and Chapter 15, ATM, which is viewed by various token ring managers as the logical migration path for classic token ring LANs. In addition to these chapters, you also might want to review Chapter 5, which contains a general discussion and comparison of random accessing protocols and token passing protocols.

CHAPTER REVIEW MATERIALS

SUMMARY

- A token ring network is an IEEE LAN technology that was developed by IBM and uses a token passing scheme for media access control. The node, called a lobe in the token ring world, that possess the token is permitted to transmit data. Only one lobe at a time can possess the token.
- A token is a special three-byte frame that is transmitted around the ring in either a clockwise or counterclockwise direction. If a lobe that receives the idle token has data to transmit, the lobe expands the token frame into a complete data frame, which is then transmitted around the ring en route from source to destination. As part of this expansion, the access control field is set to "busy," which specifies that the transmitted frame is a data frame and not an idle token.

- A token ring network can be designed as either a physical ring or as a physical star. In the former, lobes are physically connected to each other in a ringlike structure; in the latter, lobes are connected to a hub called a multistation access unit (MAU) that electronically incorporates a logical ring topology.
- Conventional token ring data rates are 4 Mbps and 16 Mbps. The difference between the two is the number of frames that can be transmitted during a single transmission. In a 4-Mbps token ring, only one frame can be transmitted, whereas a 16-Mbps token ring permits multiple frames to be transmitted.
- The encoding scheme of a token ring network is a variation of Manchester coding called differential Manchester.

• Token ring networks are governed by a special lobe called the active monitor, which oversees the operation of the network. All other lobes are called standby monitors.

• Token ring networks support a priority scheme, which enables data transmissions to be assigned a priority level. Eight priority levels are available ranging from zero (lowest) to seven (highest).

• Token ring networks support token reservations, which enable nodes to reserve the token at a specific priority level. Thus, nodes with higher-level priority data can usurp a lower-level data transmission.

• Second-generation token ring networks improve overall network performance by using LAN switches, dedicated lobes, full-duplex transmissions, and higher data transmission rates.

• Compared to token ring, a token bus LAN is a broadcast network (i.e., bus topology) based on a physical ring. Token bus data transmissions are similar to Ethernet/802.3, but media access control is similar to token ring.

VOCABULARY CHECK

active monitor

differential Manchester encoding

lobe

multistation access unit (MAU)

standby monitor

token bus

token ring

REVIEW EXERCISES

1. What is the difference between a physical ring topology and a physical star configuration relative to a token ring network?

2. Explain the difference between Manchester and differential Manchester encoding schemes.

3. What must the clock speed be of a 100-Mbps token ring LAN? How does this compare to the clock speed of 100BASE-T?

4. Compare the manner in which Ethernet/802.3 and token ring receiving nodes send receipt of data acknowledgments back to the sending node. Which method do you think is more efficient and why?

5. What happens to the operation of a token ring LAN if the intended recipient of a frame copies the frame into memory and then immediately crashes before it has a chance to set the A and C bits of the frame?

6. If the token holding time is 10 ms, what is the largest-size frame that can be transmitted on a 16-Mbps token ring LAN?

7. Explain how token ring lobes with low-priority data can effectively be shut out from ever transmitting their data. Give an illustration of how this can occur and what recourse lobes have to transmit their low-priority data.

8. In IEEE 802.5, it is the sending lobe and not the recipient that removes the frame from the ring after a successful transmission. What happens to the operation of the ring if the sending lobe crashes before it can remove the frame from the ring? (*Hint:* Look at Figure 10.4.)

9. Suggest a contention protocol that could be implemented by the standby monitors to elect a new active monitor in the event that the current monitor station fails. (*Hint:* Look at Figure 10.5.)

10. In what way(s) does switched token ring improve token ring LAN performance?

11. Go to the High-Speed Token Ring Alliance's home page at `http://www.hstra.com` to learn what the latest information is regarding high-speed token ring's future.

12. Compare token ring's and token bus's priority schemes.

13. IEEE 802.5's MAC protocol is known as *release after reception* (RAR) since the sending node waits until it has received the frame it transmitted before it releases the token. Another version of this protocol is *release after transmission* (RAT). In what ways do you think this

protocol differs from RAR in terms of operation and efficiency?

14. Another variation of the IEEE 802.5 MAC protocol is the *recipient release after reception* (RRAR). In what ways do you think this protocol differs from RAR and RAT in terms of operation and efficiency?

SUGGESTED READINGS AND REFERENCES

BALDWIN, C. 1994. *High Speed Networking Technologies: Options and Implications.* Southborough, MA: Chipcom Corporation.

FEIBEL, W. 1995. *The Network Press Encyclopedia of Networking.* 2nd ed. San Francisco: Sybex.

FRANK, A. 1995. Flocking to a Faster Network. *LAN Magazine,* August, 67–77.

———. 1996. Multimedia LANs and WANs. *LAN Magazine,* July, 81–86.

GALLO, M., and W. HANCOCK. 1999. *Networking Explained.* Boston: Digital Press.

GAW, S. 1996. Token Ring Flips the Switch. *LAN,* July, 67–72.

GORALSKI, W., and G. KESSLER. 1996. Changing Channels. *LAN Interoperability: Quarterly Supplement,* May, 6–12.

HELD, G. 1996. The LAN Guessing Game. *LAN Magazine,* May, 93–100.

KARVÉ, A. 1995. Lord of the Ring. *LAN Magazine,* August, 107–114.

———. 1996. Multimedia Takes the Stage. *LAN Magazine,* May, 123–127.

KRIVDA, C. 1995. Another Swipe at Switching. *LAN,* October, 129–134.

LIPPIS, N. 1997. The Token Ring Trap. *Data Communications,* February, 23–24.

LOVE, R. D. 1998. The Fast Track to High-Speed Token Ring. *Data Communications,* February, 95–100.

MARTIN, J. 1989. *Local Area Networks: Architectures and Implementations.* Upper Saddle River, NJ: Prentice-Hall.

ROBERTS, E. 1998. A Slow Start for High-Speed Token Ring. *Data Communications,* February, 85–92.

STALLINGS, W. 2000. *Data and Computer Communications.* 6th ed. Upper Saddle River, NJ: Prentice-Hall.

TANENBAUM, A. S. 1996. *Computer Networks.* 3rd ed. Upper Saddle River, NJ: Prentice-Hall.

UNGERMANN-BASS NETWORKS. 1995. *LAN Switching Buyer's Guide.* Santa Clara, CA: Ungermann-Bass Networks.

Fiber Distributed Data Interface (FDDI)

CHAPTER OBJECTIVES

After studying this chapter, you will be able to do the following:

1. Explain the concept of FDDI.
2. Describe the operation of an FDDI network.
3. Understand the rationale behind the development of FDDI.
4. Describe FDDI's "position" relative to other LAN, MAN, and WAN technologies.
5. Describe FDDI's encoding scheme.
6. Compare and contrast FDDI's frame format with that of token ring.
7. Compare and contrast FDDI's MAC sublayer with that of token ring.
8. Understand FDDI's design and configuration rules.
9. Describe the manner in which FDDI networks can coexist with Ethernet/802.3 networks.

CHAPTER OUTLINE

In this chapter, we present information about a network technology called fiber distributed data interface (FDDI). FDDI employs a ring topology, with fiber-optic cabling as its physical layer medium. We also discuss a "sister" standard called copper distributed data interface (CDDI), which uses copper instead of fiber. We begin the chapter with a general overview of FDDI networks. FDDI's physical and data link layers are then discussed in Sections 11.2 and 11.3, respectively. Sections 11.4 and 11.5 provide design and configuration considerations, including interconnecting FDDI with Ethernet/802.3 or ATM networks. We conclude the chapter with a brief presentation about FDDI's future as a LAN networking technology.

11.1 What Is FDDI?

FDDI stands for *fiber distributed data interface.* FDDI networks are described by ANSI standard X3T9.5 created in 1986 for interconnecting computer systems and network devices typically via a fiber ring topology at 100 Mbps. Figure 11.1 shows where FDDI networks fit in the hierarchy of network architectures. (For information about the other network architectures listed in this figure, see the appropriately named chapters.)

FDDI's bandwidth gives it considerable flexibility in how an organization allocates its resources. Its applications include directly connecting workstations and servers in workgroups and serving as a high-speed backbone to connect other networks in a building, in a campus environment, or in a city. An example of the first

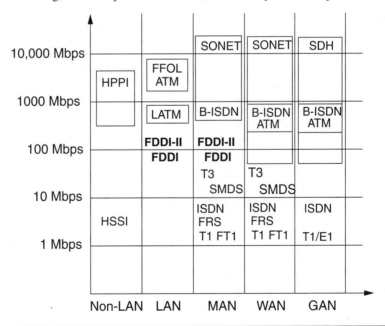

FIGURE 11.1 How the various networking technologies compare against each other in terms of bandwidth.

application is the connection of high-speed servers to other high-speed servers. For instance, a very large video server system cannot be effectively connected to a broadcast video server at 10-Mbps Ethernet/802.3 or token ring speeds, but at FDDI's data rate of 100 Mbps, the connection is adequate for server transmission. As a backbone network, FDDI interconnects network devices such as routers, bridges, switches, and concentrators to create a large network environment consisting of smaller networks. FDDI networks are not used for wide area networks where network radii typically exceed 100 km.

FDDI was very popular in networks that required 100-Mbps capability prior to 1996. At that time, FDDI's data transmission rate of 100 Mbps was ten times faster than 10-Mbps Ethernet/802.3 systems. Since 1996, however, 100-Mbps Ethernet/802.3 (Fast Ethernet) and 1000-Mbps Ethernet/802.3 (Gigabit Ethernet) technologies have displaced new FDDI installations. This does not preclude us from studying FDDI, though. FDDI networks are installed in just about any large company, and many telecommunications companies operate metropolitan area networks (MANs) that consist largely of FDDI or FDDI emulations over faster networks such as the synchronous optical networks, SONET (see Chapter 3).

Compared to other 100-Mbps networks, FDDI has several redeeming attributes. First, FDDI can be configured as two independent *counterrotating* ring networks, called a Class A configuration (Figure 11.2). This greatly increases network reliability. If the physical topology of the network is designed such that both fiber paths for both networks are physically "diverse" (this is a networking term for putting the two fiber paths for the two networks in completely different physical locations so that one backhoe does not ruin both networks at the same time while trenching up the lawn), then it is very difficult to destroy the network with a single or even multiple fiber cuts to the network cable plant. Second, FDDI is much less susceptible to a network disruption; it has the ability to "self-heal" if the ring topology is cut in a single spot. This is called *autowrapping*. The break in the active ring is corrected by establishing a loopback connection to the inactive ring. This creates a single virtual ring and allows the FDDI network to continue to function at full speed (Figure 11.3). Self-healing resembles the expression, "Physician, heal thyself." The network hardware is capable of detecting a fiber path failure between connection points on the rings. Since there are two fibers (one transmitting clockwise, the other counterclockwise) in the configuration, the stations that detect the failure join the two rings together and effectively "wrap" together to make a single fiber network twice as long as the original two-fiber network (hence the term autowrapping). If the network fiber path is destroyed in two different spots, the result is two healed network rings. Thus, self-healing is very beneficial for a single location failure because the network continues to function. In the case of two failures, the network components that will maintain connectivity are determined by which nodes need to talk to whom and how the network was designed. Self-healing is not for all situations in which the network could be disrupted. A third feature is that FDDI transmits information in frames up to 4500 octets (bytes). This increases network efficiency and lowers protocol overhead. Finally, FDDI encodes data quite a bit differently from other types of networks to increase transmission efficiency.

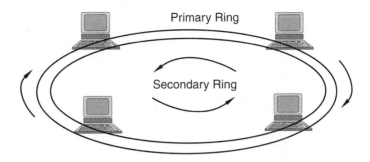

FIGURE 11.2 Example of FDDI's counterrotating ring architecture. The primary ring is active in normal operation; the secondary ring provides redundancy. All devices on the ring are dual-attachment stations (Class A nodes) or dual-attachment hubs.

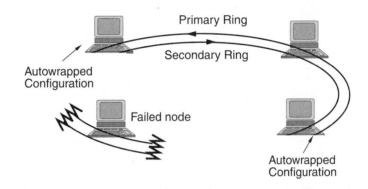

FIGURE 11.3 Example of FDDI's "self-healing" capability. In the event of a fiber cut or an inoperative node, an FDDI network automatically "heals" itself by wrapping the ring at the point of failure. This is done by interconnecting the primary and secondary rings into a single functional ring. Source: adapted from Daniels, 1990.

11.2 Physical Layer Specifications

Obviously, FDDI's physical layer is based on fiber-optic cable. FDDI uses either 62.5/125-μm or 85/125-μm multimode fiber or 8.7/125-μm single-mode fiber. Other specifications include 50/125 μm and 100/140 μm. Smaller fibers allow higher speeds but also cause higher connector loss. Further, the fiber must be specified for light transmission at the 1300-nm wavelength. Since most fiber can support light transmissions of 850 nm, 1300 nm, or 1550 nm, finding compliant fiber is usually not a problem for a network manager. Usually, in networks less than 1 km in length, 850 nm is adequate; however, as the need for performance of the medium increases, the 850-nm light source becomes inadequate. Light transmission above 1550 nm usually requires a sophisticated and expensive light source, such as a laser system. Fiber runs cannot be longer than 2 km between nodes for multimode fiber (up to 60 km with single-mode fiber), and there is a total allowable distance of 100 km per FDDI ring (two rings are allowed). Each ring consists of two fibers. Thus, two rings obviously use four fibers. (See Chapter 4 for additional information about fiber-optic cable.)

In addition to fiber, FDDI also supports copper cable via a related technology called CDDI, which stands for copper distributed data interface. CDDI supports both unshielded twisted-pair (UTP) and shielded twisted-pair (STP). As for which type of UTP, the familiar and popular EIA/TIA-568 Category 5 cabling, already installed in many buildings' wiring closets, may be used for CDDI. Similarly, IBM Type 1 STP is acceptable for CDDI use; occasionally, you may encounter the abbreviation SDDI, which is sometimes used in reference to CDDI networks employing shielded cabling. At one time, there was also a proprietary CDDI product that supported ThinWire coaxial cable. CDDI and SDDI began as de facto standards created by a group of five vendors. In 1995, ANSI issued a standard for copper-based FDDI, X3.263-1995, entitled *Fibre Distributed Data Interface (FDDI)—Token Ring Twisted Pair Physical Layer Medium Dependent (TP-PMD)*.

FDDI's physical layer does not use Manchester encoding, which is used in Ethernet/802.3 and 802.5 LANs. (See Chapter 3 for additional information about digital coding techniques.) Recall that in Manchester encoding, each bit requires at least two signal transitions or baud. This means that a 16-Mbps token ring network requires a signaling rate of 32 MHz. Ethernet/802.3 running at 10 Mbps requires 20 MHz. If we were to use Manchester encoding on an FDDI network, more than 200 MHz would be required to provide the FDDI rated speed of 100 Mbps. Instead, FDDI uses a "group" encoding scheme known as the 4B/5B method, which stands for four bits in five baud, or four-bit to five-bit. The 4B/5B encoding method takes data in four-bit codes and maps them to corresponding five-bit codes. These five-bit codes are then transmitted using a technique called *NRZI,* which stands for *nonreturn to zero, invert on ones.* By transmitting five-bit codes using NRZI, a logical 1-bit is transmitted at least once every five sequential data bits, resulting in a signal transition. The 4B/5B-NRZI scheme makes it possible for FDDI to operate at a rate of 125 MHz and provides a data rate of 100 Mbps. The use of one extra bit for every five bits translates to only 20% overhead for every clock encoding. In contrast, Manchester coding requires 50% bandwidth overhead for clock encoding because it guarantees at least one signal transition for every bit transmitted. The 4B/5B-NRZI scheme allows FDDI networks to provide high-speed capability over less optimal media and data symmetry that allows for simpler implementation of analog capture circuitry for receiving nodes.

11.3   Frame Formats and Medium Access Specifications

Frame Formats

FDDI networks employ two types of "frames." The first is the token, which is a special frame that enables a node to access the ring; the second is the frame itself. FDDI token and frame formats are quite different from a token ring frame format. Instead of bit def-

TABLE 11.1 FDDI Symbols and Codes

FDDI Code	Bit Encoding
0	1 1 1 1 0
1	0 1 0 0 1
2	1 0 1 0 0
3	1 0 1 0 1
4	0 1 0 1 0
5	0 1 0 1 1
6	0 1 1 1 0
7	0 1 1 1 1
8	1 0 0 1 0
9	1 0 0 1 1
A	1 0 1 1 0
B	1 0 1 1 1
C	1 1 0 1 0
D	1 1 0 1 1
E	1 1 1 0 0
F	1 1 1 0 1
S (Set)	1 1 0 0 1
R (Reset)	0 0 1 1 1
Q (Quiet)	0 0 0 0 0
I (Idle)	1 1 1 1 1
H (Halt)	0 0 1 0 0
T (Terminate)	0 1 1 0 1
J (Start 1)	1 1 0 0 0
K (Start 2)	1 0 0 0 1

initions, FDDI networks use "symbols," which are defined by at least four bits (Table 11.1). Following is a summary of the token and frame formats.

Token   An FDDI token consists of a preamble (PA) of 16 or more I symbols, a starting delimiter (SD) consisting of a JK symbol pair, a frame control (FC) of two symbols, and an ending delimiter (ED) field of two T symbols. The FDDI token format is shown in Figure 11.4. There also are two classes of tokens. A *restricted token* enables two specified nodes to use all of the unused or unreserved bandwidth of the network for the duration of their data transmission. A *nonrestricted token* is used for normal operation. Only one token is permitted on the ring. Thus, only one node is permitted to transmit data.

Frame   An FDDI frame consists of a preamble (PA) of 16 or more I symbols, a starting delimiter field consisting of a JK symbol pair, a frame control field of two symbols, destination and source addresses (DA and SA) each consisting of four or twelve symbols, an info field of zero or more symbol pairs for user data, a frame check sequence (FCS) of eight symbols, an ending delimiter of one T symbol, and a frame status of three or more R or S symbols. The format of an FDDI frame is shown in Figure 11.5.

Preamble	Starting Delimiter	Frame Control	Ending Delimiter

FIGURE 11.4 FDDI token format. The preamble consists of 16 or more I symbols; the starting delimiter consists of one JK symbol pair; the frame control consists of two symbols; and the ending delimiter consists of two T symbols.

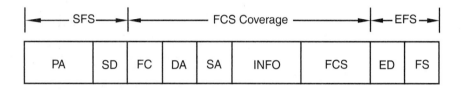

FIGURE 11.5 FDDI frame format. The preamble (PA), starting delimiter (SD), frame control (FC), and ending delimiter (ED) are the same as for a token (Figure 11.4). The destination address (DA) and source address (SA) are four or eight symbols. The info field is user data and consists of zero or more symbols. The frame check sequence (FCS) consists of eight symbols and uses a 32-bit CRC checksum. The frame status (FS) consists of three or more R or S symbols. The status can be E for error detected in frame, A for destination address recognized, or C for frame copied. The entire frame can be grouped into three primary fields: start of frame sequence (SFS), frame check sequence (FCS) coverage, and end of frame sequence (EFS).

Note that the first two fields (PA and SD) are collectively called the *start of frame sequence* (SFS); the next five fields (FC, DA, SA, info, and FCS) are collectively known as the *frame check sequence* (FCS) *coverage;* and the last two fields are collectively referred to as the *end of frame sequence* (EFS). Also note that addresses can be either 16 or 48 bits in length. Finally, the FCS uses a 32-bit CRC checksum for error control.

MAC Sublayer: FDDI versus Token Ring

FDDI uses a token passing scheme as its MAC sublayer protocol similar to that of IEEE 802.5 token ring type networks. However, FDDI does not operate like a "classic" token ring network. We described a few differences between token ring and FDDI earlier. We'll summarize them here and include some additional ones. (You might want to review Chapter 10's discussion on token ring networks at this time.)

• FDDI networks can have two counterrotating fiber-optic rings. This allows configurations of redundant topologies for highly reliable networks. IEEE 802.5 networks operate on a single ring topology (see Figure 11.2).
• On IEEE 802.5 token ring type networks, it is possible for stations to implement a priority scheme whereby token ring lobes can "reserve" a token for access to the medium. This scheme does not exist on FDDI networks because it would not work properly in the FDDI environment. FDDI nodes usually send a token at the end of a data transfer, which

means that reservation techniques do not work. This is referred to as "new token after send," which is different than IEEE 802.5's "new token after receive."

• FDDI networks have an explicit maximum data size of 4500 octets per frame. There is no such explicit data frame size for IEEE 802.5 networks. Specification of an explicit frame size precludes a node from "hogging" the cable.

• FDDI networks have the capacity to support a distributed recovery capability in case of ring failure. This means that if the ring is cut, nodes on the FDDI network automatically isolate the fault and actively reconfigure the network to provide maximum availability.

• FDDI does not use bit definitions for various fields. All FDDI fields are defined by at least four bits and may be defined by a byte of information so that the various fields can easily be modified or replaced by the nodes on the network as the frames and token travel through the ring(s).

• An optional technique in token ring networks, but implemented as a feature in FDDI, is the concept of *early token release* (ETR). ETR places a token on the network *before* the generated frame has had the opportunity to circulate throughout the entire network.

• FDDI tokens are not modified to a start of frame (SOF) as on other token ring networks. Tokens are absorbed and regenerated after a message has been sent. Tokens in an FDDI network also react differently from those of other token ring networks in that there are more accommodations for statistical network interconnections than on classic token ring architectures.

• On token ring networks, one clock on the network is responsible for providing clocking signals for all nodes on the cable. The main clock node also provides an "elastic" buffer capability that slides to compensate for speed differentials that appear on the network; this is referred to as *jitter*. In a 100-Mbps FDDI environment, this type of clocking mechanism is impractical and difficult to maintain. At 4 Mbps, the bit-time is 250 ns as compared to 10 ns per bit-time at 100 Mbps. Consequently, FDDI nodes provide their own clock (hence a "distributed" clocking scheme) and correct for timing jitter via each node's own internal elastic buffer.

Operation

To access the ring, a node must first gain possession of the token. Once it has the token, the node is permitted to transmit multiple frames until a timer expires. When its time is up, the node retransmits the token on the ring. Only one token is permitted; thus, only one node can access the ring at any time. As frames circulate around the ring, if the bits do not match a specific pattern, then the receiving station is aware that the token is used and that this frame should be examined to see if it is to continue being passed along the ring. If the node examining the frame is not the intended recipient, then the frame is regenerated to the next station in the path. If the current station is the intended recipient, then the station "snapshots" the data, passes them to the host system, and marks the bit pattern at the beginning of the frame to signify that the data were received and read into the receiving node. The frame is then passed along to the next node, continuing until it eventually reaches the sending node, which "strips" the frame by not retransmitting it. This scheme is really critical in view of the potential size of FDDI networks–1000 or more systems. It would take a very long time for frames in a classic token ring network to traverse such a large network (most token ring networks have fewer than

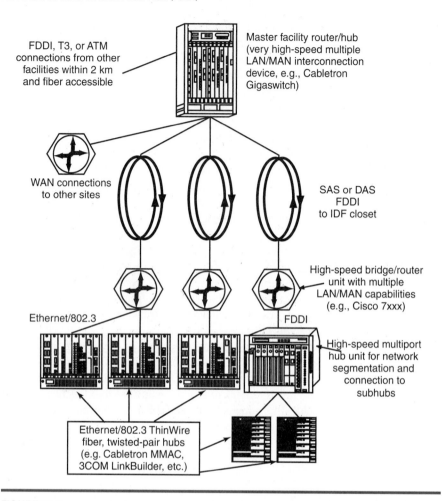

FIGURE 11.6 An example of a typical high-speed network backbone that uses FDDI to inter-connect several different types of LANs and WANs.

250 stations). It's not uncommon to find FDDI networks with over 400 connections in a single campus environment, although most FDDI networks have fewer than 100 connections to ensure good performance (Figure 11.6). Having such a large number of nodes on a single network implies that if it is not carefully designed to avert network outages, a very large number of people who rely on the network will find themselves unable to accomplish anything.

11.4   Configuration and Design Issues

The rules for configuring an FDDI network are relatively simple. A few specific fiber types are supported, and specific lengths are required between optical interconnections depending on the vendor hardware selected. The two individual fiber rings' total length must not exceed 200 km when autowrapped. The ANSI standard specifies that a maximum of 500 nodes is permitted on an FDDI network with a maximum ring circumference of 100 km and a maximum distance of 2 km between hardware devices. Some vendors allow a greater number of nodes depending on their hardware and configuration rules. Some allow fewer. As stated earlier, FDDI networks of over 1000 nodes are not uncommon.

As simple as the rules are, making the actual physical connections can be quite difficult for the inexperienced because of FDDI's fiber-based design. Within FDDI, there are two types of network connections (nodes): Class A and Class B. Class A nodes are connected to two full dual-fiber rings and have the ability to reconfigure the network to form a valid network from components of the two rings in case of a failure. Class B nodes only connect to the primary pair of fibers and can be isolated from the network in the case of some types of failure. Class A nodes are called *dual-attachment stations* (DAS); Class B nodes are called *single-attachment stations* (SAS). Some Class B nodes are equipped with bypass connections, which allow light source continuation even if the node connection fails. These bypass connections serve to maximize uptime of the network. An FDDI network designed with Class A nodes is called a Class A configuration.

In most FDDI wiring configurations, the network designer configures a main backbone to be set up as a series of Class A nodes for reliability purposes. The length of the backbone is a function of how widely distributed a network is in a building, on a campus, or in a metropolitan area. In a building environment, the backbone may be located in a single room with all segments connecting to it. The backbone may be located vertically throughout telephone closets in the building. There may be other variations as well. In all these cases, the FDDI backbone network is contained within the building. In a campus environment, the backbone could also be in a single room in a single building, but most likely runs from building to building on the campus. In this configuration, each building has a main network control closet, so there is only one fiber coupler (tap) on the network backbone at each building location. In any case, the backbone network may vary in size and number of connection points depending heavily on where the network is located and how it is used. An FDDI network also may appear as a subsidiary backbone within a building that is connected to the main FDDI backbone. In this example, there are two FDDI network levels: the main backbone and a separate FDDI network per building. This may be expanded further to an FDDI network on a floor connected to the building hub, which is in turn connected to the main backbone in a campus building environment. In this configuration, we run the fiber to the actual machine(s) on the network; other networks may or may not be bridged onto the FDDI.

For a node to be connected to a fiber-optic network, the network must have a tap attached to it. These couplers require that the cable be cut and terminated properly with approved connectors. These are typically the SC or media interface connector (MIC) variety of fiber connectors. (MICs are designed to be used by untrained personnel.) Splices in fiber may be done via a "score and break" technique where the fiber is scored, broken with special tools, and the ends of the two fibers connected with epoxy. A second method is to use a fusion splicer, which may employ an electrical arc to connect the ends of two fibers together. Splices are reasonably straightforward. Termination of cable, however, requires that the ends be cut and polished before they are inserted into terminating hoods. Polishing is typically done in a coarse way with a hand tool and completed with a polishing machine. This allows a smooth, flawless end that will properly pass the light from the source to the destination transceiver or repeater. This polishing effort may take up to 40 minutes per fiber strand (imagine this on a 48-fiber run!), which accounts for the high cost of fiber installation. Improper polishing and connection of the termination points on a fiber will at most render the fiber useless or will at the very least result in poor network performance. After it is terminated, the fiber must be tested to ensure proper installation. This normally involves using an optical time domain reflectometer (OTDR), an expensive testing device.

Typically, FDDI networks implement backbone configurations for buildings and campus environments. In this design, a master FDDI "switch" connects separate FDDI networks on each floor in the building. This configuration is called a *collapsed backbone design,* where the master backbone is the switch and all major connections have been connected to the network switch (thus "collapsed" into a single box). This enables expansion and traffic isolation between the networks and reduces network failure potential. If the switch is "intelligent," it further isolates traffic and may include redundant facilities to keep the switch operational in adverse conditions such as motherboard failure or power supply failure.

The master "hub" switch of the building is generally a very high-speed multinetwork concentration facility. Some hubs can support up to 36 FDDI networks (in the extended configuration) and can support T3 and asynchronous transfer mode (ATM) technologies in the same box. (See Chapter 3 for information about T3 circuits and Chapter 15 for information about ATM.) This tiered interconnection scheme using a very high-speed concentrating device is essential in developing high-speed, high-reliability networks. As is the case with other LANs, in a switched FDDI environment, the only traffic viewed by a specific FDDI is that which originates on it or is destined to it. Thus, traffic on all other FDDI segments is isolated to each individual segment by the switch. This reduces overall traffic between the segments, reduces unnecessary traffic between networks, and improves overall network performance since all connected systems do not "see" all data frames on the network. (See Chapter 6 for additional information about switches.) The master switch manages and sorts traffic between other switches so that it is sent only where it needs to go.

11.5 Interconnecting FDDI with Ethernet/802.3 or ATM Networks

Interconnecting FDDI and Ethernet/802.3 is easier than ever today, especially given the communications hub technologies available from vendors. What is normally required is an Ethernet/802.3 to FDDI bridge unit. Such bridge units are available in many varieties, including a card in a hub or a dedicated box that does nothing but interconnect the two networks. Most manufacturers of hub units produce Ethernet/802.3 and FDDI cards that allow interconnecting the two types of networks.

One thing to be careful about is the issue of frame size conversion. Frames headed from Ethernet/802.3 networks to the FDDI network are not a problem because the frame formats have nearly identical addressing and data containers. However, machines on the FDDI network that use the maximum frame size of 4500 bytes will cause the Ethernet/802.3 network to be very unhappy. Therefore, the bridge must segment the network frame when moving it from the FDDI network to the Ethernet/802.3 network. This segmenting can cause all sorts of problems. If this situation exists, we recommend that you restrict the maximum frame size generated by a FDDI system to 1500 octets of data, which will reduce the magnitude of the problem. While this decreases the efficiency of the FDDI network, the hassle of large-frame to small-frame conversion would otherwise offset any potential performance benefits.

Another option is to use a router to interconnect the two network types. The benefit here is that the router can also handle frame conversions for specific protocols and automatically segment the traffic for routable protocols such as TCP/IP, AppleTalk, Novell's IPX, DECnet, SNA, and others. The downside is that routers are usually substantially slower than switching bridges and can be quite pricey depending on the model and features.

A good example of an Ethernet/802.3-FDDI interconnected network is the Boeing 777 jetliner, which has an FDDI network that serves as its backbone with Ethernet/802.3 connections at the passenger seats. The Boeing 777 is one of the most technologically advanced commercial airplanes in the world, so it is fitting that it is delivered with advanced networks installed. Its designers implemented an MLAN (mobile local area network) consisting of two complete FDDI rings, one in the cabin and one in the cockpit. The FDDI network in the cabin is connected to Ethernet/802.3 LANs in the three compartments (economy, business class, and first class) by brouters (see Chapter 7). The purpose of these LANs is to transmit information to the multimedia units at each of the seats. The FDDI ring in the cockpit conveys data from two redundant servers to multimedia instrumentation units and navigation displays while it collects and stores maintenance information. The Litton FiberCom Avionics Bridge/Router (brouter) is the main internetworking device on the Boeing 777 aircraft. The brouter is a networking bridge that supports FDDI and Ethernet/802.3 network interfaces. It has the built-in capacity to internetwork among three dual FDDI networks, a 10BASE2 Ethernet, and two 10BASE-T Ethernet hubs with eight ports each. The brouter is designed to be the boundary device for the two main aircraft FDDI networks on the 777 aircraft: the Optical LAN (OLAN, formerly called PlaneNet) and the Cabin LAN (CABLAN). Its design also provides a Gatelink connection via the third FDDI interface. The brouter allows the aircraft maintainer easy access to the aircraft's on-board maintenance system via multiple Ethernet ports. These Ethernet ports are tapped by portable maintenance access terminals via connectors located at various points around the aircraft (wheel well ports, tail port, electronic equipment bay port, etc.). The brouter can support both software and hardware upgrades for additional capabilities (e.g., OSI, TCP/IP, IPX protocols). It is data loadable on board the aircraft via the FDDI interface to support future brouter software upgrades. If you would like to play with network configuration and deployment on a Boeing 777 jetliner, you can purchase one from Boeing for about $150 million. At that price, the networks are included.

FDDI also can interconnect with asynchronous transfer mode (ATM) networks. (See Chapter 15 for information about ATM networks.) In fact, high-speed technologies such as Cabletron's Gigaswitch and the Cisco Catalyst series of switches support not only FDDI networks but also ATM networks in the same box at the same time. The only "gotcha" with these technologies is that anytime large data frames, such as those of FDDI, must traverse an ATM network, the frames must be pared to the payload size of ATM cells, which is 44 octets. (The overall cell is 53 octets, with the remainder keeping track of such things as where the cell is going.) Taking a full 4500-octet FDDI network connection frame and chopping it up into 53 octet cells is time-consuming and demanding of the networking hardware. Therefore, even if the ATM network is faster than the FDDI (e.g., an OC-12 622-Mbps ATM connection), the effective throughput may actually be lower due to the additional processing required to "cellify" the FDDI frames to ATM and then deliver the cells to their destination. If the connection is an ATM network interconnecting two or more FDDI networks, then the workload is even greater on the link path between the two locations.

11.6 The Future of FDDI

The introduction of other faster network technologies such as Gigabit Ethernet and ATM have caused a halt to any development efforts on FDDI follow-ons. For example, a technology called FDDI-II was intended to handle not only traditional FDDI network traffic, but also synchronous, circuit-switched PCM data for voice or ISDN systems. Development has all but ceased, and no commercial systems have been deployed in the FDDI-II environment, especially given the growth of other more popular technologies such as ATM and SONET. As we mentioned earlier in this chapter, FDDI is now rarely used as a direct-system connection network platform, being primarily relegated to backbone deployments. Other network types, such as Ethernet/802.3, have impinged upon the applicability of FDDI, displacing it because of less expensive implementation, interconnection, and upgrade paths. Therefore, any implementation of an FDDI network needs an upgrade strategy to provide for the day when it will be too slow for its applications. Current network designers looking toward FDDI for expansion may find cheaper methods to provide 100-Mbps connectivity with greater longevity and expansion capabilities than FDDI.

Summarizing, although FDDI is still a viable and ubiquitous network technology, its days are numbered as less expensive IEEE 802.3 100-Mbps and 1000-Mbps systems supplant what were traditionally FDDI network environments. ATM also is encroaching on FDDI deployments with its scalability and support of isochronous transmission (used for video). FDDI still has its fans, however, and will not be leaving anytime soon–especially given its ability to provide very-high bandwidth and redundancy failover capabilities, while remaining stable for all types of networking applications.

End-of-Chapter Commentary

FDDI was one of the first "second-generation" LAN technologies designed specifically to meet the needs of users with high bandwidth requirements. Other second-generation LAN technologies discussed in this book are the various evolutions of Ethernet, including full-duplex Ethernet, switched Ethernet, Fast Ethernet, and Gigabit Ethernet (see Chapter 9). We also look at a revolutionary "Ethernet" technology called 100VG-AnyLAN, which at one time competed against Fast Ethernet for the 100-Mbps marketplace (Chapter 9). In Chapter 10, we examine some evolutionary changes to traditional 4/16-Mbps token ring networks, including dedicated token ring, switched token ring, full-duplex token ring, and 100-Mbps token ring. Finally, in Chapter 15, asynchronous transfer mode (ATM) networks are discussed from both LAN and WAN perspectives.

CHAPTER REVIEW MATERIALS

SUMMARY

- FDDI is a 100-Mbps fiber-based LAN/MAN technology that is designed as a ring topology.
- FDDI was developed expressly to meet the needs of network users who required data transmission rates greater than what was available from conventional Ethernet/802.3 and token ring networks. This was done prior to the development of Fast and Gigabit Ethernet.
- Physically, FDDI can be configured as two independent counterrotating rings that are capable of autowrapping themselves into a single ring in the event one ring fails.
- FDDI uses a group encoding scheme called 4B/5B, which takes data in four-bit codes, maps them to corresponding five-bit codes, and then transmits these five-bit codes using nonreturn to zero, invert on ones (NRZI). The 4B/5B-NRZI method requires only 20% overhead and enables FDDI to support data transmission rates of 100 Mbps at 125 MHz. This is more efficient than Manchester coding, which is used in Ethernet/802.3 LANs and requires 50% overhead.
- FDDI supports token and data frames. As is the case with token ring networks, only one token is permitted on the ring, and thus, only one node at a time is permitted to transmit data. Token frames are transformed into data frames during a data transmission.
- Although FDDI's MAC sublayer uses a token passing scheme similar to that of token ring, it does not operate in exactly the same way as a token ring network. Several key features that are different include the use of a dual counterrotating ring, no token reservation support, a maximum payload of 4500 octets per frame, the use of symbols instead of bit definitions for frame fields, and different encoding and clocking methods.
- FDDI supports two types of nodes: Class A nodes, called dual-attachment stations, are connected to both rings; Class B nodes, called single-attachment stations, are connected to only the primary ring.
- FDDI networks can be interconnected to Ethernet/802.s networks using an Ethernet/802.3-to-FDDI bridge. Given its relatively large payload size of 4500 octets, it is recommended that FDDI's payload size be restricted to 1500 bytes to minimize interoperability problems. Similarly, FDDI and ATM networks can be interconnected using switches, but once again, FDDI's large payload will have to be segmented into 53-byte cells to accommodate ATM.

VOCABULARY CHECK

autowrapping
collapsed backbone
dual-attachment station (DAS)

FDDI
nonreturn to zero, invert on ones (NRZI)
single-attachment station (SAS)

REVIEW EXERCISES

1. In what way(s) does FDDI's counterrotating rings promote network reliability?
2. Explain the concept of autowrapping relative to an FDDI network.
3. In what way(s) does FDDI's maximum frame size of 4500 bytes increase network efficiency and lower protocol overhead?
4. Describe how FDDI is able to maintain a 100-Mbps data rate at 125 MHz.
5. What advantages (if any) does FDDI's use of symbols for frame formats have over the use of bit definitions?
6. FDDI uses five-bit encoding, which implies there are a total of $2^5 = 32$ possible symbols.

Examining Table 11.1, note that only 24 symbols are listed: 16 data symbols (0–F) and 8 control signals (S, R, Q, I, H, T, J, K). In what way(s) do you think the remaining 8 symbols are used? (*Hint:* See `http://www.iol.unh.edu/training/fddi/htmls/symbols.html`.)

7. Compare the manner in which bits are transmitted on a fiber-based FDDI network to that of a copper-based FDDI network.

8. Compare and contrast the MAC sublayers of token ring and FDDI networks.

9. Describe the operation of an FDDI network.

10. What is the difference between Class A and Class B nodes?

11. When interconnecting an FDDI LAN with other networking technologies such as Ethernet/802.3 or ATM, one concern of paramount importance is frame size. Why is this a concern, what types of problems can the frame size issue cause, and how can this problem be addressed?

SUGGESTED READINGS AND REFERENCES

AMERICAN NATIONAL STANDARD. 1986a. FDDI Token Ring Physical Layer Medium Dependent PMD. *American National Standard,* ASC X3T9.5, February, rev. 7.

———. 1986b. FDDI Token Ring Media Access Control MAC. *American National Standard,* ASC X3T9.5, July, rev. 10.

———. 1986c. FDDI Token Ring Station Management SMT. *American National Standard,* ASC X3T9.5, September, rev. 12.

———. 1986d. FDDI Token Ring Physical Layer Protocol PHY. *American National Standard,* ASC X3T9.5, October, rev. 14.

BURR, W. 1986. The FDDI Optical Data Link. *IEEE Communications Magazine,* May.

COOPER. S. 1989. Joining the Next LAN Generation. *UNIX Review,* 72: 48–59.

DANIELS, G. 1990. Implementing and Managing FDDI Networks. *Networking Management,* November, 56–61.

GALLO, M., and W. HANCOCK. 1999. *Networking Explained.* Boston: Digital Press.

HANCOCK, B. 1989. *Network Concepts and Architectures.* Wellesley, MA: QED Information Sciences.

JOSHI, S. 1986. High-Performance Networks: A Focus on the Fiber Distributed Data Interface FDDI Standard. *IEEE Micro,* June.

ROSS, F. 1986. FDDI—A Tutorial. *IEEE Communications Magazine,* May.

STERLING, D. 1987. *Technicians Guide to Fiber Optics.* Albany, NY: Delmar Publishers.

THE INSTITUTE OF ELECTRICAL AND ELECTRONICS ENGINEERS. 1985a. Logical Link Control. *American National Standard ANSI/IEEE Std. 802.2.* The Institute of Electrical and Electronics Engineers.

———. 1985b. Token Ring Access Method and Physical Layer Specifications. *American National Standard ANSI/IEEE Std. 802.5.* The Institute of Electrical and Electronics Engineers.

WOLTER, M. S. 1990. Fiber Distributed Data Interface FDDI–A Tutorial. *Connexions: The Interoperability Report,* 4(10): 16–26.

———. 1991. ANSI X3T9.5 Update: Future FDDI Standards. *Connexions: The Interoperability Report,* 5(10): 21–23.

12 | Integrated Services Digital Network (ISDN)

The integrated services digital network (ISDN) represents the overhaul and redesign of our conventional telephone network from an analog system to an end-to-end digital network. This completely digital-based network is capable of transmitting voice and data communications over a single telephone line using inexpensive and conventional twisted-pair cable (i.e., standard copper telephone wire). A brief overview of various fundamental ISDN concepts was provided in Chapter 3 as part of our discussion of WAN technologies and services. In this chapter, we extend this discussion and provide more detailed information about ISDN. We begin with a brief history of ISDN and present a general overview of the technology. Section 12.2 introduces the various components of an ISDN network, including ISDN adapters and interfaces. ISDN channel types are discussed in Section 12.3, and this discussion is then expanded to include basic and primary rate interfaces (BRI and PRI) in Section 12.4. Section 12.5 provides a brief overview of ISDN protocols, including the Link Access Protocol-*D* channel (LAP-*D*). Several ISDN features, services, and applications are profiled in Section 12.6. This section also contains information about ISDN Internet connections. We conclude the chapter with information about two other ISDN initiatives: always on/ dynamic ISDN (AO/DI) and broadband ISDN (B-ISDN).

12.1 What Is ISDN?

History

The integrated services digital network is a carrier service that is offered by telephone companies (telcos) and designed to transmit voice and nonvoice (e.g., computer data, fax, video) communications on the same network. The advantage ISDN offers over other services is that separate connections are not needed for these different transmissions. Thus, instead of having a telephone line for voice communications, a second telephone line for fax or computer dialup connections, and a coaxial cable link for video communications, a single ISDN connection will support all of these transmissions. That is, ISDN *integrates* all of these services into a single system. ISDN service (and hence an ISDN connection) is completely digital from end to end. This represents both a departure from and an improvement in today's conventional telecommunication services, which use a hybrid of analog and digital technologies (Figure 12.1). Furthermore, ISDN's technology permits standard twisted-pair wiring to carry circuit- or packet-switched digital data. ISDN also provides a cost-effective strategy for internetworking. Instead of paying for dedicated leased lines, remote sites (i.e., user workstations or LANs) can interconnect with other sites via dialup links.

The advent of digital technology in the telephone industry in the 1970s marks the roots of ISDN. During this time, telcos modernized their central offices (COs) with digital switching equipment, replacing the analog-based public switched telephone network (PSTN) that was originally designed for voice transmission with one predicated on digital signaling and circuitry. What emerged was an *integrated digital network* (IDN), which engendered a vision of a network capable of transmitting any information source—voice, video, graphics, images, and text—directly to customers regardless of their location. In today's jargon, this vision was to treat all of these information

(a)

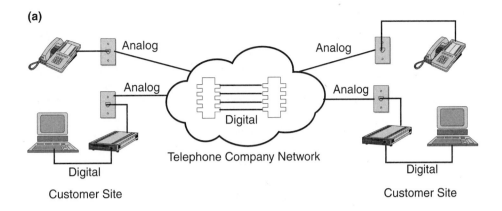

(b)

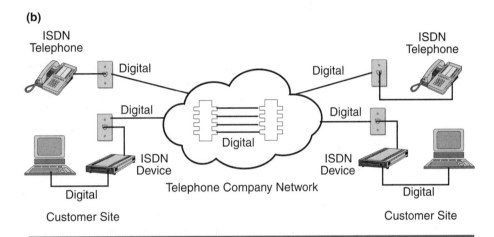

FIGURE 12.1 Today's conventional telephone network (a) is a hybrid of analog and digital technologies. Note that a computer connection requires four conversions: digital to analog from the PC, which is digital, to the customer's phone system, which is analog; analog to digital from the customer's site to the telephone company's site, which is all digital; digital to analog from the telephone company's site to the customer's site; and analog to digital from the customer's phone system to the PC. An ISDN connection (b), however, which uses special ISDN-compatible devices, is all digital from end to end. In the case of the computer connections, no digital-to-analog or analog-to-digital conversions are necessary, which result in faster connections.

sources as data, market them as services needed by businesses and consumers (e.g., videoconferencing), and then deliver these services directly to the desktop or home. There was one problem, though: Delivery of these services required end-to-end digital connectivity. Although IDN was digitally based and capable of voice, data, and video transmissions, it was not end to end. Delivery of these services was restricted because the *local loop* (the circuit between a user and the telco's nearest point of presence) was still analog. In the 1980s, standards for digital end-to-end connectivity and transmission of both voice and nonvoice services to the user were approved. This new network was named the *integrated services digital network,* or ISDN.

Standards

The development, approval, and acceptance of ISDN standards spurred widespread deployment of ISDN services throughout Europe, where the telcos were, at the time, mostly government owned. (More on this later.) In the United States, though, ISDN essentially became a product looking for a market and laid dormant for nearly 10 years. It wasn't until the Internet achieved critical mass in the mid-1990s before ISDN came to life in the United States. Given this 10-year period, from the approval of ISDN standards to its widespread availability and ultimate implementation in the United States, alternative interpretations of the ISDN acronym emerged. These included, among others, I Still Don't Need it, Innovative Services users Don't Need, I Still Don't kNow, and It's Still Doing Nothing. Today, ISDN has emerged as a viable, cost-effective solution for remote and WAN applications, and its acronym for some now represents Innovations Subscribers Do Need.

ISDN standards development is conducted under the auspices of the International Telecommunications Union (ITU), which is the former Consultative Committee for International Telephony and Telegraphy (CCITT). A subgroup of ITU, Telecommunications Standardization Section (ITU-TSS), is responsible for communications, interfaces, and other standards related to telecommunications. ITU also works in cooperation with other accredited standards committees such as the American National Standards Institute (ANSI).

The initial set of ISDN recommendations, formally called the I-series recommendations, was published by CCITT in 1984. These recommendations were published in CCITT's *Red Books,* which comprises all CCITT standards. Additional work on the I-series recommendations continued after 1984, and in 1988, an updated and more complete set of ISDN standards was incorporated into CCITT's *Blue Books.* Although subsequent updates have been made, the 1988 publication still adequately describes the basic principles and model of ISDN. A summary of the I-series recommendations is given in Table 12.1, and a copy of the ISDN model is shown in Figure 12.2.

TABLE 12.1 Summary of ISDN I-Series Recommendations

Series Number	Description
I.100	Describes the general concepts of ISDN. It addresses fundamental ISDN principles, objectives, and vocabulary.
I.200	Specifies the various services ISDN provides.
I.300	Discusses ISDN network requirements—including its architecture and addressing scheme—and specifies the manner in which an ISDN network is to provide the services described in I.200.
I.400	Addresses issues related to the user interface from the perspective of the first three layers of the OSI model. Examples include data transmission rates, hardware configurations, and data link and network layer protocols.
I.500	Discusses interconnectivity issues (e.g., interconnecting ISDN networks with non-ISDN networks).
I.600	Devoted to ISDN maintenance issues.

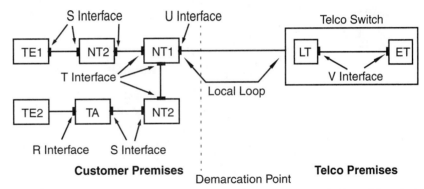

FIGURE 12.2 An ISDN reference diagram showing the relationship between ISDN equipment and interfaces. The local loop (also called the subscriber loop) is the access line between the telco's central office (CO) and the customer's site. This link is terminated at the customer's site via an NT1 device. In the United States, NT1 devices are purchased by the customer. This makes the demarcation point (the point that separates customer premises equipment from the telco equipment) the U interface. In Europe, the telcos own NT1 devices and install them on the customers' premises. In this setting, NT1 devices are considered telco equipment, and the demarcation point is now the T interface. (Source: adapted from Frank, 1995, and Leeds, 1996.)

NT1 Network Termination 1—provides connectivity between a customer's site and the telco's site. It converts the two-wire U Interface into a four-wire S/T Interface. NT1 modules can support up to eight connections (TEs, TAs, or NT2s).

NT2 Network Termination 2—converts the T interface into the S interface. NT2 provides data link and network layer functions. Connectivity to ISDN devices (TE1 or TE2) is via an S interface, and connectivity to an NT1 unit is via the T interface. An example of an NT2 device is a PBX system.

TE1 Terminal Equipment 1—an ISDN-compatible device. TE1s have built-in ISDN network interfaces and can connect directly to NT1 units via an S/T interface. Examples of TE1 devices include ISDN telephones and ISDN fax machines.

TE2 Terminal Equipment 2—a non-ISDN-compatible device. TE2s can be connected to an ISDN network via a terminal adapter (TA) through an R interface. TAs are then connected to NT2 units via an S/T interface. Examples of TE2 devices include analog telephone or fax machines and computers without an ISDN connection.

TA Terminal Adapter—provides ISDN connectivity to non-ISDN devices (TE2s).

LT Line Termination—represents the local loop connection; that is, it is where a circuit from a customer's NT1 module terminates at the telco's switch.

ET Exchange Termination—connects a telco's ISDN switch to other ISDN switches within the telco's network.

Speaking of standards, in the United States, the *regional Bell operating companies* (RBOCs)—which are now called *incumbent local exchange carriers* (ILECs) or "baby Bells"—established a national ISDN initiative to foster end user equipment interoperability. A presumption of this initiative is that any ISDN end equipment that is national ISDN-compliant should be able to connect to any telco switch. The initiative's first protocol, National ISDN-1 (NI-1), was ratified in November 1992 with a better than 80% compatibility rate. (Some RBOCs opted not to upgrade to NI-1.) The goal of subsequent protocols (e.g., NI-2) is 100% compatibility.

12.2   ISDN Components

Modules, Equipment, and Adapters

Figure 12.2 shows the basic components of an ISDN connection from the perspective of a reference or block diagram. These components, which do not necessarily correspond to actual pieces of equipment, include two types of network termination modules (NT1 and NT2), two types of terminal equipment (TE1 and TE2), and terminal adapters (TA).

The NT1 module provides the interface between the customer's premise equipment and the telco's equipment. It consists of a two-wire U interface at one end and up to seven T interfaces at the other end. Its purpose is to convert the two-wire ISDN link provided by the telco into four-wire ports that connect ISDN devices. From an OSI model perspective, NT1 is a layer-1 device since it deals with the physical and electrical termination of the circuit at the customer's site. An NT1 module also performs synchronous time division multiplexing (TDM—see Chapter 2) to combine more than one channel. (More on this later.)

The second network termination unit, NT2, is a secondary termination module that converts the T interface from the NT1 module into S interfaces that connect terminal equipment or adapters (TE or TA). An example of an NT2 unit is a *private branch exchange* (PBX), which is a telephone switching system that provides telecommunication services throughout an organization's private network. If an organization's PBX is a digital switch, which implies that the telephones connected to it are digital, then ISDN connectivity can be provided throughout the enterprise by connecting the PBX to an NT1 module. Another example of an NT2 unit is a LAN device such as a router. An NT2 module performs functions that operate up to the third layer of the OSI model.

The terminal equipment (TE) represents specific communication devices that connect to the network. Two TEs are referenced TE1 and TE2 to distinguish between compatible and incompatible ISDN equipment. TE1 examples include digital telephones and computers with built-in ISDN ports (e.g., a Sun SparcStation 10 was one of the first computers to have built-in ISDN capability). TE2 examples include analog telephones (i.e., those with RJ-11 jacks) and computers without built-in ISDN ports (e.g., RS-232C or equivalent serial ports). Most ISDN compatible devices have built-in NT2 modules and connect directly to an NT1. Some ISDN TE1 devices also have built-in NT1 and NT2 modules (sometimes referred to as NT12), with U interfaces that enable them to connect directly to the local loop. Such devices eliminate the need to purchase a separate NT1 unit. They also eliminate the capability of connecting more than one device to the network.

From a technical perspective, all ISDN devices must go through an NT2 unit.

Finally, a terminal adapter (TA) is a device that connects incompatible ISDN devices to an ISDN network. If a TA is used for an ISDN dialup connection, then it can be thought of as a modem (see Chapters 3 and 16); if a TA is used to connect a device to a LAN, then it can be thought of as a network interface card (NIC) (see Chapter 6). It should be noted that although a TA is frequently referred to as an ISDN modem or digital modem in the context of an ISDN dialup connection, this reference is incorrect. By definition, a modem performs analog-to-digital and digital-to-analog conversions.

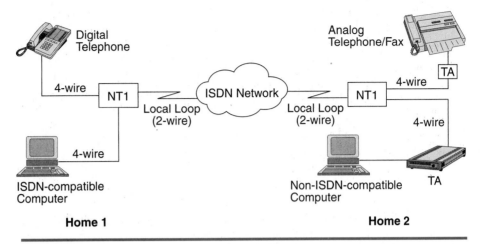

FIGURE 12.3 A home-based ISDN connection consists of a four-wire circuit that connects the home to the telco's ISDN network. This circuit physically and electrically terminates at each house's demarcation point, which is an NT1 module. All of the communication devices at home 1 have built-in NT2 modules with ISDN connector ports that provide an S/T interface to connect directly to the NT1 module. The devices at home 2, however, are not ISDN compatible. They do not comply with ISDN interface requirements and hence require terminal adapters (TA) to connect to the NT1 module. The devices at home 1 are TE1 devices; those at home 2 are TE2 devices. (The TA connected to the computer at home 2 is commonly, although incorrectly, called an ISDN modem.)

Since ISDN is completely digital, no such conversions are necessary, which makes the expressions *ISDN modem* or *digital modem* incongruous. Nevertheless, both expressions are frequently used because the general public can better relate to them than the term *terminal adapter.*

A conceptual illustration of ISDN-related components will help put the relationship among the various devices into a more concrete perspective. Figure 12.3 provides examples of two typical home-based ISDN connections. In this figure, several home-based telecommunication devices are connected to an ISDN network. The devices at home 1 are ISDN terminal equipment (TE1). They have built-in NT2 modules and ISDN ports with the proper S/T interfaces that enable them to connect directly into an NT1 module. The devices at home 2 in Figure 12.3 are not ISDN-capable. Thus, they require terminal adapters to connect to an ISDN network. These devices connect to their respective TAs via an R interface. TAs can be external units (as shown in Figure 12.3) or internal adapter cards that plug into a device's motherboard.

Interfaces

ISDN defines three primary interfaces to foster global interoperability of ISDN equipment: R, S, and T (see Figure 12.2). The U and V interfaces are U.S. specific.

The R interface provides a mechanism for non-ISDN devices to connect to an ISDN network. The ISDN device that supports the R interface is the ISDN terminal adapter, which is similar to and functions like a network interface card (see Chapter 6) or an analog modem (see Chapter 3). For example, to connect a computer to the Internet via a conventional (i.e., analog) dialup line requires either an internal or external modem. An internal modem is connected directly to the computer's logic board and provides an RJ-11 port for the telephone line, and an external modem provides two interfaces—a serial port (e.g., RS-232C or equivalent) and an RJ-11 port. To connect this same computer to an ISDN network via a dialup line, a TA is used to provide the necessary interfaces (e.g., serial and R) to connect the non-ISDN compatible computer (or other device) to an ISDN network. As we stated previously, in this capacity, a TA is often referred to as an ISDN modem or digital modem. As a completely digital service, ISDN eliminates the need for traditional modems, which perform analog-to-digital and digital-to-analog conversions. This provides extremely fast connections. For example, a traditional modem connection over analog lines requires anywhere from 30 to 60 seconds to establish a connection; an ISDN connection takes approximately 2 seconds.

The S and T interfaces are standard ISDN digital interfaces that are electronically equivalent. They are four-wire connections that partition the two-wire access line provided by the telco into separate transmit and receive lines. All ISDN-compatible equipment has S interfaces and plug directly into an NT1 module via a T interface. A distinction between these two interfaces is made because, in Europe, the T interface serves as the point of demarcation that separates the customer premises equipment (CPE) and the telco provider's equipment. In the United States, the demarcation point is the U interface. The reason for these two points of demarcation has to do with the way providers in the United States and Europe deliver ISDN service. U.S. customers are expected to purchase their own NT1 modules, which makes them CPE, whereas in Europe, NT1 modules reside at the customer's site but are owned by the telcos, which makes them part of the telco's premises equipment. NT units usually label their interfaces as S/T.

As indicated earlier, the U and V interfaces are U.S. specific. The U interface, in addition to representing the point of demarcation, is where the telco's access line from its switch is terminated at the customer's site. This access line is commonly referred to as the *local loop* or *subscriber loop*. The V interface is used to connect the exchange and line terminations (ET and LT) within an ISDN switch.

12.3   ISDN Channel Types

ISDN defines several different channel types, which provide a logical separation of user data (voice and nonvoice) from signaling and control information. ISDN uses *bearer* or *B channels* for transmitting data, and a *signaling* or *D* (delta) *channel* for transmitting signaling and control information. There is also an *H channel* that is used for transmitting user data at higher transmission rates than the *B* channel. All three channel types are discussed in the following subsections. ISDN is also a connection-oriented service, which implies that fixed virtual circuits are established between source and destination nodes. A virtual connection is first established between sender and receiver prior to transmission, the circuit remains in effect and dedicated exclusively to this session for the duration of the transmission, and the circuit is then disconnected after the transmission ends (see Chapter 2).

Although call setups between source and destination nodes are nailed up and torn down by the ISDN provider, the customer's access line (the connection between a customer's site and provider) is fixed and physical. To reduce call charges between a customer site and provider, most ISDN hardware devices support automatic dial-on-demand connections. Instead of continuously keeping the customer-provider circuit up, dial-on-demand establishes a connection only when data frames have to be transmitted. After a certain period of time (which is user configurable) in which no traffic is being transmitted from the customer's site to the provider's network, the device automatically terminates the call (hangs up). This is analogous to the way we use our telephone—whenever we need to talk to someone, we place the call; in all other situations, the phone is kept on the hook. ISDN also supports both circuit- and packet-switched connections and is an international standard based on the concepts and principles of the OSI model (see Chapter 2).

B Channel

A clear channel means no signaling information is sent on the channel.

The *B* channel is a 64-kbps clear channel used to transmit computer data (text and graphics), digitized voice, and digitized video. *B* channel transmissions are either circuit- or packet-switched. Data also can be exchanged via frame relay (Chapter 13) or through a dedicated leased line arrangement. Since ISDN uses a separate channel (the *D* channel) for signaling information, 100% of the bandwidth allocated for an ISDN *B* channel is used for data transmission. This offers an advantage over traditional T1 service where control information is in-band. For example, a 128-kbps fractional T1 line (two DS-0 circuits) provides only 112 kbps for data because 8 kbps per DS-0 channel are used for control. A 128-kbps ISDN circuit (two *B* channels), however, provides a clear 128 kbps because both *B* channels are free of any signaling overhead. (See Chapter 3 for additional information about T1 circuits.) Most basic ISDN services are based on multiple *B* channels.

D Channel

Telemetry applications involve obtaining measurements remotely and relaying them to another site for recording or display purposes.

The *D* channel is either a 16-kbps or 64-kbps channel depending on the specific service level provided. (More on this later.) It is used to carry signal and control information for circuit-switched user data. The *D* channel transmits information related to call initiation (call setup) and termination (call tear down) between an ISDN device and the telco's central office for each B channel. Thus, when a telephone call is made between two sites, the *D* channel handles all of the call-related information for the *B* channels. This is why the *B* channels are clear 64-kbps channels. The *D* channel also can be used to transmit packet-switched user data (provided that no signal or control information is needed), data from security alarm signals of remote sensing devices that detect fire or intruders, and low-speed information acquired from telemetry services such as meter reading. In a leased line configuration, no call-control information needs to be transmitted on the *D* channel.

H Channel

The *H* channel is used for transmitting user data (not signal or control information) at higher transmission rates than the *B* channel provides. Four *H* channels are defined: *H0, H10, H11,* and *H12. H0* comprises six *B* channels for a total capacity of 384 kbps. The *H10* channel is U.S. specific and aggregates 23 *B* channels for a total capacity of 1.472 Mbps. The *H11* channel is the equivalent of the North American DS-1 (see Chapter 3) and consists of 24 *B* channels for an aggregate bandwidth of 1.536 Mbps. The *H12* channel, which is European specific, comprises 30 *B* channels and has an aggregate bandwidth of 1.920 Mbps. Examples of applications that might use an *H* channel include videoconferencing, high-speed fax or high-speed packet-switched data, and high-quality audio.

12.4 Basic and Primary Rate Interfaces

B and *D* channels are generally combined (i.e., multiplexed using TDM) by ISDN service providers and offered to customers in different bundled configurations. The most common package is the $2B + D$ arrangement, which consists of two *B* channels and one *D* channel. This channel structure is known as *basic rate interface* (BRI). Two other common basic interface structures are $B + D$ and *D* only. In the BRI structure, the *D* channel is 16 kbps. A second type of channel structure is called *primary rate interface* (PRI), which has a general configuration of $nB + D$. The two most common PRIs are $23B + D$, which is equivalent to the North American DS-1 rate of 1.544 Mbps, and $30B + 2D$, which is equivalent to the European E-1 rate of 2.048 Mbps. In the PRI structure, the *D* channel is 64 kbps.

Basic Rate Interface (BRI)

Some telcos might still use older signaling software that requires ISDN signaling to be done in-band. In such instances, 8 kbps per *B* channel must be reserved for signaling, resulting in a BRI service that provides 112 kbps instead of 128 kbps.

The ISDN basic rate interface (also known as *basic access*) is a 192-bit channel that consists of two 64-kbps *B* channels, one 16-kbps *D* channel, and 48 bits of overhead used for framing and other functions. (See Figure 12.4. See also Chapter 5 for more information about framing.) The two *B* channels and the *D* channel are combined into a single pair of standard copper telephone wires. Both *B* channels can support any combination of voice or data transmissions (e.g., both voice, both data, one voice and the other data). BRI provides a full-duplex data rate of 128 kbps. If call or signal information is not being carried by the *D* channel (e.g., transmitting data via packet-switching), then the rate increases to 144 kbps if the *D* channel is carrying data. Data rates also can be increased anywhere from four to eight times more through data compression (Chapter 16).

ISDN BRI has two telephone numbers assigned to it—one for each *B* channel—and hence effectively provides consumers with two telephone lines via a single con-

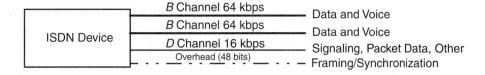

FIGURE 12.4   ISDN's basic rate interface (BRI) is a $2B + D$ package provided by the telcos. BRI consists of two 64-kbps B channels used for transmitting data or voice (or both) and one 16-kbps D channel used for transmitting signaling and control information. If no signal or control information is present, then the D channel can be used for transmitting data as well. BRI also consists of an additional 48 bits used for framing and synchronization.

nection. Thus, at home, one B channel can be used for standard voice service (except here it is digital and not analog) and the other B channel for a fax machine. Alternatively, one B channel can be for standard voice and the other B channel for an Internet connection. Also at home, the D channel can be used for telemetry services. For example, utility companies could use this channel to obtain readings from the electric, gas, or water meter.

ISDN BRI B channels, through inverse multiplexing (Chapter 2), also can be combined to form a single channel with an effective bandwidth of 128 kbps. This process is called *BONDING,* a protocol named *Bandwidth ON Demand Interoperability Network Group.* An inverse multiplexer (imux) enables the two B channels to be used simultaneously. When a standard BRI connection is first established, the receiving device negotiates various communications parameters with the sending device for the current session. In a BRI BONDING scenario, these parameters include two connections and a 128-kbps transmission rate. Once the receiving device receives and accepts these parameters, it instructs the sending device to establish a second connection by calling its second telephone number. An alignment process then occurs that effectively combines the two lines into a single channel.

Primary Rate Interface (PRI)

As noted earlier, the primary rate interface (also known as *primary access*) has two standard configurations. The first is based on the North American DS-1 (1.544-Mbps) format, and the second is based on the European E-1 (2.048-Mbps) format (see Chapter 3). PRI service is essentially the same as BRI except PRI has 23 (or 30) B channels instead of 2, and PRI's D channel operates at 64 kbps instead of 16 kbps (Figure 12.5). Unlike BRI, which is appropriate for the home or small office, PRI is more appropriate for organizations that have to provide telecommunication services to a large number of sites. For example, large corporations with various satellite offices or remote sites, corporations with PBXs, and Internet service providers are more likely to subscribe to PRI service than to BRI. With PRI, it is possible to have up to 23 (or 30) separate, independent, simultaneous ISDN connections.

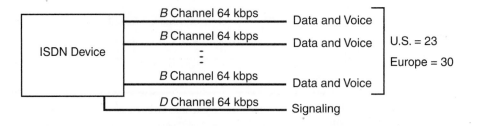

FIGURE 12.5 ISDN's primary rate interface (PRI) is packaged in two forms. The first is a 23*B* + *D* configuration, which is based on the North American DS-1 format and rated at 1.544 Mbps. The second is a 30*B* + 2*D* configuration, which is based on the European E-1 format and rated at 2.048 Mbps.

12.5 ISDN Protocols

Overview

ISDN relies on many different protocols, all of which conform to the layers of the OSI model. These protocols are defined in the ISDN I-series (see Table 12.1)—specifically the I.400 series—and are applicable to the first three layers of the OSI model. At the physical layer, the physical interfaces for both BRI and PRI are specified in I.430 and I.431. These specifications are applicable to *B, D,* and *H* channels. At the data link layer, the *D* channel is based on the ITU-T standard, Q.921, known as the *Link Access Protocol-D channel* (LAP-D). The *B* and *H* channels rely on frame relay protocols (see Chapter 13) for circuit-switched connections and an X.25 protocol called *Link Access Protocol-Balanced* (LAP-B) for packet-switched connections. At the network layer, the *D* channel relies on the ITU-T standard, Q.931, for call control, and X.25 protocols for packet data. The *B* and *H* channels also use X.25 protocols for packet-switched connections. No layer-3 protocols are necessary for circuit-switched connections. A summary is given in Table 12.2. (See Appendix E for more information about X.25.)

From Table 12.2, note that the *D* channel uses different protocols at layers 2 and 3 than *B* and *H* channels. This is because the *D* channel is a multipurpose channel. It is used for call setup and call tear down when the *B* channel is used to transmit circuit-switched user data. If no signaling or control information is needed—for example, a dedicated leased line connection is used or the *B* channel is transmitting packet-switched user data—then the *D* channel can be used to transmit packet-switched user data as well. Finally, the *D* channel can be used to transmit information from telemetry services. These applications require different protocols at the data link and network layers than the *D* and *H* channels, which simply transmit circuit- or packet-switched data.

TABLE 12.2 Summary of ISDN Protocols

OSI	D Channel			B and H Channels	
Layer	Call-control	Packet Data	Telemetry	Circuit-switched	Packet-switched
3	ITU-T Q.931 / I.451	X.25 Protocols	——	N/A	X.25 Protocols
2	ITU-T Q.921 / (LAP-D) I.441			Frame Relay Protocols	LAP-B
1	ISDN I-series: 1.430 (BRI) and 1.431 (PRI)			ISDN I-series: 1.430 (BRI) and 1.431 (PRI)	

Source: adapted from Stallings, 1997.

Link Access Protocol-*D* Channel (LAP-D)

The frame format for the Link Access Protocol for *D* channel is shown in Figure 12.6. Note that the frame carries encapsulated layer-3 data (information field). Following is a brief explanation of the various fields:

Flag—Signals the beginning or ending of the frame.

Address—Provides addressing information. The service access point identifier (SAPI) identifies where the layer-2 protocol provides service to layer 3. Specific addresses identify specific services. For example SAPI = 16 is for X.25 packet data transmissions. The command/response (C/R) bit specifies whether the frame is a command or response. The extended address (EA) bits specify the beginning and ending of the address field. If EA is 0, then another byte of address information follows. An EA of 1 implies that the current byte is the last byte of the address. Thus, given a two-byte address, EA = 0 in the higher-order byte and EA = 1 in the lower-order byte. The terminal endpoint identifier (TEI) represents the specific address or ID assigned to each ISDN terminal equipment connected to an ISDN network via an S/T interface.

Control—Provides layer-2 control information (e.g., specifies the type of frame being transmitted, maintains frame sequence numbers).

Information—Provides layer-3 protocol information and user data. The protocol discriminator (PD) identifies the specific layer-3 protocol. The length (L) byte specifies the length of the CRV field, which is either one or two bytes. The call reference value (CRV) is the number assigned to each call. Once a call is completed, this number can be reassigned to a new call. Message type (MT) identifies specific messages related to circuit-switched connections. For example, during call setup, the message CONNECT indicates that the receiving terminal equipment end node has accepted a call by the initiating TE. When a call has been completed, the message RELEASE COMPLETE is sent to indicate that the channel has been torn down (call tear down). The mandatory and optional information elements (MOIE) field carries additional information specific to the message type being transmitted.

CRC—Provides for data integrity (error control) via CRC checksums.

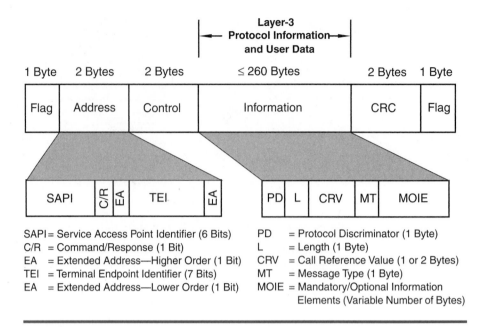

SAPI = Service Access Point Identifier (6 Bits)
C/R = Command/Response (1 Bit)
EA = Extended Address—Higher Order (1 Bit)
TEI = Terminal Endpoint Identifier (7 Bits)
EA = Extended Address—Lower Order (1 Bit)

PD = Protocol Discriminator (1 Byte)
L = Length (1 Byte)
CRV = Call Reference Value (1 or 2 Bytes)
MT = Message Type (1 Byte)
MOIE = Mandatory/Optional Information Elements (Variable Number of Bytes)

FIGURE 12.6 Frame format of ISDN's Link Access Protocol-*D* channel (LAP-D). Note that the information field contains encapsulated layer-3 data.

12.6 ISDN Features, Services, and Applications

Service Profile Identification (SPID) Numbers

The telephone numbers assigned to ISDN *B* channels have *service profile identification* (SPID) numbers associated with them. SPIDs are provided by the telcos and are usually defined by adding a prefix, a suffix, or both (it depends on the telco's switch) to an assigned telephone number. For example, assume the number assigned to a *B* channel is 4075551469. If the telco uses a prefix of 05, then the SPID is 054075551469. SPIDs are used to identify the various processes of an ISDN device. By assigning a SPID to a device, the telco's ISDN switch can identify the processes associated with each device. This prevents contention among the processes. Thus, each device connected to an ISDN line must be assigned a unique SPID. Normally, if only one ISDN device is connected, a SPID is not needed. However, if more than one ISDN device is connected, then SPIDs are required. Some ISDN equipment manufacturers support an auto-SPID function that acquires the telco's assigned SPID to a particular connection and configures the end equipment automatically.

> SPIDs are used only in North America.

Line and Feature Sets

The term *line set* is used by the North American ISDN Users' Forum (NIUF), which is an organization that provides users with a voice in the implementation of ISDN applica-

See http://sup-
port.intel.com/
support/isdn and
http://www.niuf
.nist.gov

tions. Line set describes two specific characteristics of ISDN service: the number of multiplexed B and D channels and the type of service supported. For example, line set 1 specifies a D configuration that supports packet-switched data transmissions on a single D channel. Line set 4 specifies a $1B$ configuration that supports alternate voice and data transmissions on a single B channel. Line set 27 specifies a $2B + D$ configuration that supports alternate voice and data on two B channels and packet-switched data transmissions on the D channel.

Associated with each line set is a *feature set,* which identifies specific ISDN features that can be ordered as part of the service. ISDN supports various telephone-related services including call forwarding, calling number identification (i.e., caller ID), call transfer, call waiting, and call hold. These services are similar to their non-ISDN counterparts that are offered through the telcos. There is one exception, though. With call waiting, when a second call comes in, you do not get interrupted, as is the case with non-ISDN call waiting. This is because the D channel handles all the call control information, keeping it separate from the B channels. Additional information about line and feature sets can be acquired via http://www.niuf. nist.gov/docs/428-94.pdf

Teleservices

ISDN also supports several teleservices, including capability for 64-kbps Group IV fax, teletext, and videotex. *Teletext* and *videotex* are electronic information utilities that use computers or standard television sets equipped with adapters to display information. Teletext is a one-way communication system; videotex is a two-way (i.e., interactive) system. Teletext broadcasts data as part of a television signal; videotex uses cable television or telephone lines to transmit data. Typical applications available from these services include information retrieval (news, weather, sports, access to medical databases), electronic transactions (airline reservations, electronic funds transfer, shop-at-home services), interpersonal messaging (e-mail), computing, and telemonitoring (remote sensing, telemetry services). Clearly, many of these applications are now available via the Internet's World Wide Web. However, teletext and videotex services have been available in countries such as France, Canada, and Great Britain since the early 1980s. Furthermore, trials of these two services were conducted in the United States during the 1983–1984 time period. Examples include Videotron by Knight-Ridder Newspapers in southeastern Florida, Keyfax by Keycom Electronic Publishing in Chicago, and Gateway by Times Mirror Videotex Services in southern California in 1984.

ISDN versus Regular Phone Service

An ISDN telephone can be used to call someone whose phone service is provided by the analog-based plain old telephone system (POTS). The reverse is also true. However, we will not be able to achieve high-quality connect sessions because only one part of the connection is digital; the other is analog. Thus, there will not be any improvement in line performance. As for any differences in telephones, ISDN telephone sets have many more built-in functions and capabilities than conventional analog phones. Aside from that, both types of phones function similarly, with one exception. The analog-based

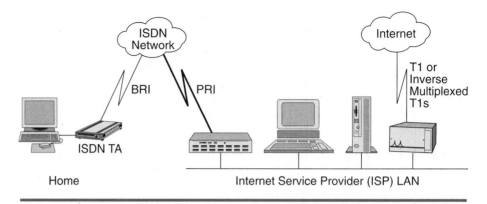

FIGURE 12.7   A typical home-based ISDN Internet connection consists of a BRI connection from the home to the telco's ISDN network and a PRI connection between the ISP and the telco's ISDN network. The entire connection, from home to ISP, is completely digital. Home-based ISDN Internet connections are an alternative to conventional analog dialup connections using 28.8-kbps or 56-kbps modems.

POTS provides power to its telephones, which is why the telephone system is still able to operate during power outages. This is not the case with ISDN, which does not provide power to its telephones (or to any ISDN terminal equipment). Thus, unless the ISDN TE is protected by an uninterruptable power supply (UPS) or its equivalent, a power outage will also bring down your telephone connection.

ISDN and the Internet

Undoubtedly, the services and capabilities available via the Internet today make ISDN less attractive. There is no need to subscribe to ISDN simply to have information retrieval, electronic transaction, or interpersonal messaging capabilities. All of these applications, and more, are available via the Web. Even ISDN's telephone-related services are now available for analog telephones via the telcos. Nevertheless, ISDN has become quite popular as an Internet dialup alternative to traditional analog modem service. A dialup ISDN Internet connection requires ISDN service for both the user and the Internet service provider. This is usually BRI for the home and PRI for the ISP. At home, an ISDN terminal adapter is needed for any computer that does not have a built-in ISDN port. At the ISP side, an ISDN communications server (or equivalent) is needed to support remote ISDN connections. The ISP link to the Internet is generally a T1 circuit, inverse multiplexed T1 circuits, or T3 or fractional T3 circuits. This is illustrated in Figure 12.7.

Many people are subscribing to ISDN, not for its applications, but because it provides a faster gateway to the Internet. For example, an ISDN BRI service, with BONDING, provides a 128-kbps connection. With compression, this connection increases to over 500 kbps. Compared to a 56-kbps modem, which provides a data transmission rate of over 200 kbps with compression, an ISDN connection wins out. Furthermore, if the

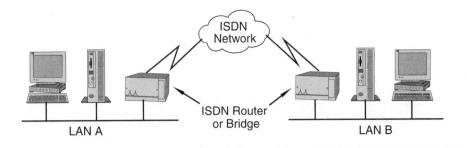

FIGURE 12.8 ISDN can be used for LAN-to-LAN connectivity. To reduce call charges, a dial-on-demand feature available in most ISDN routers and bridges will automatically call the telco's ISDN switch only when data need to be transmitted. When no traffic is seen on the port, the router or bridge will then hang up the call. This setup is exactly the same that is used for connecting a LAN to the Internet. The only difference is that one of the LANs would have a link to the Internet, as shown in Figure 12.7.

end user equipment supports Multilink PPP (MP), both *B* channels can be combined into a single 128-kbps channel. MP (formally called *Multilink Point-to-Point Protocol*) is an alternative to BONDING. It aggregates two or more *B* channels and runs PPP across these multiple *B* channels. MP is an IP protocol that combines multiple physical links (i.e., telephone lines) into a single high-capacity channel. The development of this protocol was precipitated by the desire to aggregate multiple ISDN *B* channels. Unlike BONDING, which is implemented in hardware, MP is achieved via software. MP is also applicable to analog dialup connections. For example, if each of three separate phone lines is connected to 33.6-kbps modems, then MP can aggregate these lines into a single 100.8-kbps channel. Both ISDN and analog MP solutions are supported by various Internet service providers. Thus, if your ISP offers MP dialup service, then you too can achieve higher-capacity connections to the Internet. For more information about MP, see RFC 1990.

> Although PPP is normally associated with IP, it nevertheless is a general purpose link layer protocol that supports several upper-layer protocols.

LAN-to-LAN Connections

ISDN is also ideal for the small office/home office (SOHO). With an NT1 module, you can connect a fax machine, a computer, and your telephone directly to an ISDN network via a single connection. Furthermore, if two *B* channels are inadequate, ISDN's flexible packaging scheme enables you to purchase additional *B* channels. ISDN also provides LAN-to-LAN connectivity, enabling an organization's remote LANs to be connected to each other or to its corporate LAN (Figure 12.8). This implementation of ISDN is a cost-effective solution if remote sites do not have to be in continuous communication with one another. If this is not the situation, then frame relay is a better alternative because ISDN phone charges can become exorbitant. Even in situations where frame relay is used for LAN-to-LAN communication, though, ISDN still can play a role. ISDN has proven to be an effective backup strategy to frame relay (see Chapter 13). ISDN can also be integrated with frame relay using fall-back switches. If the frame relay network fails, the ISDN network automatically takes over. Although the transmission rate is less than what is available via frame relay, it nevertheless keeps the data flowing. Finally, ISDN provides affordable desktop-to-desktop videoconferencing. So you see, there are several niche applications that can be filled quite nicely by ISDN.

12.7   Other ISDN Initiatives

Always On/Dynamic ISDN

Always on/dynamic ISDN (AO/DI) is an initiative from the Vendor's ISDN Association (VIA). The concept of AO/DI is to use a portion of the *D* channel, which is always active and constantly connected to the provider's switch, to transmit user packet data. Given that most ISDN implementations assess a charge whenever a *B* channel is active—usually so much per minute for every minute the link is up—keeping a channel up can be quite expensive. For example, a 5-cent per minute charge translates to $3 per hour, which is $72 per day. With AO/DI, transmitting user data across the *D* channel is free.

AO/DI uses 9600 bps of the *D* channel's 16-kbps capacity; the remaining bandwidth (6400 bps) is used for control and signaling information. If user data transmission rates exceed the 9600 bps reserved for AO/DI, then one of the *B* channels is automatically activated (i.e., a circuit-switched connection is established) to carry the load, and the *D* channel assumes its normal role of providing control and signaling information. If additional capacity is required, then Multilink PPP is used to automatically activate and combine the second *B* channel with the first to get an aggregate bandwidth of 128 kbps. Once bandwidth requirements drop to the point where neither *B* channel is needed, then the channels automatically become inactive, and the *D* channel resumes its low-capacity packet data transmission function. Thus, you can receive data without paying for any *B* channel usage until one of the *B* channels becomes active.

The primary application of AO/DI is transmitting IP packets. This offers several advantages to end users. For example, AO/DI provides users with a free, permanent connection to the Internet. As long as the IP packet transmissions can be carried satisfactorily via a 9600-bps link, then the connection is free. Examples of such transmissions include e-mail, small text files, stock quotes, and sports and headline news information. Furthermore, since the connection is permanent, users do not have to make a manual connection to the Internet every time they want to check for e-mail or stock quotes. AO/DI is also appealing to telcos because it reduces the number of *B* channels they have to nail up.

The telcos might assess a nominal monthly charge for AO/DI service, though, since it will be considered part of ISDN's feature set.

AO/DI was deployed in early 1998, and AO/DI products are available from major Internet equipment manufacturers. Implementing AO/DI requires that both your telco and ISP support it. Your ISP also must have a connection to the telco's X.25 network because *D* channel packet data transmissions are carried via the telco's X.25 network (see Table 12.2). Packets are first transmitted from the end user to the telco via the *D* channel, where they are placed on the telco's X.25 network and transmitted to the ISP. The ISP then transmits these packets to their destination via the Internet. Similarly, packets arriving from the Internet are transmitted to the telco via the ISP's X.25 net-

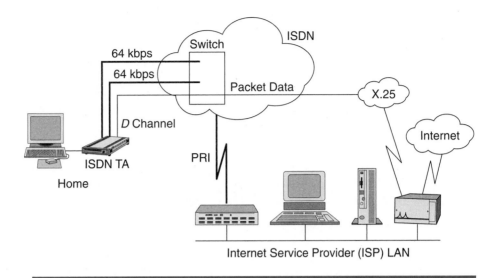

FIGURE 12.9 Always on/dynamic ISDN (AO/DI) is ideal for Internet applications. Implementing AO/DI at home requires AO/DI support from both the telco and ISP. Furthermore, the ISP must have a connection to the telco's X.25 network because this is the network that handles *D* channel packet data transmissions.

work connection. From there, the telco transmits the packets to the end user across the *D* channel (Figure 12.9).

In short, AO/DI represents a technology that satisfies users and telcos. Users, at best, get free service and, at worst, reduce the cost of their service. Telcos, on the other hand, still get to provide the service, but their switches become less saturated because the amount of *B* channel transmissions is reduced. AO/DI is a win-win solution for everyone.

Broadband ISDN

Broadband ISDN (B-ISDN) is an extension of ISDN, which is sometimes called *narrowband ISDN* (N-ISDN). B-ISDN provides full-duplex data transmission at OC-12 rates (622.08 Mbps) and is designed for delivery of two primary types of services: interactive services (e.g., videoconferencing and video surveillance) and distribution services (e.g., cable TV and high-definition TV). B-ISDN is also the basis for ATM (see Chapter 15). The topic of broadband is discussed in Chapter 18 on convergence.

End-of-Chapter Commentary

In this chapter, we presented an overview of ISDN. Many of the concepts discussed can be found in other chapters throughout this book. For example, a discussion of circuit- and packet-switching, as well as information about standards organizations, is given in Chapters 1 and 2. The concepts of bandwidth and channel capacity are discussed in Chapter 2. Issues related to the data link layer are discussed in Chapter 5, and Chapter 8 contains information about the Internet. ISDN also serves as the basis for other WAN technologies and services, including frame relay, which is the subject of the next chapter (Chapter 13), SMDS (see Chapter 14), and ATM (see Chapter 15). Chapter 16 presents information about home networking and examines various networking strategies (e.g., 56K modems, cable modems) relative to ISDN. Finally, Chapter 18 provides information about broadband ISDN from the perspective of convergence technologies.

CHAPTER REVIEW MATERIALS

SUMMARY

• ISDN is an end-to-end digital network capable of transmitting both voice and nonvoice data, including video, fax, and computer communications. Although developed in the 1970s, ISDN did not gain acceptance in the United States until the Internet was commercialized. Today, ISDN is used as a fast connection to the Internet, provides a cost-effective solution for connecting remote sites, and serves as an effective backup service for frame relay.

• ISDN connections involve network termination modules (NT1 and NT2), terminal equipment (TE1 and TE2), and terminal adapters (TAs). NT1s connect customer premise equipment to the ISDN network, and NT2s provide a connection point for TEs and TAs. Terminal equipment consists of network devices such as telephones and computers. TE1s are ISDN-compatible; TE2s are not ISDN-compatible and require TAs for connectivity.

• ISDN defines several different interfaces, which enable global interoperability of ISDN devices. The R interface is used in TAs to provide connectivity to non-ISDN devices. The S interface provides direct connectivity between TE1s and NT1s, which support a T interface. S and T interfaces are electronically equivalent and are typically designated as S/T. In the United States, two additional ISDN interfaces are defined. The U interface represents the point of demarcation and terminates the ISDN carrier's switch at the customer site; the V interface connects ISDN lines within a switch.

• ISDN supports three different channel types: B channels are clear 64-kbps channels that transmit user data; D channels are either 16-kbps or 64-kbps channels that carry signal and control information; and H channels transmit user data at higher transmission rates than B channels—$H0$ comprises 6 B channels, $H10$ channel is U.S. specific and aggregates 23 B channels, $H11$ channel is the equivalent of the North American DS-1 and consists of 24 B channels, and $H12$ channel is European specific and comprises 30 B channels.

• ISDN BRI service consists of two B channels and one D channel multiplexed into a $2B + D$ package. ISDN PRI service commonly consists of either a $23B + D$ package (North America) or a $30B + 2D$ package (Europe). The BRI D channel is 16 kbps; the PRI D channel is 64 kbps. The two BRI B channels can be combined into a single 128-kbps BONDED channel. An alternative to BONDING is Multilink PPP, which aggregates two or more B channels for PPP connections.

• ISDN protocols are defined in the ISDN I-series and represent the first three layers of the OSI model. Layer 1 defines the B, D, and H channel physical interfaces. D channel layer-2 specifications are defined by LAP-D; B and H channel layer-2 specifications are defined by frame relay protocols for circuit-switched connections and LAP-B for packet-switched connections. At layer 3, all three channels rely on X.25 protocols for packet-switched connections. The D channel also uses a separate protocol for call control at this layer.

• In North America, ISDN B channels are assigned SPID numbers, which identify specific processes associated with an ISDN device.

- ISDN supports line sets and feature sets. A line set identifies the specific configuration bundle of *B* and *D* channels and describes the type of service this package supports. A feature set identifies specific ISDN features such as call waiting or caller ID that are part of the service. ISDN also supports teletext and videotex, which provide electronic services comparable to what is available via the Internet's World Wide Web.
- A relatively new ISDN initiative is AO/DI, which takes advantage of the *D* channel's "always on" feature. Using a portion (9600 bps) of the *D* channel's bandwidth, AO/DI enables the ISDN provider to transmit user data at no cost to the subscriber. If the transmission rate exceeds 9600 bps, then one of the *B* channels is automatically activated.
- B-ISDN is designed for broadband services such as videoconferencing and provides full-duplex service at OC-12 rates.

VOCABULARY CHECK

always on/dynamic ISDN (AO/DI)
B channel
basic rate interface (BRI)
BONDING
broadband ISDN (B-ISDN)
D channel
H channel

integrated services digital network (ISDN)
Link Access Protocol-*D* channel (LAP-D)
local loop
Multilink PPP (MP)
primary rate interface (PRI)

service profile identification (SPID)
terminal adapter (TA)
terminal equipment (TE)

REVIEW EXERCISES

1. What advantages does an all-digital connection provide ISDN subscribers over a conventional analog–digital hybrid connection?
2. Speculate why you think it took 10 years for ISDN to achieve widespread deployment in the United States but was almost immediately embraced in Europe. What impact do you think the Internet would have had on U.S. society if ISDN gained widespread acceptance in the 1980s as it did in Europe?
3. What purpose does all the various ISDN interfaces provide and why are there so many of them?
4. Revisit the concepts of circuit- and packet-switching from Chapter 2 and briefly describe their advantages and disadvantages relative to ISDN.
5. Describe the differences among ISDN *B, D,* and *H* channels.
6. In ISDN terminology, the prefix kilo (k) implies $10^3 = 1000$ and not $2^{10} = 1024$. Thus, a 64-kbps channel has a data transmission rate

of 64,000 bits per second and not 65,536 bits per second. This confusion in terminology was addressed by the International Electrotechnical Commission (IEC), which approved in December 1998 a new set of standard names and symbols for binary multiple prefixes commonly used in the data processing and data transmission fields. (IEC is the leading international organization for worldwide standardization in electrotechnology.) See http:// physics.nist.gov/cuu/Units/binary. html for more information and prepare a report that describes this new standard.
7. Provide examples of the type of signaling information handled by ISDN *D* channels.
8. Explain the concept of BONDING relative to ISDN.
9. What function do ISDN *H* channels provide?
10. Describe the primary differences between ISDN BRI and PRI services.
11. Although only two *B* channels are available via a BRI connection, it is possible for the

connection to support more than two calls. How do you think this is handled?

12. Besides cost, what do you think is one of the primary benefits of PRI service?

13. How would you classify ISDN relative to the OSI model? For example, does ISDN operate at layers 1, 2, and 3 or is it simply a physical layer technology? Defend your response.

14. What role does the TEI and SAPI fields of an LAP-D frame play relative to an ISDN connection?

15. Describe some of the features that ISDN service provides relative to conventional telephone service.

16. Compare ISDN service to 56K modem service (see Chapters 3 and 16) relative to the following: synchronous versus asynchronous communications, fax service, and analog–digital conversions.

17. What advantage(s) does multilink PPP have over BONDING?

18. Describe the concept of AO/DI.

SUGGESTED READINGS AND REFERENCES

ALVICH-LOPINTO, M. 1990. Piecing Together the ISDN Puzzle. *Today's Office,* October, 21–23.

ATKINS, J., and M. NORRIS. 1995. *Total Area Networking: ATM, Frame Relay and SMDS Explained.* New York: Wiley.

BATES, R. J., and D. GREGORY. 1998. *Voice and Data Communications Handbook.* New York: McGraw-Hill.

BIRENBAUM, E. 1994. A Trio of Access Devices Aggregates ISDN. *Data Communications,* June, 147–148.

BROWN, D. 1996. Blazing with Inverse Multiplexed ISDN. *Network Computing,* 1 December, 164–167.

CRANE, E., and R. RAUCCI. 1995. Going Digital. *Open Computing,* February, 93–94.

DORTCH, M. 1990. UNIX and ISDN: Partners on the Same Line. *UNIXWorld,* 55–59.

DURR, M. 1994. ISDN Reemerges. *LAN Magazine,* January, 103–112.

FITZGERALD, S. 1994. Global Warming: ISDN Heats Up. *LAN Magazine,* June, 50–55.

FOGLE, D., and A. FRANK. 1996. The Ascent of ISDN. *LAN,* March, 120–125.

FRANK, A. 1995. Lesson 82: The ISDN Connection. *LAN Magazine,* June, 21–22.

———. 1998. Lesson 117: Always On/Dynamic ISDN (AO/DI). *Network Magazine,* April, 23–24.

GALLO, M., and W. HANCOCK. 1999. *Networking Explained.* Boston: Digital Press.

HURWICZ, M. 1996. On-Line from a LAN. *LAN,* May, 85–90.

JOHNSTON-TURNER, M. 1991. Evaluating ISDN Options. *Network World,* 18 March, 40.

LEEDS, F. 1996. Plugging in to ISDN. *LAN,* April, 93–96.

LEVITT, J. 1993. Speed Is Only One Benefit of Installing an ISDN Link. *Open Systems Today,* 23 January, 1.

MILLER, K. 1994. ISDN and Internetworking: Made for Each Other? *Data Communications,* February, 23–24.

MOSKOWITZ, R. 1996. Bracing for the Last and Longest Mile Home. *Network Computing,* 1 April, 35–36.

PARNELL, T. 1997. *LAN Times Guide to Wide Area Networks.* Berkeley, CA: Osborne McGraw-Hill.

PETROSKY, M. 1992. Momentum Builds for ISDN as a Data Pipe. *LAN Technology,* August, 15–17.

QUIAT, B. 1994. V.FAST, ISDN or Switched 56: Which Remote Solution Is the Right One? *Network Computing,* 1 March, 70–87.

ROBERTSON, B. 1993. Telecommuting via ISDN: Out of Sight, Not Out of Range. *Network Computing,* July, 134–138.

———. 1994. Choose an ISDN Flavor: NIC or Digital Modem. *Network Computing,* 1 September, 174–176.

————, and J. NEWMAN. 1995. ISDN Does It All! *Network Computing,* 1 May, 62–80.

SCHNAIDT, P. 1993. Lesson 55: An ISDN Issue. *LAN Magazine,* March, 24–25.

STALLINGS, W. 1991. Broadband ISDN: A Standards Update. *Network World,* 18 March, 49–52.

————. 2000. *Data and Computer Communications.* 6th ed. Upper Saddle River, NJ: Prentice-Hall.

UBOIS, J. 1993. The Big Pipe. *SunWorld,* November, 86–91.

WILLIS, D., and J. NEWMAN. (1996). ISDN: Prime for the Enterprise. *Network Computing,* 15 May, 45–65.

WROBEL, L. 1997a. ISDN: Innovations Subscribers Do Need—Part I. *Technical Support,* April, 41–44.

————. 1997b. ISDN: Innovations Subscribers Do Need—Part II. *Technical Support,* May, 34–38.

13

Frame Relay

In this chapter, we examine the various concepts related to frame relay from both conceptual and technical perspectives. We begin the chapter by explaining frame relay's origins. In Section 13.2, we examine the various type of circuits available with frame relay connections. These include private and switched virtual circuits, as well as the concept of committed information rates applied to these circuits. Section 13.3 provides a technical overview of frame relay. This overview comprises frame relay's basic operation as well as a discussion of several frame relay data link layer issues, including the structure of frame relay frames, congestion control, and link management. The last section of the chapter presents some miscellaneous information about frame relay. This includes transmitting voice via frame relay, a comparison of frame relay to competing LAN-to-LAN technologies such as SMDS and ATM, and two high-profile frame relay events that made the news.

13.1   What Is Frame Relay?

Frame relay is a public WAN packet-switching protocol that provides LAN-to-LAN connectivity. Its name implies what it does, namely, relays frames across a network between two sites. Frame relay was originally part of the ISDN standard. As we noted in Chapter 12, ISDN was developed in the 1970s to eventually replace the public switched telephone network (PSTN). As part of its development, ISDN was designed to provide both voice and data service. Although ISDN was considered a significant improvement to the PSTN, it was still an evolution of the PSTN and hence was circuit-switched. This did not bode well for providing data applications efficiently. If data applications were going to be supported in an efficient manner, then a packet-switching component needed to be included with the ISDN standard. (See Chapter 2 for additional information about circuit- and packet-switching.) The only packet-switching technology available at the time was X.25. This technology, however, did not support the ISDN model of keeping user data separate from control data. Consequently, frame relay was developed specifically as a packet-switching technology component of ISDN for data applications. (See Appendix E for more information about X.25.)

Prior to frame relay's development, LANs were primarily interconnected by dedicated (i.e., private) leased lines using point-to-point protocols or X.25. This design was acceptable if only one or two LANs required interconnectivity. However, as internetworking became more prevalent, multiport routers were needed to provide multi-LAN connectivity, and additional dedicated leased lines had to be installed (Figure 13.1a). LAN-to-LAN connectivity became a more expensive endeavor with the addition of each dedicated circuit. These costs were further escalated, and the network design became more complex, especially when a partially or fully meshed network design was needed (Figures 13.1b and 13.1c). Since frame relay's role in ISDN was to provide connectivity between routers, ISDN developers realized that traditional LAN-to-LAN connectivity costs could be reduced substantially if frame relay is used in place of dedicated leased lines. What frame relay provides is a single connection into a public network instead of multiple interconnections (Figure 13.2). This reduces both the cost and complexity of the network, especially in a fully meshed

In a fully connected network, the number of links is always one fewer than the number of interconnected nodes or LANs. Thus, if five LANs are fully interconnected, then each LAN requires four links.

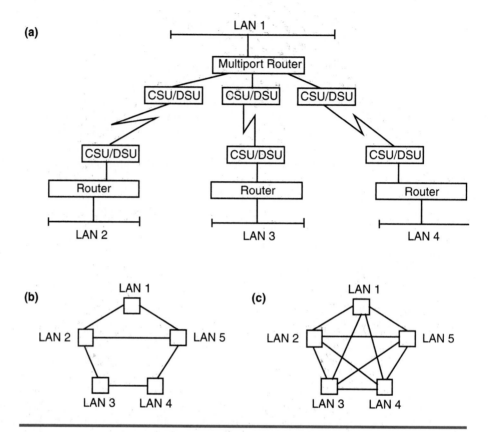

FIGURE 13.1 In a standard private line network, at least one circuit is required for LAN-to-LAN connectivity. Several topologies are possible including (a) a star configuration, (b) a partially meshed configuration, and (c) a fully meshed configuration. Note that the star configuration is the least expensive because only one LAN requires a multiport router and multiple circuits. All other LANs require a single-port router and one circuit. This configuration is also the least reliable because it has a single source of failure. An improvement in reliability calls for partially meshed or fully meshed designs. These topologies significantly increase the cost and complexity of the overall network design, though, because more than one LAN requires multiport routers and multiple circuits for LAN interconnectivity. Source: adapted from Fitzgerald & Kraft, 1993.

design. For example, in the frame relay configuration shown in Figure 13.3, each LAN only needs one link into the cloud for full interconnectivity among the five LANs. In a comparable fully meshed private leased line network, each LAN would require four links (Figure 13.1c). Furthermore, unlike traditional private leased line service, frame relay's circuit costs are not distance based, and the circuits themselves do not necessarily have to be permanent. This led to frame relay being offered and further developed as a separate protocol.

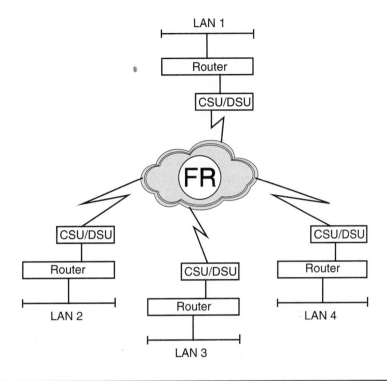

FIGURE 13.2 In a frame relay network, a single access into a frame relay "cloud" is all that is required. This simplifies the network design and makes it a less expensive endeavor.

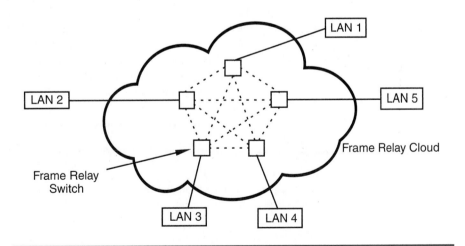

FIGURE 13.3 Frame relay provides a single connection into a public network instead of multiple connections. This translates into considerable savings in connectivity cost as well as complexity in network design, maintenance, and analysis.

13.2   Frame Relay Circuits

In a black-and-white networking world, there are only two types of telecommunications links: private and virtual. Private links (also commonly referred to as standard leased lines) provide dedicated connectivity between two sites. Virtual links, on the other hand, are shared among several sites. Frame relay is a connection-oriented protocol that employs virtual links. (See Chapter 2 for additional information about virtual circuits.) As a connection-oriented protocol, frame relay must first establish a connection before two nodes can communicate. Instead of establishing and maintaining a permanent, dedicated link between a source and destination, frame relay relies on *permanent virtual circuits* (PVCs) to interconnect two sites. Thus, PVCs establish a logical connection between two sites instead of a physical one. This is what distinguishes a frame relay network from one that uses standard leased lines. Through the use of virtual circuits, data from multiple sites can be transmitted over the same link concurrently. Frame relay also supports *switched virtual circuits* (SVCs), which enable circuits between source and destination nodes to be established dynamically. Let's examine these circuit types separately.

Permanent Virtual Circuit (PVC)

When first reading the description of a permanent virtual circuit, it is sometimes confusing trying to distinguish a PVC from a private leased line because both appear to use permanent circuits. PVCs do indeed have a predetermined link between a source and destination just as private leased lines. In fact, PVCs appear as private circuits because frame relay, as a connection-oriented protocol, must first establish circuits (i.e., "nail them up") between end nodes prior to data communications. The difference is that PVCs are virtual circuits, not dedicated ones. This means that the bandwidth is shared among multiple sites instead of being dedicated between two sites. Thus, PVCs provide nondedicated connections through a shared medium. This is done by multiplexing a physical link so that it can be shared by multiple data transmissions (see Chapter 2).

Here's an example. When you subscribe to frame relay service from your telecommunications carrier, a PVC is assigned between your LAN and all of your organization's other LANs that require interconnectivity. For example, in the network shown in Figure 13.4(a), four PVCs are used to provide connectivity respectively from LANs 2, 3, 4, and 5 to LAN 1. These PVCs are shown as one-way arrows, which imply that the PVCs are simplex links (i.e., data transmissions are unidirectional). Note that the links that connect a LAN to the frame relay network are not PVCs. Only the links within the cloud are PVCs. If two-way connectivity is needed, then duplex PVCs are used. A fully meshed design is also possible. This is shown in Figure 13.4(b). A fully meshed design involving five LANs is accomplished using either 10 duplex PVCs or 20 simplex PVCs. The use of duplex or simplex PVCs for meshed designs is a function of the local exchange carrier providing the frame relay service. Regardless of the assignment, though (simplex or duplex), a fully meshed design still only requires a single network connection from each LAN. Simple and fully meshed designs are not the only two choices available when configuring a frame relay network. A partially meshed design in which some nodes are fully interconnected and others are not is also possible. Configuration decisions are based on customer needs and network traffic requirements.

(a)

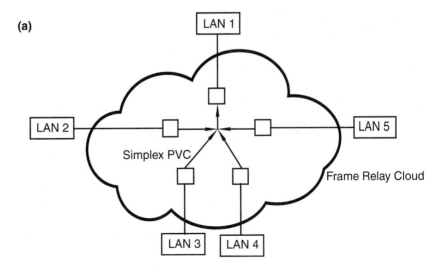

(b)

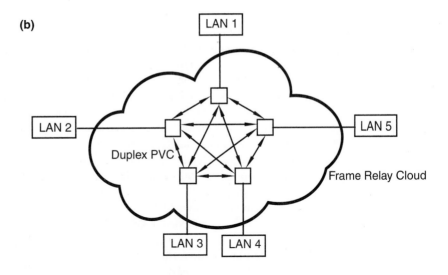

FIGURE 13.4   A frame relay network consisting of five LANs requires at least four simplex PVCs for LAN interconnectivity. In (a), simplex PVCs are used to connect LANS 2, 3, 4, and 5 to LAN 1. In this illustration, LANS 2, 3, 4, and 5 might be remote sites and LAN 1 might be corporate headquarters. In (b), a fully meshed design using duplex PVCs is shown. Here, every LAN can communicate with every other LAN using only a single connection to the frame relay network. (A fully meshed design requires $\dfrac{n(n-1)}{2}$ full-duplex PVCs, where n is the total number of LANs to interconnect.) Source: adapted from Fitzgerald, 1993.

Committed Information Rate (CIR)

Another difference between a private leased line and a PVC is bandwidth cost. The cost of a PVC is substantially less because PVCs have associated with them a *committed information rate* (CIR). A CIR is the amount of throughput a frame relay provider guarantees to support under normal network loads. A CIR, which can range from 16 kbps to T3 (44.8 Mbps), is assigned to a PVC as part of network configuration. It is the minimum guaranteed throughput of a PVC.

Unlike a private leased line, which commits a fixed amount of bandwidth, a frame relay provider calculates the average amount of traffic that has been transmitted across a PVC over a specified period of time (e.g., 1 second). Using this information, the provider then determines the average amount of bandwidth that has been used. This serves as the basis of the CIR on the provider's part. If a PVC's assigned CIR (which, again, was set when the network was first configured) is greater than or equal to this average, then data transmissions are guaranteed. If the assigned CIR is less than this average (i.e., the "pipe" is not big enough), then data transmissions are not guaranteed. Thus, the assignment of a CIR to a PVC is extremely critical to both network cost and performance. If a PVC's CIR is too little, then when the network becomes congested, frames may be dropped. On the other hand, if the CIR is too high, then you are paying for excessive bandwidth. This is analogous to the way banks calculate the monthly maintenance fee of a checking account. If the monthly average of the funds in the account is less than a prescribed minimum, then a fee is assessed. If, however, the monthly average grossly exceeds the minimum average, then you probably have too much money in the account. The penalty for having too much money in a checking account is usually lost interest, since many checking accounts pay no or little interest.

A CIR also can be assigned to a PVC either symmetrically or asymmetrically. A symmetric CIR guarantees the same amount of bandwidth in each direction of a duplex PVC; an asymmetric CIR permits different bandwidth guarantees to be committed in each direction. This flexibility in CIR assignments is one of frame relay's greatest features. The support of asymmetric PVCs makes frame relay an ideal service for client/server applications. For example, Internet or intranet-based Web servers could be configured to have inbound CIRs two or three times (or more) greater than their outbound CIRs. This accommodation of different data transmission rates for inbound and outbound traffic can result in considerable savings for an organization (Figure 13.5).

Data transmissions that exceed the CIR will be transmitted by the frame relay service provider on a "best effort" basis. This means the service provider will attempt to deliver the data but will not guarantee delivery. At best, data frames that require more bandwidth for delivery than what is called for by the CIR will be transmitted without any problem. At worst, the frames will be discarded and will have to be retransmitted. When a data transmission exceeds the CIR, it is referred to as a *burst*. Two types of bursts are defined in frame relay. The first, called the *committed burst* (B_c), is the maximum amount of data the provider guarantees to deliver within a specified time period, T. Note that $CIR = B_c/T$. Given that most providers use a 1-second time interval to calculate the average amount of bandwidth utilization, CIR is usually equal to B_c. The difference between these two parameters is their units. CIR is measured in bps; B_c is measured in bits. The second type of burst, called the *excessive burst* (B_e), is the maximum amount of *uncommitted* data a provider will attempt to deliver within a specified

Internet/Intranet Web Servers

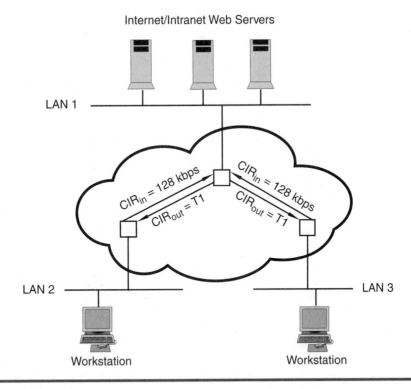

FIGURE 13.5 A frame relay network can be configured with asymmetric PVCs to accommodate different traffic flows. In this figure, LAN 1 consists of a configuration of Web servers and LANs 2 and 3 consist of workstations that access these servers. Client Web requests usually consist of small URLs, but Web server responses are usually large graphic files. Thus, LAN 1's outbound link is configured to have greater bandwidth than its inbound links. Source: adapted from Wu, 1997.

time period. In other words, a provider will guarantee a committed burst of B_c bits and will attempt to deliver (but not guarantee) a maximum of $B_c + B_e$ bits. For example, a PVC assigned a 128-kbps CIR might have associated with it an excessive burst rate of 64 kbps. This means that the provider will attempt to support data transmissions requiring a capacity of up to 192 kbps (Figure 13.6).

CIR and Oversubscription

You might be asking yourself how is it possible to burst to a higher rate than the CIR, which is supposed to be the maximum link capacity. This is a good question, and we can understand any confusion you might be experiencing. We forgot to mention one other parameter—*port speed.* In addition to defining logical connections (PVCs) and bandwidth requirements (CIRs), we must also determine the appropriate port speed of the physical link that connects our LAN to our provider's frame relay network. This link, called the *port connection* or *access line,* is the local loop connection between our LAN's frame relay end node (usually a router) and the provider's frame relay switch. At

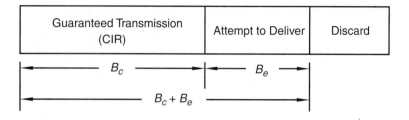

FIGURE 13.6 Data frames that fall within an agreed-upon committed information rate (CIR) are guaranteed transmission. This is called the *committed burst* (B_c) and represents the maximum amount of data the frame relay service provider guarantees to deliver within a specified time. Under normal conditions, the provider will also attempt to deliver (but not guarantee) an additional amount of data beyond the CIR. This extra amount is called the *excessive burst* (B_e). Thus, a provider will guarantee delivery of B_c bits, but will attempt to deliver a maximum of $B_c + B_e$ bits. Anything greater than this sum will be discarded.

the customer's site, the access line is connected to the end node's interface and is called the user-to-network interface (UNI). Depending on the carrier's policy, port speeds can be less than, equal to, or greater than the sum of the CIRs for a particular port. For example, in Figure 13.7, LAN 1 consists of Internet/intranet Web servers, which must serve up Web pages to the clients on LANs 2 and 3. Note that the sum of LAN 1's originating CIRs is 256 kbps + 256 kbps = 512 kbps. Further note that LAN 1's port speed is T1, which is more than twice the capacity of the sum of its CIRs. LAN 2, however, demonstrates a condition known as *oversubscription.* Its port speed (128 kbps) is less than its aggregate CIRs (192 kbps). LAN 2 has oversubscribed its connection—the capacity of its connection into the frame relay network is less than the total bandwidth guaranteed by the provider. Finally, LAN 3's port speed is equal to the aggregate of its originating CIRs.

Frame relay service providers will attempt to deliver frames that exceed a CIR if two conditions are met. First, the data bursts cannot be greater than the port speed, and second, the provider must have sufficient bandwidth available within its own network to accommodate the burst. Burst rates are only supported by a carrier for a limited time period (e.g., 2 seconds). The actual time period in which burst rates are supported varies among carriers. Thus, given the configuration of Figure 13.7, the provider will attempt to support data transmissions from LAN 1 up to T1 capacity.

In a private leased line network, the issues of port speed and CIR are irrelevant—if a T1 line is provisioned, the port speed is 1.544 Mbps and it is a fixed rate. With frame relay, though, we now have considerably more flexibility in configuring the bandwidth requirements of our LAN-to-LAN connections. The trade-off for this flexibility is more detailed knowledge and understanding of the traffic patterns and flows of these connections. Given the typical bursty nature of LAN traffic, it is usually prudent to set the CIR below the port speed to accommodate for data bursts. One rule of thumb is to ensure that the total CIR of a connection does not exceed 70% of the port speed. Thus, if the total CIR is 256 kbps, then the port speed should be no less than 384 kbps. It is also im-

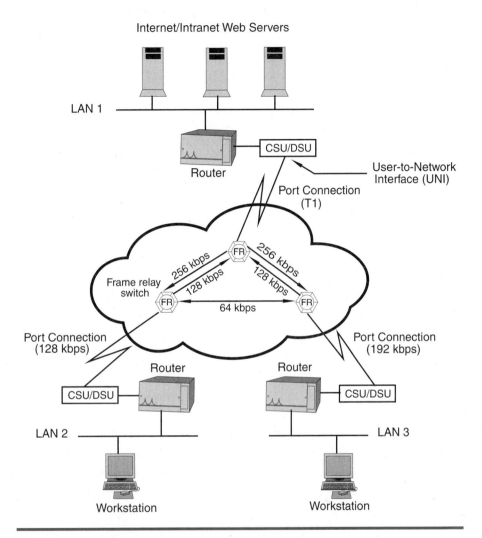

FIGURE 13.7 In a frame relay network, the port connection is the local loop circuit that connects a LAN's frame relay node (usually a router) to the service provider's switch. The capacity of this connection, called the *port speed*, can be less than, equal to, or greater than the sum of the CIRs. In this illustration, LAN 1's port speed is 1.544 Mbps, which is more than twice as great as the sum of its originating CIRs. Thus, LAN 1 can support data bursts of up to T1 speeds. In LAN 2, however, the sum of the originating CIRs (192 kbps) exceeds the port speed (128 kbps). This is a situation known as *oversubscription*. LAN 2 has oversubscribed its service since its aggregate guaranteed bandwidth is greater that its port speed. LAN 3's port speed is equal to the sum of its originating CIRs. Source: adapted from Wu, 1997.

portant to note that some providers place a restriction on the maximum burst rate permitted. The bottom line is that we need to discuss these issues with our provider.

The concept of oversubscription is interesting because a provider guarantees a certain amount of bandwidth but also provisions a link between a LAN and the frame relay network that contains less capacity than what is guaranteed. The way this is accomplished is via multiplexing and buffers. Frame relay uses statistical multiplexing (see Chapter 2) for channel allocation, and providers' frame relay switches have large buffers. Given a sufficiently large buffer size, coupled with a low probability that not every user will need the channel at the same time, it is possible for a provider to deliver data frames successfully to a LAN that has oversubscribed its service. Not all frame relay providers permit oversubscription, though. Some mandate that the port speed be at least equal to the aggregate CIRs.

Another interesting point about oversubscription is that a customer can establish a CIR of zero and effectively steal bandwidth from the provider. In fact, some service providers offer a CIR of zero as an option and even encourage customers to subscribe to this service to get an accurate assessment of bandwidth needs. In some cases, this might be a little more expensive than establishing nonzero CIRs, but it also can be beneficial if traffic rates between sites are unknown. After a few months, specific traffic usage patterns will emerge and appropriate CIRs and ports speeds can then be set. We must be careful, though. Remember that a CIR is *contractual* bandwidth. It represents the maximum data transmission rate a service provider *guarantees* to provide. A CIR of zero implies that every data frame transmitted on the network is considered a burst, and hence, delivery is not guaranteed. If the provider has surplus bandwidth (e.g., unused capacity from customers who are paying for a certain CIR but are not using all of it) available within its network, then you might not experience any network transmission problems with a CIR of zero. However, as this surplus diminishes, expect to see pronounced degradation in the performance of your LAN-to-LAN connections. The beauty about CIR is that if a higher-capacity circuit is needed, only the PVC's assigned CIR has to be changed in the provider's database; a new circuit does not have to be provisioned (as is the case with private leased lines) because the circuits are virtual.

Switched Virtual Circuit (SVC)

In addition to PVCs, frame relay also supports *switched virtual circuits.* SVCs can be thought of as cousins of PVCs—they share certain similarities (e.g., they are both virtual circuits, and everything we discussed earlier about CIRs applies to SVCs as well) but have enough dissimilarities to make them different. As we discussed earlier, frame relay is a connection-oriented protocol, and hence, a circuit must first be established (i.e., nailed-up) between end nodes prior to data communications. With PVCs, two sites are permanently interconnected with a circuit similar to the way two sites are interconnected using private leased lines. The difference is that PVCs are shared by other subscribers within a provider's frame relay network. With SVCs, however, circuits between source and destination nodes are established on the fly and then removed after data communications have ended. This makes SVCs logical *dynamic* connections instead of logical permanent connections, as with PVCs. Thus, SVCs provide switched, on-demand connectivity.

An SVC-based frame relay network is analogous to the public switched telephone network. When a node on LAN *A* needs to send data to a node on LAN *B,* the frame relay switches within the frame relay network automatically nail-up a circuit from source to destination prior to data communications. This circuit remains in effect only for the duration of a transmission. When the transmission is over, the switches then tear down the circuit. Thus, the path of every communication between source and destination nodes is not necessarily the same with SVCs as it is with PVCs. Furthermore, frame relay switches that support SVCs can automatically configure a path on demand between two sites and then remove this path from their tables at the end of a transmission. With SVCs, any frame relay subscriber can communicate with any other frame relay subscriber provided both have SVC capabilities.

PVCs and SVCs have their own set of advantages and disadvantages. PVC advantages include widespread availability (every frame relay provider supports PVCs), less complex network designs (any two sites that want to communicate must have a permanent connection between them), and less expensive equipment (switches do not have to automatically configure and remove paths dynamically). On the other side of the coin, PVCs are permanent. This implies that regardless of use, you are always paying for a specific amount of bandwidth. A second disadvantage is that every time a new connection is required, a new permanent circuit must be established. Thus, the number of PVCs a customer might need may increase dramatically, making the PVCs difficult to manage. This is especially true if a fully meshed design is required. For example, an organization with 50 sites will require $(50)(49)/2 = 1225$ PVCs for a fully meshed network. If full connectivity is required among 100 sites, the number of PVCs needed increases dramatically to 4950.

Compared to PVCs, SVCs are more versatile. Customers do not have to establish permanent circuits between any two sites because connectivity is provided on an as-needed basis, and as a usage-based service, bandwidth is only used when needed. This can translate to considerable savings for customers. On the other hand, PVCs' advantages are currently SVCs' primary disadvantages. First, widespread SVC availability among frame relay service providers is lacking (although MCI World-Com and Sprint have announced plans to deploy SVCs). SVC-based frame relay networks are also more complex in design, and switches are more sophisticated and hence expensive.

13.3 Technical Overview and Data Link Layer Issues

Basic Operation

Frame relay is a data link layer protocol. It is synchronous in nature and is based on the concept of packet-switching. Thus, every frame relay frame carries source and destination addresses. As indicated earlier, frame relay also uses statistical multiplexing. This enables multiple subscribers to share the same backbone. Although frame relay operates at the data link layer, it does not provide flow control, error detection, frame sequencing, or acknowledgments. These tasks, which represent overhead, are performed by frame relay end nodes (usually a router) at the customer's site and not by the frame relay switches. If the network becomes congested and a frame relay switch's buffers get filled, the switch will discard any subsequent frames it receives until its buffers are free. Recovery from these lost frames is left to the frame relay end nodes. Transmission errors are also ignored by the switches. All frame integrity checks are, once again, performed by the customer's end nodes. Freeing the protocol from these tasks makes frame relay a very fast and highly efficient LAN-to-LAN connection.

The physical components of a frame relay network include end nodes, frame relay switches, and communication links. End nodes serve as the interface between a customer's site (LAN) and the service provider's network; switches are responsible for transmitting data from the source LAN's end node to the destination LAN's end node. End nodes are then connected to switches via an access line (i.e., a port connection), and switches are interconnected via PVCs or SVCs.

Frame relay end nodes include bridges (see Chapter 6), routers (see Chapter 7), special concentrators, and workstations or personal computers. Of these devices, the most common implementations use frame relay-capable routers or conventional routers with frame relay-capable CSUs/DSUs. Collectively, end nodes are known as frame relay access devices (FRADs). Regardless of the type of device used, end nodes assemble or disassemble frame relay frames between two LANs. FRADs accept data frames from the local network (e.g., an Ethernet/802.3 frame) and assemble them into frame relay frames (Figure 13.8) by encapsulating the data contained in layers 3 through 7. This new frame is then placed on the access line for transmission across the network. When a FRAD receives a frame relay frame, it disassembles it by stripping off the frame relay headers and trailers, does any necessary reassembly of the LAN frame, performs an integrity check on the frame, and (assuming the frame is valid) places it on the local backbone for delivery to the destination node. Frame relay is also protocol independent. Thus, different LAN protocols such as Ethernet/802.3 and token ring, and different network protocols such as TCP/IP, SNA, and IPX, can run over frame relay.

> The term FRAD once meant special frame relay devices that were used for simple implementations. Today, however, the term is all-encompassing and implies any frame relay end node.

Frame Relay Frames

The frame relay frame (Figure 13.8) is of variable length; the standard does not specify a frame size limitation. The maximum size is set by (and is different among) providers and is generally a function of hardware limitations. Typical implementations range from 1600 to 4096 bytes. This implies that frame relay can fully support Ethernet/802.3 and token ring frames without having to segment (and reassemble) LAN frames for transmission across the frame relay network. Although this variable size feature makes the protocol compatible with the type of bursty traffic inherent in LANs, it also makes it susceptible to data processing delays across the network.

As shown in Figure 13.8, a frame relay frame consists of the following fields: start and end frame delimiters (SFD and EFD), address, user data, and frame check sequence (FCS). The SFD and EFD fields are one byte each and consist of the bit pattern 01111110 to indicate the beginning and ending of a frame. The address field is two bytes and can be extended to either three or four bytes. The components of a two-byte address are shown in Figure 13.8. These components include a 10-bit *data link connection identifier* (DLCI) that is split between the two bytes, two 1-bit *extended address* (EA) fields (one per byte), and 1 bit each for *command/response* (C/R), *forward and backward explicit congestion notification* (FECN and BECN), and *discard eligibility* (DE). The user data field is of variable length. This field contains encapsulated data from the sending node. The FCS field is used to check the integrity of the frame.

Focusing on the two-byte address field, the DLCI represents the network address of the frame and includes the virtual circuit number that corresponds to the destination port

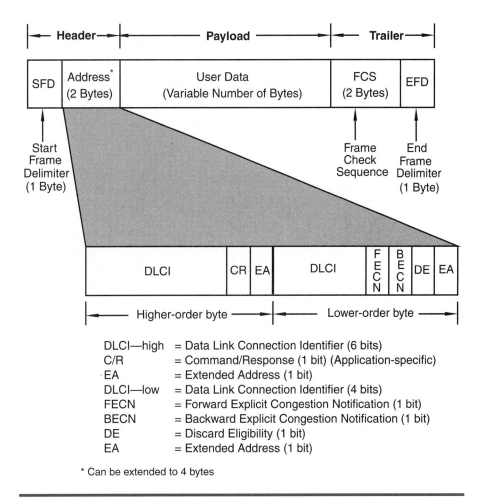

DLCI—high = Data Link Connection Identifier (6 bits)
C/R = Command/Response (1 bit) (Application-specific)
EA = Extended Address (1 bit)
DLCI—low = Data Link Connection Identifier (4 bits)
FECN = Forward Explicit Congestion Notification (1 bit)
BECN = Backward Explicit Congestion Notification (1 bit)
DE = Discard Eligibility (1 bit)
EA = Extended Address (1 bit)

* Can be extended to 4 bytes

FIGURE 13.8 The contents and format of a frame relay frame. Source: adapted from Parsons & Beach, 1996.

of the destination LAN's end node (more on this later). The C/R bit is application-specific and not used by the protocol. It is passed transparently from switch to switch. The EA bits specify whether the address is extended to three or four bytes. If EA is 0, then another byte of address information follows; an EA of 1 implies that the current byte is the last byte of the address. Thus, a two-byte address has EA = 0 in the higher-order byte and EA = 1 in the lower-order byte. The FECN and BECN bits are used to convey congestion information to end nodes in either direction. These bits are set by frame relay switches as the frame is being transmitted across the network from source to destination. If FECN or BECN is set to 1, then a sending or receiving end node, upon receipt of a frame, will know that the frame encountered congestion and can take whatever action is necessary to enact flow control. The DE bit specifies whether or not a frame should be discarded when the network gets congested. Frames with the DE bit 1 are considered low priority. When the network becomes congested, if a customer's capacity exceeds its CIR, frames with DE = 1 are the first to be dropped by frame relay switches.

Data Link Connection Identifier (DLCI)

DLCIs are virtual circuit addresses assigned to PVCs or SVCs. DLCIs enable multiple virtual circuits, which represent logical connections, to be multiplexed using a single network link. For a two-byte address, DLCIs are 10 bits in length (see Figure 13.8). This implies there are 2^{10} = 1024 possible circuit numbers. Of these, however, only 992 are available for use. The remaining 32 are reserved. For example DLCI 0 is reserved for call control, which establishes and releases a logical connection, and DLCI 1023 is reserved for exchanging information about the virtual circuits that have been established. To accommodate larger networks, the frame's address field can be extended to three or four bytes. A three-byte address field supports a 17-bit DLCI, and a four-byte address field supports a 24-bit DLCI. Outside of the frame relay cloud, DLCIs represent the destination network's end node's port number. End nodes maintain a cross-connect table that maps their port's DLCI to a specific network address. For example, in a TCP/IP-based network, the end node (e.g., a router) is configured so that each IP address assigned to the WAN interface corresponds to the correct DLCI. An illustration is shown in Figure 13.9.

DLCIs are assigned at call set-up time, or they are premapped to a destination node when PVCs are initially established with a service provider. This latter approach is used in the majority of frame relay networks. Although DLCIs must be unique within the cloud, end nodes may use the same DLCIs. For example, in Figure 13.9, the UNIs of LANs 2 and 3 are assigned the same DLCI (83). In this context, DLCIs have only local significance, and care must be exercised to ensure that the DLCI is not announced outside the local arena. In contrast to local addressing, global addressing is also available. In this context, a DLCI is assigned on a universal basis throughout the entire network. Thus, a globally assigned DLCI would identify the same destination regardless of where the originating end node is located in the network. Although global addressing simplifies the management of DLCIs, it also reduces further the number of DLCI numbers available for use since no DLCIs can be reused by different networks.

Data transfer in a frame relay network involves first establishing (i.e., nailing-up) a logical connection between the source and destination nodes and assigning a unique DLCI to the connection. Data frames are then transferred across the network, with each frame containing the assigned DLCI. The same circuit is used for the duration of the transmission. At the conclusion of the transmission, the circuit is released. Logical connections are established and released in frame relay by using frames with DLCI = 0. These frames, called *call control frames,* are exchanged between the sending and receiving nodes and include information related to the proposed connection. Among this information is the DLCI that will be assigned to the connection. Either the sending node includes this DLCI in its connection request, or it can be assigned by the receiving node at the time it accepts the sender's connection request.

To understand the process of frame relaying, let's assume that a frame of data is transmitted from LAN 2 to LAN 3 in Figure 13.9. When LAN 2's router constructs the frame for transmission, it will assign a DLCI of 83. The router places the frame on its

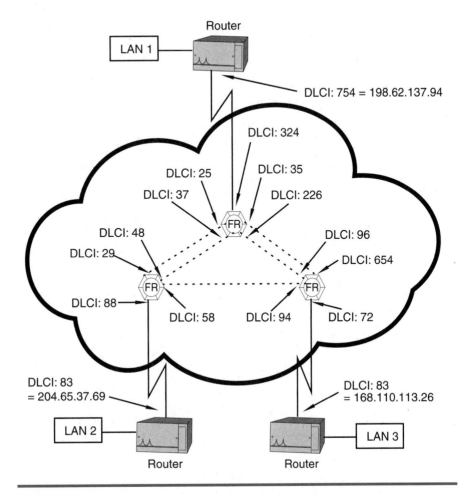

FIGURE 13.9 The virtual ports (PVCs and SVCs) of a frame relay network are uniquely identi-fied by the data link connection identifier. Cross-connect tables within the frame relay switches map incoming DLCIs to corresponding outgoing DLCIs. For example, the virtual connection between the switches connecting LANs 2 and 3 maps DLCI 58 to DLCI 94. End nodes (routers) also must maintain tables that map port addresses (i.e., the user–network interfaces) to the correct DLCIs. Although DLCIs must be unique within the cloud, end nodes can use the same DLCIs. For example, the UNIs of LANs 2 and 3 are assigned the same DLCI (83). Thus, DLCIs have only local, not global, significance. Source: adapted from Parsons & Bahr, 1996.

access line, and the frame is transmitted to the switch connected at the other end of the link. When the switch receives the frame, it checks the frame's integrity via the two-byte FCS contained in the frame's trailer. If any errors are found, the switch discards the frame. If the frame is valid, the switch then checks its routing table to determine the channel on which the frame should be placed. (We will assume the frame is valid throughout this illustration.) Let's agree that the switch's routing table shows that frames arriving via circuit 88 must go out the port assigned DLCI = 48. The switch then rebuilds the frame to include this new DLCI and ships it out the appropriate port. The next switch (a) receives the frame on the port assigned DLCI = 37, (b) does its integrity check, (c) consults its routing table and discovers that frames arriving on circuit 37 get transmitted to the port assigned DLCI = 35, (d) rebuilds the frame to include a DLCI of 35 and then transmits the frame via circuit 35. This process continues until the destination LAN's end node (in this case, LAN 3's router) receives the frame.

Congestion Control and Management

If acknowledgments are not received within a certain time interval, the source end node assumes that the frame was discarded. It will then retransmit the frame. One thing we can count on frame relay to do is discard frames. It is a no-nonsense protocol. Frame relay also does not operate too well in a noisy environment. If there is any line noise during a transmission, bit errors will occur and frame relay will drop those frames. If transmission errors occur frequently and frame relay starts discarding frames, which causes retransmissions, a vicious circle of sorts starts to develop: Discarded frames lead to retransmission, which leads to more network traffic, which leads to network congestion, which causes more frames to be discarded.

Congestion is addressed in frame relay from two perspectives. The first perspective is grounded in management and design issues. Frame relay service providers should always strive to provide an agreed upon quality of service. To do so, though, and to do it consistently, service providers should: (a) design their networks so that sufficient bandwidth is provisioned, (b) ensure that all links are clean, (c) keep customers from establishing connections where the aggregate CIRs exceed 70% of the port speed, (d) ensure that any one end node is kept from monopolizing the network at the expense of other end nodes, and (e) distribute resources across the network in a fair and equitable manner. Unfortunately, these considerations are carrier dependent and vary from one provider to another.

FECN and BECN Bits   The second perspective is standards based. The frame relay protocol provides a mechanism for addressing congestion. This is done via the forward and backward explicit congestion notification bits (see Figure 13.8). FECN and BECN are designed to inform (i.e., notify) end nodes that a frame has experienced network congestion. If congestion emerges along a virtual circuit, these bits are set to 1 by the frame relay switch connected to that circuit as the frame passes through the switch. The FECN bit is set in frames going toward the destination node; the BECN bit is set in frames going toward the sending node.

Of the two bits, congestion notification via BECN produces the most direct action. If the sending end node receives a frame with BECN = 1, it can simply reduce (or temporarily suspend) its transmission rate. This action is direct and effective. A different strategy needs to be employed by the destination end node if it receives frames with FECN = 1. Since the destination node cannot directly slow down the sender's data transmission rate, it must rely on indirect methods. One method is to increase the length of time receipt-of-frame acknowledgments take when sent to the sender. This will slow down acknowledgment transmissions. After the sending node's acknowledgment timers have expired several times, it will eventually increase the timer interval to accommodate the new rate being used by the destination node. This action indirectly causes the sender to reduce its transmission rate. A second method is to effect flow control in the higher layers. For example, if a TCP-based application such as FTP is running over TCP, and IP is being used as the network layer protocol (layer 3), then the destination node can reset its transmission window value to zero. Doing so informs the sender that the maximum number of bytes the receiver can accept is zero. Thus, a zero window informs the sender to stop transmitting data to the receiver until a nonzero window size is received from the receiver.

In TCP/IP, the transmission window represents the maximum number of bytes a remote node can accept.

Incorporating the FECN and BECN bits in the frame relay frame produces shared responsibility between the network and the end nodes for congestion control: The network's role is to monitor itself for congestion and then notify the end nodes that congestion exists. Upon notification, the end nodes then take the necessary action to reduce the flow of frames onto the network.

Discard Eligibility Bit   Besides FECN and BECN, the discard eligibility (DE) bit can be used as another strategy for congestion control. Its role is to give the network guidance in determining which frames should be discarded. This is important because setting FECN and BECN bits does not guarantee that end nodes will respond to this notification or, if they do, that the response will be in a timely manner. Furthermore, the implementation of FECN and BECN in frame relay is not mandatory. Without any guidance, the network (i.e., frame relay switches) will discard frames arbitrarily at the onset of congestion. Although discarding frames randomly produces the desired effect—it helps reduce congestion—it does not give any consideration to frames that have a "contractual right" to remain. For example, frames transmitted within the parameters of a contracted CIR are just as likely to be dropped as frames transmitted at a burst rate above the CIR. This situation can be resolved by configuring end nodes to set the DE bit to 1 for all frames transmitted at a rate higher than the CIR. Now, in the presence of congestion, network switches will discard frames with DE = 1 before they discard frames that do not have their DE bit set. Discarded frames will then be retransmitted at a later time when congestion has subsided. The DE bit also can be used to distinguish between high- and low-priority frames. For example, if e-mail data are considered more important than Web data, then the end node can be configured to set the DE bit of all Web-based frames. This gives e-mail frames a higher transmission priority than Web frames because, if congestion occurs, switches will drop Web frames first. The DE bit enables frame relay customers to adopt a frame-discard strategy that is predicated on their preferences. Although this provides a fairer and more equitable approach to discarding frames than arbitrary selection, it does not guarantee that only DE-flagged frames will be dropped.

Retransmission occurs after the sending node has detected that the packet was dropped, that is, after it failed to receive an acknowledgment.

The topics of congestion and congestion management strategies are part of a bigger picture called network performance, which includes metrics such as network uptime, delays, and frame or packet loss. These metrics vary from one provider to another. For example, network uptime guarantees can range from 99% to 99.95% to 99.99% among different providers. Although these rates are relatively close to one another, the difference in the number of minutes (or hours) of downtime is staggering. For example, uptimes of 99%, 99.5%, and 99.99% translate to downtimes of 1%, 0.5%, and 0.01%, respectively. Table 13.1 shows the differences in these rates measured daily, monthly, and yearly. Thus, a network provider that guarantees a 99% uptime measured on a monthly basis means that the guarantee does not become effective until the network has been down for more than 432 minutes (7.2 hours) over a 30-day period. If the guarantee is on an annual basis,

TABLE 13.1 Network Downtime Comparisons at Different Levels of Uptime Guarantees

	99% Uptime	99.5% Uptime	99.99% Uptime
Measured Daily 24 hr/day × 60 min/hr = 1440 minutes/day	1440 × .01 = 14.4 minutes downtime/day	1440 × .005 = 7.2 minutes downtime/day	1440 × .0001 = 0.144 minute downtime/day
Measured Monthly 1440 min/day × 30 days/ month = 43,200 minutes/month	43,200 × .01 = 432 minutes = 7.2 hours downtime/month	43,200 × .005 = 216 minutes = 3.6 hours downtime/month	43,200 × .0001 = 4.32 minutes downtime/month
Measured Yearly 1440 min/day × 365 days/year = 525,600 minutes/year	525,600 × .01 = 5256 minutes = 87.6 hours downtime/year	525,600 × .005 = 2628 minutes = 43.8 hours downtime/year	525,600 × .0001 = 52.56 minutes downtime/year

then it does not take effect unless downtime exceeds 5256 minutes (87.6 hours) over the 365-day period. These same downtimes for a 99.99% guarantee are 4.32 minutes per month and 52.56 minutes per year. As you can see, there is quite a difference. The bottom line is that customers who are subscribing to frame relay service need to investigate, probe, and negotiate network performance issues with their provider.

Link Management

The frame relay protocol specifies a *link management interface* (LMI) for link control. LMI provides an interface for link status information to be exchanged between an end node (e.g., router or switch) and the network. LMI's functions are quite basic, though, and limited to activities such as PVC notification (end nodes are notified whenever PVCs are added to or removed from the network), PVC monitoring (circuits are monitored so end nodes know which ones are available), and link establishment between an end node and the network. Given frame relay's ISDN roots, link management is provided out-of-band; thus, a separate virtual circuit is used for transmitting link status information messages.

13.4   Additional Frame Relay Information

Voice Over Frame Relay

Frame relay has evolved from a data-only service to one that can support voice, fax, and video transmissions. *Voice over frame relay* (VOFR) has benefited from the development of voice-capable FRADs, which have been designed with advanced technologies to accommodate the nuances associated with transmitting voice traffic. These technologies include voice compression, echo cancellation, and delay control techniques. Voice compression eliminates pauses and redundant information typical of human communication. This reduces the amount of bandwidth required to transmit voice signals. Voice compression also permits voice transmissions over lower-speed channels. Voice compression methods include two international standards, ITU G.729 and ITU G.728, as well as propri-

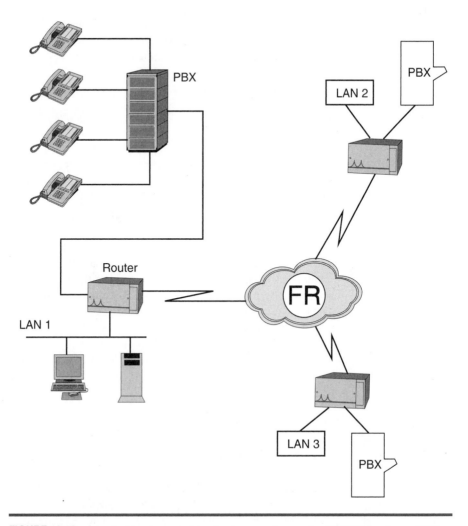

FIGURE 13.10 A typical implementation of *voice over frame relay* (VOFR) involves a PBX system connected to a voice-capable FRAD, which also links a LAN.

etary solutions. Echo cancellation eliminates voice echoing, which occurs when propagation delays reflect voice traffic back to its point of transmission. In addition to echoing, delays can also cause voice distortion. For example, if jitter is high, then the receiving-end equipment will not be able to satisfactorily regenerate the voice signal. Delay control techniques that have been developed to eliminate problems related to delay include traffic prioritization and fragmentation. With prioritization, voice transmissions are assigned a higher priority than data frames, which are buffered until voice traffic has been transmitted. Fragmentation minimizes delay by segmenting large data frames into smaller-sized frames so that voice transmissions are not impeded by the transmission of large data frames. In a typical VOFR application, a customer's PBX is connected to a FRAD, which is connected to the data network. In most cases, additional PVCs are needed, and CIRs will have to be increased to accommodate voice traffic. Frame relay service provider switches also must be capable of transmitting voice traffic. A typical implementation is shown in Figure 13.10.

In addition to voice, several vendors have also produced FRADs that are capable of supporting real-time video. Once again, attention needs to be paid to adequate bandwidth and CIRs. (See Chapter 18 for additional information about convergence technologies.)

Frame Relay versus Other LAN-to-LAN Technologies

During the late 1980s to early to mid-1990s, frame relay, SMDS, ATM, and broadband ISDN (B-ISDN) were all in the spotlight as new fast packet-switching technologies or services. Frame relay, which originally was a subset of ISDN, was defined initially to transmit data at rates ranging from 56 kbps to T1/E-1. It was considered an interim technology, lying somewhere between X.25 and ATM relative to their respective data transmission rates. Frame relay data rates dovetailed nicely with the local loop—the link between a customer's site and the telco's nearest point of presence (POP). SMDS and B-ISDN were initially designed to transmit data, fax, graphics, video, and voice at speeds from 45 to 155 Mbps. ATM was designed initially to offer the same kinds of services as SMDS and B-ISDN, but its transmission rates were from 45 Mbps to 2.4 Gbps.

Much has changed in such a short period of time. In the United States, frame relay has essentially pushed SMDS and B-ISDN out of the spotlight (see Chapters 12 and 14). Frame relay now operates at T3, and telcos are upgrading their networks to support rates greater than DS-3. In fact, frame relay's evolution took another giant step forward when the ITU approved a new version of frame relay recommendations in 2000. The new recommendations—Recommendation X.36, which defines the user–network interface, and Recommendation X.76, which defines the network–network interface—are applicable to data rates up to OC-12 (622 Mbps), making frame relay competitive with ATM for WAN connections. Additionally, frame relay is now capable of supporting services such as on-demand connections, multicast communications, data compression, and CoS/QoS, all of which enable it to transmit multimedia data such as voice and video. This makes frame relay a viable option for LAN-to-LAN and WAN connections, as well as a broadband service. Furthermore, frame relay frames can be encapsulated within ATM's 53-byte cell and transmitted across ATM links. Perhaps more important, though, given frame relay's variable frame size, a single frame can carry a minimum-sized Ethernet/802.3 frame (64 bytes), whereas ATM needs two cells for the same transmission. Thus, when it comes to transmitting Ethernet frames, frame relay is more efficient than ATM because it uses less bandwidth. Collectively, all of these issues and developments ensure that frame relay will either compete or coexist with ATM.

Frame Relay in the News

In the recent past, two frame relay outages made the news. The first occurred on April 13, 1998, when AT&T's frame relay network crashed as a result of a firmware upgrade to a core switch. According to a report in the June 1998 issue of *Data Communications,* a technician performed the upgrade on a live switch that was connected to the network and then entered incorrect commands. This generated spurious administrative messages, which would not have been a problem if the switch was off-line. However, because the switch was on-line, these messages propagated to other switches throughout the network, and within a half-hour, the entire network was down. This left AT&T's frame relay customers without connectivity for more than a day. The second outage was

If a customer's service uptime was guaranteed at either 99% to 99.5% and based on a yearly rate, the guarantee would not have applied. See Table 13.1.

on August 5, 1999, and involved MCI WorldCom's frame relay network. In this incident, only about 15% of the network infrastructure was affected, but this still translated to approximately 30% of MCI WorldCom's customers experiencing network failure. Some customers' connectivity was disrupted for as long as 10 days. The MCI World-Com outage was the result of a software error.

Although frame relay is regarded as a highly reliable and cost-effective network, the AT&T and MCI WorldCom crashes demonstrated that as little as a single hardware or software error can disrupt frame relay connections. Consequently, it is prudent for frame relay customers (and all users of network services) to give serious attention to the issue of disaster recovery. For example, AT&T and MCI WorldCom customers who had secondary (i.e., backup) ISDN circuits in place, or redundant frame relay circuits from a different provider, were able to maintain connectivity. Given the additional cost of these measures, one might be tempted to ask, "Why bother?" The answer to this question can be given by paraphrasing the edict used to explain why George Bush lost his bid for a second term as president of the United States in 1992: "It's technology, stupid."

End-of-Chapter Commentary

In this chapter, several concepts and technologies related to frame relay were discussed. These included circuit- and packet-switching, virtual circuits (PVCs and SVCs), bandwidth (CIRs), design and topology issues, and ISDN. Additional information about these concepts can be found in earlier chapters within this book. For example, circuit- and packet-switching are discussed in Chapter 2; network design and topology issues, as well as virtual circuits, are discussed in Chapters 1 and 2; bandwidth is discussed in Chapter 2; and ISDN is discussed in Chapter 12. Other technologies and services that were also discussed are addressed in subsequent chapters. These are SMDS, which is the topic of the next chapter (see Chapter 14), and ATM (see Chapter 15), which follows our discussion of SMDS.

CHAPTER REVIEW MATERIALS

SUMMARY

• Frame relay is a public wide area network packet-switching protocol that provides LAN-to-LAN connectivity. It also provides a single point of network access for multiple LAN-to-LAN connections, which is not true in networks using private links. This feature offers considerable savings on local loop charges. Frame relay can be implemented using existing bridges or routers.

• Frame relay uses virtual links instead of permanent, dedicated connections. Two types of virtual links are supported: Permanent virtual circuits (PVCs) provide a logical connection between two sites, and switched virtual circuits (SVCs) enable circuits to be established dynamically. Unlike dedicated links, bandwidth can be shared on virtual circuits.

• The minimum amount of bandwidth a frame relay service provider guarantees to provision for frame relay circuits is called the committed information rate (CIR). Data transmissions that exceed a circuit's assigned CIR are called bursts. Two types of bursts exist. A committed burst is the maximum amount of data guaranteed to be delivered within a specified time frame; an excessive burst is the maximum amount of uncommitted data a provider will attempt to deliver, but delivery is not guaranteed. A zero CIR implies that every transmission is a burst.

• Associated with CIR is the concept of oversubscription, which refers to a condition in which a LAN's port speed (the transmission rate of the link that interconnects a site's LAN to the frame relay network) is less than the aggregate CIRs of the LAN's frame relay links. Thus, a LAN oversubscribes its connection when the capacity of its frame relay link is less than the total amount of bandwidth a service provider guarantees to deliver.

• As a data link layer protocol, frame relay relies on higher-level protocols to do error correction and to request retransmissions if packets are lost or discarded. To address congestion, frame relay supports the forward and backward explicit congestion notification (FECN, BECN) bits that convey congestion information to either the sending or receiving node depending on the direction of traffic. The frame relay frame also employs a discard eligibility bit, which identifies frames that can be discarded in the presence of congestion.

• Frame relay addressing is performed using virtual circuit addresses known as data link connection identifiers (DLCIs). When a logical connection is first established between source and destination nodes, a unique DLCI is assigned to the connection. This DLCI is then included with each frame transferred between the two nodes.

• In addition to CIR considerations, when subscribing to frame relay service, the subscriber should be cognizant of service level agreements (SLAs), which address network performance issues, including network uptime guarantees. Although there appears to be little difference among 99%, 99.95%, and 99.99% uptime guarantees, the length of downtimes can be significant depending on if they are measured daily, monthly, or yearly.

• Although frame relay began as a data-only service, it is capable of supporting voice, fax, and video transmissions.

• When compared to other LAN-to-LAN technologies or services such as ATM, SMDS, or ISDN/B-ISDN, frame relay is very economical and efficient.

VOCABULARY CHECK

access line

backward explicit congestion notification (BECN)

committed burst

committed information rate (CIR)

data link connection identifier (DLCI)

discard eligibility

excessive burst

forward explicit congestion notification (FECN)

oversubscription

permanent virtual circuit (PVC)

port connection

port speed

switched virtual circuit (SVC)

voice over frame relay (VOFR)

REVIEW EXERCISES

1. Discuss the major benefits of frame relay's design, that is, the advantages of a virtual packet-switching instead of dedicated end-to-end circuits.

2. Frame relay is considered to be more *scalable* than a fixed point-to-point network. What do you think this means?

3. Given that frame relay is essentially an outsourced network, what effect do you think subscribing to frame relay will have on an organization's network management operations?

4. From a technical management perspective, what effect does frame relay's packet-switched design have on the physical layer?

5. Explain the concept of frame relay's committed information rate (CIR).

6. Explain the concept of oversubscription; give an example as part of your explanation.

7. What impact do you think bursting has on overall network performance? For example: (a) Does bursting increase latency? (b) Does bursting cause packets to be discarded? (c) Can the network absorb any bursts so they do not negatively affect network performance? Explain your responses to each part of the question.

8. Describe the differences between frame relay PVCs and SVCs.

9. Discuss the main issues related to a frame relay network subscription that should (must?) be addressed as part of the planning process.

10. Frame relay employs a simple link layer protocol and hence operates only at layer 2 of the OSI model. What benefit does this provide frame relay relative to overall network performance?

11. Although frame relay is a layer-2 technology, it does not provide all of the functions commonly done at layer 2. Briefly describe the layer-2 functions frame relay does provide.

12. Compare the contents of a frame relay frame (Figure 13.8) to the contents of an IPv4 frame (Figure 8.20). Which do you think is the more efficient protocol, frame relay or IPv4? Why?

13. Compare frame relay's frame format (Figure 13.8) to that defined for ISDN's LAP-D (Figure 12.6). What difference do you notice between the two frames? How does this difference relate to overall network performance between frame relay and ISDN?

14. Explain how frame relay handles congestion control.

15. Explain the concept and function of frame relay's data link connection identifier (DLCI).

16. Of what significance is frame relay's variable size payload?

17. Frame relay operates under the following simple rule: "If there is a problem in the network, discard the data." Under what conditions do you think this rule is invoked? Compare this simple rule to the manner in which other technologies such as Ethernet handle network "problems."

18. What impact do you think noisy transmission lines have on frame relay? Why?

19. Consider the concept of forward and backward explicit congestion notification, which are implemented by frame relay via FECN and BECN bits. Is it possible for frame relay to invoke FECN and BECN simultaneously? If so, under what conditions would this be done? If not, why?

20. Frame relay uses bandwidth on demand, which implies that the bandwidth can be allocated to users at call setup. What advantage does this have to a technology such as X.25, which uses fixed bandwidth?

21. What features does frame relay provide as a backbone network?

22. One measure of frame relay's network performance is based on the number of frames discarded above CIR. Do you think it is also important to measure the number of dropped frames transmitted *under* CIR as well? Why?

23. Which do you think provides a more accurate measurement of frame relay performance: Calculating throughput and latency measurements on a one-way basis or on a round-trip basis? Why?

24. When subscribing to a frame relay service, it is critical that the end user negotiate a service level agreement (SLA) with the frame relay service provider. Why do you think this is important? What components do you think should be included in a frame relay SLA?

SUGGESTED READINGS AND REFERENCES

ATKINS, J., and M. NORRIS. 1995. *Total Area Networking: ATM, Frame Relay and SMDS Explained.* New York: Wiley.

BATES, R. J., and D. GREGORY. 1998. *Voice and Data Communications Handbook.* New York: McGraw-Hill.

BROWN, D., and D. WILLIS. 1998. Videoconferencing on Frame Relay Networks. *Network Computing,* 15 September, 47–62.

CLARK, E. 1998. Frame Relay Goes Public. *Network Magazine,* April, 68–73.

FEIBEL, W. 1995. *The Network Press Encyclopedia of Networking.* 2nd ed. San Francisco: Sybex.

FITZGERALD, S., and L. KRAFT. 1993. A New Model for Frame Relay. *LAN Magazine,* August, 61–67.

———. 1993. Outfit Your WAN with Frame Relay. *LAN Magazine,* August, 52–59.

———. 1995. Designing Your Frame Relay Network. *Network Computing,* 15 January, 152–154.

GALLO, M., and W. HANCOCK. 1999. *Networking Explained.* Boston: Digital Press.

GAREISS, R. 1996. Don't Take No for an Answer. *Data Communications,* November, 67–82.

———. 1997. Frame Relay vs. IP: It's Your Move. *Data Communications,* February, 89–96.

———. 1998. Frame Relay. *Data Communications,* June, 76, 78–86.

HARBISON, R. W. 1992. Frame Relay: Technology for Our Time. *LAN Technology,* December, 67–78.

HELD, G. 1997. Shopping for Frame Relay. *Network Magazine,* December, 83–87.

KRIVDA, C. 1996. Frame Relay Comes of Age. *LAN,* November, 117–124.

MERRITT, J. 1992. Frame Relay Technology: The Right Link for Wide Area Backbones. *Network Computing,* 1 November, 75–76.

NEWMAN, D., T. GIORGIS, and F. YAVARI-ISSALOU. 1998. FRADs: Halfway There. *Data Communications,* 21 September, 43–54.

NEWMAN, J. 1997. Frame Relay Makes Its Voice Heard. *Network Computing,* 15 March, 134–138.

PARNELL, T. 1997. *LAN Times Guide to Wide Area Networks.* Berkeley, CA: Osborne McGraw-Hill.

PARSONS, T., and D. BAHR. 1996. Acing the Frame Relay Race. *LAN,* June, 95–104.

———, and T. Beach. 1996. Rapid Transit: Frame Relay to ATM. *LAN,* August, 115–120.

REARDON, M. 1998. Frame Relay. *Data Communications,* June, 77, 90–97.

STALLINGS, W. 2000. *Data and Computer Communications.* 6th ed. Upper Saddle River, NJ: Prentice-Hall.

WILLIS, D. 1997a. Make Room for Frame Relay. *Networking Computing,* 15 February, 73–86.

———. 1997b. Framing the Perfect WAN Contract. *Network Computing,* 15 September, 136–140.

WU, D. 1997. Client–Server over Frame Relay. *Network Magazine,* October, 105–109.

14 Switched Multimegabit Data Service (SMDS)

CHAPTER OBJECTIVES

After studying this chapter, you will be able to do the following:

1. Explain the concept of SMDS.
2. Discuss SMDS's history.
3. Discuss the rationale for SMDS's development.
4. Describe SMDS's physical layer specifications.
5. Describe the DQDB protocol.
6. Identify and describe the different levels of the SMDS Interface Protocol (SIP).
7. Explain SMDS addressing.
8. Compare and contrast SMDS to other LAN-to-LAN technologies such as ATM and frame relay.
9. Discuss SMDS's current status and understand the circumstances that led to it.

CHAPTER OUTLINE

In this chapter, we present information about switched multimegabit data service (SMDS), a data service that never achieved popularity in the United States. Our main purpose in discussing SMDS is twofold. First, the service is interesting in its own right and deserves attention. Perhaps more important, though, is SMDS's technical design and specifications. SMDS is based on IEEE 802.6, a data link layer protocol for metropolitan area networks (MANs). Called *Distributed Queue Dual Bus* (DQDB), this protocol is quite different from other protocols we have considered and merits examination. We begin the chapter with an overview of SMDS that includes its history and rationale for development. Section 14.2 presents the physical and data link layers of SMDS. This discussion is then followed by the SMDS Interface Protocol in Section 14.3 and SMDS addressing issues in Section 14.4. A comparison of SMDS to frame relay and ATM is the topic of Section 14.5. We conclude the chapter with an examination of SMDS's current status.

14.1   What Is SMDS?

Overview

SMDS stands for *switched multimegabit data service*. It is a wide area network service designed for LAN-to-LAN connectivity. In a mouthful, SMDS is a cell-based, connectionless, high-speed, public, packet-switched, broadband, metropolitan area data network. SMDS is also a data service, which means that it can only transmit data (although it is capable of transmitting voice and video).

SMDS uses fixed-length *cells* as its basic unit for transmitting data. These cells are similar to ATM cells, namely, they contain 53 bytes—a 44-byte payload plus a 7-byte header and a 2-byte trailer. (See Chapter 15 for more information about ATM.) As a connectionless data service, SMDS does not establish a connection between sending and receiving hosts prior to data transmission. Instead, an SMDS switch establishes a virtual circuit between sending and receiving machines. Cells are placed on the medium when they are ready for transmission and then transmitted independently of each other. Thus, data cells are transmitted without delay and in no particular order. This provides bandwidth on demand for the kind of bursty traffic inherent in LAN applications. (In contrast, ATM and frame relay are connection-oriented.) SMDS is available from telco providers as a shared public network that uses an international standards-based addressing plan known as E.164. Operating like a shared LAN (e.g., Ethernet/802.3), each SMDS cell contains a destination address enabling any SMDS subscriber to exchange data with any other SMDS subscriber—only those nodes with the correct destination address respond to the transmission.

SMDS can support several data rates including DS-1, DS-3, and SONET OC-3. Low-speed SMDS (56 kbps/64 kbps) is also available from some telcos. Since SMDS is a technology-independent service, customers can subscribe to SMDS at a specific data rate for guaranteed throughput. The broadband aspect of SMDS comes from its compatibility with broadband ISDN (B-ISDN) and its potential for supporting voice and video. (See Chapters 12 and 18 for additional information about B-ISDN and broadband.) SMDS also is based on and compatible with the IEEE 802.6 metropolitan area network (MAN) standard.

History

SMDS was developed by Bellcore and the Regional Bell Operating Companies (RBOCs) to address customer demand for interconnected multimegabit LANs within a major metropolitan area. It was designed to be a high-performance, reasonably priced, switched service to provide connectivity and extend LAN-like performance. SMDS is implemented by local exchange carriers (LECs), which are companies that provide local telephone and telecommunications services within the same local access and transport area (LATA).

In contrast to a LEC, an interexchange carrier, IEC or IXC, is any company that provides long-distance telephone and telecommunications services. Examples include AT&T, Sprint, British Telecom (BT), and MCI WorldCom. See Chapter 1 for additional information about LATAs, RBOCs, LECs, and IECs.

Prior to the Telecommunications Act of 1996, LECs were prohibited by law from carrying any type of traffic across LATA boundaries. This caused a problem with SMDS if a LAN-to-LAN connection involved LANs located in different LATAs. To address this issue, a service called *exchange access SMDS* (XA-SMDS) was deployed in 1993. Through XA-SMDS, LECs offered SMDS service to IECs for delivery across LATAs. Connectivity was usually established via a private link where standard SMDS routers transferred traffic from one network to another. XA-SMDS also specified a standard intercarrier interface (ICI) for the LEC-IEC connection.

Today, as a result of the Telecommunications Act of 1996, LECs and IECs can compete in each other's business, so this is no longer an issue. The only restriction is that LECs are regulated separately by each state's public utilities commissions. Thus, if the LEC providing SMDS service operates in two different states, then the types, cost, and rules of the service might vary considerably. MCI WorldCom also has established a national SMDS network that provides connectivity among SMDS networks located in different parts of the country. In this context, SMDS is considered both a MAN and WAN service.

Development Rationale

Prior to SMDS's development in the late 1980s and early 1990s, the only method network administrators had for interconnecting their LANs within a metropolitan area was via leased lines at either 56 kbps or T1 rates. Given the LAN data rates of the time (4 Mbps/16 Mbps for token ring and 10 Mbps for Ethernet/802.3), the leased line approach was insufficient from three perspectives. First, the leased lines represented a bottleneck for LAN-to-LAN transmissions. Data frames being transferred between two Ethernet/802.3 nodes residing on separate LANs interconnected by a 56-kbps or T1 line resulted in congestion and transmission delays. The LAN data rates simply overwhelmed the capacity of the leased circuit. Second, leased line costs were nontrivial. If an organization wanted to interconnect multiple LANs at different locations across a metropolitan area (e.g., within a local county), it would need multiple leased lines. Depending on the topology used, the cost of multiple T1 service can be exorbitant. Although 56-kbps service would be more affordable, the inherent delays and congestion would make it unacceptable. Finally, private leased lines did not scale up well economically. If congestion and delays of T1 service were unacceptable, the next step up was

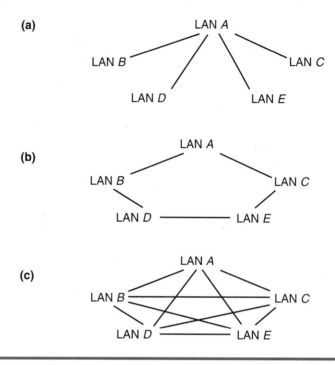

FIGURE 14.1   The traditional method of establishing metropolitan area networks (MANs) is to interconnect LANs within a metropolitan area using dedicated leased circuits. Several methods are possible, and each has its own advantages and disadvantages. In (a), LANs *B, C, D,* and *E* are indirectly connected via LAN *A.* One problem with this design is that if LAN *A* fails, then the remaining LANs cannot communicate with one another. In (b), the single source of failure of design (a) is removed and all neighboring LANs are directly interconnected. However, non-neighboring LANs are still indirectly connected. The design in (c) represents a fully meshed MAN in which every LAN is directly connected to every other LAN. Although more robust, this design is extremely expensive.

T3 service, which was too expensive for many organizations. Figures 14.1 and 14.2 compare traditionally designed MANs to an SMDS network. With SMDS, however, an organization can create a corporate LAN internet (i.e., a corporate network of LANs) across a metropolitan area cost-effectively.

14.2   SMDS Technical Overview

Physical Layer Specifications

SMDS is based on a subset of the IEEE 802.6 physical layer and MAC sublayer standard, which specifies a high-speed network protocol similar to token ring. At the physical layer, IEEE 802.6 specifies a dual bus design using fiber-optic cable (Figure 14.3). The buses, which are labeled *A* and *B,* transmit in only one, but opposite, direction. This

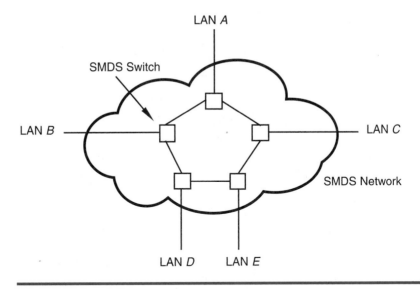

FIGURE 14.2 In contrast to traditionally designed MANs (Figure 14.1), an SMDS network provides direct connectivity among LANs within a geographical region using only a single link for each LAN.

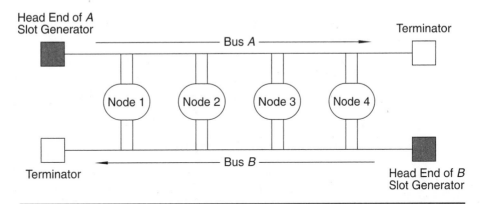

FIGURE 14.3 The physical layer of an SMDS network has two fiber-optic buses, *A* and *B,* which transmit data in opposite directions. The direction of data flow is from the head of the bus, which acts as a slot generator, to the terminator. Nodes are connected to both buses in a logically adjacent manner and read all transmitted data. Source: adapted from Bates & Gregory, 1998.

is similar to FDDI's counterrotating ring (see Chapter 11). Together, the buses provide full-duplex operation. IEEE 802.6 networks can be designed as either an open or looped bus. The difference between the two topologies is where each bus begins and ends. In the open design, the buses begin and end at different nodes; in the loop design, the buses begin and end at the same node. Both designs are illustrated in Figures 14.4(a) and 14.4(b), respectively. SMDS uses the open bus topology.

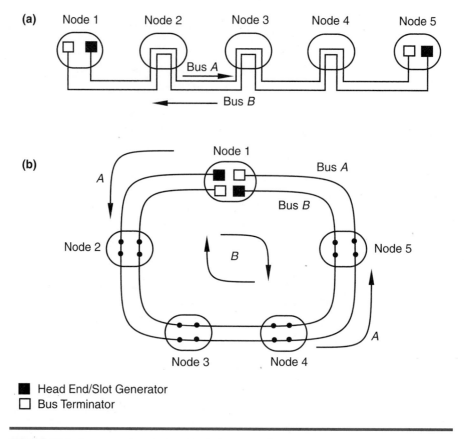

FIGURE 14.4 In an open bus design (a), the head end of the buses is located in two different nodes. In the closed loop design (b), the head of both buses is located in the same node. Source: adapted from Bates & Gregory, 1998.

Data Link Layer Specifications: DQDB

At the data link layer, access to the SMDS network is governed by the IEEE 802.6 *Distributed Queue Dual Bus* (DQDB) protocol. This protocol partitions each bus into time slots, which are used to transmit data. Each slot contains a busy bit and a request bit. If the slot contains data, then the busy bit is set to 1. A slot with its request bit set implies that a node is requesting to send data. If the busy bit is not set (i.e., busy bit = 0), then the slot is considered empty. Nodes can only transmit data using empty slots.

The DQDB protocol works as follows: Prior to sending data, a node must first reserve slots on one bus to be used on the second bus. For example, in Figure 14.3, if node 1 wants to send data to node 3, it must use bus A because A transmits in the direction of node 3. This implies that node 1 must reserve a slot on bus B. Similarly, if node 3 wants to send data to node 1, it must use bus B, which implies that it must reserve a slot on bus A. As we have mentioned, slots are reserved by setting the request bit of an empty slot.

Reserving slots on one bus to be used on the second bus enables nodes to notify their neighbors that they have data to transmit. The process of reserving slots also prevents nodes from monopolizing the bus. Without a reservation system, upstream nodes can continuously fill empty slots with data and hence deny downstream slots from ever seeing an empty slot. For example, in Figure 14.3, slots are generated at the head end of bus *A* and flow from left to right. Thus, node 1 will always see an empty slot first, followed by node 2, then node 3, and finally node 4. Similarly, on bus *B,* slots are generated and flow from right to left. Thus, node 4 will always see an empty slot on this bus before any of the other nodes.

Once a node has requested a slot, it then monitors both buses and maintains a request counter. The purpose of the counter is to maintain an accurate count of the number of unfilled data transmission requests made by downstream nodes. (Unfilled requests are identified whenever a slot has its request bit set.) This counter specifies the number of empty slots a requesting node must let pass before it can access an empty slot itself. Each time a slot that has its request bit set passes by, the counter is increased by 1; each time an empty slot passes on the second bus, the counter is decreased by 1. When the counter reaches 0, the node is permitted to transmit data—that is, it can access the next empty slot on the other bus. This procedure permits nodes to essentially transmit data on a first-come first-served basis and enables nodes to know the state of queued requests throughout the entire network. This process also represents a form of CSMA/CA, *carrier sense multiple access with collision avoidance* (see Chapter 5), which prevents nodes from sending data at the same time.

Time slots are sampled by connected nodes at a rate of 8000 per second. This makes the timing of an SMDS network consistent with the T1/E-1 and SONET/SDH hierarchies (see Chapter 3). The number of slots on a network is also a function of bus speed. For example, if the transmission rate is 34 Mbps, then there are eight slots available per frame. DQDB supports both connectionless and connection-oriented service and is capable of transmitting data, voice, and video. As a subset of IEEE 802.6, though, SMDS is connectionless based and transmits only data.

14.3   The SMDS Interface Protocol (SIP)

The *SMDS Interface Protocol* (SIP) was defined by Bellcore, which is the research branch of the RBOCs. SIP consists of three protocol levels, formally called SIP level 3, SIP level 2, and SIP level 1. As we describe these protocol levels, you will detect a similarity between their functions and the first three layers of the OSI model. It is important to note that although these protocol levels are based on the first three OSI layers, they do not directly correspond to them. Instead, the three protocol levels represent SMDS's MAC sublayer and hence operate at the data link layer. Before we get into any detail about SIP, it might help first to identify the components of an SMDS network. A simplified diagram is provided for this purpose in Figure 14.5. LANs are interconnected via SMDS using three components: SMDS routers, SMDS DSUs (SDSUs), and SMDS switches. Collectively, these three components form the basis of an SMDS network and support the DQDB protocol. Router, DSU, and switch connections are established as in any LAN–WAN configuration, and the major router manufacturers (e.g., Cisco) support SMDS routing. The point of demarcation, called the *subscriber network interface* (SNI), separates the router and SDSU, which are called the *customer premises equipment* (CPE), from the telco's SMDS network equipment. An SMDS switch represents the head end of one of the buses

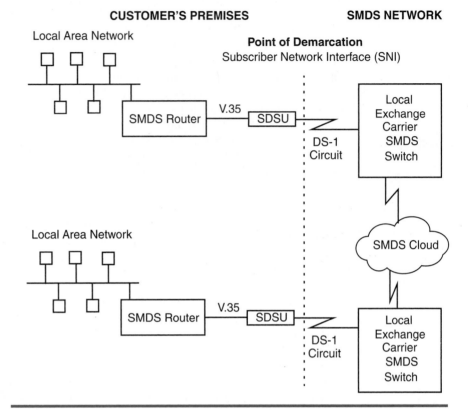

FIGURE 14.5 The components of an SMDS network consist of a router that supports the SMDS Interface Protocol, an SMDS CSU/DSU, a circuit, and an SMDS switch. The point that separates the customer's equipment from the SMDS network is called the point of demarcation and is the interface between the circuit and the SDSU. This is usually a punch-down block located at the customer's telecommunications office. This interface is formally called the subscriber network interface (SNI). Source: adapted from Sharer, 1993.

(e.g., bus *A*), and all other nodes are CPE nodes. For example, in Figure 14.4(a); node 1 is the SMDS switch, and nodes 2 through 5 are CPE nodes. The end CPE node, which is node 5 in Figure 14.4(a), serves as the head end of the second bus (i.e., bus *B*).

When data frames destined for a remote LAN are received by the SMDS router from the local LAN, the router encapsulates these frames into special SMDS frames via SIP level 3. Called SIP level-3 PDUs (short for *protocol data units*), these frames are then transmitted across the V.35 interface between the router and SDSU. SIP level-3 PDUs provide the connectionless service of SMDS and contain up to 9188 bytes of user information plus related header and trailer information (Figure 14.6). At the SDSU, SIP level 2 accepts the level-3 PDUs and partitions them into fixed-length segments of 53 bytes each (Figure 14.7). The various length and tag fields contained in the level-3 PDUs provide the necessary information for this partitioning (and eventual reassembly). These 53-byte cells, called SIP level-2 PDUs, consist of 44 bytes of user information (called the payload or segmentation unit), a 7-byte header, and a 2-byte trailer (Figure 14.8). SIP level-2 PDUs

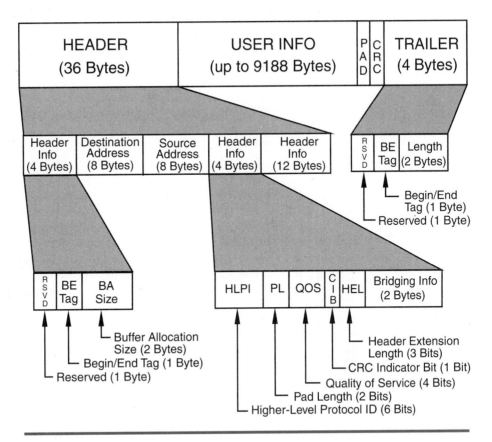

FIGURE 14.6 Contents of an SMDS Interface Protocol level-3 PDU. This frame is partitioned into a 53-byte fixed-length cell by SIP level 2 (see also Figures 14.7 and 14.8). The PAD and CRC fields vary from 0 to 3 bytes and 0 to 4 bytes, respectively. Source: adapted from Bates & Gregory, 1998.

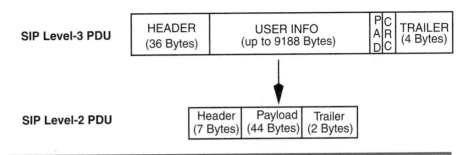

FIGURE 14.7 SIP level-3 PDUs are fragmented into 53-byte cells by SIP level 2. These level-2 PDUs are the slots that are placed on the medium. SMDS nodes read all slots placed on the bus and write to empty slots. The number of slots placed on the bus is a function of the bus's data rate. The expanded version of an SIP level-2 PDU is shown in Figure 14.8.

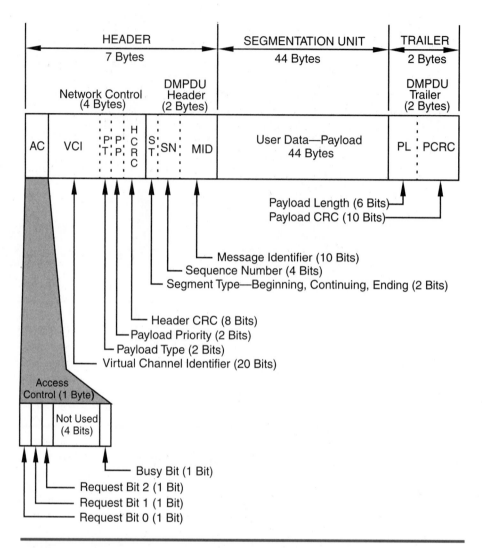

FIGURE 14.8 The basic data unit on an SMDS network is a 53-byte cell. This cell, which consists of a 7-byte header, a 44-byte payload, and a 2-byte trailer, is the result of a fragmentation process that is performed by the SMDS Interface Protocol level 2 (see Figure 14.7). SIP level 2 receives from a router (via SIP level 3) an initial MAC frame that contains up to 9188 bytes of user data plus related header and trailer information. This frame, called the *initial MAC protocol data unit* (IMPDU), is then partitioned into 53-byte cells for transmission over the network via SIP level 1. At the receiving end, cells are then reassembled into their original form. Key to this reassembly process is the header and trailer information of the IMPDU. This information is also partitioned as part of the fragmentation process and carried via the 2-byte derived MAC protocol data units (DMPDU), which are included as part of the 53-byte cell (see also Figure 14.6). Source: adapted from Bates & Gregory, 1998.

represent the basic data unit on an SMDS network. These data units are then processed by SIP level 1, which provides the physical interface to the SMDS network. This last level of SIP consists of two sublayers: the *transmission system* and the *physical layer convergence protocol*. The transmission system specifies how cells are to be placed on the medium; the physical layer convergence protocol formats the 53-byte cells for actual delivery across the network. The cells are then reassembled into level-3 PDUs at the receiving end. Thus, an SMDS router provides SIP-3, and the SMDS DSU provides SIP-2 and SIP-1.

Note that SMDS also supports three request bits—Req0, Req1, and Req2—as part of its access control field. Each request bit corresponds to a different level of priority. Priority levels are similar to those of token ring. Regardless of which priority is used, request bits indicate that a node has data to transmit.

When SMDS was initially deployed, the LECs required their customers' SMDS interface equipment to deliver level-2 PDUs to the LECs' SMDS switches. This meant that customers could not use standard CSU/DSUs; they had to purchase special SMDS DSUs. This made SMDS an expensive service because SDSUs, in some cases, cost three times more than conventional CSU/DSUs. Today, however, the level-3 to level-2 conversion is performed within the LECs' SMDS switch, enabling subscribers to use conventional CSU/DSUs.

14.4 SMDS Addressing

SMDS addresses are based on the standard ISDN global numbering addressing format specified by ITU-T standard E.164. These addresses are just like telephone numbers. They are 15 decimal digits long and include a country code, area or city code, and a local number. Country codes are two or three digits long and consist of a zone code followed by a one- or two-digit national identifier. Area or city codes are up to four digits long. For example, country codes for the United Kingdom (UK), Australia, and Taiwan are 44, 61, and 886, respectively. Sample city codes within the UK include 171 and 181 for London, 141 for Glasgow, 151 for Liverpool, and 1232 for Belfast. Sample city codes in Taiwan include 2 for Taipei and 37 for Chunan. There are no city codes for Australia. In the United States and Canada, country codes are not used. Instead, these countries use the zone code 1, which is followed by a three-digit area code and a seven-digit local number.

There are also two types of SMDS addresses. *Individual addresses* are used for unicast transmissions; *group addresses* are used for multicast traffic. To distinguish between the two, individual addresses begin with a hexadecimal C and group addresses begin with a hexadecimal E. If an address contains fewer than 15 digits, then it is padded with hexadecimal Fs. Thus, the SMDS address C14075557235FFFF identifies an individual location in the 407 area code within the United States, and E160462284422961 is a group address in British Columbia, Canada. The SMDS service provider (i.e., the LEC) assigns a block of up to 16 individual addresses to each subscriber network interface (SNI), which can exchange data among 128 individual or group addresses. More than one SMDS node can be assigned the same group address in addition to an individual address. There are restrictions, though. For example, an individual address cannot belong to more than 32 groups, and a group address cannot represent more than 128 individual addresses.

Group addressing also can be used as a filtering mechanism. For example, assume five LANs (*A, B, C, D,* and *E*) within a local county are interconnected via SMDS. Further assume that all five LANs are running IP; *A, B,* and *C* are also running IPX; and *D* and *E* are also running AppleTalk. Using group addressing, IPX traffic can be isolated from LANs *D* and *E,* and AppleTalk traffic can be isolated from LANs *A, B,* and *C.* Group addressing also can be used to create virtual ports over SMDS.

Since data transmission in an SMDS network occurs via the subscriber network interface, there is often a question of whether the customer or LEC is responsible for configuring what addresses get to exchange data. This configuration is done by the service provider based on customer specifications. Thus, the customer simply informs the LEC which addresses are to communicate with each other, and at what rate, and the LEC does all the configurations.

14.5 SMDS versus Other LAN-to-LAN Technologies

Companies that can benefit from SMDS include organizations that have at least four remote sites across a metropolitan area that: (a) need to be interconnected in a seamless, cost-effective manner; (b) require high-speed bulk data transfers at a reasonable cost; (c) need to transfer quickly large files, including video and high-resolution images such as blueprint schematics, MRIs, CAT scans, and x-rays. In short, SMDS is appropriate for any enterprise with distributed sites that uses bandwidth-intensive applications. Prime candidates include hospitals, publishing companies, graphic design houses, insurance companies, police departments, automobile manufacturers, colleges and universities, and municipal governments. Applications include CAD/CAM, LAN-to-LAN connectivity, telemedicine and teleradiology, collaborative printing and publishing, image and multimedia file transfers, distance education, videoconferencing, and high-speed access to the Internet.

SMDS versus Frame Relay and ATM

When comparing SMDS to other LAN-to-LAN technologies such as frame relay and ATM, it is important to understand that SMDS is a service, not a technology; frame relay and ATM are technologies. Since it is technology independent, SMDS can operate over frame relay or ATM. Technology independence also implies protocol independence. Thus, SMDS can support any LAN protocol such as token ring and Ethernet/802.3, as well as various network protocols including TCP/IP, OSI, IPX, and AppleTalk. Second, SMDS is a packet-switching, connectionless service; frame relay and ATM are connection-oriented. This means that it is not necessary to establish a connection through the network prior to data transmission. Instead, packets are transmitted without any delay for setting up or tearing down a circuit. There also is no need to define permanent virtual circuits (PVCs) or committed information rates (CIRs), as is the case with frame relay. Thus, an SMDS network is simpler to design than frame relay. Third, SMDS's bandwidth range (56 kbps to SONET rates) provides a better range at

TABLE 14.1 SMDS Features and Related Benefits

Feature	Related Benefit
1. Service, not a technology	1. Can operate over frame relay or ATM
2. Protocol-independent	2. Supports multiple LAN or network protocols
3. 56/64 kbps to SONET speeds	3. Complete range of speeds for all applications
4. Connectionless	4. Obviates need to define PVCs as with frame relay
5. Packet-switched	5. Packets transmitted without delay
6. Logical, fully meshed connectivity	6. Reliable and robust LAN-to-LAN connectivity
7. Shared public network	7. Subscribers can exchange data with each other
8. Uses 53-byte cells similar to ATM	8. Smooth migration to ATM
9. No CIRs as with frame relay	9. Guaranteed bandwidth; pay only for usage
10. Built-in management	10. Provides usage-based billing and statistics

TABLE 14.2 SMDS Disadvantages

1. Restricted availability—the number of LECs offering SMDS is very limited.
2. Limited nationwide/global service—MCI WorldCom is the only IEC to offer inter-LATA SMDS.
3. Perceived as an expensive service.
4. Overshadowed by frame relay and ATM.
5. Although capable, SMDS does not provide voice or video support.
6. Private networks via public backbone are now provided by the Internet and VPNs.

the low end than ATM and a better range at the high end than frame relay. Furthermore, unlike frame relay, an SMDS circuit is fully committed to its specified rate, and you only pay for the bandwidth used. Fourth, SMDS provides several network management features including usage-based billing and users' usage statistics. SMDS's addressing scheme also provides a type of built-in security measure by restricting data transfers to nodes assigned a specific group address. Many of these features are not available from SMDS's competition. Table 14.1 summarizes many of the features and benefits of SMDS; Table 14.2 lists some of SMDS's disadvantages.

14.6   Status of SMDS Today

At this stage, you are probably asking yourself why you haven't heard of SMDS before or why it is not as popular as frame relay or ATM. Given all of its features and benefits, surely SMDS must be used somewhere. You are right in your observation that SMDS seems to have been overshadowed by frame relay and ATM. However, this is only true in the United States. In Europe, SMDS is popular. (More on this later.) Many reasons have been cited in the trade publications explaining why SMDS got off to a slow start in the United States and then never did materialize into a universally compelling and accepted service. We will summarize them here for you.

First, as is the case in trying to sell any new technology or service, success depends on proper planning and marketing. It has been speculated that the LECs failed in both of these areas when it came to SMDS. Poor planning on the LECs' part resulted in expensive equipment, which gave SMDS the reputation of being an expensive service. Contributing to this reputation was SMDS's initial lack of support for low data rates (less than DS-1). Many organizations that could have benefited from SMDS service were locked out because they could not afford (or justify) the high cost associated with high speeds and the potential wasted bandwidth. Although some LECs now offer low-speed SMDS, which makes the service more attractive to companies with limited resources and bandwidth requirements, it's a matter of too little too late since these companies are opting instead for frame relay.

From a technology perspective, insufficient attention also was given to how neighboring LECs would interconnect their SMDS networks. This led to incompatible methods that made customers with LANs that crossed LATA boundaries hesitant to subscribe to SMDS. Although this issue also has been addressed, it is once again a matter of too little too late. Since the SMDS market never materialized, commitment to SMDS among the LECs has been spotty at best. LECs have been opting instead to concentrate on frame relay and ATM. For example, in the United States, among the various LECs, Verizon Communications (formerly Bell Atlantic) offers SMDS service. Furthermore, among the major IXCs (AT&T, MCI WorldCom, and Sprint), only MCI WorldCom offers nationwide SMDS service. This lack of support makes customers wary of the service and less likely to subscribe to it. In fact, the final nail in SMDS's coffin was AT&T's decision to provide frame relay and ATM instead of SMDS.

Another reason for SMDS's lack of market share in the broadband community is it was never designed to support isochronous data, which is needed to transmit real-time digital voice and video applications. SMDS was to eventually support voice and video in addition to data. Its DQDB access method provides the necessary technology for this support. However, it doesn't appear that SMDS will be further developed to incorporate support for isochronous services. Finally, although SMDS has built-in security that enables it to use a shared public network as the backbone for a private network, this concept has been overshadowed by the Internet and virtual private networks (VPNs).

From all accounts, SMDS is probably "dead" in the United States. Consider, for example, the following:

1. The SMDS Interest Group, which was the biggest promoter of SMDS, folded in 1997.
2. In *Data Communications'* 25th anniversary issue (October 21, 1997), SMDS was identified as one of the top 25 flops. "Switched multimegabit data services were designed to deliver LAN-like performances over the wide area. And it's just what they did, to the dismay of users who got high bandwidth, lots of flexibility—and the variable delays associated with Ethernet. Now the SMDS Interest Group has folded, presumably for lack of interest" (p. 143).
3. MCI WorldCom is the only interexchange carrier that offers SMDS.
4. Some local exchange carriers have discontinued offering SMDS service. US West, for example, cited a dearth of customer demand as its reason for canceling SMDS.

On the other hand, since it is a service, SMDS can coexist with ATM and frame relay. That is, SMDS subscribers can migrate to ATM or use ATM or frame relay as the underlying technology for their SMDS service. It is uncertain, though, whether this will ever come to fruition on a large-scale basis in the United States. From all accounts, it is unlikely that SMDS will grow in market share or be developed further. It might, however, survive as a niche market.

Although SMDS is not in widespread use in the United States, it is still popular in Europe. Providers include British Telecommunications (United Kingdom), Telecom Eireann (Irish Republic), France Telecom (France), Belgacom (Belgium), and Deutsche Telekom (Germany). Other countries in which SMDS deployment is high include Denmark, Switzerland, Austria, Italy, Sweden, and Australia.

End-of-Chapter Commentary

This concludes our brief discussion on SMDS. For additional information about this service, you are encouraged to consult the Suggested Readings and References at the end of the chapter. You also might want to review Chapter 13 (Frame Relay) and Chapter 15 (ATM) to compare SMDS to these two technologies.

CHAPTER REVIEW MATERIALS

SUMMARY

- SMDS is a connectionless WAN data service designed for interconnecting LANs. It was developed by the Regional Bell Operating Companies and their research organization, Bellcore, to provide customers with a multimegabit, high-speed LAN-to-LAN technology that could transmit video and graphics applications within a metropolitan area.
- SMDS uses 53-byte fixed-length cells as its basic unit for data transmission. Cells comprise a 44-byte payload, a 7-byte header, and a 2-byte trailer. Cells are transmitted immediately and without regard to order.
- SMDS's physical layer is based on two unidirectional fiber-optic cables called buses, and SMDS's data link layer is based on IEEE 802.6, Distributed Queue Dual Bus (DQDB) protocol.
- The SMDS Interface Protocol (SIP) consists of three levels: SIP level 3 provides the specifications for encapsulating data frames into SMDS frames for transmission between the SMDS router and its attached CSU/DSU; SIP level 2 provides the specifications for partitioning SMDS frames into 53-byte cells; and SIP level 1 provides the physical interface to the SMDS network and processes these cells for transmission.

- SMDS addresses are based on the ITU-T E.164 standard. Addresses are 15 decimal digits long and include a country code, area or city code, followed by a local number. Individual SMDS addresses are used for unicast transmissions, and group addresses are used for multicast transmissions.

- As a data service, SMDS can operate over and coexist with technologies such as frame relay or ATM. This is important since SMDS use is quite limited in the United States, where frame relay is the preferred choice for LAN-to-LAN connectivity.

VOCABULARY CHECK

cell
customer premises equipment
    (CPE)

Distributed Queue Dual Bus
    (DQDB)
exchange access SMDS (XA-
    SMDS)

SMDS Interface Protocol (SIP)
switched multimegabit data ser-
    vice (SMDS)

REVIEW EXERCISES

1. In our introduction to SMDS, we stated that SMDS operates like a shared LAN such as Ethernet/802.3. What advantages and disadvantages does this provide SMDS?
2. In the DQDB protocol, how can a station tell how many downstream reservations have been made?
3. Describe how DQDB can be implemented as a ring.
4. What is the function of SMDS's SNI?
5. What is a SIP level 3 PDU?
6. SMDS can operate at DS-1 and DS-3 rates. This implies that SIP level 1 provides the physical link protocol for these rates. In the text, we stated that SIP level 1 comprises two layers: the transmission and the physical layer convergence protocol (PLCP). Explain the function of these two sublayers relative to DS-1 and DS-3 links.
7. Assume that one DS-1 PLCP frame can support the transmission of ten SMDS SIP level-2 PDUs.

Further assume that a six-byte trailer is attached to the end of each PLCP frame. If it takes 3 ms to transmit this structure, what is the effective transmission rate?
8. Consider Figure 14.8, which depicts the fields of the SMDS SIP level-2 PDU. Explain the purpose of the segment type field. Provide a two-bit arrangement that can be used for this field. Compare your bit arrangement with the one that is actually used by SMDS.
9. Describe SMDS group addresses and explain their purpose.
10. SMDS is considered a service and not a technology. Distinguish between these two concepts (service vs. technology).
11. Compare and contrast SMDS and frame relay.
12. Explain why SMDS is not widely deployed in the United States.

SUGGESTED READINGS AND REFERENCES

ATKINS, J., and M. NORRIS. 1995. *Total Area Networking: ATM, Frame Relay and SMDS Explained.* New York: Wiley.

BATES, R. J., and D. GREGORY. 1998. *Voice and Data Communications Handbook.* New York: McGraw-Hill.

BELLCORE. 1990. Exchange Access SMDS Service Generic Requirements. *Bellcore Technical Advisory,* TA-TSV-001060, December.

————. 1991. Generic System Requirements in Support of Switched Multi-megabit Data Service. *Bellcore Technical Reference,* TR-TSV-000772, May.

Data Communications. 1994. SMDS Is Here: Where Are the Customers? *Data Communications,* October, 55–56.

————. 1997. The Top 25 Flops. *Data Communications,* 21 October, 142–143.

FITZGERALD, S. 1993. Packing Them In. *LAN Magazine,* September, 77–86.

GALLO, M., and W. HANCOCK. 1999. *Networking Explained.* Boston: Digital Press.

HUGHES, L., and S. STARLIPER. 1990. Switched Multimegabit Data Service (SMDS). *Connexions: The Interoperability Report,* 4(10): 34–37.

KRISHNASWAMY, P., and M. ULEMA. 1991. Developments in SMDS. *Connexions: The Interoperability Report,* 5(10): 24–31.

KUMAR, B. 1995. *Broadband Communications: A Professional's Guide to ATM, Frame Relay, SMDS, SONET, and BISDN.* New York: McGraw-Hill.

MENDES, G. 1996. SMDS: A WAN Alternative. *LAN Interoperability: A Quarterly Supplement to LAN Magazine,* August, 22–27.

MILLER, M. 1994. *Analyzing Broadband Networks: Frame Relay, SMDS, and ATM.* San Mateo, CA: M&T.

MINOLI, D. 1991. The New Wide Area Technologies: SMDS and BISDN. *Network Computing,* August, 88–92.

PARNELL, T. 1997. *LAN Times Guide to Wide Area Networks.* Berkeley, CA: Osborne McGraw-Hill.

SHARER, R. 1993. The SMDS Express. *LAN Magazine,* July, 51–58.

———. 1994. Lighten Up. *LAN Magazine,* March, 109–112.

The Institute of Electrical and Electronics Engineers. 1990. Distributed Queue Dual Bus (DQDB) Subnetwork of a Metropolitan Area Network (MAN). IEEE Standard 802.6-1990. The Institute of Electrical and Electronics Engineers.

15

Asynchronous Transfer Mode (ATM)

In this chapter, we provide an introduction to asynchronous transfer mode (ATM), which is a high-speed switching network architecture created in the late 1980s/early 1990s. ATM was designed expressly to combine the delivery of a wide range of services (data, voice, and video) over a single network. We begin the chapter with an overview and history of ATM. This is followed by an explanation of various ATM concepts and a description of how ATM operates. Section 15.3 provides a description of various ATM interface standards. ATM cells, virtual connections, and the adaptation layer are then presented in Sections 15.4 and 15.5. Section 15.6 provides a brief overview of ATM's attributes relative to the concept of convergence technology (which is discussed in more detail in Chapter 18). Finally, the last section of the chapter compares ATM to other technologies such as Ethernet, frame relay, and SONET. Included in this section is a description of how ATM can be implemented as an emulated LAN.

15.1 What Is ATM?

Overview

Asynchronous transfer mode (ATM) is a sophisticated multispeed network environment that provides a variety of complex network services for applications requiring various types of network solutions. It can be used to carry data, voice, and video—separately or simultaneously—over the same network path and is one of the most complex communications technologies available today for public or private network infrastructures. ATM can be used in LANs, MANs, and WANs, all at the same time if needed. Using terminology developed in previous chapters, ATM might also be considered a "hyphenated" protocol—it is connection-oriented, full-duplex, point-to-point, and cell-switched.

The concepts of connection-oriented, full-duplex, and point-to-point were discussed in Chapters 1 and 2. However, this is our first introduction to cell-switched, so an explanation is in order. The concept of cell-switched is very similar to frame relay (Chapter 13), which uses switches to transfer variable-length frames within the frame relay cloud from source to destination. Instead of using frames, ATM uses fixed-length *cells,* which contain exactly 53 bytes—48 bytes for user data and 5 bytes for overhead. As a result, ATM is sometimes referred to as *cell relay,* which dates back to the late 1960s. The concept of cell relay is predicated on time domain multiplexing (TDM) and packet-switching (see Chapter 2). The term *asynchronous TDM* (ATDM) was coined in 1968 to describe cell relay. We will discuss ATM cells in more detail later in the chapter.

History

In the presence of B-ISDN, "standard" or "first-generation" ISDN is called *narrowband ISDN.* See Chapter 12.

ATM has its roots in broadband ISDN (B-ISDN), which some people refer to as second-generation ISDN. In 1986, the standards organization CCITT (now part of ITU) decided to make cell relay the transfer mode of B-ISDN. The CCITT also decided to change the name of this cell-based technology from ATDM to ATM. CCITT's decision meant that broadband networks throughout the world would be based on ATM. Two

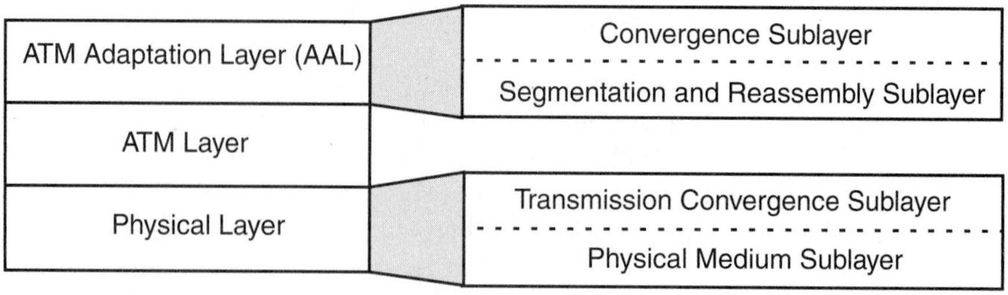

Physical Layer
- Transports cells from one interface to another via a communications channel.
- Supports both optical and electrical communications channels.
- LAN support ranges from 25 to 155 Mbps for copper and fiber.
- WAN support includes SONET/SDH rates over fiber.
- Contains two sublayers: The *physical medium sublayer* function is restricted to only medium-dependent functions such as bit transfer, bit alignment, and electrical-to-optical conversions. The *transmission convergence sublayer* performs functions related to converting cells from the ATM layer into bits on the sending node and converting bits into cells on the receiving node.

ATM Layer
- Performs cell multiplexing/demultiplexing and switching.
- Provides virtual connections between endpoints.
- Generates appropriate cell headers on a sending node based on information received from higher layers; extracts cell header on a receiving node and passes cell payload to higher layers.

ATM Adaptation Layer (AAL)
- Partitions higher-level user data into 48-byte cells plus necessary overhead.
- Defines five different adaptation types to support different service classes:
  - *AAL1:* Supports Class A services, which are connection-oriented constant-bit rate (CBR) (e.g., voice transmissions).
  - *AAL2:* Supports Class B services, which are connection-oriented variable-bit rate (VBR) (e.g., synchronized data, packet-based video).
  - *AAL3/AAL4:* Supports Class C and Class D services, which are, respectively, connection-oriented VBR (e.g., bursty data used for file transfers) and connectionless VBR (e.g., LAN data).
  - *AAL5:* Supports Class C and Class D services; known as the *simple and efficient adaptation layer* (SEAL) and used for bursty data transfers in which higher-layer protocols perform error control. AAL5 is a modification of connection-oriented VBR.
- Consists of two sublayers. The *convergence sublayer* (CS) provides a specific AAL service at an AAL network service access point (NSAP). The *segmentation and reassembly sublayer* (SAR) segments higher-level messages into an ATM's cell's 48-byte information field on the sending node and reassembles this information for delivery to the higher layers on the receiving node.

FIGURE 15.1 The ATM layers. The physical layer corresponds to OSI's physical layer; the ATM layer generally corresponds to OSI's data link and network layers; the AAL generally corresponds to OSI's higher-level layers (transport, session, and application). Source: adapted from Atkins & Norris, 1995; and Bates & Gregory, 1998.

years later, in 1988, a three-layered reference model for ATM was defined by CCITT. These layers, which represent the first three layers of the B-ISDN reference model, include the physical layer, the ATM layer, and the ATM adaptation layer. It is important to note that the ATM layers do not necessarily correspond to the layers of the OSI model. The ATM layers are summarized in Figure 15.1. (Much of the information presented in Figure 15.1 is discussed later in this chapter.) After much discussion, the CCITT also defined ATM's cell format to consist of 53 bytes, with 48 bytes for user data and 5 bytes for overhead. Finally, in 1990, the CCITT issued its first set of recommendations that specified the details of ATM for B-ISDN. For a good overview of ATM's history, see Gould (1994).

15.2   General Concepts and Operation

General Concepts

ATM operates as a "network within a network" concept. It has its own internal hand-shaking and management protocols, quality of service (QoS) facilities, performance and flow-control facilities, and many other components that are usually separated on network technologies such as frame relay. ATM is very much like building a subway system that can support other transportation systems on top of it. The "upper" transportation systems do not know that ATM is acting as an independent subsystem and are oblivious of the complex nature of ATM networking.

One of ATM's features is that it can guarantee delivery of time-sensitive information over the designed network. For instance, typical video as seen on a television set transmits 30 frames of video per second over the airwaves. Not 29, not 31—30 only. That's it. No more, no less. Therefore, it is critical for the network to be able to move exactly 30 frames of video information per second over the network. This means that the network must be able to properly reserve bandwidth space on the network to accommodate delivery of the 30 frames per second without degrading the throughput between the source and destination locations. To do this, all intermediary locations (typically ATM switch devices) between the source and the destination must allocate network "space" to move the information efficiently in the required time frame. (This is called *isochronous* communications.) This requires various handshaking between systems, bandwidth allocation and management facilities, QoS delivery facilities, and a host of other technologies, algorithms, and techniques to ensure the path between source and destination is clean, fast, and efficient. All this adds up to the need to have a "network in a network" so that ATM devices can properly manage the path of activity between the source and destination systems on the network. This implies that communication protocols such as TCP/IP and SNA do not know all of this work is taking place in the ATM hardware.

If viewed from the perspective of other LAN technologies such as Ethernet/802.3, ATM can provide many services that are somewhat equivalent to Ethernet/802.3. It can also be used in a LAN for desktop connectivity instead of Ethernet/802.3. In this context, networking software "thinks" that the ATM environment reacts like OSI layer-2 hardware, as do Ethernet/802.3, token ring, or FDDI. In terms of functionality, ATM can "be" like Ethernet/802.3 or, more specifically, can be used where Ethernet/802.3 might be used. How it works, however, is a completely different story and is not at all similar in function to other standard LAN technologies.

Operation

An ATM network fundamentally resembles a frame relay network. Cells are transmitted from source to destination via an ATM switched subnet. End nodes communicate with an ATM device via a user-to-network interface (UNI), and ATM switches communicate with each other via a network-to-network interface (NNI). The UNI and NNI components are just two of a wide variety of ATM component standards. A typical configuration is shown in Figure 15.2, and a simplified example of how ATM facilitates multiservice networking is shown in Figure 15.3.

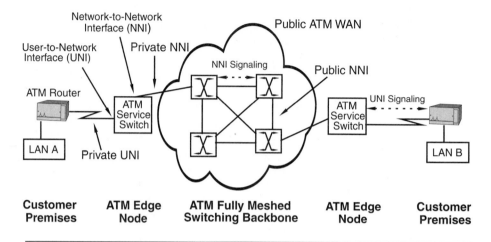

FIGURE 15.2 In an ATM connection, end nodes communicate with an ATM device via a user-to-network interface (UNI), and ATM devices communicate with each other via a network-to-network interface (NNI). Source: adapted from Mehta, 1996.

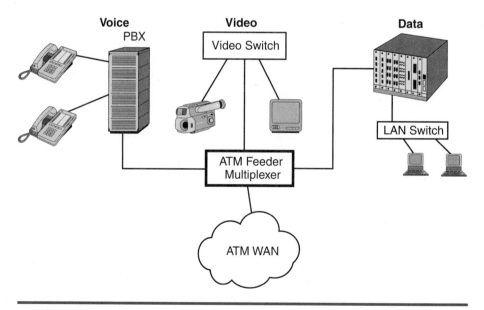

FIGURE 15.3 A simplified example of how ATM facilitates multiservice networking. ATM is the only network that was built from the ground up to support data, voice, and video at the same time. Therefore, an ATM network can be used for almost any type of network environment in use today and in the future.

15.3   ATM Interface Standards

In ATM, there is a hierarchy of standardized interfaces called the *Anchorage Accord.* The basic hierarchy, as defined by the accord, is shown in Figure 15.4. Separate standards define the manner in which network components are interconnected and how they interact. Working from left to right in Figure 15.4, the various components of the ATM environment are defined by the functional specifications listed. At this writing, the various numbers indicate current versions of the specifications. These version numbers, however, will be ever increasing over time as the standards mature and change. Shaded components are presently under development; all others are complete.

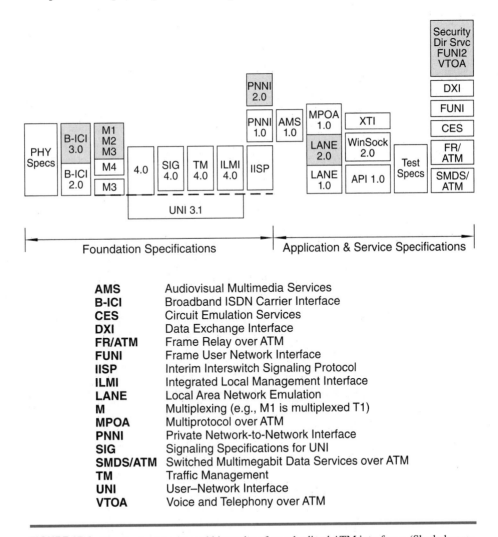

AMS	Audiovisual Multimedia Services
B-ICI	Broadband ISDN Carrier Interface
CES	Circuit Emulation Services
DXI	Data Exchange Interface
FR/ATM	Frame Relay over ATM
FUNI	Frame User Network Interface
IISP	Interim Interswitch Signaling Protocol
ILMI	Integrated Local Management Interface
LANE	Local Area Network Emulation
M	Multiplexing (e.g., M1 is multiplexed T1)
MPOA	Multiprotocol over ATM
PNNI	Private Network-to-Network Interface
SIG	Signaling Specifications for UNI
SMDS/ATM	Switched Multimegabit Data Services over ATM
TM	Traffic Management
UNI	User–Network Interface
VTOA	Voice and Telephony over ATM

FIGURE 15.4   The Anchorage Accord hierarchy of standardized ATM interfaces. (Shaded components are presently under development; all others are complete.)

Note that the standards are divided into two basic groups: (a) foundation specifications and (b) application and service specifications. The former define ATM base function sets; the latter define how other networks and applications interoperate with ATM network components. It is outside the scope of this book to explore the massive details of each functional component due to their complexity and also the amount of time it takes to properly define and illustrate every item. However, we do need to spend a little time on some of the components to understand how ATM works and why the functional layers are necessary.

In an ATM network, the type of computer being used is irrelevant to the network transportation capabilities. This means that PBXs and data networks from computer-to-computer or video-to-display facilities can all share the same network infrastructure simultaneously. This is done by using all the functional standards shown in Figure 15.4 to provide exact interfaces for different data types to the network infrastructure. In this manner, the network supports all the different types of interconnection services required as well as all the different types of transmission requirements.

Just like any other type of network, ATM uses addresses for each connection point. Two types of addresses are used. For private networks, ATM uses OSI's (see Chapter 2) network service access points (NSAPs) for its addressing mechanism. NSAPs are 20-byte addresses and include a 13-byte prefix that can be used to identify a specific location, including a country, region, or end system. Public ATM networks, however, use E.164, the standard ISDN global numbering addressing format specified by ITU-T (see Chapter 14). There is a move underfoot to standardize on NSAP-based addresses for all devices, public or private.

For a device to be connected to an ATM network, it must first have an ATM-based network interface card (NIC) installed. (See Chapter 6 for more information about NICs.) These NICs, which are layer-2 devices and contain on-board ATM circuitry, are then connected to a local switch that is usually provided by the corporate networking people. The physical connection between the workstation and the local switch (also called a "private switch") can be copper (typically UTP Category 5 running at 25 Mbps or 155 Mbps), fiber (at various speeds from 155 Mbps to terabit ranges), or wireless (10 Mbps or greater). The specification for a NIC to "talk" to a switch is the user-to-network interface (UNI) functional specification, which was mentioned earlier. The purpose of the UNI specification is to define exactly how an end station communicates to the next level of network interface, which is a private switch at a site. This specification is quite large and complex. Among others, it specifies the handshaking between the NIC and switch, the quality of service requirements for traffic between the NIC and switch, and all the other connection-oriented facilities ATM requires to ensure that the NIC and switch are content with each other when connected on the network. Furthermore, UNI also specifies sections of the hardware physical attributes such as copper interface issues, fiber interface issues, and wireless component functionalities. These collective specifications and functions are generally referred to as UNI signaling (see Figure 15.2). Thus, UNI is specifically intended for endpoint communication to the ATM switch environment.

Given this description (and the information provided in Figure 15.2), if your inclination is to imply that switches and other components communicate with each other differently, then you are correct. Switch-to-switch communication in a private (premises) network is called *private network-to-network interface* (PNNI). PNNI provides some specific functionality that switches need between each other but that end stations could not care less about. Other specifications exist as well. Two in particular are the broadband ISDN intercarrier interface (B-ICI) and the LAN user-to-network interface (LUNI). B-ICI is used for connecting two public ATM networks between different network service providers; LUNI specifies how an emulated LAN user connects to an ATM environment. For example, if we have an existing Ethernet/802.3 or other LAN, then there is a specification called LANE (local area network emulation) to help us connect to an ATM network. Similarly, if we have an existing frame relay WAN facility that needs to interoperate with ATM, then the frame user network interface (FUNI) is used. There are many others. Thus, wherever there is a network connection point on an ATM network that connects to a dissimilar connection point, a functional specification (and related abbreviation, of course) associated with the connection method is defined (see Figure 15.4).

ATM switches are responsible for transmitting data within an ATM network (see Figure 15.2). An ATM switch implements a routing method called a switch fabric. Switch fabric algorithms come in a wide variety of implementations, but the most common types are called *Batcher-Banyan* and *delta* switching environments. The algorithms in the switch exchange information with other interconnected switches to learn where source and destination SAP locations are in the overall network. By using these high-speed methods, a very large network of components can quickly be mapped and discovered when traffic hits the physical network and needs to be forwarded to the proper location. When first powered-up, switches configure themselves by going into an autodiscovery mode, which enables them to automatically learn about other connected switches. They also provide temporary NSAP addresses to ATM connection points that may need one to interoperate and help manage the overall network environment from a configuration and traffic management perspective.

15.4 ATM Cells, Virtual Connections, and Addressing

To understand how ATM switches transport data across the network from source to destination, we need to discuss, from a more technical perspective, the three main concepts of an ATM network: ATM cells, virtual connections, and addressing. These three concepts represent the essential building blocks of all ATM networks and are highly interrelated. Let's begin with cells.

ATM Cells

As we stated earlier in the chapter, ATM uses 53-byte (octet) cells comprising a 5-byte header and a 48-byte payload (user data). ATM cells are the basic unit of data that cross the UNI, and they are fixed in length. Thus, cells are *always* the same size—never larger, never smaller. It is set up this way for throughput and buffer management reasons (video gets very unhappy when the network is slow). The structure of a cell is shown in Figure 15.5. The cell's header carries the information needed to transport a cell across an ATM network.

As a point of information, in the ATM world, the term *octet* is used instead of byte. This is because octet means exactly 8 bits. The term *byte,* however, does not necessarily mean 8 bits to some people. During the early days of computing, byte was used to represent a unit of information composed of some number of consecutive

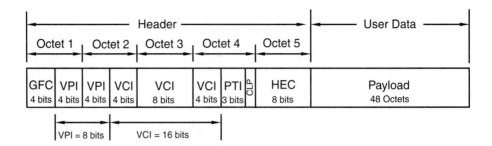

GFC Generic Flow Control—controls the flow of data across the user-to-network interface (UNI) permitting multiple ATM devices to be attached to the same network interface. GFC bits are reassigned and become VPI bits at the network-to-network interface (NNI), thus providing additional support for more virtual paths.

VPI Virtual Path Identifier—part of the network address used to identify a grouping of channels between network entities. The first 4 bits of the VPI are in the first octet; the remaining bits are in the second octet.

VCI Virtual Channel Identifier—a pointer that identifies the virtual channel the system is using on a particular path. The VPI/VCI combination makes up the data link running between two network nodes. The VCI is 16 bits long and uses the second 4 bits of octet 2, all 8 bits of octet 3, and the first 4 bits of octet 4.

PT Payload Type—indicates the type of information contained in the cell. Because cells are used for transporting different types of information, several types of payload type indicators have been defined:
— A 0 in the most significant bit (000, 001, 010, and 011) denotes that the cell is carrying *user information*. User information cells with a middle bit of 1 (010 and 011) indicate that the cell has experienced congestion.
— A 1 in the most significant bit (100, 101, 110, and 111) denotes that the cell is carrying *control* or *resource management information*.
 • 100 and 101 represent network maintenance and control.
 • 110 is for resource management.
 • 111 is reserved for future definition.

CLP Cell Loss Payload—specifies whether or not to discard the cell in the presence of congestion. If set to 1, the network can discard the cell. If set to 0, then the cell might not be discarded.

HEC Header Error Control—provides error correction for single-bit errors and error detection for multiple-bit errors in the cell header.

FIGURE 15.5 Structure and contents of an ATM UNI cell. Note that an NNI cell is nearly identical to the UNI cell. The only difference is that there is no need for the GFC field. In the NNI cell, GFC is subsumed by VPI, which totals 12 bits instead of 8. Source: adapted from Atkins & Norris, 1995.

bits. Thus, depending on the system, we could have 4-bit bytes, 8-bit bytes, 16-bit bytes, 32-bit bytes, and so forth. As the computer industry matured, most people accepted a byte to have exactly 8 bits. ATM, however, uses octet instead of byte. The use of octet in ATM instead of byte can be viewed from two perspectives. The first perspective is one of definition: Octet is the better term because it is well-defined—it has always represented exactly 8 bits of information. The second perspective is one of snobbishness: Some people use the word octet to remind others that they have been around systems a long time and that some systems used bytes of varying sizes.

Let's get back to ATM cells. One question that sometimes emerges at this point of our discussion involves a cell's size and its ability to carry routing information. For example, LAN addresses used for Ethernet or token ring are 6 bytes. Thus, source and destination addresses must occupy 12 bytes. How does this fit into a cell? Our response is simple. This is true *if* ATM were using LAN-type addressing schemes. Remember: ATM networks are based on a "network within a network" concept and, therefore, can do some clever things that don't require each cell to carry complete source and destination addresses as a LAN frame does. To better understand this, we first need to introduce the second of ATM's basic building blocks, namely, virtual connections.

Virtual Connections

In ATM, two types of virtual connections are defined: *virtual channel connection* (VCC) and *virtual path connection* (VPC). A virtual channel connection is a virtual circuit that provides a logical connection between a source and destination. These virtual circuits can be either permanent (PVC) or switched (SVC). (PVCs and SVCs are discussed in detail in Chapter 13.) A *virtual channel identifier* (VCI), which is contained within the header of a cell (see Figure 15.5), is used to identify the channel. VCIs are similar to frame relay's data link connection identifiers (DCLIs), which were discussed in Chapter 13.

A virtual path connection is semipermanent and provides a logical collection of virtual channels that have the same endpoints. In other words, a VPC carries a group of virtual channels, all with the same endpoints. For example, a multimedia application between two physicians' workstations might consist of a single path that supports two virtual channels: one for computer conferencing and a second channel for transferring large image files such as x-rays. Thus, in this illustration, a single virtual path supports two virtual channels. For another application, consider the common situation of an organization providing connectivity to a remote site. In a non-ATM environment, separate links are needed for voice, data, and video support. With ATM, though, a single virtual path can be established that supports several virtual connections. For example, one VCC could be for telephone service, a second VCC could be for a frame relay connection, and a third VCC could be for videoconferencing. Thus, virtual paths enable any connection that uses the same network path from source to destination to be bundled into a single unit. A virtual path identifier (VPI) is used to

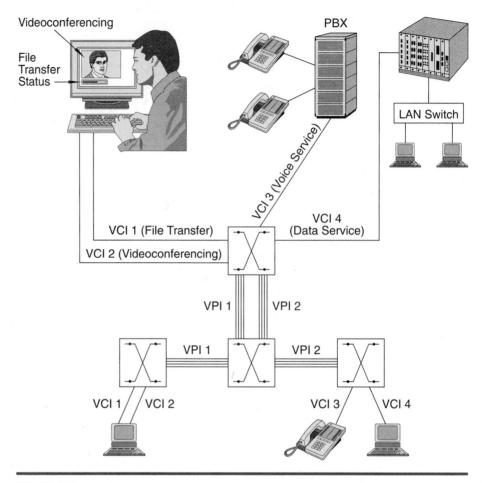

FIGURE 15.6 In an ATM network, a virtual path connection is a logical collection of virtual channels that have the same endpoints. Virtual paths indicators (VPIs) and virtual connection identifiers (VCIs) are used to label these respective connections. In this illustration, virtual channels 1 and 2 are carried by the same virtual path (VPI 1), and virtual channels 3 and 4 are carried by the same virtual path (VPI 2). (VPI 1 and VPI 2 between the two central ATM switches *could* be combined into a single path and still carry all four virtual circuits and their corresponding VCIs). Source: adapted from Minoli, 1992b.

denote a virtual path and is included in a cell's header (see Figure 15.5). A virtual channel can only be established after a virtual path connection is in place. An illustration of VCCs, VPCs, VPIs, and VCIs is given in Figure 15.6. Note that on each physical link, a VPI specifies a virtual path and a VCI specifies a specific virtual channel. Further note that VCIs only have local significance. Thus, different virtual paths may reuse VCIs. However, VCIs on the same virtual path must be different. Finally, virtual paths can be used to establish a logical network topology independent of the physical topology.

Addressing

The last statement of the previous paragraph implies that there does not have to be a physical link between switches. Two switches can be interconnected via a VPC without a direct physical link between them. Remember: ATM is connection-oriented, which means that a circuit is first established prior to data transmissions. Thus, as part of a call setup, two nonadjacent switches without a physical link can be included as part of a virtual path for a particular session. Note further that virtual paths can also provide a form of traffic control by logically (not physically) partitioning network traffic based on the type of data being carried and associated quality of service.

By using virtual path information to move data between connection points on the network, a full addressing scheme is not necessary. This means that much smaller "addresses" can be used to move information between connecting points on the network. By using such a scheme, full addressing information for the source and destination is not required in each cell, and this reduces overall overhead in the cell formats. The process (albeit simplified) is as follows: An ATM switch receives a cell at an incoming port. The switch examines the cell's header to identify the values contained in the VPI/VCI fields and then consults its translation table to determine the appropriate outgoing port based on the VPI/VCI values. Once the correct port is identified, the switch transmits the cell out the port.

Thus, instead of carrying source and destination addresses as TCP/IP packets do, ATM relies on VPIs and VCIs to transport cells across the network. In a nutshell, ATM switches are switched based on information contained in the cell header. In other words, ATM transports data via fixed-length cells based on the VPI/VCI values contained within a cell's header. During call setup, a route from source to destination is established by ATM end nodes and switches. As this path is being established, VPIs and VCIs are assigned. Thus, the determination of a route is made only once. Furthermore, unlike TCP/IP internetworking devices (routers or layer-3 switches), ATM switches do not have to decode large and relatively complicated headers to determine the appropriate output port. A direct consequence of this simplification is that forwarding decisions are implemented in silicon, thus enabling them to be implemented at wire speed. ATM also avoids collisions by having users negotiate throughput and quality of service in advance. Using these parameters, ATM can multiplex several users, each on a separate virtual channel, onto a single virtual path. Additional virtual paths can then be added by increasing the size of the switch.

At one time, this was considered an ATM advantage. However, ASIC technology has since enabled routers to perform traditional table lookups and packet forwarding at hardware speeds, thus providing them with switchlike performance. See Chapter 7 for more information about ASIC-based routers.

This is a rather simplified summary of ATM addressing concepts and does not include issues such as looping, multicasting, or routing protocols.

Let's summarize the various concepts related to ATM addressing. Each ATM station has a unique hardware address—called a *station identifier*—that is part of its network interface card. A station identifier is similar to a MAC sublayer address used in Ethernet/802.3 and token ring LANs. In addition, an ATM station also has a network layer address (or equivalent) that provides the station with a global address. The addressing method used for these network layer address equivalents is either NSAP (for private ATMs) or E.164 (for public ATMs). These two addresses are the only addresses that actually bind an ATM station to a physical link. Finally, when a connection is established from source to destination, VPIs and VCIs assignments are made that specify the virtual connection path. It is these VPI/VCI assignments that get incorporated into a cell's header and are used for route determination.

15.5 ATM Adaptation Layer (AAL)

ATM accommodates different types of traffic via the *ATM Adaptation Layer (AAL)* protocol (see Figure 15.1), which consists of two sublayers: (a) convergence and (b) segmentation and reassembly (SAR). On the sending side, the convergence sublayer accepts data messages from higher-layer application protocols, interprets the type and format of the messages, and then prepares them for processing by the SAR sublayer. The SAR sublayer then translates the messages into ATM format by packaging them into the 48-byte payload portion of an ATM cell. The reverse is done on the receiving side.

The convergence sublayer's interpretation of data type and format is based on the specific *class of service* (CoS) assigned to the data by the application. The AAL provides support for four different service classes. These are summarized in Table 15.1. When the SAR sublayer receives data from the convergence sublayer, it processes the data so they are consistent (i.e., meet the transmission needs) with the specified type and format. Depending on the data type, the AAL protocol provides five different AAL types to accommodate a particular service class. For example, AAL1 is used for data that require connection-oriented constant-bit rate transmissions. An example of this data type is traditional voice service. AAL2 is used for data types that require connection-oriented variable-bit rate data transmissions. An example of this data type is packet video, which might be used in a videoconferencing application. AAL3 and AAL4 are used for connection-oriented or connectionless variable-bit rate transmissions. Examples of these data types include bursty data typical of LAN applications such as those found on frame relay (connection-oriented) and SMDS (connectionless) networks. Lastly, AAL5, which initially was labeled the simple and efficient adaptation layer (SEAL), is used for transmissions in which higher-layer protocols provide error recovery. AAL5 is an improvement to AAL3. As a result, through the AAL protocol and its adaptation layers, an ATM transmission is able to accommodate different types of transmissions simultaneously on the same network. The correspondence between AAL types and service classes is summarized in Table 15.2.

Reviewing the information in Tables 15.1 and 15.2, you might notice that there appears to be a one-to-one correspondence between service class and AAL type. The initial design was to have a different AAL type for each service class. Specifically, AAL1 through AAL4 were designed, respectively, to support service Classes A through D. As in most cases, though, reality got in the way. When AAL3 and AAL4 were being developed, it was observed that there was considerable overlap between the two specifications. Consequently, they were combined into a single type, which is now referred to as AAL Type 3/4. AAL5 was developed to provide a less complex Type 3/4 AAL. Many of the services supported in Classes C and D did not warrant the level of sophistication that was incorporated into Type 3/4. As a result, a simpler and more efficient adaptation layer (hence AAL5's original name, SEAL) emerged.

TABLE 15.1 ATM Service Classes and Descriptions

Service Class	Description
Class A	Constant-bit rate (CBR) connection-oriented transmissions that require a strict timing relationship between source and destination nodes (e.g., circuit emulation and voice transmissions).
Class B	Variable-bit rate (VBR) connection-oriented transmissions that require a strict timing relationship between source and destination nodes (e.g., synchronized data transmissions or packet-mode video for videoconferencing).
Class C	Connection-oriented VBR transmissions that do not require a strict timing relationship between source and destination nodes (e.g., LAN data transfer applications such as frame relay).
Class D	Connectionless VBR transmissions that do not require a strict timing relationship between source and destination nodes (e.g., LAN data transfer applications such as SMDS).

TABLE 15.2 ATM Adaptation Layers (AAL) Types and Corresponding Service Classes

AAL Type	Service Class
AAL1	Class A
AAL2	Class B
AAL3	Classes C and D
AAL4	Classes C and D
AAL5	Classes C and D

Recall that a block of higher-level data is encapsulated in a PDU at the convergence sublayer. This PDU is then passed to the SAR sublayer where it is segmented into 48-byte "chunks" so that it can be transported in the payload area of an ATM cell. What is shown in Figure 15.7 is the format of AAL5's SAR PDU.

Presently, only AAL5 is widely implemented and used. The reason is that one of the ATM standards bodies, the ATM Forum, originally defined AAL5 for efficient transmission of TCP/IP. Because AAL5 uses a very small amount of the cell for its overhead, it is very popular in its use by vendors and ATM technology implementors. Whether AAL is used or not in a connection is up to the vendor of the protocol stack that uses the ATM hardware in a network topology. Some of the other AAL layers might be implemented over time. New layers probably also will be invented and older ones discarded. It's the Zen of Networking at work. Given the popularity of the AAL5 protocol, the format of its protocol data unit (PDU) at the segmentation and reassembly (SAR) level is shown in Figure 15.7. As can be seen, a cell can have many additional fields besides the general ATM format.

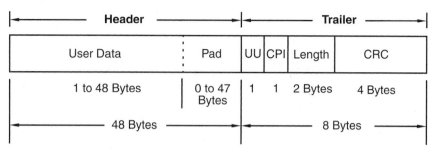

User Data This field is the actual user information being transported across the network. Although it can range in length from 1 byte to 65,535 bytes, it is segmented into 48-byte chunks.

Pad This field is used to pad the data unit to 48 bytes. Its length varies from 0 to 47 bytes.

UU This 1-byte *user-to-user* field allows 1 byte of information to be conveyed transparently between users.

CPI This 1-byte *common part indicator* is intended to identify subsequent fields, but it is not currently being used.

Length This 2-byte field stores the length of the transmitted data. This field is necessary to distinguish between user data and padding.

CRC The *cyclic redundancy check* field uses a 32-bit checksum to provide data integrity of the entire PDU.

FIGURE 15.7 Format and contents of the AAL5 segmentation and reassembly (SAR) protocol data unit (PDU). Source: adapted from Atkins & Norris, 1995.

15.6 ATM and Convergence Technology

As with any network environment, there is change. If we look at the direction of overall network trends, we see a strong movement toward the convergence of data, voice, and video applications. (See Chapter 18 for more information about the concept of convergence technology.) To satisfy all three network types, some basic functions must be created to allow all three types of network technologies to coexist. Data networking allows traffic characteristics that can be bursty in nature, and data can have variable-length packets or frames. Data traffic also can tolerate a certain amount of transmission delay, especially for non-real-time traffic. This implies that data arrival rates can be variable in nature, which suggests that *variable-bit rate* (VBR) transmissions are acceptable to data applications.

Voice traffic, on the other hand, is more sensitive to the arrival time of traffic. It's a good idea for packets carrying part of a conversation to arrive quickly enough to avoid blank spots of time ("dead air") in the conversation. This suggests a *constant-bit rate* (CBR) transmission be used for voice. There also is a problem with full-duplex speech, where two or more people speak at exactly the same time and can be heard simultaneously. Networks don't necessarily agree with this concept very well. Voice, however, is not a big bandwidth hog, as a rule, so fast data networks with VBR can support voice communications as long as the network is swift and does not suffer congestion or loss delays.

Video is even more sensitive to timing. Such transmissions expect the number of frames transmitted from one site to another to arrive in order and in a very specific time frame (usually measured in milliseconds). Technologies such as constant-bit rate, where the number of arrival bits in a transmission are constant and consistent, are essential to making a standard traffic arrival rate possible. However, CBR is not enough. The frames must be transmitted in the proper order and must arrive at the correct speed within a specific time frame. To do this, the network must reserve bandwidth in the path from the source to the destination to ensure that all the bits arrive in order and on time. This general method of providing CBR with a guaranteed delivery sequence in a specific time frame while reserving path "space" is called *isochronous communications* and is common to all ATM networks.

When you add to the discussion that different network applications will ultimately require more and more bandwidth in the future to satisfy consumer needs, ATM is the only network presently on the drawing board that provides the transmission technologies, transmission rates, and quality of service (QoS) required to address user needs . . . at least for now. (See Chapter 5 for more information about QoS.) What we are saying, then, is that the merging of network functions, which seems to be the "wave of the future," requires technologies only ATM can currently deliver. Furthermore, these are issues of which the industry is aware. There will be plenty of applications in the future where ATM as we know it will probably not be sufficient to provide all the capabilities required, and a new "super ATM" will be needed to solve those problems. That is some time off from now, though.

> There was a brief push for something called "isochronous Ethernet," which is discussed in Chapter 9. IsoEthernet never gained widespread support in the industry.

15.7   ATM versus Other Technologies and Services

ATM versus Fast and Gigabit Ethernet

ATM was initially designed as a WAN technology for use in B-ISDN. This has not stopped its encroachment, however, as a technology for LANs (or for MANs). ATM's infiltration on the LAN front was designed to serve as a 155-Mbps backbone technology and deliver 25 Mbps (called "low-speed" ATM) to the desktop. This grand scheme of a unified ATM WAN, MAN, and LAN, however, got hijacked by Ethernet, specifically, Fast Ethernet, which delivers 100 Mbps to the desktop, and Gigabit Ethernet, which provides a 1000-Mbps backbone. Thus, compared to Fast and Gigabit Ethernet, ATM data rates are low, and the deployment of ATM is quite expensive. However, the ATM Forum is working on a 2.5-Gbps ATM specification for the LAN backbone. So just when you thought Gigabit Ethernet has emerged victorious as the only logical choice for the high-speed LAN backbone, it appears as if another ATM contender is among us.

Although Gigabit Ethernet is probably capable of transmitting data and voice at acceptable levels, it is still a VBR technology and has great problems with video equipment. This becomes acutely evident in the presence of network congestion or when a specific delivery time frame is required. A good example of this is high-definition television (HDTV), which will eventually appear on global networks as a standard transmission method.

Presumably, new protocols such as the Resource Reservation Protocol (RSVP) and the Realtime Transport Protocol (RTP) (see Chapter 8) will remedy Gigabit Ethernet's QoS shortcomings. Both protocols permit applications to reserve a specific amount of bandwidth for data transmission. However, when we consider what the incorporation of these protocols with Gigabit Ethernet brings to the table and then compare their functions to ATM, several problems emerge. First, Ethernet/802.3 frames are of variable length ranging from 64 to 1518 bytes. This alone suggests that the delivery rate will not be consistent. ATM uses fixed-size cells, which does guarantee a constant delivery rate. Second, in an Ethernet/802.3 transmission, frames are queued in a switch on a first-in first-out basis. (See Chapters 6 and 9 for information about Ethernet switches.) Furthermore, before a switch transmits queued frame n, the entire contents of queued frame $n - 1$ must be transmitted. Thus, a switch transmits queued frames sequentially and in the order in which they were buffered. The problem with this scheme is that if two frames, both of which are reserving bandwidth, arrive at a switch port simultaneously (within a few microseconds of each other), the frame arriving first gets transmitted first, and the frame arriving second gets buffered. ATM switches, on the other hand, can simultaneously create and service multiple independent queues having different priorities (class of service) and different transmission needs based on data type (i.e., quality of service). Moreover, these simultaneous and multiple transmissions are performed with a constant delivery rate. (Additional information about the Gigabit Ethernet–ATM debate is provided in Chapter 9.)

Thus, just making the network faster will not solve the convergence problems. Even the work on Terabit Ethernet, currently underway at this writing, will yield a network faster than the currently fastest commercially available ATM network (today). However, it is not slated to have the proper traffic controls and network reliability factors that are inherent in an ATM environment. It is also not expected to provide a network larger than that used in a campus environment or possibly around a city (in a metropolitan network environment).

ATM versus Frame Relay

Recall that ATM is similar to frame relay. In fact, ATM is sometime referred to as cell relay to distinguish it from frame relay. The key difference is that frame relay uses variable-length frames as its main transmission unit, whereas ATM uses fixed-length packets of exactly 53 bytes) known as cells. Although ATM's use of smaller fixed-length cells results in higher overhead than frame relay incurs, it also provides two critical advantages over frame relay, namely, speed and traffic type. Since all ATM cells are exactly the same size, they are much easier (and hence, faster) to process. Second, by using short cells with predictable transmission delay, ATM can combine cells carrying delay-sensitive traffic, such as interactive video and voice, with data cells. This concept, called *interleaving,* isn't possible with frame relay because longer data frames create longer and unpredictable delays when processing voice and video traffic. Thus, frame relay is less suitable for real-time videoconferencing, for example.

ATM versus SONET

When discussing ATM and SONET, it is important to realize two things. First, SONET is nothing more than a transport mechanism (see Chapter 3), and second, ATM does not require the use of any specific physical layer protocol. As a high-bandwidth carrier service, SONET can serve as the transport facility for any network technology or service, including ATM, FDDI, SMDS, and ISDN. SONET also can support various topologies including point-to-point, star, and ring. Frequently, though, SONET is used to carry ATM traffic. The two can be thought of as linked to each other to the point where they can be considered "words that come in pairs" (e.g., hue and cry, table and chair, salt and pepper)—ATM and SONET. There is a reason for this. Instead of developing a new physical layer, the designers of ATM borrowed SONET's link-level technology and used it for ATM switching. Furthermore, the ATM Forum has defined 622-Mbps ATM (OC-12) (and higher) to run over only SONET. This does not mean, though, that OC-12 is ATM. As we discussed in Chapter 3, OC-12 is simply the label given to denote the concatenation of 12 DS-3 channels, which provides an aggregate bandwidth of 622.08 Mbps. So, in a nutshell, SONET is a carrier service that transports bits from a source to a destination, and ATM is a technology and protocol that was designed to use SONET as its carrier service.

ATM as an Emulated LAN Technology

In addition to serving as a WAN backbone, ATM can also emulate Ethernet/802.3 or token ring networks through its *local area network emulation* (LANE) interface (see Figure 15.4). LANs that incorporate LANE are called *emulated local area networks* (ELANs). In ATM's protocol hierarchy, LANE is above AAL5 in the ATM adaptation layer. The LANE protocol defines a service interface for the network layer that functions identically to the one used by Ethernet/802.3 and token ring LANs. Data that cross this interface are encapsulated in the appropriate MAC sublayer format. In an ELAN environment, LAN end nodes are connected to a special LAN emulation device that runs a LAN emulation client (LEC) process. The LEC functions as a proxy ATM end node. In addition, a native ATM end node runs a LAN emulation server (LES) process, which is responsible for resolving MAC hardware addresses to ATM addresses.

As an example of this process, consider the situation where an Ethernet/802.3 source node wants to transmit a data frame to an Ethernet/802.3 destination node across an ATM switch fabric. To do this, the source node transmits a frame of data to the LEC process that resides on a LAN emulation device. The LEC then issues an ARP (address resolution protocol) broadcast requesting a MAC-to-ATM address resolution. (See Chapter 8 for more information about ARP.) The MAC address is the hardware address of the transmitting Ethernet/802.3 end node. An LES process, which resides on a native ATM device, responds to the ARP broadcast and returns to the LEC the ATM address of the remote LAN emulation device (and residing LEC) to which the destination node is connected. The source LEC then establishes a virtual circuit to the destination LEC. The LAN emulation device then translates the Ethernet/802.3 frame into an ATM cell via the SAR sublayer (Figure 15.8). Note that implementing this scheme does not involve modifying any higher-layer protocols. Note further that in this implementation, the ATM network is effectively operating as a fast data link layer for the Ethernet/802.3 network.

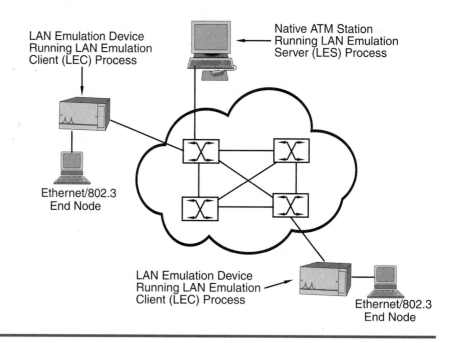

FIGURE 15.8   A typical ATM local area network emulation (LANE) configuration in an Ethernet/802.3 environment. Source: adapted from King, 1994.

In addition to resolving MAC-ATM address issues, another issue that needs attention is connection type. LAN protocols are connectionless; ATM is connection-oriented. Thus, if ATM is going to emulate an Ethernet/802.3 or token ring LAN, then it must be able to carry full source and destination addresses in every frame transmitted. This poses quite a challenge given ATM's five-byte header. Furthermore, a connection-oriented technology does not adequately support bidirectional broadcast or multicast transmissions, which are inherent in Ethernet/802.3 and token ring LANs. To address these issues, a special UNI (user-to-network interface) was developed for LANs. This LAN UNI (called LUNI) enables ATM to emulate the connectionless nature of LANs across the ATM switch fabric.

A second strategy ATM provides for desktop support is a technology called *cells in frames* (CIF), which defines a method for transporting ATM protocols over Ethernet and token ring LANs. CIF is a LAN technology that provides LANs with ATM features including QoS and the seamless integration of data, voice, and video. CIF extends ATM's virtual connections to the desktop via a special CIF attachment device, which provides an interface similar to ATM's frame user-to-network interface (FUNI). This device performs most of the segmentation and reassembly (SAR), but the Ethernet/802.3 or token ring node still must build the ATM layer's PDU. See the Web site at `http://cif.cornell.edu` for more information available from the CIF Alliance. A second resource for CIF is the document `http://www.ziplink.net/~lroberts/Atmf-961104.html`

End-of-Chapter Commentary

This concludes our discussion of ATM. The information contained in this chapter provides only a working overview of the technology. For detailed technical information, you are encouraged to visit the ATM Forum Web site (`http://www.atmforum.com`) or consult some of the Suggested Readings and References at the end of the chapter. You might also want to revisit other chapters within this book that included ATM as part of their discussion, most notably: Chapter 3, which includes a discussion of SONET; Chapter 9, which examines Gigabit Ethernet and its relationship to ATM; and Chapters 13 and 14, which provide a comparison of frame relay, SMDS, and ATM. The Glossary also provides definitions of additional ATM terms, and the Web site `http://www.techfest.com/networking/atm.htm` is a terrific resource for ATM information. Finally, as is the case with many technologies, ATM continues to evolve, and there is one evolving technology that has caught the eye of WAN operators. It is CIF, which was mentioned earlier as a technology for transporting ATM protocols over Ethernet and token ring LANs. The CIF Alliance is actively modifying CIF to work over SONET and PPP links. This proposed WAN version of CIF presumably maintains all of native ATM's key features but requires less overhead. The ATM Forum is working with the CIF Alliance to bring the concept of using CIF to carry ATM protocols to fruition.

CHAPTER REVIEW MATERIALS

SUMMARY

- Asynchronous transfer mode is a high-speed switching network architecture created in the late 1980s/early 1990s to apply circuit-switching concepts to data networks.
- ATM is also known as cell relay to distinguish it from frame relay (see Chapter 13).
- In many regards, ATM is considered a "universal" network because it can combine the delivery of a wide range of services (data, voice, and video) over a single network, has a robust quality of service (QoS) facility, can provide seamless interconnectivity between local and wide area networks, and supports a wide range of data rates—from 25 to 155 Mbps over copper and from 100 to 622 Mbps (OC-12) and higher over fiber (multimode or single mode).

- A common implementation is 155-Mbps ATM over SONET (see Chapter 3).
- ATM is specified via a three-layer reference model: the physical layer, the ATM layer, and the ATM adaptation layer.
- ATM relies on two broad classes of interface standards. Foundation specifications define the manner in which network components are interconnected. Examples include ATM physical layer specifications, the user–network interface (UNI), and the network-to-network interface (NNI). Application and service specifications define how other networks and applications interoperate with ATM network components. Examples include the frame user-to-network interface (FUNI), the WinSock interface, and local area network emulation (LANE) interface.

- ATM's operation is similar to that of frame relay. Data cells are transferred from a user site to an ATM switch. The data are then transmitted from switch to switch throughout an ATM network until they reach the final destination switch. ATM addressing is also based on the E.164 standard ISDN global numbering format.
- The fundamental building blocks of all ATM networks consist of cells, virtual connections, and switches. ATM cells are always 53 bytes long and partitioned into a 5-byte header, which contains addressing information, and a 48-byte payload containing user data. ATM virtual connections consist of either permanent or switched virtual circuits that logically connect source and destination sites. Virtual circuits are identified by specific virtual channel identifiers (VCIs). A collection of virtual channels that all have the same endpoints is called a virtual path connection (VPC), and VPCs are specified by virtual path identifiers (VPIs). Virtual connections are established (and VCI and VPI assignments are made) dynamically by ATM end nodes and switches at the time data are to be transmitted.
- The ATM adaptation layer (AAL) enables ATM to support different traffic types, including data, voice, and video. Of the various AAL types specified, only AAL5—which defines ATM transmission of TCP/IP data—is widely implemented.
- ATM supports variable-bit rate (VBR) transmissions used for data applications, constant-bit rate (CBR) transmissions used for voice applications, and isochronous communications, which guarantees a specific delivery sequence within a specific time frame so that data bits arrive in order and on time. In short, ATM provides the transmission technologies, transmission rates, and quality of service (QoS) required of all present-day network applications and functions.
- Compared to Gigabit Ethernet, ATM guarantees a constant delivery rate, but Gigabit Ethernet does not because Ethernet uses variable-length frames. In a switched environment, queued frames within an ATM switch are transmitted neither sequentially nor in the order they were buffered, as is the case with Ethernet switches. Instead, ATM switches can create and service multiple independent queues with different priorities and transmission needs and still provide a constant delivery rate.
- Compared to frame relay, ATM uses fixed-length cells as its main transmission unit, whereas frame relay supports variable-length frames. This provides ATM with higher transmission rates than frame relay and the capability to interleave cells carrying different data types.
- Compared to SONET, ATM is a technology and protocol that was designed to use SONET as its carrier service. SONET, on the other hand, is simply a carrier service that transports bits from source to destination and can be used as the transport facility for other technologies or services, including FDDI, SMDS, and ISDN. Higher-speed (at least 622-Mbps) ATM is designed to run only over SONET.
- Through its local area network emulation (LANE) interface, ATM can provide a service interface for the network layer that functions exactly the same as Ethernet/802.3 and token ring. LANs that use this interface are called emulated LANs and involve a special client/server process that enables native MAC-to-ATM address resolution. Emulated LANs also employ ATM's LAN user-to-network interface (LUNI) so that ATM, which is connection-oriented, can support the connectionless nature of local area networks.

VOCABULARY CHECK

asynchronous transfer mode (ATM)
ATM adaptation layer (AAL)
cell
cells in frames (CIF)

class of service (CoS)
isochronous communications
LAN emulation (LANE)
quality of service (QoS)
virtual channel connection (VCC)

virtual channel identifier (VCI)
virtual path connection (VPC)

REVIEW EXERCISES

1. What is the big fuss over ATM? In other words, "Why ATM?"
2. List and briefly describe some high-speed network applications that lend themselves to delivery via ATM networks.
3. What role does the Anchorage Accord play in an ATM network?
4. Visit the ATM Forum Web site at `http://www.atmforum.com` and review the specifications that comprise the Anchorage Accord.
5. Explain the following concept relative to ATM networks: Delay in the transmission of traditional data services is tolerable, but data loss is unacceptable. On the other hand, the loss of video transmission is tolerable, but delay is unacceptable.
6. Does ATM's connection-oriented feature make routing cells through an ATM network simple or complex? Why?
7. Given a continuum from simple to complex, with fixed bit rate at the simple end and variable bit rate at the complex end, in what order would you place the following switching strategies: circuit-switching, packet-switching, frame relaying, and cell relaying (ATM)? Why?
8. What purpose does ATM's UNI serve?
9. Given the structure of ATM's UNI cell (see Figure 15.5), explain how ATM establishes data transmission priorities.
10. Identify some of the primary differences between ATM and conventional LANs such as Ethernet/802.3.
11. Compare and contrast the concepts of continuous bit rate and variable bit rate. Given these two transmission types, what do you think the concept of available bit rate means relative to ATM networks?
12. What is the difference between a virtual channel connection (VCC) and a virtual path connection (VPC)?
13. ATM supports two basic types of connections: point-to-point and point-to-multipoint. Furthermore, these connections are unidirectional only. (Why?) What is absent from ATM is multicasting or broadcasting support similar to that found in shared-media LANs such as Ethernet/802.3. (a) Do you think it is necessary for ATM to support multicasting/broadcasting? Why or why not? (b) If ATM were to support multicasting or broadcasting, in what way(s) do you think this can be done?
14. Describe three QoS parameters that can be established on an ATM network during call setup.

SUGGESTED READINGS AND REFERENCES

ASKINS, J. 1996. Migrating to ATM? Learn Before You Leap. *Data Communications,* December, 79–80.

ATKINS, J., and M. NORRIS. 1995. *Total Area Networking: ATM, Frame Relay and SMDS Explained.* New York: Wiley.

BATES, R. J., and D. GREGORY. 1998. *Voice and Data Communications Handbook.* New York: McGraw-Hill.

CHIPCOM. 1993. *ATM: The Frontier of Networking.* Southborough, MA: Chipcom.

CHOLEWJA, K. 1996. Affordable ATM. *Data Communications,* December, 94–102.

CLARK, E. 1997. Real-World ATM. *Network,* July, 42–53.

CONOVER, J. 1996. ATM Access Is Ready, Willing and Able to Fly on Your Backbone. *Network Computing,* 15 November, 70–95.

FELTMAN, C. 1993a. ATM Takes Off. *Interoperability,* 19–46.

———. 1993b. ATM: The Grand Unifier. *LAN Magazine,* November, 52–70.

FRITZ, J. N. 1998. ATM WAN Services: Picking a Winner. *Data Communications,* 21 April, 77–80.

GALLO, M., and W. HANCOCK. 1999. *Networking Explained.* Boston: Digital Press.

GOULD, J. 1994. ATM's Long, Strange Trip to the Mainstream. *Data Communications,* June, 120–130.

GOULD, W. 1997. Fast Ethernet Pairs with ATM. *Network Magazine,* September, 74–77.

HURWICZ, M. 1997. ATM for the Rest of Us. *Network Magazine,* November, 75–79.

KING, S. 1994. Switched Virtual Networks. *Data Communications,* September, 66–80.

MEHTA, S. 1996. Telcos: Answering the Call for ATM. *LAN,* March, 46–52.

MINOLI, D. 1992a. ATM: The Future of Local and Wide Area Networks. *Network Computing,* 15 October, 128–134.

———. 1992b. ATM Protocols: Let's Get Technical. *Network Computing,* 15 November, 156–163.

NEWMAN, D. 1997. ATM: The Last Word. *Data Communications,* April, 105–133.

PARIKH, A. 1993. The Challenge of Migrating to ATM. *Networking Management,* June, B11–B15.

PARNELL, T. 1997. *LAN Times Guide to Wide Area Networks.* Berkeley, CA: Osborne McGraw-Hill.

ROBERTS, L. G. 1997. CIF: Affordable ATM, at Last. *Data Communications,* April, 96–102.

RUIU, D. 1993. ATM at Your Service? *Data Communications,* November, 85–88.

STALLINGS, W. 2000. *Data and Computer Communications.* 6th ed. Upper Saddle River, NJ: Prentice-Hall.

TAYLOR, M. 1996. Voice Over ATM: A Sound Assessment. *Data Communications,* December, 86–92.

TAYLOR, S. 1994a. ATM and Frame Relay: Back to the Basics. *Data Communications,* April, 23–24.

———. 1994b. Making the Switch to High-Speed WAN Services. *Data Communications,* July, 87–94.

WITTMAN, A. 1993. Local ATM: Is ATM Ready for the Desktop? *Network Computing,* September, 160–166.

ZEICHICK, A. 1997. Glossary: Asynchronous Transfer Mode. *Network,* July, 28.

IV

RELATED NETWORKING CONCEPTS, APPLICATIONS, AND TECHNOLOGIES

16

Dialup and Home Networking

CHAPTER OBJECTIVES

After studying this chapter, you will be able to do the following:

1. Explain the concept of dialup networking.
2. Compare and contrast terminal and network dialup connections.
3. Understand the role of modems in dialup networking.
4. Identify the various standards for modems, compression, and error control relative to dialup connections.
5. Explain the difference between DCE and DTE rates.
6. Understand the concept of data compression relative to modems.
7. Compare and contrast conventional analog modems and 56K modems.
8. Explain the concept of xDSL.
9. Discuss the advantages and disadvantages of ADSL.
10. Understand the design issues relative to deploying cable modem service.
11. Compare and contrast cable modems, conventional analog and 56K modems, and xDSL service.
12. Analyze the various home-based Internet connection options, including the issues surrounding these different connection methods.
13. Understand the manner in which home-based computer networking can be implemented, including some of the problems inherent with this type of environment.

In this chapter, we discuss the concepts and methods of extending networking to the home. This discussion involves both dialup networking, which entails using the telephone system to dial into a network, and creating a home-based LAN, which we called a personal area network (PAN) in Chapter 1. We begin the chapter by examining various concepts and issues related to dialup networking, including a distinction between terminal-based dialup and network-based dialup connections. Section 16.2 presents the topic of modems. Modems, which were first introduced in Chapter 3, are an integral part of dialup connections because they place the digital data of a computer into analog form for transmission across that part of the telephone network that is still analog-based. Two alternatives to conventional analog modem dialup service are then discussed in Sections 16.3 and 16.4, respectively. They are asymmetric digital subscriber line (ADSL), a service that is provided by the telephone carriers, and cable modem service, which is provided by cable TV operators. We conclude the chapter with a discussion of home networking concepts and issues. This section contains information about connecting a home computer to the Internet, interconnecting more than one home computer, network security issues relative to home networks, and sources of potential problems related to home networking.

16.1   What Is Dialup Networking?

Dialup networking refers to a network connection that is established by "dialing" into the network through the public telephone system. Dialup connections can be analog or digital. Analog connections involve the use of a modem; digital connections require end-to-end digital connectivity. (See Chapter 12 on ISDN for more information about end-to-end digital connections.) Dialup connections generally can be classified as either terminal-based or network-based.

Terminal Dialup Connection

A *terminal dialup connection* involves the use of special terminal emulation software, which makes the local system a terminal of the remote machine. This type of connection is sometimes called a *tty* connection, which is an acronym for *teletype,* a term used in the early days of computing to denote a terminal connection between a device and a centralized host. In a tty dialup connection, terminal emulation software is used to make the local system (the one dialing in) appear as a terminal to a centralized host. There are many different kinds of terminal emulation software available, each with its own capabilities. Two in particular are Kermit and ProComm. Windows 3.1 and Windows 95/98/2000 also come bundled with terminal emulation software, and modem manufacturers usually include a version of their own emulation software with their modems. Commonly emulated terminals are vt100 and vt102. In a dialup tty environment, control of the local machine is transferred to that of the remote system. The emulation software converts the local node into a terminal of the centralized host. A consequence of this conversion is that some keyboard functions or mouse capabilities do not work correctly if they are not mapped properly and supported by the remote system.

In a tty dialup connection, the remote system (the one being dialed into) can be another computer, as shown in Figure 16.1(a), or it can be a specialized device called a

(a)

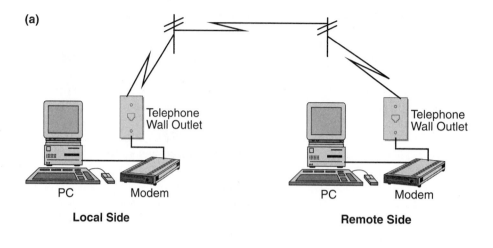

(b)

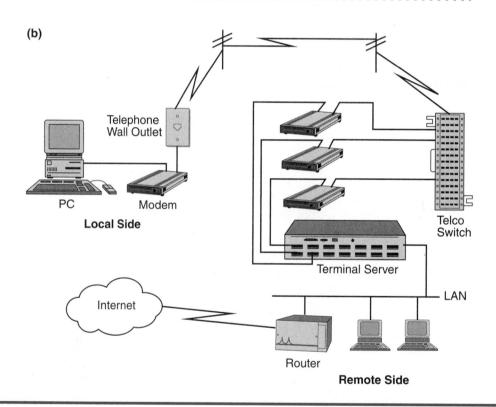

FIGURE 16.1 A typical dialup connection uses a standard telephone line as the medium for providing a computer-to-computer connection (a) or a computer-to-network connection (b) via a terminal server.

terminal server or communications server that is connected to a LAN, as in Figure 16.1(b). When a terminal or communications server is used, the server acts as an intermediary node that establishes a terminal connection between the local system and a networked machine. For example, in Figure 16.1(b), the PC client dials into the terminal server, which then enables the PC to connect to any machine on the local network or (assuming proper authorizations are in place) any machine connected to the Internet.

Although it is possible to dial into a computer that is connected to a network and gain access to the network via this system, a dialup tty connection is not a network connection. This is because the local machine is considered nothing more than a terminal of the remote system. Anything you do through this connection (e.g., read e-mail, transfer files) is all done relative to the remote system, not the local host. For example, let's assume that in Figure 16.1(b) a terminal connection is established from the local PC to one of the networked hosts via the terminal server. If you read e-mail on this host and save it, it will be saved on the host, not the PC. Similarly, if you transfer a file from the Internet and save it, it will be saved on the host, not the PC.

> This is the basis of what is referred to as a UNIX "shell account" available from some Internet service providers.

Network Dialup Connection

In a *network dialup connection,* special networking software makes the local machine become a true networked host. A network dialup connection transforms the local machine into a networked node and provides it with the same capabilities of any other networked node exactly as if it were directly connected to a LAN. A Point-to-Point Protocol (PPP) link, which is common among home-based Internet users, is an example of a network-based dialup connection. PPP enables a local machine to become a directly connected Internet host via a telephone line. Thus, in Figure 16.1(b), a networked dialup connection effectively makes the local PC appear as if it were directly connected to the LAN. Furthermore, all actions performed on the local machine are now done relative to the local machine and not to some remote node, as is the case with a tty connection. Networked dialup connections are established using special networking software such as PPP or SLIP (Serial Line Internet Protocol). On the local side, the client version of PPP or SLIP makes a connection to a remote machine running the server version of PPP or SLIP. The remote machine can be another computer or it can be a terminal server. Once the connection is established, the local machine is assigned a network address. Depending on the configuration, the server either selects from a pool of available addresses and dynamically assigns the remote machine a network address, or the server issues a preassigned address. Regardless of the type of assignment, the network address remains in effect for the duration of the session.

16.2 Analog Modem Concepts

Overview

In Chapter 3, we learned that transmitting digital data (output from a computer) across an analog-based communications network (the plain old telephone system, POTS) requires representing the digital data in analog form. We further learned that this representation is done by modifying (i.e., modulating) a continuous analog signal (called a carrier) at the source so that the signal conforms to the digital data being transmitted and then convert-ing the signal back into digital form at the destination. Thus, the modulation process in-volves coding and decoding data for transmission, and we stated that the device that performs these functions is called a *modem,* which is a contraction of the words *modula-tor* and *demodulator.*

Since a dialup network connection involves "dialing" into the network through the public telephone system, dialup connections require modems—one at each end of a transmission line—and both modems must use the same modulation technique. A mo-dem transforms a computer's digital signal into analog form at the sending side so the signal can be carried across a standard telephone line. On the receiving side, the mo-dem demodulates the signal; that is, it reconverts the transmitted analog signal from the phone line to digital form before it is passed to the computer. (See Chapter 3 for spe-cific information about the various modulation techniques that are available.)

> Wireless modems
> are used for wireless
> dialup connections.

Modem Standards

There are many industry standards for modems. Some are defined by international com-mittees, others by modem manufacturers. For universal interoperability, though, mo-dems should be compliant with standards formalized by the telecommunications sector of the International Telecommunications Union (ITU-T), which establishes worldwide communications standards. ITU-T is the former Consultative Committee for Interna-tional Telephony and Telegraphy (CCITT). Modem standards defined by ITU-T are known as the V-series (ITU-T prefaces these standards with the letter V) and specify techniques for modulation, error control, and compression. A brief description of some of these standards is given in Table 16.1. Note that a second or revised version is de-noted by *bis,* and a third version is denoted by *ter.*

DCE, DTE, Compression, and Error Control

When a dialup connection is first initialized, the two modems at each end of the connec-tion begin screaming at each other—a negotiation process, called *handshaking,* that the modems engage in so they can come to some agreement on certain communication pa-rameters. One parameter is the data transmission rate, which is formally known as the *DCE rate* and informally referred to as "speed." The modulation technique determines this speed. DCE stands for *data communications equipment.* In a dialup connection, the modem is a DCE device, and the telephone line connects the DCE device to the phone jack. Furthermore, the DCE-to-DCE rate is the data transmission rate between the two end modems. That is, it is the speed at which the two modems will exchange data. The ITU-T protocols specify modulation standards for modem speeds. The most widely used speeds (and their corresponding protocols) today are 14,400 bps (V.32 *bis*), 28,800 bps (V.34), 33,600 bps (V.34 with software enhancement), and 57,600 bps (V.90) (see Table 16.1). Note that the DCE-to-DCE rate is fixed because modems must agree on a specific modulation technique.

Although modems will always try to negotiate the fastest link possible, speeds are dependent on line quality. For example, if two V.34-compliant modems are trying to communicate with each other, they will try to negotiate a 33,600 bps connection. If this

TABLE 16.1 Selected V .*x* Modem Protocols

Protocol	Description
V.21	Standard for 300-bps modems using full-duplex transmission over a dialup line.
V.22	Standard for 600-bps and 1200-bps full-duplex modems over dialup and two-wire leased lines. Compatible with the Bell 212A standard used in the United States.
V.22 *bis*	Standard for 2400-bps full-duplex modems over dialup and two-wire leased lines; cycles to 1200- and 600-bps operation.
V.23	Standard for 600-bps or 1200-bps synchronous or asynchronous half-duplex modems used on dialup lines. Used in the United Kingdom.
V.29	Standard for 9600-bps facsimile service.
V.32	Standard for 9600-bps modems, cycles to 4800 bps when line quality degrades, and cycles forward when line quality improves.
V.32 *bis*	Standard that extends V.32 to 7200, 12,000, and 14,400 bps; cycles to lower rate when line quality degrades; cycles forward when line quality improves.
V.32 *ter*	Pseudostandard that extends v.32 *bis* to 19,200 bps and 21,600 bps.
V.34	Standard for 28,800-bps modems. (Some V.34 modems were enhanced with new software that provided them with the capability to achieve data rates of 31,200 bps or 33,600 bps.)
V.FAST	Proprietary, pseudostandard from Hayes and Rockwell for modems transmitting at data rates up to 28,800 bps; served as a migration path for V.34.
V.42	Standard for error correction instead of for a modem. Uses LAPM as the primary error-correcting protocol, with MNP Classes 1 through 4 as an alternative (see Table 16.2).
V.42 *bis*	Standard that enhances V.42 by incorporating the British Telecom Lempel Ziv data compression technique to V.42 error correction. Most V.32, V.32 *bis*, and V.34-compliant modems come with V.42 or V.42 *bis* or MNP.
V.44	A compression technology originally developed for the satellite industry to maximize available bandwidth. Approved by ITU as an industry standard in mid-2000, V.44 can generally yield download speed improvements of 20% to 60% when compared to V.42bis. In cases where data are highly compressible, a 200% improvement in download speeds can be expected. The actual amount of improvement is dynamic and depends on the data content.
V.90	Standard for 57,600-bps modems (commonly called "56K modems") in which asymmetric data rates apply (i.e., the send and receive rates are different). Depending on telephone line conditions, upstream rates (send) are restricted to 33,600 bps, and downstream rates (receive) are restricted to 57,600 bps. V.90 modems are designed for connections that are digital at one end and have one digital-to-analog conversion.
V.92	A new 56K modem standard approved by ITU in mid-2000. V.92 offers a maximum upstream rate of 48,000 bps, faster connection time, and call-waiting. The 48k upstream rate is an improvement over V.90's 33.6k, although achieving it might be as problematic as achieving a 56k downstream rate. The faster connection time feature will reduce the time it takes a modem to complete its handshaking process by one-half. The call-waiting feature will allow the modem to place an Internet connection on hold while you take another call on the same line. The total wait-time will be controlled by your ISP and can range from 0 to 16 minutes, or indefinitely.

is not possible, the modems will then try to connect at the next highest rate the line can support. If the line quality deteriorates during an established connection, then the modems will cycle down ("fall back") to a lower speed. When line quality improves, the modems will fall forward to a higher speed. Modem speed is also limited by the slower modem in the connection. Thus, if a V.34 modem is trying to establish a connection with a V.32 *bis* modem, the fastest link possible is 14,400 bps regardless of line quality.

Another parameter modems negotiate is *compression,* which is a process that codes repetitive patterns within a data set. For example, if a text message contains the string XXXXXX, then instead of using six bytes to represent the data (one for each character), a compression technique might code the string so that only two bytes are used to represent it, with one byte to identify the repetitive character and one byte to specify the number of times it is repeated. Compressed files can be sent at a faster rate than uncompressed files. For example, a 1 Mbyte uncompressed file transferred at 28,800 bps takes nearly 5 minutes depending on the file transfer protocol used. If this same file is compressed by a 4 to 1 ratio, then the time it takes to transmit the compressed file is one-quarter of the original time, which effectively quadruples the data transfer rate to 115,200 bps. Remember, though, compression is only achieved if there is redundancy in the data set. The two primary standards used for data compression involving modems are V.42 *bis* and the Microcom Networking Protocol (MNP) level 5. V.42 *bis* defines a technique that can generate a 4 to 1 data compression ratio depending on the type of file being transmitted. MNP 5 uses a data compression algorithm that compresses data by a factor of 2 to 1. MNP was initially a proprietary protocol developed by Microcom Incorporated that became an industry standard for data compression and error control in the 1980s. A brief summary of the various MNP levels is given in Table 16.2.

To benefit from compression and the potentially higher effective throughput rates, the computer must be able to transmit with its connected modem at a rate that is equal to the possible speed that can be achieved by the compression ratio. This speed is called the *DTE-to-DCE rate* and is commonly referred to as the computer's "port speed" or "serial port rate." *DTE* stands for *data terminating equipment.* In a dialup connection, the computer is the DTE device. Thus, the DTE-to-DCE rate is how fast the computer can talk to its modem, and the *DCE-to-DCE rate* is how fast the two modems can talk to each other. The DCE-to-DCE rate is a function of the modem standard and cannot be changed. However, the DTE-to-DCE rate is user configurable through the modem's communications software. Thus, a computer that is connected to a V.34 modem should maintain a port speed of 115,200 bps to benefit from a 4 to 1 compression ratio. Similarly, a computer using a V.90 modem should maintain a port speed of 230,400 bps.

A third parameter, *error control,* refers to error detection and correction. Modem standards for error control are specified by V.42 and MNP levels 1 through 4. Note that V.42 includes MNP 1–4. V.42 also includes something called link access procedure for modems (LAPM), which uses cyclic redundancy check (CRC) and automatic repeat request (ARQ) for error control. CRC is used for error detection, and ARQ prevents the modem from accepting any more data until the defective frame has been retransmitted successfully. V.42's default is LAPM. Thus, if a connection is being initialized between two V.42-compliant modems, they will use LAPM for error control. If one of the modems is not V.42 compliant, then the modems will negotiate to use MNP 1–4.

This is calculated as follows: Assuming 8 bits per byte, 28,800 bits per second = 28800/8 = 3600 bytes per second. Furthermore, given that 1 Kilobyte = 1000 bytes, 1 Megabyte = 1000 × 1000 = 1,000,000 bytes. Thus, the time it takes to transfer 1 Megabyte at 28,800 bps is equal to 1000000/3600 = 278 seconds, which is approximately 5 minutes.

A new standard, V.44, recently approved by ITU, provides a 6 to 1 compression ratio. See Table 16.1 for more information.

On PCs, serial ports are more commonly known as the *universal asynchronous receiver/transmitter,* or *UART.*

TABLE 16.2 The MNP Protocols

Protocol	Description
MNP 1–4	Used for hardware error control. All four levels are incorporated into V.42.
MNP 5	Incorporates the first four levels of MNP. Also uses a data compression algorithm that compresses data by a factor of 2 to 1.
MNP 6	Supports both V.22 *bis* and V.29.
MNP 7	Same as MNP 5 except it employs a data compression algorithm that compresses data by a factor of 3 to 1.
MNP 8	Extension of MNP 7; lets half-duplex devices operate in full-duplex mode.
MNP 9	Used for a variety of different circuits.
MNP 10	Used in cellular modems and poor line quality settings.

To summarize, modems are DCE devices that convert between analog and digital signals. Modem standards, as defined by ITU-T, specify modem speeds (called the DCE-to-DCE rate), the type of error-correction methods they will use (V.42), and the data compression technique (V.42 *bis*). Given redundancy in the data set, the effective throughput of a modem connection can be doubled, tripled, or even quadrupled depending on the compression technique used. To take advantage of this increase in effective throughput, though, the speed at which the PC talks to the modem (called the DTE-to-DCE rate) must match the potential compression ratio. Thus, if the DCE-to-DCE rate is 28,800 bps, then the DTE-to-DCE rate must be 115,200 bps to benefit from a 4 to 1 compression rate.

56K Modems

A 56K modem is a hybrid modem that involves a path consisting of both analog and digital connections. To understand this, let's consider a standard analog modem. According to Shannon's limit (see Chapter 2), the highest possible speed a modem can achieve over an analog line is somewhere between 33,600 bps and 38,400 bps depending on line conditions. Analog modems require four analog-digital conversions in each direction. This conversion process was discussed in Chapter 3 and illustrated in Figure 3.7. It is summarized here: (a) digital to analog so data from the local PC can be transmitted from home to the telco's switching station; (b) analog to digital so the data can be transmitted across the telco's digital network; (c) digital to analog so the data can be transmitted from the switching station to the remote site; and (d) analog to digital so the data can be processed by the remote computer.

We use the term *analog–digital* to represent either an analog-to-digital conversion or a digital-to-analog conversion.

In contrast to a standard analog modem, a 56K modem requires only two analog–digital conversions in each direction. Both conversions occur at the local site (conversions a and b above). This is because the path is analog from the client site to the central office switching station, but it is completely digital from the switching station to the server site (see Figure 3.8). This hybrid analog–digital circuit restricts "upstream" transmission rates (i.e., from client to server) to 33,600 bps. However, "downstream" rates (i.e., from server to client) can be as high as 57,600 bps depending on line conditions. Users of 56K modems should set their DTE-to-DCE rate to 230,400 bps.

The standard for 56K modems is called V.90 (see Table 16.1). Prior to standardization, two early, competing, and incompatible proprietary 56K modem standards were developed: x2 from USRobotics (3Com) and K56flex from Lucent Technologies. Both standards have since been absorbed by the de jure V.90 ITU-T standard. Thus, as long as both ends of a transmission link have V.90-compliant 56K modems, we do not have to be concerned with x2 or 56Kflex. If this is a concern because the type of modem at the remote end is unknown, some 56K modems employ all three technologies: V.90, x2, and 56Kflex. This way, when the modems begin their handshaking process, if the remote modem is not V.90 compliant but instead uses one of the proprietary 56K standards, then the local modem will cycle through and connect with a compatible standard. You should note that 56K modems cannot be used for global connectivity because the signaling schemes used on international connections reduce speeds to a maximum of 33.6 kbps.

> In the United States, an FCC regulation limits the highest data rate to a little less than 56K.

> V.90 was recently upgraded to the new ITU standard, V.92. See Table 16.1 for more information.

16.3   DSL Service

Overview

In our discussion of modem modulation schemes in Chapter 3, we learned that the circuit between a home and the telephone company's nearest switching station is called the *local loop* or, more formally, the digital subscriber loop. Unless a digital circuit is installed (as is the case with ISDN), the local loop is a predominately copper-based (i.e., twisted-pair) analog circuit that restricts the telephone company from having digital end-to-end connectivity among its customers. As a result, the local loop represents a bottleneck to high-speed home-based dialup networking and has become figuratively known as "the last mile." Given the cost constraints involved in rewiring local loops, the focus of resolving the bottleneck issue has been addressed by technology. One technology currently being deployed is DSL service and is discussed here. The second, cable modems, is discussed in the next section.

DSL, which stands for *digital subscriber line,* is a technology that enables data, voice, and video to be mixed and carried over standard analog (copper) telephone lines. This is accomplished by using the unused frequencies that are available on a telephone line. DSL can deliver data services without interfering with voice transmissions. Since DSL supports digital data transmissions, there is no need for any analog-to-digital or digital-to-analog conversions, as is the case with conventional dialup lines that employ analog modems. Furthermore, a DSL signal can be partitioned so that part of the channel's capacity is used for analog voice transmissions concurrently with higher-frequency data transmissions.

DSL is an "always-connected" or "always-on" technology. This means that unlike ISDN and conventional analog modem service, which are circuit-switched, you do not have to dialup a service provider to establish a connection. Instead, a DSL connection apes a leased line connection, and hence, the service is always available for transmitting or receiving data. Furthermore, DSL connections are dedicated point-to-point links. This is in contrast to cable modem service, which is bus-based and involves multiple subscribers contending for a channel's bandwidth. Since the local loop's bandwidth is not shared, DSL offers better security and dedicated bandwidth between the telco's switching station and a customer's premises.

Another feature of DSL is that it keeps data traffic off the voice network. With an analog modem service, dialup users use the public switched telephone network (PSTN) to call up their Internet service provider to gain access to the Internet. This ties up a port on the telco's voice switch, which reduces the number of voice ports available for voice calls. With DSL service, voice calls (i.e., signals) are segregated from data traffic via a line splitter and directed to the telco's voice switch for transmission across the PSTN. Data signals, however, are aggregated via a DSL access multiplexer (DSLAM), which feeds directly into a data switch for transmission across the telco's data network backbone. Thus, data signals bypass the voice switch, thereby freeing up ports for voice calls (Figure 16.2).

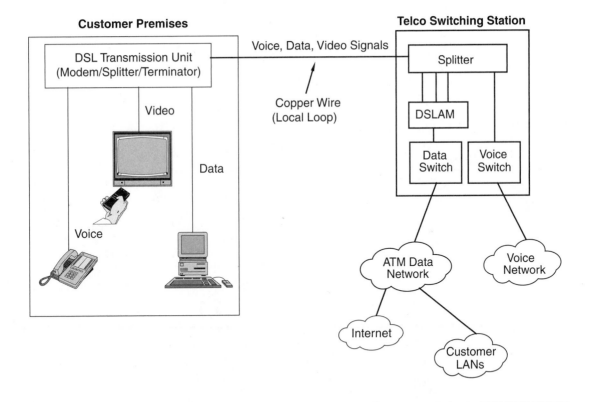

FIGURE 16.2 Generic illustration of a DSL-based connection. Voice, data, and video signals from the customer's premises are split into separate signals and transmitted across the local loop to the provider's site. Voice signals are directed to the telco's voice switch for transmission through the public switched telephone network (PSTN). Data and video signals are aggregated by the DSL access multiplexer (DSLAM) and directed to the telco's data switch for transmission through the telco's data network. Source: adapted from Aber, 1997.

DSL is commonly written with a leading x (e.g., xDSL) to collectively represent the family of digital subscriber line technologies. The leading x is a variable that specifies a descriptor, which, when combined with DSL, defines the different DSL variants. Presently, there are nine variants, which range alphabetically from asymmetric DSL (ADSL) to very-high data rate DSL (VDSL). A summary of these variants is provided in Table 16.3, and the various DSL technologies are briefly discussed later in this section. Many regard DSL technology as the telephone companies' answer to cable modems in competing for "the last mile."

DSL Transmission Rates and Circuit Quality

Depending on the specific variant used and the direction of transmission (upstream or downstream), DSL transmission rates range from 128 kbps to 52 Mbps. These rates are a function of the distance a customer's site is from the local switching station (i.e., the local loop length) as well as the quality of the local loop circuit. The longer the local loop distance, the lower the data rate; likewise, the poorer the quality of the local loop circuit, the lower the data rate.

The local loop distance is important because a cable's length has a direct effect on a signal's strength as it travels along the cable. As we noted in Chapter 4, the longer the cable, the greater the attenuation, which is a decrease in signal strength. Furthermore,

TABLE 16.3   The Digital Subscriber Line (DSL) Variants

Type	Name	Description
ADSL	Asymmetric DSL	ADSL is a high-bandwidth local loop technology that provides higher data transmission rates from the service provider to the customer (downstream) than from the customer to the service provider (upstream). Downstream rates range from 1.5 to 6 Mbps and are provided in T1 increments. Upstream transmissions are provided over a bidirectional channel with rates ranging from 64 to 640 kbps, which are provisioned in 64-kbps increments. A separate 4-kHz channel is also partitioned from the link to provide basic analog telephone service. Data transmission rates depend on line quality and local loop distance. Maximum local loop distance is approximately 10,000 feet (2 miles or 3 km). ADSL is suitable for Internet or intranet access, video-on-demand, 3-D images, database access, and remote LAN access. ADSL is an ANSI standard (T1.413).
ADSL Lite	ADSL Lite, G.Lite, Universal ADSL, Splitterless ADSL	Known by many names, this DSL variant is a slower version of ADSL that does not require a line splitter at the customer site. Instead, the ADSL link is split for the customer remotely at the service provider's site. Downstream data rates "max out" at 1.5 Mbps, and upstream rates are 384 kbps or less. Maximum local loop length is 18,000 feet, or about 3.5 miles. ADSL Lite is an official ITU-T standard (G-992.2), and its use is intended primarily for residential homes.

TABLE 16.3 The Digital Subscriber Line (DSL) Variants

Type	Name	Description
HDSL	High Bit Rate DSL	HDSL is a symmetrical DSL service that delivers T1 rates over two pairs of UTP and E-1 rates over three pairs of UTP. HDSL provides a more cost-effective strategy for provisioning T1-based local loops over existing UTP cable by separating the cable pairs into two full-duplex channels with each pair operating at 784 kbps. (In contrast, T1 cable pairs are simplex; one pair is used for downstream and the other for upstream transmissions, and each operates at T1 speed.) This provides less signal loss and less electromagnetic radiation, which result in distances twice that of T1 circuits in which a signal can travel without the need for repeaters. Maximum local loop distance is 12,000 feet (3.5 km). Applications include connecting PBXs and serving as an alternative to T1/E-1. It is also suitable for campus networks and ISPs.
HDSL2	High Bit Rate DSL 2	HDSL2 is second-generation HDSL that supports T1 transmission rates over a single UTP cable pair but still maintains a maximum distance length of 12,000 feet.
IDSL	ISDN-like DSL	IDSL is a symmetrical DSL service that delivers a maximum data rate of 144 kbps each way. It is based on ISDN technologies and uses ISDN BRI service. Unlike ISDN, which is circuit-switched, IDSL is an always-on service. However, also unlike ISDN, which supports voice, data, and video, IDSL supports only data transmissions. The maximum local loop distance for IDSL is 18,000 feet (5.4 km).
RADSL	Rate-adaptive DSL	RADSL is a nonstandard ADSL technology that determines the rate at which a signal can be transmitted across the local loop and then automatically adjusts this rate accordingly. Various proprietary solutions support downstream rates ranging from 640 kbps to 2.2 Mbps and upstream rates ranging from 120 kbps to 1 Mbps. Maximum distances range from 15,000 feet to 18,000 feet, depending on whether 24- or 26-gauge copper is used for the local loop.
SDSL	Symmetric DSL, Single-Line HDSL	SDSL is an HDSL variant that uses a single wire pair to support maximum transmission rates ranging from 384 to 768 kbps. Maximum local loop distances range from 12,000 feet to 18,000 feet. Telephone service is not supported.
UDSL	Universal DSL	UDSL is a proposed standard for the European community that will deliver symmetrical DSL service at 2 Mbps.
VDSL	Very High Data Rate DSL	VDSL is an asymmetric DSL service that is currently being defined. Transmission rates are expected to range from 13 to 52 Mbps downstream, with upstream rates ranging anywhere from 1.5 Mbps to an upstream rate equivalent. Maximum distances will range from 1000 feet (300 m) to 4000 feet (1200 m). VDSL will most likely be deployed as part of a fiber-copper hybrid local loop in which fiber is used for the service provider–neighborhood link and VDSL over UTP is used for the neighborhood–residential home link. Applications include Internet or intranet access, video-on-demand, database access, remote LAN access, and high-definition television (HDTV).

the higher the frequency of the signal, the greater the attenuation. In the "old" days, attenuation was not as great a concern for copper-based local loop circuits conditioned to operate within a 4 kHz range for analog voice transmissions. The presence of attenuation becomes much more acute when using these same circuits to support *x*DSL technologies, which operate at relatively high frequencies. Generally, the maximum distance *x*DSL technologies were designed to operate over is 18,000 feet (approximately 3.5 miles).

Although the majority of customer premises are located within 18,000 feet of their service provider's nearest switching office, this does not guarantee that the local loop circuits are capable of supporting high data transmission rates. Circuit quality can also impact a signal's strength. For example, most local loops comprise a mix of 24- or 26-gauge cable and have several cable splices or bridged taps. Mixing cables of different gauge can lead to signal reflection or distortion, and the presence of cable splices and taps can increase signal loss. Another area of concern is electrical noise. As we noted in Chapter 2, electrical noise occurs in two forms: ambient and impulse. Ambient noise can be induced by external sources such as fluorescent light transformers, electrical facilities, and heat. If ambient noise is present, receiving equipment can have problems distinguishing between incoming signals. Impulse noise consists of intermittent, undesirable signals induced by external sources such as lightning, switching equipment, and heavy electrically operated machinery such as elevator motors and photocopy machines. Impulse noise increases or decreases a circuit's signal level, which causes the receiving equipment to misinterpret the signal. Regardless of the type or source, noise degrades the quality and performance of a circuit. Electrical interference in the form of near-end crosstalk (NEXT) can also lead to signal degradation. Finally, the inside wire of a customer site cannot be overlooked. In most instances, this wire has been in place for many years and most likely has been spliced in several locations so that phone jacks could be installed in different rooms. Consequently, the internal wiring infrastructure can also have a negative impact on *x*DSL transmission rates.

It is also important to keep in mind that DSL data rates represent the speed at which data are delivered across the local loop. If there is congestion at the switching station, or if there is congestion at some point within the network cloud, it doesn't matter how fast the connection is because a bottleneck exists somewhere beyond the loop. Something else to be cognizant of is the DTE-to-DCE rate, which we discussed earlier. Most current model PCs or Macintoshes are not equipped with serial ports that have the capacity to keep up with a DSL connection. The bottom line is that DSL data rates are certainly impressive. However, these are the *theoretical maximum rates possible,* which do not reflect real-world constraints.

Types of DSL Service

As noted earlier and summarized in Table 16.3, DSL supports different types of technologies. A brief description of each follows.

Asymmetric DSL (ADSL)   ADSL is an ANSI standard that was initially developed in 1987 by Bell Communications Research (Bellcore, which changed its name to Telcordia Technologies in 1999) to deliver video-on-demand and interactive TV over UTP-based local loops. The term *asymmetric* means that more bandwidth is reserved for downstream transmissions (i.e., from service provider to customer) than for upstream connections (i.e., from customer to provider). ADSL connections require an

The term *modem* used in this context is really misapplied because ADSL is a digital technology. Hence, there is no modulation or demodulation of analog and digital signals. Nevertheless, modem is accepted and understood by the general public as any device that provides a dialup connection.

ADSL modem at the local end and at the telco switching office. ADSL service also needs to be purchased from a local phone service provider. Service might be available directly from an Internet service provider as well. Since ADSL operates over the same copper wire currently used for phone service, a second line or a new termination unit (which is required for ISDN) does not have to be installed. To use the service, you essentially connect the ADSL modem to your computer (or network) and telephone line (Figure 16.3). It is quite similar to using an analog modem except you can now transmit different types of data (voice, data, and video) simultaneously over the same circuit.

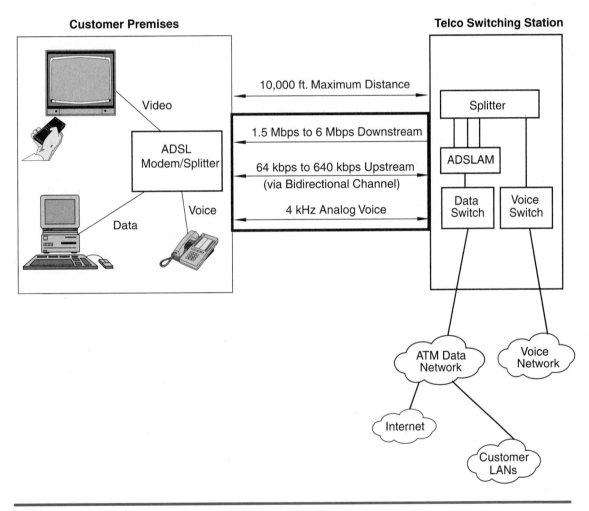

FIGURE 16.3 An ADSL connection involves ADSL modems at the local site and a "splitter" and ADSL access multiplexer (ADSLAM), which incorporates an ADSL modem, at the telco switching station. (The splitter can also be incorporated within the ADSLAM device along with the ADSL modem.) The splitter is used to separate voice and data signals. ADSL's maximum local loop distance is approximately 2 miles, its downstream rates range from 1.5 to 6 Mbps, and its upstream rates range from 64 to 640 kbps, which is provided via a bidirectional channel. A 4-kHz channel is also partitioned from the DSL link for conventional analog voice service. Source: adapted from Aber, 1997.

ADSL is also powered like conventional telephone service so during a power outage voice service will still be available. Other ADSL-connected devices such as a computer, however, still require power to run.

The biggest problem with an ADSL connection is local loop distance restrictions. To get an idea of what kind of data rate to expect, we need an accurate measurement of the local loop distance. A second potential issue is the quality of copper on which the local loop circuit is based. Both issues were discussed earlier. A third potential problem is interoperability of ADSL equipment from different manufacturers. However, this is not as much of a problem as it was before ADSL became an ANSI standard. A fourth potential issue is service availability. Deployment of ADSL service is not widespread yet. Consequently, many telco carriers might not offer it or might not have knowledgeable and skilled people onboard yet to help design or implement an ADSL-based connection. One final potential problem is relieving the headache you are sure to get trying to sort through all the rhetoric and hyperbole about DSL-service, cable modem service, ISDN, and 56K modem service.

ADSL Lite   Commonly known as G.Lite, ADSL Lite is an ITU-T standard that is similar to ADSL except it does not require a line splitter at the customer site. Instead, the link is split for the customer at the service provider's site (Figure 16.4). The maximum downstream rate ranges up to 1.5 Mbps, and upstream rates are 384 kbps or less. Maximum local loop distance is 18,000 feet. Of all the DSL variants, G.Lite is the most popular among residential home subscribers.

High Bit Rate DSL (HDSL)   HDSL is the most established of the DSL technologies. Unlike ADSL or ADSL Lite, HDSL service is symmetrical, providing T1 transmission rates over two pairs of UTP and E-1 rates over three pairs of UTP. HDSL was developed as an alternative to T1/E-1 service, and it provides a more cost-effective strategy for provisioning T1-based local loops over existing UTP cable. Unlike T1 service, which provides T1 data rates over simplex UTP cable pairs, HDSL separates the cable pairs into two full-duplex channels with each pair operating at 784 kbps. HDSL's maximum local loop distance is 12,000 feet, which is twice that of T1. The increased loop distance is a direct result of HDSL's technology, which provides less signal loss and less electromagnetic radiation.

HDSL2   This is second-generation HDSL, which provides the same performance as HDSL, but it does so over a single UTP cable pair.

ISDN DSL (IDSL)   IDSL represents a hybrid ISDN/DSL technology. It is a symmetrical DSL service that delivers a maximum data rate of 144 kbps each way that uses ISDN BRI service. Unlike ISDN, which is circuit-switched, IDSL is an always-on service. However, also unlike ISDN, which supports voice, data, and video, IDSL supports only data transmissions. The maximum local loop distance for IDSL is 18,000 feet.

Rate-Adaptive DSL (RADSL)   RADSL is a nonstandard ADSL technology that determines the rate at which a signal can be transmitted across the local loop and then automatically adjusts this rate accordingly. Various proprietary solutions support downstream rates ranging from 640 kbps to 2.2 Mbps and upstream rates ranging from

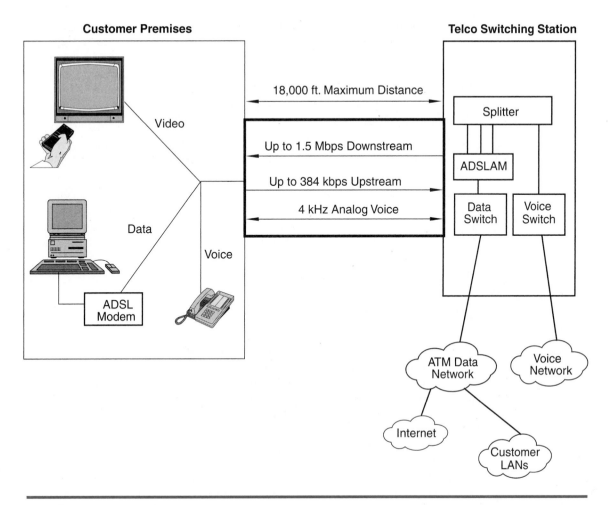

Customer Premises

Telco Switching Station

18,000 ft. Maximum Distance

Video

Up to 1.5 Mbps Downstream

Up to 384 kbps Upstream

4 kHz Analog Voice

Data

Voice

ADSL Modem

Splitter

ADSLAM

Data Switch

Voice Switch

ATM Data Network

Voice Network

Internet

Customer LANs

FIGURE 16.4 A G.Lite DSL connection is similar to that of ADSL except it is "splitterless." Here, high-speed data communications are provided by an ADSL modem connected to a PC, and the "splitting" of signals is performed at the service provider's end and not at the customer site. The maximum local loop length is 18,000 ft. (3.5 miles), upstream rates range up to 384 kbps, and downstream rates range up to T1 speeds.

120 kbps to 1 Mbps. Maximum distances range from 15,000 to 18,000 feet, depending on whether 24- or 26-gauge copper is used for the local loop.

Symmetric DSL (SDSL)   Also called *single-line HDSL*, SDSL provides symmetric data transmission rates over a single wire pair to support maximum transmission rates ranging from 384 to 768 kbps. Maximum local loop distances range from 12,000 to 18,000 feet. Telephone service is not supported.

Universal DSL (UDSL)   UDSL is a proposed standard for the European community that will deliver symmetrical DSL service at 2 Mbps.

Very-High Data Rate DSL (VDSL)   VDSL is an asymmetric DSL service that is expected to provide downstream data transmission rates ranging from 13 to 52 Mbps and upstream rates ranging from 1.5 Mbps to an upstream rate equivalent. Maximum distances will range from 1000 to 4000 feet (300 to 1000 m). VDSL will most likely be deployed as part of a fiber-copper hybrid local loop in which fiber is used for the service provider–neighborhood link, and VDSL over UTP is used for the neighborhood–residential home link.

Web sites that provide detailed information about *x*DSL include the ADSL Forum site at `http://www.adsl.com` the Universal ADSL Working Group site at `http://www.uawg.org` and the *x*DSL site at `http://www.xdsl.com`. The *DSL Sourcebook* is also available from `http://www.paradyne.com/sourcebook_offer/index.html`. One final site that should be of interest to many readers is the DSL Reports site at `http://www.dslreports.com`. In addition to the wealth of DSL-related information at this site, you can also find out if DSL service is available in your area, how far you are from the nearest provider's POP, who your DSL providers are, and what the service will cost.

16.4   Cable Modems

Cable modems represent the cable companies' infiltration into the telecommunications business, courtesy of the Telecommunications Act of 1996 (see Chapter 1). Cable modems use cable television lines for data communications. These lines use broadband coaxial cable (see Chapter 4), which has a multitude of frequencies available and significantly higher bandwidth than the UTP cable used by the telcos. Cable operators specify a frequency range within the cable and run data over it. Cable modems provide the interface (i.e., connection point) between a computer and the cable. Specifically, this interface is an Ethernet/802.3 network interface card. Thus, a PC must have an Ethernet/802.3 NIC installed to be connected to a cable modem. Once connected, it is as if the PC were connected to an Ethernet/802.3 LAN. The connection is always "up," and multimegabit data rates are possible. (See Chapter 9 for more information about Ethernet/802.3.)

Prior to deploying cable modem service, which involves two-way communication, cable operators had to upgrade their cable plants. Cable networks originally were designed specifically for downstream transmission only—they serve as a one-way broadcast facility for transmitting television signals. They were never designed for two-way transmissions. The original network design is a tree topology that consists of a signal source (called the head end), a local neighborhood distribution site, and a collection of amplifiers. The head end aggregates signals from different locations and modulates them to the frequencies that are assigned to the destination sites. (The head end usually receives a master signal from a satellite dish or a fiber backbone.) These modulated signals are then piped along the cable to a neighborhood distribution site, where they are delivered directly to a customer's home. En route from the head end to the neighborhood distribution facility, and then again to the customer's site, the signal is regenerated via one-way amplifiers. (This is similar to the use of repeaters in an Ethernet/802.3

CATV originally stood for Community Antenna Television, which was designed to provide television broadcasts in areas where broadcast reception was poor.

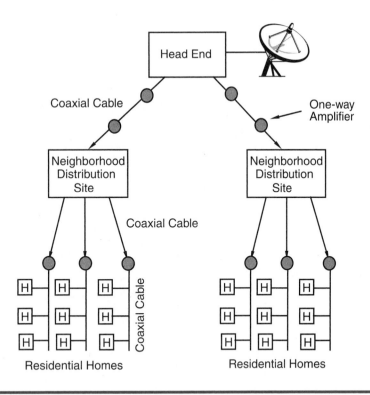

FIGURE 16.5 A coaxial-based cable television network is treelike in nature and designed for one-way transmission. Amplifiers are used to maintain signal quality while increasing distances. Source: adapted from Fitzgerald, 1996.

network.) This is necessary to maintain signal quality while increasing cable distances. A simple diagram illustrating this design is shown in Figure 16.5.

To provide for two-way transmission, cable networks had to be upgraded. Upgrade plans included replacing the one-way amplifiers with two-way amplifiers and replacing the coaxial cable with fiber-optic cable. The cable plant upgrade is occurring in two phases. The first phase involves replacing the coaxial cable with fiber at the head end. This eliminates the need for amplifiers but yet still allows the network diameter to increase without signal degradation. The fiber-optic cable also will carry more data. This resulting network is called a *hybrid fiber-coaxial (HFC) network.* The second phase involves replacing the coaxial cable at the neighborhood distribution site. Once fiber is deployed to the neighborhood, optical-to-electrical converters can replace the amplifiers, resulting in less amplification and a more robust cable plant (Figures 16.6 and 16.7).

Until two-way amplifiers are installed, cable operators can only offer high-speed downstream (from head end to customer site) data transmissions. Upstream transmissions (from customer site to head end) are restricted to 33.6 kbps via an analog modem

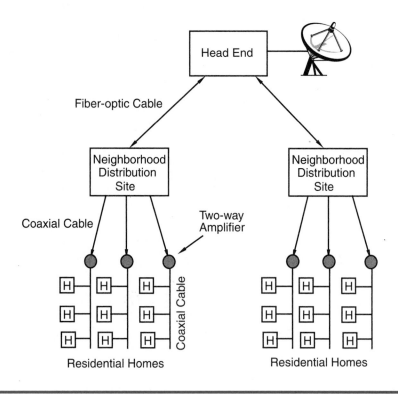

FIGURE 16.6 A hybrid fiber-coaxial (HFC) cable network consists of fiber-optic cable between the head end and neighborhood distribution sites. Coaxial cable is still deployed to the neighborhood, however. Source: adapted from Fitzgerald, 1996.

dialup connection through the telephone network. Even in those areas where two-way amplifiers are in place, because coax is still deployed to the neighborhood, upstream transmission rates are considerably less than their downstream counterparts. Depending on the cable operator and service, current upstream rates are somewhere from 500 kbps to 3 Mbps; downstream rates range between 10 to 30 Mbps.

Although these transmission rates are considerably higher than 56K modem service, we have to remember that the cable network is still a shared system. It is very similar to 10-Mbps Ethernet/802.3, which is a broadcast technology. Thus, as more subscribers come on-line, there will be more contention for the available bandwidth. (Contrast this with ADSL, which is a point-to-point topology. See also Chapter 9 for more information about Ethernet/802.3 LANs.) Most cable systems today support around 5000 users from the head end and serve somewhere between 500 and 2500 homes on a single line. One cable modem service in the United States that has been receiving attention is the @Home network by Tele-Communications, Incorporated (TCI), which was acquired by AT&T. Another is Time Warner's Road Runner Service. For more information, we suggest you start at TCI's Web site: http://www.tci.com.

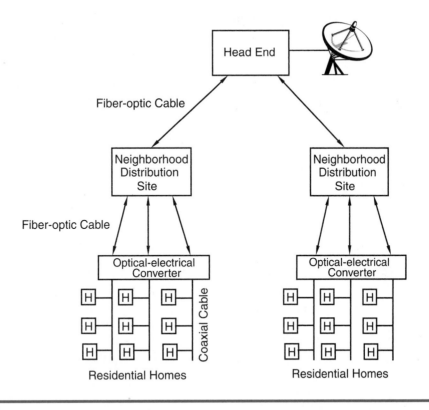

FIGURE 16.7 When completed, the upgraded cable network will be able to provide high-speed two-way transmissions for data, voice, and video service. Source: adapted from Fitzgerald, 1996.

16.5 Home Networking Concepts and Issues

The latest trend in computer communications and networking is home networking, which has become a popular solution due to the growth of multicomputer households worldwide. In the United States, for example, studies claim that over 64% of all households have a personal computer. A recent study also reported that 39% of all households have two or more computers. It's rapidly becoming the norm to be a networked house with more than one computer.

A network at home is really no different than a network at the office or at school. In fact, many times, the same technologies are used for both. Home networks are used to connect multiple computers together, to access common printers, to share files, and a rash of other requirements. One of your favorite author's (Hancock) home network is fairly comprehensive. It has switched 100-Mbps capability to all systems at home, a Windows-NT cluster, some fiber-optic cabling, and a high-speed cable modem connection to the Internet. Albeit, this home network is more advanced than most, but it does show where things are going rather quickly.

Although there are some products on the market today that make designing and configuring a home network easy, we once again issue the following proclamation: Networks are nontrivial systems. As is the case with any network installation, some advanced planning relative to the network's functions and its flexibility is in order. Even a "simple" home-based Internet connection requires careful consideration of several issues. These include the type of service you should subscribe to (e.g., 56K, ISDN, cable modem, ADSL, wireless), network security, potential line problems, and providing access to more than one computer within the home. Let's examine some of these issues in a little more detail.

Connecting to the Internet

If all you want is a home-based Internet connection, then one issue that needs to be addressed is service type. That is, you need to determine which service will best accommodate your needs. In this chapter alone, we presented several options, including traditional analog modem connections, 56K modem connections, *x*DSL connections, and cable modem connections. Other strategies were also discussed in previous chapters, including ISDN and frame relay. Following is a brief summary of some of the most common methods used to connect a home computer to the Internet.

Analog Modem   This is by far the most common and most popular method. A modem is connected via a phone line to the ISP, and you can get access to the Internet at whatever speeds the modem and ISP support. At this writing, the most popular modem for sale is the ITU-TSS standardized V.90 56-kbps modem or the dual-56-kbps load-balanced modem. This second type of modem provides a dialup via two phone lines and load balances between them, yielding a throughout of about 112 kbps if everything goes as planned. In any case, a modem, phone line, access software (e.g., PPP), and ISP account are required for connectivity. Analog modem connections are both relatively easy and inexpensive to implement. There are also nearly no equipment compatibility issues to be concerned with either. However, analog modems have reached their technical upper limit at 56K and hence offer the slowest Internet access method when compared to the other services available.

ISDN   ISDN provides a faster connection method for Internet access than analog modems. Of course, you pay more for it. There are two connection modes: dialup and permanent ISDN. To make an ISDN connection work, an ISDN-compatible phone line and an ISDN terminating device (commonly, but incorrectly, called an ISDN modem) are required with software and an ISP connection account. (See Chapter 12 for more information about ISDN.) ISDN is a viable alternative for relatively high-speed Internet connections, particularly if no other high-speed access is available within your area. ISDN works over copper phone wires, provides multiple channels that can be combined for higher transmission rates, supports voice, video, and data transmissions, and can be implemented in an always-on mode with always-on/dynamic ISDN.

Cable Modem   Cable modems offer high-bandwidth Internet access over standard coaxial cable TV lines. In this scenario, the local cable company installs a cable set-top box that has the ability to connect to your PC. Your PC will "think" it's connected to an Ethernet/802.3 LAN. An Ethernet/802.3 NIC is required. The set-top box provides a broadband access capability to the cable company, and they in turn have a router connection somewhere to the Internet. A cable modem provides an always-on connection; thus, you will be "live" on the Internet 24 hours a day, 7 days a week, just like a corporate Internet connection. Except for the PC, the cable vendor will usually provide everything needed to establish a cable modem connection (e.g., cable modem, software, Ethernet/802.3 card, and cables). Although cable modems and DSL service both provide high-speed Internet access, the method in which they provide access is quite different. For example, cable modems subscribers share bandwidth and hence must contend for access to the channel. DSL subscribers, on the other hand, have a dedicated point-to-point local loop link. Thus, during periods of peak activity, cable modem subscribers will see a degradation in overall throughput. Shared access is also not as secure as a dedicated point-to-point link. Some cable modem providers also restrict video access via a cable modem connection and instead require their subscribers to view video via their cable TV service. Finally, cable modem connections do not provide dialtone service (yet); hence, a separate telephone circuit is still needed for conventional voice communications.

Asymmetric Digital Subscriber Loop (ADSL)   ADSL in general, and ADSL Lite in particular, are two DSL variants that are applicable for residential homes. ADSL is similar to a leased line connection and, as with cable modem service, provides an always-on connection. ADSL service is asymmetric, meaning that upstream and downstream data transmission rates are different. (See Table 16.3 for more information about ADSL service.) Normally, the ADSL service provider will provide all the necessary hardware and software (except the PC) for an ADSL connection. Advantages ADSL has over other high-speed Internet connectivity strategies include high data transmission rates, its relatively lower cost, and the ability to use the existing UTP-based local loop for voice, video, and data transmissions across a single line.

High-Speed Wireless   A high-speed wireless Internet strategy involves installing wireless relay stations in a local neighborhood. These stations have a wireless relay to a small dish or flat data collector unit attached to a home. A wire from the dish goes to a relay system in the home, and the PC is connected to the network similar to an Ethernet/802.3 LAN (a NIC in the PC is required). Some commercial systems provide up to 10-Mbps symmetric connectivity to your home and do not depend on wire from the telephone company or a cable provider. Again, the vendor will provide the connection hardware and software. What is needed includes service in the area, a dish on the home, a decoder system, cables, an Ethernet NIC in the PC, software, and an ISP account. The most widely available service is currently Direct Broadcast Satellite (DBS), which is also known as Digital Satellite Service (DSS). Download speeds are approximately 350 kbps. Don't forget, though, that satellite communication services have a pronounced propagation delay.

So, which one is best? Often, it's not a question of "which is best" as much as "what is available." Telephone lines and modems are ubiquitous and easy to install and configure. The other four described methods vary in availability depending on where you live. Thus, some research will need to be done. We have used all five methods and find that they work okay once they are mature (the technology, not the authors—we never claimed to be mature). The biggest differentials are the cost per month for service, reliability issues, and one-time capital equipment costs to implement the service. You will need to shop around for what works best for you.

Interconnecting More Than One Home Computer

Interconnecting more than one computer at home involves designing a network to connect the systems together and then connecting that network to your Internet provider. This is true home networking, and hooking up computers very cheaply has never been easier. The cost of network hardware has dropped dramatically in the past few years to the point where network hardware is very inexpensive. For instance, to connect two PCs to each other via Ethernet in a home, you need two 10-Mbps Ethernet cards ($20 each), two 15-feet long Category 5 UTP cables ($11 each), and one 5-port 10BASE-T "hublet" and power supply ($40). Thus, the total expenditure is $102. Even better, some companies offer what is called a "starter kit," which contains all the hardware for about $20 less.

The software that is required for the network depends largely on the operating system being used. If you are using Windows 95/98/2000 or MacOS, then you already have the software needed on your system as part of the operating system. The same applies to many UNIX environments, including freeware versions such as Linux and FreeBSD. To make the two systems talk to each other, you must set up a peer-to-peer connection (see Chapter 2). This is when one system connects directly to the other with no intermediate router or server. On most systems, you must configure a protocol that is not dependent on a router or naming service to discover route paths or the name translation of addresses to get things to work. For instance, on a PC running Windows, you enable the NetBEUI protocol and adapter services in the network Control Panel in the Windows operating system version you are using. You must also select File and Print Sharing and allow the system to install the software (have your system CD-ROM nearby). Once you do this and reboot the systems, all you have to do is enable disk sharing on your systems. This is usually via the disk's Properties facilities; select the Sharing tab at the top. You will also need to decide on what security features you want to implement. By enabling Sharing mode, you can now access the hard disks of the remote system. In Windows, you can double click on Network Neighborhood to find out what is on the network. Connectivity to a particular system is effected by simply clicking on the system icon. You are now sharing disks from your systems over your little Ethernet in your home just as you would at the office.

Print sharing is even easier to implement than disk sharing. In Windows, just select the printer you want to share from the Printers folder on the system disk, select the target printer's icon to highlight it, and then select Sharing from the File menu. Once you enable Sharing, the other system can "see" your printer on the network and access it. Don't forget to install the printer software and drivers on the remote system so it prints correctly.

Sharing an Internet connection takes a bit more work, but nothing major. There are several ways to do it. If you are using Windows 95, you can use a variety of packages such as WinGate. These act as routers and allow multiple systems to be connected to a single dial-out over a network. If you are using Windows NT/2000 or UNIX, these operating systems are equipped with routing kernels that can be configured to allow your Internet-attached node to route packets from the Internet connection to your other systems on the mini-Ethernet. If you read the system manager's documentation, there are instructions on how to configure the routing kernel on both operating system environments. If you are using Windows 98, Microsoft includes the RIP routing protocol for IP on the distribution kit CD-ROM. By installing RIP, you can configure the system as a router for other IP nodes on your network and share your connection with them. Other operating systems will or will not have similar capabilities. Of course, another option is to purchase a small dialup router. This will cost between $200 and $1000 depending on connection type, speed, and router configuration required. So, as you can see, getting your systems configured to route to and from your Internet connection is not very hard or expensive.

The Home Network Infrastructure

Recently, there has been a move within the industry to develop standards for home-based network infrastructures. Three groups leading these efforts include the Home Phoneline Networking Alliance (HomePNA), the HomePlug Powerline Alliance (HomePlug), and the wireless networking groups. The HomePNA has developed a standard for linking multiple PCs within a home via an existing phone line. The current standard supports a 2-Mbps data rate, but a soon to be approved standard will increase this to 10 Mbps. Several products by equipment makers Intel, Dell, 3COM, and SMC are presently available that conform to the proposed standard. The HomePlug Powerline Alliance is currently developing a standard that will enable a home networking infrastructure to be based on a home's current electrical outlets. Thus, a home's AC power outlets will serve as a network connection similar to the way RJ-45 connector plates provide a UTP Ethernet connection. In this scenario, a device plugs directly into a power outlet, and the computer equipment in turn plugs into the HomePlug device. Finally, as we mentioned in Chapter 4, IEEE's recently approved wireless LAN standards (802.11 and 802.11b) are expected to spur product development for wireless home-based networking projects, which will enable a homeowner to establish a WLAN infrastructure. For additional information about HomePNA and HomePlug, visit `http://HomePNA.com` and `http://homeplug.com`.

Home Network Security

It is a fantasy to think that small-site connections are not vulnerable to attack. A home-based Internet connection is just as vulnerable to attack as a corporate connection. This is especially the case with Internet connections that are always "on," such as cable modem connections, residential regional wireless links, ISDN permanent connections, and most ADSL connections. All the protocols work the same whether you are a large company or a one-bedroom apartment location, and all locations can be compromised by an unauthorized user.

Nothing can stop an attack from happening. The best you can do is put in safeguards to keep someone from getting to your systems and their files. Tools like personal firewalls on your system, encryption software for files and disk drives, and virtual private network (VPN) software to safely connect to corporate resources all help keep prying eyes away from your systems.

Attacks on home networks do not happen that often, but when they do, they can get ugly. One of the authors had a friend who was fortunate enough to be one of the first in his neighborhood to get a cable modem connection. He installed the proper hardware and software on the system, and life was good. In the first week of operation, he left the PC on at all times and was effectively hooked into the Internet 24 hours a day. In that time frame, an unauthorized user got onto his system and set up an Internet relay chat (IRC) redirection program that allowed the hacker to get on to chat groups, be as rude and obnoxious as desired, and seriously disturb the chat groups that the hacker was attacking. In the process of this, the various larger chat bulletin board systems traced the IP address back to the friend's PC. Then a lawyer got involved. The friend first found out that something was amiss when he and his ISP received a "cease and desist" letter that threatened a lawsuit. Since the friend had been out of town that whole time, and since no one else had touched the system, it was investigation time. Examination of the system showed that the hacker really had been there and how he gained access. The software was deleted, the ISP helped explain things to the lawyer, and all went back to normal. So, in a home networking environment, you have to take security seriously and use the proper precautions, just as in the company environment, unless you want to lose your data, allow someone to set up camp on your system, or possibly have your privacy compromised in an ugly way. (See Chapter 17 for more information about network security.)

Potential Problems When Configuring a Home Network

There are several things that cause people to have trouble when they configure a home network. Most are pretty straightforward to solve if you think ahead. The most common ones we have seen are summarized here.

Phone Line   In this situation, the phone company does not properly install a phone line in the residence to the proper noise level allowances as posted by the FCC in the United States and organizations that set phone standards in other countries. When the line voltages, attenuation, crosstalk, and other settings are out of specification on the line, you get noise, signal degradation, and a myriad of other problems. Sometimes, especially when there is a lack of phone lines in a community, the phone company will put an electronic box on a single pair of lines called an "active multiplexer," which allows the phone company to put the equivalent of more phone signals on the same pair of lines. These boxes are notorious for introducing serious noise and reduced signal strength on telephone connections, which degrade a modem's capabilities and the speed of the link. Phone line noise is a very common problem with home networks and can be very irritating.

Cable   This is a problem area even for seasoned network professionals. Because there are so many ways to connect devices and so many standards for different devices, there are a plethora of cable connectors, pinouts, pair matches, and so forth that plague the well-connected network. It is therefore extremely easy to get the wrong cable in the wrong configuration between two systems when trying to configure a network. Other cable problems include trying to get the right connector type for a connection port, proper cable length, and proper cable type (e.g., shielded, unshielded, coaxial). Cables can be a real hassle when configuring home networks. (See Chapter 4 for additional information about cables.)

NIC Settings   In some NICs, there are various jumpers (small wire pins on the board) or dual in-line package (DIP) switch blocks. You must configure the jumpers or DIP switches to match the type of network connectivity options required for the network type you are using. You might also have to specify DIPs or jumpers for bus speeds, memory utilization, and other parameters. Many network cards now are software configurable, so more and more equivalent DIP switch settings are done in software, but the aggravation factor is about the same. If you get DIPs, jumpers, or internal software settings wrong, the card will not work as planned or desired.

Network Protocols   Problems involving network protocols will always emerge when establishing any network connection. Although recent versions of popular operating systems are making it easier to identify and correctly configure the required protocols, the problems that emerge can still be related to complex issues that will need to be resolved before things can work correctly. The bottom line is: If you are not comfortable working with network protocols, then get help from someone who is.

Power   In most homes, the circuit where the PC is plugged into is usually shared with other devices such as ceiling fans, lights, toaster ovens, and so forth. Most homes are not configured for "clean" power. Furthermore, the circuit breaker serving a set of electrical outlets is not always of sufficient capacity to support a computer, its peripherals (e.g., monitor, scanner, printer, modem), and noncomputer appliances such as fans, lights, and toaster ovens. If the power output of a circuit drops below what a device requires, a "brown out" results and the computer will reboot as if a power failure occurred. Consequently, it is usually a good idea to invest about $75 and purchase a battery backup power conditioning unit (sometimes called an uninterruptible power supply, or UPS) to ensure that the system and components will continue to function properly during power fluctuations.

End-of-Chapter Commentary

On this note, we conclude our discussion of dialup and home networking. Please note that there are many other issues related to dialup and home networking. That's one of the curses of networking—you can never know enough, and trying to keep current is almost a full-time job in itself. The material presented here represents some of the more salient aspects of the topic and should give you a good understanding of the concepts and issues related to dialup and home networking. Also note that additional information about some of the material presented here is available in other chapters. For example, Chapter 1 provides a discussion of network standards that is quite relevant to the discussion of modem and *x*DSL standards. Chapter 2 provides a discussion of Shannon's limit and how it is applied in determining the maximum speed of analog modems. Specific information about the analog-to-digital conversion process is provided in Chapter 3. Chapter 4 contains detailed information about hardware and cables, and the concept of error control is explained in Chapter 5. The discussion in Chapter 9 on Ethernet/802.3 networks might also be beneficial in further understanding some of the inherent restrictions of cable modem service. Chapter 12 provides information about ISDN, which is considered one of the solutions to the local loop bottleneck problem. Finally, the next chapter, Chapter 17, presents a discussion on network security issues that you might find enlightening relative to home network security.

CHAPTER REVIEW MATERIALS

SUMMARY

• Dialup networking involves establishing an analog or digital network connection through the public telephone system. Analog dialup connections require a modem at each end to modulate a computer's digital signal into analog form at the sending side and to demodulate the signal at the receiving side to reconvert the transmitted analog signal from the phone line to digital form before it is passed to the computer. Digital dialup connections do not use conventional modems but instead require special digital devices for signal conversions and translations.

• Terminal dialup connections require terminal emulation software such as Kermit or ProComm to allow a local machine to function as a terminal of the remote system. A common emulation is vt100. Network dialup connections require special networking software such as PPP to allow a local machine to become a networked node.

• Modem standards are defined by ITU-T and specify techniques for modulation, error control, and compression. Examples of these standards include V.34, which is the standard for 28.8 kbps modems, and V.90, which is the standard for 56K modems.

• Data compression refers to representing a repetitive pattern within a data set with a smaller set of bits. Compressed files can be transmitted faster than uncompressed files. Two modem compression standards are V.42 *bis* and MNP 5, which compress data by factors of 4 to 1 and 2 to 1, respectively.

• The speed two modems communicate with one another is called the DCE-to-DCE rate, and the speed a modem communicates with the computer it is connected to is called the DTE-to-DCE rate. The former is fixed and depends on the modem standard that is supported; the latter is user configurable.

• Modem standards for error control are defined by V.42 and MNP 1–4. V.42 includes MNP1–4 and LAPM, which uses CRC for error detection and ARQ for error control.

• 56K modems involve a mix of analog and digital connections. Compared to conventional modems, which require four analog–digital conversions, 56K modems require only two such conversions.

• *x*DSL refers to various digital subscriber line technologies that permit different data types such as data, voice, and video to be transmitted simultaneously over standard telephone lines. DSL transmission rates range from 128 kbps to 52 Mbps and depend on line quality and local loop distances. The most popular DSL service is ADSL, which is a digital technology standard that provides downstream rates ranging from 1.5 to 9 Mbps and upstream rates ranging from 16 kbps to 1 Mbps.

• Cable modems use conventional broadband coaxial television cable for data communications. A cable TV-based data communications network is designed as an Ethernet/802.3 LAN and hence has the same features, advantages, disadvantages, and network design issues as Ethernet/802.3. To support this type of facility, cable networks are being upgraded from a downstream-only design to a two-way interactive configuration. The cable plant is also being upgraded from coaxial cable to fiber-optic cable.

• Home-based networking involves establishing a computer network within a home. Home networks enable multiple computers to be interconnected so they can share common peripherals, files, and Internet connections.

• Home-based Internet service can be established using conventional analog modems, ISDN, cable modems, ADSL, and high-speed wireless links. Determining an appropriate connection type depends on availability, costs, reliability and security issues, and expected usage.

• Home computer networks can be established by connecting devices to an Ethernet/802.3 LAN and configuring the operating system to support a specific network protocol. Current operating systems such as Windows 95/98/2000 and MacOS 8.x (or higher) have built-in networking support, thus making it relatively easy to share files and printers. Sharing a home-based Internet connection involves configuring the operating system to support an IP routing protocol such as RIP in addition to supporting a network protocol. Routing can also be accomplished independent of the OS by installing a dialup router.

• Network security issues should be an integral part of any home-based network configuration. This is especially important if ADSL or cable modems are used for home-based Internet access since these connections are always "up."

• Potential problem areas common to establishing home-based networks include telephone lines, network cable, NIC settings, network protocol configurations, and electrical power.

VOCABULARY CHECK

compression	DCE-to-DCE rate	hybrid fiber cable (HFC)
data communications equipment (DCE)	digital subscriber line (DSL)	local loop
data terminal equipment (DTE)	DTE-to-DCE rate	modem
	error control	

REVIEW EXERCISES

1. Explain the differences between a tty dialup connection and a network dialup connection.

2. What is the purpose of terminal emulation software relative to a tty dialup connection?

3. Unlike a network dialup connection, network file transfers initiated via a tty dialup connection require a two-step process to store the file on the local PC. Explain what this two-step process involves and compare it to file transfers using a network dialup connection.

4. What purpose does a modem serve relative to a conventional (i.e., analog) dialup connection?

5. Explain the difference between the DCE-to-DCE rate and the DTE-to-DCE rate.

6. Which type of file do you think is more conducive to modem compression: text files or graphic images? Why?

7. Assume you are using a V.90 modem over a noisy line to transfer a 5-MB graphic image. Further assume that the DCE-to-DEC rate fluctuates between 14,400 and 53,000 bps. Explain why the DCE rates fluctuate. Over what time range (from low to high) can you expect the file transfer to take?

8. A network-based PPP dialup connection reveals the following information when the connection is established: 28800/ARQ/V34/LAPM/V42BIS. What does all of this mean?

9. Establish a dialup connection using your modem and record the parameters at which a connection is made. For example, most current dialup connections will identify the DCE rate, the V standard, any compression standards, and error controls.

10. A V.90 modem is commonly expressed as having a data rate of 57,600 bps. Furthermore, the symbol K when used in this context (e.g., 56K) represents 1024. Why is it, then, that the product of 56 × 1024 is equal to 57,344 and not 57,600?

11. Research the genesis of the United States's FCC regulation that limits the data rate of 56K modems to less than 56K. Do you think this regulation should remain in effect today? Why?

12. Explain the concept of the local loop.

13. Locate your neighborhood telephone switching station and determine approximately how far your home is from it. Given this distance, do you think you can benefit from a DSL connection from your home? Why?

14. Establish a link to the Web site `http://dslreports.com/prequal` and determine whether DSL service is available in your neighborhood and, if so, from whom. While at this site (`dslreports.com`), you might also want to review some of the information provided about DSL.

15. As of this writing, most telcos and CLECs provide some form of xDSL service (see Table 16.3). The most common residential service is ADSL Lite. Unfortunately, it is estimated that as many as 75% of U.S. residents cannot get DSL service. Research and report on some of the barriers to DSL service and what can be done to deliver some form of DSL service to these residents.

16. Compare cable modem service to xDSL service. As part of your comparison, discuss advantages and disadvantages of each type of service.

17. Given the choice of receiving broadband access from your local telephone company (e.g., Bell-South, Verizon Communications, PacBell), a nontelco DSL provider (e.g., Rhythms, Covad, NorthPoint), an Internet service provider (e.g., AOL, EarthLink/MindSpring), or a cable company, which would you choose and why?

18. Explain the concept of the cable company's HFC network.

19. Discuss with your classmates the type of Internet connection you presently have at home. Is this connection sufficient for your needs? If not, what type of connection are you considering or would you like to establish?

20. Compare the advantages and disadvantages among the following types of connectivity solutions: analog modem, cable modem, ISDN, xDSL, and wireless.

21. Review the list of potential problems of setting up a home network given in the text. Of those listed, which have you personally experienced (either at home, at school, or at work) and how did you resolve it?

22. Discuss the pros and cons of having a business or school provide high-speed Internet access directly to its employees/students versus outsourcing the service to an Internet service provider, cable company, or telco.

SUGGESTED READINGS AND REFERENCES

ABER, R. 1997. xDSL Supercharges Copper. *Data Communications,* March, 99–105.

AMATI COMMUNICATIONS CORPORATION. 1996. *ADSL Field Guide.* San Jose, CA: Amati Communications Corporation.

ANGEL, J. 1999. High-Speed Internet Access Comes Home. *Network Magazine,* February, 42–47.

BOLLES, G. A. 1991. Modem Talk. *Network Computing,* August, 73–81.

———. 1992. Modem Talk: What's My Line. *Network Computing,* 1 October, 85–89.

BURKES, R. E. 1991. Making a Case for Dial-up LAN Links. *LAN Technology,* March, 49–54.

CHOLEWKA, K. 1997. 56K Modems: The New Spin on Speed. *Data Communications,* May, 93–103.

CLARK, E. 1996a. Data Meets the Dial Tone. *Interoperability: Supplement to LAN,* February, 20–33.

———. 1996b. PC, Phone Home! *LAN,* October, 125–132.

———. 1999. Pricing the Last Mile. *Network Magazine,* February, 36–41.

FITZGERALD, S. 1996. Reshaping the Digital Landscape. *LAN Interoperability: A Quarterly Supplement to LAN Magazine,* August, 14–20.

FREZZA, B. 1996. Cable TV: Giving Us the Broadband Business. *Network Computing,* 15 May, 31–32.

GALLO, M., and W. HANCOCK. 1999. *Networking Explained.* Boston: Digital Press.

KALMAN, S. 1997. The Bright Future of CTI. *LAN,* January, 85–92.

LIEBMANN, L. 1996. Free Market Theory. *LAN,* July, 60–64.

MACLEAN, P. 1993. V.FAST and V.32TERBO: Faster Modems, Slower Standards. *Network Computing,* July, 110–130.

MAKRIS, J. 1998. DSL: Don't Be Duped. *Data Communications,* 21 April, 39–52.

NEWMAN, D., M. Carter, and H. Holzbaur. 1998. DSL: Worth Its Wait. *Data Communications,* June, 101–112.

NEWMAN, J. 1997. ADSL: Putting a Charge into Your Copper Cable. *Network Computing,* 1 May, 139–142.

RICHARDSON, R. 1996. Tone Dialing, SOHO Style. *LAN,* October, 107–114.

———. 1997. Betting WAN Access Technology. *Network Computing,* 1 July, 43–56.

STEINKE, S. 1996. Competition Comes to the WAN. *LAN,* July, 52–58.

———. 1997. Rehab for Copper Wire. *LAN,* February, 57–62.

———. 1999. A Lineup of Local-Loop Contenders. *Network Magazine,* February, 30–35.

TADJER, R. 1996. 56-kbps Modems Are in Search of a Home. *Network Computing,* 15 November, 24–26.

ZEICHICK, A. 1997. LAN Glossary: Computer Telephony. *LAN,* January, 138.

ZGODZINSKI, D. 1996a. The Cable Chase. *Internet World,* June, 63–66.

———. 1996b. Enter ADSL. *Internet World,* October, 72–75.

17

Network Security Issues

CHAPTER OBJECTIVES

After studying this chapter, you will be able to do the following:

1. Recognize internal and external security threats to an organization.
2. Describe the common methods of threat assessment.
3. Explain the concept of risk analysis.
4. Understand employees' role in helping maintain their organization's security measures.
5. Identify common LAN and WAN network hazards.
6. Recognize security weaknesses within your organization.
7. Understand common barriers to network security and the major issues involved in implementing proper security measures.
8. List common security measures that can minimize or prevent network security compromises.
9. Discuss the role firewalls play relative to network security.
10. Compare and contrast the various types of firewalls.
11. Describe the data encryption process.
12. Compare and contrast DES, PGP, and RSA.
13. Describe the purpose and function of public and private keys.
14. Explain the concept of authentication.
15. Compare and contrast digital certificates and smart cards.
16. Illustrate how Kerberos works.
17. Compare and contrast the various VPN-related security protocols.
18. Describe the manner in which IP has been modified to incorporate security measures.

CHAPTER OUTLINE

In this chapter, we discuss various concepts of network security, including techniques, issues, and problems involved in implementing a safe and secure network environment. It is important to note that the material in this chapter represents an overview of network security, not a detailed treatise. We begin the chapter by defining network security and present a sidebar that distinguishes between security and ethics (See Box 17.1). Section 17.2 introduces the subject of threat assessment. Included with this discussion is information about how to assess network assets that might be the target of an attack. This discussion is then followed by examples of network attacks and various security measures that should be considered to prevent such attacks. In the next three sections, specific network security measures are discussed: Section 17.4 provides information about firewalls, Section 17.5 examines various encryption methods, and Section 17.6 addresses authentication and access control measures. We end the chapter with a discussion of virtual private networks (VPNs) and the security protocols VPNs use to provide secure data transmissions via the Internet.

17.1 What Is Network Security?

Network security is defined as the proper safeguarding of all components associated with a network, including data, media, and infrastructure. A comprehensive approach to network security involves three essential elements, namely, accurate threat assessment, use of the best cryptographic tools available, and deployment of effective network access control products (e.g., firewalls). Perhaps most important, network security may only be achieved by ensuring that all network resources are used in compliance with a prescribed corporate policy and only by authorized personnel.

In light of ongoing hacker attacks and the proliferation of viruses, most people agree that network security is one of the most pressing issues in e-commerce today. Every organization requires it, but few have a firm grasp on how best to achieve it. There are many ways to achieve varying levels of network security, however, these methods can be extremely expensive or may not completely protect users from the many hazards that emerge on a daily basis. Proper implementation of network security is neither trivial nor inexpensive, and it requires expertise that encompasses most areas of network science.

17.2 Threat Assessment

A challenge inherent to network security is determining the right level of security required for proper control of system and network assets. This concept, known as *threat assessment,* identifies the assets you have and who may attempt to access them. Organizations can best assess corporate network threats by using a structured approach. To illustrate, there are many *threats to hardware* (e.g., theft of computers or related equipment, destruction of computer equipment), *threats to software* (e.g., viruses or software bugs, software deletions from a hard disk, theft of CD-ROMs), *threats to information*

BOX 17.1 Network Security and Ethics

Network security involves the various measures to protect a network's components and resources from various threats, including physical (e.g., fire, natural disasters, environmental, and sabotage) and illegitimate uses by personnel. There are no simple solutions to the issue of network security. It is prudent, however, for organizations to have established policies in place to protect themselves from security threats. Examples of such policies include a disaster recovery plan, a data backup policy, giving users access to only those areas or levels of a system warranted by their job requirements, setting file permissions to reflect authorized access, using personnel to monitor or test a network's security, and encrypting data. Of all these measures, however, none compares to making users cognizant of their role in security. It is critical that employees be made aware of security policies and the reason for these policies.

Network ethics refers to specific standards of moral conduct by network users for the responsible use of network devices and resources. Access to these devices and resources is a privilege and should be treated as such by all users. Responsible, ethical behavior should be the rule rather than the exception and is perhaps the ultimate security measure that an organization can establish. The issue of ethics is important because people are usually the weakest link in any network security scheme. People are susceptible to threats or bribes, they can make mistakes (e.g., writing down a password and leaving it on top of a desk), and they can suddenly subscribe to some new ideology that contradicts their company's policies. When placed in a questionable situation, users must be cognizant of what constitutes right or wrong behavior if they are to be held accountable for their actions. The Division Advisory Panel (DAP) of the National Science Foundation (NSF) Division of Networking and Communications Research and Information (DNCRI) defines as unethical "any activity which purposefully or through negligence: disrupts the intended use of the networks; wastes resources through such actions (people, bandwidth or computer); destroys the integrity of computer-based information; compromises the privacy of users, [or] consumes unplanned resources for control and eradication" (*Communications of the ACM*, June, 1989, p. 688).

(e.g., database data corruption or deletion, theft of key database files), *threats to system* or network operations (e.g., network congestion, electrical interferences, power outages), and *threats to security measures.* (e.g., theft of passwords or IDs). Once you have assessed your network's vulnerabilities you are in the best position to protect your organization's assets. (See Box 17.2 for information about creating strong passwords.)

Identifying Critical Assets

The initial challenge of threat assessment is distinguishing between critical and noncritical assets. This process is absolutely essential to protecting an e-business. For instance, pharmaceutical companies maintain an enormous amount of sensitive information, including sales figures, customer order information, clinical trial data, FDA documentation, agreements with partners and suppliers, and just about any other standard office information system facilities common among any other company. In this example, the most critical business asset is the compound database, which stores information about products and current research. This is the data source that ultimately generates the company's deliverables and, thus, the profits. Compromise this database and the business is critically injured.

BOX 17.2 Creating Strong Passwords [a]

The single most important component of any network security scheme is the password assigned to networked devices. It is important that strong passwords (i.e., difficult to guess) be created and maintained. Failure to do so can compromise the security of the entire network.

When selecting a password, avoid using: (a) any type of name, including yours or any family members or relatives (spouse, children, parents, aunts, uncles, cousins, in-laws, pets); the name of your company or colleagues; the name of an operating system such as "windows," "unix," or "macintosh"; the host name of your computer or your e-mail address; (b) anyone's home, work, cell, or fax telephone number; (c) any part of a social security or student number; (d) anybody's birth date; (e) any dictionary word (English or foreign); (f) a geographical area (e.g., city, state, county, park); (g) any string of characters comprising the same letters, numbers, or pattern of numbers or letters (e.g., xxxxx, 12345, wysiwyg); (h) any of the foregoing that begins or ends with a digit (e.g., unix1 or 5xxxxx).

Passwords that are difficult to guess include a mix of uppercase and lowercase letters, digits, punctuation marks, and special characters (e.g., =, *, ^, @) and are usually seven or eight characters in length. Three suggestions for creating strong passwords are as follows:

- Intermix the first letters of an easy to remember (short) phrase with digits, punctuation marks, or special characters. For example, *It was twenty years ago today* is represented as Iw$ty^aT.
- Combine two relatively short words with a special character, digit, or punctuation mark. For example, *buzz* and *off* combined with the tilde character produce the password BuzZ~OfF.
- Use letters, special characters, and punctuation marks to represent an English (or foreign) sentence. For example, *You are so lazy!* is represented as UrSoLaz!

Also refrain from writing down passwords. A password committed to memory is more secure than one that is written down. If it is necessary to write down a password, then: (a) do not label the written text as a password; (b) keep the corresponding username separate from the password; (c) never tape the paper on which the password is written to any part of a computer or its peripheral units; (d) do not maintain an electronic version of the password; and (e) make the written version different, yet still discernible to you, from the real password. For example, if your real password is *IMover4T* (I am over 40), then you might write down *IM>4T!!* (I am greater than 40), or vice versa.

Remember: *A single user with a weak password can compromise the security of an entire network.*

[a]Adapted from Garfinkel & Spafford, 1991.

As another illustration, let's take a look at the airline industry. In this example, the keys to managing the industry's vast operations are scheduling and load management, which implies computing. Scheduling is an enormously complex task involving the management of crews, equipment, supplies, cargo, passengers and many other tasks. While scheduling is extremely important and essential to business, a very critical problem for an airline is the computation of weights and balances. Pilots need to know the aircraft's takeoff weight based upon its load (e.g., fuel, passengers, cargo) to set the aircraft's flight systems for the calculated takeoff speed in various weather conditions. If this operation isn't handled properly, an aircraft becomes too heavy and is unable to fly very far. In this case, it's clear that the scheduling system is a mission-critical asset that must be protected at all costs.

It's easy to understand the critical nature of network security in our airline example. However, in many companies, people are much more concerned about sales figures and cash flow than network security. Isn't it just as important to safeguard strategic product plans, the exposure of which might result in a lawsuit? What if your Web server goes down resulting in a major public relations disaster? High-visibility companies are particularly vulnerable to bad press, and they have a great deal to lose if they experience a major security breach. Imagine that a bank gets hacked and this becomes public knowledge? Who would want to save their money at a bank that cannot safeguard its own information? Every business has items that are crucial to safeguard from external parties. Identifying what they are and how damaging they could be to the company is the first step toward effective threat assessment.

Who Covets Your Assets?

Now that you have an idea of which resources are crucial to a company, the next challenge is determining who would want them and how might they use these resources against you. In the case of the pharmaceutical company, the loss of a patent or patent-worthy research might, in the long term, result in millions of dollars of lost revenue. Determining who might benefit from the assets you control helps you identify potential threat locations and who might attempt to steal what a company deems vital to its operations.

Sometimes the threat to a company is not a competitor but someone who harbors a vendetta against that company. Companies that perform animal testing for product safety verification (e.g., pharmaceutical companies, cosmetic companies, food-related companies, defense contractors) are frequently under attack by activist groups. Some of these groups have paramilitary factions that break into labs destroying equipment and data. Some groups have even targeted networks and computing infrastructure with specific viruses designed to infiltrate a company's systems and subsequently attack research data. In short, the threat to your data may not always be your competition and sometimes the threats come from sources you'd least suspect.

In 1991, an FBI study found that over 80% of network crimes were committed by insiders within a company. In 1997, the number was adjusted to about 75% (direct internal and "known" dial-in users) through a joint study by the FBI and the Computer Security Institute. The change was mostly due to the fact that Internet and external break-ins were more accurately documented. In 2000, the percentage of internal attacks was refined again, this time to 50%. This refinement is primarily the result of better statistics on external attacks being maintained. However, any network security expert will probably tell you privately that they generally see more internal breaches than external attacks even today.

To root out potential threats from insiders, we must determine which employees might want to (a) threaten the company, (b) cause asset loss, (c) abuse fiscal fidelity, (d) sell to a competitor, (e) cause public relations problems for the company, (f) hurt customer relations or compromise customer information integrity, (g) cause internal outage of resources that would hurt corporate operations, or (h) do anything that might damage a company's ability to do business and generate revenue. Most companies do not take special precautions to protect internal network assets. This is a big mistake. Although most companies understand that security arrangements must protect corporate networks from external attacks, nearly nothing is done to prevent internal attacks, which is where most threats originate. In short, key assets must be protected from both external and internal threats. We must first understand the source of internal threats so that we can keep the honest folks honest and catch the criminals before they create problems.

Risk Analysis

To properly understand the threat to a company, we have to assess how much the loss of assets will cost. This concept is called *risk analysis* and can be quite complex in larger companies that control many assets. In most cases, performing some simple calculations on the cost of replacing, upgrading, repairing, or managing a threat situation will produce some startling numbers. You should compare the costs to managing a threat situation to the price of defending the situation. Specially designed risk analysis software is available to assist you in this endeavor. These tools range in cost from $100 to as much as $20,000 per license. The National Institute of Standards and Technology (NIST, formerly the National Bureau of Standards) publishes a risk analysis software guide, *Guide for Selecting Automatic Risk Analysis Tools,* Publication Number 500-174.

Following is an example of the impact poor risk analysis can have on an organization: One day a large public company with a name we all know discovered that its Web pages changed with some obscenities. Prior to this event, management did not feel the need to secure the corporate Web site and placed the Web server on the outside of a firewall system. As it turned out, while no corporate assets were lost, the security breach resulted in two major problems for the company. First, there was a great deal of negative publicity in the local and national news, which caused a great deal of embarrassment and compromised the company's standing in the industry. To manage the negative media attention, a professional "crisis management" PR firm was called in for a fee of over $300K. Next, the repairs to the Web server and addition of the security technologies had to be implemented very quickly—and at great expense. Fixing this disaster cost the company substantially more than setting up an effective security solution would have cost at the outset. The second problem was that the Web pages served as a buyer's catalog and this hurt business in two ways. First, search engines that used blocking software based on URLs placed the company's Web pages in a blocking state in their databases. This effectively locked out potential customers who might use these search engines to find the company's home page because they were denied access to the company's site. Second, confidence in the integrity of the Web site was badly compromised. Many companies that were considering using the Web site for e-commerce prior to this incident backed out of the deal for over 6 months until they were satisfied that the company had taken measures to prevent a recurrence of the problem. In short, something as simple as an unauthorized Web change caused a ripple effect, resulting in a multimillion dollar revenue loss and a serious public relations problem that took several months to cure. As you can see, a "minor" security breach can cause major problems that are expensive to correct, especially if the problem was never properly planned for in the first place.

War Games

Another threat assessment method is simulated *war games.* The Pentagon does it. Large companies do it. Kids play them on the weekends and in school. Role-playing games or "war games" in security terms are essential to truly understanding the threat environment and making sound decisions on what can and cannot be protected. In a network attack, the idea is to examine all the potential points of attack and then try some out to see if they work, how they can be detected and defeated, and how to handle the repercussions (e.g., business, political, public relations, technological) of the attack. War games, simulations, role playing, or whatever you wish to call it is extremely useful in properly identifying threats and counterthreats. It also allows proper identification of actions that any warrior must understand to launch a proper defense. These include (a) setting up information defenses, (b) monitoring for information attack, (c) delaying the attack until assessment and reinforcements are made available, (d) counterattacking and capture or destroy, and (e) cleaning up any problems discovered. By exercising the foregoing concepts, all threats can be identified and proper defenses planned.

Documentation

One final item to think about for the threat assessment part of network security is documentation and updates. All of the previous items are for naught if documentation does not follow the work. The legacy should be recorded for others and updated as the threats change. This process can take a substantial amount of time and effort but it is an essential part of any well thought-out plan for threat management.

17.3 Network Attacks and Security Measures Considerations

Examples of Network Attacks

One of the most successful and common methods of network attacks is through *social engineering,* which involves deception; it is, basically, lying your way into a facility. It takes a certain amount of self-confidence and the ability to talk your way out of situations where you might get caught. It also takes a certain amount of thinking "on your feet" so that you do not get into a situation where you will be discovered too soon. The idea is to test the facilities in your purview without getting caught too soon, if at all. From this exercise, you'll discover which improvements should be made.

The main purpose behind social engineering is to place the human element in the "network breaching" loop and use it as a weapon. For instance, having someone show up at the computer room with network hardware in hand and an appropriate vendor ID usually results in a staff person escorting you into the communications closet and, perhaps, even helping you to install hardware on the network. This is not good. By appealing to the victim's natural instinct to help a customer, it can be startlingly easy to breach the physical perimeter of a company and gain access to the network and all its treasures.

One favored technique is to walk into a customer's branch office and tell a tale of woe to employees. A popular story is that you work for the corporate office and have to kill a few hours before a flight. You might say: "Do you think that there might be an empty cubicle around where I can work for a while? I don't need anything except a place to park and work." Usually, someone finds an empty space for you, the "corporate visitor," to work and almost invariably, there is a live network connection in that space. Since most laptops have either a built-in Ethernet/802.3 controller chip or PC card—perhaps also a token ring PC card, you're good to go. With such a network-capable laptop loaded with various network analysis and protocol analysis tools, you, the intruder, can collect data from the network and gain valuable network attack information (e.g., passwords or user IDs). A further enhancement to the deception tactic is using a business card of someone else in the corporation to give the false impression that (a) the intruder is indeed that person, (b) the intruder does indeed work for the company, and (c) the title of the person on the card is "important" enough to impress employees into providing access to a work area.

Another technique doesn't even require having any technical skills. For example, one company created a rather elaborate security clearance procedure for users prior to gaining access to its network resources. An intruder, however, completely circumvented the company's established security procedures for accessing new accounts and acquired an invaluable list of accounts by simply contacting network personnel and posing as a vendor offering to demonstrate software. All this was accomplished with very little effort and without the consent of upper management, which was required by corporate policy. As you can see, there are many ways to thwart established security procedures by exploiting human nature.

It is not very difficult to find information about how to initiate a network attack. On the Internet, for example, there are, quite literally, thousands of locations that include very specific instructions on how to attack almost any type of protocol, operating system, or hardware environment. Doing a Web search using the search string `Hacker + Phreak + Anarchy` yields several hundreds of thousands of sites dedicated to these activities. The titles of some the documents that are available are quite revealing: "The Hacker's Handbook," "Novell Hacking Tools," "A Beginner's Guide to Hacking UNIX," "Hacking Answering Machines," and "Hacking CompuServe Information Services." It's really a sad commentary that there are over 300,000 locations on the Internet where hacking or security breaching information, tools, and experiences can easily be obtained. It's a big problem and it's growing.

Denial of Service (DoS) Attacks

Several years ago, some hackers began writing small programs that would "flood" a network address by sending as many packets as possible to the address using network utilities such as *ping* (see Chapter 8). Continuously "pinging" a machine causes it to crash or to stop accepting connections because of traffic overload. This particular type of attack, in fact, was called "Ping of Death." Variants on this idea were written to take advantage of protocol weaknesses, system bugs, or holes or application problems with high traffic volumes. These types of attacks collectively became known as *denial of service* (DoS) attacks. They were so named because users were denied access to the services of the system that was attacked.

A variant of a DoS attack is a "stateful" attack, which exploits the handshaking process that various protocols implement when establishing connections. An example of this handshaking process is TCP's three-way handshake, which we discussed in Chapter 8, and an example of a stateful attack is the TCP SYN attack. Recall from Chapter 8 that a TCP SYN message is required during a session activation as part of a normal connection setup. In a SYN attack, the receiving system is connected to by random source addresses that never respond. In this manner, the attacker can create thousands of "half" sessions on the destination system until all the memory or network connection slots are expended and the system stops accepting new connections. Thus, system services are denied by "ghost" sources that never acknowledge the next state of the connection handshake. So instead of denying services by overwhelming a system continuously with packets as a ping attack does, a stateful attack such as TCP SYN causes a system to wait until the protocol times out for a response, effectively rendering the system and its resources inaccessible. In fact, if an attacker is persistent, the destination system can time out all incoming connections after a short time so the system is unusable to anyone attempting a connection.

An extension to DoS attacks is the *distributed denial of service* (DDoS) attack. A DDoS attack involves placing hundreds or thousands of small programs on different computers connected to a network. These programs are called agents or, in common terms, Trojan horses or "zombies." From a master console somewhere on the network, a hacker activates them by sending a command to the zombies and forcing them into attack mode. The zombies then begin sending messages to the specified destination, completely overwhelming the destination system as well as the network pathways to get to the system. In a DoS attack, single systems are usually targeted, and the network resources in the path are usually not adversely affected except for slow links. A DDoS attack, however, results in a "scorched earth" from a network perspective. Because of the distributed nature of the attack, the many networks used by the zombies to get to the destination system are totally overwhelmed by traffic and are effectively disabled.

Although some DDoS attacks can be stopped, it depends on the type of attack. For example, some DDoS attacks have specific profiles and use specific protocols, which can be detected by firewalls and, in some cases, router filters. Some types actually generate what appears as legitimate traffic to the network. These "legit" traffic profiles are extremely difficult to detect and defeat. As a result, the only option for some types of attacks is placing packet rate limiters on routers. A packet rate limiter is a type of router filter that detects certain elevated traffic levels for specific conditions and then slows the packet rate down to keep from overwhelming the network connections. In this manner, the attack is throttled back to a condition where it is more of an annoyance and not destructive. Another method for stopping DDoS attacks is by reverse engineering the zombie command set so that the equivalent of an OFF command can be issued to the zombies just as the master console would do to stop the attack. These are not always successful, though, and are not appropriate for detecting the attack.

Yet another variant of a DoS attack is an application-level denial of service (ADoS) attack such as the "ILOVEYOU" e-mail worm, which began appearing in mid-2000. Launching this program eventually caused loss of e-mail services (and hence a denial of application service). These types of worms can be filtered by e-mail server virus killers and e-mail string filters, so they are not as insidious as DDoS. On the negative side, though, they can take up a great deal of e-mail server space with totally useless data. Furthermore, some can download a secondary component that can be extremely destructive if activated. For example, some of the Visual BASIC scripts that are downloaded can do some interesting things such as delete a hard drive's content or copy it to some public location for all to see. There are also many copycat variants of these types of attacks that usually flood networks within a very short time of the initial program's release.

All networks get attacked from time to time. Larger networks get attacked more often because, statistically, they are more active and visible to the networking world and are therefore an easier target to find and attack. Given the constant threat and inevitability of a network attack, we need to be prepared for the day our network is compromised. We call this state of preparedness *incident response,* or IR. Incident response is analogous to calling the fire department when you detect your house is on fire. It consists of preparation, prepositioning of technology, and then real-time response. Preparation involves surveying the network and thoroughly understanding the topology and components that make up the network and its vulnerabilities. This is similar to a fire department conducting a building inspection—it provides firefighters with critical information about the building, including where everything is located and any special hazards or problems the building presents in the event of a fire. Prepositioning means getting equipment and software in place to collect real-time information and to allow the IR team quick access to information that is critical to determining the attack profile and specific information about the attack. Real-time response is the ability to put technology and expertise on the attack problem in a very short amount of time, preferably while the attack is in progress, so that the IR team can isolate the attack, stop it, and assist law enforcement agencies in identifying and prosecuting the intruder.

Obstacles to Implementing Network Security

The greatest obstacles to implementing network security are lack of qualified personnel, money, tools, and upper management apathy. In a recent survey about network security, nearly 60% of respondents blamed weak security on a lack of staff to handle the issue. Another 55% said their budgets were insufficient to the task. More than 40% attributed the problem to nonexistent software tools, and 45% blamed upper management. Management claims security is extremely important because of the myriad of potential threats, including current and former employees, suppliers, customers, and competitors. However, there usually is no management support or funding to protect a company. Unfortunately, line items for personnel support (e.g., training) and security are absent from most network budgets.

Security Measures Considerations

Good network security begins with the stability of each system on the network, and in many cases, network vulnerabilities can increase a company's risk of data manipulation and destruction. Here are some examples of how data manipulations can harm an organization. On a research site, jealous co-workers might "taint" extensive research data, causing scientists to reach improper conclusions. Financial analysts might find that their carefully crafted spreadsheets produce improper computations on critical budgeting line items due to static, dynamic, or formulaic information being altered. Word processing documents containing standard contracts and procedures might be modified to weaken the document's meaning and undermine the intent of a contract.

Database demographic information may be erased or modified to produce false market data that is critical to a rollout of service or business offerings, causing much time and money to be wasted in the creation of market products and services. The list of opportunities for malicious manipulation goes on and on. Without good system security, the network can increase the opportunity for security breaches.

The nature of some businesses makes them prime targets for security breaches. For example, companies that engage in animal testing might be the targets of groups that engage in the willful destruction and infiltration of corporate assets to bring attention to the issue of animal testing and to disrupt corporate entities involved in such testing. Medical practices, such as family planning centers and abortion services facilities, are often the targets of groups formed for the express purpose of putting such operations out of business. Other companies may contain specific technologies that are of interest to industrial espionage specialists who wish to sell information about the technologies to competitors. Companies with extensive telecommunications systems are often the subject of PBX attacks that allow the intruder access to free long-distance services for their use without the corporate entity knowing about the attack for a very long time—if at all.

Network security, properly implemented, consists of a series of security barriers, not merely a single network security control point. The reality is that any single control point can be breached by an expert. However, by placing multiple security barriers in the path of a critical asset or resource, the chances of someone getting through without detection are greatly diminished. The concept is much like that of the strong castle protected by a series of moats. As the storming hoard nears the castle, it must traverse the moats. It is possible to traverse some moats by pole-vaulting, but eventually the invader is likely to fall into one of the moats and be caught. If there is only one moat and the invader is a good jumper, odds are the invader will succeed. If there are moats, trip wires, razor wires, tall fences with broken glass on them, land mines, Doberman pinschers at the gate, and other such traps placed in the path between the intruder and the "jewels," one or more of the obstacles are likely to alert the keepers of the castle that someone is trying to infiltrate it and that something must be done to protect the assets and destroy the intruder.

The notion that a singular perimeter is an effective defensive measure for network asset protection is long gone. Since many network assets are attacked by internal personnel, the need to protect the assets from external and internal attack is rapidly becoming the norm. This notion is similar to the plan advanced by the Great Wall of Texas Society in the United States. The society's intent is to build a 30-foot-high wall around the northern sections of the Texas border with New Mexico, Oklahoma, Arkansas, and Louisiana. Their whole premise is that the concern over the border with Mexico is outdated; they assert that the real enemy is to the north, not the south, and that "we have been watching the wrong border for too long." Similarly, most companies are concerned about external intruders, but the enemy within is far more dangerous. The fact is that the bulk of all network break-ins happen from inside the company. Therefore, intrusion protection for a network should never be limited to external network connections; it should always start directly with the information repository itself as the first line of defense. Box 17.3 provides some basic common-sense network security measures. In addition to the security measures listed in Box 17.3, there are many different technologies that can be implemented to help make a network more secure. These include firewalls, encryption techniques, authentication systems, and access control measures. All are discussed in subsequent sections.

BOX 17.3 Network Security Measures

Following are several measures that can enhance the security of a network:

1. Use dual power supply modules for network critical devices.
2. Connect devices to uninterruptible power supplies (UPS).
3. Ensure that all network devices are connected to "clean" power.
4. Install surge protection directly to the main circuit panels that feed the electrical outlets to which devices are connected.
5. Ensure all rooms with network devices are properly ventilated or air conditioned.
6. Do not place devices in combustible areas and restrict the use of volatile materials (e.g., cleaning supplies) in these areas.
7. Install smoke detectors and adequate fire-extinguishing equipment in all rooms with network critical devices.
8. Do not place network devices in areas that are susceptible to flooding or exposed to water (e.g., a utility closet with a sink).
9. Do not place network devices near windows.
10. Place critical devices such as servers in locked rooms with an alarm system and restrict access to these rooms to authorized personnel only.
11. Create and maintain strong passwords to all systems and educate users to do the same.
12. Educate users to the potential consequences of providing their access privileges to unauthorized users.
13. Enable, maintain, and review system accounting and log information regularly.
14. Install virus protection software and update virus definitions files regularly.
15. Enforce idle time outs for dialup connections.
16. Prevent users from uploading data to a system's hard disk. If this is not feasible, then restrict uploads to an area that is automatically virus checked.
17. Maintain proper file permissions.
18. If possible, place all critical data on a centralized server and protect the server.
19. Edit configuration files carefully and always save a copy of the current file prior to making modifications.
20. Minimize the physical exposure of copper-based cable by enclosing it in conduit; any taps that penetrate the conduit will be noticeable.
21. Maintain a physical map of your network that includes a wiring diagram so you know if any cable has been tampered.
22. Identify the location of any buried media before the ground is dug up.
23. Use a cable scanner to scan the cable and record values. Do this periodically and compare readings.
24. Maintain a secure wiring closet. This includes using a separate enclosed space with a locked door for the wiring closet.
25. Enclose all cable buried underground in metal pipe and document its location.
26. Do not use copper cable to interconnect buildings. If you must use copper, enclose it in metal conduit and place it high enough so that it is not easily accessible.
27. Use fiber-optic cable when possible, particularly in high-security locations.
28. Always encrypt data prior to transmission.
29. Use line-of-sight transmissions instead of broadcast transmissions.
30. Use optical-based links instead of RF-based links.
31. Use wired-based media instead of wireless media.
32. To minimize the effect of unauthorized packet-sniffing programs, design your network using switches so that each workstation has its own dedicated network segment. This reduces the overall amount of network traffic, and it limits the type of data that can be collected to broadcast or multicast messages. Alternatively, encrypt all messages prior to placing them on the network.
33. Educate all users about the potential security risks related to connecting their workstations to the Internet via a dialup line.
34. Train users on the differences between client and server processes and the security implications related to enabling server versions of Internet utilities.
35. Require users to virus-check all software downloaded from the Internet.
36. Ensure that users disable TCP/IP routing if their workstation is connected to a LAN and if they intend to use it for Internet access.

BOX 17.3 **Network Security Measures** **(continued)**

37. Do regular and frequent backups of all data onto tape or disk and store backups in a different location than the original data.

38. Establish and enforce acceptable use policies for all users.

39. Develop, implement, and review on a regular basis a disaster recovery plan.

40. Keep current with Computer Emergency Response Team (CERT) publications.

41. Subscribe to various network security listservs.

42. Attain network security tools and learn how to use them and interpret their output.

17.4 Firewalls

Overview

Historically, a firewall was defined as a "wall" placed between an automobile's floorboard and engine to keep an engine fire or explosion from entering the passenger compartment. In the context of network security, a firewall performs a similar function between the connections on a network. Specifically, firewalls are devices or products that allow the systems or network manager to restrict access to network components. There are various types of products that claim to be firewalls but which clearly are not firewalls. One sad aspect of firewalls is that the terminology has been overused, much like the word "virus." What can and cannot be accurately called a firewall is subject to interpretation by the vendor and the consumer.

At its most basic level, a firewall is a packet-filtering facility that can restrict the flow of packets to and from a network via a set of rules implemented in an interconnection device. Examples of this might be a filtering router unit that is capable of restricting which packets can be transmitted and which ones can be received from an Internet connection based upon packet addresses (source and destination) or a specific IP transport protocol type. Other types of firewalls might include intelligent port and socket (application) filters, session-level (user) filters, and a variety of other types of filtering tools that restrict traffic flow. In short, a firewall is frequently a sum of many different components that work together to block transmission and reception of traffic.

Types of Firewalls

There are five generally accepted types of firewalls used on Internet connections: frame-filtering, packet-filtering, circuit gateways, stateful and application gateways, and proxy servers. There are other less-known proxy firewall implementations and variants, but they all function fairly similarly, with varying degrees of performance and ease of configuration. Following is a brief description of each type.

Frame-Filtering Firewalls   A *frame-filtering firewall* has the ability to filter to the bit level the layout and contents of a LAN frame (e.g., Ethernet/802.3, token ring/802.5, FDDI, and others). By providing filtering at this level, frames that do not belong on the trusted network are rejected before they reach anything valuable, even on the firewall itself.

Packet-Filtering Firewalls A *packet-filtering firewall* is either a router with packet-filtering capabilities or a dedicated device that does packet-filtering. A packet-filtering firewall is best used as a dedicated unit in conjunction with a router. This way, the router does not have to perform a dual (and contradictory) function—it can facilitate communication as it is designed to do, and the packet-filtering firewall can provide the network security. The performance of a packet-filtering firewall will degrade considerably as more filters and conditional filter handling are set up. Packet-filtering also does not handle certain types of transactions on a network that are context sensitive. That is, many packets are required to do something, which, when taken as a whole, implies a certain (and usually ominous) condition has occurred.

Circuit Gateway Firewalls A *circuit gateway firewall* typically involves the session setup between a system and the user security options relative to that system for a particular user. For instance, a circuit gateway might check user IDs and passwords for a connection request. Other types of circuit firewalls might implement proxy connection authorization or other types of authentication services. Circuit firewalls are also responsible for logging who came from where and went to what, which is not trivial.

"Stateful" Firewalls Following the establishment of proxy firewalls (described next), the need to examine the transaction condition between two interoperating applications becomes essential to defeating certain sophisticated types of network attacks. IP address spoofing, session hijacking, piggyback session acquisition, and many other technical attacks were allowing hackers access to applications and eventually entire systems. To stop this type of attack profile, the firewall must be intelligent enough to watch all transactions between two systems and understand enough of the details of how a protocol works to identify a specific condition in the transaction between two applications, be able to predict what should transpire next in the transaction, and be able to detect when normal operational "states" of the connection are being violated. This type of firewall is called a *stateful inspection facility* and allows the network security manager to specify rules and filters for specific technical transactions between the systems and applications and what to do if they are violated by anyone. Many vendors of stateful firewall facilities also include detailed filtering capabilities similar to proxy filtering. In some cases, however, proxies do a better security job (depending on the application being secured), so stateful firewalls, for the most part, are capable of providing a full security rule-based range of services but sometimes are not as complete for specific applications as a proxy might be.

Application Gateways or Proxies Firewalls An *application gateway firewall* provides protection at the application level. If viewed from a functionality perspective, an application gateway firewall is the opposite of a packet-filtering firewall—the former is application or program specific and the latter is general purpose. For example, consider a typical file transfer session. Suppose you want users to be able to download files from the Internet using the file transfer protocol (FTP) but you do not want anyone from outside your organization placing files on any of your networked hosts. More specifically, you want to permit "get" FTP sessions but reject "put" FTP sessions. With a packet-filtering firewall, you have an all or none case—either it allows file transfers (get and put) to occur or it does not. An application gateway firewall, however, can be configured to permit "get" sessions and reject "put" sessions because it can examine the details of the application. Another example might be a Telnet firewall facility that provides security facilities, full packet content scanning, session management, session capturing, and other facilities. This type of firewall is specific to a particular IP application, Telnet, and is usually much more secure than packet and address filtering in a router–it might not only consider user IDs, passwords, and proxies, but it also might consider application-specific access methods and security issues.

An application gateway firewall uses custom programs for each protected application. If a new application that requires protection is added to the network, a new program has to be written and added to the set of other programs that reside on the firewall. These customized application programs act as both a client and server and effectively serve as proxies to the actual applications. For example, if e-mail is to be protected, a custom e-mail application is written that includes specific security rules (e.g., what type of e-mail is permitted). When users want to use e-mail, they must either log into the application gateway and use this special application or use a client application on a host that supports this secured e-mail service. Since these specially written applications act as proxies to their "real" counterparts, the collective set of these programs is commonly referred to as *proxy services,* and application gateway firewalls are often called *proxy server* or *proxy gateways.* There are two types of proxy gateways. In the first type, an incoming connection for a destination would be intercepted by the proxy, and a "new" connection from the proxy to the destination would be created. In this manner, a connection originating from outside the firewall is not able to "touch" the destination directly, and full filtering of the application is accomplished. The second variant of the proxy gateway allows the firewall to appear as the only destination for all applications to a trusted network from an untrusted network. Through this facility, the internal network is completely "hidden" from network view to any outside connections. This has the by-product of allowing an internal network to use unregistered address ranges for IP users to access the Internet and other external networks expecting valid address ranges. It also increases security by not allowing an external network direct access to an internal address or to any knowledge of what the internal address is for a specific node on a trusted network.

Firewalls and Multiprotocol Environments

In 1995 and 1996, the concept of generally accepted Internet applications (e.g., Web servers, POP- and IMAP-based e-mail) being deployed on internal networks for employee access began a steady and dramatic increase in both scope and size. Mission critical applications are now deployed on these intranets while existing network technologies continue to coexist on the same network environment. With "real" networks on corporate facilities, the existence and use of protocol suites besides the IP facilities found on the Internet represent the bulk of networking protocol use. In most corporate networks, especially those established in the 1980s and early 1990s, the common use of Novell's IPX, Digital Equipment Corporation's Pathworks environment (DECnet, LAT, LAST), IBM's System Network Architecture (SNA), Apple Computer's AppleTalk, and Banyan's VINES environment (StreetTalk) are still very active and very much a part of the culture at many companies. Other corporate environments support specialized protocols (e.g., ALC) for terminal applications that are very popular in a particular vertical industry segment (e.g., the airline industry) but are not seen in mainstream computing. Still other network types, such as industrial networks, warehouse networks, process control networks, and many other types of specialized networks, utilize custom protocols for maximum efficiency or for specialized applications where commercially accepted protocol suites are much too large or too general to solve a network problem.

The bottom line is that multiple protocols are the norm on intranet and extranet networks—not just TCP/IP. Unfortunately, most firewalls available today are designed to operate only within a TCP/IP environment. To protect only one protocol, such as IP, is ludicrous in a standard corporate network environment where the norm is to deploy between 3 and 18 protocol suites to satisfy legacy and computational requirements. Popular operating systems such as Windows NT/2000 come configurable with multiple protocols to satisfy corporate clients (e.g., NT comes with IP, IPX, NetBEUI, and AppleTalk standard on each system) and provide connectivity to the variety of systems on a corporate network. Protection of an IP application environment is fine if that is all a system is using, but many systems utilize other protocols. Protection of a single protocol on intranet or extranet environments without consideration for the other operating protocol's security needs is much like locking the front door of your house while leaving the back door open. Proper network security requires all entities to receive equal protective treatment to truly address the network security threat.

Even in locations where IP is the only or predominant protocol, there is the problem of a new version of the IP protocol stack, namely, IPv6. (See Chapter 8 for additional information about IPv6.) Sometimes referred to as IPng (for "next generation"), IPv6 is not only different in its address structure (e.g., it uses a 16-octet address compared to IPv4's 4-octet address) but it also differs in the mechanics of how a system receives its address (it is done dynamically) and what the remainder of the protocol does to address routing issues, security layer issues, and other new features of the protocol. To say that the current IPv4 is "compatible" with IPv6 is a gross mistake, particularly when the related RFCs call for IPv4 and IPv6 "coexistence" and not "compatibility." Coexistence, in technospeak, means that a machine may run both protocols at the same time to achieve the ability to use both at the same time, as opposed to running the new one and continuing to converse with the old one (compatibility). Therefore, for environments running only IPv4 at this time, they are about to become multiprotocol, like it or not, even if all that is running is the current version of IP and the upcoming upgrade to the protocol. No network manager who is cautious about the network environment will totally cut over to IPv6 without a parallel phase in which both protocol suites are running. In some cases, this will be a lengthy time period for sites where applications may require IPv4 to remain for application "survival" indefinitely. Therefore, to protect the internal network from attack by internal personnel, and to support multiple versions of a protocol such as IP with external networks such as the Internet, networks will need multiprotocol protection because, as you now know, the need to protect the internal network is as great or perhaps greater than the need to protect the external network.

Firewall Implementation Considerations

Since firewall requirements vary dramatically from company to company, there are many situations in which more than one product from more than one vendor is required to provide proper firewall facilities. A router with packet filters would be almost a necessity for each site. A user terminal security facility for Telnet users is also necessary, but no routers manufactured today can provide both the sophisticated security facilities for terminal traffic as well as swift routing facilities. Consequently, these two functions alone will result in the need for separate systems for control and access.

Each firewall architecture has its merits and drawbacks. Let's review the features of all major firewall types. Router screening is fast and allows rejection of common errors, hack attacks, and user strangeness which is part of any network connection. Application filtering firewalls provide extensive application control and monitoring of application behavior. Proxy facilities provide application control and session control between sources and destinations as well as address translation facilities. Stateful firewalls allow technical attacks from breaching a network and provide sophisticated filtering techniques that rival almost any proxy or application gateway. In short, almost all firewall approaches have strengths and weaknesses. In fact, this is a good thing for customers. What is best for the customer is security, implemented for the right reasons and in the most productive manner. This means that the optimal firewall configuration is one that can perform all the various types of rule-based filtering previously described depending on the type of application being used and the best security methodology approach to solve the security problem for the application environment. No single security rule-based approach that has been described can properly address all security issues in a networked environment. Most network security experts will tell you that it is impractical to expect one approach to be useful in all environments.

One of the difficulties of firewall implementation is the fairly high degree of technical expertise required to configure them. If one does not understand TCP/IP reasonably well, there is little hope of properly setting up a packet-filtering facility. Exactly how much technical knowledge is required depends on the model, but frankly, no firewall is easy to set up. Almost without exception, no matter how mature and well-written the software is, there are a myriad of administrative tasks involved in setting up a firewall. Even with fairly effective firewalls for Internet access, there are situations that, left unchecked, will cause defeat of the firewalls. For instance, tunneling of a protocol in a protocol from site to site can be very difficult to filter and control. Some sites, for purely political reasons, will not permit restrictions on certain applications that allow remote Internet users to gain access to critical data about a site that may be used to exploit the network. It is important to note that, even in the best environments, firewalls don't work forever and may be defeated.

17.5 Encryption Methods

Overview

Encryption is a process that converts sensitive data into a coded form. When retrieved by authorized users, this coded form is then reconverted (i.e., decoded) into meaningful text. Encryption essentially hides or disguises information from unintended recipients but enables authorized users to retrieve it. The study of secret communication is called *cryptology,* and the practice or art of encoding messages is called *cryptography.* Unencrypted data are referred to as *plaintext,* and their encrypted output is called *ciphertext.*

A simple encryption technique is a letter-substitution cipher. For example, let's agree that we will use the following "key" for coding and decoding messages:

A—O	H—P	O—E	V—Q
B—D	I—Y	P—B	W—U
C—C	J—M	Q—G	X—J
D—I	K—F	R—N	Y—T
E—S	L—R	S—K	Z—L
F—V	M—Z	T—W	,—#
G—A	N—X	U—H	

Now, the message,

DEAR JANE, NOT GETTING ANY BETTER, HURRY HOME

is coded by substituting the plaintext characters with those of our cipher. Thus, the encrypted message is,

ISON MOXS# XEW ASWWYXA OXT DSWWSN# PHNNT PEZS

This message can now be sent via public channels and decoded by an authorized person who knows the key. If the message is intercepted or finds its way into the hands of an unauthorized person, it will most likely appear as meaningless gibberish. Of course, it is always possible that an unintended recipient could crack the code.

Cryptography can be implemented either symmetrically or asymmetrically. In *symmetric cryptography,* a secure communication between two parties is effected by exchanging a secret key (also called a private key), which is used both to code (i.e., encrypt) and decode (i.e., decrypt) a message. Ideally, key exchanges should not be done electronically, though, and are best conducted in person. A feature of symmetric cryptography, which is commonly called private key encryption, is the speed in which messages are encrypted and decrypted. A disadvantage, though, is the number of keys required when more than a few people are involved. For example, only one key is needed for two people to exchange secret messages. However, if ten people are involved, then 45 private keys are needed. In general, n people require $(n)(n-1)/2$ private keys. An example of a private key encryption strategy is the data encryption standard (DES), which is described later.

In *asymmetric cryptography,* each person maintains two keys—one private and one public. The public key, which is published and available to anyone, is used to encrypt a message; the corresponding private key, which remains secret and is not given to anyone, is used to decrypt the message. For example, if Cheryl wants to send Howard a secret message, Cheryl encodes her message using Howard's public key, and Howard decodes the message using his private key. A message can also be encoded using the private key and decoded using the public key. Thus, the two keys represent a key pair that must be used in tandem. Although asymmetric cryptography significantly reduces the number of private keys that need to be exchanged, it runs much more slowly than symmetric cryptography. Two examples of asymmetric cryptography, which is commonly referred to as public key encryption, are Pretty Good Privacy (PGP) and RSA. The concepts of private key encryption, PGP, and RSA are described more fully later.

Public Key Infrastructure (PKI)

Cryptography is a critical component of a relatively new technology called *public key infrastructure* (PKI). PKI involves the process of issuing, delivering (i.e., publishing), managing, and revoking public keys. For example, secure Web transactions are built on a PKI. Web browsers (i.e., clients) and Web servers use what is known as a *secure sockets layer* (SSL) session for engaging in secure communications via the Internet. Prior to establishing a secure connection to a Web server, a browser first requests a copy of the server's security certificate, which contains the server's public key. After verifying the certificate's authenticity, the browser generates a symmetric key, which it will use to encrypt its data. This key is also encrypted using the server's public key. Both the encrypted data and the encrypted symmetric key are transmitted to the server. For the server to decrypt the coded message, it must first decrypt the encrypted key. Since the browser's symmetric key was encrypted using the server's public key, the key is decrypted by the server using the server's private key. (Remember that a private and public key pair work in tandem.) Once the server has the browser's symmetric key, it then decodes the message. It will also use this symmetric key to encode any data that it transmits to the browser. Note how secure Web transactions actually employ a hybrid cryptography strategy. A browser's symmetric key is used to encode data, and a server's public–private key pair is used to securely exchange the symmetric key between the browser and server across the network. Most SSL-enabled Web browsers have preinstalled certificates, which can be viewed by examining the security option. For example, in Netscape 4.7, go to Communicator/Tools/Security Info and then click on Signers. Any of the listed certificates can then be viewed by selecting one and clicking on Edit. In Internet Explorer 5.0, go to Edit/Preferences and under Web Browser click Security. Any of the listed certificates can then be viewed by selecting one and clicking on View. A Web server's certificates, which originate from a root certificate authority (CA), all have corresponding expiration dates and hence are only valid until this date. Once a certificate expires, it is considered revoked. Unfortunately, as of this writing, current Web browsers are not capable of detecting revoked certificates.

Data Encryption Standard (DES)

Developed by IBM and NIST in the 1970s, the *data encryption standard* (DES) is a mathematical model or algorithm that is used to encode data. It is also the most widely used commercial encryption algorithm. As with a letter-substitution cipher, a key is used to determine the transformation from plaintext to ciphertext. The key for a DES user consists of any one of 2^{56} possible keys, each one of which is a list of 56 zeros and ones (plus eight parity bits). This translates to approximately 10^{17} or 100,000,000,000,000,000 possible arrangements of 56 zeros and ones.

DES, which can be implemented in hardware or software, has been the single most thoroughly tested encryption algorithm. In over 20 years of testing, DES was never cracked. However, in 1998, John Gilmore and Paul Kocher broke the code in 56 hours using a homemade supercomputer they built for $250,000. Funding for the supercomputer, which was a configuration of hundreds of Intel processors, was provided by the Electronic Freedom Foundation (EFF). The project was sponsored by the U.S. government and carried a $10,000 prize. The time to crack DES has since been reduced to 22 hours.

Although DES stood the test of time for 20 years, it became obvious that a DES replacement was needed. To enhance its cryptographic capabilities, additional safeguards were suggested. One was to increase the number of keys from 56 zeros and ones to 1024 zeros and ones. This increased key size makes the algorithm more complex and hence more difficult to crack. A second suggestion was to replace DES with a completely different algorithm called Skipjack, which uses an 80-bit key space. A third suggestion was to replace DES with the "public key" method of cryptography (described later). A fourth suggestion was to use a variant of DES called Triple DES, which uses three DES operations instead of one. Even these strategies, however, might prove useless. Scientists at Oxford University claim that within a few years they will have a computer that can crack any-length encryption within seconds.

In 1997, NIST announced a public (and worldwide) competition for the design of an advanced encryption standard (AES) algorithm to replace DES. The final AES criteria mandated that the new algorithm implement a private key (i.e., symmetric) cryptography, be a block cipher, and operate on 128-bit blocks with the three key sizes of 128, 192, and 256 bits. Twenty-one proposals were received by the competition's June 15, 1998, deadline, with 15 of the 21 satisfying NIST's criteria. In August 1999, five finalists were selected after careful review by the global cryptographic community. The names of the proposed AES algorithms and their corresponding proposers were: MARS (IBM), RC6 (RSA Laboratories), Rijndael (Joan Daemen and Vincent Rijmen of Belgium), Serpent (Ross Anderson, Eli Biham, and Lars Knudsen), and Twofish (Bruce Schneier, John Kelsey, Doug Whiting, David Wagner, Chris Hall, and Niels Ferguson). If the AES development process continues as originally planned, it is anticipated that the standard will be completed by the summer of 2001. For additional information, see the AES home page at `http://www.nist.gov/aes`

> NIST announced in October, 2000 that Rijndael was selected as the proposed AES.

Pretty Good Privacy (PGP)

Pretty Good Privacy (PGP) is indeed a public key application. It is an e-mail encryption package written by Philip Zimmerman that combines three separate algorithms: RSA, which stands for the first initials of the last names of the designers—Ronald Rivest, Adi Shamir, and Len Adleman; IDEA, which stands for International Data Encryption Algorithm; and the Message-Digest algorithm, Version 5 (MD5). RSA is a public key encryption algorithm, which is discussed later in this chapter. IDEA is a conventional encryption algorithm similar to DES that uses a 64-bit block cipher with a 128-bit key space. MD5 is a hashing algorithm—developed in 1991 by Ron Rivest and described in RFC 1321—that takes a message of arbitrary length and generates a 128-bit message digest.

> A message digest is used for digital signature applications.

PGP provides both encryption and digital signature services. Encryption enables a user to encode files; digital signature service enables a user to "sign" a document so that the document's authenticity can be confirmed by checking the signature. Thus, encryption provides confidentiality; a digital signature proves a message was not modified. Encryption service is provided via RSA and IDEA. PGP first encrypts messages with IDEA and then uses RSA to encrypt the IDEA key that was used to encrypt the message initially. Intended recipients then use RSA to retrieve the IDEA key, which in turn is used to decode the message. PGP also uses MD5 to create a digital signature, which is then encrypted using RSA.

PGP was once the source of much attention by many U.S. legislatures. When PGP was first released, encryption algorithms with key sizes of greater than 40 bits in length were prohibited from being exported outside the United States. Since PGP incorporates IDEA, which uses a 64-bit block cipher with a 128-bit key space, it was illegal to exportation it. Unfortunately, someone made PGP available on the Internet without Phil Zimmerman's knowledge and Zimmerman was indicted for exporting PGP outside the United States. The Department of Commerce has since removed the restriction on exportation of encryption devices and algorithms with keys of 64 bits or less. Another incident involved patent infringement. Earlier versions of PGP (v2.3 or earlier) contained the RSA algorithm, which, at the time, was patented in the United States. Consequently, users of these versions risked patent infringement if they used PGP in the United States without a license. In May, 1994, however, an agreement with the RSA patent holder was reached and subsequent versions (v2.6 or later) of PGP can now be used legally, for noncommercial purposes, in the United States without a license.

Although the legal issues of PGP use within the United States have been resolved, PGP is still subject to the rules of the International Traffic in Arms Regulations and cannot be exported without an export license. Therefore, if you reside outside the United States and plan to put a cryptographic product like PGP on your notebook computer and use it for secure remote communications, it might be prudent to consult your government's regulations first. If information is to leave your country of origin, there are usually export laws regarding the use of cryptography either in or out of your country. In the United States, the cryptotechnologies that can and cannot be used are regulated by the Department of Commerce. DOC also regulates which countries can do business using cryptography with U.S. companies. The Department of Trade and Industry (DTI) helps regulate security issues in the United Kingdom and determines what can and cannot be exported or used outside the country. In France, rules on cryptographic use in communications are extremely strict, and in many cases, cryptography is not allowed at all unless your company is an approved financial institution. The rules can get pretty complex from country to country. Additional information about PGP can be found at `http://www.pgp.com`

> There is no limit on key sizes within the United States.

> The U.S. patent for the RSA algorithm, which is discussed in the next section, expired on September 20, 2000, and is now in the public domain.

RSA

As stated earlier, RSA is a public key encryption algorithm and stands for the first initials of the last names of the designers—Ronald Rivest, Adi Shamir, and Len Adleman. A description of this algorithm with an example of its implementation is provided in Box 17.4. RSA is a widely accepted and implemented method of public key encryption that requires two keys for each user, one public and the other private. Each user's public key is available to anyone, whereas the private key is secret and known only to the user. A message coded with the public key is decoded with the private key, and vice versa. This system provides three distinct methods of sending coded messages. The first method involves sending a coded message to a receiver from a sender whose identity is verifiable. To illustrate:

> If we wish to send you a coded message, we code our message using your public key. This way you can decode it using your private key.

The problem with this method is that the receiver of the message can never be absolutely certain who the sender is because it is the receiver's public key that is being used to code the message. The second method involves sending a coded message from a sender whose identity is verifiable, but the message can be decoded by anyone. To illustrate:

> If we wish to send you a coded message and we want you to be absolutely certain that it is from us, then we will code our message using our private key. You in turn decode our message using our public key. Since it is our public key that actually decodes our message, you are certain that the message came from us.

Authentication of a sender's identity, as demonstrated by this second method, is very important in certain transactions such as in electronic funds transfers. Now to be absolutely clandestine, if we want to send you a coded message that can only be decoded by you and we want you to know it is from us, a third method is used:

> We first code our message using your public key. (This makes the message secret.) We then encode this code once more using our private key. (This guarantees that the message is from us.) Upon receiving the message, you must decode it twice, first using our public key and then using your private key. Now, only you can read the message and it could only have been sent by us.

Although encrypting data provides a relatively high degree of security, this does not necessarily mean that encrypted data are secure. Nothing lasts forever, and that includes cryptography. There is always a way to exploit a weakness in an algorithm or key structure in cryptography, but it may be very difficult to do so. The real issue with the use of cryptography is economic: Is your data valuable enough to justify the computer power and people power required to decrypt whatever you are transmitting over a network? If so, you may still be a target anyway. If not, then less complex cryptography facilities may be more than sufficient for your security requirements.

The degree of cryptography "strength" is a function of several components. For example, the algorithm and key lengths are two of the more important components that help determine how difficult it is to break the cryptographic facilities being used. However, there are issues such as key exchange methods, standardized implementation of the cryptographic methods, export laws in various countries, and many other issues. The sensitivity of the data you're trying to protect will dictate how "strong" the cryptographic facility should be. For instance, current sales figures are really only valid for one quarter of the year and, in a public company, they will be published the following quarter. Therefore, the cryptographic "strength" required to protect these figures is only going to safeguard the information from general viewing for a brief period of time (assuming that the data cannot be viewed via another system on the network or easily compromised by individuals who know about the data). If you are storing patent information or data that have a long-term economic viability, more care should be exercised in the selection of the cryptographic methods used to safeguard the information.

Key exchange is the same idea as how to get new passwords in a secure way to the users—the key exchange is basically a computerized method to exchange cryptographic keys.

BOX 17.4 The RSA Public Key Cryptosystem

The RSA public key cryptosystem is a mathematical algorithm that has its roots in a branch of pure mathematics known as number theory. The algorithm's basic design involves elementary number theory concepts such as prime numbers, greatest common divisor (GCD), and modular systems. Before we present the RSA algorithm, we provide some brief mathematical background related to these fundamental number theory concepts.

Mathematical Background

Prime Numbers
The field of mathematics consists of several different classifications of numbers. One classification frequently used is the set of *integers*. The set of integers is an infinite set of numbers, which is represented mathematically as

$$I = \{\ldots, -3, -2, -1, 0, 1, 2, 3, \ldots\},$$

where the ellipsis symbol, . . ., is used to denote that the observed number pattern is to continue indefinitely. Contained within this set are several other number sets, including the set of *whole numbers*, {0, 1, 2, 3, . . .}, the set of *natural numbers* (also called the set of *counting numbers* or the set of *positive integers*), {1, 2, 3, . . .}, and the set of negative integers, {. . ., −3, −2, −1}. If an integer p is greater than 1 (denoted mathematically as $p > 1$) and is divisible by only itself and by 1, then p is called a *prime number* or, more simply, is referred to as being *prime*. For example, given the set of the first 100 positive integers, {1, 2, 3, . . ., 98, 99, 100}, the set of prime numbers contained within this set is

{2, 3, 5, 7, 11, 13, 17, 19, 23, 29, 31, 37, 41, 43, 47, 53, 59, 61, 67, 71, 73, 79, 83, 89, 97}

Note that we exclude 1 because 1 is not prime by definition and that 2 is the only even prime number. An integer $p > 1$ that is not prime is called *composite*. Given these two definitions, we observe that the set of negative integers, as well as the integers 0 and 1, are neither prime nor composite. Furthermore, around 300 B.C., a famous mathematician by the name of Euclid proved that there are an infinite number of primes or, expressed another way, that there is no single largest prime number.

Greatest Common Divisor (GCD) and the Concept of Relatively Prime
When two numbers are multiplied together, the result is called a product, and the numbers being multiplied are called factors of the product. For example, given $p = 2$ and $q = 4$, the product of pq is 8, and 2 and 4 are the factors of the product, 8. To determine if a number n is a factor of a given product, we divide the product by n. If the division yields a 0 remainder, then n is a factor of the product. Factors are also thought of as *divisors* of a product because they evenly divide (i.e., yield a 0 remainder) a product. Thus, 2 and 4 may also be thought of as divisors of 8. The *greatest common divisor* (GCD) of two natural numbers is the greatest (i.e., largest) natural number that evenly divides the given pair of natural numbers. Note that the GCD may also be thought of as the greatest common factor (GCF). For example, given the two natural numbers 12 and 16, the divisors of 12 are 1, 2, 3, 4, 6, 12, the divisors of 16 are 1, 2, 4, 8, 16, and the GCD of 12 and 16, denoted GCD (12, 16), is 4. Now consider the two numbers, 24 and 25. Note that the GCD (24, 25) = 1. If the GCD of two natural numbers p and q is 1, then p and q are said to be *relatively prime*. Thus, 24 and 25 are relatively prime. Similarly, 8 and 15 are relatively prime because the GCD (8, 15) = 1, but 15 and 36 are not relatively prime because the GCD (15, 36) = 3. The GCD (p, q) may be found readily for small values of p and q by factoring them into their prime factors. (The fundamental theorem of arithmetic states that any natural number greater than 1 is either prime or can be expressed as a product of prime factors.) For larger values of p and q, this process becomes tedious and hence is done by applying a rule known as Euclid's algorithm. (For more information about Euclid's algorithm, consult a book on number theory.)

BOX 17.4 The RSA Public Key Cryptosystem (continued)

Modular Systems

A modular system is a mathematical system that cyclically repeats itself. For example, the set, {0, 1, 2, 3, 4, 5, 6, 7}, contains only the given eight elements. It is a finite set, and only the elements within this set may be used. This means that if we were to work with these set elements in sequence, after using the number 7, we must cycle back and start with 0. A mathematical system of this nature that consists of the set of elements {0, 1, 2, 3, . . ., $m - 1$} is called a *modulo m system*, which is abbreviated mod m. Thus, our given illustration represents a modulo 8, or mod 8, system. A number that is not an element of a given modulo system set is found by dividing the number by the mod, m. This is formally denoted as $a \equiv b \pmod{m}$, where a is the given number, b is the remainder that results from dividing a by m, and m is the mod. An interpretation of this notation is that a and b have the same remainder when divided by m. For example, $23 \equiv 7 \pmod 8$ and $916 \equiv 20 \pmod{32}$.

The RSA Algorithm

The strength of the RSA algorithm is based on prime numbers. Specifically, its design takes advantage of being able to readily generate very large prime numbers, but at the same time, the algorithm's security feature relies on the difficulty in trying to factor the product of very large prime numbers. The algorithm itself is described in three stages. The first stage corresponds to the steps involved in generating two keys—one public and one private. Public keys are usually published; private keys are kept secret. The second stage encrypts a given message, and the third stage decrypts the message. A running example is provided for each stage. If a given message is encrypted via a public key, then it is decrypted using the associated private key. Similarly, if a message is encrypted using a private key, then it is decrypted using the associated public key. Hence, the two keys are inverses of each other, and manipulating a message with the two keys successively, in either order, results in the original message.

Stage 1: Key Generation

1. Randomly generate two large prime numbers, p and q

We will select $p = 5$ and $q = 11$. In practice, though, p and q should be very large (e.g., 300 decimal digits each) because small values are not secure. *Note*: At one time, numbers consisting of around 100 decimal digits each were considered sufficiently large. However, during the mid-1990s, a message that was encrypted using values of p and q such that their product yielded a 129-digit number was cracked in less than a year. Thus, larger values for p and q should be used to preserve the basic premise on which RSA was designed.

2. Find n by letting $n = pq$

Given $p = 5$ and $q = 11$, $n = (5)(11) = 55$.

3. Let $m = (p - 1)(q - 1)$

Given $p = 5$ and $q = 11$, $m = (5 - 1)(11 - 1) = (4)(10) = 40$.

Note: This step is considered an intermediate step and represents a special mathematical function known as *Euler's phi*, which is denoted as $\phi(n)$. See Cormen, Leiserson, & Rivest, 1990, p. 817, for additional information.

4. Find a small, odd integer, e, that is relatively prime to m

Recall from the earlier mathematical background information that e *and* m *are relatively prime if GCD (*e, m*) = 1.*

Since the numbers we are working with are small, we will find e by trial and error. Generally, though, Euclid's algorithm is used.

- If $e = 2$, then GCD (2, 40) = 2
- If $e = 3$, then GCD (3, 40) = 1

Since GCD (3, 40) = 1, we let $e = 3$.

BOX 17.4 The RSA Public Key Cryptosystem (continued)

5. Find an integer, d, so that $de = 1$ (mod m) and $d < m$

Finding an integer d *so that* de = 1 (mod m) *is equivalent to solving the equation,* de = 1 + am, *where* a $\geq$ 0, *for* d. *Thus,* d = (1 + am) / e. (This step formally computes d as the multiplicative inverse of e mod [$\emptyset(n)$]. See Cormen, Leiserson, & Rivest, 1990, p. 834, for additional information.)

Once again, since the numbers we are working with are small, we will find d by trial and error.

- If $a = 0$, then $d = [1 + (0)(40)] / 3 = 1/3 = 0.33\overline{3}$ (This is not an integer)
- If $a = 1$, then $d = [1 + (1)(40)] / 3 = 41/3 = 13.66\overline{6}$ (This is not an integer)
- If $a = 2$, then $d = [1 + (2)(40)] / 3 = 81/3 = 27$ (This is an integer)

Thus, $d = 27$.

6. Let the public key = (e, n)

Given $e = 3$ and $n = 55$, the public key = (3, 55). This key gets published.

7. Let the private key = (d, n)

Given $d = 27$ and $n = 55$, the private key = (27, 55). This key remains secret.

Stage 2: Message Encryption Stage:
$$E(s) = s^e \text{ (mod } n)$$

To encrypt a message, we apply the public key to the function, $E(s) = s^e$(mod n), where s is a given message, and e and n represent the public key integer pair. One example of an electronic message might be the number of sequential bits a data frame comprises. For our running example, we select the number 4 as our message, s. Thus,

$$E(s) = s^e \text{ (mod } n)$$
$$= 4^3 \text{ (mod 55)}$$
$$= 64 \text{ (mod 55)}$$
$$= 9 \text{ (mod 55)}$$

As a result, our encrypted message, $E(s) = 9$. This is what gets transmitted.

Stage 3: Message Decryption Stage:
$$s = [E(s)]^d \text{ (mod } n)$$

To decrypt a message, we apply the private key to the function, $s = [E(s)]^d$ (mod n), where $E(s)$ is the encrypted message, and d and n represent the private key integer pair. The result should equal the original message, 4. Note the various mathematical manipulations we employ so that we can work with reasonably sized numbers. These manipulations are based on laws of exponents and by continually expressing a given result in mod 55. For example, in the third step below, $9^3 = 729$, which is equal to 14 (mod 55). *Note*: The process of raising a number a, to a power, b, mod another number, m, that is, a^b (mod m), is formally called *modular exponentiation*. An efficient method used to compute this power electronically is known as *repeated squaring*, which uses the binary representation of b. See Cormen, Leiserson, & Rivest, 1990, p. 829, for additional information.

$$
\begin{aligned}
s &= [E(s)]^d &&\text{(mod 55)} \\
&= (9)^{27} &&\text{(mod 55)} \\
&= (9^3)^9 &&\text{(mod 55)} \\
&= 14^9 &&\text{(mod 55)} \\
&= (14^3)^3 &&\text{(mod 55)} \\
&= 49^3 &&\text{(mod 55)} \\
&= 4 &&\text{(mod 55)}
\end{aligned}
$$

Thus, we successfully decrypted the encrypted message.

When determining which algorithm(s) and key length(s) to use for encrypting network traffic, two aspects have to be addressed. They are (a) identifying what you are trying to protect and assessing its value and (b) taking into account any plans you might have for encrypting traffic destined for outside your county's borders and the laws governing this action. As we've said before, the algorithm and key length are important for safeguarding the information. In the United States, the ANSI data encryption standard implements a 56-bit key length and contains variants that implement 40-bit keys and 128-bit keys. The keys themselves may be protected by a variant of DES called triple DES, which essentially is the key being encrypted three times. So, 40-bit DES may be plenty strong enough for the bulk of the traffic you are going to pass around, whereas 56-bit or 128-bit may be necessary for really sensitive data such as 5-year plans and the like. Triple DES may be essential for safeguarding the keys of the cryptographic method, which is critical. If someone knows the keys for the method, then it does not matter how secure the method is—it's broken! Thus, the answer to the question, "Which is best?" depends on what you are trying to protect and where.

Speed may also be an issue. Some algorithms are much slower than others, and this may factor into the decision as to which one to use. For example, DES is faster than RSA in real-time applications. RSA, as with all public key encryption schemes, is time-consuming. Time is needed to "sign" a message and verify it at the receiving end. DES, on the other hand, requires more keys than RSA. Public key systems can do authentication and encryption, but DES can only do encryption. As you can see, there are trade-offs. One alternative is to use a combination of conventional encryption and public key methods.

A comprehensive reference guide that contains the specifications for a wide range of common public key strategies, including key agreement, digital signatures, and public key encryption is the *IEEE P1363 Standard Specifications for Public Key Cryptography.* This document provides detailed descriptions of the primary encryption algorithms, including RSA and Diffie-Hellman. IEEE P1363 represents a different type of IEEE standard in that it provides a set of tools from which implementations and other security standards can be designed. Thus, instead of defining interface specifications, P1363 defines functional specifications relative to cryptographic parameters and public key strategies. Corresponding to P1363 is IEEE P1363a, which is a supplement to the base standard and contains information that did not get published in the original document. The two documents will eventually be combined in a future revision. IEEE also is planning a second supplement, P1363b. For additional information about the P1363 series of reference guides, see http://grouper.ieee.org/groups/1363

17.6 Authentication and Access Control Measures

Another network security measure is *authentication,* which is a form of identification verification; it is a process of verifying a claimed identity. This can include not only the sender's identity, but also the sender's message as well as the receiver's identity. The concept of authentication is similar to providing someone access to a secure area. A security guard, for example, needs to verify the identity of the person who seeks admittance.

There are several ways in which this can be done. For instance, access may be granted on the basis of the person possessing a badge, by a known individual vouching for the person, or by the person reciting a secret code or phrase.

Network authentication systems are not much different from what we just described. For example, access to a network or computing resources might be granted by a user ID and password, through the use of a magnetic-strip card or badge, or via some unique human physical characteristic such as fingerprints or retinal patterns. All of these access methods, known formally as *access control measures,* are an important component of the authentication process. This is because authentication implies that the remote node believes you are who you say you are; that is, it proves the sender of a message knows the "key." Just because you have a key to the front door of the house does not mean that you have permission to go through every dresser drawer in the house. The combination of authentication and access control ensures that you are who you say you are and then allows you access to only what you are supposed to access. All of this activity might also be encrypted. Once again, there are many pieces to making sure network security works well, and no single security measure works well alone. One example of an authentication system is RSA, which was discussed in the previous section. RSA verifies to a remote node the sender's identity. Three authentication measures we discuss in this section are digital certificates, smart cards, and Kerberos.

Digital Certificates

Digital certificates are kind of an electronic passport. People use a variety of techniques to identify each other: looks, sounds, smell, and feel. Fingerprints, retinal scans, facial thermography, and other biometrics also help identify someone as being who they claim to be. In most cases, though, implementation of biometric security devices is in its infancy at this writing and expensive. A simpler method is to have someone identify certain attributes about themselves to a separate entity in which a sender and receiver both have a level of trust. This third party issues the user a numerical value, pattern, or key called a digital certificate. The certificate, in conjunction with cryptographic tools, identifies a specific user on the network, regardless of where the user is located or what application the user is using, in a reliable method. Digital certificates are available from a wide variety of trusted parties such as VeriSign. Unfortunately, there are as many ways to provide digital certificate authentication as there are vendors, and this means that their use tends to be spotty and somewhat chaotic at this writing.

Smart Cards

Smart cards are similar to digital certificates in that they represent another form of authentication. Similar to a credit card, a smart card has integrated circuits embedded in it that store information in electronic form. Smart cards use personal identification numbers, biometrics (e.g., fingerprints, voice, signature), and encryption methods to authenticate a user. Smart cards communicate with an external "reader," which can be a computer system, a cash register, or any other type of input device. The method of communication is either by direct contact or by radio signals. In either case, once contact is established, the "reader" provides the required voltage to power the card.

Smart cards have several applications besides providing authentication service for network security. For example, the medical profession uses smart cards to store patients' personal medical histories. This technology provides privacy and protection of patient records, enables the tracking of medication and medical information, and enables a patient's insurance coverage to be verified almost immediately. Smart cards can also store patient's x-rays and other graphical data. Another application is education. Many universities provide students with smart cards for meal plan authorization. These cards also can be used as credit or debit cards for purchasing campus products, as a library card for checking out books, as a "vending" card for photocopying or vending machines, and for accessing secured buildings or dormitories.

Kerberos

Cerberus was the three-headed dog in Greek mythology that guarded the gates to Hades. Its namesake is used to describe a client/server network security authentication system. Originally developed at MIT, Kerberos, which is based on DES encryption, is an Internet standard that uses a three-pronged approach for authentication: a database that contains users' rights, an authentication server, and a ticket-granting server.

To illustrate how Kerberos works, let's assume we want to access a data file stored on one of our company's primary servers. When we first log on to our workstation and request access to this file, an authentication server searches its database for our access rights. Once the server confirms that these rights include the requested service (i.e., we have permission to access the file), it generates an encrypted "ticket," which enables our workstation to access the ticket-granting server. The authentication server also returns the "key" that was used to encrypt something called an "authenticator," which contains our name, network address, and the current time. Our workstation then sends the ticket and authenticator to the ticket-granting server, which decrypts both pieces of data. If they match, the ticket-granting server generates a ticket for the requested service to be used only by us. This ticket is then returned to our workstation, which we then present to the company's server on which the file is stored. Once this server receives our ticket, it gives us access to the file.

A Kerberos-generated ticket is programmed to have a short life cycle (e.g., 1 hour or 1 day). This way, if an unauthorized person acquires a session ticket, it will only be valid for that time period. To use Kerberos, every network application has to be rewritten to support it. Additional information about Kerberos and other network security information can be obtained from `http://www.securityserver.com`. The Internet RFC that describes Kerberos is RFC 1510, which is available from `http://info.internet.isi.edu:80/in-notes/rfc/files/rfc1510.txt`

See also `http://www.rfc-editor.org/rfc.html` for information about RFCs.

17.7   Virtual Private Networks and Internet Security

In Chapter 7, we introduced the concept of a virtual private network (VPN) as a practical illustration of the network layer. A VPN is an IP connection between two sites over a public IP network that has its payload traffic encrypted so that only the source and destination can decrypt the traffic packets. A VPN enables a publicly accessible network to be used for highly confidential, dynamic, and secure data transmissions. Of course, this type of security can be mostly implemented by encrypting files and other user data before transmission, but it is not quite as secure as a VPN. VPNs provide further security because they are capable of encrypting not only the actual user data but also many of the protocol stack informational items that may be used to compromise a customer site in a technical session attack profile. The current VPN exploitation that has emerged in the industry within the last couple of years is centered mainly on IP-based networks such as the Internet. One of the major problems of VPN technologies is that there is a great variety of implementation styles and methods, which cause much confusion when trying to develop a strategy for their use in a company. (See Chapter 7 for a summary of the various VPN implementations.)

VPN Security Protocols

Another problem with VPNs is their use of the Internet. The underlying technology of the Internet (see Chapter 8), namely, the Internet Protocol (IP), was never designed with security in mind. As a result, several VPN protocols have been developed to help secure VPNs. These include the *Point-to-Point Tunneling Protocol* (PPTP), *Layer 2 Forwarding* (L2F), *Layer 2 Tunneling Protocol* (L2TP), and *IP Security* (IPSec). Following is a brief description of these protocols.

The Point-to-Point Tunneling Protocol (PPTP)   The Point-to-Point Tunneling Protocol was developed by several organizations, including the Internet Engineering Task Force (IETF), Microsoft, and U.S. Robotics (now part of 3COM). PPTP, which is integrated in Windows NT, uses Microsoft's proprietary Point-to-Point Encryption algorithm, which provides encryption and authentication for remote dialup and LAN-to-LAN connections. For dialup users, PPTP can be provided either directly by a PPTP-enabled client or indirectly via a PPTP-enabled server through an Internet service provider (ISP). Regardless of who provides the service, two connections are established. A control session is responsible for establishing and maintaining a secure tunnel from sender to receiver, and a data session provides data transmission. In LAN-to-LAN applications, a tunnel is established between NT servers. PPTP supports several network protocols including IP, IPX, NetBEUI, and NetBIOS. PPTP will eventually be incorporated into IPSec.

The Layer 2 Forward (L2F) Protocol   The Layer 2 Forward protocol provides tunneling between an ISP's dialup server and the network. In this application, a user establishes a dialup Point-to-Point Protocol (PPP) connection to the ISP's server. This server then wraps the PPP frames inside an L2F frame, which is then forwarded to a layer-3 device (a router) for network transmission. The router is responsible for users authentication and network addressing. L2F does not provide any data encryption, and its user authentication capability is weak.

The Layer 2 Tunneling Protocol (L2TP)   The Layer 2 Tunneling Protocol defines a method for tunneling PPP sessions across a network. It combines PPTP and L2F. This protocol is still being developed as a standard and as of this writing has not been fully implemented.

IKE was originally known as the Internet Security Association and Key Management Protocol with the Oakley key exchange protocol—ISAKMP/ Oakley Resolution.

IP Security (IPSec) IP Security is a suite of protocols developed by IETF. The suite includes an authentication header (AH), an encapsulating security payload (ESP), and the Internet key exchange (IKE). Operating at layer 3, IPSec provides address authentication via AH, data encryption via ESP, and automated key exchanges between sender and receiver nodes using IKE. Although PPTP, L2F, and L2TP support multiprotocol routing and provide some VPN security services, they are more applicable to remote access connections (i.e., dialup). IPSec provides end-to-end data encryption and authentication for VPNs. IPSec-complaint products are quickly becoming available, and the International Computer Security Association (ICSA) has developed an IPSec certification program to ensure products are compliant and interoperable. Many people believe that VPNs will grow rapidly once IPSec-compliant products are deployed on a full-scale basis.

It is important to note that all of the preceding VPN security strategies do not provide the same level of security. For example PPTP, L2F, and L2TP require an additional layer of encryption to provide secure data transmissions. Thus, if a VPN employs any of these security strategies, then the VPN is really only a virtual network and not a true VPN. Of the various security strategies described, only IPSec, which is discussed in more detail in the next section, creates encrypted tunnels. This is why the VPN Consortium supports only IPSec, PPTP with RC4 encryption, and L2TP under IPSec as acceptable VPN security strategies.

The IP Security Protocol (IPSec)

As indicated above, IPSec is really a suite of protocols that contains an authentication header, encapsulating security payload protocol, and Internet key exchange. The authentication header contains six fields (Figure 17.1). The *next header* field is one byte long and identifies the higher-level protocol that follows the AH. The *payload length* field is also one byte long and specifies the length of the *authentication data* field. The *reserved* field is a two-byte field reserved for future use and it is always set to zero. The *security parameters index* (SPI) field is four bytes long and identifies the security protocols (called the "security association") being used in the packet. This is followed by the four-byte *sequence number* field, which serves as a counter that identifies the number of IP AH packets it has received that bear the same destination address and SPI data. Although the sending node must include this information in outgoing packets, the receiving node does not have to process this field. The sequence number also protects against the receipt of duplicate packets. The last field is the *authentication data*. This is a variable-length field that contains the integrity check value (ICV), which is a digital signature of a packet. Authentication algorithms used to generate this signature include DES, MD5, the Secure Hash Algorithm (SHA-1), and others. The AH immediately follows the IP header in a standard IPv4 packet, but comes after the hop-by-hop, routing, and fragmentation extension in an IPv6 packet. (The destination options extension header of an IPv6 packet can precede or follow the AH.)

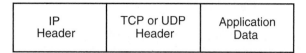

IPv4 Packet without AH

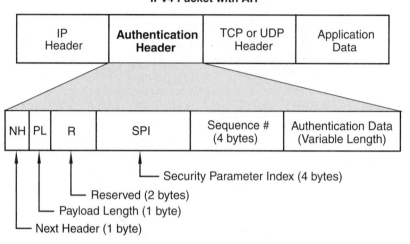

FIGURE 17.1 The authentication header, which is part of the IPSec protocol suite, provides authentication service to IP. AH safeguards data from being altered during transmission. The AH immediately follows the IP header in a standard IPv4 packet, but comes after the hop-by-hop, routing, and fragmentation extension in an IPv6 packet. NH identifies the higher-level protocol that follows the AH. PL specifies the length of the authentication data. R is reserved for future use and is set to zero. SPI identifies the security protocols (called the "security association") being used in the packet. The sequence number serves as a counter that identifies the number of IP AH packets it has received that bear the same destination address and SPI data. The sequence number also protects against the receipt of duplicate packets. The authentication data field contains the integrity check value (ICV), which is a digital signature of the packet. Authentication algorithms used to generate this signature include DES, MD5, the secure hash algorithm (SHA-1), and others. Source: adapted from Thayer, 1997.

The encapsulating security payload header contains seven fields (Figure 17.2). The first two fields, the *security parameters index* and *sequence number,* are the same as those in the authentication header. Collectively, these two fields are referred to as the control header. The next field, *payload data,* contains the encrypted version of the user's original data. It also contains optional initialization vector (IV) information if the encryption algorithm used to encrypt user data requires any type of synchronization (e.g., DES control information). The fourth field, *padding,* provides for any necessary padding requirements of the encryption algorithm or for byte-boundary alignments. This ensures that the payload data have the correct length. The *pad length* field speci-

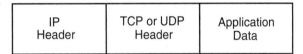

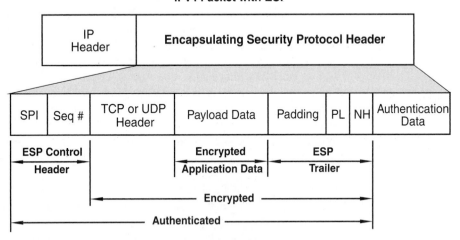

FIGURE 17.2 The Encapsulating Security Protocol header, which is part of the IPSec protocol suite, provides encryption service to IP. The ESP header immediately follows the IP header in a standard IPv4 packet, but comes after the hop-by-hop, routing, and fragmentation extension in an IPv6 packet. The security parameter index (SPI) and sequence number (Seq #) are the same as in the authentication header (see Figure 17.1). The payload data contain the encrypted version of the user's original data as well as optional initialization vector (IV) information if the encryption algorithm used to encrypt user data requires any type of synchronization (e.g., DES control information). The ESP trailer consists of padding, pad length (PL), and the next header (NH) fields. Padding provides for any necessary padding to ensure that the payload data have the correct length; PL specifies the number of pad bytes used in the padding field; and NH identifies the type of data contained in the payload data. The authentication data field is optional and contains a digital signature applied to the entire ESP (sans this field). Source: adapted from Thayer, 1997.

fies the number of pad bytes used in the padding field. The *next header* field references the payload data by identifying the type of data contained in the payload data field. These last three fields—padding, pad length, and next header—are called the ESP trailer. The last field, *authentication data,* is optional and similar to the authentication data field of the authentication header—it is a digital signature applied to the entire ESP (sans this field). The ESP header, like the AH, immediately follows the IP header in a standard IPv4 packet, but comes after the hop-by-hop, routing, and fragmentation extension in an IPv6 packet. (The destination options extension header of an IPv6 packet can precede or follow the ESP header.) If ESP and AH are to be used together, then ESP follows AH.

The Internet key exchange provides a mechanism for automating key exchanges between sending and receiving nodes when authentication (AH) and encryption (ESP) are used together. In such instances, both sender and receiver have to know their respective keys. Furthermore, to ensure secure communications across the network, these keys must be known only to the parties communicating. The IKE protocol delivers this service by using the Diffie-Hellman algorithm for key generation and provides three different methods of key exchange: *main mode, aggressive mode,* and *quick mode.* In main mode, six messages (i.e., three back-and-forth exchanges) are sent between a sender and receiver. The first two messages establish a specific security policy, the next two messages contain key information, and the two last messages provide authentication information. Aggressive mode is similar to main mode and achieves the same result. The difference is that there are only two exchanges (four messages sent between sender and receiver) instead of three. Quick mode is used to generate new keys after all necessary information has been exchanged between the communicating nodes via main or aggressive modes. IPSec essentially operates in one of two modes. In *tunnel mode,* the entire IP packet is encrypted and wrapped within a new IPSec packet (see Figure 17.2). In *transport mode,* only the data payload is encrypted. For more information about IPSec, see http://www.ietf.org/html.charters/ipsec-charter.html

Protecting VPN Connections

Multimegabit technologies such as cable modems, *x*DSL, and others enable high-speed access from home, small office, hotel, and other remote locations. With "push" technologies, personal computers at home and on the road will be connected more hours of the day and, in many cases, continuously connected to access information from providers around the world. This also means that although the system that only occasionally dials in to a public IP network is hard to hack, this might not always be the case. In the very near future, working with corporate documents at home will entail being continuously connected to public IP networks and VPNs. Although cryptography will help make a VPN connection more secure than one that is not encrypted, many implementations do not utilize cryptography facilities because they slow down the connection between the systems using the VPN. Thus, the need for protecting VPNs is greater than ever to allow for secure remote computing and distributed connectivity. (Remember that the greatest security threat originates from within). Desktop firewall products will be instrumental in securing these environments.

As network capacity continues to increase and technology continues its relentless pursuit into more segments of our lives, network security is going to get even more complex, just as network protocols and operating systems must. New technologies and new techniques to provide authentication and access control will be coming out over the next few years, and this will cause methods of implementation of network security to change. Firewall facilities will be available on desktop, workstation, and server systems just as they are provided on network-to-network connections today. More electronic access to financial facilities will be forthcoming, and this means that the entire area of electronic commerce (e-commerce) is exploding and will continue to grow.

Hackers and the threats they provide will increase as technology becomes more available to everyone. This means that the methods to provide network security must change to adapt to new threats. Consequently, the network security business will be a growing segment of the industry for a long time.

End-of-Chapter Commentary

Although we have come to the end of this chapter, there is much more to network security than what is presented here. We do not have the space to address every aspect of network security in this book. This is best left for books specifically dedicated to this topic. You are encouraged to consult the chapter Suggested Readings and References for additional information as well as the Web sites listed throughout the chapter.

CHAPTER REVIEW MATERIALS

SUMMARY

- Network security involves protecting everything associated with a network from all types of hazards, including environmental, electrical, and those perpetrated from unauthorized systems or humans.
- One of the first steps to establishing a network security policy is threat assessment. This involves identifying the critical assets of an organization—including hardware, software, data, systems, operations, and security measures—that are either attractive to unauthorized access or the potential target of an attack. A key component of threat assessment is risk analysis, which refers to assessing the price of an attack. This includes the cost associated with equipment replacement or repairs as well as the time lost in productivity to address the attack. One strategy to threat assessment is to simulate security attacks to help identify areas of vulnerability and the attack's overall effects to an organization. Regardless of what measures are taken to help assess network security threats, it is critical that everything be documented. This includes documenting all initial security measures implemented, details of any actual attacks or attempted break-ins, and any follow-up procedures conducted.
- Network attacks are very real and serious. An Internet search on network security provides access to thousands of sites that provide specific directions or

guidelines to compromising LAN and WAN security measures. Regardless of how strong an organization's security is, it only takes one weak link to compromise the network. Typically, this weakness is human and not systems oriented. One of the most common and successful methods for gaining unauthorized access to a network is through social engineering, which involves exploiting or manipulating people. Other attacks include denial of service attacks, which deny access to network resources by effectively shutting down a system. Consequently, it is important that organizations make their employees cognizant of security issues and incorporate their employees into their overall network security plans.
- Firewalls represent a common hardware approach to network security. The types of firewalls include those that filter at level 2 (frames) or level 3 (packets); monitor session setups between a system and the user security options relative to that system for a particular user (circuit gateways); monitor all transactions between two systems and are capable of (a) identifying a specific condition in the transaction between two applications, (b) predicting what should transpire next in the transaction, and (c) detecting when normal operational "states" of the connection are being violated (stateful firewalls); and provide network protection at the application level by using custom programs

for each protected application that serve as proxies to the actual applications (application gateways, also known as proxy servers).

• Encryption is the process of coding a message so that it is incomprehensible to unauthorized users. When retrieved by authorized users, encrypted messages are then reconverted (i.e., decoded) into meaningful text. Encrypted output is called ciphertext, and unencrypted messages are called plaintext.

• The data encryption standard (DES) is a specific coding technique developed by the National Institute of Standards and Technology (formerly the National Bureau of Standards) and IBM for protecting sensitive data during transmission. It is a mathematical algorithm that incorporates 2^{56} possible keys to transform plaintext to ciphertext. Improvements to DES include increasing the key size to 2^{1024} and using a variant of DES called triple DES, which uses three DES operations instead of one. Alternatives to DES include an 80-bit key space algorithm called Skipjack and public key encryption methods. A DES replacement, generically known as advanced encryption standard (AES), is forthcoming.

• Pretty Good Privacy (PGP) is a public key application developed for e-mail security. PGP incorporates both encryption and digital signatures.

• RSA is a public key encryption algorithm for encoding data that requires two keys for each user, one public and the other private. Public keys are available to anyone; private keys are known only to the user. Messages coded with public keys are decoded with private keys, and vice versa.

• Network authentication refers to verifying the identity of a specific user or device of a networked system. It can also refer to verifying that data received as a result of a networked transaction have not been modified. Network authentication methods include digital certificates, which consist of a numerical pattern, value, or key that is used for personal identification and involve a user identifying a specific personal trait to a trusted third party who issues the certificate, and smart cards, which are a type of "credit card" with embedded integrated circuits that store information in electronic form.

• Kerberos is an Internet standard client/server network security authentication system developed at MIT and based on DES encryption. Kerberos uses a three-pronged approach for authentication: a database that contains users' rights, an authentication server, and a ticket-granting server. Kerberos is named after Cerberus, the three-headed dog in Greek mythology that guarded the gates to Hades.

• Internet-related security protocols include the Point-to-Point Tunneling Protocol (PPTP), Layer 2 Forwarding (L2F), Layer 2 Tunneling Protocol (L2TP), and IP Security (IPSec). PPTP provides encryption and authentication for remote dialup and LAN-to-LAN connections. PPTP establishes two types of connections: a control session for establishing and maintaining a secure tunnel from sender to receiver and a data session for the actual data transmission. L2F provides tunneling between an ISP's dialup server and the network. L2TP is a method for tunneling PPP sessions across a network. It combines PPTP and L2F. IPSec is a suite of network security protocols that operates at layer 3 and provides address authentication, data encryption, and automated key exchanges between sender and receiver nodes.

VOCABULARY CHECK

application gateway firewall
authentication
ciphertext
circuit gateway firewall
cryptography
cryptology
data encryption standard (DES)
firewall
frame-filtering firewall

IP Security (IPSec)
Kerberos
Layer 2 Forwarding (L2F)
Layer 2 Tunneling Protocol
    (L2TP)
packet-filtering firewall
plaintext
Point-to-Point Tunneling
    Protocol (PPTP)

Pretty Good Privacy (PGP)
proxy server
public key infrastructure (PKI)
risk analysis
RSA
stateful firewall
threat assessment
triple DES

REVIEW EXERCISES

1. Do you think network security is a people issue or a technology issue? Why?

2. The concept of network security is overarching. It involves the destruction, alteration, and loss of data, as well as service disruptions or interruptions. Give two examples each of how data can be destroyed, altered, or stolen, and how network service can be disrupted or interrupted.

3. In what way(s) is ethics related to network security?

4. Defend the following statement: Maintaining the integrity and security of a computer system that is connected to a network is extremely critical to overall network security.

5. What user actions do you think can lead to someone gaining unauthorized access to a networked system?

6. Explain the purpose of conducting a threat assessment relative to network security.

7. Defend or refute the following statement: As an individual user, I am not concerned about network security because I do not keep anything on my computer that is worth stealing.

8. Why is it considered a good security measure to educate users about network security?

9. A strong recommendation made by several network security consultants is that all home network users of an "always-on" Internet connection such as cable modem service or *x*DSL should install a firewall. To get a feeling for why this is so, connect to `http://grc.com/default.htm` and download and install Shields UP! on your home system. Also see `http://networkice.com` and review the BlackICE Defender product.

10. Briefly discuss some of the primary characteristics of firewalls. As part of your discussion, describe some of the advantages and disadvantages of the different firewall types relative to level of sophistication and protection.

11. Investigate whether your organization's networking staff has an installed firewall. If so, what type is it; if not, inquiry why not.

12. Examine the concept of network security from both LAN and WAN perspectives. For example, what considerations are common between LANs and WANs, and what considerations are necessary and unique to each network type?

13. Explain the differences between authentication methods and encryption methods. Give examples of each as part of your explanation.

14. Discuss three specific access control methods relative to system or network security.

15. Although certain data encryption codes are nearly impossible to crack, what would give a person the incentive to try to crack a particular code?

16. Go to `http://www.pgp.com` and download and install the latest version of PGP Freeware.

17. Go to `http://www.pgp.com/phil/phil-key.asp` and examine Phil Zimmerman's DSS/Diffie-Hellman and RSA public keys. What is the functional difference between these two key types?

18. Describe the concept of a virtual private network. Why is security a concern when using a VPN?

19. Compare and contrast the various VPN-related security protocols described in the text.

20. What is IPSec and what does it bring to the table relative to IP?

21. Perform a security assessment of your own network and system(s). Specifically, identify your assets, the potential threats to these assets, and any known vulnerabilities. Share this list with your classmates/colleagues for completeness. Now consider the risks involved commensurate with the various levels of security implementation (ranging from "do nothing" to "disconnect from the network altogether").

22. Just how much security do you think is enough?

23. Investigate whether your school or organization has an established network security policy. (This is different from an acceptable use policy, although the security policy might be incorporated within an AUP.) If it does, review it for completeness. If not, inquire why not.

SUGGESTED READINGS AND REFERENCES

BAUM, M. 1994. *Federal Certification Authority Liability and Policy.* Cambridge, MA: Independent Monitoring.

BIRD, T. 1998. Building VPNs: The 10-Point Plan. *Data Communications,* June, 123–132.

BISHOP. M. 1992. Foiling Password Crackers. *UNIX-World,* March, 85–91.

BRYANT, B. 1988. Designing an Authentication System: A Dialogue in Four Scenes. *Massachusetts Institute of Technology,* 8 February.

CARL-MITCHELL, S., and J. S. QUARTERMAN. 1992. Building Internet Firewalls. *UNIXWorld,* February, 93–102.

CHESWICK, W. R., and S. M. BELLOVIN. 1994. *Firewalls and Internet Security: Repelling the Wily Hacker.* Reading, MA: Addison-Wesley.

CORMEN, T. H., C. E. LEISERSON, and R. L. RIVEST, 1990. *Introduction to Algorithms.* New York: McGraw-Hill.

DYSON, P. 1995. *The Network Press Dictionary of Networking.* 2nd ed. San Francisco: Sybex.

ELLIS, J., B. FRASER, and L. PESANTE. 1994. Keeping Internet Intruders Away. *UNIX Review,* September, 35–44.

FARROW, R. 1999. Public Key Infrastructure Basics. *Network Magazine,* January, 78–79.

———, and R. POWER. 1998. Is Someone Scanning Your Network? *Network Magazine,* September, 83–84.

FEIBEL, W. 1995. *The Network Press Encyclopedia of Networking.* 2nd ed. San Francisco: Sybex.

FRATTO, M. 1997. Unlocking Private Networks. *Networking Computing,* 1 November, 53–76.

———. 1998. IPSec—Compliant VPN Solutions: Virtualizing Your Network. *Network Computing,* 1 August, 72–80.

GALLO, M., and W. HANCOCK. 1999. *Networking Explained.* Boston: Digital Press.

———, and R. NENNO. 1985. *Computers and Society with BASIC and Pascal.* Boston: PWS.

GARFINKEL, S. 1991. *Practical UNIX Security.* Sebastopol, CA: O'Reilly & Associates.

———, and G. SPAFFORD. 1991. Building a Network Firewall. *LAN Technology,* December, 59–68.

HOOVER, A. 1995. Securing the Enterprise: Firewalls Can Keep You from Getting Burned. *Internet World,* February, 39–43.

KARVÉ, A. 1997a. Lesson 104: Public Key Cryptography. *LAN,* April, 23–24.

———. 1997b. Public Key Infrastructures. *Network Magazine,* November, 69–73.

———. 1998. Lesson 115: IP Security. *Network Magazine,* February, 27–28.

———. 1999. Making Sense of the PKI Puzzle. *Network Magazine,* October, 56–60.

LANDAU, S. 2000. Designing Cryptography for the New Century. *Communications of the ACM,* May, 115–120.

MORSE, S. 1994. Network Security: How to Stay Ahead of Network Explosion. *Network Computing,* 15 February, 54–63.

MOSKOWITZ, R. G. 1994. Firewalls: Building in That Peaceful, Easy Feeling. *Network Computing,* 1 June, 159–161.

QUARTERMAN, J. S., and S. CARL-MITCHELL. 1993. Tutorial: Local Protection for Networked Systems. *UNIXWorld,* July, 64–72.

RANUM, M. 1994. Internet Firewall Protection. *Open Computing,* September, 95–99.

SCHWARTAU, W. 1995. Beyond the Firewall: New Systems Watch Intruders and Strike Back. *Internet World,* February, 44–48.

SIMONDS, F. 1996. *Network Security.* New York: McGraw-Hill.

SIYAN, K., and C. HARE. 1995. *Internet Firewalls and Network Security.* Indianapolis, IN: New Riders Publishing.

STALLINGS, W. 1993. Make It Real. *LAN Magazine,* September, 105–112.

———. 1995. Getting Cryptic: PGP for You and Me. *Internet World,* February, 34–39.

———. 2000. *Data and Computer Communications.* 6th ed. Upper Saddle River, NJ: Prentice-Hall.

STEINKE, S. 1998. Authentication and Cryptography. *Network Magazine,* January, 51–55.

STEPHENSON, P. 1995. Securing Remote Access. *Network Computing,* 1 February, 130–134.

STREBE, M., C. PERKINS, and M. G. MONCUR. 1998. *NT Network Security.* San Francisco: Sybex.

THAYER, R. 1997. Bulletproof IP. *Data Communications,* 21 November, 55–60.

VAUGHN-NICHOLS, S. 1995. It's Alive: Clipper's Still Kicking. *Internet World,* February, 62–65.

18

Network Convergence

CHAPTER OBJECTIVES

After studying this chapter, you will be able to do the following:

1. Discuss the basic concepts of convergence of network technologies.
2. Understand the benefits and drawbacks of convergence efforts as applied to network environments.
3. Describe the network technological convergence of wire-based and wireless network entities into a holistic network environment.
4. Understand the components of convergence of network applications from hand-held personal digital assistants (PDAs) to mainframe computing facilities.
5. Understand the issues and problems in converting legacy networks into "converged" network environments.

6. Understand the issues of computing and network "style" changes to an organization as a result of convergence.
7. Discuss the impact to existing network resources as convergent technologies are implemented.
8. Discuss organizational and management issues of converged environments and how they affect a corporation's technical needs and staffing.
9. Discuss how a converged network more effectively interacts with Internet resources.
10. Understand how home and personal use of technologies changes as convergence leaves the corporate network and affects residential communications.

CHAPTER OUTLINE

Did you ever experiment with food combinations when you were growing up and mom wasn't around to control your actions? For example, did you put vanilla extract in a cola or mix peanut butter with vanilla ice cream? Even Elvis had a penchant for peanut butter and banana sandwiches (or "PB and 'nanner sandwich" as he was said to have called it). If you were like most of us, you were working on your own personal convergence experience at an early age. By taking different entities and combining them in a new way, an entirely new product is produced. This is the essence of convergence. Sometimes the results are powerful; sometimes they just taste bad and need to be trashed at the first opportunity (e.g., tuna and peanut butter didn't work for us). In the context of networking, convergence represents combining different technologies and applications. For example, facsimile (i.e., "fax") technology represents the convergence of several technologies and applications, including optical scanning, computer printing, and data and voice communications. A major networking convergence issue receiving much attention today is IP telephony, which involves integrating voice and data. In IP telephony, digitized voice signals are converted to IP packets, which are then transmitted over the Internet. In this scenario, packet technology and the Internet are uniting voice and data such that traditional voice communication services are being delivered over an IP data network.

In this chapter, network convergence is addressed from several different perspectives. We begin by discussing various convergence concepts. In Section 18.2, we examine some network-related issues relative to convergence, including network media, applications, and multimedia networking. Section 18.3 provides a comprehensive overview of the possible effects network convergence has on businesses, including the effects on legacy networks, computing and networking styles, network performance, organizational changes, network management, and the Internet. In the last section, we briefly describe network convergence issues relative to residential homes.

18.1   What Is Network Convergence?

Overview

Network convergence is a very powerful concept and buzzword in networking circles today. Basically, it involves the melding of dissimilar network media, protocols, and applications to provide a network environment dramatically different from what was previously available. Consider for a moment the various systems and technologies that are common among many companies today. Most organizations or their employees rely on a(n)

- mainframe system with a very large corporate database, which contains enterprise information useful for a wide variety of applications;
- departmental servers that provide database sharing and access to the mainframe;
- corporate e-mail server(s);
- LAN-based fax server(s);

- desktop PCs;
- company PBX system for in-house telephony;
- personal cell phones with digital messaging and paging facilities;
- Web servers;
- Internet connection(s); and
- personal digital assistants (PDAs) such as a Palm Pilot^{tm} system.

Without a doubt, each component on this list is useful in its own right. However, by combining different network types (e.g., LAN, WAN, wireless voice, and wireless messaging) along with the various components listed and uniting them with various applications and settings, some very powerful computational environments are possible. For instance, consider the concept of "follow me anywhere" e-mail. By converging a cell phone's capabilities with a PDA and wireless messaging, and then using the corporate e-mail server in conjunction with message forwarding and a "where am I" phone server at an Internet site, an individual could receive e-mail on the PDA, cell phone, or other devices anywhere and at any time. This is possible by converging the available technologies into a cooperative network of functionality that produces an entirely new product. This type of service is not possible without the convergence of network technologies, applications, and data resources into a single delivery stream. Extending this concept further, a new cell phone introduced in Japan contains a built-in video camera with TCP/IP and modem technologies. This phone allows a user to connect to another phone via the Internet and conduct a slow video frame conversation between wireless phones. It also is in color and has a built-in mini-Web browser. These illustrations might seem very futuristic, but they are not. Such technologies are available at this writing and have been around for some time. As convergence continues in networking and applications, the melding of techniques and facilities will continue to produce some fascinating and exciting results.

Another current illustration of network convergence is the Bluetooth wireless technology, which interconnects various devices including computers, mobile phones, mobile computers, and handheld or portable terminals using short-range (approximately 33 feet, or 10 m) radio links. The Bluetooth technology is designed to facilitate wireless LANs so that networks of different hand-held and mobile devices can communicate and exchange data. One usage example is the *three-in-one phone* concept where a telephone functions as a portable phone at home, as a mobile phone when you are on the move, and as a walkie-talkie when the phone is within range of another Bluetooth-enabled telephone. Another usage example is the *automatic synchronizer* in which Bluetooth technology automatically synchronizes a user's desktop PC, mobile computer, notebook (e.g., PDA), and mobile telephone. Thus, mobile office workers, for example, upon returning to their offices, can have their current calendar, which is stored on their notebook device, update the calendar stored on their desktop PC. This kind of synchronization, where data can be exchanged without reentering it, is only one of Bluetooth's major application goals. A second major application area is e-commerce, where users can electronically pay for parking meters, bus tickets, shopping, and movies automatically through the use of Bluetooth-enabled devices. In short, Bluetooth technology fosters *personal area wireless connectivity.* The primary members of the Bluetooth Alliance are 3COM, Ericsson, IBM, Intel, Lucent, Microsoft,

Motorola, Nokia, and Toshiba and include thousands of manufacturers throughout the world. It is the alliance's objective to embed Bluetooth technology into hundreds of millions of electronic devices by 2002 and have them operate at a globally available frequency band so they are compatible worldwide. For more information about Bluetooth, see `http://www.bluetooth.com`.

Convergence Is More Than Combining Voice and Data

To many people and to many organizations, the concept of network convergence simply means merging voice and data networking into a single networked entity. However, network convergence is much more than that. As an example, consider the following recent developments and think about how they might affect computing and the networking marketplace:

- Hewlett-Packard announced research results in early December 1999 revolving around the concept of *molecular electronics.* After several successes at H-P and other collaborating institutions of higher learning, they stated that future processor technologies would not be limited to the current physical boundaries of transistor electronics. *Molecular computing* is based on the idea that switches, transistors, and logic gates—the basic building blocks of computer chips—can be constructed out of individual molecules. Given a molecule that is designed to stop or start the flow of electricity and connect it to wires that are only a molecule or so wide, the creation of processors and memory chips millions of times smaller than the fingernail-sized silicon chips currently in production now becomes possible. This type of technology will not only lead to massively powerful processors the size of a grain of sand, but it will also revolutionize computing and networking as we currently know it. From a networking perspective, think about the technology's impact on the size and ubiquity of networking components, as well as the need for massive networks to interconnect all the potential processing systems of a molecular size. The potential uses and the networking requirements for such an implementation are many. Some illustrations follow.

  —*Medicine.* Injected into the bloodstream, tiny computers could traverse through the human body, destroying bacteria, identifying harmful cells, and diagnosing disease. Devices the size of a wristwatch, powered only by body heat, could store vast libraries of data and keep a record of images, facts, and events from a person's entire life.

  —*Space Science.* Space probes that today weigh a ton might be the size of a baseball, powered by a peanut-sized battery, and travel to other solar systems.

  —*Foreign Language.* Molecular computers could be used to translate the spoken word in any language on the fly.

  —*Automobile Industry.* Vehicles could drive themselves, avoiding traffic jams and accidents, homing in on a destination while passengers sit back and relax.

- Computers can calculate the square root of 73,324,969 in a fraction of a second. However, put your PC next to any 3-year-old child and ask the two to identify the penguin in a picture of a zoo and there's no contest: The kid wins every time. Researchers around the world are at work on sophisticated mathematical techniques that might even the odds. They're applying probability theory to those problems computers have always been deficient in solving such as evaluating large amounts of input data (e.g., photographs) and making qualitative judgments about the data. The result is that by 2010, we'll likely see increasingly smarter computers that finally achieve some of the long-discussed but never realized goals of artificial intelligence: Computers will be able to carry on a conversation with you, recognize your face, read your handwriting, and help you search for objects. What's different is that researchers are more or less giving up on teaching computers exactly how to perform each individual task. That was the near-fatal failing of earlier artificial-intelligence efforts; they required humans to generate rules for everything (e.g., "If it's round, then it's a face," with myriad other qualifications).

Today, researchers are letting mathematical algorithms do the heavy lifting, so to speak, so that computers teach themselves. Rather than try and describe what a face looks like, they give computers hundreds of digital pictures of faces and train them with software to develop their own increasingly accurate and flexible mathematical definitions of a face. These techniques have their roots in what's known as probabilistic inference, and a more recent refinement called *probabilistic networks,* which involve assigning numbers to degrees of uncertainty about each bit of data or possible outcome and drawing up rules about how you can manipulate those numbers. We're familiar with this type of probabilistic thinking when it comes to the weather—meteorologists talk about a 70% chance of rain, for example. Furthermore, our brains are thought to be constantly making decisions in a very similar manner, effectively using shortcuts to find the most likely answers, rather than perfect answers. Optical illusions offer a tangible example of this process in action: You can almost feel your brain "click" to a likelier way of seeing things when it figures out what's going on. Work in this area is not limited to obscure statistics journals or academics' offices. Already, Microsoft, for one, has incorporated a number of probability-based features into its products. Help software running in the background of some programs can determine what part of the program a user is working on and whether or not the cursor has moved recently, which might mean the user is stalled, before suggesting instructions. More sophisticated probability-based features are likely to come. At its Cambridge labs, more than half of the Microsoft researchers are working on projects that include at least some elements of probabilistic inference. Even Mr. Gates has said that probabilistic techniques are part of Microsoft's competitive advantage in Internet ventures, making its search engines and customized techniques more robust. Needless to say, probabilistic technologies are a solution to helping users communicate better with systems and software. It is quite obvious that the demand for networking will be greater than ever before. Who has all the answers to their information needs on a single machine? Also, what are the statistical odds that a user will require text-only information? Or, is the world really moving to a multimedia experience on the desktop for all types of information?

- Dressing smart will soon take on new meaning. Do you want to make phone calls on your necktie and e-mail friends by your sleeve? How about a shirt that prescribes medication or a suit that moves in response to light, heat, and pressure? Although this might sound like something James Bond's "Q" might design, this is the kind of clothing we will most likely be wearing in the new millennium. *Wearable computing,* a term coined at the Massachusetts Institute of Technology's Media Lab in the

1970s, often conjures up images of clunky headpieces or belts. However, as chip technology advances and computers get smaller, engineers say that so-called *wearables* will stop being accessories and will be woven into the fabric of our clothes. Instead of creating fabric that contains a complex network of lumpy connectors, like the keyboard of a computer, companies are creating fabrics that have a continuous field of sensitivity. The individual keys dissipate into the threads, making the cloth sensitive to touch no matter where pressure is applied. To date, a team has created a tie that doubles as a mobile telephone, with a tiny microphone lodged into the knot and a keypad woven into the silk. In the next 5 to 10 years, we can expect to see clothes that not only detect light, heat, sound, and pressure, but can also emit them. Combine this with voice recognition and fabrics that respond to gestures and you have clothing of an entirely new order.

What does all of this have to do with the concept of network convergence? Well, it's pretty straightforward to predict that convergence will include voice and data. What is not so straightforward is the further convergence of other newer technologies onto networks that either are very new or not currently in production. Some technologies being deployed at this writing, such as the Bluetooth wireless interoperability standard, will have their work cut out for them when technologies such as clothing become part of the converged networked world.

18.2 Networking Issues and Convergence

Network Media and Convergence

Convergence in networking means that multiple types of network "styles" will be integrated into common manageable entities. Overall, it is pretty easy to predict the very long-term networking methods. Long-range terrestrial networking will be predominantly fiber-based (glass and plastic), and short-range terrestrial networking will be predominantly wireless. Notice that we didn't say anything about speed. Technologies are evolving rather quickly that will allow networking speeds to keep up with computational demand as long as the research continues to be funded to develop the new networking materials. For example, TRW is using indium phosphide, which is an alternative base chemistry to the popular gallium arsenide method of chip construction. Indium phosphide is expected to have a top-end frequency range of 200 GHz; gallium arsenide is expected to peak at about 50 GHz. As a result, TRW recently announced a 69-GHz communications processor that will easily allow 40-Gbps connectivity over fiber. Wireless LANs also, over time, will be as fast as land-based technologies.

On a more short-term basis (2–5 years), we expect the following media, which are described relative to network type, to predominate the network convergence efforts in the world.

LANs The ever popular Category 5 unshielded twisted-pair (UTP) cable, as well as Enhanced Category 5 (Cat 5E), will continue to lead the pack in the under 100–m land-based networking realm. Under development are Category 6 and Category 7 cabling standards, primarily designed to enhance existing Category 5/5E cables for higher-speed LAN technologies such as Gigabit Ethernet. Phone systems, copper-based video, and almost any data network can use Category 5/5E cabling at this writing. Category 5 UTP does have its limitations, however. The most common problem is cable length. The longer the cable, the greater its ability to receive unwanted signals, and long cable lengths foster increased buildup in signal resistance. There is also the need to support faster networks such as high-speed ATM and Gigabit Ethernet. Both technologies have very short transmission wavelengths, which result in restrictive UTP cable lengths. In addition to wire-based LANs, we also expect a strong presence of wireless networking in the LAN environment so that docking station computing (e.g. laptops, notebooks, and PDAs) will interoperate via infrared wireless connectivity or microcell radio wave-oriented network facilities for short distances in an office environment.

MANs   Metropolitan area networks are still mostly fiber-based, but new wireless technologies and the strong emergence of broadband will change the complexion of this space significantly for small businesses and residential networking consumers. Already in Canada, over 20% of all residential telephone connections are via broadband connection (also known in residential circles as "cable TV connectivity"). In the United States, the massive purchasing of cable television providers in 1999 by AT&T will result in a large and steady push to provide voice and data access via broadband as well as existing broadband video facilities. This will enable broadband companies such as AT&T to bypass the traditional telephone company's copper-based local loop and establish their own self-managed cable path to the consumer. Broadband networking has the ability to provide massive network infrastructure capabilities for a variety of needs in a metropolitan area (1–100 km range). This ability will allow small companies to gain services similar to large companies. It will also enable small companies to compete in global markets historically dominated by companies that are able to provide network infrastructures for interconnection to their customers and suppliers. Ubiquity of MAN media technologies will change the way that networks will affect small- and medium-sized businesses in a profound manner.

WANs   Wide area networks currently employ several different media types, including leased lines, fractional T-carrier, T-carrier, SMDS (in Europe), and frame relay. Major growth over the next 2 to 5 years will include enhanced frame relay facilities, SONET, and synchronous digital hierarchy (SDH). In Holland, for example, a 40-Gbps SDH backbone is operational throughout the area known as Maasflacht, near Rotterdam. This very high-speed WAN provides connectivity throughout the Europort docking and terminal facilities within southern Holland at a very reduced price compared to previous connectivity options. In the United States, large companies such as AT&T and MCI WorldCom are installing or expanding existing SONET connections to provide national SONET facilities to replace or augment existing frame relay facilities. Through the use of transnational SONET, the convergence of high-speed networks becomes a reality for city-to-city and site-to-site connectivity. One interesting development is in the area of gigabit connectivity for WANs. The current 10-Gigabit Ethernet proposal (IEEE draft 802.3ae) provides for a 10-Gbps connection speed over WAN facilities. This is expected to become very popular for network service providers in lieu of using frame relay, SONET, and other high-speed network solutions due to its direct compatibility with Ethernet LANs.

GANs Global area networks are following the trend of WANs except that larger multinational network providers are taking over the predominant positions in the market to become a "one-stop supplier" of services to companies requiring multinational connections.

Long-term and very long-term networking trends are all looking toward a fiber-based terrestrial backbone with interconnections to wireless methods for various networking needs. Copper is here and will be around for many years, but there are plenty of countries (including very large ones such as Russia and China) that have no wiring infrastructure and where it does not make any sense to create one when wireless facilities will do the job nicely and with fewer problems. Some areas of the world will migrate to almost pure wireless networking environments for all converged services very quickly. For the more "wired" countries in today's market, the migration to pure wireless overall will be slower.

Network Applications and Convergence

At the heart of network convergence is applications: Content is key. In today's network environments, application technologies are usually independent of one another. For example, e-mail systems do not collaborate to a great extent with other applications used on networks. Accounting systems do not integrate with network management. Network performance and quality of service measurement facilities do not integrate with office information systems. Yet, there are useful components of all facilities, which, when abstracted among various application environments, become useful to all applications environments on a network.

In a converged environment, traditional networked applications will eventually evolve into new systems of interactivity that are radically different from those seen today. E-mail, voicemail, videomail, and hyperlinked documents are obvious candidates for convergence because they all convey specific types of information in a manner that can be understood by the same destination entity, namely, a human recipient. Microsoft's Outlook 2000 program is a good illustration of the initial steps in this direction toward the concept of *integrated messaging.* Outlook 2000 can hyperlink with MS Word, the MS Internet Explorer Web browser, contact management software, videoconferencing (via NetMeeting add-ons), and fax facilities. Third-party offerings also enable Outlook 2000 to interact and transfer voicemail between systems and e-mail delivery facilities. While neither is totally cohesive nor seamless in user interface, it is a start that shows the direction of desktop application convergence.

Many other application systems, including enterprise resource planning (ERP) facilities, accounting, electronic data interchange (EDI), business modeling, and traffic management—all of which are designed to provide intra- and intercompany assets and inventory exchanges—are becoming "Webified." That is, access to these applications is being provided in an integrated manner via Weblike interfaces that facilitate a distributed access method throughout an organization, regardless of corporate personnel or location. For example, upper management executives are able to see what they need to see, while at the same time and via the same system hierarchies and subcomponents, the loading dock personnel can manage product inflow/outflow. Thus, application information converges to the user depending on the user's perspective of the information provided.

All of these applications, and many more, will depend totally on network resources. As various communications messaging facilities are integrated into these ap-

Accenting the concept of integrated messaging, a Enum technology enables users to enter a telephone number into Web browsers to find a corresponding URL, e-mail address, or IP address. Enum-enabled applications demonstrate the convergence of the public switched telephone network and the Internet. For more information see http://www. enumworld.com or RFC 2916.

plication types, richer user interface facilities will be available to Web browsers, PDAs, and video display systems. In all cases, network resources will need to communicate data, voice, and video in disproportionate amounts depending on the application being used. Farther along in the future brings the merger of large corporate applications with personal applications. For instance, is it too farfetched for the tires on your car to set off an alarm to the car when the tread is dangerously thin, send a message to various tire marketing folks, automatically select the best candidate (based on location, cost, and quality), inform the car's autopilot to schedule a replacement visit, work with the smart card debiting facilities to pay for the tires, and send you information via voicemail or e-mail on what happened and how the low tire tread issue was addressed? We think not.

Convergence and Multimedia Networking

Another network convergence issue is multimedia networking, which involves transmitting information as a combination of full-motion video, sound, graphics, text, and animation across a network. Nearly all desktop computer models sold today are multimedia capable. They are equipped with speakers, microphones, sound cards, video cards, high-resolution monitors, and DVD drives. As stand-alone devices, PCs deliver rich, full-feature multimedia output via interactive games, music CDs, and the like. The delivery of multimedia information across a network, however, is another issue.

Multimedia applications generally can be classified as either prerecorded or interactive. Prerecorded multimedia implies that the "action" was recorded earlier and a user is simply viewing it in a non-real-time manner. Two examples include prerecorded music CDs and prerecorded DVD movies. It is also possible to download prerecorded multimedia files. In many cases, downloading these files over the Internet is time consuming and frustrating because they are usually extremely large in size (e.g., 5 or 10 megabytes) and because you cannot view the file until you receive it in its entirety. If the file is not what you wanted, then the download wasted both your time and bandwidth. Interactive multimedia, however, is in real time. Videoconferencing is one example of interactive multimedia. LAN- and WAN-based interactive multimedia networking has obvious applications in education because of its potential for delivering real-time educational content to the desktop. However, it also creates problems for the network.

There are two issues with interactive multimedia networking. First, multimedia data streams are extremely bandwidth intensive. These data streams must carry video information as well as audio information that is synchronized to the video. Second, multimedia is isochronous, which means that the data stream must be delivered as a continual and uninterrupted flow of data. Isochronous communications are normally not a problem in a circuit-switched environment. However, in a packet-switched environment such as the Internet, delivering interactive multimedia across the network requires a strategy that will guarantee regular, continuous, and timely data delivery.

During the past few years, several standards have been developed that facilitate Internet-based and LAN-based interactive multimedia networking. These standards developments, which address the bandwidth and isochronous communications issues, include the Moving Picture Experts Group (MPEG) series and the H.320 standards family. A brief discussion of each follows.

The Moving Picture Experts Group (MPEG) The MPEG series specifies compression techniques that reduce multimedia data streams into smaller-sized entities for transmission across the network. The series includes MPEG-1, MPEG-2, MPEG-4, and MPEG-7. With the exception of MPEG-7, all versions are ISO/IEC standards. MPEG-7 is expected to be ratified in mid-2001.

- *MPEG-1* provides compression levels of approximately 100 to 1 and supports VHS-quality multimedia transmissions at T1 rates.
- *MPEG-2* provides compression levels as high as 200 to 1 and is the standard for HDTV applications. MPEG-2 supports multimedia transmissions ranging from 4 to 100 Mbps. It is currently used in Direct Broadcast Satellite, which is also known as Direct Satellite Systems. MPEG-2 is the recommended standard for network convergence applications.
- *MPEG-4* is designed expressly for multimedia applications, especially in small multimedia devices such as videophones.
- *MPEG-7*, known officially as the multimedia content description interface, is designed for searching, managing, and filtering multimedia information.

H.320 The H.320 family consists of several different standards that were developed for distinct networking environments. Individually, these standards—H.320, H.321, H.322, H.323, and H.324—represent a suite of standards that specifies audio/video compression and multiplexing methods, data framing, control information (e.g., call setup), the type of communications interface, and other related issues. Collectively, though, these standards represent the H.320 family of standards.

H.320 is also known as Px64.

- *H.320* is a 1990 ITU standards suite that was developed primarily to support video-conferencing and multimedia communications over ISDN circuits.
- *H.321* is a 1995 ITU standard for adapting H.320's suite of standards to broadband ISDN networking environments, including ATM.
- *H.322* is a 1995 ITU standard designed expressly for delivering QoS capabilities to LANs such as IsoEthernet.
- *H.323* (Version 2) is a 1998 ITU standard for packet-based multimedia networking. This standard is receiving the most attention currently in multimedia networking circles since its focus is on providing QoS capabilities to Ethernet/802.3 LANs as well as the Internet. H.323 is nondevice and non-OS specific. Thus, it can be implemented in a variety of devices that support different OS platforms. H.323 supports IETF's Real-Time Transfer Protocol (RTP) for delivering packet-based audio and video streams across the Internet, as well as the Real-Time Control Protocol (RTCP) for maintaining QoS information. H.323 also supports IP multicasting, which enables multiple destinations to receive the same multimedia stream simultaneously without having to retransmit the stream multiple times to each destination node. The first version of H.323, which was approved in 1996, did not support IETF's Resource Reservation Protocol (RSVP). However, with Version 2, end nodes can now set QoS via RSVP. The second version also provides support for URL-type addressing, as well as improved audio and video capabilities.
- *H.324* is a 1996 ITU standard that specifies low-bit rate multimedia transmissions over analog modem (V.34) dialup connections.

With the release of H.323/Version 2 in 1998, the convergence of data, voice, and video via multimedia streams is spurring the development multimedia-based applications and the deployment of interactive multimedia networking. As advances in this area continue, distributed real-time multimedia will become more commonplace within the LAN/MAN/WAN environments. Furthermore, with broadband technologies such as *x*DSL and cable modems permeating the residential marketplace, interactive multimedia networking's presence will be felt in this area as well. Work on H.323 continues at this writing, with Version 3 having just been completed and Version 4 currently being drafted.

Although standards are now available that resolve the two major hurdles of true interactive multimedia networking, this does not mean that organizations are prepared to deploy this technology onto their LANs. To support LAN-based multimedia networking, organizations need to examine their local network infrastructure carefully to ensure that it can support multimedia's impact. Specifically, a review of the overall infrastructure should consider capacity and performance issues (e.g., What are the multimedia application performance requirements and does the current infrastructure have sufficient bandwidth to support the applications?) and management resource issues (e.g., Are current network management tools sufficient?). Additionally, firewall configurations should be examined to ensure that they will pass multimedia data streams, and routers should be configured (if not already) to support QoS as well as IP multicasting.

18.3 Effects of Network Convergence on Businesses

As network convergence begins to establish its presence in today's business networking environments, its effects will be pronounced and impact nearly all aspects of networking. A brief illustration of these effects follows.

Convergence Effects on Legacy Networks and Systems

In most corporate networks that have existed for more than 10 years, there are legacy systems, which comprise special purpose operating system environments or employ minicomputers, super-minicomputers, mainframes, or supercomputers. Some of these systems are highly specialized or have very large-capacity capabilities that are simply not available from other vendors, and most use non-Windows and non-UNIX-based operating systems. For example, minicomputers that use Data General's AOS or Digital Equipment Corporation's (now Compaq) RSX-11M, IAS, RSTS/E, or RT-11 operating systems provide access to 8- and 16-bit computing hardware. Super-minicomputers such as the VAX and Alpha processors use UNIX variants and OpenVMS. Specialized middle-range systems such as Tandem have operating system environments such as VLX and NonStop. IBM mainframe systems have historically employed MVS and VM/CMS as their operating systems. Cray and Fujitsu supercomputers use COS, LTCS, and a UNIX variant called UNICOS. In some cases, server-based architectures such as Novell Netware provide specialized operating environments with special purpose protocols such as Novell's IPX and SFX. Even MS Windows environments still use a proprietary protocol for file and printer sharing called Network Basic Extended

User Interface (NetBEUI). All of these systems have networking capability with vendor proprietary protocols. System protocols such as DECnet, Banyan VINES IP, Systems Network Architecture (SNA), Local Area Transport (LAT), and Local Area VAXCluster (LAVC) operate over specialized hardware or LANs such as Ethernet/802.3 and token ring. Some protocols such as DECnet and SNA have been used on hundreds of thousands of middle-ware systems for many years and are so entrenched in existing applications that only a complete replacement of the applications and system types will provide for removal of the protocols embedded in the applications. Like automobile engines, you cannot replace parts from different auto vendor's engines without a lot of compromises to the engine itself and without a lot of hassle. Over time, the only logical step is to replace the whole thing with a more holistic, unified vendor approach. Legacy networks will be profoundly affected by convergence because many components must be replaced to enable interconnectivity between new systems and legacy systems.

Convergence Effects on Computing and Networking Styles

In the not so distant past, it was commonplace to have a computer system that was self-contained, that is, no network resources whatsoever, not even for printing. Now, it is inconceivable to provide computing resources without network resources. The two have truly become inseparable. As the melding of network technologies and computing technologies progresses, so has the downward scaling of computing into hand-held personal digital assistants (PDAs). These devices are often as powerful as desktop computing systems but are physically small enough to be placed in one's pocket. With high-density storage, a PDA can contain a great deal of information. With the convergence of terrestrial and wireless networking, these units truly become limitless in their ability to supply information to the user. In fact, most PDAs now contain more computing power than the original PCs released in 1984. It is not impractical to expect these devices to become the mainstay computing power for most individuals in the future.

As noted earlier, some companies such as IBM are working on technologies called "wearable computing." Wearable computers are expected to become extremely ubiquitous over the next few years. It will not be uncommon to find computing technology located in clothing, automotive products, household appliances, and building automation devices. Potentially, even something as trivial as a candy wrapper might sport a small microprocessor to provide date of purchase and storage information. Obviously, having a desktop or mobile PC is not enough for this type of computing style. The reality is that the "network is the computer," which implies that the integration and wealth of network resources make the network the most critical element in a converged environment.

At the same time that convergence is melding networking and computing systems, there is also a convergence among copper-based, fiber-based, and wireless systems in the networking environment. Personal digital assistants are being used in environments where traditional notebook paper was used in years past. As an example, most of this chapter was written on a Palm Pilot computer prototype with a voice recognition system based on the IBM ViaVoice system. It is also possible to purchase a wireless "always-on" Internet connection that allows a Palm Pilot with the proper hardware to communicate with an Internet service provider in certain North American cities. By integrating an Internet connection with a voice recognition system, the Palm Pilot becomes a multifunctional communication system that does not require a keyboard or even a pen to input data. Keyboards, mice, and other input devices become obsolete because the system is capable of communicating via voice recognition. By adding capabilities such as infrared transmission between the Palm Pilot and a cellular telephone, data stored on the Palm Pilot can now be exchanged among the Palm Pilot, the cellular telephone, and a PC. Although this is one of the application areas of the Bluetooth technology initiative using a wireless environment, the same effect can be achieved through a variety of network media including copper and fiber. In this brief example, current technology allows the convergence of computing and networking platforms as well as a variety of networking transmission media. It does not take a large leap of logic to expect that the Palm Pilot will eventually allow all the functionality that a cell phone would allow in addition to the range of items that the PDA allows now. The original architects of the Palm Pilot have started up another company called Handspring, which makes a competing and 100% compatible system called Visor that uses the existing products and software for a Palm Pilot and attachments such as video cameras. Extrapolation of taking the Palm Pilot technology and merging it with traditional computing capabilities, extended network facilities including wireless capabilities, and adding in attachments such as video cameras all provide for the convergence of the technologies into something new that has not existed in the previous technical spectrum. This example of convergence clearly shows how data, voice, and video are on the marching path to becoming a singular technical solution in the future.

Convergence Effects on Network Performance and Growth Rate

Historically, voice, data, and video have been transmitted over separate and distinct networks within a corporate environment. With convergence, these separate networks are being merged into a single network in many organizations as a means of simplifying network management, access, and cost. Undoubtedly, this convergence will also increase network traffic. Whenever a technology causes an increase in network traffic, there's going to be a corresponding network performance problem. The question then becomes which network is affected based upon the type of technology being used. As the convergence of voice, data, and video becomes more of a reality, a single network architecture will most likely be implemented at most companies, and that network will be affected by all three application types. For example, in data networking, performance is largely governed by packet size, packet arrival rate, connection speed, and network type. Variances of any of these parameters cause the network to perform in different and often unpredictable ways. Some applications in data networking are very predictable in performance, but others are not. Some applications use stateful protocols, some use stateless protocols, and others use ACK/NAK protocols, all of which have completely different performance variances and tolerances. Some applications require continuous-bit rate (CBR) transport capabilities, others require variable-bit rate (VBR), and still others a combination of both. This makes planning and implementing a data network a rather difficult exercise in performance management. Think about how much more difficult this task will be once voice and video are a part of this network.

Voice networks, on the other hand, are usually very predictable because there are standards and other types of constructs that limit their speed and capabilities. The science of planning voice networks and predicting their performance is much more structured than that for data networks. This is rapidly changing, however, because many voice networks are now becoming Voice over IP (VoIP) networks. Voice over IP networks are configured very similarly to data networks if the data networks were created as standalone entities. The reality is that most Voice over IP networks are configured to be partnered with a data network or inserted onto an existing data network. This means that many of the performance modeling and performance estimation problems that exist for data networks now exist for voice networks. It also means that many of the problems that exist for the IP protocol now exist for voice connections as well.

Video networks to date have always been a separate network since they usually involve the use of broadband technology or the use of high-speed network connections to compensate for the video frame speed requirements. In the last several years, new video technology that reduces the frame rate from 30 frames per second to 12 to 15 frames per second has been making its way into the marketplace as an acceptable videoconferencing solution. The result is that connection speeds of approximately 384 kbps are more than adequate for the slower speed frame rate. As new compression technology begins to appear in the desktop videoconferencing area, the ability to achieve 30 frames per second over a standard data network becomes reality. This means that the days of dedicated networks for video are gone and replaced with the opportunity to operate a data network using video services. This is similar to what is happening in the voice area and brings with it the same performance and congestion issues.

One thing in common with all three network types as they converge onto a singular network path is the use of IP. By using IP, all three network application types can coexist on the same physical network structures. The key to coexistence of all three application types on the same network is the need to supply a large enough data pipe to satisfy performance requirements of the applications. Not only must the network be fast enough, but it must also support the burst rate required to keep all applications happy. Burst rate performance is the ability for the network devices in the path to deal with a constant burst rate of the highest performance rate of the network for a period of time in such a manner that the network does not lose the traffic as a congestive failure. This means that network hardware and software must have sufficient memory allocated and available to deal with the instantaneous traffic arrival rate in any particular location on the network. While doing this type of estimation is not terribly difficult, it is different from what most network managers actually do when designing and implementing a network to deal with any particular data type. Very few network managers actually use modeling software or any type of performance estimation software as part of their design criteria for the network. This means that addressing a converged network's performance requires a new set of skills to deal with the merging of the different network data types on the same physical network plant.

Organizational Changes and Convergence

Network convergence will also require organizational changes to properly plan and prepare for converged network environments. In most corporate network environments, the voice, data, and video departments rarely are part of the same networking infrastructure, nor do they talk to each other very much. Even worse, the different networking departments may report to very different management structures, which can lead to political infighting as the converged networks are deployed throughout a company. The skills sets traditionally required to manage a voice or data network are substantially different enough that separate people with separate skills sets were required to manage each network type. If both network types adopt the common use of IP, the skills sets emerge rapidly into more of a data skill set than to a voice skill set. This means that the folks working on the voice side of the network need to understand IP and all the networking capabilities associated with it.

Although there are some common areas across the two network types, for the most part, the two networks are radically different enough that neither side will fully understand some of the nuances required to make the new network function correctly. Thus, as part of organizational changes, networking departments must realize and embrace the concept of training networking personnel at a fairly substantial level. For example, if the voice network is converted to a VoIP network, there is a substantial amount of training that must happen over and above IP training. Training might include understanding the new PBX technology; system management training for working with OSs such as Windows NT or Windows 2000; basic network training to understand standard network interfaces such as Ethernet NIC cards and cabling plant issues; application management training for VoIP applications running on the operating system of choice being used for the PBX; new telephone handset training because the telephone handsets will have an IP addresses and not just a cable interface to the network; and a variety of other miscellaneous training that is required to fully understand the new VoIP environment. The collective scope of this training can be quite difficult, and hence, management cannot expect its networking personnel to assimilate all of the related information in a short period of time. Oddly enough, it might be easier to train a system manager to understand the salient voice-related aspects of VoIP than to try and educate voice people to understand the system and network management requirements of a data network.

The management structures involved in an organization must also change to deal with the convergence of voice, data, and video networking into a single network. This usually involves eliminating management positions and the consolidation of some functions into other management positions. Viewed from the perspective of a corporation's bottom line, this is definitely a desirable effect. However, these actions cause tremendous hardship on personnel and on personnel relationships in any department affected by the changes. It also causes the remaining or newly formed management structure to understand many networking types that were previously not part of the job description.

Network Management and Convergence

Network management of a combined network changes dramatically as well. Most companies will use the existing data network as the base network for combining voice and video functions in a converged networking environment. Well-managed data networks generally have a variety of tools available that enable a network manager or personnel to monitor and manage data traffic. The unfortunate part is that many companies neither purchase these tools nor know how to use them correctly. This means that, in many cases, when the voice and video functions are combined onto the data network, the network management function becomes more complex and yet does not benefit by having additional or better tools to deal with the new application types.

If a common protocol such as IP is used for the converged network, many of the standard data network management function tools, such as HP OpenView, may be used to monitor activities relative to the protocols used in the new network management environment. Even though the voice or video systems may not have support for the management station being used, since the application protocol is supported, they are easily monitored and managed just like a data network. In most situations, the video or voice systems supplier has applications or new tools to provide network management functions in the IP environment for the converged functions.

As previously described, problems of moving from three separate networks to a single network will involve a change of skill sets for the network management teams. The only solution to this is training for all parties involved and the realization that some people who are transferred from voice or video network management into the combined network will require additional training that the data networking people already have. Obviously, if wireless network technologies such as Bluetooth or other wireless microcell technologies are used, additional and specialized training will be required to satisfy the needs to keep the network operational.

Convergence and the Internet with Corporate Network Applications

It is not uncommon at all for a company to want to merge networks further together and not use an existing private network as much as use the Internet as a method of transport from site to site. In most companies, there is a gross misunderstanding of what the Internet actually is, however. The Internet is a consolidation or combination of many, many networks owned by very large companies around the world. The actual Internet backbone is, in relative terms, quite small. Most companies never connect to the backbone directly and, instead, connect to large telecommunications carriers such as AT&T, MCI WorldCom, and Sprint or to a very large hosting provider such as Exodus Communications. Therefore, what a company believes to be the Internet is actually a telecommunications company's large network that is connected to other sites located on the same network or, through peer connections, to other networks. Under ideal circumstances, the source address and the destination address between cooperating systems on the Internet would be on the same vendor's network, which would provide total control over traffic path and performance by the vendor and allow a guaranteed service level agreement (SLA). Such agreements are critical in convergence networks to ensure the performance of the network and performance of the applications using the network.

Most larger vendors that provide network connectivity capabilities to a company understand and deal with the convergence of data, voice, and video networking as part of their everyday business. It is still up to the customer, however, to ask the right questions of the vendor to ensure that the vendor is providing the proper network bandwidth, burst management capability, service level agreement, and overall performance capabilities at the connection points to ensure success. Obviously, security is a major concern when using the Internet as a connection methodology. Consequently, Internet and VPN security issues should also be addressed when negotiating with a provider for converged services.

18.4 Convergence at Home

For most readers at this time, their home network probably consists of an analog modem dialup connection via a local ISP. This is changing rapidly, however, where many homes have "always-on" Internet connections such as DSL and cable modems. In the case of a DSL connection from a residence, the same phone line providing analog support also provides a digital connection for data over the same pair of copper wires. (see Chapter 16). How fast the digital connection is depends largely on the distance from the residence to the central office and the type of DSL service provided. The most common type of DSL speed "pairing" is called medium-speed asymmetrical and usually involves a downlink speed of 1.5 Mbps and an uplink speed of 128 kbps. Asymmetrical connections, as you remember from our previous discussions in this book, are those where the transmit and receive speeds are different. On symmetrical connections, the transmit and receive speeds are the same in both directions. Since DSL signaling is at a different frequency on the same copper pair as the analog telephone, the two functions do not disturb each other on the same physical pair of wires. This is another example of convergence, at the signaling level, that most individuals would probably never recognize.

Once a DSL connection is made available in a home, there is often a desire to share the connection with more than one computer in the residence. Therefore, a "hublet" that provides LAN functions (e.g., Ethernet) will typically be connected to the DSL modem or router and then the other computers connected to the hublet. By adjusting software in all the machines or adding special network software if the machines are capable of using it, all the machines connected to the hublet can share the DSL connection. This is another type of convergence that happens in the residence: Computers that once were stand-alone devices are now communicating with each other through a standard network type (e.g., Ethernet) for local purposes only.

Many new apartment facilities in the United States are being prewired with high-speed Internet capability as well as PBX functionality built into the apartment. By providing both voice and data capability to each apartment, apartment providers can offer superior services, charge higher rents and make more money, and also attract technically literate tenants who can afford such connectivity. The same capability has not gone unnoticed to new home builders, who are now providing Category 5/5E UTP cable to each room in a residence as a means of connecting voice and data for new owners.

Networking functionality is converging very rapidly in the home market as companies become more amenable to permitting residential telecommuting a certain number of days per week. However, many companies will not allow residential telecommuting unless there is a separate voice and data entity at the residence to provide simultaneous access to voice and Internet or internal network resources. This trend is in a strong growth curve at this writing and will continue for a considerable period of time.

At the wireless level, some large network providers such as AT&T have developed neighborhood wireless repeating infrastructures to supply high-speed wireless connectivity to homes that cannot be provisioned a DSL connection due to exceeded home-to-CO distances or where cable television does not exist to provide a broadband connection to the residence. These connections are capable of providing 11-Mbps or greater connectivity and can be installed in fewer than 2 hours.

The convergence at the residence of video, voice, and data is obviously a high-growth area for telecommunications providers. Further, the agreements by large network vendors such as Cisco Systems with appliance makers such as Whirlpool mean that network and traditional industrial equipment manufacturers are obviously on the path to merging networking capabilities into traditional appliances such as refrigerators, washers and dryers, and kitchen stoves. Some demonstrations already have included the ability for a refrigerator to monitor food extraction and placement by scanning bar codes as the food is put in or removed from the refrigerator. A small processor in the refrigerator keeps track of inventory and makes this available to a residential local area network server. The server may then be available to the Internet to be scanned from work or from a remote location and find the exact contents of the refrigerator or have an on-line grocery store provider automatically deliver given items as the inventory drops to an unacceptable level. While this all seems the stuff of fantasy, it is a raging fact that this is going on and will surely be much greater than the current prototypical offerings. The convergence of services with the networking of home appliances and other technologies is inevitable. It's not a matter of if; it's a matter of when.

End-of-Chapter Commentary

As the last chapter of this book, it is fitting that the topic of network convergence was presented here because it represents the union of nearly every technology and application discussed in the previous 17 chapters. To appreciate and understand what network convergence entails requires an understanding of both past and present technologies and related applications. For example, the convergence of voice and data involves understanding basic voice communications concepts that were presented in Chapters 1, 3, 12, and 14, as well as basic data communications concepts that were presented in Chapters 2, 3, 4, and 5. This convergence also involves packet-switching technology and is being implemeted at both LAN and WAN levels. Once again, to understand the related protocols and various implementation issues—including quality of service (QoS), the differences between circuit-switching and packet-switching, Ethernet/802.3 LANs, and the Internet's ability to handle voice packets—a review of Chapters 2, 3, 5, 8, 9, 13, 14, and 15 is in order. Finally, realizing that the convergence of voice and data only begins to scratch the surface of true network convergence, we presented several examples in this chapter that should serve as the impetus for discovering other ways to merge present technology into compelling new entities. We hope that your study of *Computer Communications and Networking Technologies* has provided you with a solid foundation of networking that will enable you to do just that.

CHAPTER REVIEW MATERIALS

SUMMARY

- Network convergence involves the integration of different technologies and applications, which when combined, create powerful new entities and products; it is more than simply combining data, voice, and video.
- Converged land-based networks of the future will be primarily fiber-based, whereas short-range networking will be predominately wireless. Furthermore, as new technologies are developed, multimegabit per second data rates over fiber will be available, and wireless LANs will eventually be as fast as land-based LANs. In the short term (2–5 years), however, LANs will continue to support copper media, and MANs and WANs will support different media types, including fiber, hybrid coaxial/fiber, and wireless.
- The cornerstone of a converged network will be content. Current network applications will eventually converge to provide richer and more feature-filled applications that are limited only by the imagination. Network resources and designs will also need to evolve to support these new applications.

- The adoption of recent standards such as H.323 will advance the development of interactive multimedia applications, as well as the deployment of these applications over the network. These standards resolve interactive multimedia networking's two major problem areas: network capacity and quality of service (QoS).
- The effects of a converged network will have a pronounced effect on businesses. It will impact an organization's legacy networks and systems; it will have an effect on an organization's infrastructure and network design; it will affect overall network performance; it will foster the convergence of administrative units and functions; and it will impact the resources and manner in which a company's network is managed.
- Network convergence will also establish a presence in the home. Given broadband technologies such as xDSL and cable modems, coupled with the merging of traditional voice and data service providers with content and video providers, the delivery and structure in which we receive information in the home will change considerably.

VOCABULARY CHECK

Bluetooth	MPEG	wearable computing
H.323	network convergence	
molecular electronics	probabilistic networks	

REVIEW EXERCISES

1. Explain the concept of network convergence.
2. Using your imagination, suggest three applications that you would like to see emerge as a result of convergence.
3. Given the various technologies discussed in the previous chapters of this book, in what way(s) do you think these technologies will evolve into new, yet-to-be-defined technologies as a result of convergence? (For example, cable companies have combined several different technologies

into their backbones that changed their original one-way television broadcast facility into a high-speed broadband facility capable of two-way data, voice, and video transmission.)

4. In what way(s) do you think convergence will impact the cost and performance of current network implementations and applications?
5. Identify and discuss two outside influences you think will either spur or retard the advancement of network convergence.

6. In what way(s) do you think network convergence will impact your life? Give three examples.

7. What impact do you think each of the following will have on network convergence? (a) standards development; (b) censorship; (c) taxes; and (d) mergers, acquisitions, and strategic alliances.

8. What do we mean when we say that convergence is more than uniting data and voice?

9. Given the various network types of LAN, MAN, WAN, and GAN, what type of media is expected to support these networks in the short and long term?

10. Explain the difference between prerecorded and interactive multimedia networking.

11. What major problems does interactive multimedia networking pose in today's network environments?

12. In addition to MPEG, another compression standard is the Joint Photographic Experts Group (JPEG). Using the Web, find out what JPEG is and how it differs from MPEG relative to multimedia networking.

13. An alternative to H.323 for IP telephony, which integrates voice and data over an IP network, is called the Session Initiation Protocol (SIP). Using the Web, find out what SIP is and why some people think that it offers a more robust strategy for IP telephony.

14. Summarize the effects network convergence is expected to have on businesses.

15. In what way(s) is your organization planning/preparing for convergence, or in what way(s) has it implemented convergence concepts (e.g. IP telephony) into the company's network?

16. Describe three ways in which you think network convergence will impact you at home.

SUGGESTED READINGS AND REFERENCES

BATES, R. J., and D. GREGORY. 1998. *Voice and Data Communications Handbook.* New York: McGraw-Hill.

BROWN, D. 1999. Video Conferencing 2000: H.323's Year? *Network Computing,* 6 September, 79–98.

DYSON, P. 1995. *The Network Press Dictionary of Networking.* 2nd ed. San Francisco: Sybex.

ESSEX, D. 1999. IP Telephony: What Does the Future Hold? *Network Magazine,* January, 40–44.

FEIBEL, W. 1995. *The Network Press Encyclopedia of Networking.* 2nd ed. San Francisco: Sybex.

GALLO, M., and W. HANCOCK. 1999. *Networking Explained.* Boston: Digital Press.

HALL, E. 1999. Preparing Your Network for IP Multicasting. *Networking Computing,* 17 May, 121–122.

HANCOCK, B. 1989. *Network Concepts and Architectures.* Wellesley, MA: QED Information Sciences.

———. 1996. *Advanced Ethernet/802.3 Management and Performance.* Boston: Digital Press.

HELD, G. 1988. Modem Modulation: Techniques and Compatibility Issues. In *Handbook of Communication Systems Management,* ed. J. W. Conrad, 419–431. Boston: Auerbach Publishers.

HORAK, R. 2000. *Communications Systems & Networks.* 2nd ed. Foster City, CA: M&T Books.

JESSUP, T. 1999. Porting the PBX. *Data Communications,* July, 72–76.

LIPPIS, N. 1999. Enterprise VOIP: Two to Go. *Data Communications,* July, 19–20.

METZLER, J. 2000. The Merging of Telephony and IP: How and Why to Make the Move. *Packet,* Second Quarter, 60–65.

MICHAEL, B. 2000. DSL Solution. *Computer Telephony,* June, 88–113.

NOLLE, T. 1999. Voices on the LAN. *Network Magazine,* August, 34.

ROSENBERG, J. and R. SHOCKEY. 2000. The Session Initiation Protocol (SIP): A Key Component for Internet Telephony. *ComputerTelephony,* June, 124–139.

SCHOLL, F. 1997. Planning for Multimedia. *Network Magazine,* June, 101–105.

STALLINGS, W. 1997. *Local and Metropolitan Area Networks.* 5th ed. Upper Saddle River, NJ: Prentice-Hall.

————. 2000. *Data and Computer Communications.* 6th ed. Upper Saddle River, NJ: Prentice-Hall.

STAMPER, D. A. 1991. *Business Data Communications.* 3rd ed. Redwood City, CA: Benjamin/Cummings.

STEINKE, S. 1996. Multimedia: The I-Way Drive-In. *LAN,* August, 45–50.

TANENBAUM, A. S. 1996. *Computer Networks.* 3rd ed. Upper Saddle River, NJ: Prentice-Hall.

WILLIS, D. 1999a. Integrating Voice and Data. *Networking Computing,* 18 October, 50–73.

————. 1999b. Voice Over IP, The Way It Should Be. *Networking Computing,* 11 January, 96–99.

Appendix A
Vendor Ethernet/802.3 Prefixes

Ethernet/802.3 vendor prefixes are the first six (leftmost) hexadecimal digits of an Ethernet/802.3 address. Vendor prefixes, officially called *organizationally unique identifiers* (OUIs), are assigned by IEEE, which maintains a Web site of all publicly released OUI assignments. (Not all organizations make their assigned prefixes public.) This Web site, located at `http://standards.ieee.org/regauth/oui/index.html` is updated quarterly. Note that OUI assignments do not always match the original equipment manufacturer (OEM) of a network interface. Some organizations elect to license their vendor codes to other manufacturers. In such cases, the prefix will reflect the OEM and not the IEEE assignment. For example, the Ethernet/802.3 prefix 00400B is officially assigned to Cisco Systems, but field reports show that it appears on Crescendo devices. As a result, a second, unofficial list of prefixes has been published that contains reports of prefixes observed in the field. This second list, which is subject to errors, is available at `http://map-ne.com/Ethernet/Ethernet.txt`. Page constraints prevent us from listing a complete table that merges the official and unofficial lists in this appendix. Nevertheless, the reader is encouraged to visit either of the Web sites given to receive the most current list of vendor Ethernet/802.3 prefixes.

Appendix B
Using Parity for Single-Bit Error Correction

Let's define a *codeword* to have the following structure (each X_i is a bit in the data set):

$$X_1\, X_2\, X_3\, X_4\, X_5\, X_6\, X_7\, X_8\, X_9\, X_{10}\, X_{11}\, X_{12} \ldots$$

Also, let every bit with a subscript that is a power of 2 be a *check bit,* denoted by r_j, which will contain redundant information for error correction. Thus, X_1, X_2, X_4, and X_8 are check bits, and we replace them with r_1, r_2, r_4, and r_8, respectively.

$$r_1\, r_2\, X_3\, r_4\, X_5\, X_6\, X_7\, r_8\, X_9\, X_{10}\, X_{11}\, X_{12} \ldots$$

Since the X_i bits are predetermined (they represent user data), we need a rule for forming check bits. This rule is based on parity and is defined as follows:

> Each check bit, r_j, is formed by collecting all corresponding X_i bits. These are determined by expressing the subscript of each X_i as the sum of a power of 2. For example, X_3 corresponds to r_1 and r_2 because its subscript, 3, is equal to the sum of check bits r_1's and r_2's subscripts (i.e., $3 = 1 + 2$). Once the set of X_i bits is identified for each r_j, the check bit then forces the parity of each set to be even or odd depending on the parity selected.

This rule is implemented by first expressing the subscript of each X_i bit as a power of 2:

- X_3 corresponds to r_1 and r_2 ($3 = 1 + 2$)
- X_5 corresponds to r_1 and r_4 ($5 = 1 + 4$)
- X_6 corresponds to r_2 and r_4 ($6 = 2 + 4$)
- X_7 corresponds to r_1, r_2, and r_4 ($7 = 1 + 2 + 4$)
- X_9 corresponds to r_1 and r_8 ($9 = 1 + 8$)
- X_{10} corresponds to r_2 and r_8 ($10 = 2 + 8$)
- X_{11} corresponds to r_1, r_2, and r_8 ($11 = 1 + 2 + 8$)
- X_{12} corresponds to r_4 and r_8 ($12 = 4 + 8$)

Using the list just generated, we now identify all X_i bits that correspond to each r_j:

- r_1 corresponds to $\{X_3, X_5, X_7, X_9, X_{11}\}$
- r_2 corresponds to $\{X_3, X_6, X_7, X_{10}, X_{11}\}$
- r_4 corresponds to $\{X_5, X_6, X_7, X_{12}\}$
- r_8 corresponds to $\{X_9, X_{10}, X_{11}, X_{12}\}$

Given the preceding information, we now construct a codeword for a specific data set. Let's assume that the data string to be transmitted consists of the bit pattern 10001100. Let's further assume even parity. Our goal is to generate a single-bit error correction code for the given eight data bits. This codeword will be of the form:

		b_1		b_2	b_3	b_4		b_5	b_6	b_7	b_8
r_1	r_2	X_3	r_4	X_5	X_6	X_7	r_8	X_9	X_{10}	X_{11}	X_{12}

Substituting the data bits into this structure, we have:

		b_1		b_2	b_3	b_4		b_5	b_6	b_7	b_8
r_1	r_2	1	r_4	0	0	0	r_8	1	1	0	0

We now determine the check bits (assuming even parity).
- Since r_1 corresponds to $\{X_3, X_5, X_7, X_9, X_{11}\}$, r_1 is based on the parity of bits 10010. Thus, r_1's parity is 0.
- Since r_2 corresponds to $\{X_3, X_6, X_7, X_{10}, X_{11}\}$, r_2 is based on the parity of bits 10010. Thus, r_2's parity is 0.
- Since r_4 corresponds to $\{X_5, X_6, X_7, X_{12}\}$, r_4 is based on the parity of bits 0000. Thus, r_4's parity is 0.
- Since r_8 corresponds to $\{X_9, X_{10}, X_{11}, X_{12}\}$, r_8 is based on the parity of bits 1100. Thus, r_8's parity is 0.

As a result, the codeword is:

		b_1		b_2	b_3	b_4		b_5	b_6	b_7	b_8
0	0	1	0	0	0	0	0	1	1	0	0

This is the data string that's transmitted. Let's now assume the receiving node receives the string 001001001100. A visual inspection clearly reveals that the sixth bit (from the left) is incorrect; it's 1 when it should be 0. Unfortunately, the receiving node cannot see this. It must rely on an algorithm both to detect and then to correct the error. This is done as follows:

1. Check the parity of each check bit using the data string that was received.
   - $r_1 = 10010$. Given even parity, $r_1 = 0 =$ Correct (C)
   - $r_2 = 11010$. Given even parity, $r_2 = 1 =$ Error (E)
   - $r_4 = 0100$. Given even parity, $r_4 = 1 =$ Error (E)
   - $r_8 = 1100$. Given even parity, $r_8 = 0 =$ Correct (C)

2. Using the check bits, which are based on parity, we see that $r_1 = $ C, $r_2 = $ E, $r_4 = $ E, and $r_8 = $ C. If we let C = 0 and E = 1 and multiply the subscript of each check bit by its corresponding C or E value, then we get the following:

$$C(1) + E(2) + E(4) + C(8)$$
$$= 0(1) + 1(2) + 1(4) + 0(8)$$
$$= 0 + 2 + 4 + 0$$
$$= 6$$

Note that only check bits 2 and 4 are in error. This implies that bit 6 is incorrect since only bit 6 is checked by r_2 and r_4. Thus, the sixth bit is in error and should be complemented.

Appendix C
Guidelines for Installing UTP Cable

1. **Know and understand the related premises wiring standards.** First and foremost, it is important that you are knowledgeable of the published standards related to UTP premises wiring. Network cable installation is governed by a standard known as EIA/TIA-568. This standard was jointly developed by the Electronic Industries Association (EIA) and the Telecommunications Industry (TIA). EIA/TIA-568 is a North American standard that specifies the type of cable that is permitted for a given speed, the type of connectors that can be used for a given cable, and the network topology that is permitted when installing cables. The standard also defines the performance specifications that cables and connectors must meet. In short, EIA/TIA-568 represents a comprehensive standard for premises wiring that addresses network design and performance characteristics for physical media. Familiarize yourself with this standard as well as EIA/TIA-569 (*Commercial Building Standard for Telecommunications Pathways and Spaces*) standards. Although a nonstandard cabling system might work, this is something you should not chance. Also, do not let the issue of cost take precedence over standards. It is better to spend a little more money for something that is consistent with published standards than not. Standards were written for a purpose and should not be ignored.

2. **Check local building codes.** Prior to any wiring installation, contact the facilities people of your company to ensure that the planned cable plant is consistent with electrical and fire codes. Also consult the following: Section 800 of the National Electrical Code for telecommunications cable installations; EIA/TIA-607, the standard on the grounding and bonding of a building premises cabling plant; and IEEE 1100-1992, *Recommended Practice for Powering and Grounding Sensitive Electronic Equipment* (known as the *Emerald Book*).

3. **Think globally and locally.** If your cable installation is parochial, you are encouraged to think about how it might impact the entire organization. At the very least, and as a courtesy, contact your organization's designated network administrator and share your plans with this individual.

4. **Plan and document.** Not enough can be said about these two activities. Planning is extremely important to ensure that all factors have been considered including: who

is responsible for installation, termination, and certification of the installation; who will manage the cable plant; whether existing cable should be used; what minimum specifications the cable plant must meet; what interruptions there will be to company business prior to, during, and after the installation; what facilities modifications are needed to facilitate and support the installation; what future needs might be and how the current installation lends itself to meeting these needs; and so forth. As for documentation, it is extremely important that network maps be constructed and maintained. There should be a general topology map and a wire map that identifies cable lengths, termination points, grounding information, and so on. In our experiences, we found it easier to maintain handwritten maps than to use a software program. Copies of these maps should be in a centralized location and at key sites throughout an organization. Modifications to the cable plant should be documented at the time they are made.

5. **Be sensitive to physical security and the physical environment.** Include security issues as part of the planning process. Try to acquire dedicated space with a locked door to serve as wiring closets. Also make certain these areas are clean, air-conditioned, and free of corrosive material (see Box 17.3).

6. **Test the cable on the spool and after installation.** This is important. If you only test the cable after installing it, you cannot be certain if any detected postinstallation problems are the result of the installation process or bad cable.

7. **Label the cables.** Regardless of how diligent you are in documenting the cable plant, there will be instances when your map is not readily available when examining the cable plant. By labeling both ends of a cable with Avery stickers or their equivalent, you will have a built-in map that identifies each cable, its termination point and length, and electrical characteristics, among others.

8. **Inspect the installation, ensure the cable has been tested properly and accurately, and get a warranty from the cable installer.** Check for the following: Make certain cables have been installed neatly and securely; look for cinch marks and worn insulation (there should be none); be sure cables are not resting directly on ceiling tiles, have not been pulled near anything that radiates heat, are not near electrical fixtures, and have not been placed where people can step on them or roll over them in a chair; make sure that the minimum bend radius has not been exceeded; and ensure that cable runs do not exceed maximum recommended lengths. Also, make sure the cable plant is certified; that is, it meets all published certification standards such as those found in the EIA/TIA Technical Service Bulletin (TSB)-67. Finally, since a certified installation does not guarantee quality of work, obtain a warranty (at least 10 years) on the installed cable.

9. **Consider STP rather than UTP.** Before committing to UTP, you might want to consider installing STP. This would be prudent especially if the installation site is a source of high electromagnetic interference (EMI).

10. **Install a sufficient number of pairs.** Consider installing sixteen pairs to each location—four pairs for a LAN, four pairs for voice, and eight pairs (four each) for alternate LANs. Although using fewer pairs might be functional, it is much more difficult to manage in a live network. Most networks will be upgraded in the future, and this will mean parallel network connectivity for a period of time while the new network is tested and the old one is running.

Appendix D
Network Design and Analysis
Guidelines; Network Politics

Network design and analysis refer to the essential methods required to properly design a network. A properly generated network design provides the following benefits:

- Proper analysis of existing equipment for network installation.
- List of requirements for network installation.
- Proper configuration of network components for optimum cost savings.
- A flexible and adaptable network topology.
- Correct selection of network hardware and software.
- Documentation of the network for future enhancements and modifications.
- Migration path into future network technologies without redesign.
- A long network life cycle.
- Interconnect paths and methods for multiple network architectures.
- User analysis and configuration of network resources for optimal use.
- Network management plan and methodology to reduce downtime and allow for maximum use of available resources.
- Expectations for performance, reliability, and usability.
- Optimal programming environment for network applications.
- Training needs for programmers, users, and network managers.
- Recurring expense forecasting and budgeting methods.
- Network support needs (programming, management, user support).
- Use of mathematical modeling tools to help ensure the success of the network design and topology.
- Optimal design to prevent network congestion, queuing delay, and proper placement of routing and management resources on the network.

Unfortunately, many network administrators do not take the time to perform a network design and analysis. Instead, they rely exclusively on vendor recommendations. Network design and analysis involve much more than ordering hardware and software from a vendor. If you want to trust a vendor, that is your choice. However, few vendors are qualified network designers, and those who are do not offer this service free of charge. Be forewarned: You get what you pay for, and in the end, you will be the person who will be blamed for poor network performance or problems, not the vendor (Figure D.1). *Networks are neither trivial nor cheap.* If implemented incorrectly, expect to spend more time correcting problems, increased network downtime, and increased stress in your life.

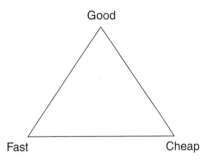

FIGURE D.1   This triangle is called "Truman's triangle," named after its inventor, Truman Reynolds. Truman's triangle serves as a good guide for anything that is network related. Pick any two vertices of the triangle and then apply the word *not* to the remaining description (vertex). For example, if you want a network that is fast and good, it will *not* be cheap.

The Steps of Network Design and Analysis

1. **Identify the Need.** Today, networks are an integral part of nearly every organization, and network managers are constantly faced with decisions to upgrade an existing network or install a new network. Before any action is taken, make sure you really need to upgrade or install a network. Don't be pressured into a new installation or an upgrade. Thus, before you swap out your token ring network for Ethernet/802.3, before you decide to replace your 10-Mbps Ethernet hubs with switches, or before you decide to upgrade your backbone from Fast Ethernet to Gigabit Ethernet, justify the need for doing so.

2. **Identify Function and Cost.** What is the network supposed to do and how much is it going to cost? The first part of this question can be answered by defining what functionality the network is to offer. If it is e-mail, file transfer, task-to-task communications, great, but write it down. In addition to functionality, there is the issue of cost. Networks are just like systems — they have a life cycle. Networks require periodic upgrading and expansion. They have recurring costs such as software and hardware maintenance, training, telco service, and replacement equipment purchases. They require personnel to manage and maintain the network components and might require custom software development, which implies costs for software engineering or application programming. Networks are expensive to install and operate over a period of time because they are service intensive.

3. **Site Survey.** A site survey involves the careful examination of company facilities, building architecture, phone facilities, and existing computer hardware and software components. It also includes the examination of existing contracts, power facilities, HVAC facilities, wireways and wire centers, electromagnetic interference possibilities, radio frequency interference possibilities, safety issues, security issues, building wiring and fire codes, electrical codes, reception and shipping facilities, building maintenance capabilities, on-site or vendor maintenance capabilities, and other related items. As a result, a thorough inspection of the network site is necessary. Furthermore, this inspection should not be done alone. You should include the director of management facilities or equivalent, as well as managers of departments that might be affected.

4. **Basic Design, Data Collection/Reduction, and Data Analysis.** This step involves the use of mathematical modeling tools (manual and computer-based) to address issues such as data flow ratios, probabilities of error, queuing delays, interconnect problems, least-cost network topological layout, routing paths, and redundancy paths. Following the modeling of the network, a financial analysis is done to determine how much the network is going to cost to implement, start up, maintain, and expand. An assessment analysis is also performed to identify networks that are most useful (closest to desired functionality) and least useful (on the right track, but not closest to desired combination of price, performance, and ease of use). Finally, an analysis of personnel needs and operational considerations is performed. This analysis describes the type of personnel necessary to get the job done, what kind of personnel will be needed for the day-to-day support of the network and its related components, and the costs associated with such personnel.

5. **Formal Design Document.** The last step in the design and analysis of a network is the formal design document. This document is a summary of all the previous steps. It documents the rationale for the network design and includes a description of the components, a network topology, a wiring diagram, expansion capabilities, expected life cycle, applications support environment, network management environment, potential problems, data throughput analysis, testing and verifications procedures, identification of network installation resources, an implementation timetable, personnel and training needs, cost analysis, and risks. This document is the backbone of the network design and serves as a guideline for implementation and expansion.

Why go through all of this? The answer is simple and complex (sort of the yin and yang of networks): It's proper business procedure and it reduces potential risk. Many people approach network design and analysis in the same manner as buying stocks—they use the "gut-feeling" approach; they rely on emotion instead of reading a prospectus, doing some research, or hiring a financial planner or stockbroker. They say that network design and analysis activities are not necessary to install wire, hardware, and software. They also "prove" this by identifying other installed networks, which did not undergo a design and analysis, but are working without any problems. This might indeed be the case. Sometimes it works, and sometimes it doesn't. However, just as you might get lucky in the stock market using a gut-feeling approach, chances are you will be less fortunate lacking the design and analysis of a network. In fact, studies have been done that indicate a gut-feeling approach works only about 25% of the time. When looking at network design and analysis, the main mistake many companies make is they approach a network in the same manner that they approach the "self-broker" methodology. This is not prudent because networks have some fairly serious restrictions that require both formal training and experience before someone is in a position to design a network properly.

Components of Good Network Design

Good network design is characterized by the following main points:

1. **It meets or exceeds the needs defined in the specification.** This is self-explanatory.
2. **It is cost effective and cost predictable.** Cost effective is obvious; cost predictable, however, is not. Over the period of life of any network, there is a need to pre-

dict the costs the network will incur upon corporate finances. Some obvious costs include component upgrades, software maintenance, hardware maintenance, and operational management tools and personnel. Some of the less obvious costs that need to be predictable are documentation, training, code maintenance, system downtime due to network component failure, productivity delays due to congestion or network failure, and consulting assistance. These costs should be part of the design so no surprises surface after the fact.

3. **Its capabilities are obvious and beneficial.** If a network is obviously useful and beneficial, the life of the network can be more easily justified, and the corporation will utilize the network and its capabilities in all appropriate areas. Thus, the capabilities of a network should be demonstrable upon demand so that its merits are recognized by management. If this can be done, then the needs of a network can be addressed properly and funding for the network is assured.

4. **It is capable of being managed by both system-manager-level and network-manager-level personnel.** This is necessary to protect a company from the eventual exit of trained network personnel. Both network and systems people should be capable of managing an organization's network.

5. **It is user transparent.** Users should not have to know the intricacies associated with the network. They should be able to use it in the easiest and most efficient manner possible.

6. **It is easily expanded.** A network should be capable of expansion without redesign. Management structures change, corporate directions change, people change. There is no reason that the network should not be able to change as well.

7. **It is well-documented.** Proper documentation of how a network was configured, why, and the politics behind it is critical to future support, expansion, and interpretation of the original goals of the network. Furthermore, any network-related activities (e.g., errors detected and how they were resolved, changes made to configuration files, breaches of security) should be logged for future reference and network history.

8. **The technology is state of the practice, not state of the art.** State of the practice means that the network architecture reflects proven, useful, current technology that is not leading edge. Why not leading edge? The reason is simple. Leading edge technology is good for daredevils, but it has no place in a business or engineering environment unless it is the only reasonable method to do a job. Leading edge technology is usually bug- and problem-laden, few people understand it, it imposes unnecessary risk upon the functionality of a network, and it might not receive wide acceptance upon review by the industry and other vendors. State of the practice technology reflects what is in use. It might not be the latest on the market, but it is proven, reliable, manageable, cost predictable, and there is plenty of talent to manage the technology that is available. When working with and configuring networks, it is essential that cost and risk constantly be kept in mind.

9. **It is supportable and maintainable at all node locations.** Regardless of where a network node is located, network managers should be able to have access to that location to provide necessary support or maintenance if needed.

10. **Network diagnostics and management are thought out and available.** If network diagnostic and management issues are not addressed a priori, then users

suffer and network managers cannot be expected to manage the network properly. As a result, attention must be given to such issues as management strategies, type of diagnostic tools needed, appropriate training and support for network managers, and disaster-recovery procedures.

11. **The network provides future interconnectivity.** Do not configure a network for one type of computer. Although the battle for the desktop essentially has been won by the Intel platform and Microsoft Windows, this does not mean that you only need to consider this hardware–software platform. The network should provide for interconnectivity among different products and architectures that either currently exist or might emerge as a result of network and corporate expansion.

12. **The network has predictable performance as loading changes.** System performance will change over the life of any system. When a network is initially configured, it is generally underutilized. As time passes, though, it becomes overutilized to the point where its performance is impacted negatively. This underutilization/ overutilization syndrome causes problems in network design. As a result, when considering network performance, it is necessary to look at not only the network topology and components, but also the loading history of critical processors and applications to ensure that there is a clear picture of how fast and how well things are going to perform.

13. **Its load on networked systems is predictable and reasonable.** Increased network use will eventually impact the performance of networked systems. For example, hub, switch, or router performance can degrade, and end user workstations (particularly those running a single-task operating system) can freeze up. A good network design will take these issues under consideration and provide some means for addressing them.

14. **It provides security adequate to the corporate or application needs.** Accept the following dictum: Networks are not secure. Although it is possible to make it quite difficult for someone to break into a network, you cannot keep out a professional. If someone wants to get into your network badly enough, there is very little you can do to stop it from happening. To ensure the success of a network, a security audit is performed during the design phase to identify sources of network and component vulnerability and what can be gained through penetration. This information is then presented to management, which will decide the resources needed to address these deficiencies.

15. **It supports system upgrades and enhancements.** It is impractical to expect network software and hardware to be upgraded simultaneously within all systems as new hardware and software become available. As a rule, any systems upgrade will disrupt operations on an entire network if the upgrades are not carefully considered networkwide. A good network design will allow for network and systems upgrades and provide for a method to do both. Good network design requires that the future be considered as well as the present.

16. **It survives the politics of the company and provides for political needs.** Network design must encompass not only the needs of the technical end, but also the needs of the practical end. That is, it must address the day-to-day needs of the corporation as well as the political needs of its management. For a network to survive the political environment, care must be taken to allow proper placement

of the network in the political environment. If the network is not properly intro-duced, placed, and controlled by the appropriate level of management, the politi-cal machine can turn on the network and associated personnel and proceed to squash everything in its path.

Network Politics

When designing and configuring networks, funny things creep in that make no logical sense, have no basis for reasonable reality, and are of questionable use. These things are called *politics*. In a networked environment, politics take on a whole new role. The more nodes of a network, the more likely politics will invade the design and operation of the network, especially when competition exists between the various departments networked together. Politics are further exacerbated if competing departments depend on each other for technical support, assistance, and worst of all, funding. Another prob-lem is that of machine ownership. Although all machines are owned by the corporation, department managers get very possessive over the systems and resources they have a day-to-day interest in using and adopt a "my machine syndrome." Avoiding network politics generally tends to increase the political problem as a whole. To help keep poli-tics to a minimum, consider the following items:

1. Spend time describing and documenting to users what you do and why.
2. Always get the local management at each location involved.
3. Do not underestimate any network user.
4. Good rapport is all-important when dealing with personnel from different depart-ments. Get to know the users and managers at all locations and keep everyone in the loop.
5. Do not take an attitude of "I'm technical and don't do politics." This will increase your political problems in the long run. In the networked environment, politics are part of the design and support. Get used to it.
6. If possible, get some sensitization training. There is nothing worse to a user than a surly answer from the support organization. Try to show some empathy toward a user, but keep the sympathy to a minimum.
7. If you do not write well, get some training. Written communication is very impor-tant to tracing problems in the political structure.

If a political situation arises, take action but do not react to the situation. Many political moves occur due to power plays, inconsideration, or just to instigate a situation. If one arises, do not let your emotions get in the way of solid, logical reasoning and fact. You also must learn to discern a political problem from a real nonpolitical problem. If there is a system down, that's a real problem; don't escalate it into a political one.

Appendix E
X.25

In 1976, the Consultative Committee for International Telegraph and Telephone (CCITT) formally approved "Recommendation X.25: Interface Between Data Terminal Equipment (DTE) and Data Circuit-Terminating Equipment (DCE) for Terminals Operating in the Packet Mode on Public Data Networks." This standard, which has been periodically revised throughout the 1980s and 1990s, corresponds (although not exactly) to OSI's first three layers. In the original standard, X.25 referred to these layers as levels, namely, level 1, level 2, and level 3. This terminology was discontinued in later revisions of the standard, but it is still occasionally used in the literature today. Although many people refer to it as one, X.25 is not a network. Instead, it is a formal set of specification for connecting data terminal equipment (e.g., a computer or a terminal) to a public packet-switched public data network (Figure E.1). The most recent version of this protocol, adopted in 1996, also specifies how this connection is established when access is made by a dedicated circuit. X.25 provides data transmission speeds up to 2 Mbps and provides error-free transmissions. X.25 is an international standard for data communications in wide area networking (it does not support voice communications, though) and is extremely robust in transmitting data over noisy lines. It is also one of the oldest WAN protocols.

X.25's Physical Layer

X.25's physical layer addresses the manner in which data are transferred across the DTE-DCE link. This includes the physical and electrical characteristics of the media, the type of connectors, and the signaling scheme. In short, it specifies the interface between the DTE and DCE. Instead of defining these interface characteristics, X.25 references the X.21 interface standard. X.25 also supports V.35 as well as the EIA RS-232C standard for the DTE-DCE interface.

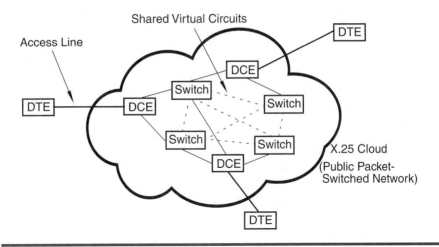

FIGURE E.1 X.25 is a set of specifications that addresses the interface between the user's equipment and the network. In X.25 terminology, the user's equipment is called data terminal equipment (DTE) and typically comprises a computer as well as any modem or line interfaces located on the customer's premises. Access to the network is provided via a physical link between the DTE and the data circuit-terminating equipment (DCE), which serves as a connection device between the user's end equipment and the network switches (i.e., the service provider's equipment). X.25 does not specify how the WAN operates; it simply provides a standard for accessing the WAN.

X.25's Link Access Layer

The link access layer of X.25 provides reliable end-to-end data transmissions across the DTE-DCE link. X.25's layer 2 is defined by the *Link Access Protocol-Balanced* (LAP-B), which provides link access specifications for frame composition, flow-control procedures, and error-checking methods. LAP-B is what ISDN's *H* channel uses for its layer-2 protocol for packet-switched connections. LAP-B is also a subset of the *High-level Data Link Control* (HDLC) protocol, which is one of the foremost and influential data link control protocols ever developed. Since many current data link control protocols are based on HDLC, the general format of HDLC frames is shown in Figure E.2.

Excluding the flag fields, which contain the start-stop bit pattern 01111110 to mark the beginning and ending of a frame (bit-stuffing is used to guarantee the uniqueness of this start-stop flag), HDLC frames are partitioned into at most four fields: address, control, information, and frame check sequence (FCS). Furthermore, all fields except the data field are of fixed length. When there are no frames being transmitted across the DTE-DCE link, the start-stop flag sequence is usually repeated indefinitely. A brief description of these fields follows:

- **Address**—The address field identifies the sending or receiving node and has a standard length of eight bits, although it can be extended in multiples of seven bits to accommodate longer address sizes. The first bit of the address octet is either 1 or 0, and the remaining seven bits specify a station's address. If the leading bit is 1, then the address field contains the last part of the address. A leading bit of 0 specifies that the

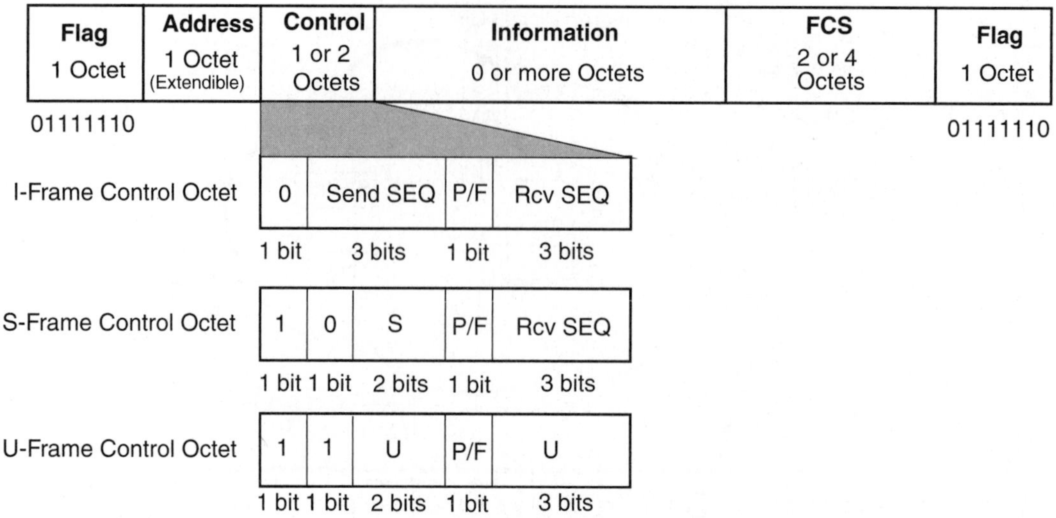

Control Field Descriptions for Each HDLC Frame Type

I-Frame Control Octet
- Send SEQ—This is the sequence number of the frame. Either a three-bit (modulo 8) or seven-bit (modulo 128) sequence number may be used. In the case of the latter, the control octet must be extended to two octets.
- P/F—(See separate description below.)
- Rcv SEQ—This is the sequence number of the first unacknowledged frame. It is determined by adding 1 to the sequence number of the last acknowledged frame.

S-Frame Control Octet
- S—This two-bit field is used to provide flow and error control. Four commands or responses are supported.
  Receive Ready (RR): Used as a positive acknowledgment or to indicate that a station is ready to receive I-frames.
  Receive Not Ready (RNR): Used as a positive acknowledgment or to indicate that a station is not ready to receive I-frames. RR and RNR together provide a "stop–go" type of flow control.
  Reject (REJ): Informs sender that specific I-frames were either not received or discarded due to errors and hence should be retransmitted. This represents a negative acknowledgment and infers a Go-Back-N protocol.
  Selective Reject (SREJ): Similar to REJ except only select frames are retransmitted instead of all the frames with sequence numbers corresponding to a particular gap.
- P/F—(See separate description below.)
- Rcv SEQ—(Same as I-frame.)

U-Frame Control Octet
- U—The U fields are used to provide additional link control information. The two- and three-bit fields are combined to provide a single five-bit field, which supports up to 32 commands or responses. Commands used to set the desired mode of operation, including extended mode for seven-bit sequence numbers, follow. (SABM and SABME are used in X.25.)
  Set Asynchronous Response Mode (SARM) and *Set Asynchronous Response Mode Extended (SARME)*
  Set Asynchronous Balanced Mode (SABM) and *Set Asynchronous Balanced Mode Extended (SABME)*
  Set Normal Response Mode (SNRM) and *Set Normal Response Mode Extended (SNRME)*
  Disconnect: Terminates a previously selected mode and places link in an idle state; used for a "normal" disconnect.
  Selected U responses include the following:
  Unnumbered Acknowledgment (UA): Acknowledges receipt and acceptance of a U command such as SARME.
  Frame Reject (FRMR): Specifies that a received frame was not formatted properly (e.g., I-frame did not contain an integral number of octets).
  Disconnect Mode (DM): "Ungraceful" link termination; used as an error-recovery procedure.

P/F Bit Description

The P/F bit is known as the *poll bit* when sent in a command; it is the *final bit* in a response. It is used as a form of handshaking: When a P bit is set in a command, it must be matched by an F bit in the corresponding response. In *normal mode*, a primary station will initially send a command with the P bit set requesting I-frames. The sender of I-frames then sets the F bit to indicate the end of a response. In *asynchronous mode*, every S or U command sent with the P bit set must have the F bit set in corresponding responses. Furthermore, an I-frame with the P bit set must have a corresponding RR, RNR, or REJ frame with the F bit set.

FIGURE E.2   Frame format of the high-level data link control (HDLC) protocol. X.25's Link Access Protocol-Balanced (LAP-B) is a subset of HDLC.

address field is being extended and contains at least one more octet. When only two devices are interconnected (i.e., there is only one station at each end of a link), then received frames will have exactly the same address. Hence, the address field is not required in this type of configuration—known as *balanced mode*—but is included primarily to maintain a standard frame format. The address field is necessary, however, in *unbalanced mode,* which involves the interconnection of multiple devices in parallel. An unbalanced mode configuration consists of a primary station that is interconnected to at least one secondary station. A primary station controls the link and issues commands; secondary stations are controlled by the primary station and issue responses to the primary station's commands. Since a primary station maintains separate logical links to secondary stations, the address field is essential for unbalanced mode configurations.

- **Control**—The control field specifies the type of frame being transmitted. As can be seen from Figure E.2, HDLC defines three different types of frames. *I-frames* are information frames that are used to send actual user data. Designated by a leading 0 bit in the control octet, I-frames are the only frames that can transport user data and hence are regarded as HDLC's principal frame type. *S-frames* are supervisory frames and contain only the flag, address, control, and FCS fields since they do not carry user data. Designated by a leading 10 bit-pair in the control octet, S-frames are used to transport sequence numbers that represent acknowledgments for received frames. S-frames are also used for flow and error control. *U-frames* are unnumbered frames that provide additional link control information. U-frames are designated by a leading 11 bit-pair in the control octet. A description of the control octets for each of these frame types is provided in Figure E.2.
- **Information**—The information field contains actual user data. Although theoretically this field can contain a variable number of bits, in practice it usually comprises an integral number of octets.
- **FCS**—The frame check sequence field provides error control via either the 16-bit CRC-CCITT or alternatively through CRC-32.

X.25's frame format mirrors HDLC's frame structure. As a subset of HDLC, X.25 only provides *asynchronous balanced mode* (ABM), which is set as part of the U-frame control octet shown in Figure E.2. HDLC-ABM is a connection-oriented service that uses seven-bit sequence numbers (modulo 128). Thus, an extended control field is used.

X.25's Packet Layer

X.25's packet layer specifies a virtual circuit service for transporting X.25 packets across the packet-switched network. Two services are available: permanent virtual circuit and virtual call. Both provide a point-to-point, connection-oriented transport mechanism. X.25's *permanent virtual circuit service* is a fixed virtual circuit that requires no call initiations. This is similar to a leased line service except the circuit is virtual, which implies a logical connection instead of a physical one. This means that the bandwidth is shared among multiple sites instead of being dedicated between two sites. X.25's *virtual call service* is similar to the permanent virtual circuit service except it represents a standard virtual circuit connection. This means that a virtual circuit between two DTEs is dynamically established. This requires a call initiation procedure in which the initiating

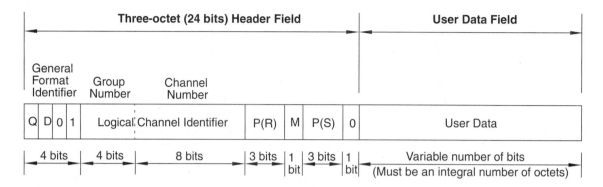

General Format Identifier This four-bit field specifies the packet format. In general, the GFI field is ??01 for packets with 3-bit sequence numbers and ??10 for packets with 7-bit sequence numbers. The field shown specifies that the packet uses 3-bit sequence numbers. The D bit is for delivery confirmation; if set, then end-to-end packet acknowledgment is required. The Q bit is a data qualifier bit.

Logical Channel Identifier This 12-bit field specifies the virtual circuit number; it is composed of a 4-bit group number and an 8-bit channel number.

P(R) This is the packet receive sequence number.

M This is the "more data" bit. If set to 1, then it indicates to the receiving DTE that the current packet was unable to support the entire user data, and hence, subsequent data packets contain the remaining part of the data.

P(S) This is the packet send sequence number.

User Data This field contains the actual user data. The maximum length of this field varies, but it is generally 128 octets. Other maximum lengths allowed vary from 16 to 4096 octets. As noted above, this field must contain an integral number of octets.

Notes

1. The packet format shown is that of a data packet. Other types of packets include control packets, as well as receive ready (RR), receive not ready (RNR), and reject (REJ) packets, which are similar to the corresponding LAP-B S-frames. The difference is that these packets operate at the packet layer.

2. X.25 headers are either 24 bits or 32 bits in length. For example, data packets that use 7-bit sequence numbers have a 32-bit header.

3. Some packet headers also contain an 8-bit *packet type identifier* field, which identifies the type of packet (e.g., a call request packet).

FIGURE E.3 Format of an X.25 data packet.

DTE transmits a request packet to the destination DTE requesting that a link be established. The destination DTE in turn responds with a call accepted packet that accepts the initiating DTE's request and confirms that the circuit is established. X.25 can support up to 4096 simultaneous DTE-DTE virtual circuits on a single DTE-DCE link. The format of an X.25 data packet is shown in Figure E.3.

Glossary

AAL   See *ATM Adaptation Layer.*

AAUI   See *Apple Attachment Unit Interface.*

Access Line   The *local loop* in *frame relay.* Also called a *port connection.*

Active Monitor   A station on a token ring network that oversees the ring and ensures that it is functioning properly. Also called a *monitor station.*

Address   A unique number assigned to a device to identify its location within a network. An address also can uniquely identify a network application process.

Addressing   A network concept that describes the process of assigning unique identification numbers (called *addresses*) to a networked device.

Address Resolution Protocol (ARP)   An Internet protocol that binds a node's *IP address* to its corresponding *MAC* sublayer (hardware) address.

ADSL   See *Asynchronous Digital Subscriber Line.*

ADSL Lite   A slower *ADSL* in which downstream rates equal 1 Mbps and upstream rates equal 128 kbps. Intended primarily for homes. Also called *G.Lite.*

Alignment Error   An Ethernet/802.3 frame that does not end on a "byte-boundary."

Always On/Dynamic ISDN (AO/DI)   An initiative from the Vendor's ISDN Association (VIA) in which a portion of the *D* channel, which is always active and constantly connected to the provider's switch, is used to transmit user packet data.

AM   See *Amplitude Modulation.*

Ambient Noise   Electrical *noise* that is always present and is generated primarily by transmission equipment such as transmitters, receivers, and repeaters. Ambient noise also can be induced by external sources such as fluorescent light transformers, electrical facilities, and heat. Ambient noise

makes it difficult for receiving equipment to distinguish between incoming signals. Also called *thermal noise.*

Amplitude   A characteristic of a carrier signal that represents the signal's strength. It is the level of voltage on a wire or the intensity of a light beam on a fiber-optic cable. Mathematically, the amplitude of a periodic function is one-half the difference between the maximum and minimum values of the function.

Amplitude Modulation (AM)   A *modulation* technique in which a carrier signal's strength is altered by varying the signal's voltage.

Amplitude-Shift Keying (ASK)   Similar to *amplitude modulation* except amplitude-shift keying is the more appropriate term when used in the context of converting digital data (or signals) into analog signals at the sending end and then back to digital form at the receiving end. The amplitude of a signal is altered so that it conforms to digital data (0s and 1s); one amplitude is used to represent a binary 0 and a second amplitude is used to represent a binary 1.

Analog   Any physical device or signal that varies continuously in strength or quantity over an infinite range of voltages or currents. An example is voltage in a circuit.

Analog Communication   Any communication method based on analog principles. In analog communications, signals flow across a wire in the form of electromagnetic waves. These waves resemble a sine curve and have the following three characteristics: *amplitude,* which is the level of voltage on a wire (or the intensity of a light beam when dealing with fiber-optic cable); *frequency,* which is the number of oscillations, or cycles, of a wave in a specified length of time; and *phase,* which is the point a wave has advanced within its cycle. Typically associated with voice transmission rather than data transmission because voice transmission facilities, such as the telephone, were initially analog based.

Analog Data Any data type that is continuous in nature and varies in strength and quantity over time. Analog data can be represented as either *analog signals* or *digital signals.*

Analog Signal Any signal that has continuously varying waveforms represented by a sine wave, which has characteristics of amplitude, frequency, and phase. Examples include conventional audio and video.

Analog-to-Digital Conversion The process that converts analog data, which is in the form of a sine wave, into digital signals, which are represented as 0s and 1s. This conversion is necessary so that analog data such as voice communications can be transmitted across a digital network. The most common approach for doing this is a process known as *pulse-code modulation.*

AO/DI See *Always On/Dynamic ISDN.*

Apple Attachment Unit Interface (AAUI) Apple Computer Corporation's proprietary *AUI.*

Appliance See *Network Appliance.*

Application Gateway Firewall See *Proxy Server.*

Application Program Software that performs a specific function such as e-mail.

Application Protocol Defines how an application is to be implemented on a network. Also includes specific user programs for interacting with an application.

ARP See *Address Resolution Protocol.*

AS See *Autonomous System.*

ASK See *Amplitude-Shift Keying.*

Asymmetric Cryptography See *Cryptography.*

Asynchronous Communication A data transmission method that requires the sending node to encapsulate special start and stop bits within each unit of data being transmitted. Thus, data can be transferred at any time by the sending node without the receiving node having any advance notification of the transfer.

Asynchronous Digital Subscriber Line (ADSL) A *DSL* variant in which traffic is transmitted at different rates in different directions. Downstream rates range from 1.5 to 9 Mbps; upstream rates range from 16 kbps to 1 Mbps. Rates depend on line quality and local loop distance. Suitable for Internet or intranet access, video-on-demand, database access, and remote LAN access.

Asynchronous Transfer Mode (ATM) A connection-oriented, full-duplex, and point-to-point high-speed cell-switched network architecture that was created in the late 1980s/early 1990s to apply circuit-switching concepts to data networks. Designed to carry data in 53-octet cells,

ATM can be used to transmit data, voice, and video—separately or simultaneously—over the same network path. Although not based on any specific physical layer protocol, ATM is generally carried over *SONET.* Also known as *cell relay* to distinguish it from *frame relay.*

ATM See *Asynchronous Transfer Mode.*

ATM Adaptation Layer (AAL) An ATM layer that interprets the type and format of user data messages and then translates these messages into ATM format by packaging them into the 48-byte payload portion of an ATM cell. The AAL's interpretation of data type and format is based on the specific class of service assigned to the data by the application. The AAL provides support for four different service classes and provides five different AAL types to accommodate a particular service class. *AAL1* is used for data that require connection-oriented constant-bit rate transmissions (e.g., voice transmissions); *AAL2* is used for data that require connection-oriented variable-bit rate transmissions (e.g., a videoconferencing application); *AAL3* and *AAL4* are used for connection-oriented or connectionless variable-bit rate transmissions (e.g., bursty data typical of LAN applications such as those found on frame relay and SMDS networks); and *AAL5*, which is an improvement to *AAL3*, is used for transmissions in which higher-layer protocols provide error recovery.

Attachment Unit Interface (AUI) A 15-pin "universal" connector that allows a device to be connected to UTP, thick or thin coax, or fiber-optic cable via an external transceiver.

Attenuation The decrease in signal strength, which occurs as the signal travels through a circuit or along a cable. The longer the cable, the greater the attenuation. Also, the higher the frequency of the signal, the greater the attenuation.

AUI See *Attachment Unit Interface.*

Authentication In the context of network security, a systematic method for confirming the identity of an entity. For example, in a secure Web transaction between a client and a server, an authentication procedure is used to establish proof of identity between the two nodes.

Autonomous System (AS) A collection of networks controlled by a single administrative authority that shares a common routing strategy. Routers connecting networks within an AS trust each other and exchange routing information using a mutually agreed upon routing protocol. Also known as a routing domain or protocol area.

Autowrapping The "self-healing" of a token or FDDI ring that has been cut in a single spot. The break in the active ring is corrected by establishing a loopback connection to the inactive ring. This creates a single virtual ring and allows the network to continue to function at full speed.

Backbone Switch One application of an Ethernet switch in which the switch serves as the backbone for the entire LAN. In this application, the network topology is called a *collapsed backbone*.

Backward Explicit Congestion Notification (BECN) A one-bit field in a *frame relay* frame that is set to 1 by a frame relay switch to denote that a frame transmitted toward the sending node experienced congestion.

Bandwidth In *analog communications,* the total capacity of a communications channel measured in hertz (Hz). It is the difference between the highest and lowest frequencies capable of being carried over a channel. The greater the bandwidth, the more signals that can be carried over a given frequency range. In *digital communications* and networking, bandwidth is the theoretical capacity of a communications channel expressed in bits per second (bps), which is called *data rate.*

Bandwidth On Demand Interoperability Network Group (BONDING) A protocol that aggregates two *ISDN B* channels into a single 128-Mbps circuit.

Barrel Connector A cylindrical shaped connector used to connect two segments of coaxial cable.

Baseband Cable Uses the entire bandwidth of the cable to carry a single signal.

Basic Rate Interface (BRI) An *ISDN* basic access channel that comprises two 64-kbps *B* channels, one 16-kbps *D* channel, and 48 bits of overhead used for framing and other functions. Commonly written as $2B + D$.

Baud A unit of signaling speed, named after the French engineer Jean Maurice Emile Baudot (1845–1903). It is another term used to express the capacity of a channel, but is different from bits per second.

Baud Rate A measure of the number of times line conditions (i.e., frequency, amplitude, voltage, or phase) change each second. At low speeds (under 300 bps), data rate (measured in bps) and baud rate are the same because signaling methods are relatively simple. As speed increases, signaling methods become more complex. Baud rate then differs from data rate because several bits are typically encoded per baud. That is, each signal can represent more than one bit of information.

B Channel A 64-kbps ISDN clear channel (no signaling information is sent on the channel) used to transmit computer data (text and graphics), digitized voice, and digitized video. Most basic ISDN services are based on multiple *B* channels. Also called a *bearer channel.*

Bearer Channel See *B Channel.*

BECN See *Backward Explicit Congestion Notification.*

Bend Radius The radius in which cable (copper or fiber) can be curved or "bent" without breaking. Fiber is much more flexible than copper cable and can be bent in much smaller radii than equivalent copper.

B-ISDN See *Broadband ISDN.*

Bit-Stuffing A data link process that is used to guarantee the uniqueness of a flag bit so that user data are not interpreted as a given start–stop bit pattern.

Bit-Time A unit of measure equal to 0.1 μs. Thus, a one-bit transmission requires 0.1 μs. Transmitting a 64-byte Ethernet/802.3 frame requires 512 bit-times, or 51.2 μs.

Bluetooth An emerging wireless convergence technology designed to interconnect various devices, including computers, mobile phones, mobile computers, and handheld or portable terminals using short-range (approximately 10 m) radio links.

BNC Connector A type of connector used with thin coaxial cable. There are several interpretations of BNC, including bayonet Neill-Concelman (named after its developers), bayonet nut connector, barrel nut connector, and British national connector.

BONDING See *Bandwidth On Demand Interoperability Network Group.*

BRI See *Basic Rate Interface.*

Bridge A layer-2 device that interconnects two or more individual LANs or LAN segments. A transparent bridge is used in Ethernet/802.3 and 802.5 (token ring) networks; a source routing bridge (introduced by IBM) is used exclusively in token ring networks. Bridges keep local traffic local, but forward traffic destined for a remote network. Forwarding/filtering decisions are based on MAC sublayer (i.e., hardware) addresses. Bridges partition Ethernet/802.3 networks into multiple collision domains.

Broadband Cable Shares the bandwidth of a coaxial cable among multiple signals.

Broadband ISDN (B-ISDN) An extension of ISDN that provides full-duplex data transmission at OC-12 rates (622.08 Mbps) and is designed for delivery of interactive services (e.g., videoconferencing and video surveillance) and distribution services (e.g., cable TV and high-definition TV). B-ISDN is also the basis for *ATM.*

Broadcast A data transmission that is destined to all hosts connected to a network. A broadcast message is a special *multicast* message.

Broadcast Design A network configuration that consists of nodes sharing a single communications channel. Every node connected to this shared medium "hears" each other's transmissions.

Broadcast Storm A network phenomenon that occurs when several broadcast messages are transmitted at the same time. Broadcast storms can use up a substantial amount of network bandwidth and in many cases can cause a network to crash or shut down.

Brouter A combination bridge-router; a bridge with routing capabilities.

Buffering Switch See *Store-and-Forward.*

Bus Design A specific design based on a broadcast topology. All nodes are directly connected to the same communications channel.

Cable See *Wire.*

Cable Modem A modem that uses cable television lines for data communications. These lines use broadband coaxial cable, which has a multitude of frequencies available and significantly higher bandwidth than the UTP cable used by the telcos. Cable modems provide an Ethernet/802.3 network interface that enables a computer to connect to the cable. Once connected, it is as if the PC were connected to an Ethernet/802.3 LAN. The connection is always "up," and multimegabit data rates are possible. Depending on the cable operator and service, current upstream rates for cable modems are somewhere between 500 Kbps to 3 Mbps; downstream rates range from 10 to 30 Mbps.

Capacitance The property of a circuit that permits it to store an electrical charge. The capacitance of a cable determines its ability to carry a signal without distortion. The lower the capacitance, the longer the distance a signal can travel before signal distortion becomes unacceptable.

Carrier Sense Multiple Access (CSMA) A protocol that serves as the basis for various *random access protocols.* CSMA-based protocols include *1-persistent CSMA, nonpersistent CSMA, CSMA with Collision Detection (CSMA/CD),* and *CSMA with Collision Avoidance (CSMA/CA).*

Carrier Sense Multiple Access with Collision Avoidance (CSMA/CA) A variant of *CSMA/CD* except that it specifies an implementation scheme for *collision avoidance* instead of *collision detection.*

Carrier Sense Multiple Access with Collision Detection (CSMA/CD) A variant of either *1-persistent* or *nonpersistent CSMA* that specifies what a node is to do upon detecting a collision. 1-persistent CSMA/CD is the MAC sublayer protocol used in Ethernet/802.3 LANs.

Carrier Sense Protocol A network protocol that requires nodes to listen ("sense") for the "sound" of another node's transmission prior to accessing a shared channel.

Carrier Signal An analog signal that can be modulated with a second data-carrying signal. The carrier does not convey any information until the signal is altered using a specific modulation technique such as *amplitude modula-*

tion, frequency modulation, or *phase modulation.* It is the modulation that conveys the information.

CCITT See *Consultative Committee for International Telephony and Telegraphy.*

CDDI See *Copper Distributed Data Interface.*

Cell A unit of data that is transmitted across a network. Similar to a data *frame.* When used in the context of *ATM,* a cell contains exactly 53-bytes, with 48 bytes for user data and 5 bytes for overhead.

Cells in Frames (CIF) A method of transporting *ATM* protocols over *Ethernet* and *token ring LANs.* CIF is a LAN technology that provides LANs with ATM features, including *QoS* and the seamless integration of data, voice, and video.

Centralized System A single computer that provides all the computing resources for all offices and departments within an organization via computer *terminals* that are connected to the centralized system.

CERT See *Computer Emergency Response Team.*

Channel Service Unit (CSU) A device used for terminating T-carrier circuits. A CSU regenerates the signal, monitors the line for electrical anomalies, provides proper electrical termination, performs framing, and provides remote loopback testing for diagnosing line problems. Usually combined with a *DSU* to form a single unit called a *CSU/DSU* or DSU/CSU.

Channel Service Unit/Data Service Unit (CSU/DSU) A device that combines the functions of a *CSU* and a *DSU.* A CSU/DSU works exclusively with digital signals; it provides an interface between a digital computing device and a digital transmission medium.

Check Bits See *Redundancy Bits.*

Checksum A parameter used to detect errors. Checksums are calculated using a predetermined *generator polynomial* and assigned to a specific checksum field of a data frame.

CIDR See *Classless Interdomain Routing.*

CIF See *Cells in Frames.*

Ciphertext A coded message. See also *Encryption.*

CIR See *Committed Information Rate.*

Circuit Gateway Firewall A device or product that involves monitoring the session setup between a system and the user security options relative to that system for a particular user. For instance, a circuit gateway might check user IDs and passwords, or it might implement proxy connection authorization or other types of authentication services. A circuit gateway firewall is also responsible for logging who came from where and went to what.

Circuit-Switched Network A network design in which a dedicated physical circuit gateway is established between the source and destination nodes before any data transmission can take place. Furthermore, this circuit must remain in place for the duration of a transmission.

Circuit-Switching A switching technique in which a dedicated circuit path is established between two entities on demand. This path is established prior to any data transmissions and is used exclusively by the connected parties until the connection is terminated. Contrast with *packet-switching*.

CIX See *Commercial Internet Exchange*.

Class I Repeater A type of repeater used in *Fast Ethernet LANs*. Class I repeaters support both of Fast Ethernet's signaling schemes—100BASE-T4 and 100BASE-TX/FX.

Class II Repeater A type of repeater used in *Fast Ethernet LANs*. Class II repeaters support only one Fast Ethernet signaling scheme—100BASE-T4 or 100BASE-TX/FX.

Classless Interdomain Routing (CIDR) A routing mechanism that allows sites to advertise multiple *IPv4* Class C networks by using a single prefix.

Class of Service (CoS) A data prioritization scheme that tags data with a specific priority level. Higher-priority data get delivered before lower-priority data.

CLEC See *Competitive Local Exchange Carrier*.

Client A networked device that requests resources from a *server*.

Client/Server A model or paradigm that describes network services and the programs used by end users to access these services. The client side (or front end) provides a user with an interface for requesting services from the network, and the server side (or back end) is responsible for accepting user requests for services and providing these services transparent to the user.

Coaxial Cable A type of cable that consists of a single-wire conductor, surrounded by a dielectric material and two types of shielding—a foil shield and a braided shield—arranged concentrically and encased in a PVC or Teflon outer jacket.

Codec A device that consists of a built-in encoder and decoder. The term itself means "coder/decoder." A codec is used for *analog-to-digital conversions* in which analog data are converted into digital signals for transmission across a digital network. A codec is also used to decode these digital signals back into analog form at the receiving end.

Codeword A data frame that comprises both user data and *redundancy bits,* which are used for *error control*.

Collapsed Backbone A network topology in which all LAN segments are interconnected via a bridge or switch, which serves as the network backbone.

Collision What happens when two or more nodes attempt to transmit data simultaneously on an Ethernet/802.3 network.

Collision Domain A "field" within a single Ethernet/802.3 network where two nodes can cause a collision. In the case of a single-segmented Ethernet/802.3 LAN, the independent segment represents the collision domain; in a multi-segmented Ethernet/802.3 LAN, the collective segments comprise the collision domain.

Commercial Internet Exchange (CIX) A subscription organization consisting of a consortium of commercial and nonprofit regional network providers that began offering Internet service independent of the NSFNET backbone and without NSF's restriction on traffic type. Today, CIX serves as an Internet interconnect site similar to a *NAP*.

Committed Burst (B_c) In *frame relay,* the maximum amount of data a provider guarantees to deliver within a specified time period, T. $CIR = B_c/T$. Most providers use a 1-second time interval to calculate the average amount of bandwidth utilization. Thus, CIR is usually equal to B_c. The difference between these two parameters is their units. CIR is measured in bps; B_c is measured in bits. See *also Excessive Burst*.

Committed Information Rate (CIR) The amount of throughput a *frame relay* provider guarantees to support under normal network loads. A CIR, which is assigned to a PVC when the network is initially configured, can range from 16 kbps to T3 (44.8 Mbps) and is the minimum guaranteed throughput of a PVC. If a PVC's assigned CIR is greater than or equal to the average amount of traffic transmitted across a PVC over a specified period of time (e.g., 1 second), then data transmissions are guaranteed. If the assigned CIR is less than this average, then data transmissions are not guaranteed.

Competitive Local Exchange Carrier (CLEC) A new telecommunication service provider formed after the Telecommunications Act of 1996 in the United States.

Compression A process that codes repetitive patterns within a data set. Compressed files can be sent at a faster rate than uncompressed files.

Computer Emergency Response Team (CERT) A formal organization operated by the Software Engineering Institute at Carnegie-Mellon University and dedicated to addressing computer and network security issues. CERT also serves as a clearinghouse for identifying and resolving security "holes" in network-related software or operating systems.

Computer Network A collection of computers and other devices that use a common network protocol to share resources with each other over a network medium.

Conductor That part of a wire which serves as the medium for the physical signal. It is composed of either copper wire, glass, or plastic fiber. In the case of copper, the wire can be stranded (composed of several thin wires) or solid (a single "thick" strand). Furthermore, the thickness of a wire is given in terms of gauge, which represents the conductor's diameter. The lower the gauge, the thicker the wire. Most often, wire gauges are expressed in terms of AWG—American Wire Gauge—which is a classification system for copper wire based on a wire's cross-section diameter.

Congestion   A situation when a network is consumed with excessive network traffic (i.e., lots of packets), resulting in performance degradation. Congestion occurs when routers are too slow, causing queues to lengthen, or when routers are too fast, causing queues to build up whenever input traffic is greater than the capacity of output lines. The ultimate level of congestion is known as *deadlock,* which occurs when one router cannot proceed until a second router does something, and the second router cannot proceed because it is waiting for the first router to do something. Congestion control is provided by layer 3 of the *OSI model.*

Connectionless Service   A type of service in which messages are partitioned into *packets* and routed through the network. Each packet is independent of the other packets that carry parts of the message, and each packet carries a destination address. Unlike *connection-oriented service,* no physical link is established between sending and receiving nodes prior to data transmission.

Connection-Oriented Service   A type of service in which prior to the transfer of data a physical (and virtual) link is established between the sending and receiving nodes. This link remains in effect for the duration of the session. After the session is completed, the link is removed. Characteristics of a connection-oriented service include wasted bandwidth (link must remain established even during idle periods of a transmission), a high potential for a hung network (there is always a possibility that a link will not be terminated), and guaranteed sequential arrival of packets at the destination node.

Connector   A layer-1 device that attaches network components together.

Consortia Standards   Network standards that are designed and agreed upon by a group of vendors who have formed a consortium for the express purpose of achieving a common goal. These vendors pledge their support for the standards being developed by the consortium and also develop and market products based on these mutually agreed upon sets of standards.

Consultative Committee for International Telephony and Telegraphy (CCITT)   An international standards organization, which is now part of *ITU.*

Contention   A phenomenon in which more than one node competes to access a shared medium simultaneously.

Contention Protocol   A network protocol that specifies the procedures nodes are to follow when competing for access to the same communications channel at the same time. Also called *Random Access Protocol.*

Content Service Provider (CSP)   An organization that provides its subscribers with designated applications or technologies via the Internet.

Copper Distributed Data Interface (CDDI)   An interface that provides a 100-Mbps data transmission rate over copper. A CDDI network is similar to an FDDI network. CDDI also is restricted to connections between concentrators on the ring and single-attachment devices, not for the ring itself.

CoS   See *Class of Service.*

CPE   See *Customer Premises Equipment.*

CRC   See *Cyclic Redundancy Check.*

CRC Checksum   The result of a polynomial division that uses a predetermined *generator polynomial* as the divisor.

CRC Error   An invalid *CRC* checksum.

Crosstalk   Electrical interference (i.e., *noise*) that occurs when energy radiated from one wire pair of a twisted-pair wire "spills over" into another pair. In one type of crosstalk, called *near-end crosstalk* (NEXT), a signal on the transmit pair is so strong that it radiates to the receive pair. A direct consequence of this spilled-over radiation is that the receiving device cannot decipher the real signal.

Cryptography   The practice or art of encoding messages into secret code or cipher. In the context of network security, cryptography can be implemented either symmetrically or asymmetrically. *Symmetric cryptography* implies that a secret (i.e., private) key is used to code and decode messages. In general, n people who want to establish a secret communication among them require $(n)(n-1)/2$ private keys. *Asymmetric cryptography* implies that each person engaged in secret communications maintains a public–private key pair. The public key is published; the private key is kept secret. The successive application of each key is then used either to code or to decode a message.

Cryptology   The study of secret communications or speech.

CSMA   See *Carrier Sense Multiple Access.*

CSMA/CA   See *Carrier Sense Multiple Access with Collision Avoidance.*

CSMA/CD   See *Carrier Sense Multiple Access with Collision Detection.*

CSP   See *Content Service Provider.*

CSU   See *Channel Service Unit.*

CSU/DSU See *Channel Service Unit/Data Service Unit.*

Customer Premises Equipment (CPE) Any telecommunication device that is owned and housed at a customer site.

Cut-Through A network switch architecture in which switches begin forwarding frames from one switch port to another as soon as the frame's destination address is read.

Cyclic Redundancy Check (CRC) An *error detection* method that constructs a polynomial whose terms' coefficients are the values of each of the bits of a data frame. This polynomial is divided by a predetermined *generator polynomial.* The remainder of this division, called the CRC *checksum,* is then assigned to a frame's checksum field. The most common CRC used in most LAN protocols is CRC-32, a 32-bit checksum.

DAM See *Demand Access Multiplexing.*

DAS See *Dual Attachment Station.*

Data Communications Equipment (DCE) Generally used as a synonym for *modem.* A DCE device is placed between *DTEs* and is responsible for establishing, maintaining, and terminating the link connecting the two DTEs.

Data Encryption Standard (DES) A specific coding technique developed by the National Institute of Standards and Technology (formerly the National Bureau of Standards) and IBM for protecting sensitive data during transmission.

Datagram A grouping of bits organized as a logical unit of data at the network layer. *IP* datagrams serve as the Internet's primary unit of information. In the OSI model, a datagram is generically referred to as a *packet.*

Datagram Packet-Switching See *Packet Switching.*

Data Link Connection Identifier (DLCI) In *frame relay,* virtual circuit addresses assigned to *PVCs* or *SVCs.*

Data Link Layer The second layer (layer 2) of the OSI model. The data link layer regulates and formats transmission of information from software on a node to the network cabling facilities. This layer is partitioned into two sublayers: the *logical link control* sublayer (LLC), which provides framing, flow control, and error control; and the *media access control* sublayer (MAC), which specifies the manner in which nodes access a shared medium.

Data Rate A measure of the amount of data that can be transferred over a communications medium in a given period. Data rate is measured in bits per second (bps) and can vary considerably from one type of channel to another.

Data Service Unit (DSU) A device used for terminating a T-carrier circuit. A DSU provides the interface (usually V.35, a type of serial interface) for connecting a remote bridge, router, or switch to a T-carrier circuit. The DSU also provides flow control between the network and the *CSU.*

DSUs are usually combined with a CSU to form a single unit called a CSU/DSU.

Data Terminal Equipment (DTE) End *devices* that communicate through their serial ports or expansion buses. Computers (PCs, workstations) are examples of DTEs. See also *Data Communications Equipment..*

DB Connector Layer-1 device that serves as an interface between a computer and a peripheral device such as a printer or external modem. DB stands for "data bus."

DCE See *Data Communications Equipment.*

DCE-to-DCE Rate The speed at which two modems "talk" to each other. This rate is fixed and is a function of a modem's speed. Typical rates are 14,400 bps (*V.32*), 28,800 bps (*V.34*), and 57,600 bps (*V.90*).

D Channel A 16-kbps or 64-kbps *ISDN* circuit that is used to carry signal and control information for circuit-switched user data. The *D* channel transmits call initiation (call setup) and termination (call tear down) information between an ISDN device and the telco's central office for each *B channel.* The *D* channel also can be used to transmit packet-switched user data (provided that no signal or control information is needed), data from security alarm signals of remote sensing devices that detect fire or intruders, and low-speed information acquired from telemetry services such as meter reading. The *D* stands for "delta."

Deadlock See *Congestion.*

Decentralized System Computer systems that are independent of each other and maintain separate databases germane to specific activities.

Decryption The process of taking an encrypted (coded) message and translating it into its original meaningful form.

De Facto Standards Network standards, placed in the public domain, that have been met with widespread industry acceptance instead of formal approval from a standards organization (*De facto* is Latin for "from the fact.")

De Jure Standards Network standards approved by a formal accredited standards organization such as ANSI or ITU. (*De jure* is Latin for "by right, according to law.")

Demand Access Multiplexing (DAM) A multiplexing technique in which a pool of frequencies is managed by a "traffic coordinator." Pairs of communications frequencies are assigned to a requesting station—one pair for transmission, a second pair for reception ("demand"). These two pairs of frequencies are connected to another set of frequencies ("access"). When one or both stations are finished communicating, the allocated frequencies are deallocated and returned to the frequency pool, where they are made available for other incoming requests ("multiplexing").

Demand Priority A *MAC* sublayer protocol used in *100VG-AnyLAN* networks. Demand priority specifies the manner in which repeater hubs poll their ports to identify which nodes have data to transmit and the order of these transmissions.

DES See *Data Encryption Standard.*

Desktop Another name for a networked device. See also *Workstation.*

Device Any entity that is connected to a network. Examples include terminals, printers, computers, or special network-related hardware units such as communication servers, repeaters, bridges, switches, and routers. Local or sending devices originate communications; remote or receiving devices are the recipients of such communications.

Differential Manchester Encoding A data transmission encoding scheme similar to *Manchester encoding*—each bit-period is partitioned into two intervals, and a transition between "high" and "low" occurs during each bit-period. In differential Manchester coding, though, the interpretation of these low-to-high and high-to-low transitions is a function of the previous bit-period. The presence of a transition at the beginning of a bit-period is coded 0, and the absence of a transition at the beginning of a bit-period is coded 1. Differential Manchester encoding is also used for clocking purposes.

Diffused IR A "broadcast" infrared transmission method in which a transmitter "floods" a specific area with a strong infrared signal that is spread over a wide angle. The IR signal is transmitted by reflecting off ceilings, walls, and other surfaces.

Digital Any device or signal that varies discretely in strength or quantity between two values, usually 0 and 1. 0 implies "off"; 1 implies "on." Digital signals are represented as binary digits called "bits" and are *discrete.*

Digital Certificate An electronic passport that consists of a numerical pattern, value, or key and is used for personal identification. Creating a digital certificate involves a user identifying a specific personal trait to a trusted third party, which issues the certificate.

Digital Communication Any type of communication in which data are represented in the form of binary digits.

Digital Data Any data that had been converted into a binary code such as ASCII.

Digital Signal An electronic signal that is represented using 0s and 1s instead of as a continuum of voltages, as is the case with *analog signals.* Analog data are usually converted to digital signals via *pulse-code modulation;* digital data are converted to digital signals using any one of several techniques, including *Manchester encoding, differential Manchester encoding,* and *NRZI.*

Digital Signature A security authorization method in which a user "signs" a document so that the document's authenticity can be confirmed by checking the signature. A digital signature proves a message was not modified.

Digital Subscriber Line (DSL) A technology that enables data, voice, and video to be mixed and carried over standard analog (copper) telephone lines. This is accomplished by using the unused frequencies that are available on a telephone line. Thus, DSL can deliver data services without interfering with voice transmissions. There are at least nine DSL variants: *ADSL, ADSL Lite, HDSL, HDSL 2, IDSL, RADSL, SDSL, UDSL,* and *VDSL.*

Digital Subscriber Loop The formal term for the *local loop,* which is the circuit between a *customer's premises equipment (CPE)* and the telco's equipment.

Digital-to-Analog Conversion A process used to convert digital data such as computer output into analog signals for transmission across an analog circuit path. Common strategies for effecting this conversion include *amplitude-shift keying (ASK), frequency-shift keying (FSK), phase-shift keying (PSK),* and *quadrature amplitude modulation (QAM).*

Digital-to-Digital Conversion A process used to convert digital data into digital signals for transmission over a suitable facility. Common strategies include *Manchester encoding, differential Manchester encoding,* and *NRZI.*

DIN Connector Similar to a *DB connector,* but circular instead of rectangular and typically used to connect a keyboard to a computer. DIN stands for "Deutsche Industrie Norm," a German industrial standard.

Directed IR A "point-to-point" infrared transmission method that requires an unobstructed line-of-sight connection between transmitter and receiver. It is basically a "point and beam" medium.

Direct Sequence Spread Spectrum (DSSS) A physical layer technology used in wireless LANs (IEEE 802.11). DSSS operates by spreading a signal over a wide range of the 2.4-GHz band.

Discard Eligibility A field in a *frame relay* frame, which, if set to 1 by an end node, denotes that the frame can be discarded in the presence of congestion. Discarded frames will then be retransmitted at a later time when congestion has subsided.

Distance-Vector Algorithm A routing algorithm that determines the distance between source and destination nodes by calculating the number of router hops a packet traverses en route from the source network to the destination network. An example of a distance-vector algorithm is the Bellman-Ford algorithm.

Distributed Queue Dual Bus (DQDB) A data link layer protocol (IEEE 802.6) that specifies the medium access method for *MANs*. Used in *SMDS*.

Distributed System Computers that are linked together to provide, in a transparent manner, the required computing resources and information-processing needs of an entire organization. Distributed systems bear the greatest resemblance to computer networks.

DLCI See *Data Link Connection Identifier.*

DNS See *Domain Name Service.*

Domain Name A logical name assigned to an *IP address* and used as another type of addressing construct for identifying Internet nodes. The translation between logical name and IP address is called name resolution, which is provided by a *domain name service.*

Domain Name Service (DNS) An Internet translation service that resolves *domain names* to *IP addresses,* and vice versa. Domain name service is provided by DNS servers.

DQDB See *Distributed Queue Dual Bus.*

DS-0 A single digital voice channel rated at 64 kbps. The notation *DS-0* stands for "digital signal at level 0," which refers to a voice channel multiplexed into a digital signal.

DS-1 A digital signal that carries 24 *DS-0* channels plus one 8-kbps channel reserved for framing for an aggregate bandwidth of 1.544 Mbps. A *T1* circuit carries a DS-1 signal.

DS-2 A digital signal that carries 4 *DS-1* channels for an aggregate bandwidth of 6.312 Mbps. A *T2* circuit carries a DS-2 signal.

DS-3 A digital signal that carries 28 *DS-1* channels for an aggregate bandwidth of 44.736 Mbps. A *T3* circuit carries a DS-3 signal.

DS-4 A digital signal that carries 168 *DS-1* channels for an aggregate bandwidth of 274.176 Mbps. A *T4* circuit carries a DS-4 signal.

DSL See *Digital Subscriber Line.*

DSL Access Multiplexer (DSLAM) A device that aggregates *DSL* signals so they can be transferred directly into a data switch for transmission across the telco's data network backbone.

DSLAM See *DSL Access Multiplexer.*

DSSS See *Direct Sequence Spread Spectrum.*

DSU See *Data Service Unit.*

DTE See *Data Terminal Equipment.*

DTE-to-DCE Rate The speed at which a computer "talks" to its modem. Typical rates include a 4:1 compression ratio between DTE and DCE speeds. Thus, for a *V.34*

modem (28,800 bps), the DTE-DCE rate is 115,200 bps. This rate is user configurable.

Dual-Attachment Station (DAS) An FDDI node that is connected to two full dual-fiber rings and has the ability to reconfigure the network to form a valid network from components of the two rings in case of a failure. A DAS is also called a *Class A* node.

E-1 The multiplexing of 30 separate 64-kbps voice channels, plus two 64-kbps control channels, into a single wideband digital signal rated at 2.048 Mbps. E-1 is the basic telecommunications service used in Europe.

E-2 A multiplexed circuit that combines 4 *E-1* circuits and has an aggregate bandwidth of 8.448 Mbps.

E-3 A multiplexed circuit that combines 16 *E-1* circuits and has an aggregate bandwidth of 34.368 Mbps.

E-4 A multiplexed circuit that combines 64 *E-1* circuits and has an aggregate bandwidth of 139.264 Mbps.

E-5 A multiplexed circuit that combines 256 *E-1* circuits and has an aggregate bandwidth of 565.148 Mbps.

E.164 An ITU-T standard network addressing format that resembles telephone numbers. E.164 addresses are 15 decimal digits long and include a country code, an area or city code, and a local number. Country codes are two or three digits long and consist of a zone code followed by a one- or two-digit national identifier. Area or city codes are up to four digits long. If an address contains fewer than 15 digits, then it is padded with hexadecimal Fs. Australia does not use city codes, and the United States and Canada use the zone code 1 followed by a three-digit area code and a seven-digit local number in lieu of country codes.

E-commerce Short for "electronic commerce," which involves using the Internet for credit card purchases of items such as automobiles, airline tickets, computer hardware and software, and books.

EGP See *Exterior Gateway Protocol.*

EIGRP See *Enhanced IGRP.*

Encapsulation A process in which a *packet* or *frame* is enclosed or "wrapped" in a specific protocol header. For example, *routers* typically perform protocol encapsulation in which packets from one network protocol are wrapped into the header of another network protocol so the packet can be transmitted to a different network. Also called *tunneling.*

Encryption The process of coding a message so that it is incomprehensible to unauthorized users. When retrieved by authorized users, encrypted messages are then reconverted (i.e., decoded) into meaningful text. Encrypted output is called *ciphertext.*

Enhanced IGRP (EIGRP)   A routing protocol designed by Cisco that combines the best features of distance-vector and link-state routing protocols.

Error Control   The process of guaranteeing reliable delivery of data. Error control can be provided through *error detection* or *error correction*.

Error Correction   The process in which a destination node, upon detecting a data transmission error, has sufficient information to correct the error autonomously. Error correction implies *error detection*.

Error Detection   The process in which a destination node detects a data transmission error and requests a retransmission from the sending node. Error detection is also called error correction through retransmission.

Ethernet   A local area network protocol developed jointly by Xerox, Intel, and Digital Equipment Corporation (DEC) at the Xerox Palo Alto Research Center (PARC) in the mid-1970s. The name "Ethernet" was derived from the old electromagnetic theoretical substance called luminiferous ether, which was formerly believed to be the invisible universal element that bound together the entire universe and all its associated parts. Thus, an "ether" net is a network that connects all components attached to the "net."

Excessive Burst (B_e)   In *frame relay*, the maximum amount of uncommitted data a provider will attempt to deliver within a specified time period. A provider will guarantee a *committed burst* of B_c bits and will attempt to deliver (but not guarantee) a maximum of $B_c + B_e$ bits.

Exchange Access SMDS (XA-SMDS)   A special *SMDS* service through which local exchange carriers offer SMDS to interexchange carriers for delivery across *LATAs*.

Exterior Gateway Protocol (EGP)   Any Internet interdomain routing protocol used to exchange routing information with other autonomous systems. Also refers to a specific EGP defined in RFC 904. Another EGP is the Border Gateway Protocol (BGP), defined in RFC 1105 and RFC 1771. Both EGP and BGP are part of the *TCP/IP* protocol suite. Of the two, however, BGP has evolved into a robust Internet routing protocol and the term "border gateway protocol" is used in favor of the term "exterior gateway protocol."

Extranet   An interconnection from an internal intranet to a customer or noncompany network that is not the Internet connection.

4B/5B   A data encoding method, which stands for *four bits in five baud,* or *four-bit to five-bit,* used in FDDI networks.

5-4-3 Repeater Placement Rule   A general rule of thumb to follow when configuring an Ethernet/802.3 LAN to ensure that it follows IEEE specifications. The 5-4-3 repeater placement rule requires no more than five segments of up to 500 m each, no more than four repeaters, and no more than three segments with end nodes connected to them. This rule is also known as the 4-repeater rule or the 5-4-3-2-1 rule. In the latter, the 2 implies that two of the five segments are used as interrepeater links, and the 1 implies that a configuration using the maximum parameters permitted results into one collision domain.

568SC Connector   See *SC Connector.*

Fast Ethernet   100-Mbps *Ethernet (IEEE 802.3u).* Three different media specifications are defined: 100BASE-TX, 100BASE-T4, and 100BASE-FX.

FDDI   See *Fiber Distributed Data Interface.*

FDDI-II   A now-defunct second-generation *FDDI* technology that was intended to handle traditional FDDI network traffic as well as synchronous, circuit-switched *PCM* data for voice or *ISDN* systems.

FECN   See *Forward Explicit Congestion Notification.*

Federal Internet Exchange (FIX)   An Internet interconnect site similar to a *NAP.*

FHSS   See *Frequency Hopping Spread Spectrum.*

Fiber Distributed Data Interface (FDDI)   An ANSI standard, X3T9.5, created in 1986 for interconnecting computer systems and network devices typically via a fiber ring topology at 100 Mbps.

Fiber-Optic Cable   A type of cable that carries data signals in the form of modulated light beams. The cable's conductor can be either glass or plastic. Fiber-optic cable is immune to electromagnetic interference (EMI) and other types of externally induced *noise*, including lightning; it is unaffected by most physical factors such as vibration; its size is smaller and its weight is lighter than copper; it has much lower attenuation per unit of length than copper; and it can support very high bandwidth. Two general types are available: *single-mode fiber* and *multimode fiber.*

Fibre Channel   A family of ANSI standards that defines a specific communications interface for high-speed data transfers between different hardware systems. Applications include the medical profession, where large images (e.g., 100-MB+ x-rays) are transferred from a scanner to a computer to a screen, and the electronic publishing industry, where large files are transferred from a designer/creator's machine to a publisher's computer. It has also become the backbone of high-speed data storage systems.

File Transfer Protocol (FTP)   An TCP/IP application protocol used for transferring files between two systems.

Firewall   A device or product that allows systems or network managers to restrict access to components on a network. Five generally accepted types of firewalls are used on Internet connections: *frame-filtering, packet-filtering, circuit gateways, stateful and application gateways,* and *proxy servers.*

FIX See *Federal Internet Exchange.*

Flow Control A process that controls the rate at which data messages are exchanged between two nodes. Flow control provides a mechanism to ensure that a sending node does not overwhelm a receiving node during data transmission.

FM See *Frequency Modulation.*

Forward Explicit Congestion Notification (FECN) A one-bit field in a *frame relay* frame that is set to 1 by a frame relay switch to denote that a frame transmitted toward the receiving node experienced congestion.

Fractional T1 *T1* service that is sold in 64-kbps increments.

FRAD See *Frame Relay Access Device.*

Fragmenting A process in which a *packet* is broken into smaller units to accommodate the maximum transmission unit a physical network is capable of supporting. Fragmented packets are sent to the destination separately and then reassembled at the destination node before they are passed to the higher levels. In *IP*, reassembly of a *datagram* occurs at the destination node and not at any of the intermediary nodes the packet traverses.

Frame A specially formatted sequence of bits that incorporates both data and control information.

Frame-Filtering Firewall A *firewall* device or product that filters (permits or denies access) at the *data link layer* by examining frames for both layout and content.

Frame Relay A public *WAN* packet-switching protocol that provides LAN-to-LAN connectivity. Its name implies what it does, namely, relays frames across a network between two sites. Frame relay was originally part of the *ISDN* standard.

Frame Relay Access Device (FRAD) Any *frame relay* end node.

Framing A *data link layer* process that partitions a bit stream into discrete units or blocks of data called *frames.*

Frequency The number of times an electromagnetic signal repeats itself (i.e., the identical signal is continuously generated) within a specific time period. A frequency rate of one cycle per second is defined as 1 *hertz* (Hz).

Frequency Division Multiplexing (FDM) A multiplexing technique that partitions the available transmission frequency range into narrower bands (subfrequencies), each of which is a separate channel. FDM-based transmissions are parallel in nature.

Frequency Hopping Spread Spectrum (FHSS) A physical layer technology used in wireless LANs (*IEEE 802.11*).

FHSS operates by transmitting short bursts of data on different frequencies. One burst is transmitted on one frequency, a second burst is transmitted on a second and different frequency, and so forth.

Frequency Modulation (FM) A *modulation* technique in which the *frequency* of an electromagnetic wave is altered so that the signal can carry more information.

Frequency-Shift Keying (FSK) Similar to *frequency modulation* except frequency-shift keying is the more appropriate term when used in the context of converting digital data (or signals) into analog signals at the sending end and then back to digital form at the receiving end. The frequency of a signal is altered so that it conforms to digital data (0s and 1s); one frequency is used to represent a binary 0 and a second frequency is used to represent a binary 1.

FSK See *Frequency-Shift Keying.*

FTP See *File Transfer Protocol.*

Full-Duplex Ethernet Ethernet/802.3 LANs that are switched-based and hence collision-free. In full-duplex Ethernet, both sending and receiving channels can operate simultaneously since the receiving channel does not have to listen for collisions.

Full-Duplex Transmission A data transmission method that involves the simultaneous sending and receiving of data in both directions.

GAN See *Global Area Network.*

Gateway A software application that converts between different application protocols. The host on which this software resides is called a *gateway machine.* Historically, this term also refers to a *router* in the *IP* community.

Geostationary Earth Orbit (GEO) Satellite A satellite placed into orbit at an altitude of 22,000 miles (36,000 km) above the equator. GEO satellites traverse their orbits at approximately the same rate as the earth rotates. Thus, the satellite appears stationary with respect to the earth's rotation. Also called *geosynchronous earth orbit.* Only eight GEO satellites are needed to provide global communications coverage.

Gigabit Ethernet 1000-Mbps Ethernet (*IEEE 802.3z*).

G.lite See *ADSL Lite.*

Global Area Network (GAN) A collection of *WANs* that spans the globe.

GOSIP See *Government OSI Profile.*

Government OSI Profile (GOSIP) A U.S. government directive that mandated all government organizations to purchase *OSI*-compliant networking products beginning in 1992. In 1995, however, GOSIP was modified to include *TCP/IP* as an acceptable protocol suite for GOSIP compliance.

Graded-Index Multimode Fiber A type of multimode fiber in which variations in the density of the core medium change its index of refraction such that light is refracted (i.e., bends) toward the center of the fiber.

H.323 An ITU standard for packet-based multimedia networking.

Half-Duplex Transmission A data transmission method in which data may travel in either direction—from sender to receiver or from receiver to sender—but only one unit can send at any one time. While one node is in send mode, the other is in receive mode.

Harmonic Motion The basic model for vibratory or oscillatory motion. Examples include mechanical oscillators such as mass–spring systems and pendulums; periodic motion found in the earth sciences such as water waves, tides, and climatic cycles; and electromagnetic waves such as alternating electric currents, sound waves, light waves, radio waves, and television waves.

H Channel An *ISDN* channel used for transmitting user data (not signal or control information) at higher transmission rates than a *B channel* provides. Four *H* channels are defined: *H0* (six *B* channels; 384 kbps); *H10* (United States specific; aggregates 23 *B* channels; 1.472 Mbps); *H11* (equivalent of North American DS-1; 24 *B* channels; 1.536 Mbps); and *H12* (European specific; comprises 30 *B* channels; 1.920 Mbps).

HDSL See *High bit-rate Digital Subscriber Line.*

HDSL 2 A modified *HDSL* designed and packaged for corporate clients.

Hertz A measure of frequency in cycles per second. A frequency rate of one cycle per second is defined as 1 hertz (Hz). Named in honor of Heinrich Rudolph Hertz (1857–1894), a German physicist who in the late 1880s was the first to produce radio waves artificially.

HFC See *Hybrid Fiber Cable.*

High bit-rate Digital Subscriber Line (HDSL) A *DSL* variant that provides symmetrical service at *T1* rates over two pairs of *UTP* and *E1* rates over three pairs of UTP. Telephone service is not supported. Applications include connecting PBXs and serving as an alternative to T1/E1. HDSL is suitable for campus networks and *ISPs.*

Hold-down A strategy used by *RIP* that requires routers not to update their routing tables with any new information they receive for a prescribed period of time, called the hold-down time. Designed to prevent routing loops. Hold-down is not standardized.

Hop The passage of a *packet* through an intermediate gateway (*router*) en route to another network. For example, if a packet transverses through two routers in reaching

its final destination, then we say the destination is two hops away.

Host A networked computer system (see *Workstation*). Also a computer system that provides service to users (see *Server*).

HTTP See *Hypertext Transfer Protocol.*

Hub Generically, any *device* that connects two or more network segments or supports several different media. Examples include repeaters, switches, and concentrators.

Hybrid Fiber Cable (HFC) A cable TV cable plant that has *fiber-optic cable* between the head end and neighborhood distribution sites, but coaxial cable between the neighborhood distribution and residential homes and businesses.

Hybrid Switching A data transmission method that combines the principles of circuit- and packet-switching. This technique first partitions a message into packets (*packet-switching*) and transmits each packet via a dedicated circuit (*circuit-switching*). As soon as a packet is ready for transmission, a circuit meeting appropriate bandwidth requirements is established between the sending and receiving nodes. When the packet reaches its destination, the circuit is broken down so that it can be used again.

Hypertext Transfer Protocol (HTTP) A TCP/IP application protocol on which the World Wide Web (WWW) is based. It is a request–response protocol in which an HTTP client program establishes a TCP connection to an HTTP server program and requests specific services from the server. Request messages are made through a *user agent* such as a Web browser, and response messages are provided by the server after it has received and interpreted the request message.

IAB See *Internet Architecture Board.*

IANA See *Internet Assigned Numbers Authority.*

IBM Cable System (ICS) A copper wire classification system established by IBM that specifies nine cable "types" (1 through 9). Of the nine types defined, specifications are available for only seven; types 4 and 7 have no specifications.

ICANN See *Internet Corporation for Assigned Names and Numbers.*

ICMP See *Internet Control Message Protocol.*

ICS See *IBM Cable System.*

IDSL See *ISDN-like Digital Subscriber Line.*

IEC See *Interexchange Carrier.*

IEEE See *Institute of Electrical and Electronics Engineers.*

IEEE 802 The primary *IEEE* standard for the 802.*x* series for *LANs* and *MANs.*

IEEE 802.1 *IEEE* standard that defines an architectural overview of *LANs*.

IEEE 802.2 *IEEE* standard that defines the logical link control, which describes services for the transmission of data between two nodes.

IEEE 802.3 *IEEE* standard that defines the *carrier sense multiple access/collision detection* (*CSMA/CD*) access method commonly referred to as *Ethernet*. Supplements include 802.3c (10-Mbps Ethernet), 802.3u (100-Mbps Ethernet, known as *Fast Ethernet*), and 802.3z and 802.3ab (1000-Mbps Ethernet, known as *Gigabit Ethernet*).

IEEE 802.4 *IEEE* standard that defines the token bus network access method.

IEEE 802.5 *IEEE* standard that defines the logical ring *LAN* that uses a token passing access method; known also as *token ring*.

IEEE 802.6 *IEEE* standard that defines metropolitan area networks (*MANs*).

IEEE 802.7 *IEEE* standard that defines broadband *LANs* (capable of delivering video, data, and voice traffic).

IEEE 802.9 *IEEE* standard that defines integrated digital and video networking—integrated services LANs (ISLANs).

IEEE 802.10 *IEEE* standard that defines standards for interoperable *LAN/MAN* security services.

IEEE 802.11 *IEEE* standard that defines standards for wireless media access control and physical layer specifications.

IEEE 802.12 *IEEE* standard that defines the "demand priority" access method for 100-Mbps LANs; known also as 100 Base-VG or *100VG-AnyLAN*.

IEEE 802.13 Defines nothing—*IEEE* was concerned about the superstitious overtones associated with 13.

IEEE 802.14 *IEEE* standard that defines a standard for cable TV-based broadband communication.

IETF See *Internet Engineering Task Force.*

IGP See *Interior Gateway Protocol.*

IGRP See *Interior Gateway Routing Protocol.*

ILEC See *Incumbent Local Exchange Carrier.*

Impedance A measure of the opposition to the flow of electric current in an alternating current circuit. Measured in ohms (abbreviated by the Greek symbol omega, Ω), impedance is a function of capacitance, resistance, and inductance. Impedance mismatches, caused by mixing cables of different types with different characteristic impedances, can result in signal distortion.

Impulse Noise Electrical *noise* that consists of intermittent, undesirable signals induced by external sources such as lightning, switching equipment, and heavy electrically oper-

ated machinery such as elevator motors and photocopy machines. Impulse noise increases or decreases a circuit's signal level, which causes the receiving equipment to misinterpret the signal.

Incumbent Local Exchange Carrier (ILEC) The contemporary name given to the seven *RBOCs* and GTE relative to the United States Telecommunications Act of 1996. With mergers, only three will remain: BellSouth, SBC, and Bell Atlantic (now Verizon).

Infrared (IR) A line-of-sight transmission method that uses electromagnetic radiation of wavelengths between radio waves and visible light, operating between 100 GHz and 100 THz (terahertz). IR transmission can occur in one of two ways: *directed* and *diffused.*

Institute of Electrical and Electronics Engineers (IEEE) A professional society of engineers, scientists, and students. One of its many activities is to act as a coordinating body for computing and communication standards.

Insulation Material surrounding the *conductor* of a wire. The insulation serves as a protective "barrier" to the conductor by preventing the signal from "escaping" and preventing electrical interference from "entering."

Integrated Services Digital Network (ISDN) A carrier service that is offered by telephone companies (telcos) and designed to transmit voice and nonvoice (e.g., computer data, fax, video) communications on the same network. In response to its long period of dormancy, ISDN is also known as I Still Don't Need it, Innovative Services users Don't Need, I Still Don't kNow, and It's Still Doing Nothing.

Interexchange Carrier (IEC) Any company that provides long-distance telephone and telecommunications services. Examples include AT&T, Sprint, British Telecom (BT), and MCI WorldCom.

Interior Gateway Protocol (IGP) Any intradomain Internet protocol used to exchange routing information within an *autonomous system.* Examples include *RIP, RIP-2, OSPF, IGRP,* and *Enhanced IGRP (EIGRP).*

Interior Gateway Routing Protocol (IGRP) A routing protocol developed by Cisco to address some of the problems associated with routing in large heterogeneous networks.

Intermediate System to Intermediate System (IS-IS) An intradomain routing protocol designed by *OSI* to run within an *AS* (called a "routing domain" in the OSI world). IS-IS uses a *link-state routing algorithm* to calculate least-cost paths and is similar in operation to *OSPF.* The formal title of this protocol is Intermediate System to Intermediate System Intra-Domain Routing Exchange Protocol.

Intermodulation Noise Electrical noise that occurs when two frequencies interact to produce a phantom signal at a different frequency. Occurs in *frequency-division multiplexed* channels.

International Organization for Standardization (ISO) An international organization that develops and promotes networking standards worldwide.

International Telecommunications Union (ITU) A global standards organization. ITU is the former *CCITT*.

Internet When used as a noun and spelled with a lowercase *i*, "internet" is an abbreviation for *internetwork,* which refers to a collection of interconnected networks that functions as a single network. When used as a proper noun and spelled with an uppercase *I*, "Internet" refers to the world's largest internetwork, which consists of hundreds of thousands of interconnected networks worldwide and based on a specific set of network standards (*TCP/IP*).

Internet Architecture Board (IAB) An organization that is part of the *Internet Society* responsible for the overall planning and designing of the Internet. Responsibilities include setting Internet standards, managing the publication of RFC documents, and resolving technical issues. Assigned to the IAB are the *Internet Engineering Task Force* and the *Internet Research Task Force.* Formerly known as the Internet Activities Board.

Internet Assigned Numbers Authority (IANA) An organization that had authority over all number spaces used in the Internet including *IP addresses.* IANA control was transferred to the *Internet Corporation for Assigned Names and Numbers (ICANN).*

Internet Control Message Protocol (ICMP) An *IP datagram* that carries messages about the communications environment of the *Internet.*

Internet Corporation for Assigned Names and Numbers (ICANN) A private, nonprofit corporation with international representation expressly formed to assume the responsibilities originally performed by *IANA* and other government organizations that provide domain name service.

Internet Engineering Task Force (IETF) An organization that is part of the *Internet Architecture Board* and primarily concerned with addressing short- or medium-term Internet engineering issues. Relies on the Internet Engineering Steering Group (IESG) to prioritize and coordinate activities.

Internet Protocol (IP) A layer-3 connectionless protocol. IP receives data bits from the lower layer, assembles these bits into packets, called IP *datagrams,* and selects the "best" route based on some metric to route the packets between nodes. This is the IP of *TCP/IP.*

Internet Registry (IR) A formal hierarchical system used for assigning *IP addresses.* From top to bottom, this hierarchy consists of *IANA,* regional Internet registries (RIRs), and local Internet registries (LIRs), and it works as follows: IANA allocates blocks of IP address space to RIRs; RIRs allocate blocks of IP address space to their LIRs; LIRs then assign addresses to either end users or ISPs.

Internet Research Task Force (IRTF) An organization that is part of the *Internet Architecture Board* and primarily concerned with addressing long-term research projects. Relies on the Internet Research Steering Group (IRSG) to prioritize and coordinate activities.

Internet Service Provider (ISP) A company that provides its customers with access to the Internet.

Internet Society (ISOC) An international organization comprised of volunteers who promote the Internet as a medium for global communication and collaboration. ISOC is considered the ultimate authoritative organization of the Internet.

Internet2 A collaborative project of the University Corporation for Advanced Internet Development (UCAID), which comprises over 100 U.S. universities, government organizations, and private sector firms. Internet2's mission is to develop advanced Internet technologies and applications that support the research endeavors of colleges and universities. Internet2 members use the *vBNS+* to test and advance their research.

Internetwork A collection of interconnected networks that function as a single network. The individual networks comprising an internetwork are called *subnetworks.*

Interoperability The degree in which products (software and hardware) developed by different vendors are able to communicate successfully (i.e., interoperate) with each other over a network.

Intranet An internal network implementation of traditional Internet applications within a company or an institution.

Inverse Multiplexing The reverse of *multiplexing.* Instead of partitioning a single communication medium into several channels, an inverse *multiplexer* combines several "smaller" channels (i.e., low-speed circuits) into a single high-speed circuit. This technique is also sometimes generically called *line aggregation.*

IP See *Internet Protocol.*

IP Address A network address assigned to a node's network interface and used to uniquely identify (locate) the node within the Internet. Two versions are currently implemented: *IPv4* and *IPv6.*

IPSec See *IP Security.*

IP Security (IPSec) A suite of network security protocols that operates at layer 3 and provides address authentication, data encryption, and automated key exchanges between sender and receiver nodes.

IPv4 An acronym for *Internet protocol version 4.*

IPv4 Address An *IP address* based on *IPv4.* These addresses consist of 32 bits (0 through 31) partitioned into four groups of eight bits each (called *octets*) and organized into five classes (A through E) based on the values of bits 0 through 3.

IPv6 An acronym for *Internet protocol version 6,* which is an evolutionary replacement to IPv4. IPv6 maintains most IPv4 functions, relegates certain functions that either were not working or were rarely used in IPv4 as optional, and adds new functionality that is missing from IPv4. Sometimes called IPng (for next generation).

IPv6 Address An *IP address* based on *IPv6.* An IPv6 address consists of 128 bits and is 4 billion $\times$ 4 billion times the size of the IPv4 address space (2^{128} vs. 2^{32}). Unlike IPv4 addresses, IPv6 addresses use a colon as their delimiter (instead of a "dot" notation), and they are written as eight 16-bit integers expressed in hexadecimal form.

IR See *Infrared* or *Internet Registry.*

IRTF See *Internet Research Task Force.*

ISDN See *Integrated Services Digital Network.*

ISDN-like Digital Subscriber Line (IDSL) A *DSL* variant that provides symmetrical service at a maximum of 144 kbps each way. Uses *ISDN* hardware.

IS-IS See *Intermediate System to Intermediate System.*

ISO See *International Organization for Standardization.*

ISOC See *Internet Society.*

Isochronous Communications The delivery of time-sensitive data such as voice or video transmissions. Networks that are capable of delivering isochronous service (e.g., *ATM*) preallocate a specific amount of bandwidth over regular intervals to ensure that the transmission is not interrupted.

IsoEthernet Short for *Isochronous Ethernet,* an IEEE standard (*IEEE 802.9a*) that is designed to support time-sensitive applications such as videoconferencing and telephony. IsoEthernet runs both conventional 10-Mbps *Ethernet* and *ISDN B channels* over the same network. The Ethernet channel is used for normal data networking needs; the ISDN *B* channels are used for time-sensitive applications.

ISP See *Internet Service Provider.*

ITU See *International Telecommunications Union.*

IXC See *Interexchange Carrier.*

Jabber An *oversized* Ethernet/802.3 *frame* and an invalid *CRC checksum.*

Jitter An irregular variation in the timing between a sender's and receiver's respective clocks or an irregular variation in the shape of a signal. In phase jitter, a signal will be out of phase, and in amplitude jitter, a signal's amplitude will vary over time.

Jumbo Frame A proprietary-based Ethernet frame that extends Ethernet's 1500-byte data field to 9000 bytes. Jumbo frame technology enables data transfer rates to approach gigabit speeds on an Gigabit Ethernet LAN, which is currently limited in performance due to the relatively small data field. For example, a 900,000-byte message requires 600 frames that support a 1500-byte data field, but only 100 jumbo frames. Thus, the amount of processing overhead for Gigabit Ethernet is six times more than the jumbo frame Gigabit Ethernet's overhead for the same message.

Kerberos A client server network security authentication system, developed at MIT and based on *DES* encryption. It is an *Internet* standard that uses a three-pronged approach for authentication: a database that contains users' rights, an authentication server, and a ticket-granting server. Kerberos is named after Cerberus, the three-headed dog in Greek mythology that guarded the gates to Hades.

LAN See *Local Area Network.*

LANE See *LAN Emulation.*

LAN Emulation (LANE) An *ATM* protocol that specifies a technology that enables ATM to emulate Ethernet/802.3 or *token ring* networks. In ATM's protocol hierarchy, LANE is above *AAL5* in the *ATM adaptation layer.* The LANE protocol defines a service interface for the *network layer* that functions identically to the one used by Ethernet/802.3 and token ring LANs. Data that cross this interface are encapsulated in the appropriate *MAC sublayer* format.

LAP-D See *Link Access Protocol-D Channel.*

LAPM See *Link Access Procedure for Modems.*

LATA See *Local Access and Transport Area.*

Latency The amount of delay a network device introduces when data frames pass through it. It is the amount of time a frame spends "inside" a network device. For example, switch latency is usually measured from the instant the first bit of a frame enters the device to the time this bit leaves the outbound (i.e., destination) port.

Layer 2 Forward (L2F) A protocol that provides tunneling between an *ISP's* dialup server and the network.

Layer 2 Tunneling Protocol (L2TP) A method for tunneling PPP sessions across a network. It combines *PPTP* and *L2F.*

Layer-3 Switch A layer-2 switch that is capable of examining layer-3 header information, which is then used to filter network protocols or broadcasts. Also a router that is capable of performing router table lookups and packet forwarding at hardware speeds via application-specific integrated circuit (ASIC) chips.

Layer-4 Switch A *router* that is capable of examining upper layer (layer-4 through layer-7) information to make routing decisions. It is more appropriate to refer to layer-4 switches as either layer-2 or layer-3 application switches because application information from upper layers is being used for routing decisions.

LEC See *Local Exchange Carrier.*

Lightwave Wireless A line-of-sight laser-based connection facility that allows long-distance light-based wireless networking without the need to install cable.

Line-of-Sight A type of wireless transmission that requires the transmitter and receiver to be able to "see" each other; that is, they must be in each other's "line-of-sight."

Line Set Used by the National ISDN Users' Forum to describe the number of multiplexed *B* and *D* channels and the type of *ISDN* service supported.

Link Access Protocol-D Channel (LAP-D) An *ITU* standard on which the *ISDN D* channel is based.

Link Access Procedure for Modems (LAPM) A *modem* protocol that uses *CRC* and ARQ for *error control.* CRC is used for *error detection;* ARQ prevents the modem from accepting any more data until the defective frame has been retransmitted successfully. *V.42's* default is LAPM. Thus, if a connection is being initialized between two V.42-compliant modems, they will use LAPM for error control. If one of the modems is not V.42-compliant, then the modems will negotiate to use *MNP 1–4.*

Link-State Algorithm A routing algorithm in which routers send each other information about the links they have established to other routers via a link-state advertisement (LSA), which contains the names and various cost metrics of a router's neighbors. LSAs are flooded throughout an entire router's domain. Thus, rather than storing actual paths (which is the case with *distance-vector algorithms*), link-state algorithms store the information needed to generate such paths. An example of a link-state algorithm is Dijkstra's shortest path algorithm, which iterates on length of a path to determine the shortest route.

Lobe A *token ring* node, as defined in the IBM world.

Lobe Length The cable length between *token ring* nodes.

Local Access and Transport Area (LATA) A specific geographical region in which a *LEC* provides local telephone and telecommunications services in the United States. There are 195 LATAs. Services that cross LATA boundaries are provided by *IECs.*

Local Area Network (LAN) A network that interconnects computing resources within a moderately sized geographical area. This can include a room, several rooms within a building, or several buildings on a campus. A LAN's range usually is no more than 10 km in radius.

Local Exchange Carrier (LEC) A telecommunications provider that provides service within a prescribed geographical area. See also *CLEC* and *ILEC.*

Local Loop The circuit that connects the telephone central office or exchange (sometimes called *POP*) with a customer's location. In frame relay, this circuit is called the *port connection* or *access line.* Formally called *digital subscriber loop.*

Logical Link Control (LLC) Sublayer The top sublayer of the data link layer that provides framing, flow control, and error control. Defined in *IEEE 802.2.*

Loop A network configuration in which nodes are connected via dedicated wiring instead of through a centralized hub (as is the case of a *star* design). Loops can be either *simple* (only one connection between any two nodes), *partial* (some nodes are interconnected by more than one link), or *complete* (every node has a connection to every other node). A loop is also referred to as a *meshed* design.

Low-Earth Orbit (LEO) Satellite A satellite placed in orbit at an altitude of 300 to 1200 miles above the earth. Depending on their orbit, a constellation of up to 48 LEO satellites is needed for global coverage.

L2F See *Layer 2 Forward.*

L2TP See *Layer 2 Tunneling Protocol.*

MAC See *Medium Access Control Sublayer.*

Manchester Encoding A data transmission encoding scheme that differs from standard digital transmission schemes. Instead of "high" equaling 1 and "low" equaling 0, a timing interval is used to measure high-to-low transitions. Furthermore, instead of a timed transmission period being "all high" or "all low" for either 1 or 0, a 1 is sent as a half-time-period low followed by a half-time-period high, and a 0 is sent as a half-time-period high followed by a half-time-period low. Consequently, the end of the last bit transmitted is easily determined immediately following the transmission of the last bit.

MAE See *Metropolitan Area Exchange.*

MAN See *Metropolitan Area Network.*

MAU See *Media Attachment Unit* or *Multistation Access Unit.*

Media The plural of *medium.*

Media Access Control (MAC) Sublayer The bottom half of the *data link layer* that provides media access management protocols for accessing a shared medium. Example *MAC sublayer* protocols include IEEE 802.3 (*Ethernet*) and IEEE 802.5 (*token ring*).

Media Attachment Unit (MAU)   Another term for a *transceiver.*

Media Converter   A layer-1 device that enables different network media to be connected to one another.

Medium   The physical environment used to connect networked devices. See also *Media.*

Medium-Earth Orbit (MEO) Satellite   A satellite placed in orbit at an altitude of 6000 to 12,000 miles above the earth. A constellation of 20 MEO satellites is needed for global coverage.

Meshed Design   The interconnectivity among multiple nodes or sites. In a fully meshed design, every node or site is connected with every other node or site. In a partially meshed design, only some nodes or sites are interconnected.

Metric   A generic term used in *routing* to represent different quantities such as distance, number of router *hops,* and *bandwidth.*

Metro-Area Satellites   A specially equipped jet that flies 50,000 feet above cities to provide wireless, broadband networking service.

Metropolitan Area Exchange (MAE)   An *Internet* interconnect site similar to a *NAP.* A NAP is funded by the National Science Foundation; a MAE is not. There are currently two MAE points, one each on the east and west coasts of the United States and known as MAE East and MAE West.

Metropolitan Area Network (MAN)   A network that interconnects computing resources that span a metropolitan area such as buildings located throughout a local county or city. MANs generally refer to networks that span a larger geographical area than *LANs* but a smaller geographical area than *WANs.*

Microcom Networking Protocol (MNP)   Defines various levels of *error correction* and compression for *modems.*

Micron   One micrometer (one-millionth of a meter) and abbreviated by the symbol μm. Used in specifying the size of fiber-optic cable.

Microwave   An *RF* transmission method that uses high-frequency waves and operates at a higher frequency in the electromagnetic spectrum (usually above 900 MHz). Microwave transmissions are considered a *line-of-sight* medium.

MIME   See *Multipurpose Internet Mail Extensions.*

MNP   See *Microcom Networking Protocol.*

MNP 1–4   The first four *MNP* levels used for hardware error control. All four levels are incorporated into *V.42.*

MNP 5   The fifth level of *MNP* that incorporates the *MNP 1–4.* Also uses a data compression algorithm that compresses data by a factor of 2 to 1.

MNP 6   The sixth level of *MNP* that supports V.22 *bis* and V.29.

MNP 7   The seventh level of *MNP* that improves *MNP 5's* data compression algorithm to a 3 to 1 compression factor.

MNP 8   The eighth level of *MNP* that extends *MNP 7;* enables half-duplex devices to operate in full-duplex mode.

MNP 9   The ninth level of *MNP* that is used in a variety of circuits.

MNP 10   The tenth level of *MNP* that is used in cellular modems and in situations where line quality is poor.

Modem   An acronym for *modulator/demodulator.* A modem transforms (modulates) a computer's digital signal into analog form at the sending side so the signal can be carried across a standard telephone line. On the receiving side, a modem demodulates the signal—it reconverts the transmitted analog signal from the phone line to digital form before it is passed to the computer.

Modulation   A method in which a characteristic of an electromagnetic wave is altered. Types of modulation include *amplitude modulation, frequency modulation, phase modulation,* and *pulse-code modulation.*

Molecular Electronics   The concept in which the current development of switches, transistors, and logic gates can be designed from individual molecules.

Moving Picture Experts Group (MPEG)   A series of compression standards used for compressing multimedia data.

MPEG   See *Moving Picture Experts Group.*

Multicast   A data transmission that is destined to a group of recipients.

Multidrop Design   A network configuration in which each system node is connected to a common cable plant and assigned a specific number that is used to communicate with the system and also to establish priority of when a system will be communicated with from a master control system. Primarily used in factories.

Multilink PPP (MP)   An *IP* protocol that combines multiple physical links (i.e., telephone lines) into a single high-capacity channel. Unlike *BONDING,* which is implemented in hardware, MP is achieved via software. MP is also applicable to analog dialup connections.

Multimode Fiber   A type of fiber-optic cable with a core diameter ranging from 50 to 100 μm. In multimode fiber, different rays of light bounce along the fiber at different angles as they travel through the core. This results in some degree of signal distortion at the receiving end. Multimode fiber can be of two types: *graded-index* or *step-index.*

Multiplexer A device that does *multiplexing.* Also called a *mux* for short.

Multiplexing A technique used to place multiple signals on a single communications channel. Multiplexing partitions a channel into many separate channels, each capable of transmitting its own independent signal, thereby enabling many different transmissions over a single medium.

Multipurpose Internet Mail Extensions (MIME) An extension to the *Simple Mail Transport Protocol (SMTP)* that extends the concept of e-mail by providing support for different data types and for complex message bodies. MIME enables users to exchange nontext files such as graphics, video, or audio in addition to plaintext files.

Multistation Access Unit (MAU) A token ring hub.

Mux Abbreviation for *multiplexer.*

NADH See *North American Digital Hierarchy.*

NAP See *Network Access Point.*

National Information Infrastructure (NII) A federal policy initiative to facilitate and accelerate the development and utilization of the nation's information infrastructure. The perception of the NII is one of a "seamless web" of telecommunications networks consisting of computers, specialized databases, radios, telephones, televisions, and satellites. The NII is expected to provide consumers with convenient and instantaneous access to nearly any kind of information ranging from research results to medical and educational material to entertainment.

NC See *Network Computer.*

Near-End Crosstalk (NEXT) See *Crosstalk.*

netstat A UNIX program that generates a local host's routing table. Similar output can be generated on a Windows NT system using the command *route print.*

Network Access Point (NAP) An *Internet* traffic exchange point that provides centralized Internet access to Internet service providers. A NAP serves as a critical regional "switching station" where all different network backbone providers meet and exchange traffic on each other's backbone.

Network Appliance Any one of several powerful computing devices designed to support a single dedicated application such as Web browsing or e-mail. In some cases, network appliances do not have keyboards or monitors.

Network Architecture A formal, logical structure that defines how network devices and software interact and

function; defines communication protocols, message formats, and standards required for interoperability.

Network Computer (NC) An inexpensive ($500 or less) network access device with functionality that allows some applications to be run, but not as complete as what would typically be found on a PC or a workstation of some sort. NCs are stripped-down systems that use the network to access their applications dynamically.

Network Convergence The integration of different network technologies and applications, which when combined, create powerful new entities and products. One example of network convergence is IP telephony, which integrates voice and data onto an IP network. Network convergence, however, involves more than simply combining voice and data.

Network Diameter The overall length between a network's two remotest nodes.

Network Ethics Specific standards of moral conduct by network users for the responsible use of network devices and resources.

Network Interface Card (NIC) A layer-2 device that performs standard *data link layer* functions, including organizing data into frames, transferring frames between the ends of a communication channel, and managing the link by providing error control, initialization, control termination, and flow control. A NIC is also known as a *LAN* adapter, network adapter, network card, and network board. When used in Ethernet/802.3 networks, a NIC is called an Ethernet card or adapter.

Network Operating System (NOS) Software that is installed on a system to make it network capable. Examples include IBM's LAN Server, Banyan's VINES, and Novell's NetWare (also known as IntranetWare). A NOS is independent of a computer's native operating system—it is loaded "on top" of the computer's operating system and provides the computer with networking capability based on a particular protocol. If an operating system provides built-in network support (e.g., Microsoft's Windows NT and Sun's Solaris), then the OS is called a *networkable* operating system.

Network Protocol A formal specification that defines the vocabulary and rules of data communication. See also *Protocol.*

Network Protocol Suite A set of related and interoperating network protocols. An example is the *TCP/IP* protocol suite, which consists of protocols for e-mail, Web service, file transfers, and routing.

Network Security The proper safeguarding of everything associated with a network, including data, media, and equipment. It involves administrative functions, such as *threat assessment,* technical tools and facilities such as cryptographic products, and network access control products such as *firewalls*. It also involves making certain that network resources are used in accordance with a prescribed policy and only by people who are authorized to use these resources.

Network Service Access Point (NSAP) An *OSI* addressing mechanism used by private *ATM* networks. NSAPs are 20-byte addresses and include a 13-byte prefix that can be used to identify a specific location, including a country, region, or end system.

Network Standards A formal set of rules, developed by and agreed upon by various organizations, defining hardware interfaces, communication protocols, and network architectures. Several standards exist, including *de jure, de facto, proprietary,* and *consortia.*

Network Termination Unit (NTU) A device that terminates *E-1* circuits. An NTU provides broadly similar *CSU/DSU* functionality.

Network Topology The basic design of a computer network that details how key network components such as nodes and links are interconnected.

NEXT See *Crosstalk.*

Next Generation Internet (NGI) An initiative to forge collaborative partnerships between the private and public sectors. The *vBNS+* serves as the medium for NGI. Funding ($100 million for 3 years) has not been approved as of this writing.

NGI See *Next Generation Internet.*

NIC See *Network Interface Card.*

NII See *National Information Infrastructure.*

Node Another name for a *device.* Usually used to identify computers that are network hosts, workstations, or servers.

Noise Any undesirable, extraneous signal in a transmission medium. There are generally two forms of noise— *ambient* and *impulse.* Noise degrades the quality and performance of a communications channel and is one of the most common causes of transmission errors in computer networks.

Nonpersistent CSMA A *CSMA*-based protocol in which a node continually waits a random period of time whenever it detects a busy channel. Once it senses an idle channel, it may then transmit data.

Nonreturn to Zero, Invert on Ones (NRZI) An encoding technique used for converting digital data into digital signals. In NRZI, encoding is based on transitions from one voltage state to another (i.e., from a low-to-high state or from a high-to-low state). Specifically, data are coded 0 if no transitions occur and 1 at the beginning of a transition.

North American Digital Hierarchy (NADH) A multiplexed *T1* structure used in North America that combines multiple T1 lines into higher-rated T-carrier circuits. For example, a *T2* circuit consists of four multiplexed T1 circuits and has an aggregate bandwidth of 6.312 Mbps; a *T3* link consists of 28 multiplexed T1 circuits with an aggregate bandwidth of 44.736 Mbps; and a *T4* channel consists of 168 multiplexed T1 circuits and is rated at 274.176 Mbps.

NOS See *Network Operating System.*

NRZI See *Nonreturn to Zero, Invert on Ones.*

NSAP See *Network Service Access Point.*

nslookup A UNIX and Microsoft NT program used to acquire the *IP address* of a *domain name.* This program can also be used for IP address resolution, which translates a numerical IP address to its corresponding domain name.

NTU See *Network Termination Unit.*

Nyquist's Theorem A sampling theorem that states that the maximum signaling rate of a noiseless channel is twice the number of samples. Thus, if we have w cycles per second (i.e., hertz), then we can have $2w$ signal states. Generalizing this concept, if a noiseless communications channel uses N values per signaling state, then the channel's maximum data transmission capacity in bits per second is given as $2w\text{Log}_2N$, where w = the number of cycles expressed in hertz and N = the number of discrete signaling states used.

1-persistent CSMA A CSMA-based protocol in which a node continuously monitors a shared channel until it is idle and then seizes the channel and begins transmitting data. The "one" in 1-persistent represents the probability that a single waiting node will be able to transmit data once it detects an idle channel ($p = 1$).

OC See *Optical Carrier.*

Open Shortest Path First (OSPF) An *interior gateway protocol* based on a *link-state algorithm.* Designed for large heterogeneous *IP* networks.

Optical Carrier (OC) A *fiber-optic* digital transmission hierarchy used for *SONET.* OC rates range from OC-1, which is the equivalent of 28 DS-1 channels (51.84 Mbps), to OC-192, which is the equivalent of 5376 DS-1 channels (9.953 Gbps). OC rates are the optical equivalent of *STS* rates.

OSI An acronym for open systems interconnection. See *OSI Model.*

OSI Model A network architecture for developing network protocol standards. The OSI model formally defines and codifies the concept of *layered* network architecture. It uses well-defined operationally descriptive layers that describe what happens at each stage in the processing of data for transmission. The OSI model consists of the following seven layers, which are numbered in descending order: application (7), presentation (6), session (5), transport (4), network (3), data link (2), and physical (1).

OSPF See *Open Shortest Path First.*

Oversized Frame An Ethernet/802.3 frame with more than 1518 bytes but a valid *CRC checksum.*

Oversubscription In *frame relay,* when the capacity of a frame relay connection into the frame relay network is less than the total bandwidth guaranteed by the provider. More specifically, the *port speed* is less than the aggregate *CIR.*

Packet The smallest unit of information that is transferred across a packet-switched network. In *TCP/IP,* a packet is called a *datagram.*

Packet-Filtering Firewall A *router* or a dedicated device that filters network access at the network layer by examining packet addresses (source and destination).

Packet-Switched Network A network design that enables nodes to share a communications channel via a *virtual circuit.* Messages are partitioned into smaller messages called *packets,* which may contain only a few hundred bytes of data, accompanied by addressing information. Packets are sent to the destination node one at a time, at any time, and not necessarily in a specific order. The network hardware delivers the packets through the virtual circuit to the specified destination node, which is responsible for reassembling them in the correct order.

Packet-Switching A switching technique in which messages are partitioned into smaller units called packets, which contain addressing information as well as sequence numbers. Packets are then sent to the destination node one at a time, at any time, and not necessarily in a specific order. Furthermore, the channel used to transmit a packet is occupied only for the duration of the packet's transmission. Two general packet-switching strategies are virtual circuit packet-switching and datagram packet-switching. In *virtual circuit packet-switching,* a nondedicated, shared path is established between sending and receiving nodes; all packets traverse this path in sequence via a store-and-forward transmission in which complete packets are first stored on an intermediate node and then forwarded to a successive node along the path en route to the destination. In *datagram packet-switching,* packets are transmitted independently of each other and not necessarily along the same path. Thus, packets can arrive out of sequence.

PAN See *Personal Area Network.*

PAR See *Positive Acknowledgment with Retransmission.*

Parallel Communication A data transmission method in which the bits representing a character of data are transmitted simultaneously on separate channels. Also called *parallel transmission.*

Parity The use of an extra bit (called a *parity bit* or a *redundancy bit*) to detect single-bit errors in data transmissions. Parity can be specified as even, odd, or none. Even parity means that there must be an even number of 1-bits in each bit string; odd parity means that there must be an odd number of 1-bits in each bit string; and no parity means that parity is ignored. The extra bit (i.e., the parity bit) is forced to either 0 or 1 to make the total number of bits even or odd.

Partitioning A network configuration strategy that involves dividing a LAN into several separate (but still interconnected) network segments. Also called *segmentation.*

PBX See *Private Branch Exchange.*

PC Card A layer-2 plug-in adapter used in portable or laptop computers. Three different "types" are available. Type 1 cards are 3.3 millimeters thick and enhance the memory capabilities of a device; Type II cards are 5 mm thick and are used for modems and network adapters for both Ethernet and token ring; Type III cards are 10.5 mm thick and are generally either miniature hard disks or wireless *NICs;* and Type IV cards, when produced, will be approximately 16 mm thick and support hard disk drives that have a capacity greater than what is currently available from Type III cards. PC cards were formerly known as *PCMCIA cards.*

PCM See *Pulse-Code Modulation.*

PCMCIA Card A layer-2 device that was originally designed to serve as memory cards for microcomputers. These cards are now known as *PC cards.* PCMCIA stands for Personal Computer Memory Card International Association.

Peer-to-Peer A model or paradigm on which some network communications and applications are based. In a peer-to-peer environment, each networked host runs both the client and server parts of an application.

Period The reciprocal of *frequency.* It is the amount of time it takes to complete a single cycle, that is, seconds per cycle.

Permanent Virtual Circuit (PVC) A communications channel that provides a logical connection between two sites instead of a physical one. In a *connection-oriented* protocol such as *frame relay,* PVCs appear as *private links* because a circuit must be established between end nodes prior to data communications. The difference is

PVCs are virtual circuits, not dedicated ones, and hence bandwidth is shared among multiple sites by *multiplexing* techniques. Thus, PVCs provide nondedicated connections through a shared medium, which enables data from multiple sites to be transmitted over the same link concurrently.

Personal Area Network (PAN) A home-based computer network.

PGP See *Pretty Good Privacy.*

Phase A characteristic of a sine wave that specifies the point a wave has advanced within its cycle. From a mathematical perspective, phase is generally expressed in degrees or radians. For example, a 90° (or $\pi/2$ radians) phase shift means that one-fourth of the wave has been shifted, which indicates that it has advanced one-fourth of the period.

Phase Modulation (PM) A *modulation* technique in which the phase angle, which is the phase difference between two signals, is manipulated in some manner. This manipulation effectively delays the natural flow of the waveform temporarily.

Phase-Shift Keying (PSK) Similar to *phase modulation* except phase-shift keying is the more appropriate term when used in the context of converting digital data (or signals) into analog signals at the sending end and then back to digital form at the receiving end. PSK modifies the phase angle of the carrier wave based on the digital data being transmitted. The changes in phase angle are what convey the data in a phase modulated signal. In its simplest implementation, one phase represents a binary 0 and a second phase represents a binary 1.

Physical Layer The lowest layer (layer 1) of the *OSI model*. The *physical layer* translates *frames* received from the *data link layer* (layer 2) into electrical, optical, or electromagnetic signals representing 0 and 1 values, or bits. Abbreviated PHY in the documentation.

ping A UNIX and Microsoft NT program used to test the communication path between source and destination nodes. ping is an *ICMP*-based application and is an acronym for "packet Internet groper."

Pinout The electrical signals associated with each pin and connector. Also called pin assignment.

PKI See *Public Key Infrastructure.*

Plain Old Telephone System (POTS) The conventional telephone network. See also *Public Switched Telephone Network.*

Plaintext An uncoded message; a message in its original, meaningful (uncoded) form.

Plastic Fiber A type of fiber-optic cable in which the fibers (i.e., conductors) are constructed of plastic instead of glass.

Plenum Cable Any type of cable that contains an outer sheath or "jacket" that is composed of a Teflon coating. Plenum cable is used for cable "runs" through a return air system. In case the cable burns during a fire, both PVC and Teflon give off nasty toxic gases when burning. Teflon, however, is fire retardant and takes much longer to get to a burning point.

PM See *Phase Modulation.*

Point of Presence (POP) A telco's central office or switching station.

Point-to-Point Network A network design in which only adjacent nodes (nodes that are next to each other and only one hop away) can communicate with one another.

Point-to-Point Tunneling Protocol (PPTP) A protocol that provides encryption and authentication for remote dialup and LAN-to-LAN connections. PPTP establishes two types of connections: a control session for establishing and maintaining a secure tunnel from sender to receiver and a data session for the actual data transmission.

POP See *Point of Presence* or *Post Office Protocol.*

Port Connection The *local loop* in *frame relay.* Also called *access line.*

Port Speed In *frame relay,* the data transmission rate in bits per second of the *local loop.*

Positive Acknowledgment with Retransmission (PAR) An error-control strategy used in TCP in which a receiver acknowledges all successfully transmitted frames. If the sender does not receive a positive acknowledgment from the receiver within a certain time frame, then it will assume the data segment did not arrive, or it arrived damaged, and retransmit the data.

Post Office Protocol (POP) A TCP/IP application protocol used for transferring e-mail from a server to a desktop PC client.

POTS See *Plain Old Telephone System.*

PPTP See *Point-to-Point Tunneling Protocol.*

Pretty Good Privacy (PGP) A *public key* application developed by Phil Zimmerman for e-mail security.

PRI See *Primary Rate Interface.*

Primary Rate Interface (PRI) An *ISDN* primary access channel that comprises either 23 (United States) or 30 (Europe) 64-Mbps *B* channels and two 64-kbps *D* channel. Commonly written as $23B + D$, or $30B + 2D$.

Private Branch Exchange (PBX) A telephone exchange used within an organization to provide internal telephone extensions and access to the public telephone network; it is the modern-day equivalent of what used to be called a switchboard.

Private Link A communications channel that provides a private, dedicated link between two sites. Also commonly referred to as standard leased line.

Private Switch One application of an Ethernet switch. A private switch supports only one *MAC* address per port, which provides each node with its own dedicated 10-Mbps segment. This eliminates contention for the cable, thereby liberating the end nodes from performing collision detection.

Probabilistic Network An artificial intelligence-network convergence strategy in which numbers are assigned to degrees of uncertainty about each bit of data or possible outcome so that a device can construct rules about how it can manipulate the numbers.

Promiscuous Mode A state in which an Ethernet interface can be placed so that it can capture every frame that is transmitted on the network. For example, an *Ethernet NIC* set in promiscuous mode collects all messages placed on the medium regardless of their destination address.

Propagation Delay The amount of time a signal takes getting from one point in a circuit to another.

Proprietary Standards Network standards that are developed in a manufacturer-specific manner. Their specifications are not in the public domain and are only used and accepted by a specific vendor.

Protocol An accepted or established set of procedures, rules, or formal specifications governing specific behavior or language. When applied to networks, a *network protocol* is a formal specification that defines the vocabulary and rules of data communication.

Proxy Server A device or product that provides network protection at the application level by using custom programs for each protected application. These custom-written application programs act as both a client and server and effectively serve as proxies to the actual applications. Also called application gateway firewall or proxy gateway.

PSK See *Phase-Shift Keying*.

PSTN See *Public Switched Telephone Network*.

Public Key A special code, available in the public domain, that can be used to code and decode messages.

Public Key Infrastructure (PKI) A network security infrastructure that involves the process of issuing, delivering (i.e., publishing), managing, and revoking public keys to effect secure transmissions across a public network such as the Internet.

Public Switched Telephone Network (PSTN) The traditional analog-based telephone system used in the United States that was originally designed for voice transmissions.

Pulse-Code Modulation (PCM) A coding technique used to convert analog signals to digital signals, and vice versa.

PVC See *Permanent Virtual Circuit*. Also an abbreviation for polyvinyl chloride.

PVC Cable Any type of cable that contains an outer sheath or "jacket" that is composed of polyvinyl chloride (PVC). Also called *nonplenum cable*.

QoS See *Quality of Service*.

Quadrature Amplitude Modulation (QAM) A modulation technique used by *modems* that involves the combined effects of *phase modulation* and *amplitude modulation*. QAM uses eight phase changes and two amplitudes to create 16 different signal changes.

Quality of Service (QoS) Parameters associated with data prioritization that specify such things as the amount of bandwidth a priority data transmission requires as well as the maximum amount of latency the transmission can tolerate in order for the transmission to be meaningful. QoS is needed for transmitting real-time voice and video traffic.

RA See *Routing Arbiter*.

Radio Frequencies (RF) Any transmission method that uses electromagnetic waveforms.

Radio Transmission Any wireless technique that uses *RF* to transmit information.

RADSL See *Rate-Adaptive Digital Subscriber Line*.

Random Access Protocol A network protocol that governs how nodes are to act in those instances where accessing a shared medium at will on a first-come first-served basis is permitted. Also called *Contention Protocol*.

Rate-Adaptive Digital Subscriber Line (RADSL) A *DSL* variant that provides transmission rates similar to *ADSL*. Transmission rates can be adjusted based on distance and line quality. Up to 7-Mbps downstream rate.

RBOC See *Regional Bell Operating Company*.

Redundancy Bits Extra bits incorporated into a data frame that provide error-correction information. A data set composed of both user data and redundancy bits is called a *codeword*. Also called *check bits*.

Regional Bell Operating Company (RBOC) A regional telephone company in the United States formed after the AT&T breakup in 1984.

Reliable Service A type of service that requires a sending node to acknowledge receipt of data. This is called an acknowledged datagram service.

Repeater A layer-1 device that provides both physical and electrical connections. Its function is to regenerate and propagate signals—it receives signals from one cable segment, regenerates, retimes, and amplifies them, and then transmits these "revitalized" signals to another cable segment. Repeaters extend the diameter of Ethernet/802.3 networks but are considered part of the same collision domain.

Request for Comments (RFC) The working notes of the Internet research and development community. RFCs provide network researchers and designers with a medium for documenting and sharing new ideas, network protocol concepts, and other technically related information. They contain meeting notes from Internet organizations, describe various Internet protocols and experiments, and detail standards specifications. All Internet standards are published as RFCs (not all RFCs are Internet standards, though).

Resource Reservation Protocol (RSVP) A layer-3 protocol developed by *IETF* to provide a mechanism to control network latency for specific applications. This is done by prioritizing data and allocating sufficient bandwidth for data transmission. RSVP can be thought of as an IP-based *QoS* protocol.

RF See *Radio Frequencies.*

RFC See *Request for Comments.*

Ring Design A network design that is based on a broadcast topology in which nodes are connected to a physical ring and data messages are transferred around the ring in either a clockwise or counterclockwise manner (or both).

RIP See *Routing Information Protocol.*

RIP-2 An updated version of *RIP,* formally known as RIP Version 2. New features include authentication, interpretation of *IGP* and *BGP* routes, *subnet mask* support, and multicasting support.

Risk Analysis The assessment of how much a loss is going to cost a company.

RJ A specific series of connectors defined in the Universal Service Order Code (USOC) definitions of telephone circuits. RJ is telephone lingo for "registered jack."

RJ-11 A four-wire modular connector used for telephones.

RJ-45 An eight-wire modular connector used in UTP-based Ethernet/802.3 LANs.

Router A layer-3 device that is responsible for determining the appropriate path a packet takes to reach its destination. Commonly referred to as *gateway.*

Routing A layer-3 function that directs data packets from source to destination.

Routing Arbiter (RA) A project that facilitates the exchange of network traffic among various independent Internet backbones. Special servers that contain routing information databases of network routes are maintained so that the transfer of traffic among the various backbone providers meeting at a *NAP* is facilitated.

Routing Information Protocol (RIP) A distance-vector algorithm that determines the best route by using a *hops* metric. RIP was at one time the *de facto standard* for IP routing.

Routing Protocol A specific *protocol* that determines the route a packet should take from source to destination. Routing protocols are a function of network protocols. For example, if your network protocol is *TCP/IP,* then several routing protocol options are available including *RIP, RIP-2,* and *OSPF.* If your network protocol is OSI's CNLP, then your routing protocol is IS-IS. Routing protocols determine the "best" path a packet should take when it travels through a network from source to destination and maintain routing tables that contain information about the network's topology. Routing protocols rely on routing algorithms to calculate the least-cost path from source to destination.

Routing Table A data structure that contains, among others, the destination address of a node or network, known router addresses, and the network interface associated with a particular router address. When a router receives a packet, it looks at the packet's destination address to identify the destination network, searches its routing table for an entry corresponding to this destination, and then forwards the packet to the next router via the appropriate interface.

RSA A *public key* encryption algorithm for encoding data. The abbreviation stands for Rivest, Shamir, and Adleman, the last names of the three individuals who designed it.

RSVP See *Resource Reservation Protocol.*

Runt Frame An Ethernet/802.3 frame that has at least 8 bytes but fewer than 64 bytes and has a valid CRC checksum.

SAN See *Storage Area Network.*

SAP See *Service Access Point.*

SAS See *Single-Attachment Station.*

Satellite Communication System An *RF*-based broadcast network design involving earth ground stations and orbiting communication satellites. Data transmissions from a land-based antenna to the satellite (called the uplink) are generally point-to-point, but all nodes that are part of the network are able to receive the satellite's transmissions (called the downlink).

SC Connector A TIA/EIA-568A standard connector for fiber-optic cable; also called a *568SC connector.*

SCSI Acronym for small computer systems interface (pronounced "scuzzy"), which is a high-speed parallel interface used to connect a computer to peripheral devices such as scanners, printers, CD-ROM drives, and mass storage devices such as ZIP drives via a single computer port. Up to eight SCSI devices can be interconnected in a daisy-chained configuration.

SDH See *Synchronous Digital Hierarchy.*

SDSL See *Symmetric Digital Subscriber Line.*

Segmentation See *Partitioning.*

Serial Communication A data transmission method in which the bits representing a character of data are transmitted in sequence, one bit at a time, over a single communications channel. Also referred to as *serial transmission.*

Server A networked device that provides resources to *client* machines. Examples include print servers, mail servers, file servers, and Web servers. Servers are shared by more than one user; clients have only a single user.

Service Access Point (SAP) Specified within the *OSI model,* a SAP refers to a location through which a process operating at one layer provides services to a process operating at the layer above it.

Service Profile Identification (SPID) Numbers assigned by the telcos and used to identify the various processes of an *ISDN* device. (Used only in North America.)

Shannon's Limit A mathematical theorem that describes a model for determining the maximum data rate of a noisy analog communications channel. Shannon's limit is given by the following formula: maximum data rate $(MDR) = H \log_2 (1 + S/N)$, where *MDR* is given in bits per second, H = bandwidth in hertz, and S/N is a measure of the *signal-to-noise ratio.* Named for the mathematician who derived it, Claude Shannon.

Shielded Twisted-Pair (STP) Twisted-pair cable in which individual wire pairs are shielded (i.e., protected from *noise*).

Signal Quality Error (SQE) A signal generated by a transceiver and read by the controller of the host to which the transceiver is connected. In V2.0 Ethernet, SQE is called *heartbeat* and is generated periodically to inform the host's controller that the transceiver is "alive." In IEEE 802.3, SQE is only generated when a real signal quality error occurs.

Signal-to-Noise Ratio (SNR) A measure of signal quality expressed in decibels (dB). It is the ratio of signal strength to background noise on a cable. More specifically, SNR is the ratio between the desired signal and the unwanted noise in a communications medium.

Simple Mail Transport Protocol (SMTP) A TCP application protocol for exchanging electronic mail.

Simplex Communication A data transmission method in which data may flow in only one direction; one device assumes the role of sender and the other assumes the role of receiver. These roles are fixed and cannot be reversed. An example of a simplex communication is a television transmission.

Single-Attachment Station (SAS) An FDDI node that is connected to only the primary pair of fibers and can be isolated from the network in the case of some types of failure. An SAS is also called a *Class B* node.

Single-Mode Fiber A type of fiber-optic cable with a core diameter ranging from 7 to 9 μm. In single-mode fiber, only a single ray of light, called the *axial ray,* can pass. Thus, a light wave entering the fiber exits with very little distortion, even at very long distances and very high data rates.

SIP See *SMDS Interface Protocol.*

Sliding Window Protocol A *flow-control* strategy that enables a sender to transmit frames continuously without having to wait for acknowledgments to these frames from the receiver. The sliding window concept is implemented by requiring the sender to sequentially number each data frame it sends and by having the sender and receiver maintain information about the number of frames they can respectively send or receive.

SMA Connector A fiber-optic cable connector that meets military specifications.

Smart Card A type of "credit card" with embedded integrated circuits that stores information in electronic form and is used for authentication. Similar to a *digital certificate.*

SMDS See *Switched Multimegabit Data Service.*

SMDS Interface Protocol (SIP) *SMDS* protocol that consists of three different levels: SIP level 3, SIP level 2, and SIP level 1. These three protocol levels are similar in function to the first three layers of the *OSI* model but represent SMDS's MAC sublayer and hence operate at the data link layer.

SMTP See *Simple Mail Transport Protocol.*

SNR See *Signal-to-Noise Ratio.*

SOHO An abbreviation for *small office/home office.*

SONET See *Synchronous Optical Network.*

Spanning Tree A single path between source and destination nodes that does not include any loops. It is a loop-free subset of a network's topology. The spanning tree algorithm, specified in IEEE 802.1d, describes how bridges (and switches) can communicate to avoid network loops.

SPID See *Service Profile Identification.*

Split-Horizon A strategy employed by *RIP* to ensure that a router never sends routing information back in the direction from which it came. Used to prevent routing loops.

Split-Horizon with Poisoned Reverse A modified *split-horizon* strategy in which routing information provided by a neighbor is included in updates sent back to that neighbor. Such routes are assigned a cost factor of infinity, which makes the network unreachable.

Spread Spectrum A radio technology that refers to a security technique. Spread spectrum transmission camouflages data by mixing signals with a pseudonoise (PN) pattern and transmitting the real signal with the PN pattern. The transmission signal is spread over a range of the frequencies in the radio spectrum.

SQE See *Signal Quality Error.*

Stackable Repeater Hub Individual repeater units "stacked" one on top of another. Instead of using a common shared backplane, stackable hubs use a "pseudobackplane" based on a common connector interface. An external cable interconnects the individual hubs in a daisy-chained manner. Once interconnected, the entire chain of hubs becomes a single logical unit that functions as a single repeater.

Stacking Height The maximum number of stackable repeater hubs permitted.

Standby Monitor A station (i.e., lobe) on a token ring network that oversees the *active monitor.* Except for the active monitor, all token ring lobes are standby monitors.

Star A network configuration characterized by the presence of a central processing hub, which serves as a wire center for connecting nodes. All data must pass through the hub in order for nodes to communicate with each other.

Stateful Firewall A device or product that monitors all transactions between two systems and is capable of (a) identifying a specific condition in the transaction between two applications, (b) predicting what should transpire next in the transaction, and (c) detecting when normal operational "states" of the connection are being violated.

Static Route A fixed route that is entered into a router's *routing table* either manually or via a software configuration program.

Statistical Multiplexing A *multiplexing* technique that allocates part of a channel's capacity only to those nodes that require it (i.e., have data to transmit). Based on the premise that, statistically, not all devices necessarily require a portion of the channel at exactly the same time.

ST Connector Similar to a *BNC connector* but used with *fiber-optic cable.*

Step-Index Multimode Fiber A type of multimode fiber in which light pulses are guided along the cable from source to destination by reflecting off the cladding.

STM See *Synchronous Transport Module.*

Stop-and-Wait Protocol A *flow-control* strategy that requires the sender to transmit one frame and then wait for the receiver to acknowledge receipt of this frame before any additional frames are transmitted.

Storage Area Network (SAN) A network dedicated exclusively for storing data. Usually involves *Fibre Channel* technology.

Store-and-Forward A method used by bridges and switches in which the contents of an entire frame are captured by the device before a decision is made to filter or forward the frame. A store-and-forward network switch is also called a *buffering switch.* A network based on this principle is called a store-and-forward network.

STP (Shielded Twisted-Pair) See *Twisted-Pair Cable.*

STS See *Synchronous Transport Signal.*

Subnet Mask A special network address used to identify a specific subnetwork. Using a unique bit combination, a mask partitions an address into a network ID and a host ID.

Subnetting The partitioning of a network address space into separate, autonomous *subnetworks.* Key to subnetting is a network's *subnet mask.*

Subnetwork A network segment. Commonly abbreviated *subnet.*

SVC See *Switched Virtual Circuit.*

Switch A network device that filters or forwards data based on specific information. A layer-2 switch (e.g., an Ethernet switch) filters or forwards frames from one node to another using MAC-level (i.e., hardware) addresses; a layer-3 switch filters or forwards packets based on network addresses; and a layer-4 (or higher) switch filters or forwards messages based on specific application protocols. Forwarding rates are usually done at *wire speed* and via "private" connections (i.e., no other node "sees" the traffic). Switches partition Ethernet/802.3 networks into multiple collision domains.

Switched Ethernet An Ethernet/802.3 LAN that is based on network switches instead of repeaters or bridges. A switched Ethernet/802.3 LAN isolates network traffic between sending and receiving nodes from all other connected nodes. It also transforms traditional Ethernet/802.3 from a broadcast technology to a point-to-point technology.

Switched Multimegabit Data Service (SMDS) A cell-based, connectionless, high-speed, public, packet-switched, broadband, metropolitan area data network.

Switched Virtual Circuit (SVC) A circuit between source and destination nodes that is established on the fly and then removed after data communications have ended. SVCs are logical dynamic connections instead of logical permanent connections, as with *PVCs*. Thus, SVCs provide switched, on-demand connectivity.

Symmetric Cryptography See *Cryptography*.

Symmetric Digital Subscriber Line (SDSL) A *DSL* variant in which traffic is transmitted at the same rate in each direction. Maximum transmission rate is 768 kbps. Uses single-wire pair. Telephone service not supported. Suitable for videoconferencing.

Synchronous Communication A data communication method that requires sending and receiving nodes to monitor each other's transmissions so that the receiving node always knows when a new character is being sent. In this instance, the sending and receiving nodes are "in sync" with each other.

Synchronous Digital Hierarchy (SDH) An *ITU physical layer* standard that provides an international specification for high-speed digital transmission via optical fiber. SDH incorporates *SONET* and uses the *STM* signal hierarchy as its basic building block. SDH is essentially the same as SONET. At OC-3 rates and higher, the two are virtually identical.

Synchronous Optical Network (SONET) An ANSI *physical layer* standard that provides an international specification for high-speed digital transmission via optical fiber. At the source interface, signals are converted from electrical to optical form. They are then converted back to electrical form at the destination interface. The basic building block of the SONET signal hierarchy is *STS-1* (51.84 Mbps). See also *Synchronous Digital Hierarchy*.

Synchronous Transport Module (STM) Represents a digital transmission carrier system used for *SDH*. STM rates range from STM-1, which is equivalent to OC-3 (155.52 Mbps), to STM-64, which is equivalent to OC-192 (9.953 Gbps).

Synchronous Transport Signal (STS) A digital transmission hierarchy used for *SONET*. STS rates range from STS-1, which is the equivalent of 28 DS-1 channels (51.84 Mbps), to STS-192, which is the equivalent of 5376 DS-1 channels (9.953 Gbps). STS rates are the electrical equivalent of *OC* rates.

T-1 The multiplexing of 24 separate voice channels, each rated at 64 kbps, plus one 8-kbps framing channel into a single wideband digital signal rated at 1.544 Mbps.

T-2 A multiplexed circuit that combines 4 *T1* circuits and has an aggregate bandwidth of 6.312 Mbps.

T-3 A multiplexed circuit that combines 28 *T1* circuits and has an aggregate bandwidth of 44.736 Mbps.

T-4 A multiplexed circuit that combines 168 *T1* circuits and has an aggregate bandwidth of 274.176 Mbps.

TCP See *Transmission Control Protocol*.

TCP/IP An acronym for *Transmission Control Protocol/Internet Protocol*. A formal network protocol suite based on its two namesake subprotocols, *TCP* and *IP*.

TDM See *Time Division Multiplexing*.

TE See *Terminal Equipment*.

Telco An acronym for *telephone company*.

Terminal Adapter (TA) A device that connects non-compatible ISDN devices to an ISDN network. If a TA is used for an ISDN dialup connection, then it can be thought of as a modem. If a TA is used to connect a device to a LAN, then it can be thought of as a network interface card. It should be noted that, although a TA is frequently referred to as an ISDN modem or digital modem in the context of an ISDN dialup connection, this reference is incorrect. By definition, a modem performs analog-to-digital and digital-to-analog conversions. Since ISDN is completely digital, no such conversions are necessary; thus, the expressions "ISDN modem" or "digital modem" are incongruous.

Terminal Equipment (TE) A specific communication device that connects to an *ISDN* network. Two TEs are referenced in the specification: *TE1* refers to an ISDN-compatible device (e.g., digital telephone or a computer with a built-in ISDN port), and *TE2* refers to a noncompatible ISDN device (e.g., an analog telephone or a computer without a built-in ISDN port).

Terminator Layer-1 device that prevents signal reflections by providing electrical resistance at the end of a cable to "absorb" signals to keep them from bouncing back and being heard again by the devices connected to the cable.

Thick Ethernet IEEE 802.3 10BASE5, which uses "thick" coaxial cable (outer diameter between 0.375 inch and 0.405 inch) as its physical medium.

Thin Ethernet IEEE 802.3 10BASE2, which uses "thin" coaxial cable (outer diameter between 0.175 inch and 0.195 inch) as its physical medium.

Threat Assessment An activity that involves determining how much security is necessary for proper control of system and network assets. Threat assessment is guided by answering the overriding question, "What assets are critical to the operation of my network and who do I think would want access to them?"

Throughput A realistic measure of the amount of data transmitted between two nodes in a given time period. It is a function of hardware/software, speed, CPU power, overhead, and many other items. Compared to *bandwidth,* throughput is what the channel really achieves, whereas bandwidth is what is theoretically possible.

Time Division Multiplexing (TDM) A multiplexing technique that assigns to each node connected to a channel an identification number and a small amount of time in which to transmit. TDM-based transmissions are serially sequenced.

Token A special frame on a token ring or token bus network. Possession of the token permits a node to transmit data.

Token Bus A local area network technology based on a token passing protocol for media access. Defined in IEEE 802.4. A token bus network is characterized as a logical ring on a physical bus—physically, the network resembles a bus topology, but logically, the network is arranged as a ring with respect to passing the token from node to node.

Token Passing Protocol A network protocol that requires nodes to possess a special frame, called a *token,* prior to transmitting data. Token passing schemes are both contention-free and collision-free.

Token Ring A local area network technology based on a token passing protocol for media access control. Defined by IEEE 802.5. A token ring LAN is implemented either as a logical ring using a physical ring topology or as a logical ring structure arranged in a physical star configuration.

traceroute A UNIX program that depicts the gateways a packet transverses. A corresponding Microsoft NT command is called *tracert.*

Transceiver A service used in Ethernet/802.3 networks to connect nodes to the physical medium. Transceivers serve as both the physical connection and the electrical interface between a node and the physical medium, enabling the node to communicate with the medium. Transceivers transmit and receive signals simultaneously.

Transmission Control Protocol (TCP) A layer-4 connection-oriented protocol that performs several functions, including providing for reliable transmission of data by furnishing end-to-end error detection and correction; guaranteeing that data are transferred across a network accurately and in the proper sequence; retransmitting any data not received by the destination node; and guaranteeing against data duplication between sending and receiving nodes. It is the TCP of *TCP/IP.*

Tree A network configuration in which nodes are connected to one another in a hierarchical fashion. A root node or hub is connected to second-level nodes or hubs; second-level devices are connected to third-level devices, which in turn are connected to fourth-level devices, and so forth.

Triple DES A variant of *DES* that uses three DES operations instead of one.

Tunneling See *Encapsulation.*

Twisted-Pair Cable A type of copper cable that uses at least two insulated copper wires that have been twisted together. There are two basic types: *unshielded twisted-pair (UTP)* and *shielded twisted-pair (STP).*

UDP See *User Datagram Protocol.*

UDSL See *Universal Digital Subscriber Line.*

UNI See *User-to-Network Interface.*

Unicast A data transmission that is destined to a single recipient.

Uniform Resource Identifier (URI) A conceptual entity used with *HTTP* to represent a universal set of names and addresses of all resources regardless of their location. URIs enable specific resources to be identified throughout the World Wide Web. They contain the name, location, or any other defining attribute of the specified resource. One example of a URI is a *URL.*

Uniform Resource Locator (URL) A specific type of *URI* that is used to identify a resource's location throughout the World Wide Web by specifying the access method needed to acquire the resource. The general form is `http://` *host:port/url-path,* where *host* is the fully qualified domain name of an Internet-connected node, *port* is the port number to which the TCP connection is made, and *url-path* provides the details of how the specified resource is accessed relative to the scheme being used.

Universal Digital Subscriber Line (UDSL) A *DSL* variant that provides symmetrical service at 2 Mbps each way.

Unreliable Service A network service type that requires no acknowledgment of receipt of data from the receiving node to the sending node. This is called a *datagram service.*

Unshielded Twisted-Pair (UTP) Twisted-pair cable in which individual wire pairs are not shielded (i.e., protected from *noise*).

URI See *Uniform Resource Identifier.*

URL See *Uniform Resource Locator.*

User Agent An entity such as a Web browser through which HTTP client request messages are made to an HTTP server.

User Datagram Protocol (UDP) A connectionless protocol providing an unreliable datagram service. UDP does not furnish any end-to-end error detection or correction, and it does not retransmit any data it did not receive.

User-to-Network Interface (UNI)   An end node's port where the *local loop* terminates at a customer's site.

Utilization   A network performance measure that specifies the amount of time a LAN spends successfully transmitting data. *Average utilization* means that over some period of time (e.g., 10-hours), on average, a certain percentage of the LAN's capacity is used for successfully transmitting data. *Peak utilization* means that, at a specific moment in time, a certain percentage of the LAN's capacity was utilized.

UTP   See *Unshielded Twisted-Pair.*

V.22 *bis*   ITU-T standard for 2400-bps full-duplex modems; cycles to 1200 bps/600 bps.

V.29   ITU-T standard for 9600-bps facsimile service.

V.32   ITU-T standard for 9600-bps modems; cycles to 4800 bps when line quality degrades, and cycles forward when line quality improves.

V.32 *bis*   ITU-T standard that extends *V.32* to 7200, 12,000, and 14,400 bps; cycles to lower rate when line quality degrades, and cycles forward when line quality improves.

V.32 *ter*   Pseudostandard that extends *V.32 bis* to 19,200 bps and 21,600 bps.

V.34   ITU-T standard for 28,800 bps modems. (V.34 modems upgraded with special software can achieve data rates of 31,200 bps or 33,600 bps.)

V.FAST   Proprietary pseudostandard from Hayes and Rockwell for modems transmitting at data rates up to 28,800 bps; served as a migration path for *V.34.*

V.42   ITU-T standard for modem *error correction.* Uses *LAPM* as the primary error-correcting protocol, with *MNP* Classes 1 through 4 as an alternative.

V.42 *bis*   ITU-T standard that enhances *V.42* by incorporating the British Telecom Lempel Ziv data *compression* technique to V.42 *error correction.* Most *V.32, V.32 bis,* and *V.34* compliant modems come with V.42 or V.42 *bis* or MNP.

V.44   ITU-T standard that provides a 6:1 compression ratio. When compared to V.42, download speeds can increase from 20% to 60%.

V.90   ITU-T standard for 57,600-bps modems (commonly called "56K modems") in which asymmetric data rates apply (i.e., the send and receive rates are different). Depending on telephone line conditions, upstream rates (send) are restricted to 33,600 bps, and downstream rates (receive) are restricted to 57,600 bps. V.90 modems are designed for connections that are dig-

ital at one end and have only two analog-digital conversions each way.

V.92   ITU-T standard for 56K modems that increases upstream rates to 48,000 bps, and provides faster connection times and call-waiting.

vBNS+   See *Very High Performance Backbone Network Service +.*

VCC   See *Virtual Channel Circuit.*

VCI   See *Virtual Channel Identifier.*

VDSL   See *Very High-Speed Digital Subscriber Line.*

very High Performance Backbone Network Service + (vBNS+)   A nationwide network that supports high-performance, high-bandwidth applications. The vBNS+ began in 1995 as the vBNS, which was a restricted access collaborative networking project between the National Science Foundation and MCI WorldCom. Today, the vBNS+ operates as a new advanced networking service and is open to the entire U.S. higher education and research community. It has an OC-48 packet over *SONET* backbone that runs parallel with the original vBNS OC-12 *ATM* backbone. In addition to the advanced networking services it offers, the vBNS+ is also a development platform for next generation *Internet* applications.

Very High-Speed Digital Subscriber Line (VDSL)   A *DSL* variant that provides asymmetric service over fiber. Downstream rates range from 13 to 52 Mbps; upstream rates range from 1.5 to 2.3 Mbps. Suitable for Internet/ intranet access, video-on-demand, database access, remote LAN access, and high-definition TV.

Virtual Channel Connection (VCC)   A virtual circuit that provides a logical connection between an *ATM* source and destination. Data can only be transmitted in one direction via a VCC. A VCC is denoted by a *virtual channel identifier (VCI),* which is included as part of the ATM cell header. Multiple virtual channels that share the same connection can be packaged into a single virtual path.

Virtual Channel Identifier (VCI)   A parameter used to identify *ATM virtual channels.* VCI information is carried within an ATM cell header.

Virtual Circuit   A nondedicated connection through a shared medium that gives the high-level user the appearance of a dedicated, direct connection from the source node to the destination node.

Virtual Circuit Packet-Switching   See *Packet-Switching.*

Virtual Local Area Network (VLAN)   A network consisting of nodes that are not physically connected to the same medium. Instead, they are connected in a virtual sense using specially designed software that groups several ports in a switch into a single workgroup. Nodes connected to these ports are considered part of a workgroup, and network traffic from any node/port is (usually) limited to only those nodes or ports assigned to the workgroup.

Virtual Path Connection (VPC)   A semipermanent connection that provides a logical collection of *ATM virtual channels* that have the same endpoints. More specifically, a VPC carries a group of virtual channels, all of which have the same endpoints. Virtual paths enable any connection that uses the same network path from source to destination to be bundled into a single unit. A *virtual path identifier (VPI)* denotes a virtual path and is included in a cell's header. A virtual path can also provide a form of traffic control by logically (not physically) partitioning network traffic based on the type of data being carried and associated *quality of service.*

Virtual Path Identifier (VPI)   A parameter used to identify an *ATM virtual path.* VPI information is carried within an ATM cell header.

Virtual Private Network (VPN)   An *IP* connection between two sites over a public IP network that has its payload traffic encrypted so that only source and destination nodes can decrypt the traffic packets. A VPN enables a publicly accessible network to be used for highly confidential, dynamic, and secure data transmissions.

VLAN   See *Virtual Local Area Network.*

VOFR   See *Voice Over Frame Relay.*

VOIP   See *Voice Over IP.*

Voice Over Frame Relay (VOFR)   Transmitting voice signals over a *frame relay* network.

Voice Over IP (VOIP)   A technology that enables users to place telephone calls across the Internet.

VPC   See *Virtual Path Connection.*

VPI   See *Virtual Path Identifier.*

VPN   See *Virtual Private Network.*

WAN   See *Wide Area Network.*

Wavelength   A measure of the length of a wave. It is the distance an electrical or light signal travels in one complete cycle.

Wavelength Division Multiplexing (WDM)   A *multiplexing* method used with fiber-optic cables. Involves the simultaneous transmission of light sources over a single fiber-optic channel. Light sources of different wavelengths are combined by a WDM multiplexer and transmitted over a single line. When the signals arrive, a WDM demultiplexer separates them and transmits them to their respective destination receivers.

WDM   See *Wavelength Division Multiplexing.*

Wearable Computing   Coined at the Massachusetts Institute of Technology's Media Lab in the 1970s, the term today indicates a network convergence strategy in which computer technology is woven into clothing fabric. To date, a team has created a tie that doubles as a mobile telephone, with a tiny microphone lodged into the knot and a keypad woven into the silk.

Web-Based Networking   A relatively new communications model that has emerged as a result of the Internet and which fosters the notion of *the network is the computer,* a phrase coined in the late 1980s by Sun Microsystems' president, Scott McNealy. "The network is the computer" implies that by making resources available to users via a network, the network essentially becomes the single most powerful computer accessible. Thus, the network gives users access to more computing power than their desktop models.

Well-Known Port Number   A port address that identifies the specific process or application a user accesses on a host. For example, *SMTP* is assigned well-known port number 25.

Wide Area Network (WAN)   A network that interconnects computing resources that are widely separated geographically (usually over 100 km). This includes towns, cities, states, and countries. A WAN generally spans an area greater than 5 miles (8 km) and can be thought of as consisting of a collection of *LANs.*

Wire   A general term for the physical layer of a network. The three main physical attributes of wire are *conductor, insulation,* and *outer jacket.* Wire also has three important electrical characteristics that can directly affect the quality of the signal transmitted across it: *capacitance, impedance,* and *attenuation.* Signal quality is affected most by the combination of attenuation and capacitance. The two primary forms of wire are copper and fiber. Also called *cable.*

Wireless Communications   A type of communications in which signals travel through space instead of through a physical cable. There are two general types of wireless communication: *radio transmission* and *infrared transmission.*

Wireless LAN (WLAN)   A *LAN* consisting of nodes that rely on *wireless communication* techniques for transmitting or receiving data. Specified by *IEEE 802.11.*

Wire Speed   A unit of measure used to describe a device's maximum (i.e., fastest) filtering and forwarding rates. In 10-Mbps Ethernet/802.3, wire speed is equal to 14,880 frames per second. This is frequently reported as 14,880 packets per second.

WLAN   See *Wireless LAN.*

Workgroup Switch   One application of an Ethernet switch. A workgroup switch partitions a single shared medium into multiple shared media and supports more than one MAC address per port. Also called *segment switches*.

Workstation   A computer system that has its own operating system and is connected to a network. A workstation can be a personal computer such as a Macintosh or Intel-based PC, a graphics workstation such as those manufactured by Sun Microsystems, a super-minicomputer such as IBM's AS/400, a super-microcomputer such as DEC's Alpha, or a mainframe such as an IBM ES-9000. Also called *host, server, desktop,* or *client.*

X.25   An early networking protocol that defines the interface between a public packet-switching data network and the device used to access this network.

XA-SMDS   See *Exchange Access SMDS.*

Index

Photo Credits

Page 51, © Bettmann/CORBIS; p. 58,
   Courtesy Lucent Technologies Bell
   Labs; p. 86, Giraudon/Art Resource,
   NY; p. 113, Courtesy DuPont; p. 127,
   Courtesy MGM Studios; p. 155,
   Property of AT&T Archives. Reprinted
   with permission of AT&T; p. 186,
   Courtesy Radia Perlman/Sun
   Microsystems; p. 244, Courtesy MCI/
   Worldcom; p. 314, Courtesy
   International Data Group.